Launching the Imagination

A Comprehensive Guide to Basic Design

Launching the Imagination

A Comprehensive Guide to Basic Design

second edition

Mary Stewart

Boston   Burr Ridge, IL   Dubuque, IA   Madison, WI   New York   San Francisco   St. Louis
Bangkok   Bogotá   Caracas   Kuala Lumpur   Lisbon   London   Madrid   Mexico City
Milan   Montreal   New Delhi   Santiago   Seoul   Singapore   Sydney   Taipei   Toronto

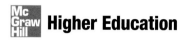

Higher Education

LAUNCHING THE IMAGINATION: A COMPREHENSIVE GUIDE TO BASIC DESIGN
Published by McGraw-Hill, a business unit of The McGraw-Hill Companies, Inc., 1221 Avenue of the Americas, New York, NY, 10020.

This book is printed on acid-free paper.

2 3 4 5 6 7 8 9 0 DOW/DOW 0 9 8 7 6 5

ISBN   0-07-287061-3

Editor in Chief: *Emily Barrosse*
Publisher: *Lyn Uhl*
Sponsoring Editor: *Joe Hanson*
Developmental Editor: *Cynthia Ward*
Editorial Assistant: *Elizabeth Sigal*
Executive Marketing Manager: *Suzanna Ellison*
Managing Editor: *Jean Dal Porto*
Project Manager: *Catherine R. Iammartino*
Art Director: *Jeanne Schreiber*
Senior Designer and Interior Designer: *Kim Menning*
Cover Designer: *Bill Stanton*
Senior Photo Research Coordinator: *Alexandra Ambrose*
Photo Research: *Photo Search, Inc., New York*
Art Editor: *Emma C. Ghiselli*
Cover Credits:
[1]   Stan Rickel, *Teapot Sketches*, 1991. Courtesy of the artist.
[2]   Detail, Jacey, *Untitled.* © Jacey, Shannon Associates.
[3]   Tanija & Graham Carr, *Untitled*, 2001. Courtesy of the artists. Photo: Victor France.
[4]   Detail, Michael James, *Rhythm/Color: Improvisation*, 1985. Photo: David Caras.
[5]   Donna Dennis, *Subway with Silver Girders*, 1981-82. The Margulies Collection at the Warehouse. Photo: Peter Aaron.
Lead Media Producer: *Shannon Gattens*
Media Project Manager: *Michele Borrelli*
Production Supervisor: *Janean A. Utley*
CD-ROM Development and Design: *Creative Myndz*
Composition: *10.5/14 Palatino by Prographics*
Printing: *70# Sterling Ultra Web Dull, R.R. Donnelley and Sons, Inc./Willard, OH*

Library of Congress Cataloging-in-Publication Data
Stewart, Mary, 1952-
    Launching the imagination : a comprehensive guide to basic design / Mary Stewart.-- 2nd ed.
      p. cm.
    Also issued in parts titled: Launching the imagination : A comprehensive guide to two-dimensional design, and Launching the imagination : A comprehensive guide to three-dimensional design.
    Includes bibliographical references and index.
    ISBN 0-07-287061-3 (softcover : alk. paper)
    1. Design. I. Title.
NK1510.S74 2006
745.4--dc22
                                                                                          2005041666

www.mhhe.com

Launching the Imagination:
A Comprehensive Guide to Basic Design
is dedicated to my teachers. Especially Garo Antreasian,
Rudy Pozzatti, Marvin Lowe, and Adrian Tió.

dedication

In the beginning of my teaching career, I had the good fortune to audit the courses of two master teachers of design, William Itter and David Hornung. Itter's fundamentals course, derived from Joseph Albers' approach, featured assignments that were methodical, systematic, and highly analytical. Hornung's course, which focused on conceptual and visual patterns, was exuberant, synthetic, and often irreverent. Despite significant differences in their assignments, both teachers brilliantly presented substantial design information.

Based on these experiences and my own teaching, I concluded that a comprehensive approach to design requires experimentation as well as analysis, and that rambunctiousness is the natural partner to rigor. Thus, when McGraw-Hill invited me to write a design textbook, I was determined to present substantial information in the liveliest possible way.

A Comprehensive Approach for 21st Century Students

Launching the Imagination treats design as both a verb and a noun—as a problem-solving process as well as a well-crafted product. It challenges students to use design to explore their own ideas while encouraging them to look closely and learn from the work of other artists. My aim was to write a book that would help students create designs that are both conceptually inventive and visually compelling. I hope that students will be inspired to see the foundations course as a launching pad for their future work, for their entry into the community of artists.

Thorough coverage of 2D and 3D design. This book covers all of the topics common to foundations courses, recognizing that artists and designers benefit from a strong shared vocabulary. By combining these topics in one volume, we are able to provide students with a coherent approach to the full-year course that also offers a savings over the cost of multiple volumes. (For instructors who only want a 2D or 3D volume, however, split volumes are available.) This second edition has benefitted from the feedback of many foundations teachers, whose suggestions are reflected in the expanded and refined discussions of 2D and 3D elements and principles.

Unique coverage of time design. *Launching the Imagination* recognizes that students in today's foundations courses have the opportunity to work in a wider range of media than ever before. I have tried to present a teachable unit on time design or "4D" (Part Four) by exploring the elements and principles at the core of such new and old forms as film, websites, graphic novels, and visual books. Time design is of great interest to our students, and this section is comparable to the 2D and 3D design sections in length and significance.

Unique coverage of creativity and concept development. Because foundations courses are as much about process as product, *Launching the Imagination* covers such topics as generating and developing ideas, managing time, and making the most of critiques. This material, found in Part Two, can be assigned any time in the course. Some instructors find it valuable to discuss the material during class time, while others prefer it as supplemental reading.

Hundreds of full-color images. An art textbook is only as good as the images it offers—and I've sought images that are diverse and compelling. The stylistic range represents both time-honored masterworks (such as Caravaggio's *Descent from the Cross*) and works by contemporary artists (such as Alfred Leslie's *The Killing Cycle*, which was inspired by Caravaggio's painting). There are examples from many different cultures, representing a wide range of two-, three-, and four-dimensional media. A Maori meeting house is included in a discussion on cultural meaning, a kinetic Japanese tower is presented in a discussion of time, and contemporary and historic masks have been analyzed throughout. Many forms of visual culture are represented, from comic books and product design to video, painting, sculpture, and more.

preface

Conversations with practicing artists. Guest speakers have enhanced my own courses, and I tried to recreate that experience in book form through the "Profiles" at the end of each chapter. In these interviews, students learn about working processes and career choices from a remarkable group of masters. The "Profiles" help students see connections between basic design and professional practice. Interviews with sculptor Todd Slaughter and photographer Abelardo Morrell have been added to the second edition.

New to the Second Edition

Working with invaluable feedback from adopters of the first edition, I have expanded, reorganized, refined, and updated the presentation—all with an eye to creating a better learning experience. The following summarizes the key changes in this edition:

- **Expanded and improved coverage of 2D design.** All three chapters of Part One have been thoroughly revised, with clearer writing, improved image choices, and larger image sizes. Chapter 1 goes into greater detail on the elements of line, shape, texture, and value. Chapter 2 offers a more precise introduction to color theory and a more thorough introduction to color schemes and composing in color. Chapter 3 has been significantly reorganized, and greater attention has been given to gestalt theory, the illusion of space, and the illusion of movement.

- **Expanded and improved coverage of 3D design.** Part Three has been expanded to four chapters, making for a more coherent and manageable presentation of 3D elements, principles, materials, and concepts. Because an understanding of the practical and expressive qualities of materials is essential to work in 3D, I have created a separate chapter (10) on construction methods and materials. Throughout Part Three, illustrations have been added and concepts have been explained in greater detail.

- **New coverage of visual communication.** The unit on Concepts and Critical Thinking (Part Two) has been strengthened by the addition of a new Chapter 7, entitled "Constructing Meaning." This new chapter provides a lively and concise introduction to the theory and practice of visual communication. In it, students will explore the role of audience in communication and consider the importance of intent, context, visual drama, and metaphor.

- **Better placement of "Key Questions."** To help students immediately see the relevance of a topic to their own studio work, the "Key Questions" now appear at the end of sections within the chapter rather than at the end of the chapter.

- **New media resource guides.** This book is supported by a website and CD-ROMs that adds another dimension to the learning environment. A page at the end of Parts One, Two, Three, and Four shows you what types of media resources are keyed to each of those parts. These guides also include lists of studio projects that are available in the Instructor's Manual.

Multimedia Resources for Students and Instructors

Please contact your local McGraw-Hill representative for details on the following supplements, including policies, prices, and availability, as some restrictions may apply. If you are not sure who your representative is, you can find him or her by using the rep locator at www.mhhe.com.

For Students:

- **The Core Concepts CD-ROM** is made up of five components to offer students essential study material in conjunction with this text. *Elements and principles of art* are illustrated with interactive exercises and animations. *Art techniques* are demonstrated and explained with brief video segments. *Chapter*

Resources include study guides and quizzes. *Internet Resources* provides a guide to using the Internet for research. *Study Skills Primer* provides students with essential advice on how to be successful when studying during college.

- **The Online Learning Center,** located at **www.mhhe.com/launching2,** offers resources for each chapter of the text, including chapter objectives, discussion questions, online testing, and links to websites for additional research of the topics covered. In addition, the site hosts links to promote getting involved in art and in conducting research on the Web.

For Instructors:

- **The Instructor's Manual** includes more than 50 studio assignments, with examples, in a consistent format that makes them easy for instructors to use as is or adapt to their own purposes. For new foundations teachers, the IM offers suggestions for constructing a syllabus. The Instructor's Manual is available on the instructor's section of the Online Learning Center, located at **www.mhhe.com/launching2,** and on the **Instructor's Resource CD-ROM.** Adopters may obtain a password and/or CD-ROM from their local McGraw-Hill representative.

Acknowledgments

Writing this book has been an enormous undertaking and I've received a lot of help from my colleagues. At Northern Illinois University, I am especially indebted to Dr. Harold Kafer, who has been encouraging and supportive throughout this process, to Professor Leif Allmendinger, who reviewed Chapter Seven and suggested improvements, and to Foundations Program secretary Florence Butler, whose reserves of energy and wit seem bottomless.

I would like to thank the following artists and designers who contributed so generously to the Profiles, which accompany each chapter:

Nancy Callahan, Professor of Art, *The State University of New York at Oneonta*

Bob Dacey, Associate Professor of Art, *Syracuse University*

Diane Gallo, Independent Writer

Sharon Greytak, Independent Filmmaker

Ann Baddeley Keister, Associate Professor of Art, *Grand Valley State University*

Heidi Lasher-Oakes, Independent Sculptor

David MacDonald, Professor of Art, *Syracuse University*

Rodger Mack, Professor of Art, *Syracuse University*

Abelardo Morell, Professor of Art, *Massachusetts College of Art*

Rick Paul, Professor of Art, *Purdue University*

Todd Slaughter, Professor of Art, *The Ohio State University*

Ken Stout, Professor of Art, *University of Arkansas*

Jerome Witkin, Professor of Art, *Syracuse University*

Phillia Yi, Professor of Art, *Hobart and William Smith Colleges*

I am also grateful for the advice of the following reviewers, who responded so thoughtfully to the project in various stages of development. Their opinions, suggestions, criticisms, and encouragement helped shape *Launching:*

For the Second Edition:

Kathleen A. Arkles, *College for Creative Studies*

Donald Barrie, *Seattle Central Community College*

Julie Baugnet, *St. Cloud State University*

Donna Bechis, *Fitchburg State College*

Nancy Blum-Cumming, *University of Wisconsin-Stout*

Debra K.D. Bonello, *Lansing Community College*

Jeff Boshart, *Eastern Illinois University*

Jacquelin Boulanger, *New College of Florida*

Stephanie Bowman, *Pittsburg State University*

Peter Brown, *Ringling School of Art*

John Carlander, *Westmont College*

Steven Cost, *Amarillo College*

Michael Croft, *University of Arizona*

Cat Crotchett, *Western Michigan University*

Claire Darley, *Art Academy of Cincinnati*

Anita M. DeAngelis, *East Tennessee State University*

Beverly Dennis, *Jowes County Junior College*

Tracy Doreen Dietzel, *Edgewood College*

Tim Doud, *American University*

James Elniski, *School of The Art Institute of Chicago*

John Ford, *Labette Community College*

Corky Gross, *Cazenovia College*

Arlene Grossman, *Art Institute of Boston at Lesley University*

Danielle Harmon, *West Texas A & M University*

Christopher Hocking, *University of Georgia*

Carol Hodson, *Webster University*

Sara M. Hong, *University of Arizona*

Lorie Jesperson, *Lake Michigan College*

Cheryl Ann Kittredge, *University of Maine, Presque Isle*

Michelle LaPerriere, *Maryland Institute College of Art*

In Shik Lee, *Tompkins Cortland Community College*

Richard F. Martin, *New York Institute of Technology*

Christine McCullough, *Youngstown State University*

Julie McWilliams, *Sussex County College*

Nancy Morrow, *Kansas State University*

Byron Myrich, *Jones Junior College*

Kelly Nelson, *Longwood University*

Lara Nguyen, *California State University, Long Beach*

Grace O'Brien, *Purdue University*

Mark O'Grady, *Pratt Institute*

William Potter, *Herron School of Art-IUPUI*

Patsy C. Rainey, *University of Mississippi*

Cherri Rittenhouse, *Rock Valley College*

Gil Rocha, *Richland Community College*

William B. Rowe, *Ohio Northern University*

Kim Schrag, *Tompkins Cortland Community College*

Jean Sharer, *Front Range Community College*

Gail Simpson, *University of Wisconsin-Madison*

Todd Slaughter, *Ohio State University*

Robert Smart, *Lawrence University*

Karen Spears, *Eastern Kentucky University*

Mindy Spritz, *The Art Institute of Atlanta*

Teresa Stoll, *Lake City Community College*

Katherine Strause, *University of Arkansas at Little Rock*

Rob Tarbell, *Limestone College*

William Travis, *Rowan University*

Gerson M. Rapaport, *New York Institute of Technology*

Linda Vanderkolk, *Purdue University*

Carolynne Whitefeather, *Utica College*

Reid Wood, *Lorain County Community College*

Marilyn H. Wounded Head, *Mesa State College*

Alice Zinnes, *New York City College of Technology, City University of New York*

For the First Edition:

Scott Betz, *Winston-Salem State University*

Jeff Boshart, *Eastern Illinois University*

Peter Brown, *Ringling School of Art and Design*

Brian Cantley, *California State University, Fullerton*

Laurie Beth Clark, *University of Wisconsin, Madison*

Michael Croft, *The University of Arizona*

John Fillwalk, *Ball State University*

David Fobes, *San Diego State University*

Albert Grivetti, *Clarke College*

Ken Horii, *Rhode Island School of Design*

Imi Hwangbo, *University of Louisville*

Michelle Illuminato, *Bowling Green State University*

Ann Baddeley Keister, *Grand Valley State University*

Margaret Keller, *St. Louis Community College*

Dan Lowery, *Southwestern Illinois College*

Karen Mahaffy, *University of Texas at San Antonio*

Richard Moses, *University of Illinois*

Gary Nemcosky, *Appalachian State University*

Helen Maria Nugent, *Art Institute of Chicago*

Rick Paul, *Purdue University*

Ron Saito, *California State University, Northridge*

Karen Schory, *Johnson County Community College*

Susan Slavick, *Carnegie Mellon University*

Paul Wittenbraker, *Grand Valley State University*

William Zack, *Ball State University*

Finally, the McGraw-Hill team has been knowledgeable, supportive, and enthusiastic. Senior Editor Joe Hanson has contributed a great deal to the book design, continually expanded the use of new technologies, and enthusiastically promoted the book at every opportunity. Developmental Editor Cynthia Ward encouraged me to pursue a wide range of revisions, and the book is greatly improved as a result. Editorial assistants Torii Yamada and Elizabeth Sigal have been prompt and helpful throughout the process. Designer Kim Menning and layout genius Glenda King greatly increased the visual impact of the book. As head of the photo research team, Alexandra Ambrose was prompt, inventive, and helpful. Project Manager Cathy Iammartino and Executive Marketing Manager Suzanna Ellison were highly accessible, enthusiastic, and consistently supportive. Bonnie Mitchell and her Creative-Myndz team have been resilient, dedicated, and endlessly inventive in their approach to the CD-ROM.

Mary Stewart

Preface   viii
Introduction   6

part one

Two-Dimensional Design

chapter one
Basic Elements   18

chapter two
The Element of Color   52

chapter three
Principles of Two-Dimensional Design   78

part two

Concepts and Critical Thinking

chapter four
Cultivating Creativity   116

chapter five
Problem Seeking and Problem Solving   128

chapter six
Developing Critical Thinking   146

chapter seven
Constructing Meaning   164

part three

Three-Dimensional Design

chapter eight
Elements of Three-Dimensional Design   180

chapter nine
Principles of Three-Dimensional Design   220

chapter ten
Materials and Methods   242

chapter eleven
Physical and Cerebral   260

part four

Time Design

chapter twelve
Aspects of Elements of Time   292

chapter thirteen
Narrative and Non-Narrative   322

chapter fourteen
Interdisciplinary Arts   345

Key Readings   371
Notes   375
Glossary   377
Photo Credits   387
Index   397

Preface   vii

A Guide to the *Core Concepts in Art* CD-ROM   xviii

Introduction: Beginner's Mind, Open Mind   6

Defining *Design*   9

Two-Dimensional Design

chapter one
Basic Elements   18

LINE   18
Defining Line   18
Line Quality   18
Actual Lines   20
Implied Lines   22
Line Networks   23
Using Line   25
Key Questions   26

SHAPE   26
Defining Shape   26
Types of Shape   28
Degrees of Representation   32
Degrees of Definition   34
Using Shape   35
Key Questions   37

TEXTURE   37
Types of Texture   37
Creating Texture   38
Texture and Space   38
Trompe L'Oeil   40
Combining Physical and Visual Texture   40
Marks and Meanings   42
Key Questions   42

VALUE   43
Contrast   43
Value Distribution   44
Value and Volume   46
Value and Space   46
Value and Lighting   47
Key Questions   48

Summary, Keywords   49

Profile: Philla Yi, Printmaker   50

chapter two
The Element of Color   52

COLOR THEORY   52

COLOR PHYSICS   53
Color and Light   54
Using Additive Color   54
Using Subtractive Color   55

COLOR INTERACTION   55

DEFINING COLOR   57
Hue   57
Value   58
Intensity   60
Key Questions   63

COLOR SCHEMES   62
Monochromatic   62
Analogous   62
Complementary   63
Split Complementary   63
Triadic   64
Chromatic Grays and Earth Colors   64
Using Disharmony   65
Key Questions   66

COMPOSING WITH COLOR   67
Creating the Illusion of Space   67
Weight and Balance   68
Distribution and Proportion   68
Color as Emphasis   69

COLOR, EMOTION, AND EXPRESSION   70
Color Keys   72
Symbolic Color   72
Expressive Color   74

Summary, Keywords   75

Profile: Ann Baddeley Keister, Fiber Artist   76

chapter three
Principles of Two-Dimensional Design   78

UNITY AND VARIETY   78
Gestalt: Theory and Application   80
Patterns and Grids   85
Key Questions   87

BALANCE   87
Weight and Gravity   87
Symmetrical Balance   89
Radial Symmetry   90
Asymmetrical Balance   90
Expressive Uses of Balance   93
Key Questions   94

SCALE AND PROPORTION   94

RHYTHM   95

EMPHASIS   96
Emphasis by Isolation   96
Emphasis by Placement   97
Emphasis Through Contrast   97
Key Questions   99

CREATING THE ILLUSION OF SPACE   99
Linear Perspective   100
Other Ways to Create the Illusion of Space   103
Using of Illusion of Space   103
Key Questions   105

DYNAMIC SPACE: CONSTRUCTING *MULAN*   105

THE ILLUSION OF MOVEMENT   107
The Kinesthetic Response   107
The Decisive Moment   107
Before and After   108
Multiplication   108
Key Questions   110

DETERMINING PRIORITIES   109

Summary, Keywords   110

Profile: Ken Stout, Painter   111

PART ONE MULTIMEDIA RESOURCES   113

part one

Concepts and Critical Thinking

chapter four
Cultivating Creativity 116

DESIGN AND CREATIVITY 116

SEVEN CHARACTERISTICS OF CREATIVE THINKING 116
Receptivity 117
Curiosity 117
Wide Range of Interests 117
Attentiveness 117
Connection Seeking 117
Conviction 117
Complexity 117

GOAL-SETTING 118
A Goal-Setting Strategy 119
Characteristics of Good Goals 120

TIME MANAGEMENT 120
Set the Stage 121
Prioritize 121
See the Big Picture 121
Work Sequentially 121
Use Parts to Create the Whole 121
Make the Most of Class Time 121
Start Early 122
When in Doubt, Crank It Out 122
Work Together 122
Reduce Stress 123

Summary 124

Profile: Nancy Callahan, Artist, and Diane Gallo, Writer 126

chapter five
Problem Seeking and Problem Solving 128

PROBLEM SEEKING 128
The Design Process 128
The Fine Art Process 130
Sources of Ideas 130
Characteristics of a Good Problem 132

CONVERGENT AND DIVERGENT THINKING 133
Using Convergent Thinking 133
Using Divergent Thinking 135

BRAINSTORMING 136
Make a List 136
Use a Thesaurus 137
Explore Connections 137
Keep a Journal 138

VISUAL RESEARCH 139
Thumbnail Sketches 139
Model Making 139

VARIATIONS ON A THEME 141

AN OPEN MIND 143

Summary, Keywords 143

Profile: Heidi Lasher-Oakes, Sculptor 144

chapter six
Developing Critical Thinking 146

ESTABLISHING CRITERIA 146

FORM, SUBJECT, AND CONTENT 147

STOP, LOOK, LISTEN, LEARN 147

TYPES OF CRITIQUES 148
Description 148
Cause and Effect 149
Compare and Contrast 149
Greatest Strength/Unrealized Potential 151

DEVELOPING A LONG-TERM PROJECT 152
Week One Assessment 152
Week Two Assessment 153
Developing A Self-Assignment 153
Self-Assignment: Jason Chin The Mythological Alphabet 154

TURN UP THE HEAT: PUSHING YOUR PROJECT'S POTENTIAL 156
Basic Arithmetic 156
Transformation 157
Reorganization 159

CONCEPT AND COMPOSITION 159

ACCEPTING RESPONSIBILITY 160

Summary, Keywords 161

Profile: Bob Dacey, Illustrator 162

chapter seven
Constructing Meaning 164

BUILDING BRIDGES 164
Shared Language 164
Iconography 165
Audience 166
Immediacy 166
Stereotypes 168
Clichés 168
Surprise 168
Key Questions 169

PURPOSE AND INTENT 169

CONTEXT 170

CONNECTIONS 171

DRAMA 173

AESTHETICS AND ANESTHETICS 173

Summary, Keywords 174

Profile: Ken Botnick, Graphic Designer 175

PART TWO MULTIMEDIA RESOURCES 177

part two

Three-Dimensional Design

part three

chapter eight

Elements of Three-Dimensional Design   180

DEFINING FORM   180

FORM AND FUNCTION   181

ORTHOGRAPHIC PROJECTION   182

DEGREES OF DIMENSIONALITY   184
  Relief   184
  Three-Quarter Works   184
  Freestanding Works   184
  Environmental Works   184

LINE   187
  Line Quality   188
  Actual Lines   191
  Implied Lines   192
  Line Networks   192
  Key Questions   193

PLANE   194
  Key Questions   195

VOLUME   195

MASS   197
  Key Questions   197

SPACE   198
  Positive and Negative   198
  Compression and Expansion   201
  Activated Space   201
  Entering Space   203
  Key Questions   203

TEXTURE   204
  Degrees of Texture   204
  Characteristic and Contradictory Textures   204
  The Implications of Texture   205
  Key Questions   206

LIGHT   206
  Value and Volume   206
  Striking a Surface   206
  Ambient and Directed Light   208
  Light as Sculpture   208
  Key Questions   210

COLOR   211
  Degrees of Harmony   211
  Contrast   212
  Color and Emotion   212
  Symbolic Color   213
  Key Questions   214

TIME   214

THE COMPLEXITY OF THREE-DIMENSIONAL DESIGN   215

Summary, Keywords   215, 216

Profile: Rodger Mack, Sculptor   217

chapter nine

Principles of Three-Dimensional Design   220

UNITY AND VARIETY   221
  Increasing Unity   221
  Combining Unifying Forces   224
  Increasing Variety   224
  Degrees of Unity   224
  Grid and Matrix   226
  Key Questions   226

BALANCE   227
  Key Questions   230

SCALE   231

PROPORTION   231
  Key Questions   232

EMPHASIS   233
  Emphasis by Isolation   233
  Emphasis through Contrast   234
  Key Questions   235

REPETITION AND RHYTHM   235
  Key Questions   238

Summary, Keywords   239

Profile: David MacDonald, Ceramicist   240

chapter ten

Materials and Methods   242

CHOICE OF MATERIALS   242
  Increasing Material Strength   243
  Methods of Construction   246

CONNECTIONS   248

TRANSITIONS   250

TRADITIONAL MATERIALS, CONTEMPORARY USES   250
  Stone   250
  Wood   251
  Metals   252
  Clay   252
  Glass   252
  Fibers   253
  Plastics   254

STUDENT MATERIALS   255
  Boards   255
  Glues   255
  Tapes   255

MATERIALS AND MEANINGS   255
  Key Questions   256

Summary, Keywords   257

Profile: Todd Slaughter, Sculptor   258

chapter eleven

Physical and Cerebral   260

CONSTRUCTED THOUGHT   261
  From Life to Art   261
  Degrees of Representation   261
  Boundaries   264
  Bases and Places   266
  Key Questions   268

PHYSICAL FORCES   269
  Weight and Gravity   269
  Compression and Expansion   270
  Tension and Torsion   271
  Presence and Absence   272
  Process and Product   273

CEREBRAL QUALITIES OF SCULPTURAL OBJECTS   275
  Building on a Tradition   275
  Reinventing Sculpture   275

CONTEMPORARY QUESTIONS, CONTEMPORARY ANSWERS   276
  Sculpture as Place   276
  Sculpture as Journey   278
  Sculpture as Time   280
  Sculpture as Self   282

EXPRESSING IDEAS IN PHYSICAL FORM   284
  Key Questions   284

Summary, Keywords   284

Profile: Rick Paul, Sculptor   285

PART THREE MULTIMEDIA RESOURCES   289

Time Design

chapter twelve

Aspects and Elements of Time   292

BUILDING BLOCKS   294
   Relationships   295
   Transitions   296
   Key Questions   298

DURATION   298
   Key Questions   299

TEMPO   299
   Key Questions   301

INTENSITY   301
   Key Questions   302

SCOPE   302
   Key Questions   304

SETTING   305
   Objects and Implications   305
   Setting and Actor   307
   Sound: The Hidden
     Dimension   308
   Key Questions   310

CHRONOLOGY   310
   Key Questions   312

SCHINDLER'S LIST: CONTENT AND COMPOSITION   313

Summary, Keywords   318

Profile: Sharon Greytak,
   Filmmaker   319

chapter thirteen

Narrative and Non-Narrative   322

TELL ME A STORY   322

WORKING WITH MULTIPLE IMAGES   323
   Multiple Image Structures   324
   From Scene to Screenplay   326

ESTABLISHING BOUNDARIES   327
   Conceptual Boundaries   327
   Developing a Story   328
   Emotional Boundaries   328
   Style   330

CAUSALITY   331

STORY AND STYLE IN *CITIZEN KANE*   333
   The Opening Sequence   333
   Conflict   334
   The Closing Sequence   335

THE 15-SECOND NARRATIVE   337

NON-NARRATIVE   341
   Key Questions   344

Summary, Keywords   344

Profile: Jerome Witkin,
   Painter   346

chapter fourteen

Interdisciplinary Arts   348

EXPLORING THE VISUAL BOOK   348
   Selecting a Text   352
   Writing a Text   355
   Text and Type Style   356
   Word and Image
     Relationships   358
   Advantages of Visual
     Books   358
   Key Questions   358

INSTALLATION ART   359
   Uses of Space and Time   359
   The Importance of Context   360
   Advantages of Installation
     Art   362
   Key Questions   362

PERFORMANCE ART   362
   Historical Background   363
   Characteristics of Performance
     Art   363
   Key Questions   365

ADVANTAGES OF INTERDISCIPLINARY ART   366

Summary, Keywords   366

Profile: Abelardo Morell,
   Photographer   367

PART FOUR MULTIMEDIA RESOURCES   369

part four

A Guide to *Core Concepts in Art* CD-ROM, Version 3.0

 GETTING STARTED

System Requirements

In order to run this CD-ROM properly, please make sure that your computer meets the minimum system requirements:

WINDOWS

- Intel Pentium II 200
- 128 MB RAM (64 MB available RAM)
- Windows 95/98, 2000, XP, or NT 4.0+
- 4x (or better) CD-ROM drive
- SVGA or higher monitor with 800x600 resolution running 16-bit color

MACINTOSH OSX

- G3 running 10.1 or better
- 128 MG of available RAM
- Color monitor with 800x600 resolution running 16-bit color

MACINTOSH CLASSIC

- Power Macintosh 180 (G3 recommended)
- 128 MG of available RAM
- System 8.6 or later
- 4x (or better) CD-ROM drive
- Color monitor with 800x600 resolution running 16-bit color
- Sound capability

QuickTime Requirements

QuickTime is required to run the program. You can click the InstallQuicktime.html file on this CD-ROM, which will bring you directly to the Apple QuickTime website, where you can download the program. The website is www.apple.com/quicktime/download

Starting the CD-ROM

Follow these steps to install the CD-ROM and begin working with the program:

WINDOWS

1. Insert the CD into the CD-ROM drive.
2. Double click on My Computer on your desktop.
3. Double click on the CD-ROM drive, most commonly called the D:/drive.
4. Double click on the Start_HerePC.exe file from the CD-ROM.

MACINTOSH

1. Insert the CD into the CD-ROM drive.
2. Double click on the "Launching the Imagination" CD-ROM.
3. Double click on the Start_Here (OSX) or Start_Here (Classic) file from the CD-ROM. Use Start_Here (OSX) for Macintosh 0SX 10.1 or higher, and Start_Here (Classic) for System 9.2 or lower.

If you need help installing this program, please call 1-800-331-5094 between 9am and 5pm EST.

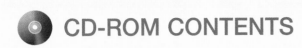

CD-ROM CONTENTS

The five icons on the main menu correspond to the five components of the *Core Concepts in Art* CD-ROM.

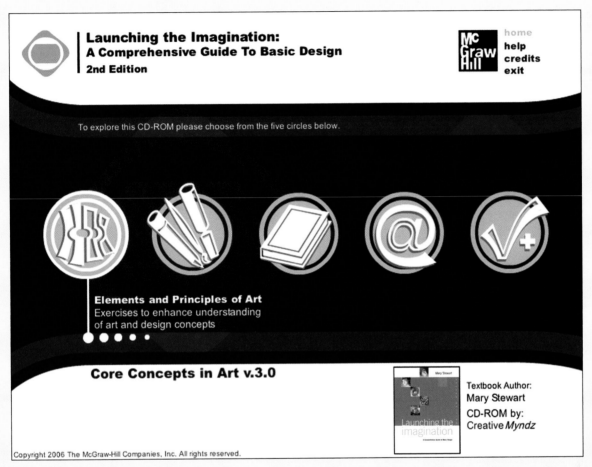

Launching the Imagination:
A Comprehensive Guide To Basic Design
2nd Edition

home
help
credits
exit

To explore this CD-ROM please choose from the five circles below.

Elements and Principles of Art
Exercises to enhance understanding
of art and design concepts

Core Concepts in Art v.3.0

Textbook Author:
Mary Stewart
CD-ROM by:
Creative *Myndz*

Main menu of *Core Concepts in Art*

Elements and Principles of Art

Explore the elements of 2D, 3D, and time design through interactive exercises and animated demonstrations. Experiment with the principles of unity and variety, pattern and rhythm, balance, scale and proportion, emphasis and focal point, and illusion of space.

Art Techniques

Observe techniques for painting, sculpture, printmaking, glass, jewelry, photography, and new media in a series of video demonstrations.

Chapter Resources

Review the content of each chapter in *Launching the Imagination*, Second Edition, in this section of the CD-ROM.

More extensive chapter review materials are also available at the McGraw-Hill **Online Learning Center** (www.mhhe.com/launching2), which can be launched from the Internet Resources section.

Internet Resources

This section is helpful if you are new to using the Internet for research. It offers basic "how-to's" on using the Web, along with an introduction to computer terminology and netiquette.

Study Skills Primer

Applicable to all your courses, this primer offers tips on study and organizational skills. It also includes advice on documenting sources.

You can also access the McGraw-Hill **Online Learning Center** through a link in this section.

EXPLORING ELEMENTS, PRINCIPLES, AND TECHNIQUES

The following screen shots are examples of the types of demonstrations and interactive exercises found in the CD-ROM. For a guide to correlating the CD-ROM with this text, see the "Multimedia Resources" pages at the end of every part.

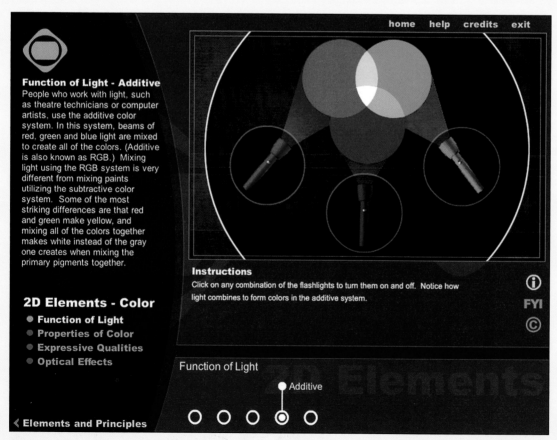

Function of Light - Additive
People who work with light, such as theatre technicians or computer artists, use the additive color system. In this system, beams of red, green and blue light are mixed to create all of the colors. (Additive is also known as RGB.) Mixing light using the RGB system is very different from mixing paints utilizing the subtractive color system. Some of the most striking differences are that red and green make yellow, and mixing all of the colors together makes white instead of the gray one creates when mixing the primary pigments together.

2D Elements - Color
● Function of Light
● Properties of Color
● Expressive Qualities
● Optical Effects

home   help   credits   exit

Instructions
Click on any combination of the flashlights to turn them on and off. Notice how light combines to form colors in the additive system.

Function of Light
● Additive

‹ Elements and Principles

An interactive activity that allows you to experiment with additive color, found in "Elements and Principles of Art"

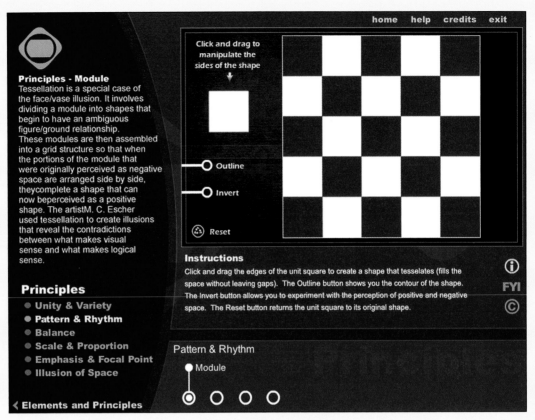

Click and drag to manipulate the sides of the shape

○ Outline

○ Invert

⊛ Reset

Principles - Module
Tessellation is a special case of the face/vase illusion. It involves dividing a module into shapes that begin to have an ambiguous figure/ground relationship. These modules are then assembled into a grid structure so that when the portions of the module that were originally perceived as negative space are arranged side by side, theycomplete a shape that can now beperceived as a positive shape. The artistM. C. Escher used tessellation to create illusions that reveal the contradictions between what makes visual sense and what makes logical sense.

Principles

- Unity & Variety
- **Pattern & Rhythm**
- Balance
- Scale & Proportion
- Emphasis & Focal Point
- Illusion of Space

⟨ **Elements and Principles**

Instructions
Click and drag the edges of the unit square to create a shape that tesselates (fills the space without leaving gaps). The Outline button shows you the contour of the shape. The Invert button allows you to experiment with the perception of positive and negative space. The Reset button returns the unit square to its original shape.

ⓘ
FYI
©

Pattern & Rhythm

● Module

◉ ○ ○ ○

An interactive activity that allows you to experiment with positive and negative space, found in "Elements and Principles of Art"

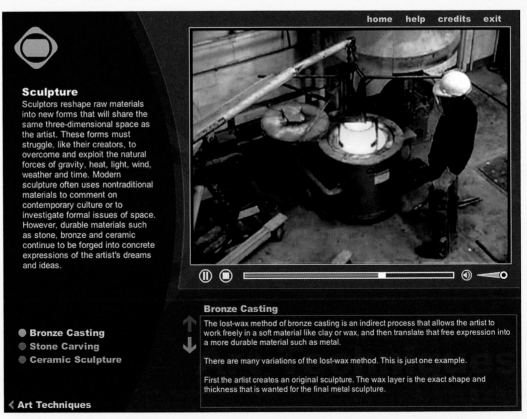

Sculpture
Sculptors reshape raw materials into new forms that will share the same three-dimensional space as the artist. These forms must struggle, like their creators, to overcome and exploit the natural forces of gravity, heat, light, wind, weather and time. Modern sculpture often uses nontraditional materials to comment on contemporary culture or to investigate formal issues of space. However, durable materials such as stone, bronze and ceramic continue to be forged into concrete expressions of the artist's dreams and ideas.

● **Bronze Casting**
● **Stone Carving**
● **Ceramic Sculpture**

⟨ **Art Techniques**

Bronze Casting

The lost-wax method of bronze casting is an indirect process that allows the artist to work freely in a soft material like clay or wax, and then translate that free expression into a more durable material such as metal.

There are many variations of the lost-wax method. This is just one example.

First the artist creates an original sculpture. The wax layer is the exact shape and thickness that is wanted for the final metal sculpture.

A video demonstration of the lost-wax method of bronze casting, found in "Techniques"

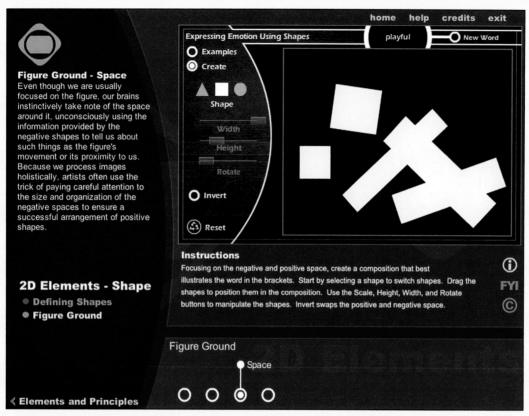

An interactive activity that allows you to experiment with positive and negative space, found in "Elements and Principles of Art"

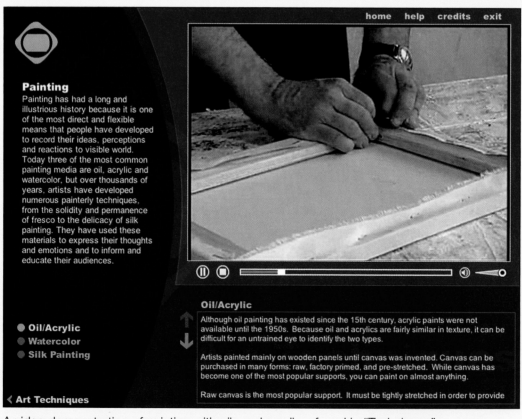

A video demonstration of painting with oils and acrylics, found in "Techniques"

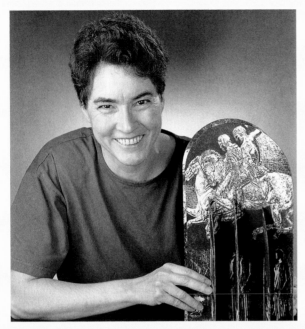

Author Mary Stewart with *Labyrinth* book.

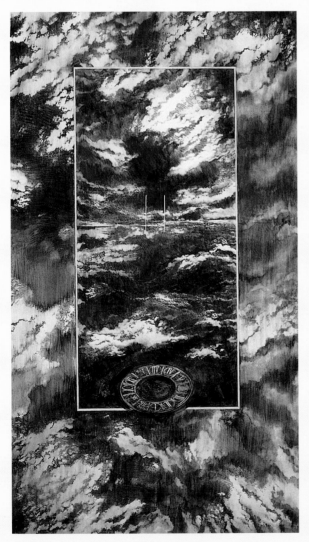

***Learning to Breathe #4,* 1999.** Photocopy transfer and colored pencil. 82″ × 42″.

Author **Mary Stewart** is currently the Foundations Program Coordinator for the School of Art at Northern Illinois University. Strongly committed to first-year students, Stewart has taught Two-Dimensional Design, Three-Dimensional Design, and Drawing for over twenty-five years. She also serves as a Regional Coordinator for Foundations in Art: Theory and Education, a professional organization devoted to excellence in college-level teaching.

As an artist, Stewart uses the dialogs of Plato as a beginning point for visual narratives using drawing, visual books, and computer graphics. *Labyrinth,* shown in the top photo, is composed of eleven etchings based on cave paintings, fragments of early writing, and Greek sculpture. When collapsed, the book presents a cohesive composition; when opened, the images become fragmented, creating a sense of mystery. The second photograph represents *Learning Series,* a twelve-part installation. The size and shape of each drawing suggest a doorway, while photocopies of train stations, water, gates, and architectural ruins suggest the universal nature of memory described by Plato. Stewart is now developing a series of computer animation projects exploring interpretations of reality.

about the author

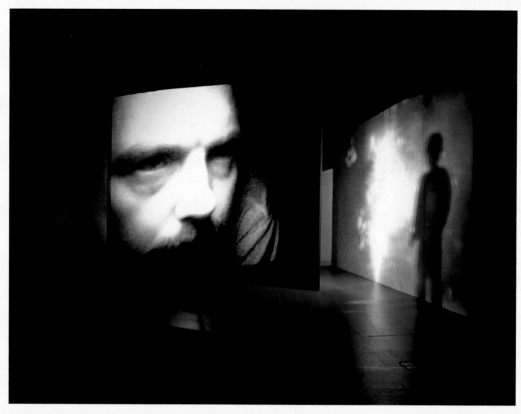

i.1 **Bill Viola**, *Slowly Turning Narrative*, **1992.** Bill Viola's *Slowly Turning Narrative* consists of a large, rotating screen onto which moving images are projected. One side of the screen is a mirror, which reflects distorted images back into the room.

Beginner's Mind, Open Mind

You are ready to embark on a marvelous journey. New technologies and exhibition venues offer dazzling new ways to produce, perform, and publicize visual ideas. Contemporary sculpture has expanded to include performance art and installations (i.1), and metalsmiths now use everything from plastics to precious metals to create inventive small-scale sculptures (i.2). Graphic designers develop many forms of visual communication, from shopping bags and exhibitions (i.3) to Websites, logos, and brochures. Film and video, the most popular forms of public storytelling worldwide, are becoming increasingly integrated with the Internet, which promises to extend visual communication even further (i.4). And, as a result of the extensive experimentation with expression and abstraction in the twentieth century,

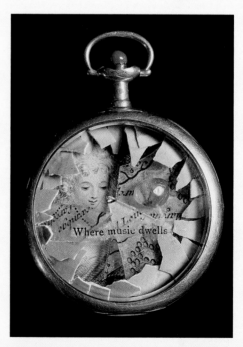

i.2 **Keith E. LoBue**, *Where the Music Dwells*, **1993.** A broken pocket watch can become an evocative artwork when images and words are added.

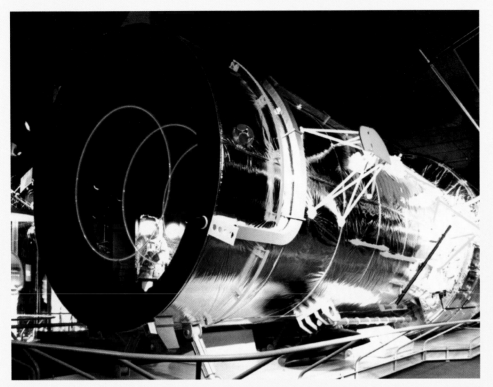

i.3 Bill Cannan & Co., NASA's Participating Exhibit at the 1989 Paris Air Show. To suggest the mystery of space travel and highlight individual displays, this NASA exhibition used dramatic pools of light within a mysterious dark setting.

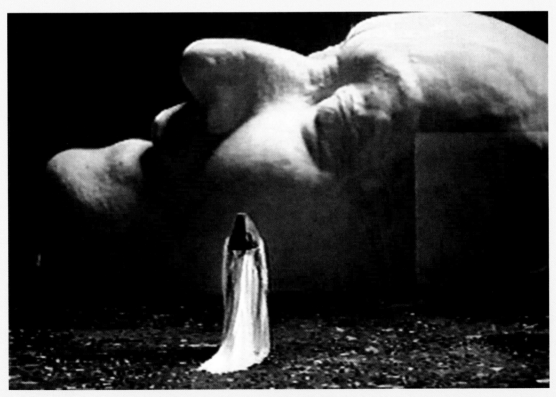

i.4 Hans-Jürgen Syberberg, *Parsifal*, 1982. Syberberg combined live actors with oversized projections of dreamlike landscapes in his filmic interpretation of Richard Wagner's opera.

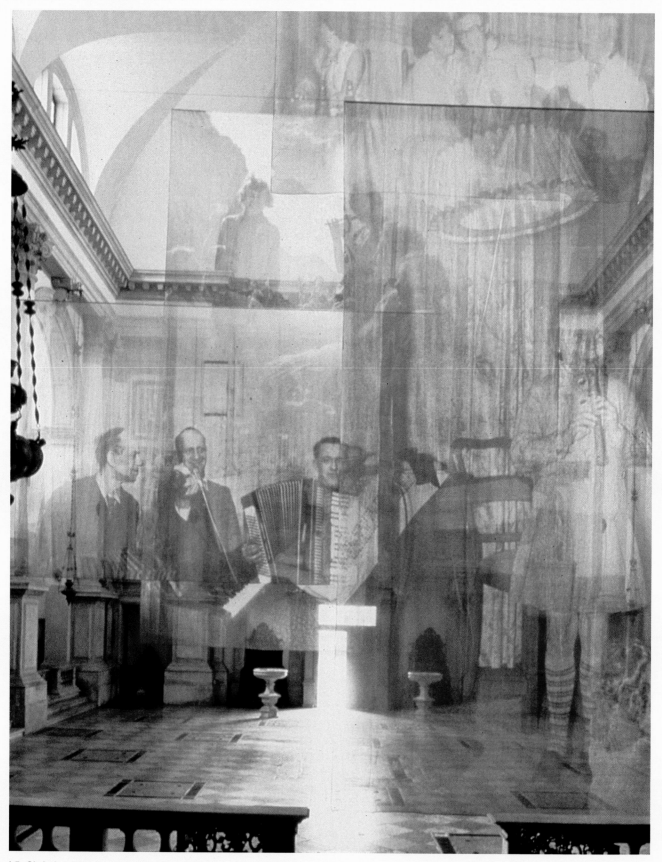

i.5 Christian Marclay, *Amplification,* 1995. The photographic images in this installation shift, fuse, and divide, depending on the position of the viewer.

the traditional arts of painting, printmaking, and photography (i.5) now offer expanded opportunities for introspective thinking and the development of a personal vision. The opportunities for exploration are endless. It is a great time to be studying art and design!

A journey of a thousand miles begins with one step. As a beginner, your first steps are especially important. Free of the preconceptions or habitual patterns that often paralyze more advanced students, beginners enter the learning experience with an open mind and an intense desire to learn. With no reputation to defend, they can more easily make the mistakes that are so essential to learning. Having taught students at all levels (from freshmen to graduate students and beyond), I have found that beginners of any age are the most courageous students by far. The open, unencumbered "beginner's mind" is wonderfully receptive and resilient. As a result, remarkable changes occur during the first year of study.

Defining Design

The ideas and implications of basic design are extensive and complex. The compositions created by fine artists and the designs used in the applied arts are all derived from the same raw material. As a verb, *design* can be defined four ways:

- To plan, delineate, or define, as in designing a building
- To create a deliberate sequence of images or events, as in developing a film storyboard (i.6)

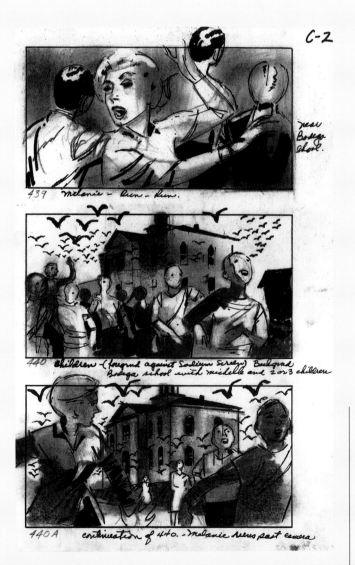

i.6 Harold Michelson, Storyboard for Alfred Hitchcock's *The Birds*. Storyboards are used to plan the sequence of events and compose the specific shots in a film. Alfred Hitchcock, who began his career as an artist, preplanned his films with exacting care.

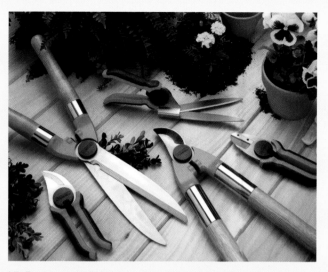

- To create a functional object, as in product design (i.7)
- To organize disparate parts into a coherent whole, as in composing a brochure

As a noun, *design* may be defined as

- A plan or pattern, such as the layout for a garden (i.8)
- An arrangement of lines, shapes, colors, and textures into an artistic whole, as in the composition of a painting or sculpture (i.9)

i.7 Designworks/USA, Home Pro Garden Tool Line. These five gardening tools are all based on the same basic combination of handle, blades, and simple pivot. Variations in proportion determine their use.

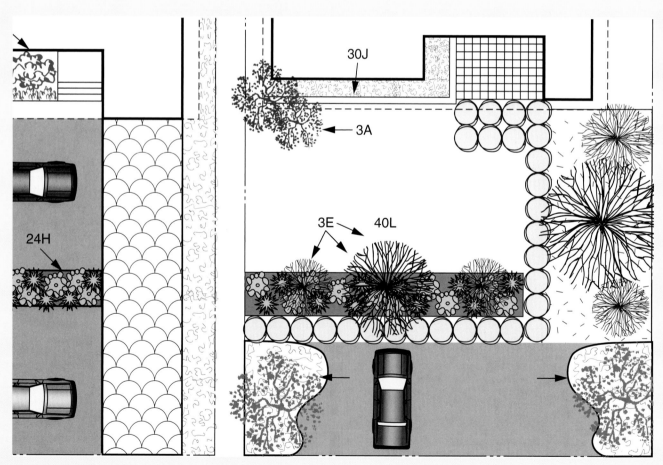

i.8 Garden Design. An extensive layout is generally used for planning a garden. Matching the plants to the soil conditions, setting, climate, and overall intent saves money and improves results. In this case, the design is not an artwork in itself but, rather, a plan of action.

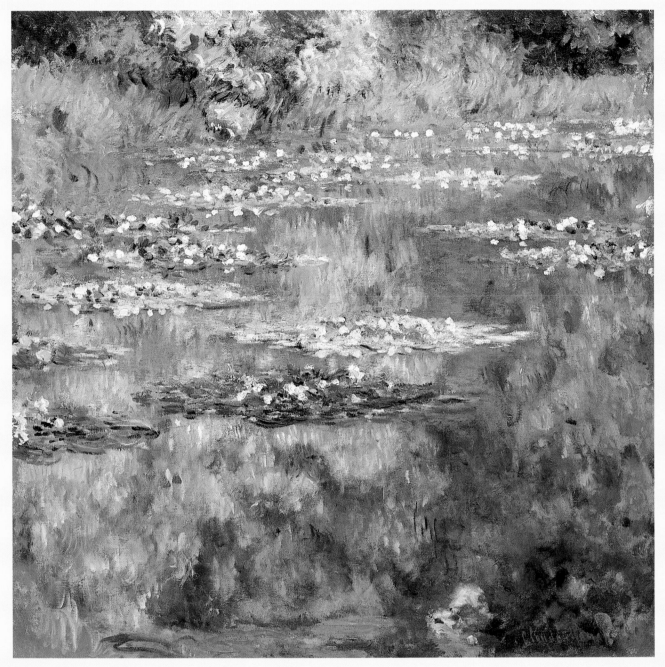

i.9 Claude Monet, *Waterlily Pond (Le Bassin des Nymphéas)*, 1904. Impressionist Claude Monet moved to the village of Giverny in 1883 and built an extensive water garden. The waterlilies he grew there inspired his last major series of paintings. Monet combined lines, shapes, textures, and colors to create a compelling illusion of a shimmering space.

Design is deliberate. Rather than hope for the best and accept the result, artists and designers explore a wide range of solutions to every problem, then choose the most promising option for further development. Even when chance is used to generate ideas, choices are often made before the results are shown. Design creates a bridge between artistic intention and compositional conclusion. As painter Joseph Albers noted, "To design is to plan and to organize, to order, to relate and to control."

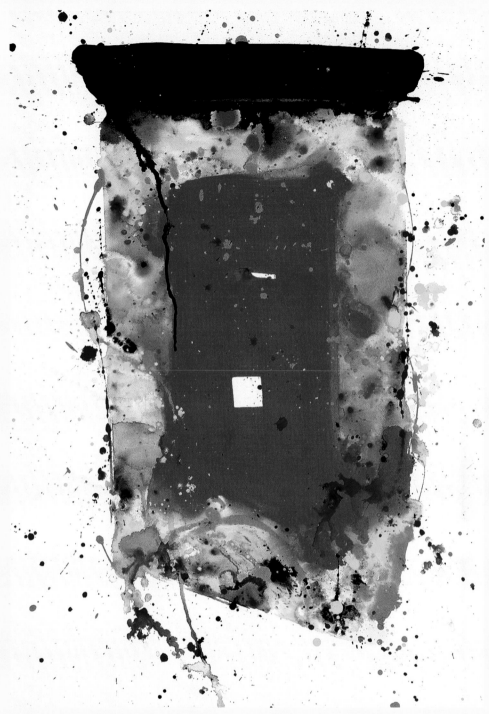

i.10 Sam Francis, *Flash Point,* **1975.** Surrounded by explosive energy, the white square in the center of this painting provides a unifying focal point.

Two-dimensional compositions are constructed from lines, shapes, textures, values, and colors that have been arranged to create a unified whole (i.10). Lines, planes, volumes, masses, and space are the basic components of a three-dimensional composition (i.11). Time design, including video, photography, performance, kinetic sculpture, and the book arts (i.12), is based on the juxtaposition of images and events. A great idea never saved a bad painting. Art and design are visual forms of communication: without careful composition, a great idea may be lost.

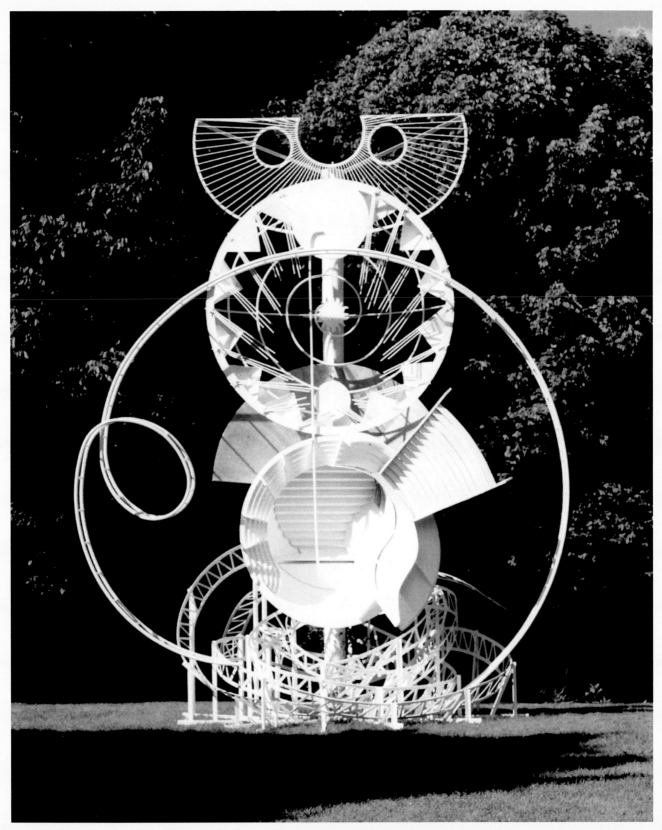

i.11 Alice Aycock, *Tree of Life Fantasy: Synopsis of the Book of Questions Concerning the World Order and/or the Order of Worlds,*
1990–92. Inspired by the double-helix structure of DNA and by medieval illustrations representing the entrance to paradise as a spinning hole in
the sky, Aycock has combined a linear structure with a series of circular planes and a lot of open space. The resulting sculpture is as open and
playful as a roller coaster.

i.12 **Paul Jenkins and Jae Lee, from** *Inhumans:* **"First Contact," March 1999.** Comic books, like films, rely on the development of characters, the use of "camera" angles, and the organization of multiple images.

Developing a wide range of solutions to every problem is the quickest way to master composition. Small, quick studies are often used to explore the possibilities. By translating a mental image into a rough sketch, you can immediately see whether the idea has potential. Furthermore, the best way to have a good idea is to have a lot of ideas (i.13). If you explore only one idea, you are far less likely to produce an inventive image. By selecting the best rough composition from 20 sketches, you will have a good beginning point for your final design.

In the pages that follow, the basic elements, principles, and implications of design are ex-

plored in depth. Over 600 images supply visual examples from many cultures and in all areas of art and design. Fourteen interviews with living artists provide insight into the creative process.

Reading this book, however, is just the first step. True understanding comes through your own efforts, combined with the direction your teachers can provide. Remember that basic drawing and design courses provide the foundation on which all subsequent courses are built. You are only a beginner once in your entire life: this is not a rehearsal. By using your time well, you really *can* get the rocket off the launching pad.

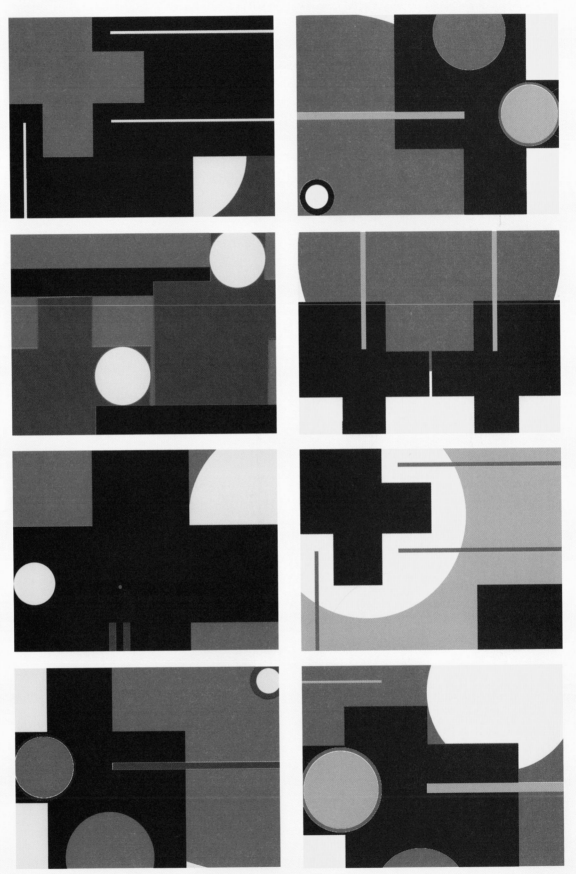

i.13 Mary Stewart, *Formal Relationships* **(Exercise), 2001.** The relationships among the parts and the whole determine the visual quality of a design. To explore a wide range of relationships, artists and designers often complete many small studies before developing more elaborate work.

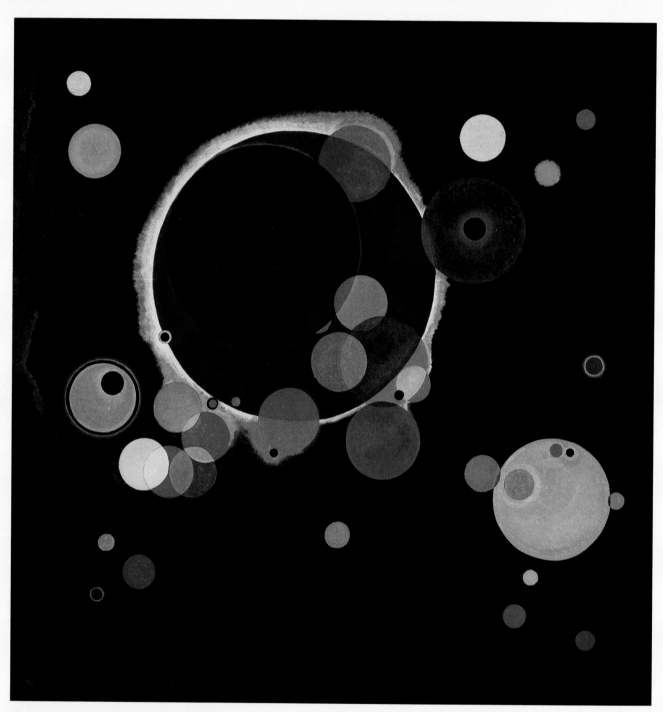

Wassily Kandinsky, *Several Circles,* **1926.** Oil on canvas, 55¼ × 55⅝ in. (140.3 × 140.7 cm).

Two-Dimensional Design

The careful observation required for drawing, the understanding of color required for watercolor painting, and the craftsmanship required for metalsmithing can increase awareness of ourselves and our world. On a personal level, making art heightens our attention, engages our emotions, and provides a sense of accomplishment. Creating objects and images is engrossing and exhilarating. These personal rewards make art one of the most popular hobbies.

The professional artist or designer must translate personal insights into public communication. No one will pay for the production of meaningless images. The ideas and emotions a professional wishes to express must engage an audience, whether the communication occurs in the silence of a museum or in the chaos of a city street.

This ability to communicate visually is developed through years of study plus relentless practice. Artists and designers must develop their visual awareness, develop engaging ideas, and master various techniques. They spend hours in the studio, refining ideas and inventing alternative solutions to visual problems.

A journey of one thousand miles begins with one step. In the chapters that follow, we will define the elements and principles of two-dimensional design and explore their expressive qualities. Line, shape, texture, and value are presented in Chapter One. Chapter Two is devoted to the characteristics and compositional impact of color. Chapter Three is devoted to the organization of all the elements of design into increasingly complex compositions. These readings can help you build the base of visual knowledge needed for art and design at a personal as well as a professional level.

Part One

chapter one
Basic Elements

chapter two
The Element of Color

chapter three
Principles of Two-Dimensional Design

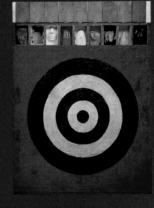

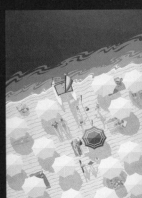

Basic Elements

Line, shape, texture, value, and color are the basic building blocks from which two-dimensional designs are made. Just as oxygen and hydrogen are powerful both individually and when combined as H_2O, so these visual **elements** are powerful both independently and in combination. In this chapter, we will explore the unique characteristics of the four basic elements and analyze their uses in art and design. Color, the most complex element, will be discussed in Chapter Two.

LINE

Defining Line

Line is one of the simplest and most versatile elements of design. Line may be defined as

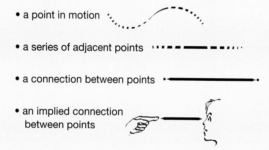

- a point in motion
- a series of adjacent points
- a connection between points
- an implied connection between points

1.1 Despite its apparent simplicity, line can be created in many ways and can play many roles in a design.

The inherent dynamism of line is embodied in the first definition. The remaining three definitions emphasize the connective power of line. Lighter and more fluid than any of the other visual elements, line can add a special energy to a design. Simply by drawing a line, we can activate a space, define a shape, or create a bridge between visual elements.

Line Quality

Each line has its own distinctive quality. This quality is largely determined by the line's orientation, direction, degree of continuity, and by the material used.

    Orientation refers to the line's horizontal, vertical, or diagonal position. Diagonal lines and curving lines are generally the most dynamic (1.2A, 1.2D). Charged with energy, they suggest movement and change. Horizontal lines are typically the most stable, or static (1.2B). Vertical lines imply *potential*

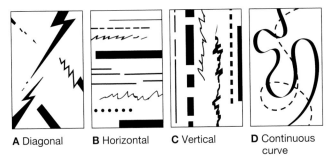

chapter one

A Diagonal   **B** Horizontal   **C** Vertical   **D** Continuous curve

1.2 Line orientation and continuity.

action, and can be static or dynamic, depending on the context in which they are placed (1.2C).

Direction refers to the implied movement of a line. Line weight is often used to accentuate direction. Generally, a swelling line suggests forward or outward movement, while a shrinking line suggests inward movement. Notice how the top and bottom diagonal lines in figure 1.2A seem to push forward as they become thicker.

Continuity, or linear flow, can enhance or reduce direction. As shown in figure 1.2D, a continuous line tends to generate a stronger sense of direction than a broken or jagged line.

Each material can be used to produce a range of distinctive lines. Metallic graphite can be used to produce modulating lines of varying thickness. A felt pen produces a crisp, clean, emphatic line. Charcoal and chalk are black, soft, and highly responsive to each change in pressure and direction. Brush and ink offers even wider variation in line width, continuity, and darkness. By experimenting with the range of marks each instrument can produce, we can use each material more expressively.

A match between line quality and the expressive intent is essential. The network of agitated lines Giacometti used in figure 1.3 suggests anxiety, while the fluid lines in figure 1.4 express movement and energy. Barnett Newman used two very different lines in *Stations of the Cross: Lema Sabachthani, the First Station* (1.5). The solid black line gains stability through its parallel position along the left edge of the painting. In contrast, the line on the right is agitated and exposed, surrounded by open space. In this painting, Newman used just two lines to express both spiritual strength and human fragility.

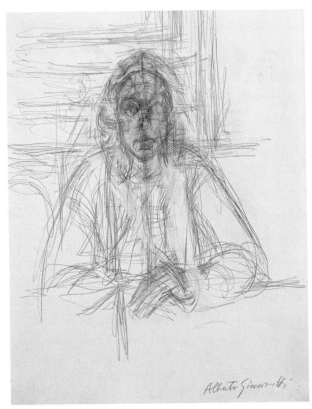

1.3 Alberto Giacometti, *Annette*, 1954. Pencil on paper, 16⅜ × 11¾ in. (41.59 × 29.85 cm).

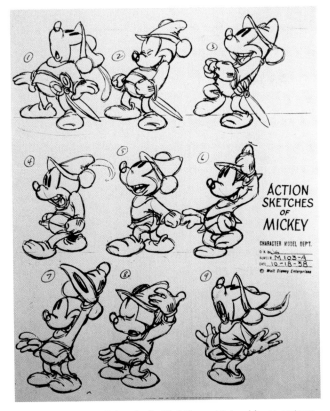

1.4 This is an original sketch of a Walt Disney Mickey Mouse cartoon done by Walt Disney artists Frank Thomas and Ollie Johnston.

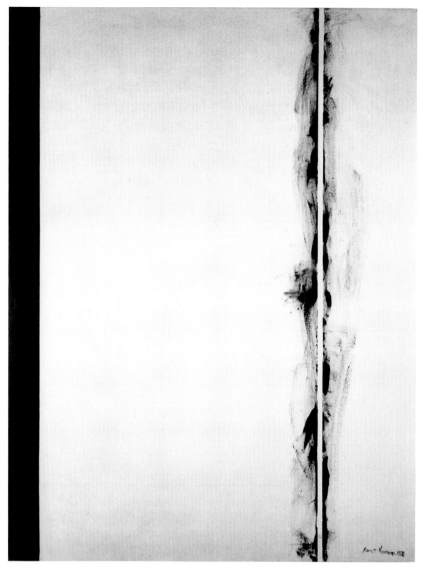

1.5 Barnett Newman, *Stations of the Cross: Lema Sabachthani, The First Station,* 1958. Magna on canvas, 6 ft 5⅝ in. × 5 ft ½ in. (1.98 × 1.54 cm).

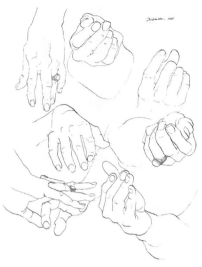

1.6 Eleanor Dickinson, *Study of Hands,* 1964. Pen and ink, 13⅛ × 10⅛ in. (34 × 26 cm).

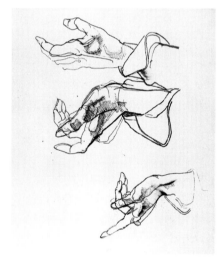

1.7 Rico Lebrun, *Hand,* 1964. Pen and ink.

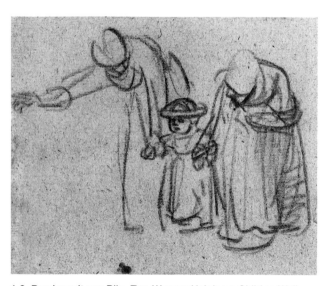

1.8 Rembrandt van Rijn, *Two Women Helping a Child to Walk,* c. 1635–37. Black chalk.

Actual Lines

Actual lines can describe complex forms simply and eloquently. In figure 1.6, Eleanor Dickinson used pen and ink **contour lines** to define both the inner and outer edges of a woman's hands. Through contour drawing, the complex anatomy was distilled down to a few simple lines. Similarly, Rico Lebrun's **gesture drawing** of a hand (1.7) captures essential action rather than describing anatomical detail. We focus on what the hand is *doing* rather than on what the hand *is*. As shown in figure 1.8, Rembrandt often used economical lines to describe

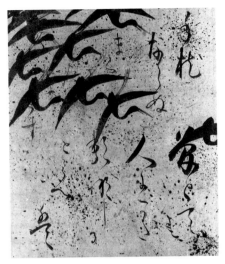

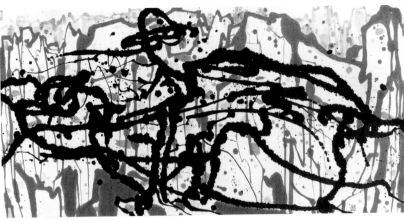

1.10 Wu Guanzhong, *Pine Spirit*, **1984.** Chinese ink, color on paper, 2 ft 3⅝ in. × 5 ft 3½ in. (70 × 140 cm).

1.9 Attributed to Tawaraya Sôtatsu, calligraphy by Hon'ami Koetsu, *Flying Cranes and Poetry*, Edo period (1615–1868). Ink on gray-blue paper, gold flecked, 7⅝ × 6⅜ in. (19 × 16 cm).

the spheres and cylindrical volumes from which figures are made. Because it communicates information using basic volumes, this type of line drawing is often called a **volume summary.**

Calligraphic lines can add even more energy to a drawing or a design. The word *calligraphy* is derived from two Greek words: *kalus*, meaning "beautiful," and *graphein*, meaning "to write." Like handwriting, the calligraphic line is both personal and highly expressive. In figure 1.9, words and images are combined in a celebration of flight. Painter Tawaraya Sôtatsu and calligrapher Hon'ami Koetsu used variations in line weight and continuity to suggest the graceful motion of birds. This exploration of movement is pushed even further in *Pine Spirit*, by Wu Guanzhong (1.10). Fluid ink lines record the movement of the artist's hand while simultaneously creating an abstract landscape. There is a wonderful economy in each of these drawings. Like poetry, the story is told using minimal means.

Organizational lines are often used to create the loose linear "skeleton" on which a composition can be built. Ideas can be developed quickly through line, and compositional changes can be made easily. As shown in the Giacometti drawing in figure 1.3, these skeletal drawings have great energy and may be presented as artworks in themselves. In other cases, organizational lines provide the framework for elaborate compositions. When we analyze Alfred Leslie's *The Killing Cycle* (1.11), we can discern

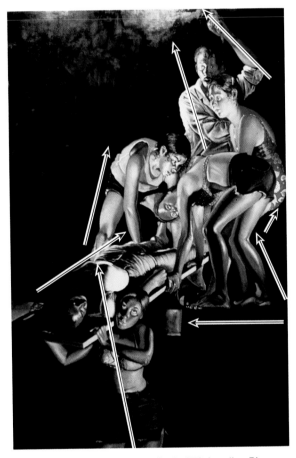

1.11 Alfred Leslie, *The Killing Cycle (#5): Loading Pier*, **1975.** Oil on canvas, 9 × 6 ft (2.7 × 1.8 m).

an underlying framework. A dead man on a diagonal board connects a single woman in the lower left corner to the four figures in the upper right. A horizontal line supports these four figures, while their bent arms and legs create even more diagonal lines. The diagonal lines add energy to the composition, while the horizontal line adds stability.

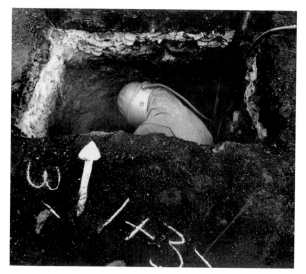

1.12 A series of dots can create an implied line.

1.13 Minor White, *Sandblaster*, San Francisco, 1949. Gelatin silver print, 10⁷⁄₁₆ × 11⁷⁄₁₆ in. (26.51 × 29.05 cm).

Implied Lines

Lines can play a major role in a design even when they are **implied** or suggested, rather than actually being drawn. Because **implied lines** simply *suggest* connections, the viewer must become actively involved in compositions that are constructed using this type of line.

Fortunately, we have a natural inclination to seek visual unity. Given enough clues, we will connect separate visual parts by filling in the missing pieces. The visual clues may be quite obvious. For example, we can easily link the 16 circles in figure 1.12 to create a linear spiral. In other cases, the clues are subtle. In Minor White's *Sandblaster* (1.13), the white arrow implies a connection between the numbers in the foreground and the worker's helmet.

This inclination to connect fragmentary information is called **closure**. "Lost and found" contours require an elegant form of closure. In a "lost and found" composition, the edges of some shapes are clearly defined, while other shapes appear to merge with the background. When presented with such an image, the viewer must create a mental bridge between the resulting islands of information.

The Killing Cycle is an example of a "lost and found" composition. The top four figures are clearly delineated, while the lower two figures begin to merge with the surrounding space. This effect is even more pronounced in Caravaggio's *The Deposition* (1.14A), the painting from which Leslie derived his inspiration. A line drawing of this image has many gaps, as details are lost in the shadows (1.14B). Used skillfully, this loss of definition becomes a strength rather than a weakness. Connections made through closure can stimulate the viewer's imagination by encouraging a more personal interpretation.

A

B

1.14 Caravaggio, *The Deposition*, 1604. Oil on canvas, 9 ft 10⅛ in. × 6 ft 7⅞ in. (3 × 2.03 m).

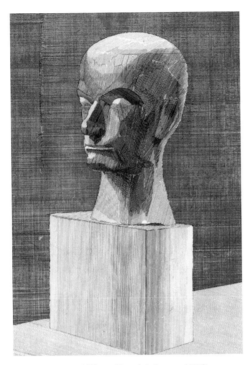

1.15 Jacques Villon, *Baudelaire,* c. 1918. Etching, printed in black, plate 16⅝₁₆ × 11 in. (41.4 × 28 cm).

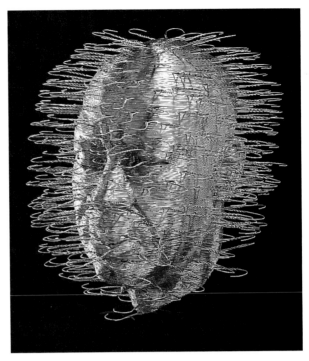

1.16 David Mach, *Eckow,* 1997. Coathangers, 2 ft 2¼ in. × 1 ft 11½ in. × 2 ft 5½ in. (67 × 60 × 75 cm).

Line Networks

Multiple lines and line networks can add detail to a design and create a convincing illusion of space. **Hatching** produces a range of grays through straight parallel lines. Even a wider range of grays can be produced through **cross-hatching,** which creates a more complex network of lines. Jacques Villon used both hatching and cross-hatching in his portrait of poet Charles Baudelaire (1.15). The head is divided into a series of faceted planes. Hatching defines each shift in the surface of the head, while cross-hatching creates the shadows.

Cross-contours can create an even more powerful illusion of three-dimensionality. Often created using curving parallel lines, cross-contours "map" surface variations across shapes or objects. In figure 1.16, David Mach created a cross-contour sculpture by bending coat hangers into the shape of a human head. In two-dimensional design, we can use drawn lines to produce a similar effect.

Hatching, cross-hatching, and cross-contour are often combined. In *Head of a Satyr* (1.17), Michelangelo used all of these techniques to visually carve out the curves and planes of the head.

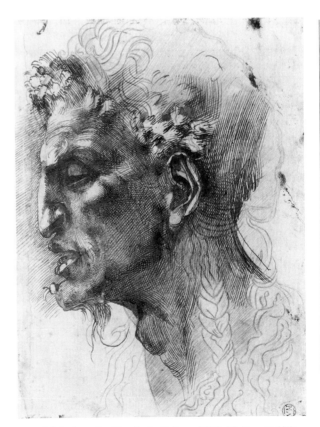

1.17 Michelangelo, *Head of a Satyr,* c.1620–30. Pen and ink over chalk, 10⅝ × 7⅞ in. (27 × 20 cm).

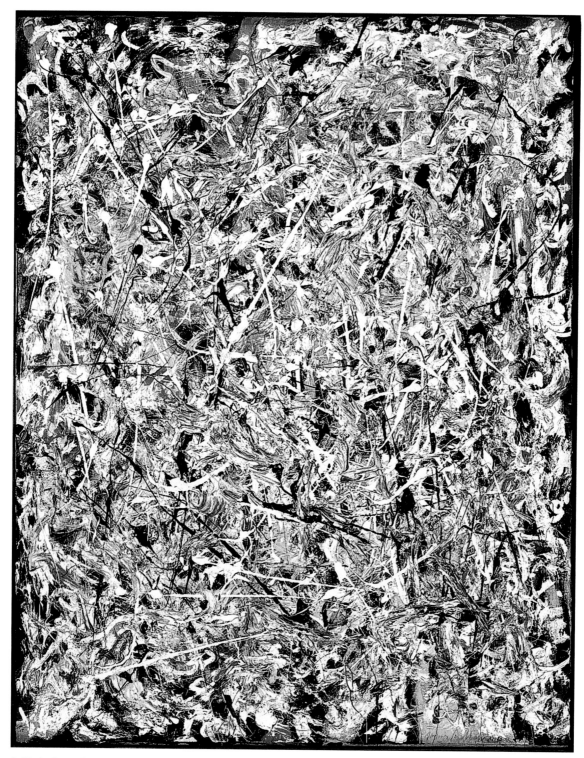

1.18 Jackson Pollack, *White Light,* **1954.** Oil, enamel. aluminum paint on canvas, 48¼ × 38¼ in. (122.4 × 96.9 cm).

Line networks play an equally important role in abstract and nonobjective art. Jackson Pollock dripped and spattered house paint to produce *White Light*, shown in figure 1.18. Seeking universal meaning rather than conventional representation, Pollock spontaneously generated many layers of lines on a large piece of canvas. He then trimmed the canvas, discarding the weaker sections of the design. The remaining lines seem to flow in and out of the painting. Clusters of silvery enamel form swirling, textural masses that are punctuated by explosions of red and yellow.

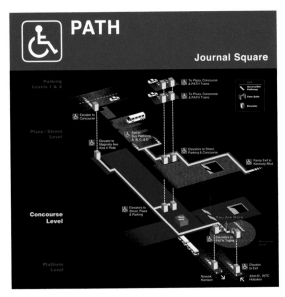

1.19 PATH Station Maps, Louis Nelson Associates, Inc., NY. Graphic designer: Jennifer Stoller.

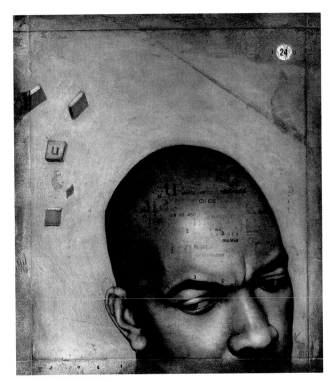

1.20 Joel Peter Johnson, *Self Portrait.* Oil on board, 9 × 8 in. (22.86 × 20.32 cm).

Using Line

Line can be used to define, enclose, connect, or dissect. Line serves all of these purposes in a New York City subway map (1.19). A curved line has been combined with an angular line to define the wheelchair shape. Another line encloses this logo within a square, emphasizing its importance. Diagonal lines connect the subway entrance to the elevators, while vertical lines dissect the drawing to show the location of the elevators. This seemingly simple design communicates complex information clearly. Using this map, a person in a wheelchair can navigate through a busy station and catch the right train.

Careful use of the four edges of a sheet of paper can strengthen any design. In a sense, the first line we draw is actually the *fifth* line in the composition. In his *Self-Portrait* (1.20), Joel Peter Johnson used drawn lines to repeat the four edges of the composition. The resulting box encloses four small shapes on the left and the number on the right. Johnson's head breaks out of this boundary. As a result, the portrait appears to extend beyond the painting's edge and into the world of the viewer.

Lines can serve many purposes at once. In an advertisement for the American Institute of Graphic Artists (1.21), vertical dotted lines at the upper left and lower right highlight the speaker's schedule. A horizontal line creates a connection between the *D* and *B* in the "design to business" logo, and separates the top and bottom of the overall layout. Even

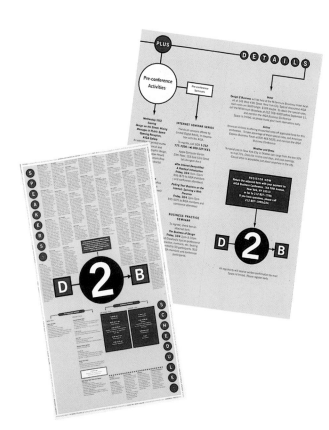

1.21 Brochure from an American Institute of Graphic Arts conference "Design 2 Business, October 5–6 '96 NYC."

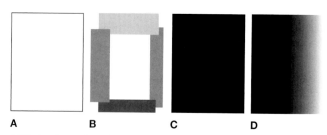

1.22 Any form of enclosure can create a shape.

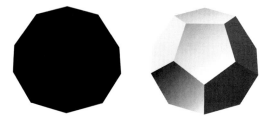

1.23 Variations in lighting can transform a shape into an illusory volume.

the columns of text can be read as vertical and horizontal lines. Despite their apparent simplicity, lines can add structure, movement, and cohesion to all forms of two-dimensional design, from paintings to posters.

SHAPE

Defining *Shape*

A **shape** is a flat, enclosed area (1.22A–D). Shapes can be created by

- Enclosing an area within a continuous line
- Surrounding an area by other shapes
- Filling an area with solid color or texture
- Filling an area with broken color or texture

A three-dimensional enclosure is called a **volume.** Thus, a square is a shape, while a cube is a volume. **Gradation,** or **shading,** can be used to make a two-dimensional shape appear three-dimensional, or volumetric. For example, in figure 1.23, a flat, angular shape becomes a faceted polyhedron when a series of gray tones is added.

Flat or gradated shapes can be used to create an arresting image. In Aaron Douglas' *From Slavery Through Reconstruction* (1.24), flat shapes and transparent targets create an energetic panorama. We can almost hear the speaker in the center

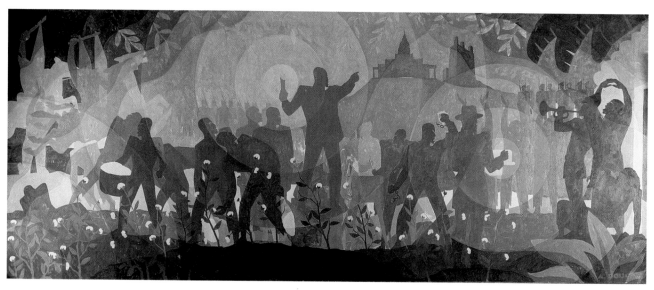

1.24 Aaron Douglas, *Aspects of Negro Life: From Slavery Through Reconstruction*, 1934.
Oil on canvas, 5 ft × 11 ft 7 in. (1.52 × 3.5 m).

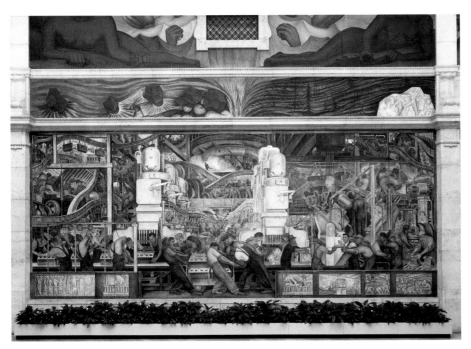

1.25 Diego M. Rivera, *Detroit Industry, north wall,* 1932–33. Fresco, 17 ft 8½ in. × 45 ft (5.4 × 13.7 m).

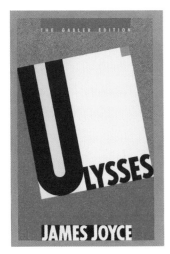

1.26 Cover of *Ulysses,* by James Joyce, 1986. Designer: Carin Goldberg.

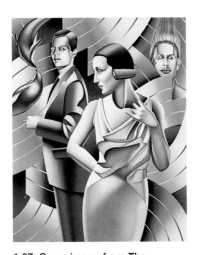

1.27 Cover image from *The Penguin Pool Murder,* a Hildegarde Withers Mystery, by Stuart Palmer. Art Director & Designer: Krystyna Skalski, Illustrator: John Jinks.

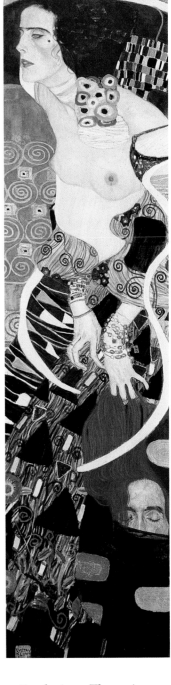

1.28 Gustav Klimt, *Salomé,* 1909. Oil on canvas, 70⅛ × 18⅛ in. (178 × 46 cm).

and feel the movement of the crowd. In Rivera's *Detroit Industry* (1.25), shading and size variation have been combined to suggest volume and increase the illusion of space. One-point perspective (which will be discussed at length in Chapter Three) has been used to increase visual depth in the painting.

Graphic designers are equally aware of the power of both flat and gradated shapes. In a cover for *Ulysses* (1.26), Carin Goldberg used crisp, simple shapes to create a dramatic design. The primary colors of red, yellow, and blue combined with the tilted title block immediately attract attention. Krystyna Skalski and John Jinks used a very different approach for their cover for a mystery novel (1.27). Gradation now suggests a light source and helps to create the illusion of space.

Gustav Klimt combined flat and volumetric shapes to create *Salomé* (1.28). In this horrific tale from the biblical New Testament, John the Baptist has been imprisoned for his criticism of the royal family. Salomé, the king's niece, performs a stunning dance and the delighted king grants her a single wish. In revenge, Salomé asks for John's head. The tall, vertical shape of the painting is similar to the size and shape of a standing viewer. Flat patterns and color surround the volumetric figures, while two curving lines add a sinuous energy to the center of the design.

Types of Shape

The size and shape of a soccer field are very different from the size and shape of a tennis court. In both cases, the playing area defines the game to be played. It is impossible to play soccer on a tennis court or to play tennis on a soccer field.

Similarly, the outer edge of a two-dimensional design provides the playing field for our compositional games. The long, horizontal rectangles used by Douglas and Rivera can create an expansive

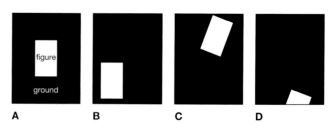

1.29 Various figure/ground relationships.

panorama, while the vertical rectangle used for *Salome* compresses the sordid drama into a narrow, claustrophobic shape. Thus, creating a dialogue between compositional shapes and the surrounding format is our first area of concern.

Figure and Ground, Positive and Negative

As shown in figure 1.29A, a shape that is distinguished from the background is called a **positive shape,** or **figure.** In design, the area around a positive shape is called the **negative shape,** or **ground.** Depending on its location relative to the ground, the figure can become dynamic or static, leaden or buoyant (1.29 B–D).

In highly realistic paintings, the entire composition is treated like a window into an imaginary world. A smooth surface tends to increase this illusion. The canvas texture is sanded down before the paint is applied, and heavy brushstrokes are often kept at a minimum. We are invited to see *into* the painting, rather than focusing on the surface.

When a shaped format is used, we become more aware of the artwork's physicality. The 9-foot-tall teacup in Elizabeth Murray's *Just in Time* (1.30) is monumental in size and loaded with implication. The painted shapes connect directly to the shaped edge, emphasizing the crack running down the center of the composition. This is no ordinary teacup. For Murray, a crack in everyday reality invites entry into an alternative world.

When the figure and ground are equally well designed, every square inch of the composition becomes highly charged. In Bill Brandt's photograph (1.31), the brightly lit arm, face, and breast dramatically divide the black ground,

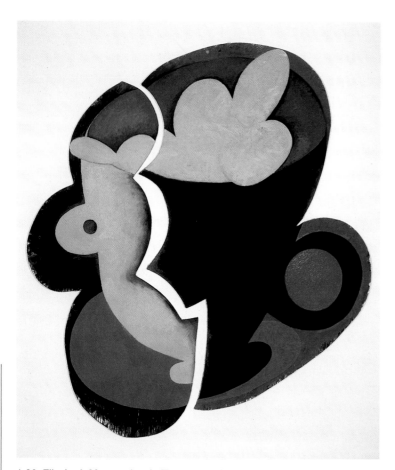

1.30 Elizabeth Murray, *Just in Time,* **1981.** Oil on canvas in two sections, 106 × 97 in. (269.24 × 246.38 cm).

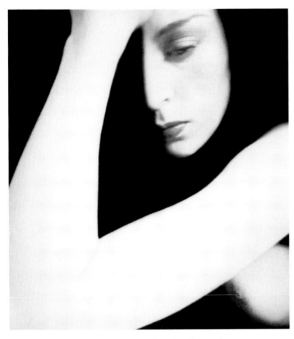

1.31 Bill Brandt, *Nude,* 1952. Gelatin silver print.

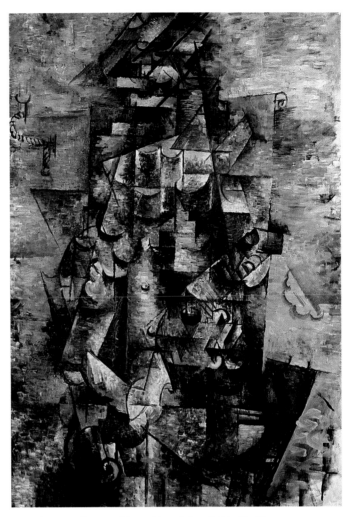

1.32 Georges Braque, *Man with a Guitar,* 1911–12. Oil on canvas, 45¾ × 31⅞ in. (116.2 × 80.9 cm).

creating three strong, triangular shapes. These triangles energize the design and heighten our awareness of the compositional edge.

In a Cubist painting, such as Georges Braque's *Man with a Guitar* (1.32), the figure and ground merge and shift, further activating the dialogue between figure and ground. Seeking a fresh interpretation of time and space, the Cubists shattered the fixed viewpoint required for traditional perspective drawing. Painting this image shortly after Einstein published his general theory of relativity, Braque visually deconstructed solid matter, then reconstructed the composition from the fragments.

Figure/ground reversal occurs when first the positive then the negative shapes command our attention. As shown in a fragment from *Metamorphosis II* (1.33), M. C. Escher was a master of figure/ground reversal. The organic shapes on the left become an interlocking mass of black and white lizards. The lizards then evolve into a network of hexagons. Combined with the figure/ground reversal, this type of metamorphosis animates the entire 13-foot-long composition.

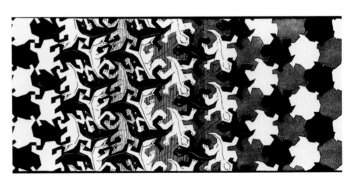

1.33 M. C. Escher, part of *Metamorphosis II,* 1939–40. Woodcut in black, green, and brown, printed from twenty blocks on three combined sheets, 7½ × 153⅜ in. (19 × 390 cm).

SHAPE

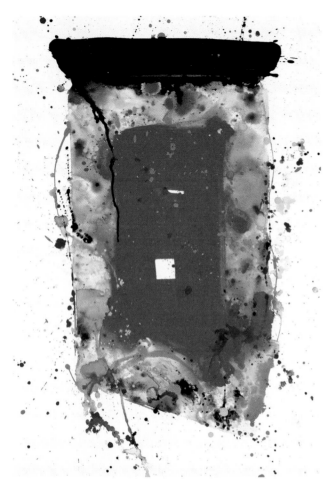

1.34 Sam Francis, *Flash Point*, 1975. Acrylic on paper, 32¼ × 22⅞ in. (82 × 59 cm).

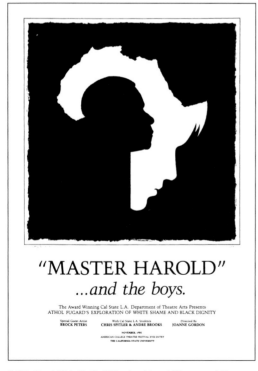

1.35 David McNutt, *"Master Harold" . . . and the Boys*, 1985. Poster.

Figure/ground reversal requires interaction between opposing forces. Escher generally achieved this balance by using light and dark shapes of similar size. In figure 1.34, Sam Francis achieved a similar balance between a small white square and a much larger red rectangle. The crisp boundary and central location strengthen the square. Despite its small size, it holds its own against the much larger mass of swirling red paint.

Graphic designers often use figure/ground reversal to create multiple interpretations from minimal shapes. In figure 1.35, David McNutt used a single white shape on a black ground to create the head of a master and a servant within the outline of Africa. Used to advertise a South African play, the poster immediately communicates a dramatic human relationship within a specific cultural context.

Rectilinear and Curvilinear Shapes

Rectilinear shapes are composed from straight lines and angular corners. **Curvilinear shapes** are dominated by curves and flowing edges. Simple rectilinear shapes, such as squares and rectangles, are generally cooperative. When placed within a rectangular format, they easily connect to other shapes and can run parallel to the compositional edge (1.36A). Curvilinear shapes, especially circles, are generally less cooperative. They retain their individuality even when they are partially concealed by other shapes (1.36B).

Aubrey Beardsley (1.37) combined rectilinear and curvilinear shapes to create another interpretation of the Salome story, described on page 27. The

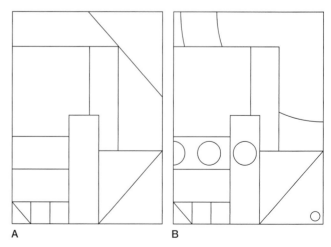

A   B

1.36A-B Rectilinear and curvilinear shapes. Rectilinear shapes can easily be fit together to create a unified design. Curvilinear shapes tend to be more individualistic.

rectangular shape of the format is reiterated by an additional boundary line. Within this boundary, curving black and white shapes create a complex composition, dominated by the bubble pattern in the upper left corner. In the upper right corner, Salomé clutches Saint John's head. Extending from the head down to the flower, a white line follows the transformation of the dead saint's blood into a living plant. This line creates a conceptual and compositional connection between the top and bottom edges.

A very different combination of rectilinear and curvilinear shapes activates Robert Rauschenberg's *Brace* (1.38). The central image of three baseball players is surrounded by layered rectangles to the right, left, and bottom, while a solid line extends from the catcher to the top edge. Bold brushstrokes add power to the painting. Occupying only a small fraction of the composition and surrounded by vigorously painted shapes, the circle *still* dominates the design: we *have* to keep our eyes on the ball!

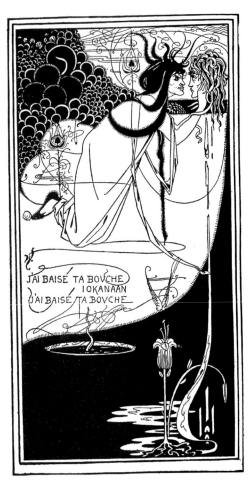

1.37 Aubrey Beardsley, *Salomé with the Head of John the Baptist,* **1894.** Line block print, 11 × 6 in. (27.9 × 15.2 cm).

1.38 Robert Rauschenberg, *Brace,* **1962.** Oil and silkscreen on canvas, 60 × 60 in. (152.4 × 152.4 cm).

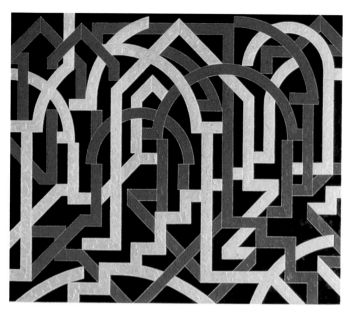

1.39 Valerie Jaudon, *Tallahatchee*, 1984. Oil and gold leaf on canvas, 6 ft 8 in. × 8 ft (2 × 2.4 m).

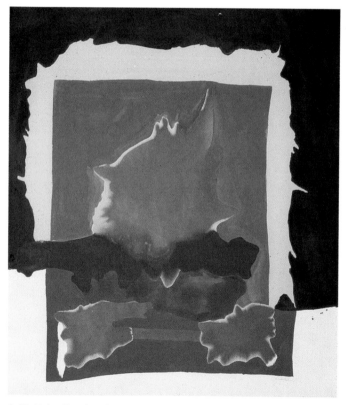

1.40 Helen Frankenthaler, *Interior Landscape*, 1964. Acrylic on canvas, 8 ft 8⅞ in. × 7 ft 8⅞ in. (266 × 235 cm).

Geometric and Organic Shapes

Geometric shapes are distinguished by their crisp, precise edges and mathematically consistent curves. They dominate the technological world of architecture and industry, and they appear in nature as crystalline structures and growth patterns, such as the spiral. In Valerie Jaudon's *Tallahatchee* (1.39), geometric shapes provide a clarity, harmony, and universality comparable to a musical composition. **Organic shapes** are more commonly found in the natural world of plants and animals, sea and sky. As shown in Frankenthaler's *Interior Landscape* (1.40), organic shapes can add unpredictable energy, even when the composition as a whole is based on rectangular shapes.

Degrees of Representation

Nonobjective shapes, such as circles, rectangles, and squares, are **pure forms.** Pure forms are shapes created without reference to realistic subject matter. *No. 15* (1.41), by the Zhou brothers, is a nonobjective painting. A vertical line echoes the left edge of the painting, while the right side is dominated by an open, rectilinear shape. Vigorous white and gray brushstrokes fill the background. A spherical shape at the top pulls our eyes upward, while a curving red line seems to dance around the large gray oval. As an exploration of spirituality, this painting is both energetic and intuitive, exploring feeling rather than recording vision.

Representational shapes are derived from specific subject matter and strongly based on direct observation. Most photographs are representational and highly descriptive. For example, in Ansel Adams' *Monolith, the Face of Half Dome, Yosemite Valley* (1.42), each variation in the cliff's surface is clearly defined.

Between these two extremes, **abstract shapes** are derived from visual reality but are distilled or transformed, reducing their resemblance to the original source. In *Seventh Sister* (1.43), Robert Moskowitz deleted surface details from the rocky mountain. His abstracted cliff is a universal representation of a vertical surface rather than a descriptive painting of a particular cliff.

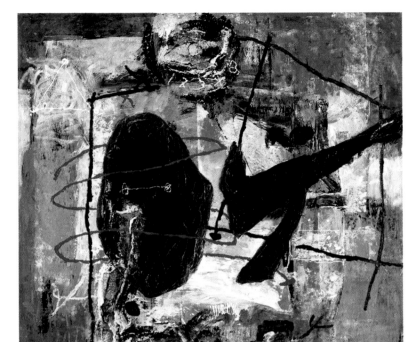

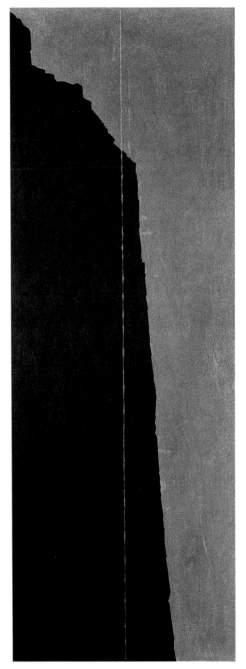

1.41 Zhou Brothers, *The Stone Heart,* **1990.** Mixed media on canvas, 48 × 48 in. (121.92 × 121.92 cm).

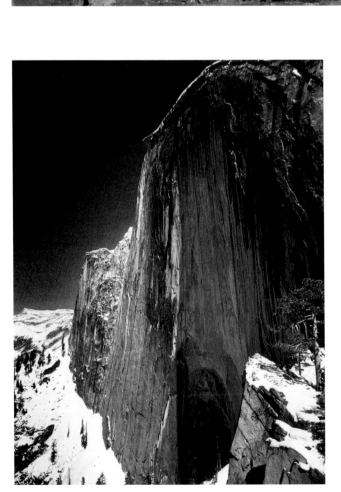

1.42 Ansel Adams, *Monolith, The Face of Half Dome, Yosemite Valley.* Photograph.

1.43 Robert Moskowitz, *Seventh Sister,* 1982. Oil on canvas, 108 × 39 in. (274.3 × 99 cm).

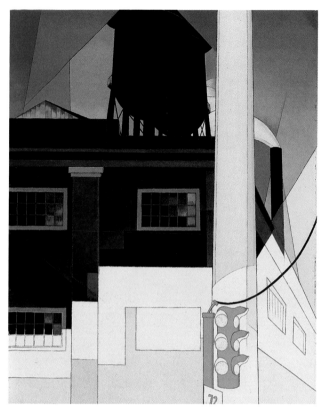

1.44 Charles Demuth, . . . *And the Home of the Brave,* 1931. Oil on composition board, 29½ × 23⅜ in. (74.8 × 59.7 cm).

Reference to reality is a traditional way to increase meaning in an artwork. Drawing on their experience in the physical world, viewers can connect to the illusion of reality presented in the painting. In a nonobjective image, lines, shapes, textures, and colors generate all of the meaning. Because there is no explicit subject matter, some viewers find it more difficult to appreciate a nonobjective image.

By working abstractly, the artist can combine the power of association with the power of pure form. Charles Demuth's . . . *And the Home of the Brave* (1.44) demonstrates the power of abstraction. A factory has been turned into a series of lines and geometric shapes. Variations on red, white, and blue add a symbolic connection to the American flag. Painted during a period of nationwide unemployment, the factory is dark and forbidding. The ironic title (which is based on a line from the American national anthem), adds a subtle political statement.

Degrees of Definition

Definition is the degree to which a shape is distinguished from both the ground area and the positive shapes within the design. **High-definition** creates strong contrast between shapes and tends to increase clarity and immediacy of communication. For this reason, the diagrams used in this book generally feature black figures on a white ground. **Low-definition** shapes, including soft-edged shapes, gradations, and transparencies, can increase the complexity of the design and encourage multiple interpretations.

Definition is an inherent quality in photography. In addition to variations in focus, the photographer can choose finer-grained film and slick paper to create a crisper image and coarser-grained film and textured paper to create a softer image.

Variations in photographic definition can substantially affect meaning. We normally expect to see high-definition in the foreground and low-definition in the background. In *Movie Premier, Hollywood* (1.45), Robert Frank reversed this expectation. He focused on the faces of the worshiping crowd rather than the somber actress, trapped by her fans. This photograph challenges the clichéd image of a glamorous celebrity and suggests the darker side of fame.

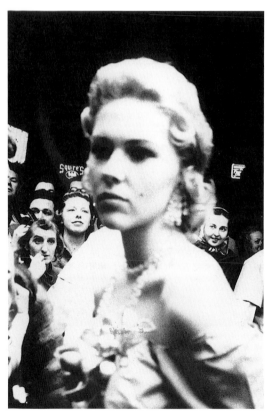

1.45 Robert Frank, *Movie Premiere, Hollywood,* from *The Americans,* 1955–56. Gelatin silver photograph, 12½ × 8⅜ in. (31.75 × 21.27 cm).

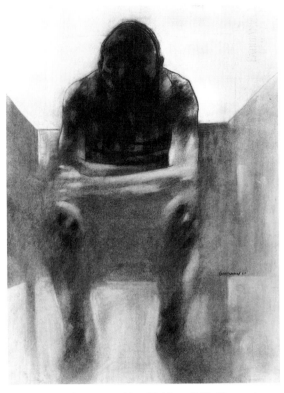

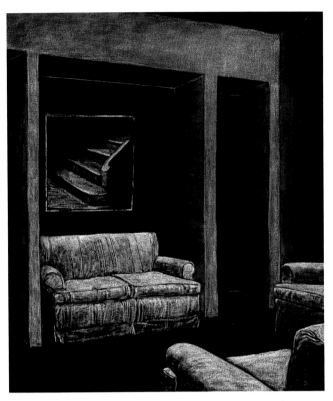

1.46 Sidney Goodman, *Man Waiting*, 1961. Charcoal on paper, 25⅝ × 19⅛ in. (65.1 × 48.7 cm).

1.47 Juan Muñoz, *Raincoat Drawing*, 1992–93. Mixed media on fabric, 49³⁄₁₆ × 40⅛ in. (124.94 × 101.92 cm).

Definition also plays an important role in drawing. Many media, including graphite and charcoal, can be used to create strong, clear lines as well as soft, fuzzy shapes. In Sidney Goodman's *Man Waiting* (1.46), charcoal is used to create a mysterious figure in a threatening space. The darker, more clearly defined shapes in the upper torso seem to push toward us, while the legs, hips, and chair dissolve into the background. Similarly, in Juan Muñoz's *Raincoat Drawing* (1.47), simple white lines define a boundary and suggest an interior space. The shading used in the staircase increases the illusion of space and invites us to ascend. Encouraged to fill in the details, the viewer becomes actively involved in both drawings.

Using Shape

Simple shapes are often used when clear, direct communication is needed. For example, Gary Goldsmith used just two shapes in an ad for an antidrug campaign (1.48). The text on the left reads "The average high induced by cocaine lasts thirty minutes." The text in the black shape on the right reads "The average death induced by cocaine lasts slightly longer." When these two sentences are compositionally combined, the narrow white band and the large black rectangle create a division between life and death.

1.48 Ad by Citizens Against Cocaine Abuse: "The average high induced by cocaine lasts thirty minutes. The average death induced by cocaine lasts slightly longer." Art Director & Designer: Gary Goldsmith, Copywriter: Neal Gomberg, Agency: Goldsmith/ Jeffrey, Client: Citizens Against Cocaine Abuse.

SHAPE

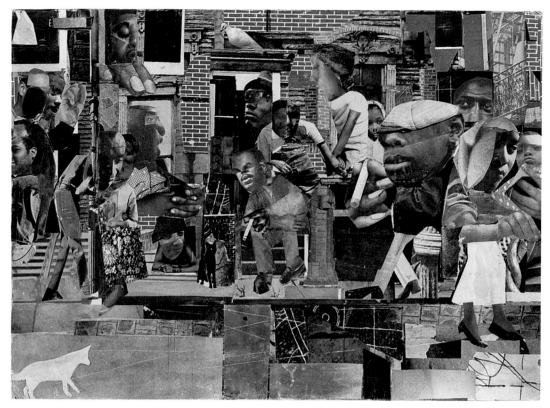

1.49A Romare Bearden, *The Dove,* 1964. Cut-and-pasted paper, gouache, pencil, and colored pencil on cardboard. 13⅜ × 18¾ in. (34 × 47.5 cm).

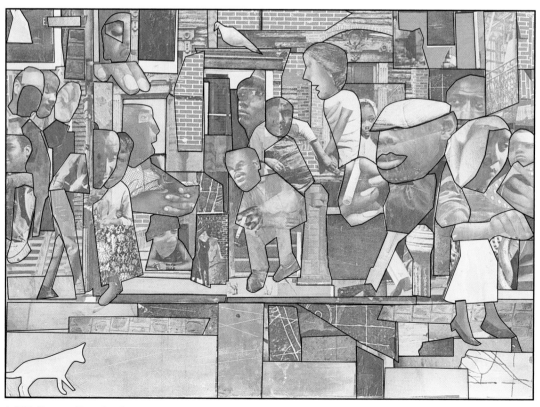

1.49B Romare Bearden (compositional diagram). Printed and cut shapes work together to create a complex composition.

More complex shapes are often used when the message is subtle or contradictory. **Collage** is one method for creating such complex shapes. Constructed from visual fragments initially designed for another purpose, a collage combines two kinds of shapes. In Bearden's *The Dove* (1.49A), the outer edges of each collage fragment create one set of shapes. A second set of shapes is created by the lines and textures *printed* on these photographic fragments. A linear diagram of this artwork demonstrates the complexity of the resulting composition (1.49B). Combining his perceptions of contemporary Harlem with childhood memories, Bearden used this interplay of the cut edges and printed textures to create a pattern of shifting shapes.

In *Target with Plaster Casts* (1.50), Jasper Johns combined simple shapes with sculptural objects to create an equally complex composition. A series of concentric circles creates a clearly defined target at the center of the painting. Nine sculptural fragments of a human figure line the upper edge—an ear, a hand, a mouth, and so forth. To add further complexity, scraps of newspaper were embedded in the colored wax from which the painting was constructed. Equally attracted to the representational body parts above and the symbolic target below, we must reconcile two very different forms of visual information.

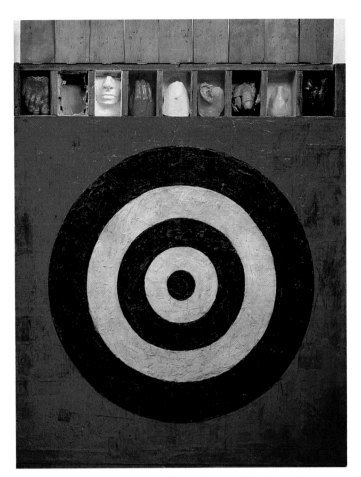

1.50 Jasper Johns, *Target with Plaster Casts*, 1955. Encaustic and collage on canvas with objects, 51 × 44 × 2½ in. (129.5 × 111.8 × 6.4 cm).

TEXTURE

The surface quality of a two-dimensional shape or a three-dimensional volume is called **texture.** Texture can create a bridge between two- and three-dimensional design. It engages our sense of touch as well as our vision, and it can enhance both the visual surface and the conceptual substance of any design.

Types of Texture

Physical texture creates actual variations in a surface. The woven texture of canvas, the bumpy texture of thickly applied paint, and the rough texture of wood grain are common examples. **Visual texture** is an illusion. It can be created using multiple marks or through a descriptive simulation of physical texture. **Invented texture** is one form of visual texture.

Key Questions

- Experiment with rectilinear, curvilinear, geometric, and organic shapes. Which shape type will best express your idea?
- What happens when negative and positive shapes begin to fuse together?
- What happens when you combine flat, solid shapes with gradated shapes?
- Representational, nonobjective, and abstract approaches are discussed in this section. Which approach will best express your idea?

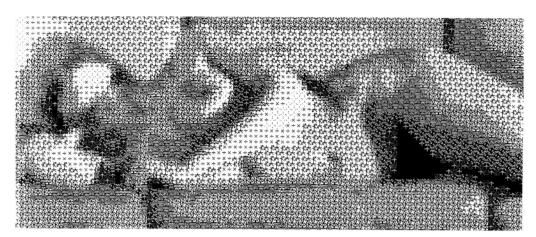

1.51 Kenneth Knowlton and Leon Harmon, *Computerized Nude,* **1971.** Computer-generated image.

Using invented texture, the artist or designer can activate a surface using shapes that have no reference to perceptual reality (1.51).

Creating Texture

When creating any type of texture, we must take two basic factors into account.

First, every material has its own inherent textural quality. As shown in figure 1.46, charcoal is characteristically soft and rich, while a linocut, such as Beardsley's Salomé (see figure 1.37) creates crisp, distinct edges. It is difficult to create soft, atmospheric textures using linocut or crisp, distinct textures using charcoal.

Second, the support surface contributes its own texture. This surface may be smooth, as with most photographs, or quite bumpy, as with the canvas and embedded collage Jasper Johns used for his *Target* (see figure 1.50). Thus, work with texture requires a heightened sensitivity to materials.

Texture and Space

Visual texture is created whenever lines, dots, or other shapes are repeated. Variations in the size, density, and orientation of these marks can produce different spatial effects. Larger and darker marks tend to advance outward (1.52A). Finer marks, tightly packed, tend to pull us inward (1.52B). In figure 1.52C, the marks have been organized into a loose spiral. The overall impact is strongest when size, density, and orientation are combined, as in figure 1.52D.

In figure 1.53, Douglas Smith combined texture and linear perspective to produce a dramatic illusion of space. The lines of mortar between the bricks all point toward the truck in the center, while the

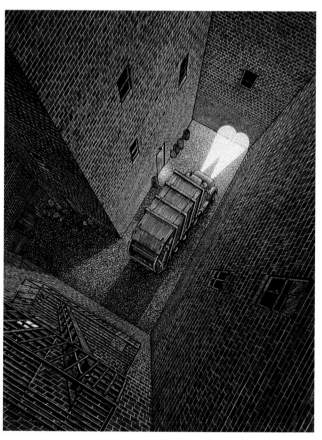

1.53 **Douglas Smith,** *No Turning,* **1986.** Scratchboard and watercolor, 11½ × 15 in. (29.2 × 38.1 cm).

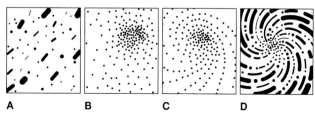

A   B   C   D

1.52 **Examples of textural size, density, and orientation.**

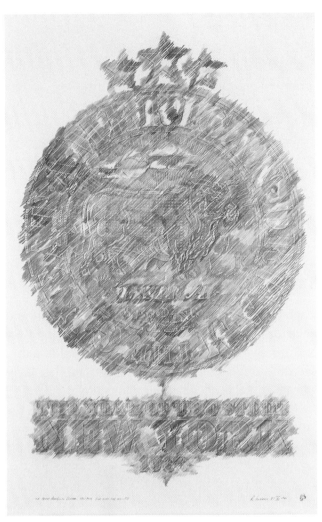

1.54 Robert Indiana, *The Great American Dream: New York*, **1966.** Colored pencil rubbing on paper. 39½ in. × 26 in. (100.33 cm × 66.04 cm).

1.55 Glenn Ligon, Untitled (*I feel most colored when I am thrown against a sharp white background*), **1990.** Oilstick and gesso on wood, each panel 6 ft 6 in. × 30 in. (2 m × 76.2 cm).

bricks themselves diminish in size as the distance increases. The truck at the bottom of the wall of bricks seems to be trapped in a claustrophobic space.

By contrast, Robert Indiana's *The Great American Dream* (1.54) is spatially shallow. Indiana constructed a three-dimensional model of a coin or medallion from layers of cardboard. He then laid his drawing paper on top of the construction and made a rubbing, using colored pencils. This seemingly simple composition can be interpreted in at least three ways. First, creating a design through rubbing can remind us of the coin rubbings we may have made as children. Second, in many cultures, rubbing coins evokes wealth or good luck. Finally, the rubbing itself creates the *illusion* of the coin or medallion, not the reality. Perhaps the Great American Dream is an illusion, ready to dissolve into economic disarray.

Both spatial and flat textures can be created using letters, numbers, or words. Variations in the size, density, and orientation can strongly affect the meaning of these verbal textures. In figure 1.55, African-American painter Glenn Ligon repeatedly wrote, "I feel most colored when I am thrown against a sharp white background," on a gallery wall. As the density of the words increases, the words begin to fuse together, creating variations in the visual texture while reducing verbal clarity.

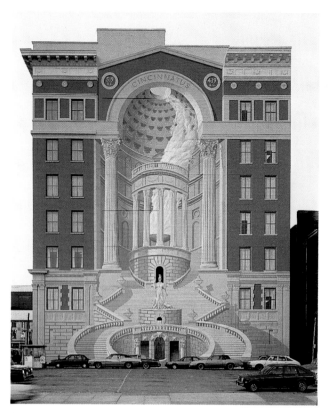

1.56 Richard Haas, *trompe l'oeil* mural on Brotherhood Building, Cincinnati, OH.

Trompe L'Oeil

Taken to an extreme, visual texture can so resemble reality that a deception occurs. This effect is called **trompe l'oeil,** from a French term meaning "to fool the eye." Trompe l'oeil can become a simple exercise in technical virtuosity or can significantly alter our perception of reality. By simulating architectural details, Richard Haas created an amazing dialogue between illusion and reality in figure 1.56. This wall-sized trompe l'oeil painting actually appears to expand architectural space.

Combining Physical and Visual Texture

Each material has a distinctive physical texture, and each drawing method creates a distinctive visual texture. By combining physical and visual textures, we can unify a composition and add another layer of conceptual and compositional energy.

Blended graphite, pastel, or charcoal creates the smooth surface often favored for highly representational images. Claudio Bravo developed the visual textures in *Package* (1.57) using pastel and charcoal. By carefully drawing every fold, he created a convincing simulation of a three-dimensional object.

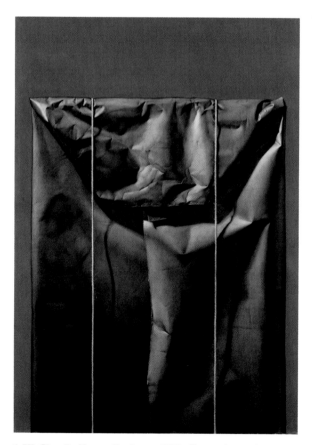

1.57 Claudio Bravo, *Package,* 1969. Charcoal, pastel, and sanguine chalk, 30⅞ × 22½ in. (78.42 × 57.15 cm).

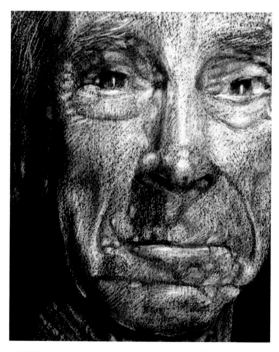

1.58 Bertrand Russell for the New York Times Book Review.

Cross-hatching creates a more active visual texture. Dugald Stermer's portrait of mathematician Bertrand Russell (1.58) is constructed from a network of vigorous lines. The bumpy texture of the paper adds more energy to this lively drawing.

Albrecht Dürer's engraving of a horse (1.59) is even more highly textured. Each line in this image was carefully carved into a thin sheet of copper, then filled with ink and printed on an etching press. The resulting lines are slightly raised, or embossed. Thus, the cross-hatching creates a distinctive visual texture, while the embossed ink adds a subtle physical texture.

Physical and visual textures are combined in *Nigredo* (1.60). Artist Anselm Kiefer began by gluing an enormous photograph to the surface of the canvas. He then added perspective lines to accentuate spatial depth. Torn fragments from a woodcut, bits of straw, and generous layers of paint fill the foreground. All of the materials were used to express a concept from medieval alchemy. Through the symbolic union of male and female forces, the alchemist sought to transform ordinary materials into gold. In the nigredo stage, opposites dissolve into powerful

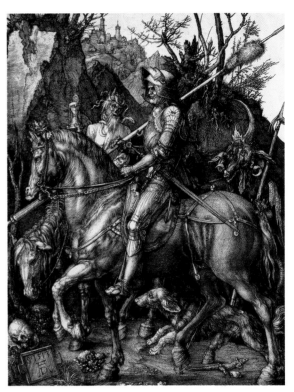

1.59 Albrecht Dürer, *The Knight, Death and the Devil,* **1513.** Engraving, 11 × 14 in. (28 × 36 cm).

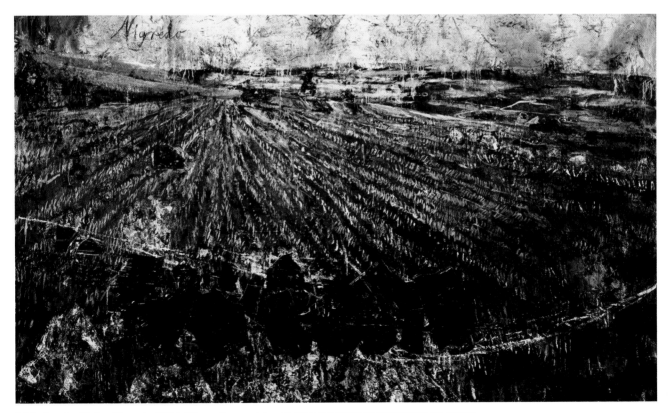

1.60 Anselm Kiefer, *Nigredo,* **1984.** Oil, acrylic, emulsion, shellac and straw on photograph on canvas, with woodcut. 130 × 218½ in. (330.2 × 555 cm).

black material from which this transformation will occur. In this painting, Kiefer used texture to enhance the concept and activate the composition.

Marks and Meanings

Every mark we make can add or subtract from the composition as a whole. When the texture is random or inappropriate, the composition becomes cluttered and confused. On the other hand, deliberate use of texture can enhance the illusion of space and increase compositional unity.

For example, each brushstroke in Ben Marra's *Self-Portrait* (1.61) describes a different facet of the face. Just as a sculptor carves out a portrait in plaster, so Marra used bold brushstrokes to carve out this portrait in paint. There are no random marks. Using both visual and physical texture, Marra increased the painting's immediacy and dimensionality.

Chuck Close's *Self-Portrait* (1.62) offers a very different interpretation of the head. Working from a photograph, Close methodically reduced the face to a series of squares within a grid. He then painted

circles, diamonds, and other simple shapes inside each square. The grid provides structure, while the loosely painted interior shapes create an unexpected invented texture.

In Van Gogh's *Starry Night* (1.63), the texture of oil paint serves three distinct purposes. First, it creates a physical texture, suggesting the actual texture of the trees in the foreground. Second, it brings great energy to every painted shape: we feel the wind; we become mesmerized by the glowing whirlpools of light. Finally, we become connected to the artist himself. Van Gogh's hand is clearly evident in every brushstroke he made.

Key Questions

- How many ways can texture be created?
- How can texture be used to increase the illusion of space?
- What happens to your design when flat shapes and textured shapes are combined?

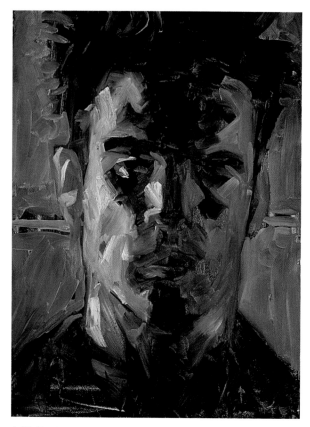

1.61 Benjamin Marra, *Self-Portrait*, **1998.** Oil, 8½ × 11 in. (21.6 × 28 cm).

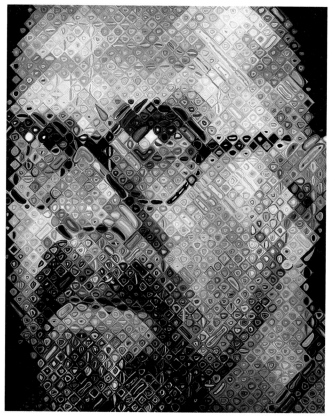

1.62 Chuck Close, *Self-Portrait*, **1997.** Oil on canvas, 8 ft 6 in. × 7 ft (2.59 × 2.13 m).

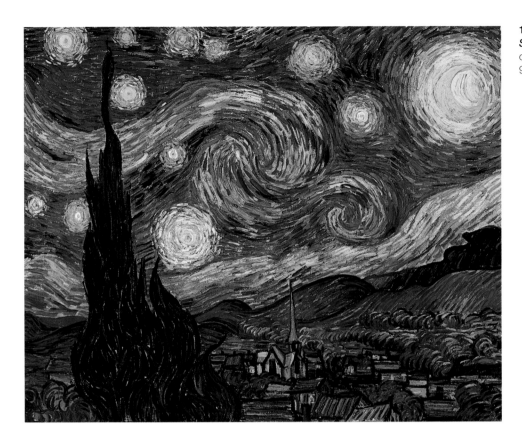

VALUE

Value refers to the relative lightness or darkness of a surface. The word *relative* is significant. The lightness or darkness of a shape is largely determined by its surroundings. For example, on a white surface, a gray square appears heavy and imposing (1.64A). The same gray square has less visual weight and seems luminous when it is surrounded

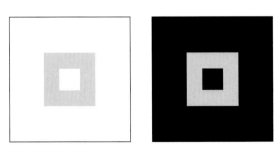

1.64 Relative Value.

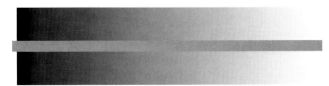

1.65 Value Scale.

by a black ground (1.64B). A 12-step **value scale** further demonstrates the importance of context (1.65). The solid gray line appears luminous when it is placed on a black background. As it crosses over the middle grays and into the white area, it seems to darken. In the center, it merges with the gray background and seems to disappear.

Contrast

Both communication and expression are affected by **contrast,** or the amount of difference in values. High contrast tends to increase clarity and improve readability. That is why the diagrams in this book are generally in black and white. Low contrast is often used for shapes of secondary importance or when the message is subtle. As demonstrated by Deborah Remington's *Capra* (1.66), value gradation can suggest a light source, create a sense of volume, or enhance the illusion of space.

Photographers are especially aware of the importance of contrast. By using a filter or changing the print paper, they can quickly modify contrast. High contrast gives the *Alice in Chains* Website (1.67) a gritty immediacy. Each word and each shape are

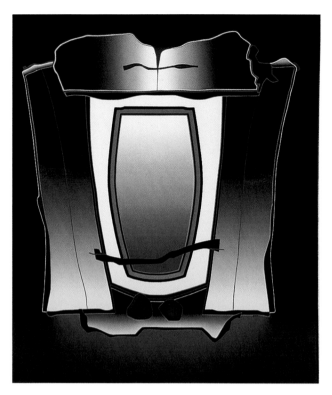

1.66 Deborah Remington, *Capra*, 1974. Oil on canvas, 6 ft 4 in. × 5 ft 7 in. (1.93 × 1.7 m).

clearly defined and confrontational. The city in Steiglitz's photograph (1.68) is quieter and more atmospheric. This low-contrast photograph invites the viewer into a preindustrial world of horses and carriages.

Value Distribution

Value distribution refers to the proportion and arrangement of lights and darks in a composition. Careful use of value distribution can increase emotional impact. A composition that is 80 percent black simply has a different "feel" than a composition that is 80 percent white.

Darker values are often used to create a sense of mystery or increase dramatic tension. For example, Ray K. Metzker's *Philadelphia* (1.69) is dominated by dark values. Surrounded by somber buildings in a silent city, the commuters huddle together under the brightly lit bus shelter like actors in a mysterious play.

Lighter values may suggest openness, optimism, and clarity. For example, lighter values dominate the bottom and right edges of Conley Harris' landscape (1.70), creating an expansive effect. The darker values at the center of the composition then pull us inward.

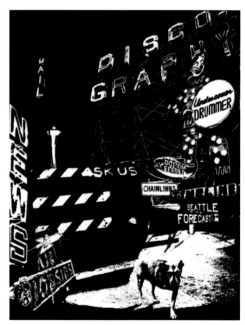

1.67 Alice in Chains, "Dog's Breath" Website. Sony Music Creative Services, Santa Monica, CA. Graphic Interface Designer: Mary Maurer.

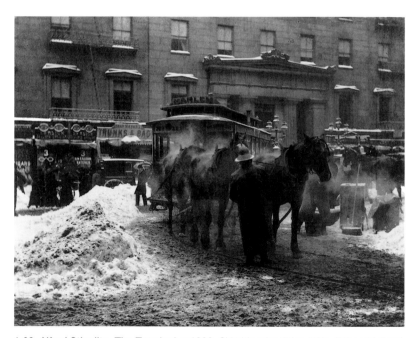

1.68 Alfred Stieglitz, *The Terminal*, c.1892. Chloride print, 3½ × 4½ in. (8.8 × 11.3 cm).

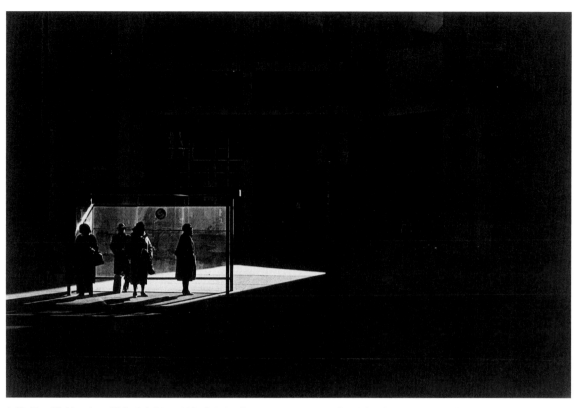

1.69 Ray K. Metzker, *Philadelphia,* **1963.** Gelatin silver print on paper, 6⅛ × 8¾ in. (15.4 × 22.3 cm).

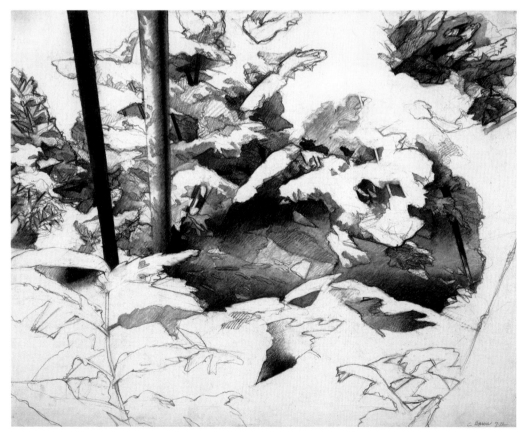

1.70 Conley Harris, *Doubles/Triples, Italy*. Charcoal drawing, 23 × 30 in. (58.42 × 76.2 cm).

VALUE

Value and Volume

When a full range of values is used, a two-dimensional shape can seem three-dimensional, or volumetric. Figure 1.71 shows the transformation of a circle into a sphere. We begin with a simple outline, then add the **attached shadows,** or values that directly define the basic form. Addition of a **cast shadow** in the third image grounds the sphere. In the fourth drawing, the separation between the shadow and the sphere creates a floating effect.

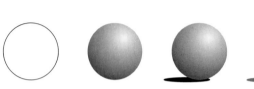

1.71 From shape to volume through use of lighting.

This illusion of space is so convincing that objects can appear to extend out from a two-dimensional surface. The earliest oil painters used **grisaille,** or a gray underpainting, to create this illusion of space. Color was then added, using transparent glazes or layers of paint. A detail from van Eyck's *Ghent Altarpiece* (1.72) shows both the grisaille painting and the full-color painting. The two statues in the center were painted using a range of grays, while color has been added to the kneeling figures on the right and left. Variations in value give all of the figures a remarkable dimensionality.

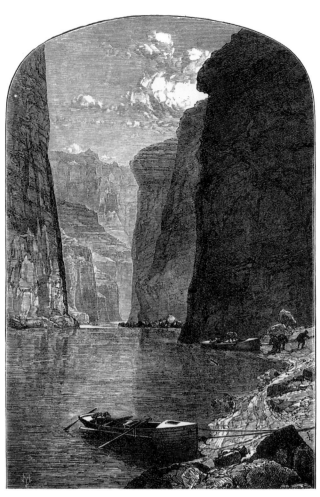

1.73 Thomas Moran, *Noon-Day Rest in Marble Canyon*, from *Exploration of the Colorado River of the West*, by J. W. Powell, **1875.** Wood engraving after an original sketch by Thomas Moran, 6½ × 4⅜ in. (16.5 × 11 cm).

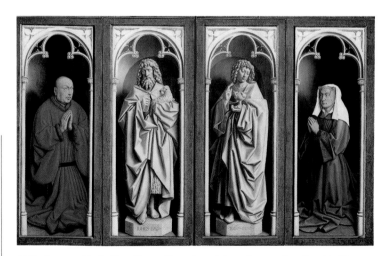

1.72 Jan van Eyck, The *Ghent Altarpiece* (closed), completed 1432. Oil on panel, approx. 11 ft 6 in. × 7 ft 7 in. (3.5 × 2.33 m).

Value and Space

When combined in a composition, very dark shapes tend to advance spatially, while gray, blurry shapes tend to recede. For example, in Thomas Moran's *Noon-Day Rest in Marble Canyon* (1.73), the dark values in the foreground gradually fade until the cliffs in the background become gray and indistinct. This effect, called **atmospheric perspective,** is one of the simplest ways to create the illusion of space.

Chiaroscuro (literally, "light-dark") is another way to create the illusion of space. A primary light source is used to create six or more values. A dark background is added to increase contrast. In *Judith and Her Maidservant, with the Head of Holofernes* by Artemesia Gentileschi, (1.74), the highlighted areas are clearly delineated, while darker areas seem to dissolve into the background. The resulting image is as dramatic as a theatrical stage.

Value and Lighting

Filmmakers and set designers are especially aware of the expressive uses of value. Working with a wide range of lights, including sharply defined spotlights and more diffused floodlights, they can increase or decrease the illusion of space, emphasize an object or an action, and influence our emotional response to a character.

Four common forms of lighting are shown in figure 1.75. As described by Herbert Zettl in *Sight, Sound, Motion: Applied Media Aesthetics,* a key light is the primary source of illumination. Placing this light at a 45-degree angle can enhance the illusion of space. Addition of a backlight separates the actor from the background and adds definition. When a fill light is added, the contrast between light and dark becomes less harsh, and the actor may appear less formidable. In theatrical performances, powerful side lighting is often used to increase drama while enhancing dimensionality.

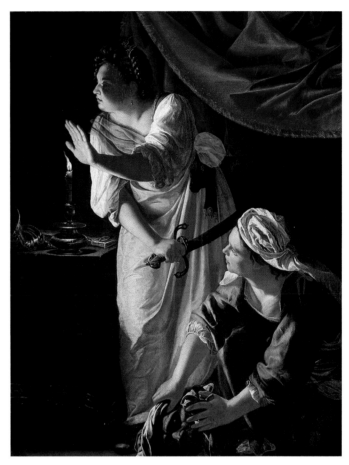

1.74 Artemesia Gentileschi, *Judith and her Maidservant with the Head of Holofernes,* c. 1625. Oil on canvas, 72½ × 54¾ in. (1.84 × 1.42 m).

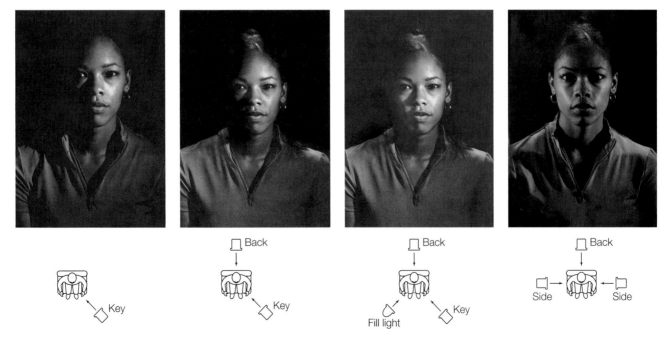

1.75 John Veltri, Lighting Techniques from *Sight, Sound, Motion: Applied Media Aesthetics,* 3rd ed., by Herbert Zettl, 1999.

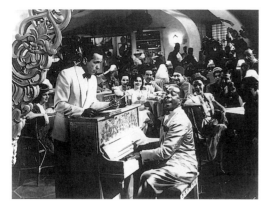

1.76A

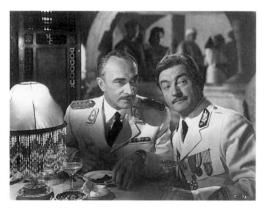

1.76B

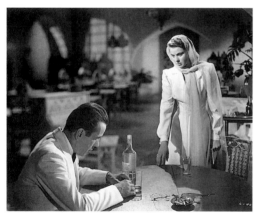

1.76C

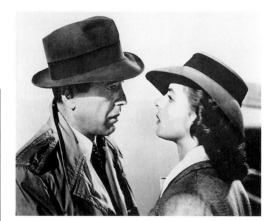

1.76D

All of these aspects of lighting are used expressively in the film *Casablanca*, directed by Michael Curtiz. The lighting is fairly dark when we first enter Rick's Cafe Americain, the saloon where most of the action occurs. In this dark and mysterious place, a man will be shot, a seduction will be thwarted, and a romance will be rekindled. The piano player, Sam, and the audience members closest to the stage are brightly lit as he sings an optimistic song (1.76A). The two villains in the film, Major Strasser and Captain Renault, are often strongly side-lit (1.76B), which makes them appear more formidable and enhances the texture in their faces. By contrast, much softer light is used for the face of the heroine, Ilsa, who is emotionally and politically fragile.

Indeed, value and lighting is used to accentuate Ilsa's emotions throughout the film. When she tries to explain to Rick the reason she had left him in Paris two years earlier, Ilsa wears a pure white dress and enters the darkened saloon like a virginal beam of light (1.76C). Later, when she visits Rick in his apartment, shadows cover her face, accentuating her conflicted emotions as she tries to decide whether to remain with her husband, Victor, whom she idealizes, or return to Rick, whom she loves. In the final scene at the airport, diffused lighting again emphasizes Ilsa's vulnerability (1.76D). She and Victor disappear into the foggy night, escaping from Casablanca, while Rick and a reformed Captain Renault stroll away together to join the Foreign Legion.

Key Questions

- What is the advantage of a wide value range? What is the advantage of a narrow value range?

- What happens when you invert the values — that is, the black areas become white and the white areas become black?

- Would your design benefit from a stronger illusion of space? If so, how can value be used to increase the illusion of space?

SUMMARY

- The elements of two-dimensional design are line, shape, texture, value, and color.

- Lines can contain, define, dissect, and connect. Line networks can be created using hatching, cross-hatching, and cross-contours.

- A shape is created whenever an area is enclosed. The figure is the primary shape, while the ground, or negative shape, provides the surrounding context.

- When figure and ground shapes are equally strong, figure/ground reversal can occur.

- There are many types of shapes, including rectilinear, curvilinear, geometric, organic, representational, nonobjective, and abstract. When gradated, shapes can appear three-dimensional.

- Texture is the visual or physical surface of a shape. Visual texture can be created through multiple marks, while actual variations in the surface create physical texture.

- Relative lightness or darkness in an artwork is called value. Value can be used to create the illusion of space, suggest volume, shift compositional balance, and heighten emotion.

Keywords

actual line
abstract shape
atmospheric
  perspective
attached shadow
calligraphic line
cast shadow
chiaroscuro
closure
collage
continuity
contour line
contrast
cross-contour

cross-hatching
curvilinear shape
definition
direction
dynamic
elements
figure/ground reversal
geometric shape
gesture drawing
gradation (shading)
grisaille
hatching
high-definition

implied line
invented texture
line
low-definition
negative shape
  (ground)
nonobjective shape
organic shape
organizational line
orientation
physical texture
positive shape
  (figure)

pure form
rectilinear shape
representational shape
shape
texture
trompe l'oeil
value
value distribution
value scale
visual texture
volume
volume summary
volumetric

Profile:
Phillia Yi, Printmaker

Energy and Expression Using Woodcut
on a Large Scale

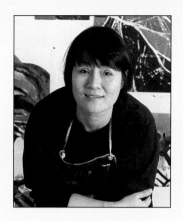

Phillia Changhi Yi has revitalized the ancient process of woodcut through her large-scale prints. Drawing directly on luan plywood, Yi cuts away the negative shapes and inks the raised positive shapes to create abstract images that vigorously combine line, color, texture, and movement. Yi has exhibited widely, with over 20 solo shows and numerous international group shows to her credit. She lectures widely and has taught workshops at Manhattan Graphics Center, Women's Studio Workshop, and the Southern Graphics Council Conference.

MS: The energy in all of your images is impressive. What is its source?

PY: Conflict is my primary source, conceptually and compositionally. As a woman from Korea living in the United States, I find myself caught between cultures. This isolates me in an interesting way and gives me a unique perspective. My work reflects the day-to-day dilemmas and tension of my multicultural experience.

Crisis moments often trigger ideas, but historic events are never treated literally. I combine abstract imagery with representational elements in my prints. Both flat and illusory space is created, suggesting an altered sense of time and scale. "Tight" movement is juxtaposed with fluid shapes, and both warm and cool colors are used in opaque and translucent layers. This activates the psychological space and creates a complex, highly charged composition.

MS: Many members of your family are doctors. How did you become an artist?

PY: Getting the right encouragement at the right time gave me the confidence to pursue art. All of my five siblings are talented, I think, but choosing an art career seemed too risky. My father encouraged me to study graphic design, but I found that printmaking was my real passion. My mentor, Professor Romas Viesulas at Tyler School of Art, said that I had the commitment and ability for a career in art. His confidence gave me confidence.

MS: How do you develop your images?

PY: I begin with a month of drawing, usually in charcoal, on 29" × 41" sheets of printmaking paper. In the drawings, I work out my images and ideas. Social and political themes dominate. For example, the beating of Rodney King by members of the Los Angeles Police Department and the subsequent burning of Koreatown inspired *Dance*.

The Other Side, shown here, deals with the power of women, who must prevail in a world dominated by men. The whole composition is based on the intersection between these two forces, near the center of the print. In a sense, the large black shape represents the unconscious, while the curving red shape suggests that which is conscious, palpable, and real. I am interested in the uneasy alliance or balance between complex life forces, rather than a simple battle between adversaries. Each corner is treated differently, adding more variety and energy to the print.

MS: The size of this piece is extraordinary. Using eight panels, you have created a print that is 12 feet long!

PY: When I was studying printmaking at SUNY–New Paltz, I was surrounded by printmakers. The size of the press, acid trays, rollers, and other equipment seemed to limit the size of the print. When I went to Tyler in Philadelphia, my roommate, who was a painter, introduced me to her friends. Some were completing a 5' × 7' painting a day! I realized that the small size and slow process of printmaking had historically given it a "second-class" status. I was determined to overcome this perception, so I developed a working method that is forceful, spontaneous, and direct. There is still a great deal of deliberation, but the cutting and printing processes are relatively fast.

MS: Some artists work very methodically over a long period of time, while others work in short, intensive bursts. What is your approach?

PY: I adapt my method to my situation. I have obligations as a teacher, a mother, and an administrator, so summer is my only solid block of work time. A regular schedule is best for me. At the beginning of the summer, I go to the studio for a few hours each day. I soon increase this to about 6 hours a day for drawing. When I am cutting the blocks and printing, I often work for 8 to 10 hours a day. I am very consistent.

MS: What is the best work method for your students?

PY: Success is primarily based on commitment. I would say that art-making is about 5 percent talent and inspiration and 95 percent hard work. A professional or a serious student continues to work despite obstacles. It is important for students to explore ideas and make mistakes: that is the best way to learn.

MS: What is the purpose of your artwork?

PY: Art is expression, not explanation. Artists must be attentive, noticing every detail of experience. Art both reflects and influences society and culture. In that sense, I feel that artists have a responsibility to their generation, not just to create objects of beauty but to create objects of truth—whether they are beautiful or not. My ideas come from my daily life and my personal experience, both good and bad. The most important characteristic is my belief that art should be expressed in terms of human experience. My work is essentially optimistic: I embrace all that the world has to offer.

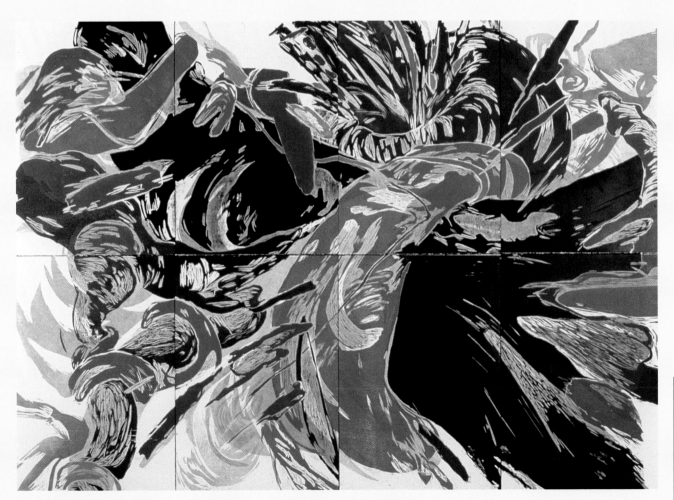

Phillia Changhi Yi, *The Other Side*, 1993. Color woodcut, 84 × 120 in. (213 × 305 cm).

chapter two

The Element of Color

Color immediately attracts attention. When presented with a collection of bottles filled with liquid in various colors, very young children will group the objects by color rather than by size or shape. An interior designer may use rose-red walls in a restaurant to increase emotional warmth, while using light blue walls in a day-care center to encourage calm. Bright yellow and magenta red add pizzazz to an eye-catching poster in figure 2.1. Designed to call attention to the disparity in the number of exhibitions granted to male and female artists, this poster had to compete with other posters displayed on walls throughout New York City. Color is both the most elusive and most emotionally complex design element. By harnessing its power, we can substantially expand our compositional capabilities.

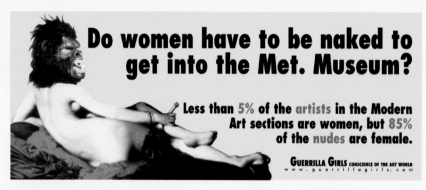

2.1 Guerrilla Girls, "Do women have to be naked to get into the Met. Museum? Less than 5% of the artists in the Modern Art sections are women, but 85% of the nudes are female," 1989. Poster, 11 × 28 in. (27.9 × 71.1 cm).

COLOR THEORY

Color theory is the art and science of color interaction and effects. In *The Art of Color*,[1] Johannes Itten lists the following approaches to color theory:

- The physicist studies electromagnetic wavelengths in order to measure and classify color.
- The chemist, working with the molecular structure of dyes and pigments, seeks to produce highly permanent colors and excellent paint consistency.
- The physiologist investigates the effects of color and light on our eyes and brain.
- The psychologist studies the expressive effects of color on our mind and spirit.

An artist combines all these areas of knowledge. Like the physicist, the artist uses color wavelengths to create various effects. Like the chemist, the artist must be aware of the safety and permanence of dyes and pigments. When using color to create the illusion of space, the artist puts into practice theories developed by the physiologist. And both communication and expression are strongly affected by the psychological effects of color.

COLOR PHYSICS

Two major color systems are used in art and design. **Additive color** is created using beams of light (2.2). Red, green, and blue, the familiar RGB on a computer screen, are the primary colors in this system. Many additional colors can be mixed from these primaries. **Subtractive color** is created when white light is reflected off a pigmented or dyed surface (2.3). The subtractive primaries are blue, red, and yellow.

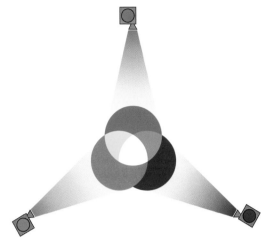

2.2 Light itself creates additive color.

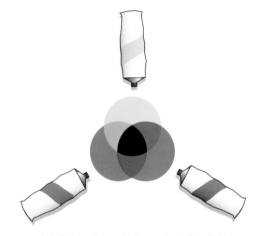

2.3 Subtractive color is created when light is reflected off a surface.

This book was printed using cyan blue, magenta red, and yellow, the transparent primaries (or **process colors),** commonly used in mass production. As viewers, we optically combine thousands of cyan, magenta, and yellow dots to create a coherent image. Black (abbreviated as *K* in the CMYK printing system) was then added to enhance detail and increase contrast (2.4).

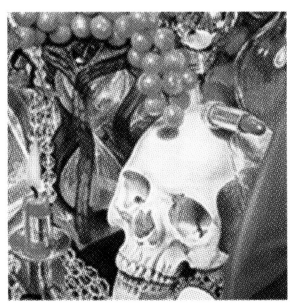

2.4 Color printing detail of *Wheel of Fortune*, showing dot pattern used in CMYK printing.

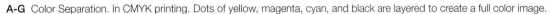

A-G Color Separation. In CMYK printing. Dots of yellow, magenta, cyan, and black are layered to create a full color image.

A Yellow **B** Magenta **C** Yellow and magenta **D** Cyan **E** Yellow, magenta, and cyan **F** Black **G** Full color printing

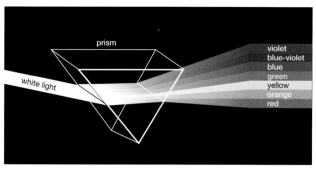

2.5 When white light passes through a prism, the spectrum becomes visible.

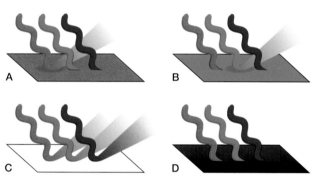

2.6 We see color when the primaries of light are reflected off a colored surface. A red surface absorbs the green and blue wavelengths, while reflecting the red. All wavelengths are reflected by a white surface. All wavelengths are absorbed by a black surface.

Color and Light

When white light passes through a prism, it is refracted, or bent. This creates a wide spectrum of hues, which is dominated by red, orange, yellow, green, blue, blue-violet, and violet (2.5). Each hue, or separate color, is defined by a specific electromagnetic wavelength, with red as the longest and violet as the shortest. When white light hits a colored surface, some wavelengths are reflected, while other wavelengths are absorbed. As shown in figure 2.6A, a red surface reflects the red wavelengths while absorbing the blue and green wavelengths. Similarly, a green surface reflects the green wavelengths while absorbing the red and blue (2.6B). All wavelengths are reflected off a white surface (2.6C); all wavelengths are absorbed by a black surface (2.6D). Color reflection and absorption are rarely total. As a result, we can often see hints of various colors within a dominant color.

Using Additive Color

Lighting designers, videographers, and website artists use additive color extensively. Beams of red, green, and blue light are used to create a full-color video projection. The mixture of adjacent beams creates cyan, magenta, and yellow, which are the secondary colors in the additive system. When all three beams are combined, white light results.

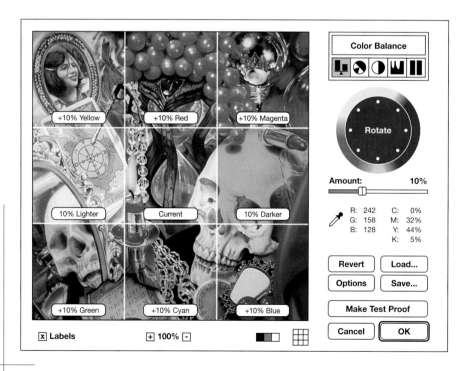

2.7 Color variations using a computer.

We can quickly and easily create variations in additive color on a computer. In figure 2.7, the current color choice is shown in the center. Variations are shown in the eight surrounding squares. Even a 10 percent increase in a given color produces a very different result.

Our perception of additive color is influenced by

- The intensity (or wattage) of the projected light
- The light source, from incandescent light and fluorescent light to daylight
- The surface quality of the illuminated object; projected light behaves very differently on transparent, translucent, and textured surfaces
- The ambient (overall amount of) light in the environment

Using Subtractive Color

Painters, printmakers, and illustrators use subtractive color in various forms, including acrylics, oils, pastels, and inks. Each pigment or dye used in the manufacture of such materials is chemically unique. Quinacridone red and pthalocyanide blue are transparent and intense. The cadmiums and earth colors are generally opaque. **Color overtones** complicate matters further. Color theorist David Hornung defines an overtone as "a secondary hue bias in a primary color." For example, alizarin crimson is a red with violet overtones, while scarlet is a red with orange overtones. To create the widest range of mixtures, artists and designers may use a six-hue palette, including two reds, two yellows, and two blues, plus **achromatic** black and white, which have no hue. Since most foundation color projects are done using paint, ink, or colored paper, the remainder of this chapter will focus on subtractive color.

COLOR INTERACTION

Color interaction refers to the way colors influence one another.

Colors are never seen in isolation. The blue sheet of paper we examine in an art supply store reminds us of the blue of the sky, the ocean, or the fabrics in a clothing store. Lighting also affects our perceptions. Incandescent light creates a warm

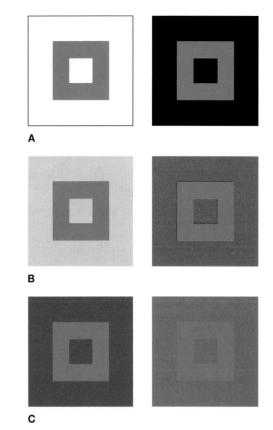

2.8 Examples of simultaneous contrast. Light/dark contrast is shown in figure A, a complementary reaction is shown in figure B, and subtle variations are shown in figure C.

orange glow, while standard fluorescent lights produce a bluish ambiance. And, when our blue paper is added to a design, it is profoundly affected by the surrounding colors.

This effect is called **simultaneous contrast.** Three principles of simultaneous contrast are shown in figure 2.8A-C. Light/dark contrast is shown in the first pair of images. A blue-green square appears much lighter when it is placed on a black background. A complementary reaction is shown in the second pair. The same blue-green square appears to glow when it is surrounded by red rather than a neutral gray. In the third example, the same blue-green square appears almost green when it is surrounded by solid blue, yet it appears almost blue when surrounded by green.

The **Bezold effect** demonstrates the profound influence of color interaction. Color theorist Wilhelm Bezold (1837–1907) realized that change in a single color can substantially alter our perception of an entire pattern. In figure 2.9A-D, changing the

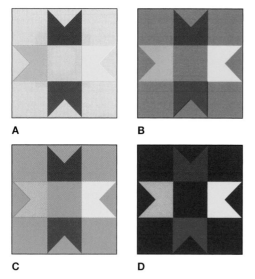

A   B

C   D

2.9 *The Bezold effect.* Changing a single color alters the entire design.

background color from gray to red adds an electric energy to the design. A light green background accentuates the darker shapes while diminishing the brightness of the orange shape. A blue-black background creates a strong contrast in value and pushes the orange and yellow shapes forward. The compositional impact can be substantial, even when the amount of changed color is small.

Color interaction becomes especially dramatic when complementary colors, such as red-orange and blue-green, are used in a composition. In the human eye, two types of cells, known as rods and cones, are arranged in layers on the retina. These cells serve as photoreceptors. The rods record lightness and darkness, while the cones are used to distinguish the hues, such as red and blue. According to **opponent theory,** the cones can register only one color in a complementary pair at a time. Constant shifting between the opposing colors creates a visual overload at the edges of the shapes, resulting in an electric glow. In *Inner Lhamo Waterfall* (2.10), Pat Steir used this effect to suggest the majesty and mystery of the falling water.

A similar characteristic of human vision can be used to create an **afterimage.** If we stare at a red square for 30 seconds (2.11), then stare at a white sheet of paper, a blue or green shape will seem to appear. This is due to fatigue in the cones, the color sensors in our eyes. Overloaded by the intense red, our eyes revert to the blue and green cones, creating the afterimage.

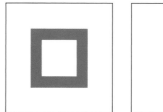

2.11 Afterimage exercise.

2.10 Pat Steir, *Inner Lhamo Waterfall,* **1992.** Oil on canvas, 114 × 90¼ in. (289.6 × 229.2 cm).

DEFINING COLOR

Hue

The **hue,** or name of a color, is determined by its wavelength. Red, blue, green, yellow, and so forth are all hues.

Physicists, painters, and philosophers have devised numerous systems to organize hues. Johannes Itten's 12-step color wheel (2.12) is a clear and simple example. Red, blue, and yellow **primary colors** are in the center. These colors can be mixed to produce many other colors. The **secondary colors** of green, orange, and violet follow. These colors are mixed from adjacent primaries. A circular spectrum of **tertiary colors** completes the wheel. The mixture of a secondary color and the adjacent primary color creates a tertiary color.

Artists often use a wide range of hues to capture the richness of reality. In *Wheel of Fortune* (2.13), Audrey Flack used a full spectrum of hues to define a collection of symbolic objects in relentless detail. The makeup and mirrors symbolize vanity; the candles, hourglass, and skull suggest the passage of time; the grapes suggest passion. Reds, blues, and yellows dominate the painting. Hints of orange, violet, and green complete the spectrum.

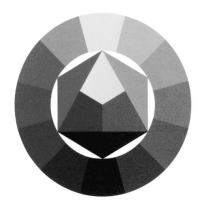

2.12 The 12-step Itten color wheel.

A limited number of hues can be equally effective. *Thoughts of Summer* (2.14) was composed using a narrow range of solid and gradated reds. The blocks of color shimmer with energy, suggesting the oppressive heat of a summer day. Using a limited palette, Robert Lazuka created a quiet yet hypnotic image.

Temperature is an especially important aspect of hue. **Temperature** refers to the heat a color generates, both physically and psychologically. Try laying six colored squares of equal value on fresh snow on a sunny day. By the end of the day, the warm-colored oranges, reds, and violets will sink into the melting snow, while the blue and green squares will remain

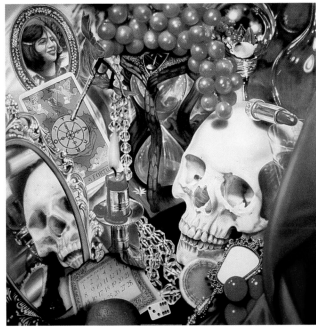

2.13 Audrey Flack, *Wheel of Fortune*, 1977–78. Oil over acrylic on canvas, 8 × 8 ft.

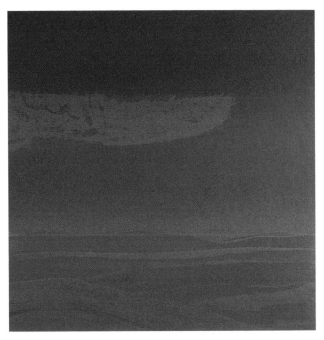

2.14 Robert Lazuka, *Thoughts of Summer,* 1999. 21 × 21 in. (53 × 53 cm).

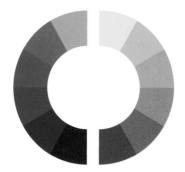

2.15 Separation of the color wheel by temperature.

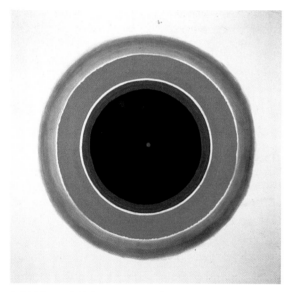

2.16 Kenneth Noland, *A Warm Sound in a Gray Field,*
1961. 6 ft 10½ in. × 6 ft 9 in. (2.1 × 2.06 m).

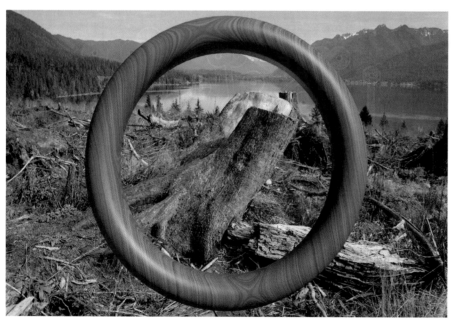

2.17 MANUAL (Suzanne Bloom and Ed Hill), *Quinault,* from *A Constructed Forest,* **1993.**
Chromogenic print, 24 × 36 in. (61 × 91.4 cm).

closer to the surface. Figure 2.15 shows a simple division of the color wheel by temperature.

Color temperature can help create the illusion of space. Under most circumstances, warm colors advance, while cool colors recede. This effect is demonstrated very clearly in Kenneth Noland's *A Warm Sound in a Gray Field* (2.16). The red ring with its yellow halo pushes toward us, while the blue-black circle pulls us inward. The small red dot in the center of the composition further activates the void by creating another advancing shape. In *Quinault* (2.17), Suzanne Bloom and Ed Hill used a similar combination of warm and cool colors to create a very different illusion of space. A warm brown ring dominates the image, targeting the tree stump in the center. The cool blue lake and mountains recede into the background.

Value

Value refers to the relative lightness or darkness of a color. By removing hue from the equation, we can create a simple value scale (2.18A) that shifts from white to black through a series of grays. As shown in figure 2.18B, hues such as violet, blue, and green are inherently darker in value than pure yellow or orange. Translation of color into value is shown in the final column. Despite the wide variety of hues, all the colors in 2.18C have essentially the same value.

Three basic variations in value are shown in figure 2.19. When white is added to a hue, the resulting **tint** will be lighter in value. The addition of gray produces a **tone.** The addition of black creates a darker **shade.** One of the simplest ways to unify a design is to limit the colors used to the tints, tones, and shades of a single hue.

Using a full range of values, we can create a very convincing representation of reality. In *Vision* (2.20), Nicora Gangi transformed a simple still life into a dramatic drawing. A bright light in the background pushes the dark

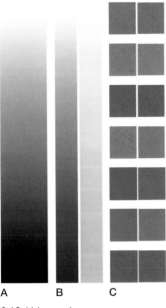

2.18 Value scales.

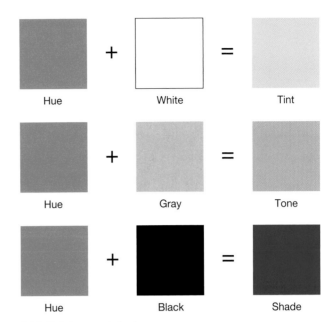

2.19 Tint, tone, and shade.

foreground vessels toward us. The limited value range in David Hockney's *Mist* (2.21) is equally effective. The gray-green palm trees dissolve into the peach-colored fog as quietly as a whisper. By making a black-and-white photocopy, we can easily check the range of values in a design. The photo-

copied image will be quite readable when the value range is broad. When a very narrow range of values is used, the photocopy will produce a solid black or gray image.

Value is the dominant force in some paintings, while hue is the dominant force in others. Romaine

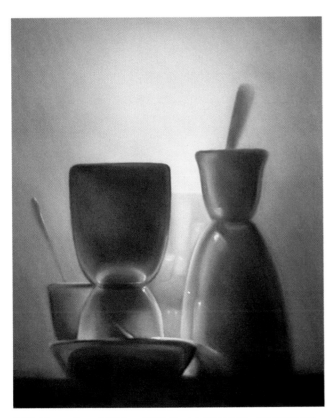

2.20 Nicora Gangi, *Vision,* **1994.** Pastel, 10 × 14 in. (25 × 36 cm).

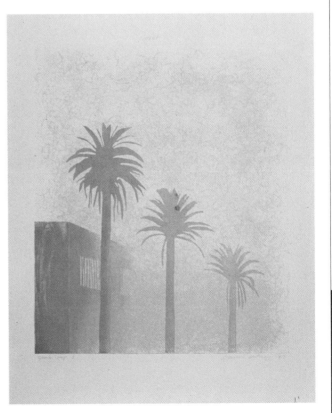

2.21 David Hockney, *Mist,* **1973.** From The Weather Series. Lithograph in 5 colors, edition 98, 37 × 32 in. (93.9 × 81.2 cm).

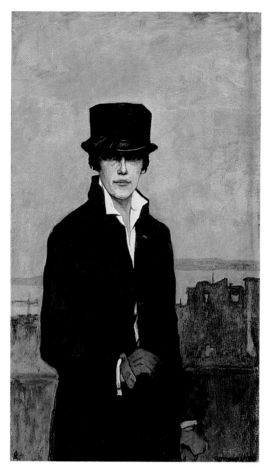

2.22 Romaine Brooks, *Self-Portrait*, 1923. Oil on canvas. 46¼ × 26⅞ in. (117.5 × 68.3 cm).

Brooks' *Self-Portrait* (2.22) is essentially a value painting. Blacks, whites, and grays dominate the image. On the other hand, hue dominates Henri Matisse's *Green Stripe* (2.23). Surrounded by bold blocks of red, green, and blue, the lime-green line provides the focal point as well as the painting's title.

Intensity

Intensity, saturation, and **chroma** all refer to the purity of a color. The primary colors are the most intense. This intensity generally diminishes when colors are mixed.

Figure 2.24A-C presents three intensity scales. Column A shows the most intense primary and secondary colors. Column B demonstrates the loss of intensity when black is added. In column C, two complementary colors are mixed, producing a range of elegant, low-intensity colors.

High-intensity colors are often used to maximize impact. Grace Hartigan's *City Life* (2.25) explodes with energy, as the rich blues, reds, and yellows dance across the canvas.

A combination of high- and low-intensity colors can be equally effective. Arshile Gorky combined primary hues and subtle earth colors in figure 2.26. Surrounded by low-intensity colors, the brilliant yellow and red shapes seem to glow with energy.

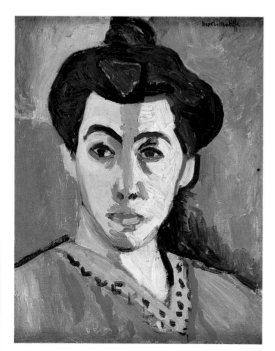

2.23 Henri Matisse, *Green Stripe (Madame Matisse)*, 1905. Oil on canvas, 16 × 12¾ in. (40.6 × 32.4 cm).

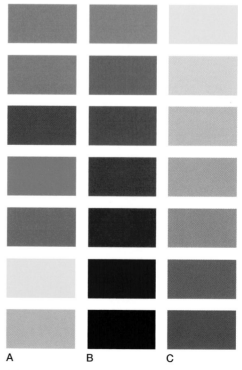

A   B   C

2.24 Intensity scales.

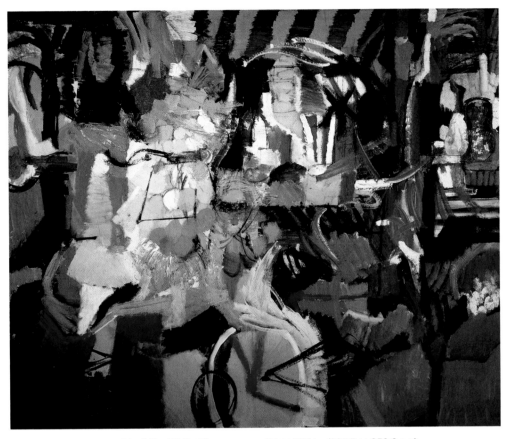

2.25 Grace Hartigan, *City Life,* 1956. Oil on canvas, 81 × 98½ in. (205.7 × 250.2 cm).

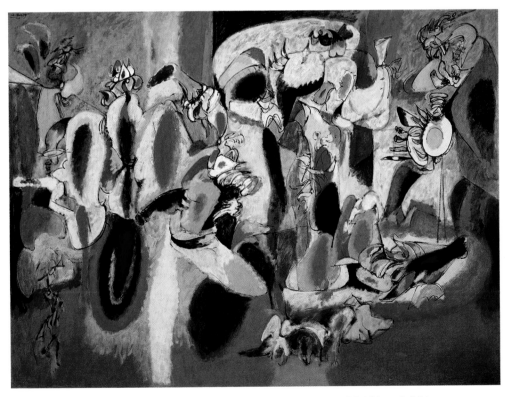

2.26 Arshile Gorky, *The Liver Is the Cock's Comb,* 1944. Oil on canvas, 6 ft 1¼ in. × 8 ft 2 in.
(1.86 × 2.49 cm).

COLOR SCHEMES

Relationships among colors are critical to the success or failure of a design, and many theories of **color harmony** have been developed to help artists, architects, and designers make good choices. A basic color wheel can help illustrate five common approaches.

Monochromatic

Variations on a single hue are used in a **monochromatic** color scheme (2.27). The advantage of this system is a high level of unity: all the colors are strongly related. Boredom, due to the lack of variety, is a potential disadvantage. In *Tracers–Side Order* (2.28), Guy Goodwin used various textures, patterns, and words to add interest to the monochromatic image.

Analogous

Adjacent colors on the color wheel are used in an **analogous** color scheme (2.29). As with monochromatic harmony, a high degree of unity is ensured, but the wider range of hues offers greater variety and can increase interest.

Houses in Provence (2.30), by Paul Cézanne is dominated by analogous blues and greens. Oranges, yellows, and yellow-greens help to emphasize the houses. Variations on green were used for the surrounding hills. Soft blue brushstrokes energize the landscape and fill the sky.

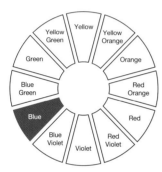

2.27 Monochromatic color system.

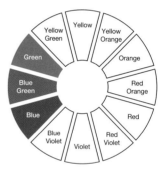

2.29 Analogous color system.

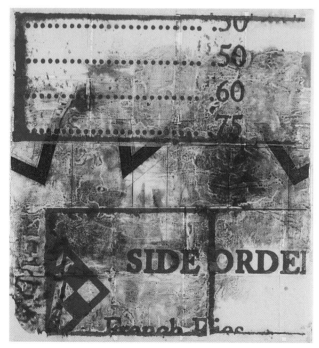

2.28 Guy Goodwin, *Tracers–Side Order,* 1999. Resin, polyurethane, ink on polycarbonate, 51 × 54 × 4 in. (130 × 137 × 10 cm).

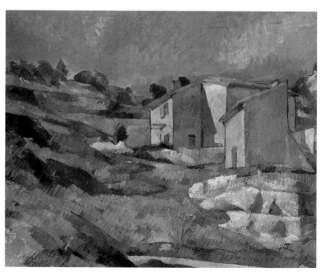

2.30 Paul Cézanne, *Houses in Provence (Vicinity of L'Estaque),* 1880. Oil on canvas, 25⅝ × 32 in. (65 × 81 cm).

Key Questions

- Which will work better in your design, a limited or a wide range of hues?

- What proportion of warm and cool colors best communicates your idea?

- What happens when you combine low-intensity colors with high-intensity colors?

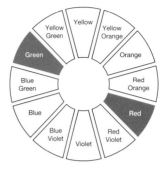

2.31 Complementary color system.

Complementary

The palette dramatically expands in a **complementary** color scheme (2.31). Complementary colors are opposites on the traditional color wheel. When mixed together, they can lower intensity and produce a wide range of browns. When paired in a composition, complementary colors become ideal partners. Each increases the power of the other.

Bacon's *Four Studies for a Self-Portrait* (2.32) is dominated by the complements of red and green. The design is unified by browns, including the reddish brown filling the background. Vigorous slashes of pure green and red add visual energy and create the illusion of movement.

Each complementary pair has its own distinctive strengths. Violet and yellow provide the widest value range, while orange and blue provide the widest range of variations in temperature. Red and green are closest in value and create extreme agitation when placed side by side. By mixing two complements plus black and white, we can create a range of colors that begins to suggest the power of a full spectrum.

Split Complementary

An even wider range of possibilities is offered by the **split complementary** color scheme (2.33). Rather than pair colors that are in opposite positions on the color wheel, the artist completes the scheme using the two colors on either side of one of the complements. Georgia O'Keeffe's *Jack in the Pulpit No. V* (2.34) is dominated by rich greens and violets, with accents of yellow at the top of the composition and a vertical line of red just to the left of the center.

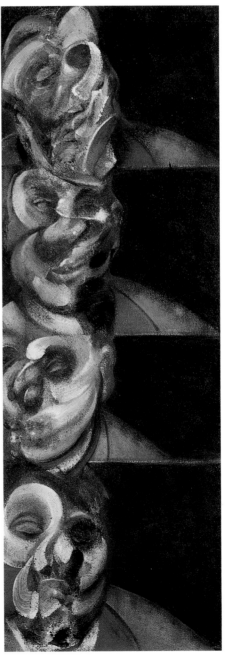

2.32 Francis Bacon, *Four Studies for a Self-Portrait,* **1967.** Oil on canvas, 36 × 13 in. (91.5 × 33 cm).

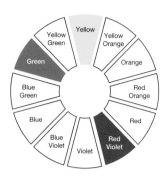

2.33 Split complementary system.

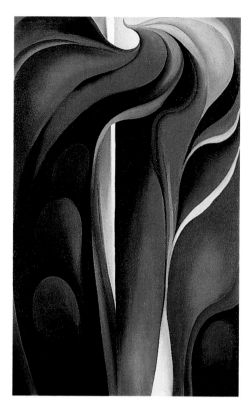

2.34 Georgia O'Keeffe, *Jack in the Pulpit No. V*, 1930. Oil on canvas, 48 × 30 in. (122 × 76 cm).

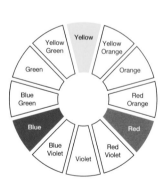

2.35 Triadic system.

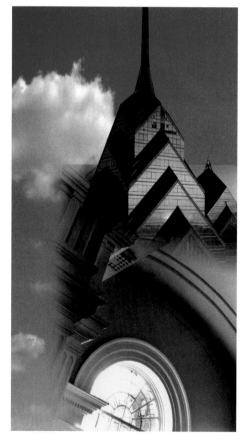

2.36 Joel Katz Design Associates, Cover of *Philadelphia Architecture: A Guide to the City*, 2nd ed., 1984.

Triadic

The **triadic** color scheme pushes the choices even farther apart, so that they are now located in a triangular position, equally spaced around the wheel (2.35). This scheme is often used when variety and a strong impact are essential. In a cover for *Philadelphia Architecture* (2.36), variations on red, blue, and yellow bring energy to the design, while the dark gray values provide detail.

Chromatic Grays and Earth Colors

While the basic color wheel can help us identify many kinds of relationships, two important types of colors are not included: chromatic grays and earth colors. A **chromatic gray** is made from a mixture of various hues, rather than a simple blend of black and white. The result is both subtle and vibrant. In *The Magpie* (2.37), the grays vary widely, from the purples and blue-grays in the shadows to the golden-gray light in the foreground and the silvery grays for the snow-covered trees. This is not a dark, sullen winter day. Through the use of chromatic grays, Claude Monet makes the warm light and transparent shadows sparkle in the crisp air.

Earth colors, including raw sienna and burnt sienna, raw and burnt umber, and yellow ochre, are made generally from pigments found in soil. Often warm in temperature, when used together they create a type of analogous harmony. For example, browns, oranges, and tans accentuate the gestural energy and organic shapes in *Bush Cabbage Dreaming at Ngarlu* (2.38), by Australian artists Cookie Stewart Japaljarri, Alma Nungarrayi Granites, and Robin Japanangka Granites. This acrylic painting was inspired by traditional aboriginal artworks, which are literally made from earth colors. When used alone, earth colors can unify even the most agitated composition. When used in combination with high-intensity colors, earth colors can provide a balance between subdued and overt colors.

Using Disharmony

Selecting the right colors can make the difference between a visual disaster and a visual delight. As a result, color harmony is the subject of endless books offering advice to artists, architects, and surface pattern designers. Monochromatic, analogous, complementary, split complementary, and triadic systems are traditional forms of color harmony.

However, cultural definitions of harmony are as changeable as popular music. In a search for fresh

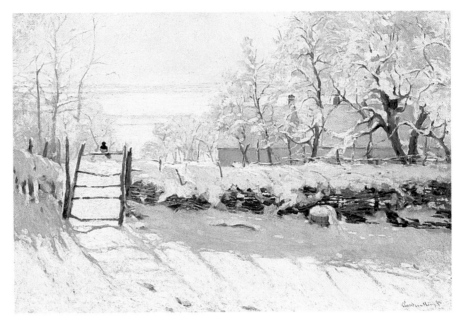

2.37 Claude Monet, *The Magpie*, 1869. Oil on canvas, 35 × 51 in. (89 × 130 cm).

and eye-catching images, designers in all fields invent new color combinations each year. For example, the pink, gray, and black prized by designers in one year may seem passé in the next. Consequently, definitions and uses of color harmony are actually quite fluid.

Furthermore, when skillfully used, color **disharmony** can be as effective as color harmony.

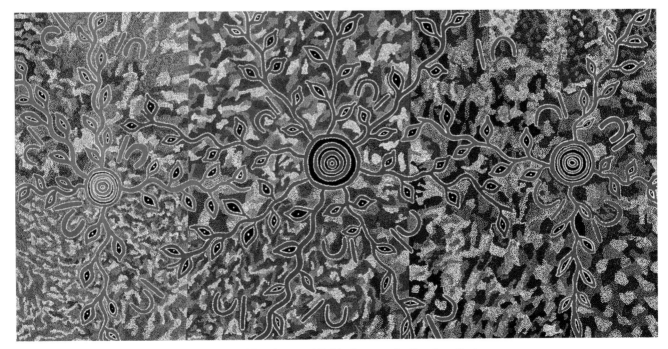

2.38 Cookie Stewart Japaljarri, Alma Nungarrayi Granites, and Robin Japanangka Granites; *Bush Cabbage Dreaming at Ngarlu;* Yuendumn, Central Australia, 1986. Acrylic on canvas, 47½ × 93½ in. (120.5 × 237.5 cm).

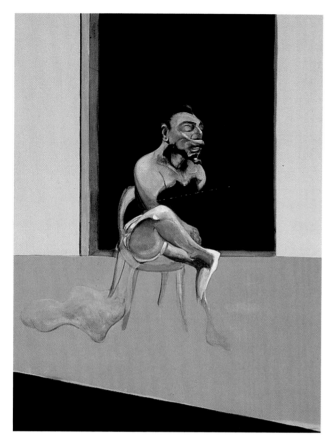

2.39 Francis Bacon, *Triptych*, 1972. Oil on canvas, one of 3 panels, each 78 × 58 in. (198.1 × 147.3 cm).

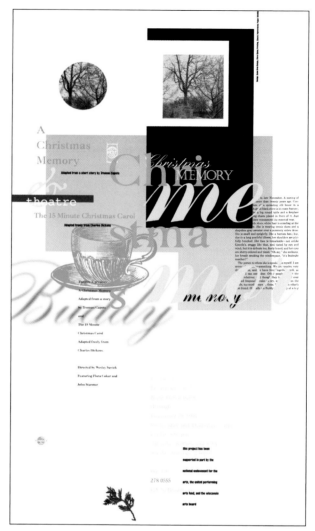

2.40 Steve Quinn, *A Christmas memory*, 1991. Photoshop, 11 × 17 in. (27.94 × 43.18 cm).

Disharmony is often used when the subject matter is disturbing or when an unusual visual approach is needed. In figure 2.39, Francis Bacon used pinks, grays, greens, and blacks to produce a painting that is as disturbing as it is beautiful. The colors in the body suggest disease, while the blocks of black, green, and gray create a room that is bleak and disorienting. Using a similar pink, gray, and black plus yellow-orange, Steve Quinn created a gentle evocation of memory in his Christmas poster (2.40). Here, the words and images shift back and forth in space, as fluid as a dream. As these examples demonstrate, the degree and type of harmony used must depend on the ideas behind the image and on the visual context in which an image will appear.

Key Questions

- What are the advantages of each of the traditional color schemes?

- When a limited palette is used, how can a few colors create the greatest impact? When a full palette is used, how can the colors become unified?

- What will happen if your composition is dominated by earth colors or chromatic grays?

- Which is more suitable for the idea you want to express: traditional color harmony or some form of disharmony?

COMPOSING WITH COLOR

Composition may be defined as the combination of multiple parts into a harmonious whole. The effect of color on composition is profound. Color can shift visual balance, create a focal point, influence our emotions, and expand communication. In this section, we will consider four major compositional effects of color.

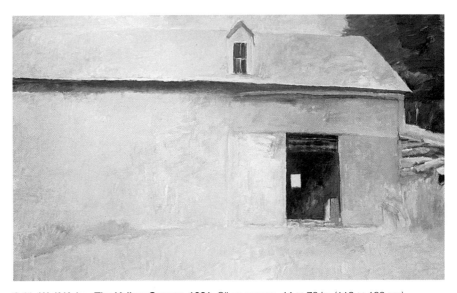

2.41 **Wolf Kahn,** *The Yellow Square,* **1981.** Oil on canvas, 44 × 72 in. (112 × 183 cm).

Creating the Illusion of Space

Pictorial space is like a balloon. When we "push" on one side, the other side appears to bulge outward. Through our color choices, we can cause various areas in a composition to expand or contract visually. In most cases, cool, low-intensity colors tend to recede, while warm, high-intensity colors tend to advance. In Wolf Kahn's *The Yellow Square* (2.41), the greens and violets defining the exterior of the barn gently pull the viewer into the painting, while the blazing yellow window inside the barn pushes out as forcefully as the beacon in a lighthouse.

This effect can play an even more important role in nonobjective paintings. As described by painter Hans Hofmann, the "push and pull" of color can be a major source of energy in a nonobjective composition. For example, a large block of intense red dominates Hofmann's *Magnum Opus* (2.42). The blue rectangle at the left side pulls us inward, while the crisp yellow shape on the right pushes outward.

2.42 **Hans Hofmann,** *Magnum Opus,* **1962.** Oil on canvas, 84⅛ × 78⅛ in. (213 × 198 cm).

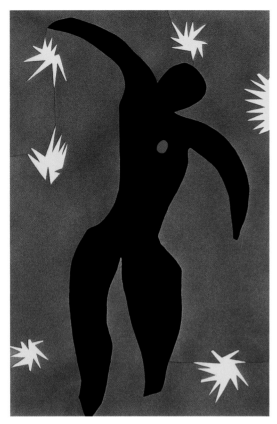

Weight and Balance

The effect of color on visual weight and balance is equally dramatic. In *Icarus* (2.43), Henri Matisse visually tells the story of the boy who flew too close to the sun, melting his wax wings and plunging into the ocean. The black body "falls" into the surrounding blue background, while a red heart seems to pull the figure upward, away from death. Six bursts of yellow surround the figure. Equally suggestive of the stars above the boy and of light shimmering on the water below, these simple shapes add energy to the composition and meaning to the myth.

Distribution and Proportion

Through careful distribution, even the most disharmonious colors can work together beautifully. Four rectilinear gray shapes dominate Nancy Crow's *Double Mexican Wedding Rings 1* (2.44). Gradated values extend outward, creating a subtle glow. Twelve small multi-colored squares accentuate the edges of the four large squares and frame up the composition as a whole. In most compositions, the earth colors, chromatic grays, and high-intensity reds, blues, and yellows would clash. In this composition, an even distribution of colors creates a unified and vigorous composition.

Proportional distribution is another way to harmonize seemingly incompatible colors. Willem de Kooning's *Door to the River* (2.45) is dominated by a large mass of brilliant yellow. Five small patches of blue-gray create a **subordinate accent color.** Vigorous strokes of olive and grays create essential connections between major compositional shapes, adding both energy and unity to the design.

2.43 Henri Matisse, *Icarus,* from *Jazz* series, 1947. Gouache on paper, cut and pasted, 17⅛ × 13⅜ in. (43.6 × 34 cm).

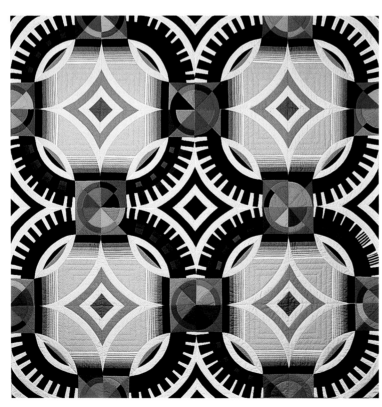

2.44 Nancy Crow, *Double Mexican Wedding Rings 1,* © 1988. Hand quilted by Marie Moore. 72 × 72 in. (183 × 183 cm).

Color as Emphasis

Graphic designers often use color to create a focal point within a composition. The subway map in figure 2.46 provides a good example. Cooler areas of gray, green, and blue, placed on a black background, provide basic structural information. The bright yellow lines show the path through the subway. Red, which is used at only one point in the diagram, clearly locates the viewer on the map.

Color can also be used to increase the compositional importance of a visual element. A small red astronomical observatory dominates Vernon Fisher's *Objects in a Field* (2.47). Located just above the center of the painting, it commands our attention while echoing the curved shape of the white parachute in the foreground.

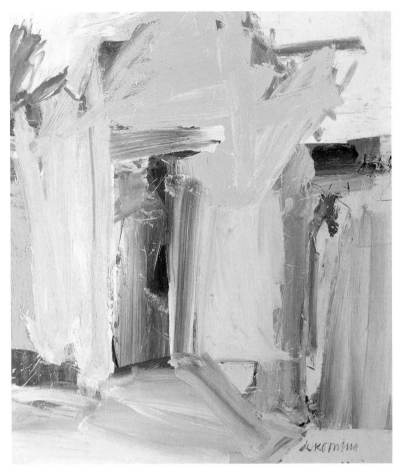

2.45 **Willem de Kooning,** ***Door to the River,*** **1960.** Oil on canvas, 80 × 70 in. (203.2 × 177.8 cm).

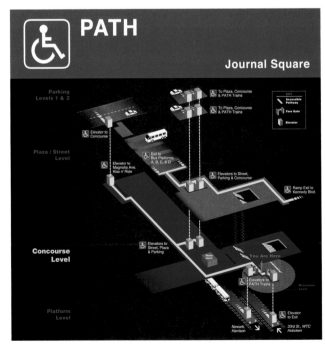

2.46 **PATH Station Maps, Louis Nelson Associates, Inc., NY.** Graphic designer: Jennifer Stoller.

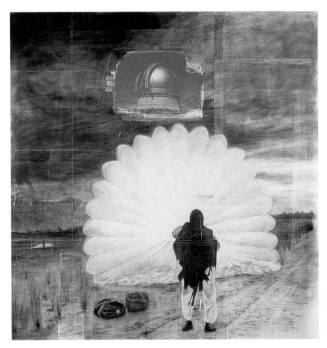

2.47 **Vernon Fisher,** ***Objects in a Field,*** **1986.** Acrylic on canvas, 8 × 8 ft (2.4 × 2.4 m).

COLOR, EMOTION, AND EXPRESSION

Colors are never emotionally neutral. The subtle browns and greens in Andrew Wyeth's *Wind from the Sea* (2.48) suggest the sepia color of a nineteenth-century photograph and evoke the slow pace and serenity of a countryside at rest. Richard Diebenkorn's *Interior with Book* (2.49), painted just 12 years later, provides a very different interpretation of a similar interior scene. The intense yellows and oranges in the background push toward us, while the solid blocks of blue pull inward, flattening the image. The tension and power thus generated create a California landscape that is a world apart from Wyeth's New England. The color in Sandy Skoglund's *Radioactive Cats* (2.50) creates yet another interpretation of an interior space. The gray walls, furniture, and clothing suggest a world that is lifeless and coated in ash. In contrast, the lime-green cats glow with an inquisitive energy that may be toxic!

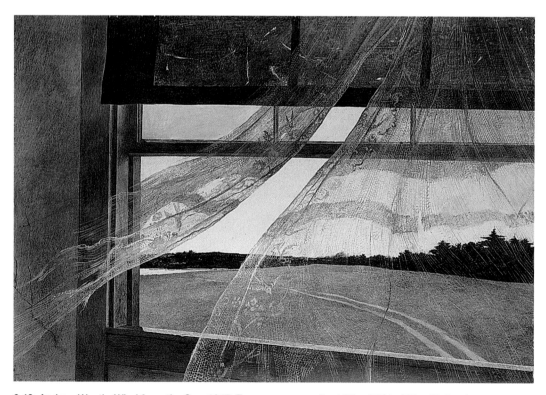

2.48 Andrew Wyeth, *Wind from the Sea*, 1947. Tempera on masonite, 18½ × 27½ in. (47 × 69.9 cm).

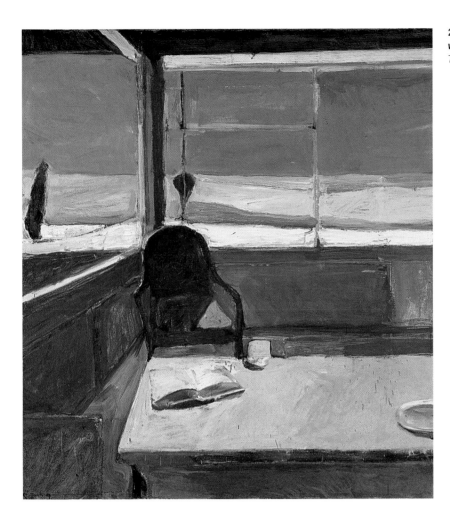

2.50 Sandy Skoglund, *Radioactive Cats,* 1980. Cibachrome print, 30 × 40 in. (76.2 × 101.6 cm).

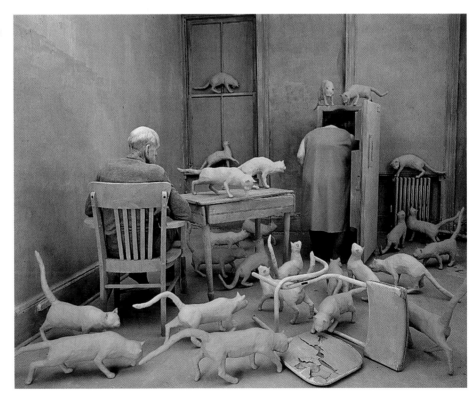

COLOR, EMOTION, AND EXPRESSION

Color Keys

A dominant color, or **color key,** can heighten psychological as well as compositional impact. The blues that dominate Joe Spadaford's *Illustrated Man* (2.51) suggest both magic and melancholy. Based on Ray Bradbury's collection of stories by the same name, Spadaford had to suggest the torment of a man whose tattoos come to life at night. At the other extreme, in Egon Schiele's *Portrait of Paris von Gütersloh* (2.52), the flaming orange around and within the figure places the anxious man in an emotional electric chair. In both cases, color was used to heighten emotion rather than represent reality.

Symbolic Color

Colors are often assigned symbolic meaning. These meanings may vary widely from culture to culture. In *The Primary Colors*, Alexander Theroux writes

> [Blue] is the symbol of baby boys in America, mourning in Borneo, tribulation to the American Indian and the direction South in Tibet. Blue indicates mercy in the Kabbalah and carbon monoxide in gas canisters. Chinese emperors wore blue to worship the sky. To Egyptians it represented virtue, faith, and truth. The color was worn by slaves in Gaul. It was the color of the sixth level of the Temple of Nebuchadnezzar II, devoted to the planet Mercury. In Jerusalem a blue hand painted on a door gives protection . . . and in East Africa, blue beads represent fertility.[2]

In Hopi culture, colors symbolize spatial location and geographic direction. The Kachina doll in figure 2.53 represents Butterfly Maiden, a benevolent spirit. Red represents a southerly direction; white, the east or northeast; blue or green, the west.

Symbolic color also plays a major role in *Flag* (2.54) by Jasper Johns. Part of a series of images based on the American flag, this print presents a reversal of the usual colors at the top. If we stare at this flag, then shift our attention to a white sheet of paper, we will once again see the familiar red, white, and blue. In this painting, an afterimage was used to suggest the contradictory nature of patriotism.

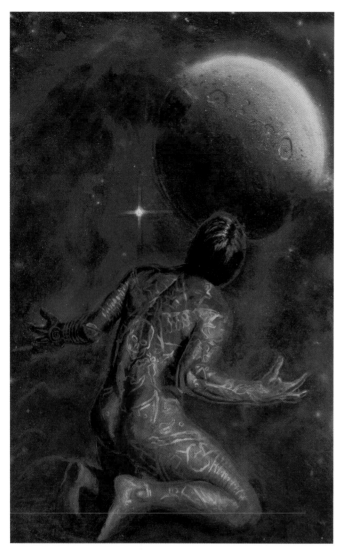

2.51 Joseph Spadaford, *Illustrated Man,* **1998.** Acrylic and airbrush on illustration board.

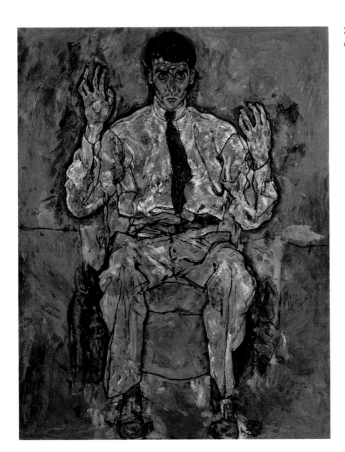

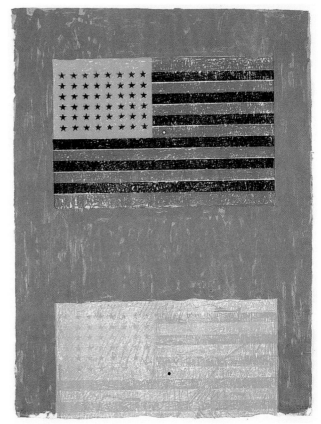

2.54 Jasper Johns, *Flag,* 1968. Lithograph, printed in color, composition: 34⅝ × 25⅞ in. (87.9 × 65.7 cm).

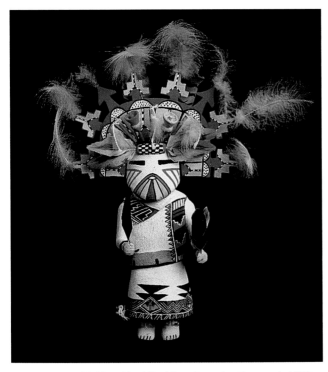

2.53 Butterfly Maiden, Hopi Kachina. Carved cottonwood, 13½ in. (35 cm).

COLOR, EMOTION, AND EXPRESSION

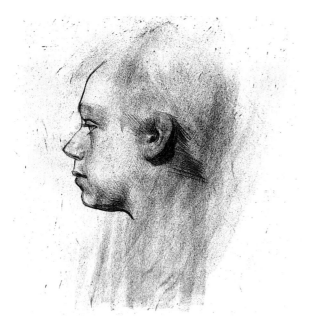

Käthe Kollwitz, *Self-Portrait in Profile, Facing Left, I,*
1889. Lithograph, 5⅞ × 5⅞ in. (15 × 15 cm).

Expressive Color

Color and value each have unique strengths. A group of self-portraits by Käthe Kollwitz demonstrates three possibilities. The black-and-white value study on cream-colored paper (2.55) has a simple eloquence, while a more developed value drawing (2.56) adds drama and definition to the figure. The last portrait (2.57) places the warm figure against the cool background and makes her seem more accessible.

Color can increase the power of a given shape, shift compositional weight, and create a focal point. It can enhance the illusion of space, suggest volume, and heighten emotion. Well used, color is one of the most expressive elements of art and design.

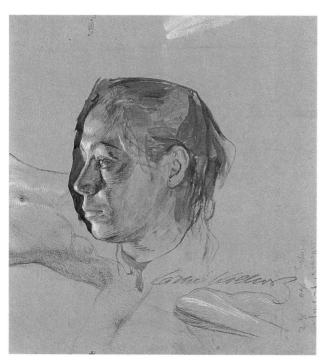

2.56 Käthe Kollwitz, *Selbstbildnis und Aktstudien (Self-portrait and Nude Studies),* **1900.** Pencil, dark gray ink wash, with white and yellowish highlights, on heavy brown paper, 11 × 17½ in. (27.8 × 44.5 cm).

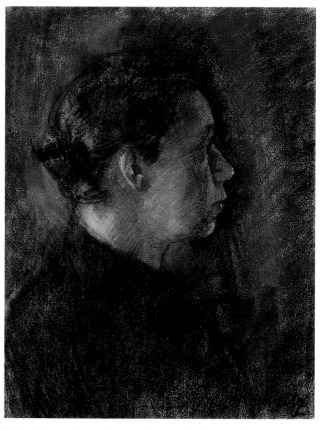

2.57 Käthe Kollwitz, *Selbstbildnis im Profil Nach Rechts,* **c. 1900.** Pastel on laid paper, 19 × 14⅜ in. (46.8 × 36.5 cm).

SUMMARY

- Color immediately attracts attention. Its emotional and physiological impact strengthens communication and heightens expression.

- Red, green, and blue are the additive color primaries. Blue, red, and yellow are the subtractive color primaries.

- The three basic qualities of color are hue (the name of the color), value (its lightness or darkness), and intensity (its purity).

- Using a monochromatic, analogous, complementary, split complementary, or triadic color scheme can increase harmony in your design.

- The level of color harmony must match the expressive intent. In the right context, disharmony can be more expressive than harmony.

- In a composition, color can enhance the illusion of space, shift visual weight and balance, and help emphasize compositional details.

- Distribution and proportion can help unify disharmonious colors.

- Colors are never emotionally neutral. A dominant color key can heighten psychological impact, while a symbolic color provides a cultural reference.

Keywords

accent color	color interaction	monochromatic	subtractive color
achromatic	color key	opponent theory	temperature
additive color	color overtone	primary colors	tertiary colors
afterimage	color theory	process colors	tint
analogous	complementary	saturation	tone
Bezold effect	composition	secondary colors	triadic
chroma	disharmony	shade	value
chromatic gray	hue	simultaneous contrast	
color harmony	intensity	split complementary	

Profile:
Ann Baddeley Keister, Fiber Artist

Color, Construction, and Communication:
Designing a Tapestry

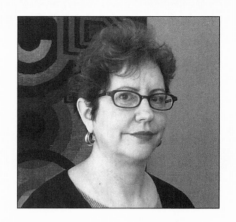

Ann Baddeley Keister is a nationally renowned fiber artist. She has a BFA and MFA degree from the University of Kansas and received further training in Aubusson tapestry techniques from Jean Pierre Larochette at the San Francisco Tapestry Workshop. Her work has been exhibited both nationally and internationally and is in many private and corporate collections, including The Vanguard Group, The Discovery Channel, and the Indianapolis Museum of Art. In this interview, we discussed a large-scale tapestry Ann designed for the downtown campus for Grand Valley State University in Michigan.

MS: When I look at your work, I am impressed by the very deliberate use of design in these complex narrative tapestries. These images could be painted or done on a computer so much more quickly. What is the advantage of weaving? What attracted you to fiber arts?

AK: My undergraduate degree actually was a general degree in design, which allowed me to explore a number of different craft and fine art media, including textiles. The University of Kansas has a great fiber facility, and since I had learned how to knit and sew at the age of seven, the materials of textile art just felt natural and familiar to me. I love making the structure through the repetitive action of weaving. And I'm attracted to the pliability of the material. For me, metals are too unforgiving, clay is too messy—fiber, as a material, just feels "right" to me. I feel that there is a strong symbiosis between the images that I am interested in making and the material from which those images are constructed. One seems to feed off of the other.

MS: Designer Paul Rand said, "Art is an idea that has found its perfect form. Design is the means by which this is realized." And it is often said that art is about expression, while design is about communication. Is your work both art and design?

AK: Yes, and it is also craft and decoration. Contemporary fiber arts is such a diverse field. I love pure pattern AND I love storytelling. I love looking at beautiful colors, and want to offer the viewer a visual feast through my work!

MS: What is your usual work process?

AK: Many of my projects begin with a commission. I determine the client's requirements and puzzle over possible solutions. With *Memory*, during a walk along the Grand River, I saw a historical marker describing the late nineteenth-century flood. I began to think about this terrible storm that washed away bridges and created piles of logs careening through the city. I immediately realized that this event could provide my image.

I made a number of pencil sketches, exploring compositional possibilities. I then developed these sketches in color, using the Adobe Illustrator. I have an extensive knowledge of color theory and this actually gives me the freedom to choose my colors very intuitively. I am using a lot of blue in this piece, since it is one of the school's colors, and I have a lot of discordant colors, which seem appropriate for such a devastating event.

A full-size, 6' × 10' computer print comes next. I match colors from my collection of approximately 200 colors of wool yarns. One strand on the loom is made up of six strands of yarn. I use a lot of optical mixing to create very subtle gradations. Finally, I weave the piece. The most useful thing I learned from my teachers is this: DO YOUR WORK! There is no substitute for action. Weaving is slow and simply has to be done consistently. During my summer work time, I am in the studio from about 9 to 6 an average of five or six days a week. Since weaving is an activity that makes demands on the body and the concentration, I do take breaks in my daily work with forays into the garden or other household chores. This is one reason that I find working at home so satisfying. My domestic interests in cooking, the garden, and my home often find their way into the imagery in my work as well.

MS: What are your criteria for excellence?
AK: I seek unity between concept and composition. Each of the formal elements: line, shape, texture, and color—is essential. There is almost always a dynamic sense of space in my work, which makes the tapestry read well in an architectural setting. I seek an inseparable connection between imagery, technique, and material.

MS: Do you have any advice for my students?
AK: Take this time to be inventive. Try out many possibilities. If you don't like an image, don't do it! Invent another way to solve the problem. The joy you bring to the creative process will be apparent in the final design.

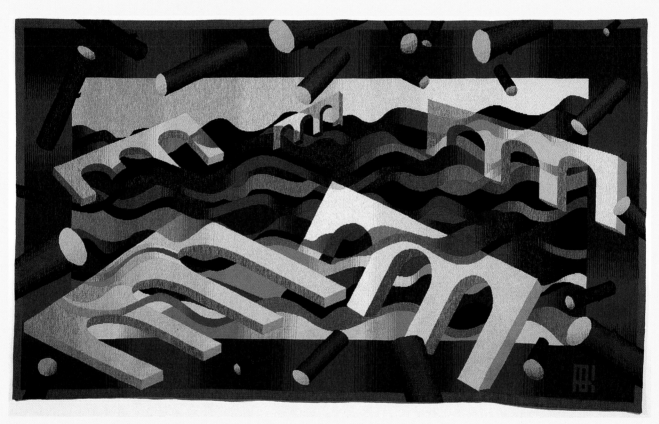

Ann Baddeley Keister, *Memory,* **2000.** Wool tapestry, 6 × 10 ft (1.83 × 3.1 m).

Principles of Two-Dimensional Design

Imagine yourself practicing jump shots on a deserted basketball court. By focusing all of your attention on the basket, you can master the sequence of moves needed to score. Now, imagine yourself playing in a high-paced game. You are now surrounded by skillful and cooperative teammates. The skills you practiced alone become heightened as you take passes and make shots. The complexities increase and the stakes rise when 10 players fill the court.

Developing a compelling composition can be equally exhilarating. **Composition** can be defined as "the combination of multiple parts into a unified whole."[1] In a well-composed design, line, shape, texture, value, and color work together, as a team. As one element becomes dominant, another element becomes subordinate. A dialogue is created between positive and negative shapes, and opposing forces add vitality rather than creating confusion. Through composition, we can create order, emphasize critical information, and evoke an emotional response.

We will begin this chapter with a discussion of unity and variety, the basis on which all design is built. We will then define and discuss balance, scale, proportion, emphasis, and rhythm. The chapter ends with a discussion of the illusion of space and the illusion of movement. Relationships between concept and composition will be emphasized throughout.

UNITY AND VARIETY

Unity can be defined as similarity, oneness, togetherness, or cohesion. **Variety** can be defined as difference. Unity and variety are the cornerstones of composition. When they are combined effectively, we can create compositions that are both cohesive and lively.

Mark Riedy used three major strategies to unify figure 3.1. First, all of the major shapes are organized diagonally, from the lower left to the upper right. A series of parallel lines in the sand and sea emphasizes this diagonal structure. Second, the top third of the painting is filled with the blue water, while the beach fills the bottom two-thirds. This proportional relationship has been used since antiquity to create a dynamic form of balance. Third, one shape is repeated 19 times, creating the graceful collection of umbrellas. Repetition in any form tends to increase unity.

A sailboat, 9 groups of bathers, and especially the single red umbrella add variety. The red umbrella breaks the pattern set by the 18 white umbrellas. The resulting focal point attracts our attention to a particular spot on the beach. As

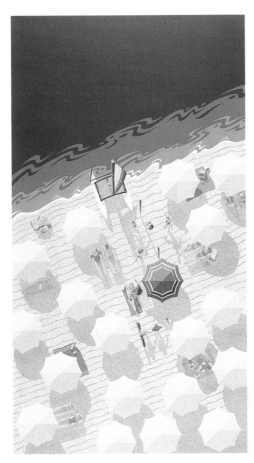

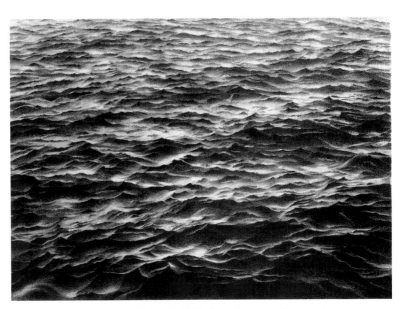

3.2 Vija Celmins, *Untitled (Ocean)*, 1969. Graphite on acrylic ground on paper, 14 × 18 in. (35.6 × 45.7 cm).

3.1 Mark Riedy, *Day at the Beach*, 1988. Acrylic airbrush.

we begin to notice the number of people clustered around this umbrella, we are pulled into the painting and the miniature world it represents. One small red circle dramatically changes our visual and emotional response to the entire painting.

We face a new compositional challenge with each design we make. There are no simple formulas: each idea has its own expressive requirements. For example, in figure 3.2, Vija Celmins used a highly unified drawing to create a quiet, contemplative image. The size and shape of the waves are the only variations. At the other extreme, Hannah Höch's *Cut with a Kitchen Knife* (3.3) is crowded with conflicting images and fragmentary words. Created shortly after the end of World War I, this collage reflects the tumultuous economic and political conditions in postwar Germany. Celmins used a highly unified pattern of waves to suggest the ocean's hypnotic power, while Hoch used a collection of conflicting images to suggest chaos. Using very different approaches, each artist created an appropriate composition for the concept she wished to convey.

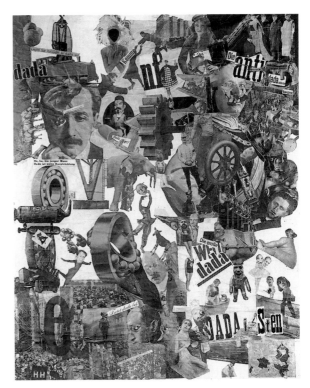

3.3 Hannah Höch, *Cut with a Kitchen Knife*, 1919. Collage, 44⅞ × 35½ in. (114 × 90 cm).

Creating an effective partnership between unity and variety is essential. Excessive unity can be monotonous, while excessive variety can be chaotic. In the following section, we will analyze these and other unifying forces in depth, consider ways to increase variety, and explore ways to create a partnership between the two.

Gestalt: Theory and Application

Artists and designers use many strategies to create compelling compositions. **Gestalt** psychology offers a fascinating analysis of these strategies. According to this theory, visual information is understood holistically before it is examined separately. We first scan the entire puzzle, then analyze the specific parts. Because the human mind can absorb only a limited number of separate bits, an image composed of units that are unrelated in size, style, orientation, and color will appear chaotic and unresolved. The implications of Gestalt are complex, and many books have been written on the subject. In this introduction, we will focus on six essential aspects.

Grouping

When presented with a collection of separate visual units, we immediately try to create order and make connections. **Grouping** is one of the first steps in this process. We generally group visual units by location, orientation, shape, and color. For example, the units in figure 3.4A form two distinct groups despite their dissimilarity in shape. Orientation

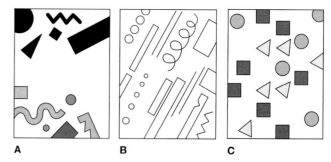

3.4A–C Examples of grouping by location, orientation, and shape.

creates group cohesion in figure 3.4B. The diagonal orientation of the various elements creates unity despite the shape variations. Grouping by shape is shown in figure 3.4C. We mentally organize this set of units by shape in spite of their similarity in size and value.

Rama and Laksmana Bound by Arrow-Snakes (3.5) demonstrates the compositional and conceptual power of grouping. We first see the complete composition. Multiple groups of humans and animals fill the long, horizontal rectangle. Next, we may notice that the composition is divided into three sections, each dominated by a distinctive background color.

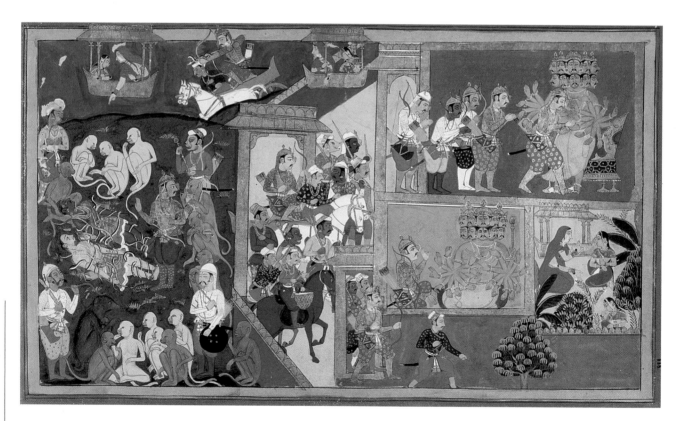

3.5 Sahibdin and workshop, *Rama and Laskshmana Bound by Arrow-snakes,* from the *Ramayana,* Mewar, c. 1650–52. Opaque watercolor on paper, 9 × 15⅛ in. (22.86 × 38.42 cm).

Blue and gray dominate the section on the left; red and orange dominate the section on the right, and a yellow background fills the center. Within these major groups, we can discern further subdivisions, including the two clusters of monkeys on the right, the four compositional boxes on the left, and the throng of horsemen in the center.

Like a comic book, this painting tells a complex story of prophecy, magical transformation, imprisonment, and escape. It begins in the rose-colored box on the right, as Indrajit devises a defense against Rama and Laskhmana, who are about to attack the palace. On the left, Indrajit's arrows turn into snakes, binding the attackers. Indrajit's triumphal march dominates the center of the composition. By grouping the various events, the artist was able to present complex visual information effectively.

Containment

As we can see from figure 3.5, groups are most easily created when visual units are placed inside a container. **Containment** is a unifying force created by the outer edge of a composition or by a boundary within a composition. A container encourages us to seek connections among visual units and adds definition to the negative space around each positive shape. In figure 3.6A, a random collection of shapes becomes more unified when a simple boundary is added (3.6B). Any shift in the location of this boundary creates a new set of relationships. A vertical rectangle is often used when a rising or sinking movement is needed, while a horizontal format can create an expansive effect (3.6C). The circular container in figure 3.6D draws our attention to both the center and the outer edges of the composition.

Larry Moore's illustration in figure 3.7 uses containment in an especially inventive way. Three containers are used in this composition: the edge of the drawing provides the first container; the curtains provide the second; and the face itself provides the third container. A wide variety of corporate logos cover the face. Logos must attract attention, regardless of the context in which they are placed, and each of these logos was originally designed as a distinct visual unit. In this composition, however, the individualistic logos become a cooperative team. The connections created by the three levels of containment are stronger than the separations created by the individualistic logos.

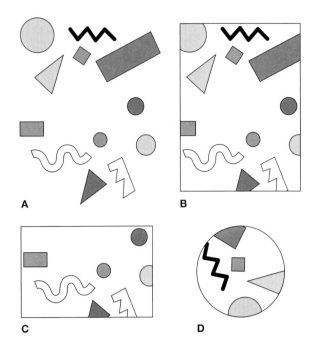

A   B

C   D

3.6 A–D A container of any kind helps unify disparate visual units.

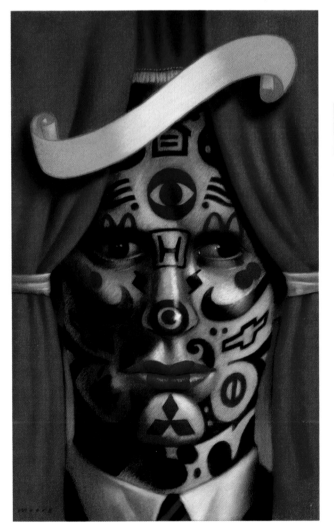

3.7 Larry Moore, for Creative Club of Orlando. Pastel on paper, 10 × 15 in. (25.4 × 38.1 cm).

Repetition

Repetition occurs when we use the same visual element or effect over and over. By leafing through Chapter One, we can find many examples of unity through repetition. Kandinsky's *Several Circles* (page 16) is unified by shape. The repeated circles create a cohesive design despite the wide range of colors used. Repeated textures unify many works,

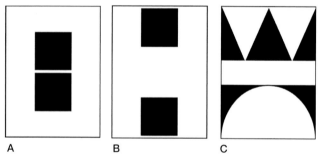

3.8 Aaron Macsai, *Panels of Movement.* Bracelet, 18K gold, sterling, copper, ⅞ × 7 in. (2 × 18 cm).

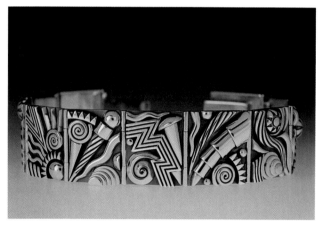

A   B   C

3.9A–C Variations in proximity.

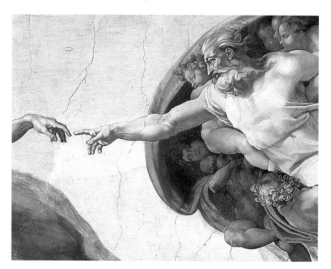

3.10 Michelangelo, *Creation of Adam* (after cleaning, 1989), c. 1510. Sistine Chapel, Rome.

including the Villon portrait on page 23, the Durer engraving on page 41, and the Moran landscape on page 46.

In Aaron Macsai's *Panels of Movement* (3.8), similar lines, shapes, textures, and colors were used in each of the 10 panels from which the bracelet was constructed. A spiral shape, an undulating line, a sphere, and at least one triangular shape appear in each of the panels. Despite their variations in size, texture, and location, these repeated shapes create a strong connection from panel to panel.

Proximity

In design, the distance between visual elements is called **proximity.** As shown in figure 3.9A, close proximity helps increase unity. More distant shapes read as separate events (3.9B). **Fusion** occurs when shapes or volumes are placed so close together that they share common edges. When shapes of similar color and texture fuse, new negative shapes can be created as the surrounding area becomes more clearly defined (3.9C).

Careful use of proximity can create visual tension, adding energy to the design. A detail from Michelangelo's *Creation of Adam* (3.10) demonstrates the expressive power of visual tension. Jehovah's hand, on the right, nearly touches Adam's hand, on the left. As we gaze upward at the ceiling of the Sistine Chapel, less than 6 inches of space separate the two. In this cosmology, all of human history begins when the spark of life jumps this gap. If the hands had been placed too far apart or too close together, the spark that animates both the man and the painting would have been lost.

Continuity

Continuity may be defined as a fluid connection among compositional parts. As shown in figure 3.11, this connection can be actual or implied. With actual continuity, each shape touches an adjoining shape. With implied continuity, we mentally make the connections. Actual continuity helps to unify the flowers at the top of the drawing, while implied continuity helps connect the hands of the clock to the flowers on the lower right.

Skillful use of continuity can add visual movement to a design. **Movement** creates deliberate visual pathways and helps direct the viewer's attention to areas of particular interest. In Frank

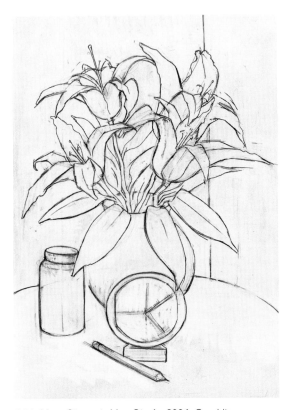

3.11 Mary Stewart, *Line Study*, 2004. Graphite, 12 in. × 9 in.

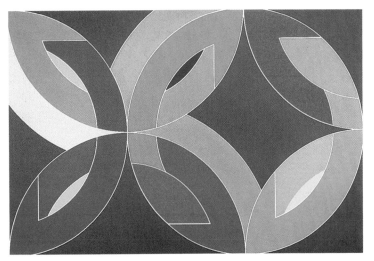

3.12 Frank Stella, *Lac Laronge IV*, 1969. Acrylic polymer on canvas, 9 ft ⅛ in. × 13 ft 6 in. (2.75 × 3.11 m).

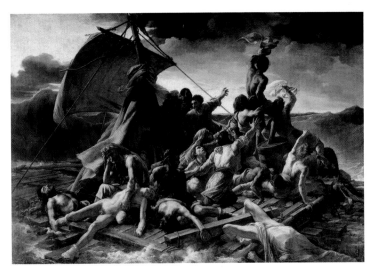

3.13A Théodore Géricault, *Raft of the Medusa*, 1818–19. Oil on canvas, 16 ft 1 in. × 23 ft 6 in. (4.9 × 7.2 m).

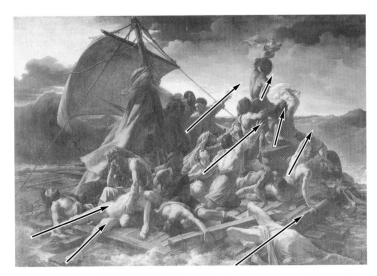

3.13B Diagram of *Raft of the Medusa*, showing eye movement toward focal point.

Stella's *Lac Laronge IV* (3.12), curving lines and shapes flow from one circle to the next, creating continuous visual flow. Color distribution enhances this effect. The upward curve of blue in the upper left corner is echoed by a quarter turn of blue in the lower right corner. The downward curve of reds in the lower left corner is echoed by a quarter turn of scarlet in the upper right corner. The hints of olive and ochre add a further spin to the wheel.

Movement can play an equally important role in a representational design. In Géricault's *Raft of the Medusa* (3.13A), a pattern of diagonal lines (3.13B) directs our attention to a single **focal point,** or primary point of interest. The arms and legs of the sailors, the floorboards of the raft, and even the angle of the sail all lead us toward the rescue ship in the upper right corner. This dramatic use of movement greatly increases the emotional power of this historical painting. One hundred forty-nine survivors from a sinking ship began a desperate journey on the raft.

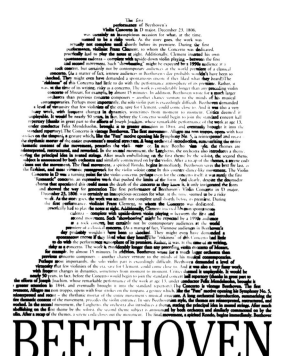

BEETHOVEN

3.14 Because of closure, hundreds of separate shapes can be combined to create a face.

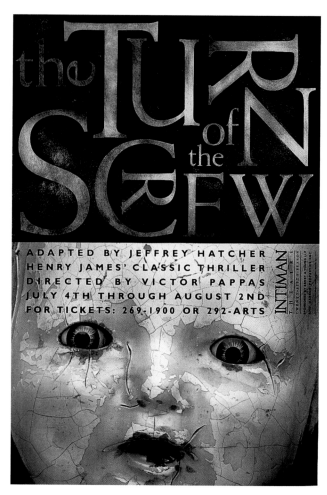

3.15 Cyclone Design, *Turn of the Screw.* Theater poster.

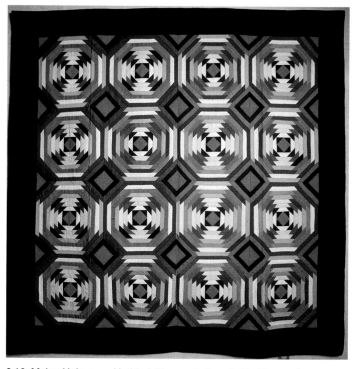

3.16 Maker Unknown, *Untitled*, Mennonite Log Cabin Pineapple Variation quilt, c. 1880–1900. Wool, 82 × 82 in. (208 x 208 cm). International Quilt Study Center, University of Nebraska-Lincoln, 1997.007.0691.

When rescued two weeks later, only 15 had survived. The pattern of bodies and extended arms pulls us irresistibly toward the sailor at the front of the raft, whose very life depends on the attention he can attract.

Closure

Closure refers to the mind's inclination to connect fragmentary information to produce a completed form. In figure 3.14, thousands of letters have been connected to form words, and hundreds of words have been connected to create a portrait of composer Ludwig von Beethoven.

Closure makes it possible to communicate using implication. Freed of the necessity to provide every detail, the artist or designer can convey an idea through suggestion, rather than description. When the viewer completes the image in his or her mind, it is often more memorable than an explicit image.

Combining Gestalt Principles

Artists and designers often combine all of the principles of Gestalt in a single composition. In figure 3.15, closure and containment help us read the disoriented words at the top of the composition. Proximity then helps us connect these words to the doll's face that fills the bottom half of the design. In *Turn of the Screw,* a play by Henry James, two children turn the tables on their governess, with devastating results. The turning text and frightened face convey both the title and the feeling perfectly.

Patterns and Grids

A **pattern** is created when any visual element is systematically repeated over an extended area (3.16). Many patterns are based on a module, or basic visual unit. A **grid** is created through a series of intersecting lines. Both can be used to create containment, increase continuity, strengthen proximity, and encourage closure. As a result, patterns and grids tend to increase compositional unity.

Patterns are often used to decorate walls, books, or fabrics. In his *Canterbury Tales,* designer William Morris used complex floral patterns to create multiple borders and backgrounds. Four major patterns are shown in figure 3.17. Curvilinear patterns of grape vines, flowers, and oak leaves fill the borders. The flowing text at the top of the page echoes these curving shapes and creates an additional pattern. There are even more patterns in the main drawing. The standing man is surrounded by two distinct leaf patterns, and a linear pattern suggests wood grain.

Multiple fragments of visual information can also be unified through pattern. In *Tar Beach* (3.18), Faith Ringgold used a pattern of repeating squares to organize blocks of printed fabric into a distinctive border. Based on Ringgold's own memories of sleeping on an apartment roof during hot weather, this pattern refers to the quilt depicted in the painting and to the magical expanse of buildings and lights visible from the rooftop.

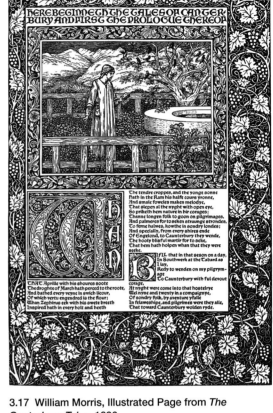

3.17 William Morris, Illustrated Page from *The Canterbury Tales*, 1896.

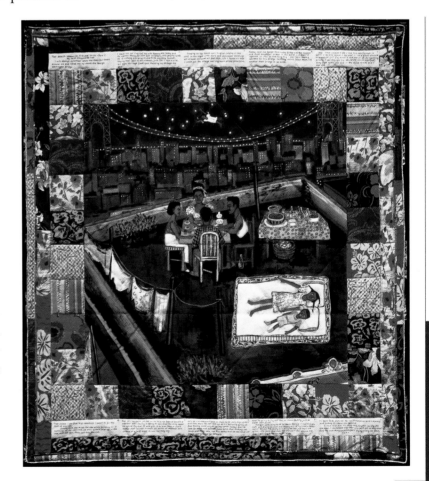

3.18 Faith Ringgold, *Tar Beach*, 1988. Acrylic on canvas, fabric border, 74 × 69 in. (187.96 × 175.26 cm).

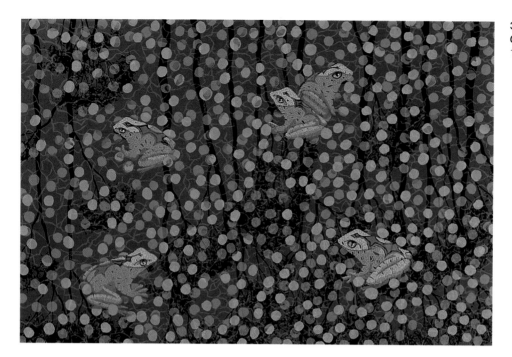

3.19 Lin Onus. *Gumiring Garkman.* 1994. Screenprint, 19⅝ × 29½ in.

Patterns can add energy as well as unity to a design. Hundreds of small circles provide a unifying pattern in figure 3.19. The circles are unified by their similarity in size and organization, while slight variations in color cause subtle shifts in visual space. The location of the five frogs within this pattern is unconventional. They sit like the corners of a skewed square, just to the left of center. As with na-

ture itself, an underlying pattern has been combined with unexpected variety to create a memorable image.

Grids are most commonly created using vertical and horizontal lines. The unifying power of a grid is so great that even the most disparate information gains cohesion when a grid is used. In Dobkin's Amnesty International leaflet (3.20A), commercial

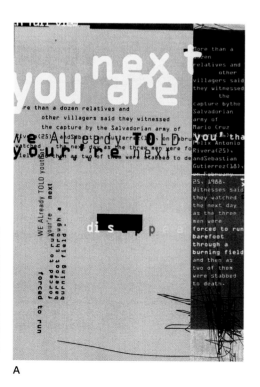

A

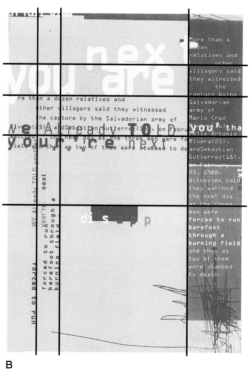

B

3.20A Joan Dubkin. Informational leaflet for Amnesty International, 1991.

3.20B Diagram of Amnesty International poster, showing organizational structure.

and handmade letterforms tell the story of political repression and governmental terror in El Salvador. Disoriented words and menacing phrases convey the helplessness and fear of the victims. Fragments of sentences appear and disappear unexpectedly. An underlying grid, shown in figure 3.20B, brings just the right amount of order to this poignant design.

Grids can be used to expand ideas as well as increase order. For example, in *Death by Gun* (3.21), Felix González-Torres used a grid to organize hundreds of photographs of weekly victims of gunfire in America. The large sheets were then photocopied and distributed to gallery visitors. The grid provides structure for the collection of images while emphasizing the sheer number of weekly deaths. As units with the grid, each victim was presented more as a statistic than as an individual.

Key Questions

- What strategies have you used to unify your composition?
- What gives your composition variety?
- Is the balance between unity and variety appropriate for the ideas you want to express?
- What would happen if your composition were constructed using a pattern or grid?

BALANCE

In design, **balance** refers to the equal distribution of weight or force among visual units. Visual balance creates equilibrium among compositional units, regardless of their size, weight, or shape. Negative and positive shapes work together to create balance.

Weight and Gravity

Visual weight can be defined in two ways. First, *weight* refers to the inclination of shapes to float or sink. Second, *weight* can refer to the relative importance of a visual element within a design.

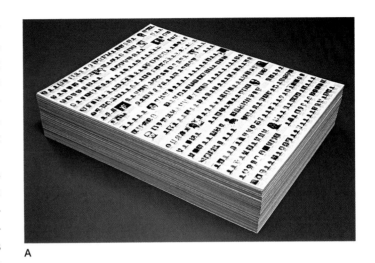

A

B

3.21 A–B. Felix González-Torres, *Untitled (Death by Gun)*, 1990. Offset print on paper, 44½ × 32½ in. (113.03 × 82.55 cm).

The compositional forces that most influence visual weight are size, value, type of shape, texture, location, and orientation. The context in which a visual unit is placed strongly affects each of these forces. For example, when a shape is placed on a neutral white ground, darker values and vigorous textures generally increase its visual weight. As noted in Chapter One, circles tend to stand out when placed in a rectangular format, while squares fit in more easily. Location within the format also affects visual weight. Shapes that appear to extend beyond the upper edge tend to rise, while shapes that appear to extend below the bottom appear to sink.

The vertical, horizontal, or diagonal orientation of a line or shape also affects visual weight. Try this simple experiment. Which is the most dynamic and which is the most static position for the box in fig-

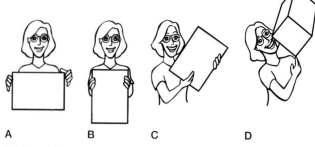

3.22 Which box is the most static? Which is the most dynamic?

ure 3.22? Most viewers find positions A and B the most static, or stable. In these positions, the box is at rest, with the vertical and horizontal edges reconfirming the stability we experience when objects are at rest in the real world. By contrast, position C and position D place the box in a dynamic position, halfway between standing and falling. A composition that is dominated by diagonals tends to be visually dynamic, while a composition that is dominated by horizontals tends to be more stable, or static.

Bernice Abbott's photograph of New York skyscrapers (3.23) demonstrates the power of orientation. Using dramatic vertical shapes within a tall vertical format, she captured the soaring energy of Wall Street within a small image. Even the most abstract design is governed by gravity. In figure 3.24, a rectangle filled with horizontal lines suggests the stability and tranquility of a landscape. Image stability would have increased if a horizontal format had been used. Instead, by using a vertical orientation and devoting the upper half to a gradated blue shape, Tetsurō Sawada combined the serenity of a landscape with the expansive feel of the soaring sky.

Visual weight can also refer to the relative importance of a visual element within a

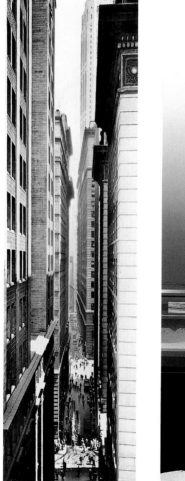

3.23 Bernice Abbott, *Exchange Place,* **New York, 1934.** Photograph.

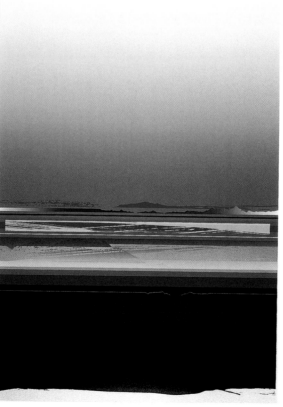

3.24 Tetsurō Sawada, *Brilliant Scape (Blue),***1985.** Silkscreen, 22⅞ × 15¾ in. (58 × 40 cm).

design. In *Moonrise, Hernandez, New Mexico, 1941* (3.25), Ansel Adams combined balance, gravity, and movement to create an image that is both tranquil and dramatic. A squarish format dominated by horizontal lines provides stability. The quiet village sinks to the bottom of the design. The tiny moon, positioned just to the right of compositional center, pulls us into the velvety black sky at the top half of the image. As the focal point for the image, the moon has the most visual weight in this photograph.

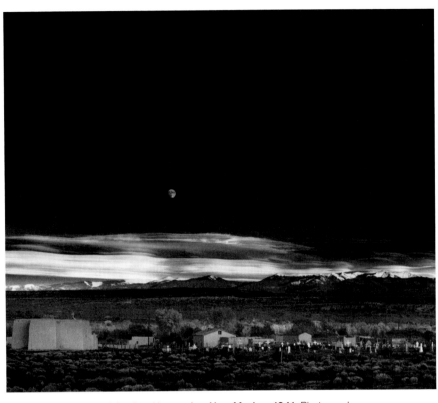

3.25 Ansel Adams, *Moonrise, Hernandez, New Mexico, 1941.* Photograph.

Symmetrical Balance

Symmetrical balance occurs when shapes are mirrored on either side of an axis, as in a composition that is vertically divided down the center (3.26A). A shift in this axis (3.26B) creates symmetry between the top and bottom of the design.

A symmetrically balanced design can appeal to our desire for equilibrium and communicate calm and stability. The Taj Mahal (3.27) was built by a seventeenth-century Indian emperor as a tomb for his beloved wife. The three white marble domes and the four flanking towers create architectural symmetry. In the reflecting pool, a mirror image appears, increasing visual symmetry. The building is both graceful and serene.

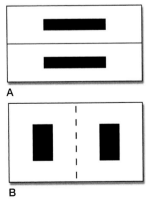

3.26 Examples of symmetrical balance.

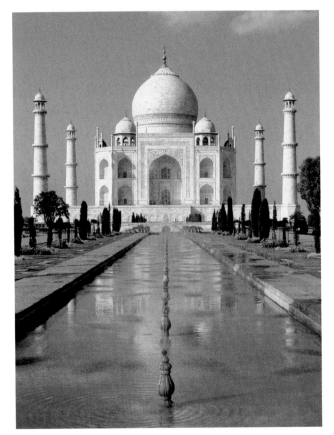

3.27 Taj Mahal, Agra, India.

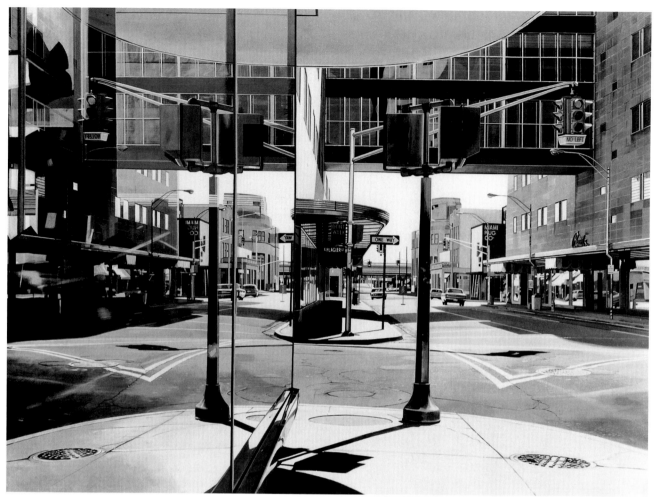

3.28 Richard Estes, *Miami Rug Company,* **1974.** Oil on canvas, 40 × 54 in. (101.6 × 137.16 cm).

Approximate symmetry is created when similar imagery appears on either side of a central axis. For example, in Richard Estes' *Miami Rug Company* (3.28), actual and reflected light poles divide the space as decisively as a gate. Radiating from the center of the composition, a network of diagonal lines pulls us into the painting. At the same time, the large pane of glass on the left side pushes toward us, shimmering with darkened reflections of the buildings on the right side. The overall effect is unnerving. The seemingly symmetrical shapes are actually quite different, and the resulting image is disorienting rather than serene.

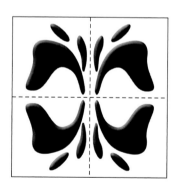

3.29 Radial symmetry can be created when lines and shapes are mirrored both vertically and horiontally.

Radial Symmetry

With **radial symmetry,** lines and shapes are mirrored both vertically and horizontally, with the center of the composition acting as a focal point (3.29). An expanded approach to radial symmetry is shown in Judy Chicago's *Rejection Quintet: Female Rejection Drawing* (3.30). Because the format is now divided diagonally as well as vertically and horizontally, the entire design radiates from the center.

A popular variant on radial balance is the spiral. A spiral can increase energy in a circular format or add

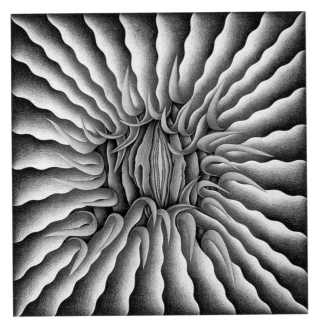

3.30 Judy Chicago, *Rejection Quintet: Female Rejection Drawing,* **1974.** Prismacolor and graphite on rag/board, 39⅝ × 29⅝ in. (101 × 75 cm).

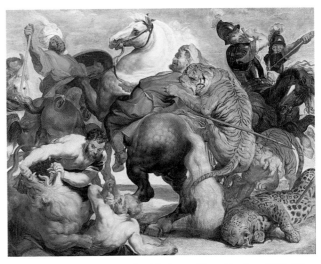

3.31A Workshop of Peter Paul Rubens, *Tiger Hunt,* **c. 1616.** Oil on canvas, 38⅞ × 49¼ in. (98.8 × 125 cm).

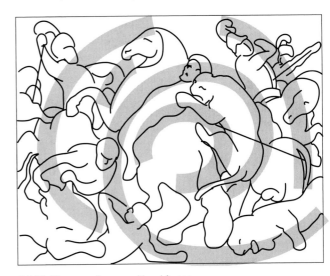

3.31B Diagram of compositional forces.

movement to a rectangular composition. In Rubens' *Tiger Hunt* (3.31A–B), the spiral pulls the tiger and the hunters together in the center of the painting. It then spins outward, breaking apart near the edges.

Asymmetrical Balance

Asymmetrical balance creates equilibrium among visual elements that do *not* mirror each other on either side of an axis. Depending on the degree of asymmetry, the resulting design may be quite stable, very dynamic, or nearly chaotic.

Many strategies can be used to create asymmetrical balance:

- A large shape is placed close to the fulcrum, while a small shape is placed farther away. Just as a child at the end of a seesaw can balance an adult near the center, so large and small shapes can be balanced in a design (3.32A).

- Multiple small squares, acting together, can balance a large square (3.32B).

- A small, solid square can balance a large, open circle. The solidity and stability of the square give it additional weight (3.32C).

- A textured shape placed near the fulcrum can be balanced by a distant open shape (3.32D).

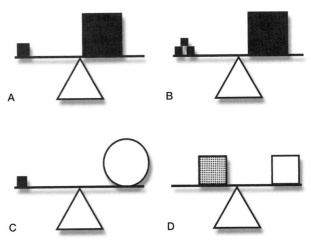

3.32A–D Creating assymetrical balance.

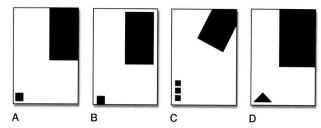

A   B   C   D

3.33 Examples of asymmetrical balance.

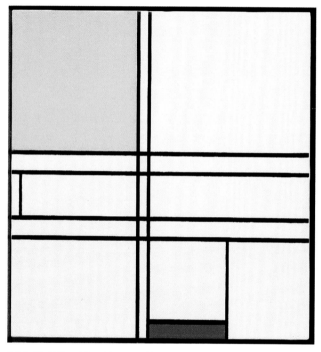

3.34 Piet Mondrian, *Composition with Blue and Yellow,* **1935.** Oil on canvas, 28¾ × 27¼ in. (73 × 69.2 cm).

Asymmetrical balance becomes even more interesting when a boundary is added. Because the negative space is just as important as each positive shape, more complex compositions can now be created:

- A small shape placed near the bottom of the format balances a large shape placed along the top. Especially within a tall rectangle, shapes placed near the top tend to rise, while shapes placed near the bottom tend to sink (3.33A).

- When the small square intersects the bottom edge and the large square moves away from the edge, the differences in weight become even more pronounced (3.33B).

- The top shape now gains energy through its diagonal orientation. Three bottom shapes are needed to create balance (3.33C).

- Finally, a small, aggressive shape can balance a large, passive shape (3.33D).

Balance in a composition shifts each time a visual element is added or subtracted. A complex network of negative and positive lines and shapes creates the balance in Mondrian's *Composition with Blue and Yellow* (3.34). The large yellow square positioned along the top edge is easily balanced by the small blue rectangle, which sinks to the bottom. Very minor changes can substantially shift compositional balance.

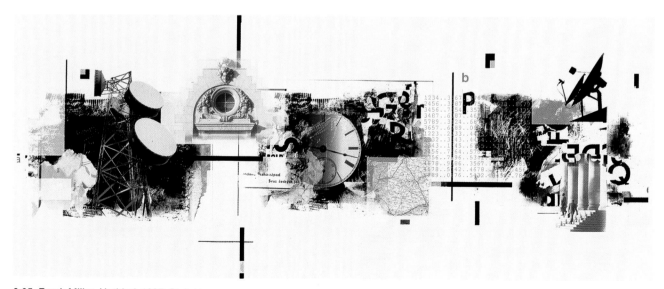

3.35 Frank Miller, *Untitled,* **1997.** Digital image.

The balance in Frank Miller's digital design (3.35) is even more complex. A horizontal line extends from the left to the right, in slightly descending steps. Four broken vertical lines divide the design into three major sections, each roughly one-third of the total length. Within these sections, the curving satellite dishes, clock, and letters add a series of repeated curves. Multiple lines, shapes, and clusters of information have been balanced in this image.

Expressive Uses of Balance

Each type of balance has its advantages. The approximate symmetry Frida Kahlo used for her double self-portrait (3.36) is symbolically appropriate and compositionally effective. Painted in response to her divorce from painter Diego Rivera, it presents the beloved Frida in a native costume on the right and the rejected Frida in European dress on the left. A linear vein connects the women's hearts. In figure 3.30, Judy Chicago used radial symmetry to pull the viewer into the composition. In figure 3.1 (see page 63), Mark Riedy used asymmetrical balance to animate his beach scene and accentuate the red umbrella.

There are even some cases in which a degree of **imbalance** is necessary. Eric Fischl used imbalance very deliberately in *Barbeque* (3.37). The table in the foreground is tilted and the bowl of fish is impossi-

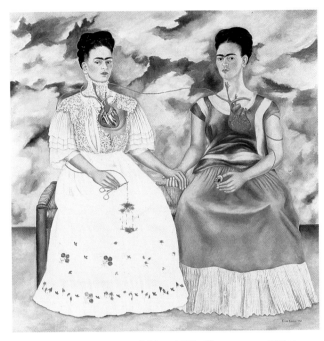

3.36 Frida Kahlo, *Las Dos Fridas*, 1939. Oil on canvas, 69⅛ × 69⅛ in. (176 × 176 cm).

bly large. Pulled by the diagonal lines leading to the house, the pool seems strangely distorted, while the tiny women are more like dolls than people. Manning the grill, the father looks on approvingly as his son engages in a little recreational fire-breathing. Spatial distortion combined with a bizarre collection of objects and events turns a family picnic into a suburban nightmare.

3.37 Eric Fischl, *Barbeque.* 1982. Oil on canvas. 5 ft. 5 in. × 8 ft. 4 in.

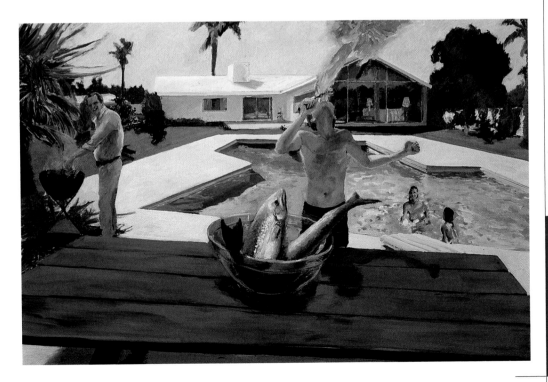

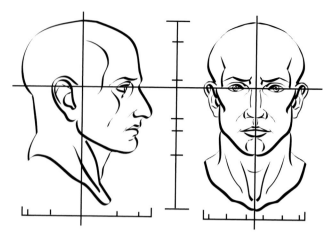

3.38 Proportion is an essential part of figure drawing.

SCALE AND PROPORTION

Scale and proportion strongly affect compositional balance and emotional impact. **Proportion** refers to the relative size of visual elements *within* an image. When we compare the width of the head with its height or divide a composition into thirds, we are establishing a proportional relationship (3.38). **Scale** commonly refers to the size of a form when compared with our own human size. Thus, a 50-foot-long painting is a large-scale artwork, while a 10-square-inch square painting is an example of small scale.

Most designs distribute information fairly evenly within the format, with only modest size variation among the parts. Exaggerating these proportions can be eye-catching, because the image immediately stands out from the norm. In *Save Our City*, by Michael Bierut (3.39), the large black rectangle at the top presses down on the white shape below, covering the top part of the word *Save*. Meanwhile, the vertical white text suggests a city skyline and helps pull the white section of the poster upward. This tension between the upper and lower sections of the design perfectly matches the urgency of the message.

Likewise, various expressive possibilities occur when scale is exaggerated. *Intermission* (see page 97) presented many challenges to painter Ken Stout. The 50-foot-long format had to become an asset, rather than a liability. We visually enter the theater through the pink doorway at the far left. Cool blue light bathes the restless audience. Two men in the balcony add to the action, as one aims a peashooter

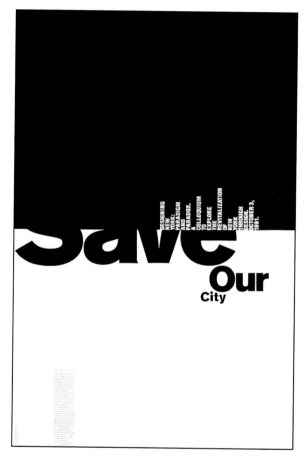

3.39 Michael Bierut, *Save Our City*. Design Firm: Pentagram, NYC.

and another launches a paper airplane. On the stage, a tiny actor creates a transition between the audience and the stage crew. The painting ends in a final burst of red, at the far right side. Taking advantage of each square inch, Stout created a swirling panorama of figures engaged in a wide variety of activities, onstage, backstage, and in the audience.

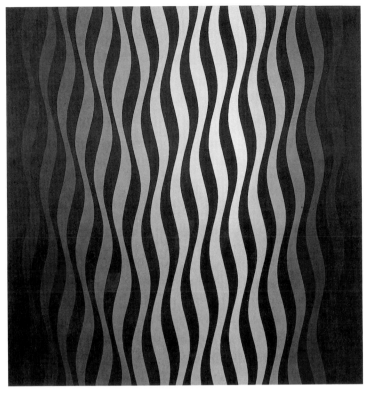

3.40 Bridget Riley, *Drift No. 2,* 1966. Acrylic on canvas, 7 ft 7½ in. × 7 ft 5½ in. (2.32 × 2.27 m).

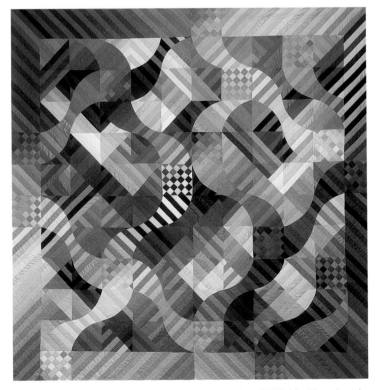

3.42 Michael James, *Rhythm/Color: Improvisation,* 1985. Machine-pieced and -quilted cotton and silk, 99½ × 99½ in. (253 × 253 cm).

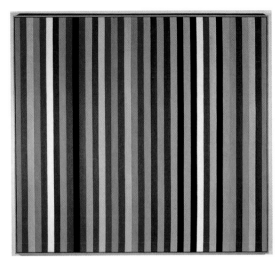

3.41 Gene Davis, *Billy Budd,* 1964. Acrylic on canvas, 5 ft 8½ in. × 6 ft 4⅞ in. (2.32 × 2.27 m).

RHYTHM

Rhythm is created when multiple units are presented in a deliberate pattern. Visual rhythm is similar to musical rhythm. In music, rhythm is created through the organization of sound in time. Meter (the basic pattern of sound and silence), accents (which emphasize specific notes), and tempo (the speed with which the music is played) can be combined to create a dazzling array of compositional possibilities.

As with music, the rhythm in a visual composition can take many forms. In Bridget Riley's *Drift No. 2* (3.40), a simple line has been repeated to create an undulating rhythm similar to the waves on the surface of a pond. Stripes of various colors create a spatial rhythm in Gene Davis' *Billy Budd* (3.41). Warm and cool colors in various values and intensities were used, causing some stripes to advance while others recede.

Michael James combined undulating and spatial rhythms in his *Rhythm/Color: Improvisation* (3.42). A series of square blocks creates a unifying grid. Diagonal lines within each block and the curving shapes between blocks add another layer of movement. Fifteen blocks covered with diamond shapes provide accents, while a pattern of radiating diagonals energizes the border.

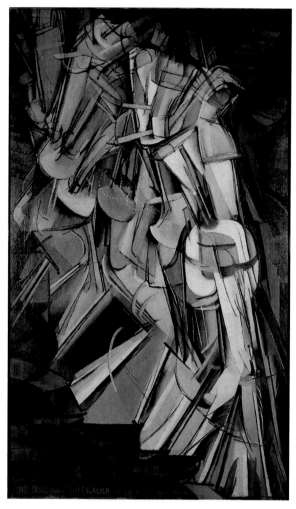

3.43 Marcel Duchamp, *Nude Descending a Staircase, No. 2*, 1912. Oil on canvas, 58 × 35 in. (147.3 × 88.9 cm).

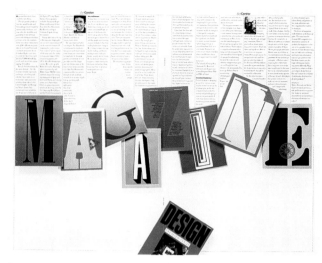

3.44 Pentagram Design, **Magazine.** Publisher: Art Center College of Design, Pasadena, CA.

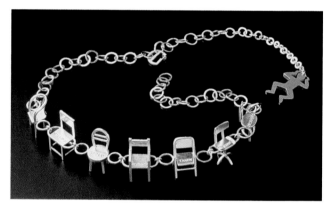

3.45 Joana Kao, *I Never Liked Musical Chairs.* Bracelet, sterling, 24K, 2¾ × 1¾ in. (7 × 4 cm).

Visual rhythm can be as regular as a waltz or as syncopated as jazz. Multiplication, fragmentation, and superimposition propel the nude descending Duchamp's staircase (3.43). The jerking rhythm demonstrates the alternating stability and instability of human locomotion, rather than physical grace.

EMPHASIS

Each player in a basketball game has a particular role to play. The guards primarily focus on defense, the forwards on offense. The point guard plays a dominant role, calling plays and controlling the action. Likewise, the various visual elements in a composition must work together as a team. In most cases, a few carefully selected visual elements dominate, or stand out, while others are subordinate, or supportive.

Emphasis gives prominence to part of a design. A focal point is a compositional device used to create emphasis. Both emphasis and focal point are used to attract attention and increase visual and conceptual impact.

Emphasis by Isolation

Any **anomaly,** or break from the norm, tends to stand out. Because we seek to connect the verbal and visual information we are given, a mismatched word or an isolated shape immediately attracts our attention. In figure 3.44, the word *design* is emphasized through its separation from the word *magazine*. Its placement right at the bottom edge makes this shape even more eye-catching.

Just as a pattern tends to increase connection among visual elements, so any break in the pattern emphasizes isolation. In figure 3.1 (page 63), 18 white umbrellas establish the pattern that is so beautifully broken by the single red umbrella. In *I Never Liked Musical Chairs* (3.45), metalsmith Joana Kao created a pattern using 7 tiny chairs connected by a silver chain. The figure at the end of the chain breaks the pattern. This break conveys the isolation felt by a child ejected from the game.

Emphasis by Placement

Every square inch of a composition has a distinctive power. As a result, placement alone can increase the importance of a selected shape.

The compositional center is especially potent. In his *The Power of the Center*, psychologist Rudolph Arnheim discusses **centricity** (compressive compositional force), and **eccentricity** (expansive compositional force). Both centricity and eccentricity activate *Flash Point*, shown on page 30. The central white square pulls us into the middle of the painting, while the explosive red rectangle pushes toward the outer edge.

This effect is even more pronounced in figure 3.46. Any representation of another human attracts our attention, and faces are of particular interest. Four major lines and a series of concentric circles direct us inward, toward the man's left eye. Fragments of text extend outward, beyond the edge of the composition. Continually compressing and expanding, the seemingly simple image pulls the viewer inward while simultaneously appearing to extend outward, beyond the boundary.

Emphasis Through Contrast

Contrast is created when two or more forces operate in opposition. By reviewing the elements and principles of design discussed in this section, we can quickly create a long list of potential adversaries, in-

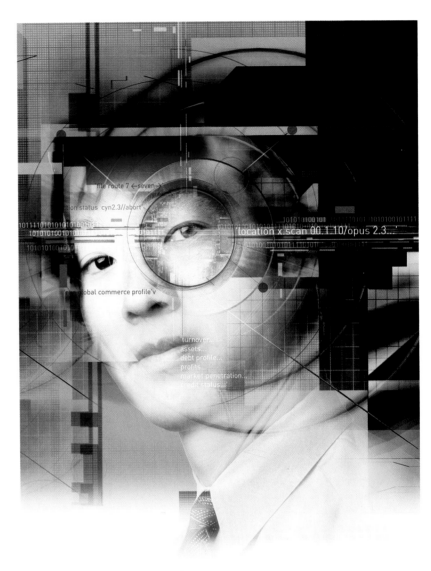

3.46 Jacey, *Untitled*, computer graphics. Example of centricity and eccentricity.

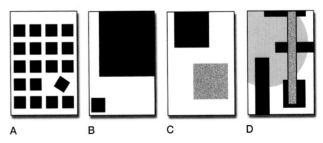

A   B   C   D

3.47A–D Examples of contrast.

cluding static/dynamic, small/large, solid/textured, and curvilinear/rectilinear (3.47A–D).

When the balance is just right, powerful compositions can be created from any of these combinations. Devoting about 80 percent of the compositional space to one force and about 20

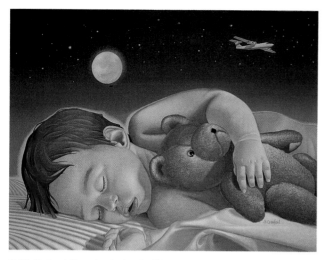

3.48 Robert Crawford, *Jamie Sleeping*, 1988. Acrylic on canvas, 20 × 14 in. (50.8 × 35.5 cm).

percent to the other is especially effective. The larger force sets the standard, while the smaller force creates the exception. Just as a single basketball player wearing a blue uniform will stand out if the other four players wear yellow, so a smaller force can dominate a design. Consider these examples:

- *Contrast in scale.* In figure 3.48, the small airplane and the moon become charged with meaning when combined with the image of the sleeping child. Dreams take flight.

- *Contrast in shape.* Zurbarán's *Saint Serapion* (3.49) provides a brilliant example of contrast by shape as well as emphasis by separation. The small note pinned at the right edge of the canvas gains so much power that it easily balances the large figure filling the rest of the frame.

- *Contrast in color.* One of the most compelling uses of emphasis by color occurs in *Schindler's List,* by Steven Spielberg (3.50). Midway through the black-and-white film, a small girl in a red coat is shown walking toward her death. She breaks away from the line and runs back to hide under a bed in a nearby house. This is the only use of color in the main body of the film. When her red coat appears again, her body is being transported to a bonfire. This simple use of color creates one of the most emotional moments in a remarkable film.

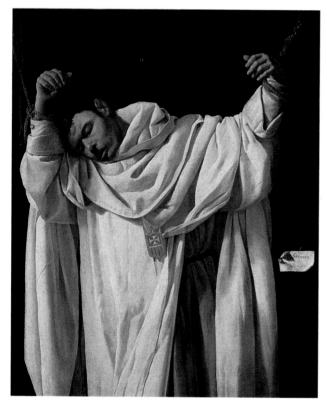

3.49 Francisco de Zurbarán, *Saint Serapion*, 1628. Oil on canvas, 47½ × 41 in. (120.7 × 103.5).

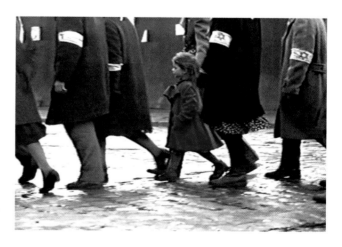

3.50 Still from *Schindler's List,* by Steven Spielberg.

Key Questions

- What would happen to your composition if you dramatically changed its scale or shifted its proportions?
- Is there a dominant shape in your composition? If so, is it the shape you most *want* to emphasize?
- Is there a focal point in your composition? If not, should there be?

Now, let's return to our basketball game for a moment. First, place yourself in the bleachers, high above the court. As a spectator, you can easily observe the overall distribution of players and follow the flow of the game. Now, mentally place yourself in the middle of the game, passing the ball and making shots. As a player, you are physically engaged in a complex and ever changing event. The game swirls with activity as players advance and recede in space.

In the preceding section, we focused on the overall distribution of compositional elements and analyzed the basic structure of a visual game. In this section, we will explore ways to create the illusion of space and the illusion of movement. By pulling viewers into our compositions, we can create a very different type of engagement.

CREATING THE ILLUSION OF SPACE

Just as symmetrical balance is appropriate for some images while asymmetrical balance is appropriate for others, so each type of space offers distinct advantages. The opening page of the medieval *Book of Kells* (3.51) is spatially shallow. Assorted human figures huddle to the right of the dominant vertical shape, while intricate border patterns flatten the space. At the other extreme, the spatial depth in Altdorfer's *Battle of Alexander* (3.52) is so convincing that we almost feel we can enter this battle between Alexander the Great and King Darius of Persia. The flat wooden panel has been transformed through the illusion of space.

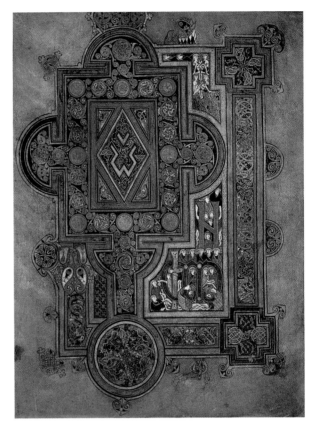

3.51 Book of Kells: Opening page, St. Luke's Gospel. Trinity College, Dublin, 9½ × 13 in. (24 × 33 cm).

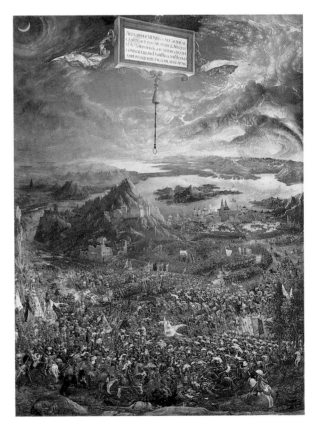

3.52 Albrecht Altdorfer, *Battle of Alexander*, 1529. Limewood, 47¼ × 62¼ in. (120 × 158 cm).

Linear Perspective

Linear perspective is a mathematical system for projecting the apparent dimensions of a three-dimensional object onto a flat surface. This surface, called the **picture plane,** is comparable to a window overlooking a city street. By tracing the outlines of the buildings on the pane of glass, you can make a simple perspective drawing.

Developed during the Renaissance, perspective offered a methodical approach to depicting the rational reality perceived by artists in the fifteenth century. It soon gained wide acceptance as a means of systematically diminishing the size of objects as they recede in space. Raphael's *School of Athens* (diagram 3.53) is one example. A broad arch in the foreground frames the compositional stage. Three additional arches diminish in size, pulling us into the painting. The diagonal lines in the buildings and floor converge at a point in the center of the painting. The viewer is invited to enter a vivid illusory world.

Even though many recent philosophical and aesthetic theories challenge this conception of reality, perspective remains the most pervasive Western system for suggesting three-dimensionality on the two-dimensional surface. Linear perspective is based on five fundamental concepts, shown in figure 3.54:

1. Objects appear to diminish in size as they recede into the distance. This diminishing effect persists until all objects disappear. Perspective is possible because the rate at which objects appear to diminish is regular and consistent.

2. The point at which objects disappear entirely is called a **vanishing point.** Sets of parallel lines (such as train tracks) converge at a vanishing point as they go into the distance, creating deep space.

3. In basic one- and two-point perspective, all vanishing points are positioned on the **eye level,** or **horizon line,** which is level with the artist's eyes.

4. Because all proportional relationships shift with each change in position, a fixed viewing position is an essential characteristic of linear perspective.

5. Only a limited area is clearly visible from a fixed position. To accommodate a larger viewing area, you must move farther away from the object to be drawn. This expands the **cone of vision** and increases the area being viewed.

Using a simple cube, we can explore three basic types of linear perspective.

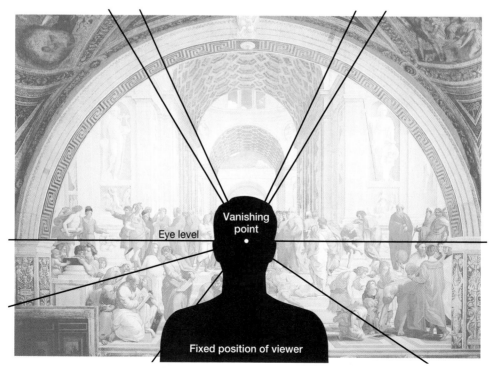

3.53 Perspective used in Raphael's *School of Athens*.

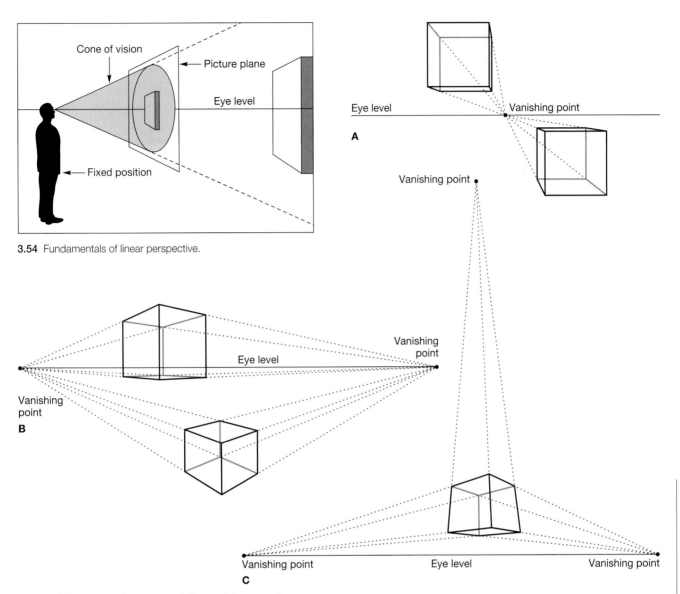

3.54 Fundamentals of linear perspective.

3.55 A-C. Examples of one, two and three-point perspective.

One-point perspective occurs when the lines receding into space appear to converge at a single point on the eye level. This occurs when the viewer is confronted with the flat front of the cube, and results in a drawing in which vertical lines and horizontal lines run parallel to the edges of your sheet of paper (3.55A). One-point perspective is relatively simple and can be very dramatic. However, as we move to the far right or left of the cube being drawn, many of the horizontal lines appear to shift, becoming more diagonal. They are no longer parallel to the top and bottom edges of your rectangular sheet. At this point, a second vanishing point is needed.

Two-point perspective is used when the lines receding into space appear to converge at two vanishing points on the eye level. This occurs when the

viewer is confronted with the vertical edge of the cube, rather than the flat front (3.55B). Now, only the vertical lines remain parallel to each other and the edge of the paper. All other lines recede back to the two vanishing points on the eye level. Because it clearly shows two sides of an object, two-point perspective is often used for diagrams and architectural renderings.

Three-point perspective is used when the lines receding into space appear to converge at two vanishing points on the eye level, plus a third point placed above or below the eye level. This occurs when the artist is positioned far above or below the cube, creating a "bird's eye" or "worm's eye" view (3.55C). Now, all the lines converge at the various vanishing points: none of the sets of lines parallel the edge of the paper.

UNITY AND VARIETY

101

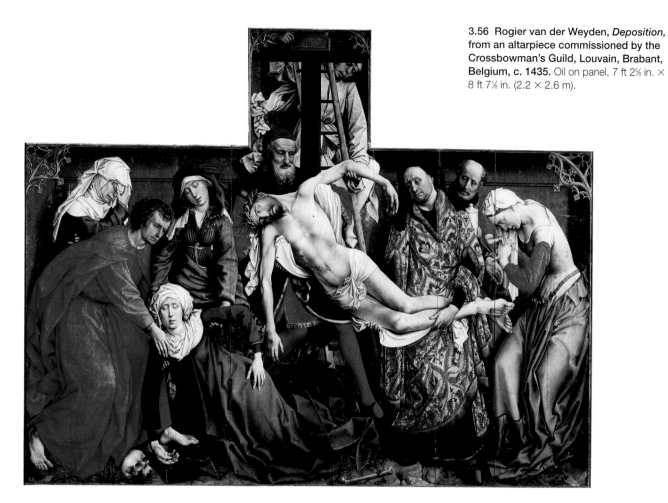

3.56 Rogier van der Weyden, *Deposition,* from an altarpiece commissioned by the Crossbowman's Guild, Louvain, Brabant, Belgium, c. 1435. Oil on panel, 7 ft 2⅝ in. × 8 ft 7⅛ in. (2.2 × 2.6 m).

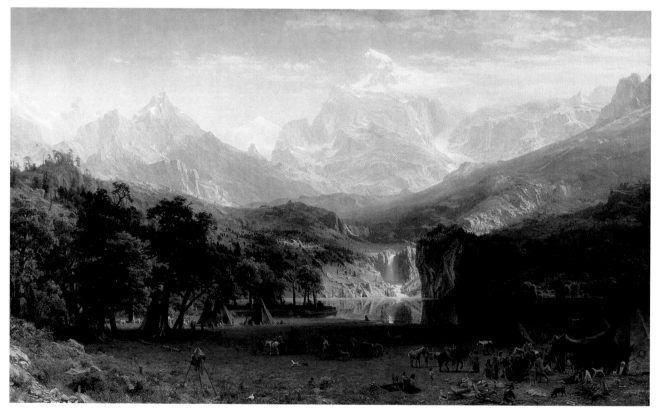

3.57 Albert Bierstadt, *The Rocky Mountains, Landers Peak.* 1863. Oil on canvas 6 ft 1¼ in. × 10 ft ¾ in.

Other Ways to Create the Illusion of Space

- *Overlap.* Overlap is the simplest way to suggest space, and it can be especially effective when combined with size variation. In *Deposition* (3.56), Rogier van der Weyden used overlap combined with value to create a convincing drama within a crowded compositional space.

- *Size variation.* Because the diminishing size of distant objects is a basic characteristic of human vision, any systematic variation in size can enhance the illusion of space. This effect is demonstrated most clearly when the distance is great. In Ansel Adams' *Monolith: The Face of Half Dome* (see page 33), the imposing cliff in the foreground rapidly diminishes in size as it moves back in space.

- *Definition.* Sharply focused shapes also tend to advance, while blurred shapes tend to recede. When we look at a landscape, dust and water droplets in the air blur outlines and add a blue-gray color to distant shapes. This effect is known as **atmospheric perspective.** In *The Rocky Mountains: Lander's Peak* (3.57), Albert Bierstadt combined dramatic lighting with atmospheric perspective to increase the illusion of space.

- *Location.* Visual elements placed near the top of the page tend to recede, while shapes placed at the bottom tend to advance. In *A Thousand Peaks and Myriad Ravines* (3.58), the mountains at the top of the scroll appear more distant, despite their large size.

- *Color.* As noted in Chapter Two, the spatial implications of color are profound. Under most circumstances, high-intensity colors tend to advance, and contrast in hue, value, or temperature can be used to create a push/pull effect.

Using the Illusion of Space

Through the illusion of space, artists invite viewers to enter an imaginary world. Expression can be heightened when the world so created is particularly intriguing or when the spatial illusion is especially dramatic.

Amplified perspective can be defined as the exaggerated use of linear perspective to achieve a dramatic and engaging presentation of the subject.

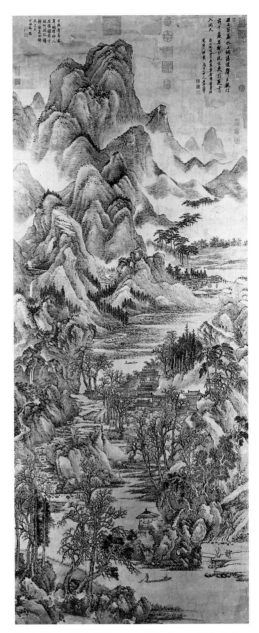

3.58 Wang Hui, *A Thousand Peaks and Myriad Ravines*, Qing dynasty, 1693. Hanging scroll, ink on paper, 8 ft 2½ in. × 3 ft 4½ in. (2.54 × 1.03 m).

Amplified perspective is often created using an unusual viewing position, such as a bird's eye view, accelerated convergence, or through distortion.

In Dali's *Christ of St. John of the Cross* (3.59), amplified perspective changes our interpretation of the crucifixion of Jesus. Dramatic three-point perspective emphasizes the importance of the note pinned at the top of the cross. As we look down, the vulnerability of Jesus emphasizes his humanity, while the hovering position of the figure suggests his divinity.

Fractured space can be created when multiple viewpoints are combined in a single image. In his

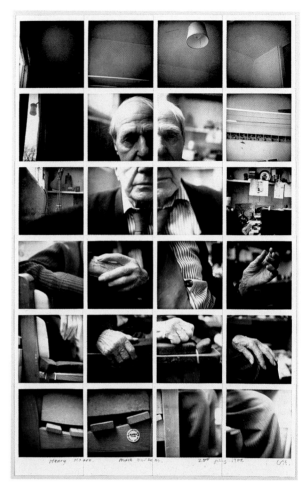

3.60 David Hockney, *Henry Moore Much Hadham 23rd July 1982*, **1982.** Composite Polaroid, 21 × 14 in. (53 × 36 cm).

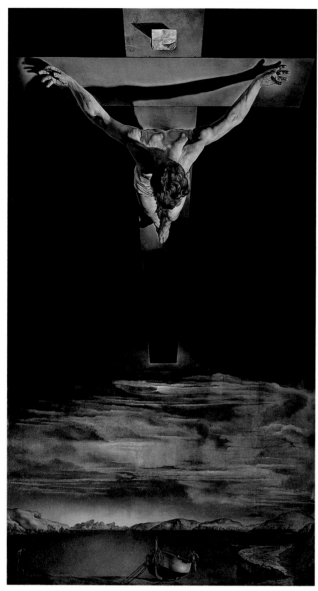

3.59 Salvador Dali, *Christ of St. John of the Cross*, **1951.** Oil on canvas, 80⅞ × 45⅝ in. (204.8 × 115.9 cm).

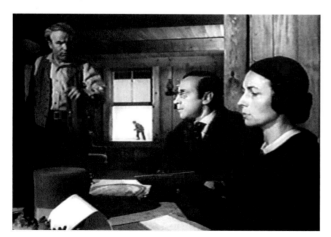

3.61 Scene from *Citizen Kane.* Three layers of space divide this shot from *Citizen Kane:* the mother in the foreground, the father in the middleground, and the child in the background.

portrait of sculptor *Henry Moore* (3.60), David Hockney used multiple photographs to manipulate space and suggest the passage of time. The repeated hands gesture to us as we visually converse with the old master.

Layered space can be created when the foreground, middle ground, and background are clearly defined. Layered space is used extensively in the film *Citizen Kane.* In figure 3.61, young Charlie Kane plays in the background, while his mother in the foreground signs over his care to a lawyer. His father, who is opposed to this action, occupies the middle ground, caught between the mother and the child. The tensions in the family, the determination of the mother, and the innocence of the child are heightened when Charlie shouts, "The Union forever!" as part of his game. When the lawyer takes charge of him, the family will be split apart forever. These three compositional layers communicate complex emotions while telling a story.

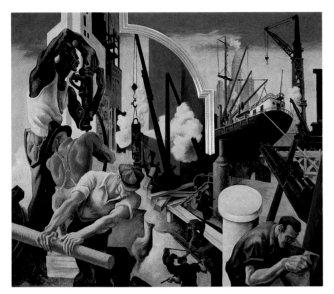

3.62 Thomas Hart Benton, *City Building*, from the mural series *America Today*, 1930. Distemper and egg tempera on gessoed linen with oil glaze. 7 ft 8 in. × 9 ft 9 in. (2.3 × 3 m).

Spatial complexity tends to expand when multiple spatial systems are compositionally combined. The swirling space in Thomas Hart Benton's *City Building* (3.62) was constructed using conflicting spatial systems. The size variation between the figures in the foreground and the ship in the background creates a strong sense of space, which is extended even further by the faint skyscrapers in the distance. The dark cranes and pulleys, however, tend to push forward in space, creating a conflict between the background and the foreground. The curving white line extending from the center of the painting to the upper edge complicates matters even further. Part of the wall itself, this bit of molding disrupts the illusion of space by drawing our attention to the flat surface. In this mural, Thomas Hart Benton orchestrated contrasting compositional forces to create an explosive image.

Key Questions

- How can depth be increased or decreased in your composition?
- How will spatial depth affect the meaning of your work?
- What happens when flat and spatially deep areas are combined?

DYNAMIC SPACE: CONSTRUCTING *MULAN*

Animators use the illusion of space with great inventiveness. Freed from the restrictions of reality, they can invent and explore space with abandon. Indeed, every type of space is used beautifully in Disney's *Mulan*. From the opening shots to the grand finale, the illusion of space is of critical importance to the visual and conceptual power of the film.

- *Overlap.* After a brief battle with Shan-Yu and his men, a Chinese soldier lights a signal fire to warn of the invasion. With Shan-Yu filling the foreground, we see six towers, with signal fires gradually blazing forth from each (3.63A). Here, overlap and size variation enhance the illusion of space.

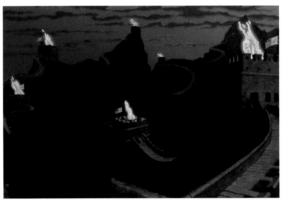

3.63A

- *Linear perspective.* Linear perspective is used in the next sequence, when General Li enters the imperial palace to inform the emperor of the invasion. One-point perspective is used to create the large, majestic hall (3.63B). As the general

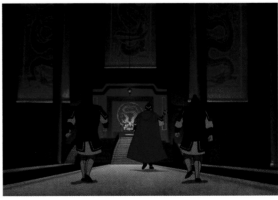

3.63B

approaches the throne, the angle of vision shifts to an aerial view. Three-point perspective is now used to emphasize the insignificance of the figures within this great hall (3.63C).

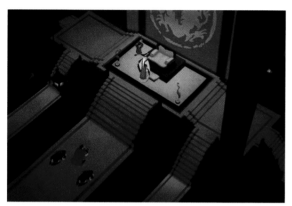
3.63C

- *Atmospheric perspective.* Atmospheric perspective is often used as the troops travel through the mountains. After learning of the death of his father in battle, Captain Shang walks to the edge of a cliff. Like the massive mountains in the background, his seemingly invincible father has dissolved in the mist. A small figure within a large landscape, Captain Shang remains sharply focused, dignified, and powerful, even as he grieves (3.63D).

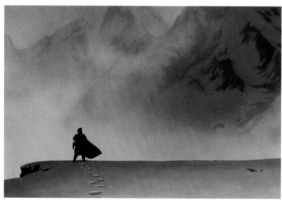
3.63D

Camera angles help orient the viewer and can determine the amount and type of space in each shot. An aerial view can provide the sweeping panorama needed to convey the enormity of a battle, while a low camera angle can provide an expansive view of the sky. The major battle scene in *Mulan* beautifully demonstrates the critical role camera angle can play in a film. The enormity of the enemy

army is shown in figure 3.63E. A low camera angle positions the Mongols along a ridge, above the

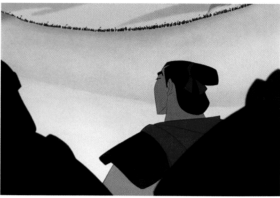
3.63E

small company of Chinese soldiers. As the Mongols pour over the ridge and gallop toward Mulan, the camera angle shifts to a slanted, oblique view (3.63F), then to a complete aerial view (3.63G). The shifting perspectives give us a more comprehensive

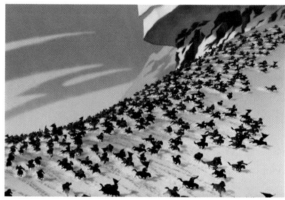
3.63F

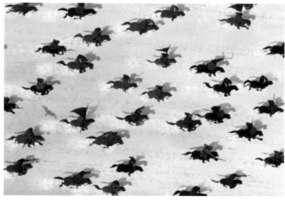
3.63G

view of the extent of the battle and emphasize the hopelessness of the emperor's warriors, who are confronted with an apparently invincible enemy

When Mulan grabs the one remaining cannon and races forward to create an avalanche, an aerial view is again used to show her vulnerability against the advancing enemy. Throughout the battle, shifts in camera angle provide the emotional and compositional power needed to create a dramatic battle sequence using the fewest number of shots.

THE ILLUSION OF MOVEMENT

Mulan is constructed from thousands of tiny frames. When run through a film projector, they create the fluid movement that is a hallmark of Disney animation. Animation is possible because we have the perceptual ability to integrate the sequential images into a continuous flow.

Substantial audience involvement is also required to create the illusion of movement within a drawing or sculpture. When presented with multiple images on a single surface, we must feel the movement, complete the action, or anticipate the next event. Based on our day-to-day experience in an ever changing world, we use our imagination to connect static images to create the illusion of movement.

The Kinesthetic Response

Kinesthetics is the science of movement. Through the very process of walking, we consistently engage in a complex balancing act as we fall forward, then catch ourselves with the next step. When confronted by a life-sized figure, such as the man from Robert Longo's *Men in Cities* series (3.64), the lunging movement of the model resonates on a physical level. Based on our personal experience, we feel as well as see the gesture. Capturing the gesture at the right moment is critical. In Myron's *Discus Thrower* (3.65), the athlete is caught at the moment *before* the whirling vortex of energy explodes, releasing the disc. By capturing this moment rather than the moment of release, the sculptor has trapped within the marble the energy of the throw.

The Decisive Moment

Photographer Henri Cartier-Bresson used his understanding of impending change to formulate a theory of photography he called "the decisive moment." A pioneer in the use of the 35-mm camera, he specialized in capturing the most telling moment in time. The space, emotions, and events he recorded in *Valencia* (3.66) are both fascinating and disturbing. Sharply focused and framed by the window, the policeman's fierce face dominates the foreground. Squeezed between the target shapes and the wall on

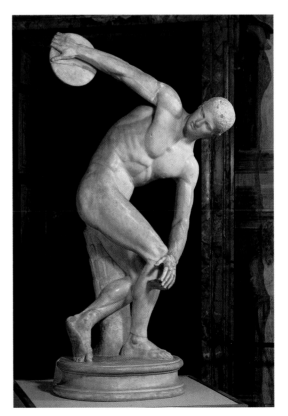

3.65 **Myron,** *Discus Thrower (Diskobolos).* Roman copy after the original bronze of c. 450 B.C. Marble, height 5 ft 1 in. (1.54 m).

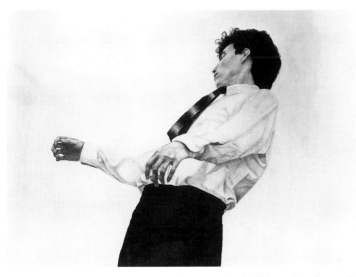

3.64 **Robert Longo,** *Untitled,* **1980.** From the *Men in Cities* series. Crayon & graphite on paper, 40½ × 28 in. (102.9 × 71.1 cm).

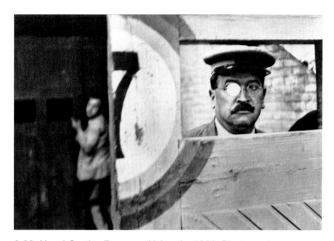

3.66 Henri Cartier-Bresson, *Valencia*, 1933. Photograph.

the left, a boy turns toward us apprehensively. A dissected target shape is balanced by the man's monocle on the right and the boy's face on the left. Horizontal rectangles compress three of the four corners of the composition. The resulting interplay of shapes creates a complex dialogue between childhood fears and adult authority.

Before and After

The kinesthetic response and the decisive moment both rely on our past experience. Based on our physical experience, we can feel the awkward position of the Longo figure; through our emotional experience, we realize that the Cartier-Bresson photograph is just one moment in a more extensive story. Likewise,

to create a story through a single image, many illustrators deliberately plan the moment *before* and *after* the actual drawing. For example, anticipation plays a major role in Chris Van Allsburg's *The Mysteries of Harris Burdick* (3.67). Each drawing is accompanied by a title and an abbreviated text. Based on the clues, we can invent all sorts of stories.

Multiplication

As an object moves, it sequentially occupies various positions in space. Visual multiplication can be used to simulate this effect. For example, the superimposed figures in Thomas Eakins' *Double Jump* (3.68) record the multiple positions the man occupies dur-

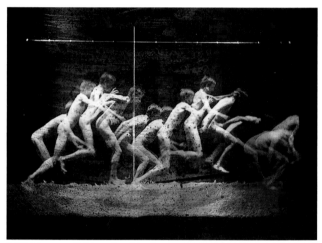

3.68 Thomas Eakins, *Double Jump*, 1885. Modern print from a dry-plate negative.

3.67 Chris Van Allsburg, "Under the Rug" from *The Mysteries of Harris Burdick*, Houghton-Mifflin, 1984.

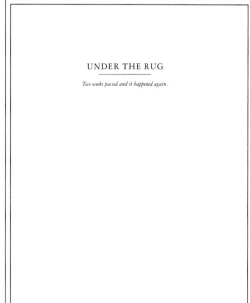

UNDER THE RUG

Two weeks passed and it happened again.

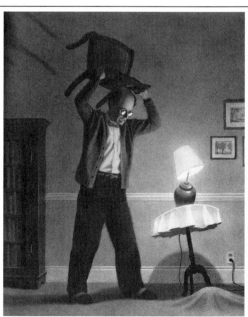

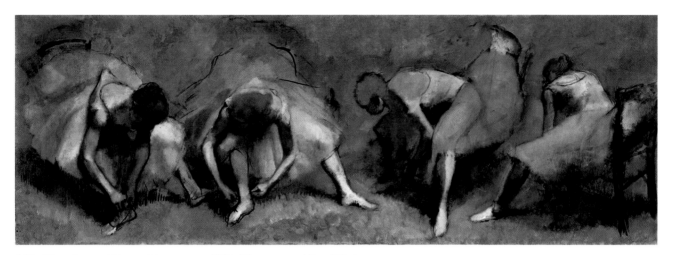

3.69 Edgar Degas, *Frieze of Dancers, c.* **1895.** Oil on canvas. 70 × 200.5 cm.

ing an athletic event. Even when figures are simply repeated, as in Edgar Degas' *Frieze of Dancers* (3.69), movement is strongly suggested.

As shapes lose definition, they often gain dynamism. Shifts can occur in both time and space. Francis Bacon's self-portrait (figure 2.32, page 63) retains its volumetric form while simultaneously dissolving any conventional sense of anatomy. The blurred boundaries and repetition create a strong illusion of movement.

DETERMINING PRIORITIES

Clear priorities can help us make appropriate compositional decisions. Just as a play will become gibberish if 10 actors speak different lines simultaneously, so a design will become chaotic when all aspects are given equal prominence. The following websites provide wonderful examples of both chaos and clarity.

The site in figure 3.70 is overloaded with competing information, beginning with the banner ads at the top of the screen. Multiple type styles, colors, buttons, and layers of information all compete for attention. There are no supporting actors in this play; each visual element is accorded star status, regardless of its importance.

In contrast, the GTS Companies website (3.71) is a model of simplicity, clarity, and restraint. Information is sized and organized according to its significance. The company name is prominently displayed, followed by a description of services provided. By clicking on three simple boxes, viewers can get

detailed information on major divisions in the company and additional links are provided in a column on the left. An update on company activities appears in an open box when the visitor enters the site. The blues that dominate the design provide unity, while a single red header is used for emphasis.

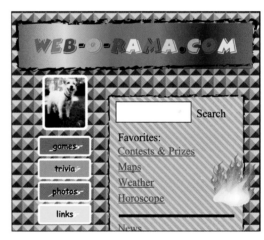

3.70 An example of bad website design.

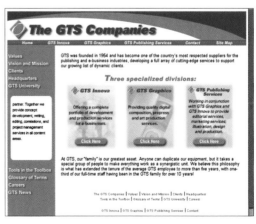

3.71 GTS Companies Website.

By determining compositional priorities, we can emphasize the most important aspects of a design. Knowing what to leave out is as important as knowing what to include. Using visual economy, we can distill a design down to its true essentials.

Key Questions

- Can the illusion of movement enhance the idea you want to express? If so, how can you create the illusion of movement?

- What happens when static (unmoving) and dynamic (moving) shapes are used together in a design?

- To what extent is the illusion of movement affected by the illusion of space?

SUMMARY

- Using composition, we can organize multiple parts into a harmonious whole. In a well-composed design, visual elements work together as a team.

- Gestalt psychology describes six unifying strategies: grouping, containment, repetition, proximity, continuity, and closure.

- Effective design requires a dialogue between unity and variety. Too much unity can lead to boredom, while too much variety can lead to chaos.

- Any similarity between visual elements tends to increase unity; any difference between visual elements tends to increase variety.

- Symmetry, radial symmetry, and asymmetry are three common forms of balance. Visual balance creates equilibrium among compositional units, regardless of their size, weight, or shape.

- Scale and proportion are two types of size relationships. Proportion refers to the size relationships within an image, while scale involves a size comparison with our physical reality.

- Emphasis is most commonly created through isolation, placement, or contrast. A focal point can strengthen emphasis.

- The illusion of space can be created through linear perspective, overlap, size variation, location, definition, atmospheric perspective, and use of color.

- The illusion of movement is often created by selecting the most telling moment in an event or through various types of multiplication.

- By determining our priorities, we can emphasize the most important aspects of a design. Using visual economy, we distill a design down to its true essentials, create an appropriate visual hierarchy, and increase overall impact.

Keywords

amplified perspective	eye level (horizon line)	picture plane
anomaly	focal point	proportion
approximate symmetry	fractured space	proximity
asymmetrical balance	fusion	radial symmetry
atmospheric perspective	Gestalt	repetition
balance	grid	rhythm
camera angle	grouping	scale
centricity	imbalance	space
closure	isolation	symmetrical balance
composition	kinesthetics	three-point perspective
cone of vision	layered space	two-point perspective
containment	linear perspective	unity
continuity	movement	vanishing point
contrast	one-point perspective	variety
eccentricity	pattern	visual weight
emphasis		

Profile:
Ken Stout, Painter
Immediacy and Energy in Large Scale

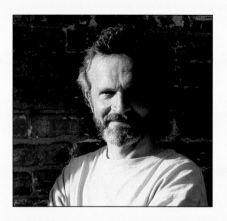

Ken Stout is an internationally renowned figurative painter. He has shown his work widely, including group shows at the Nelson-Atkins Museum of Art in Kansas City and the Butler Museum of American Art, as well as solo shows at the Goldstrom Gallery in New York City and the Cité Internationale des Arts in Paris. Stout has received numerous awards, including a National Endowment for the Arts Painting Award in 1990 and the Arkansas Arts Council painting award. *Intermission* was commissioned by the Walton Arts Center in Fayetteville, Arkansas, funded by Saatchi and Saatchi in 1992 and permanently installed in 1994.

MS: How did *Intermission* begin?

KS: I actually began work on the mural in 1989. During visits to Paris and Madrid, I was bowled over by a Toulouse-Latrec mural I saw at the Orsay Museum and by a mural by Delacroix at St. Sulpice. Both were vibrant with energy, and the strident reds and greens in the Delacroix sent the viewer's eyes hurtling around and through the composition. I also loved Velasquez's *Las Meninas* and Goya's frescos for their immediacy and fearlessness. I was interested in the mural project because it gave me an opportunity to combine the immediacy of drawing with the richness of painting.

MS: Why show the intermission, not the play?

KS: It is a moment in time that is highly charged. The mural depicts a cross section of the theater, from backstage to stage and from audience to lobby. The performer on stage is like a toggle switch, connecting the audience to the action backstage. As he bows through the closing curtain, the audience begins to break apart, dissolving into its own private plays. Applause fills the theater, children begin to awaken, and neighbors discuss the performance. I wanted to pull the viewer into a scene bursting with energy, as if all things were in orbit, pushing and pulling, as in dance. The whole painting is a gesture, an embodiment of bodies in motion, with both the volumes and voids ignited with energy.

MS: I know that you love art history and that your preliminary research on this project was extensive. What did you learn from the masters?

KS: Mostly, I learned ways to increase compositional complexity without sacrificing gestural energy. These compositional lessons helped me sustain a vigorous visual pace for all 50 feet of the painting.

Technically, though, my work method was more exploratory and direct than is the usual practice.

First, the 300 preliminary drawings and paintings I did stand as autonomous images in themselves. I learned from all of them — but didn't copy any of them when I painted the mural. I confronted the painting directly, rather than replicating ideas I had worked out beforehand.

Second, I didn't graph out, slide project, or otherwise draw the outlines on the canvas. I just drew blue lines to divide the canvas into halves, quarters, and eighths, then drew freehand, using a brush attached to a 3-foot-long bamboo pole, starting with light washes in earth colors, then building up more layers as necessary.

Finally, every figure was painted from life, using over 50 community members as models. They were amazingly generous and patient, considering it wasn't putting a penny in their pockets. This process increased the connection between the audience and the artwork, and we had a great party for everyone when the painting was installed. I continue to meet these townspeople on the street, and, as participants in the project, they have a continuing relationship with the painting.

MS: So it sounds like you didn't really know what would happen when you began to paint each day.
KS: Each model, each pose, and each prop provided variations and surprises. I actually used at least two models for each figure in the painting, which basically means that there is another 50-foot-long painting underneath the one that you see!

MS: What advice do you have for my students?
KS: Take risks. Without daring — indeed, without great daring — there is no beauty. We must go beyond ourselves if we are ever to fulfill our real potential.

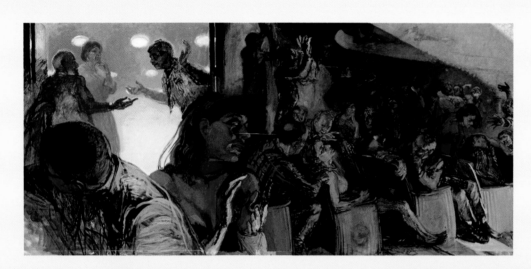

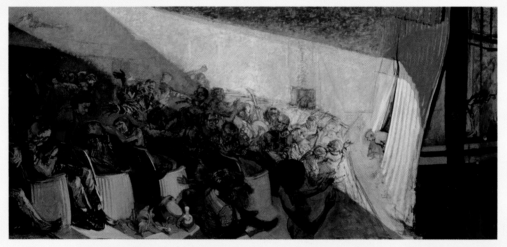

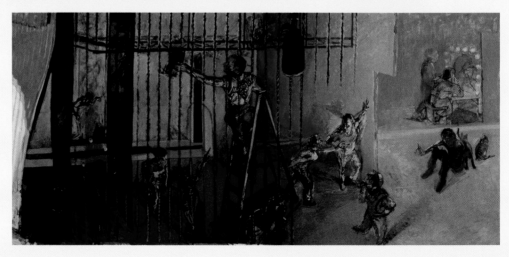

Part One
Multimedia Resources

Take advantage of the multimedia resources that accompany this book in order to test and expand your understanding of two-dimensional design elements.

Resources

Contents

www.mhhe.com/launching2

Student Center
Chapter 1
Chapter 2
Chapter 3

Learning objectives for each chapter
Study outlines for each chapter
Quizzes with instant feedback
Flashcards for studying art vocabulary
Internet exercises for developing critical viewing skills
Book suggestions for your professional library and research projects

Core Concepts in Art CD-ROM

An Internet guide to help you maximize connectivity and avoid problems
A study skills primer to help you make the most of your courses

Studio projects for Part One are described and illustrated for teachers on the Web and on a CD-ROM.

Resources

Projects

www.mhhe.com/launching2

Instructor Center
IM Part One

Instructor's Resource CD-ROM

Part One

Line Inventory: An introduction to the vocabulary and power of line
Four Lines, Four Times: Sixteen linear compositions
Line Dynamics: Using line in complex design, plus creating illusion of space
Shape Inventory: Sixteen compositions using shape
The Parts and the Puzzle: Exploring the design process
Balancing Act: How format affects weight and balance
Pushing Proportion: How proportion affects meaning
Texture Inventory: Sixteen texture studies
Object Lesson: Exploring an everyday object in a three-part series
Exploring Abstraction: Creating an abstract composition from a complex still life
Architectural Abstraction: Abstracting lines and shapes from a 3D object
Labyrinth Collage and Book: Developing a complex composition
The Transformative Effects of Value: Light and its emotional impact
Concealing/Revealing #1: Closure, figure/ground relationships, and balance
Concealing/Revealing #2: The impact of value on composition and communication
Concealing/Revealing #3: Color and communication
Dualities: Integrating line, shape, texture, and color in a special kind of self-portrait
True Lies: Designing Fiction: An exploration of linear narrative

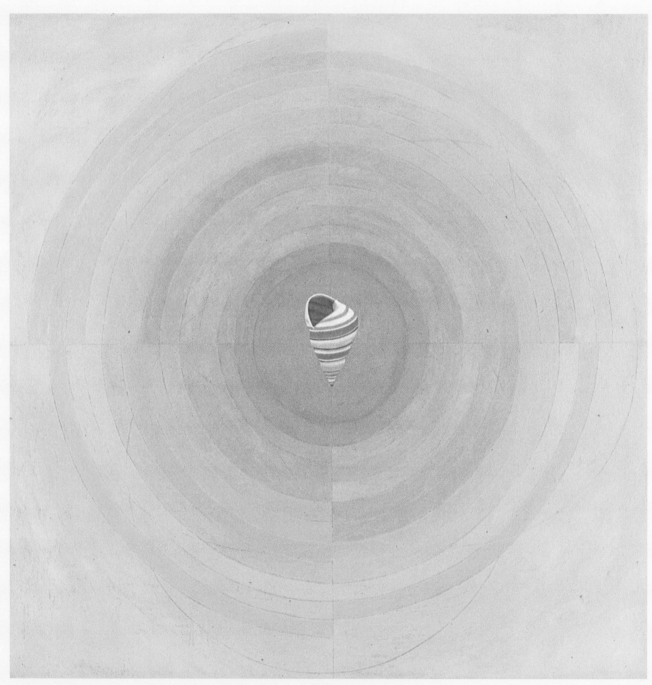

Georgiana Nehl, *Sun/Star* **(Detail), 1996.** Oil paint on gessoed wood, 25¾ in. w. × 13¼ in. h. × 1 in. d. (65 × 34 × 3 cm).

Concepts and Critical Thinking

chapter four
Cultivating Creativity

chapter five
Problem Seeking and Problem Solving

chapter six
Developing Critical Thinking

chapter seven
Constructing Meaning

In *A Kick in the Seat of the Pants,* Roger Von Oech identifies four distinct roles in the creative process.

First, the *explorer* learns as much as possible about the problem. Research is crucial. Ignorance of a topic may result in a superficial solution, while finalizing the first solution envisioned often results in a cliché.

Second, the *artist* experiments with a wide variety of solutions, using all sorts of combinations, proportions, and materials. By creating 10 answers to each question, the artist can select the best solution rather than accepting the only solution.

Third, the *judge* assesses the work in progress and determines what revisions are required. Innovative ideas are never fully developed when first presented; most need extensive revision and expansion. Rather than discard an underdeveloped idea, the judge identifies its potential and determines ways to increase its strength.

Finally, the *warrior* implements the idea. When the project is large and complex, implementation can be a challenge. When obstacles appear, the warrior assesses the situation, determines the best course of action, and then completes the project.

We will explore each of these roles in the next four chapters. Strategies for cultivating creativity and improving time management are discussed in Chapter Four. Chapter Five deals with concept development and visual problem solving. Chapter Six is devoted to critical thinking and provides specific ways to improve any design. In Chapter Seven, we expand our discussion of visual communication and consider ways to make more meaningful designs.

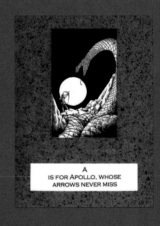

A
IS FOR APOLLO, WHOSE
ARROWS NEVER MISS

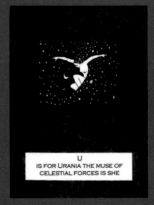

U
IS FOR URANIA THE MUSE OF
CELESTIAL FORCES IS SHE

Cultivating Creativity

"The heart of all new ideas lies in the borrowing, adding, combining or modifying of old ones. Do it by accident and people call you lucky. Do it by design and they'll call you creative."

Michael LeBoeuf, in *Imagineering*

chapter four

DESIGN AND CREATIVITY

Design and creativity are natural partners. The quality of a design is determined by the integration of its parts into a cohesive whole. The design will work when the parts fit together well. Many compositional possibilities are invented and discarded during the design process. Likewise, creative thinking requires extensive exploration and experimentation. Old ideas are recombined to create new structures. These new structures suggest new questions, which then suggest new answers. By looking at familiar elements in a new way and by combining ideas that have traditionally been separate, we can cultivate a cycle of creativity.

Once viewed as peripheral, creativity and innovation have become highly valued in the current business climate. In the Information Age, intellectual property can be the most important asset in a business. Innovation in art and design, always highly valued in Western culture, has accelerated. New technologies have expanded the range of approaches available, and new ideas drawn from literature, science, philosophy, and history inspire contemporary artists and designers. The sky is the limit. An effective artist or designer cannot simply follow instructions. Cultivating creative thinking is as fundamental as mastering any technical skill.

SEVEN CHARACTERISTICS OF CREATIVE THINKING

Creativity is inherently unpredictable. Through creative thinking, old habits are broken and familiar patterns of thought are transformed. Anything can happen. Predicting the future based on past experience becomes inadequate when a creative breakthrough occurs. Like a shimmering drop of mercury, creativity eludes capture.

We can actively encourage creative thinking, however. Rather than waiting for inspiration, we can set up the conditions favorable to creativity. Based on observation and on interviews, various researchers have noted the following characteristics in many creative people.

Receptivity

Creative people are open to new ideas and welcome new experiences. Never complacent, they question the status quo and embrace alternative solutions to existing problems. Listening more and talking less is helpful. As journalist Larry King says, "I never learn anything new when I'm the one talking!"

Curiosity

A good designer brings an insatiable curiosity to each project. Researching unfamiliar topics and analyzing unusual systems is a source of delight rather than a cause for concern. Like a child, the designer is eager to learn new things and explore new places. "How does it work?" and "How can it work better?" are frequently asked questions.

Wide Range of Interests

With a broad knowledge base, a creative person can make a wider range of connections. Consider the number of words you can create from the letters in the word *image:*

age, game, gem, am, aim, a, I, me

Try the same game with the word imagination:

gin, nation, gnat, ton, tan, not, man, again, gain, oat, got, tag, am, aim, ant, no, on, tin, gamin, inn, ingot, main, a, I

With more components, the number of combinations increases. Likewise, an artist who has a background in literature, geology, archery, music, and history can make more connections than a single-minded specialist.

Attentiveness

Realizing that every experience is potentially valuable, creative people pay attention to seemingly minor details. Scientists often develop major theories by observing small events, which they then organize into complex patterns. Artists can often see past superficial visual chaos to discern an underlying order. Playwrights develop dramatic works by looking past the surface of human behavior to explore the substance of the human condition. By looking carefully, creative people see possibilities that others miss.

Connection Seeking

Seeing the similarity among seemingly disparate parts has often sparked a creative breakthrough. For example, Egyptian hieroglyphs became readable when a young French scholar realized that they carried the same message as an adjacent Greek inscription on a slab of stone. By comparing the two and cracking the code, Jean-François Champollion opened the door for all subsequent students of ancient Egyptian culture.

Conviction

Creative people value existing knowledge. Since new ideas are often derived from old ideas, it is foolish to ignore or dismiss the past. However, creative people also love change. Never satisfied with routine answers to familiar questions, they constantly consider new possibilities and often challenge the authorities. Convinced of the value of their ideas, they tenaciously pursue an independent path.

Complexity

In lecture classes, we must accurately take notes, memorize facts, and collect and analyze data. We are encouraged to think rationally, write clearly, and present our ideas in a linear progression. In studio classes, exploration, experimentation, and intuition are encouraged, especially during brainstorming sessions. Synthesis, emotion, visualization, spatial perception, and nonlinear thinking are highly valued.

To be fully effective, a creative person needs to combine the rational with the intuitive. While intuition may be used to generate a new idea, logic and analysis are often needed for its realization. As a result, the actions of creative people are often complex or even contradictory. As noted by psychologist Mihaly Csikszentmihalyi,[1] creative people often combine

- Physical energy with a respect for rest. They work long hours with great concentration, then rest and relax, fully recharging their batteries. They view balance between work and play as essential.

- Savvy with innocence. They use common sense as well as intellect in completing their work yet remain open to experience. Creative people tend to view the world and themselves with a sense of wonder, rather than cling to preconceptions or stereotypes.

- Responsibility with playfulness. When the situation requires serious attention, creative people are remarkably diligent and determined. They realize that there is no substitute for hard work and drive themselves relentlessly when nearing completion of a major project. On the other hand, when the situation permits, a playful, devil-may-care attitude may prevail, providing a release from the previous period of work.

- Risk-taking with safe-keeping. Creativity expert George Prince has noted two behavioral extremes in people.[2] Safe-keepers look before they leap, avoid surprises, punish mistakes, follow the rules, and watch the clock. A safe-keeper is most comfortable when there is only one right answer to memorize or one solution to produce. Risk-takers are just the opposite. They break the rules, leap before they look, like surprises, are impetuous, and may lose track of time. A risk-taker enjoys inventing multiple answers to every question.

  An imbalance in either direction inhibits creativity. The safe-keeper lives in fear, while the extreme risk-taker lives brilliantly — but dangerously. Creative thinking requires a mix of risk-taking and safe-keeping. When brainstorming new ideas, open-ended exploration is used: anything is possible. But, when implementing new ideas, deadlines, budgets, and feasibility become major concerns. The risk-taker gets the job started; the safe-keeper gets the job done.

- Extroversion with introversion. When starting a new project, creative people are often talkative and gregarious, eager to share insights and explore ideas. When a clear sense of direction develops, however, they often withdraw, seeking solitude and quiet work time. This capacity for solitude is crucial. Several studies have shown that talented teenagers who cannot stand solitude rarely develop their creative skills.

- Passion with objectivity. Mature artists tend to plunge into new projects, convinced of the significance of the work and confident of their skills. Any attempt to distract or dissuade them at this point is futile. However, when the model or rough study is done, many will pause to assess their progress. This period of analysis and judgment may occur in a group setting or may be done by the artist alone. In either case, the emotional attachment required while creating is now replaced by a dispassionate objectivity. Work that does not pass this review is redone or discarded, regardless of the hours spent in its development. In major projects, this alternating process of creation and analysis may be repeated many times.

- Disregard for time with attention to deadlines. Time often dissolves when studio work begins. An artist or a designer can become engrossed in a project: when the work is going well, 6 hours can feel like 20 minutes. On the other hand, an acute attention to deadlines is necessary when preparing an exhibition or working for a client.

- Modesty with pride. As they mature, creative people often become increasingly aware of the contributions to their success made by teachers, family, and colleagues. Rather than brag about past accomplishments, they tend to focus on current projects. On the other hand, as creative people become aware of their significance within a field, they gain a powerful sense of purpose. Distractions are deleted from the schedule, and increasingly ambitious goals are set. When the balance is right, all these complex characteristics fuel even greater achievement.

GOAL SETTING

As humans, our behavior is strongly goal-directed. Every action occurs for a reason. When we focus our attention on a specific task, we can accomplish just about anything. Goals help us channel our energy and manage our time. When we reach our goals,

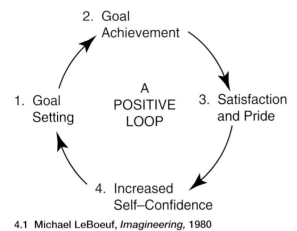

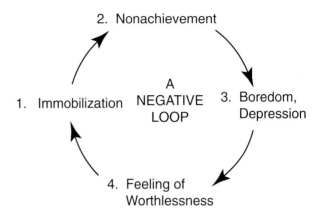

4.1 Michael LeBoeuf, *Imagineering*, 1980

our self-esteem increases, which then helps us overcome obstacles. And, with each goal met, our knowledge increases. Michael LeBoeuf has diagrammed this effect clearly (4.1).

A Goal-Setting Strategy

Self-knowledge is essential. To be effective, goals must be authentic. No matter how hard we try, we can never really fulfill our potential when pursuing goals set by others. Identifying our true interests, strengths, and objectives can be liberating. The following exercise can help clarify personal interests.

1. Get a package of small Post-it notes. Working spontaneously, write one of your characteristics on each note, such as "I am creative," "I love music," "I write well." Identify as many attributes as possible.

2. When you finish, lay out the notes on a table and look at them for a while. Consider the type of person they describe. What are this person's strengths? What additional interests might this person need to develop?

3. On a fresh stack of notes, write a new set of responses, this time dealing with the question "Why not?" as an expansion of these interests. Why not travel to Tibet? Why not learn Spanish? Why not master canoeing? Add these to the grid.

4. Then, leave the room. Go for a walk, have dinner, or head to class. Let your subconscious mind play with the possibilities suggested by your notes.

5. Next, organize the notes into four general categories: intellectual goals, personal-relationship goals, spiritual or emotional goals, physical fitness goals. If you are an extreme safe-keeper, add a category called "Adventure." If you are an extreme risk-taker, add a category called "Organization." Since a mix of activities helps feed the psyche, working with each of these categories is important. Even though spiritual, emotional, or social development is fluid and continuous, recognition of these categories can contribute to effective time management.

6. Prioritize the notes within each category. On the top note, write "This is first because _____." One the second, write "This is second because _____." Continue until you complete the grid. Discard notes that you now realize are unnecessary.

7. Choose one goal from each of the four categories. It is tempting to choose the top goal in each case, but this is unrealistic. Even the most experienced businessperson can rarely manage more than three major goals at a time. Choose one primary goal and three secondary goals.

8. Now, specify your goals. "I want to become a better artist" is too vague. Consider specific actions you can take to improve your artwork. "I need to improve my drawing" is more specific. "I want to learn anatomy" is better still. To learn anatomy, you can take a class, study an anatomy book, or draw from a skeleton. These are tangible actions: you now know what to do.

9. Determine how to achieve your goals and develop a rough timetable, listing weekly goals,

semester goals, and one-year goals. It is not necessary to list career goals just yet. Most of us explore many ideas during our first year of college, and formalizing career goals prematurely is counterproductive. After you are clearly committed to a major field of study, you can add a page of long-term goals, projecting your priorities for the next three to five years.

10. At least once a month, review your chart and add or delete information as necessary. If you realize that you are overextended this term, shift one of your minor goals to next semester or delete it altogether. This system is intended to provide you with a target, not to create a straitjacket. Make adjustments as necessary, so that your primary goals are met.

11. If you achieve all your goals, congratulate yourself—then set more ambitious goals next term. If you achieve half of your goals, congratulate yourself—then prioritize more carefully next term. You may have taken on too many tasks and thus dissipated your energy. Because there is always a gap between intention and outcome, a 70 to 80 percent completion rate is fine.

Characteristics of Good Goals

Challenging but Attainable

Too modest a goal will provide no sense of accomplishment. Too ambitious a goal will reduce, rather than increase, motivation. No one wants to fight a losing battle! Knowing your strengths and weaknesses will help you set realistic goals.

Compatible

Training for the Boston Marathon while simultaneously trying to gain 20 pounds is unwise, since you will burn off every calorie you consume. Trying to save a thousand dollars while touring Europe is unrealistic, since travel always costs more than you expect. On the other hand, by taking a dance class or joining a hiking club, you may be able to combine a fitness goal with a social goal.

Self-Directed

Avoid goals that are primarily dependent on someone else's actions or opinions. "I want to earn an *A* in drawing" is a common example. Since the grade is determined by a teacher, your control in this area is limited. Instead, focus on improving your drawing as much as possible. This will increase your receptivity to learning and will focus your attention on actions you can control. When you do your best work, good grades generally follow.

Clearly Defined

We all have "too much to do." No matter how carefully we organize our time, there are only 24 hours in a day. Identifying daily and weekly priorities can help focus attention, increase productivity, and reduce stress.

1. Identify your target. It may be a specific action (such as doing your laundry) or a broader intention (such as improving your knowledge of anatomy). Specificity is important. It is nearly impossible to hit a target you cannot see.

2. Focus. Reduce distractions as much as possible. If visiting friends have taken over your living space, plan another time for socializing; then chase them out. If you need music to improve your concentration, put on an appropriate CD. If you can't seem to focus due to an assortment of worries, try writing them down; then refocus on the task at hand. Getting worries off your mind often helps.

3. Then, hit your target with the necessary force and energy.

Temporary

Set clear target dates, get the job done, and move on to the next project. Each completed task increases your self-confidence and adds momentum. Unfinished work, on the other hand, can drain energy and decrease momentum. If you are overloaded, delete secondary goals, so that you can complete primary goals.

TIME MANAGEMENT

Time management can help you achieve your goals. Working smarter is usually more effective than simply working harder. In a world bursting with opportunity, using your work time well can increase the time available for travel, volunteer work, or socializing. The following time-management strategies have been used by many artists and designers.

Set the Stage

Choosing when and where to work can significantly increase your output. If you are a lark, bursting with energy and enthusiasm in the morning, tackle major projects before noon. If you are an owl, equipped with night vision and able to hunt after dark, work on major projects after dinner. If you are distracted by clutter, clean your desk before beginning your workday, and tidy up your desk before you leave. These seemingly minor actions can substantially increase your productivity.

Prioritize

Use your goal list to help determine your priorities. Note which tasks are most *urgent* and which tasks are most *important*. Timing can be crucial. When you pay your phone bill on time, you easily complete an urgent but unimportant task. When your phone bill is overdue and the service is cut off, this unimportant task becomes a major headache. Dispense with urgent tasks quickly. Distribute important tasks over several weeks if necessary.

See the Big Picture

Use monthly calendar pages to record your major projects and obligations. A calendar that is organized by months can help you see which weeks will be packed with deadlines and which weeks will be relatively quiet. To avoid all-nighters, distribute large, important tasks over several weeks. To avoid missing a pivotal lecture or critique, schedule out-of-town trips during "slow" weeks.

Work Sequentially

Many activities are best done in a specific sequence. If you are writing a 20-page paper, it is best to start with research, make an outline, complete a rough draft, make corrections, then write the final draft. If you are designing a poster, it is best to start with research, make thumbnail sketches, assess the results, make a full-size rough layout, consult the client, and

then complete the poster. It is tempting to try to cut out the intermediate steps and move directly to the final draft, but this is rarely effective. With most large projects, you learn more, save time, and do better work by following the right sequence of events.

Use Parts to Create the Whole

Seen as a whole, a major project can become overwhelming. In an extreme case, creative paralysis sets in, resulting in a condition similar to writer's block. Breaking down big jobs into smaller parts helps enormously. In *Bird by Bird*, Anne Lamott gives a wonderful description of this process:

> Thirty years ago my other brother, who was ten years old at the time, was trying to get a report on birds written that he'd had three months to write. [It] was due the next day. . . . He was at the kitchen table close to tears, surrounded by binder paper and pencils and unopened books on birds, immobilized by the hugeness of the task ahead. Then my father sat down beside him, put his arm around my brother's shoulder, and said, "Bird by bird, buddy. Just take it bird by bird.[3]

By doing the job incrementally, you are likely to learn more and procrastinate less.

Make the Most of Class Time

Psychologists tell us that beginnings and endings of events are especially memorable. An experienced teacher knows that the first 10 minutes of class sets the tone for the rest of the session and that a summary at the end can help students remember the lesson. A choreographer knows that the first 10 minutes of a performance can set the stage for the next 2 hours and that the end of a dance determines the overall impact. Similarly, the wise student arrives 5 minutes early for class and maintains attention to the end of class.

Be an active learner. You can use that 5 minutes before class to review your notes from the previous session and organize your supplies. This helps create a bridge between what you know and the new information to be presented. Try to end the class on a high note, either by completing a project or by clearly determining the strengths and weaknesses of the work in progress. By analyzing your progress, you can organize your thinking and provide a solid beginning point for the next work session.

Start Early

Momentum is extremely powerful. It is much easier to climb a hill when you are already moving forward, rather than reclining. When you receive a long-term assignment, such as a 20-page paper, start it right away. Even one hour of research will help focus your attention on the problem and get you going. A slow start is better than no start!

When in Doubt, Crank It Out

Fear is one of the greatest obstacles to creative thinking. When we are afraid, we tend to avoid action and consequently miss opportunities. It is difficult to act decisively or pursue the unknown potential of a new idea. Both habit and perfectionism feed fear. If you consistently repeat the same activities and limit yourself to the most familiar friendships, you will become more and more fearful of new experiences. If you insist on doing each job perfectly, you can waste time on minor defects and avoid exploring new ideas. Perfectionism is especially destructive during brainstorming, which requires a loose, open approach.

Creativity takes courage. As IBM founder Thomas Watson noted, "If you are not satisfied with your rate of success, try failing more." Baseball player Reggie Jackson is renowned for his 563 home runs—but he also struck out 2,597 times. Thomas

Edison's research team tried over 6,000 materials before finding the carbon-fiber filament used in lightbulbs.

"When in doubt, don't!" is the safe-keeper's motto. "When in doubt, do!" is the risk-taker's motto. Creativity requires risk-taking. By starting each project with a sense of adventure, you increase your level of both learning and creativity.

Work Together

Many areas of art and design, including filmmaking, industrial design, and advertising design, are often done collaboratively. Working together, artists and designers can complete projects that are too complex or time-consuming to be done alone. Collaborative thinking helps us break familiar patterns and teaches us to listen to alternative or opposing ideas.

Here is one example. Gather 20 people. Start with a copied fragment from an existing image, such as *Metamophosis II*, an 8 × 160 in. banner by M. C. Escher (4.2). In this case, students in a design class were provided with a 1-inch strip of the banner to create a beginning point and another 1-inch strip of the banner to create the ending point (4.3A). Each person invented an 8½ × 11 in. connection between the two strips. Buildings, plants, abstract shapes, chess pieces, and other images were used to bridge the gap between the strips at the beginning and the end. The images were then connected end to end, like cars in a train. When combined, they created a collaborative banner, 20 feet long (4.3B). Students had to negotiate with the person ahead of them in the line and with the person behind them,

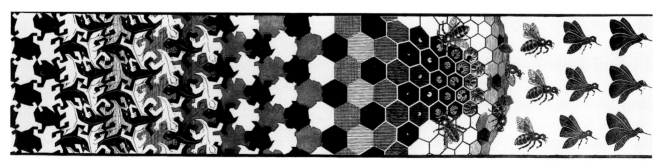

4.2 M. C. Escher, Part of *Metamorphosis II*, 1939–40. Woodcut in black, green, and brown, printed from 20 blocks on three combined sheets, 7½ × 153⅜ in. (19 × 390 cm). © 2002 Cordon Art B. V. Baarn, Holland. All rights reserved.

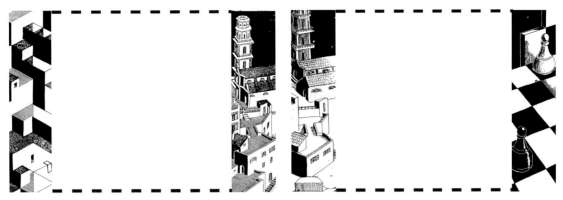

4.3A Examples of Escher Starter Images

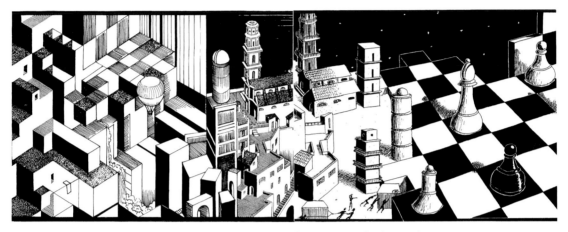

4.3B Mary Stewart and Jesse Wummer, **Expanded Escher Collaboration.** Student work.

in order to make a continuous image with graceful transitions. In effect, all 20 participants become members of a creative team. Finally, each 8½ × 11 in. section was photocopied and traded, providing each person with the completed artwork. In a collaboration of this kind, everyone gains, both in the learning process and in the sharing of the product.

Reduce Stress

Finally, good time management can help you avoid excessive stress. When you are pushing beyond familiar limits, some stress is inevitable. Excessive stress, however, leads to illness, anger, insomnia, mental paralysis, exhaustion, and depression. Here are some strategies that can help.

No Blame

No matter what happens, blaming yourself or others is never useful. Work on the solution rather than remaining stuck in the problem.

Keep Your Balance

A mix of emotional, spiritual, physical, and intellectual activities will help feed all areas of your psyche. No matter how significant a particular assignment may appear to be, remember that it is only one aspect of your life. Taking a break can often give you the fresh perspective you need to solve a difficult problem. Value rest. When the balance is right, your time off can actually increase your productivity.

Remember That Positives Attract

A creative person seeks change. Any change tends to present a combination of obstacles and opportunities. Focusing on the opportunities rather than on the obstacles increases confidence. Furthermore, an upbeat, positive attitude attracts other creative thinkers, while a negative, excessively critical attitude drives creative thinkers away. By assuming that you *can* do the job well, you start the spiral of accomplishment needed to fully realize your creative potential. Accentuate the positive!

SUMMARY

- Creativity and design both require new combinations of old ideas.

- Creative people are receptive to new ideas, are curious, have a wide range of interests, are attentive, seek connections, and work with great conviction.

- Creative people combine rational and intuitive thinking. While intuition may be used to generate a new idea, logic and analysis are often needed for its completion. As a result, the actions of creative people are often complex or even contradictory.

- Goals you set are goals you get. Establishing priorities and setting appropriate goals will help you achieve your potential. Good goals are challenging but attainable, compatible, self-directed, clearly defined, and temporary. Deadlines encourage completion of complex projects.

- Creating a good work area, completing tasks in an appropriate sequence, making the most of each work period, maintaining momentum, and reducing stress are major aspects of time management.

- Collaborative work can help us expand our ideas, explore new fields, and pursue projects that are too complex or time-consuming to do alone.

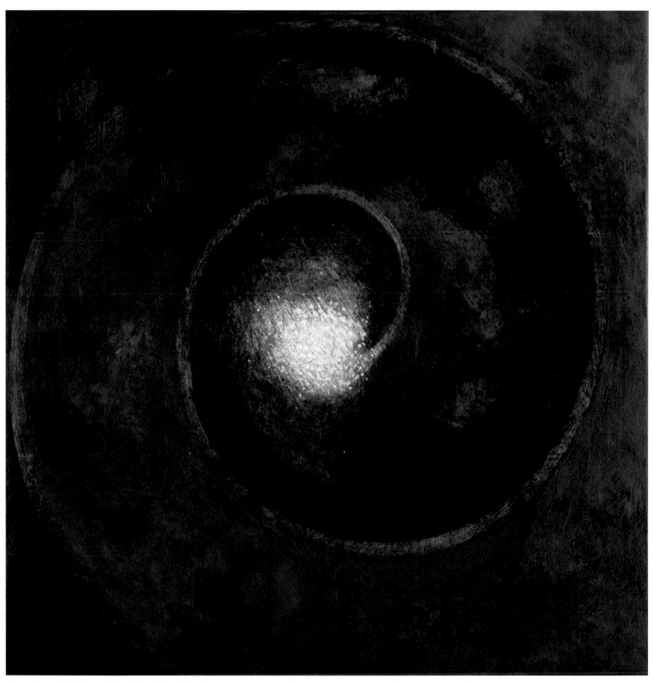

Georgiana Nehl, *Sun/Star* **(Detail), 1996.** Oil paint on gessoed wood, 25¾ in. w. × 13¼ in. h. × 1 in. d. (65 × 34 × 3 cm).

Profile:
Nancy Callahan, Artist, and Diane Gallo, Writer

Storefront Stories: Creating a
Collaborative Community

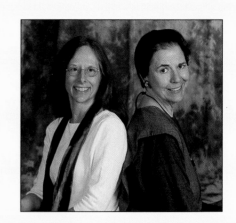

Nancy Callahan (left in photo) is a leader in the field of artists' books and is known for her creative work in screen printing. She has exhibited her work widely, and, in 1994, she was one of four artists chosen to represent the United States at the International Book and Paper Exhibition in Belgium. In 1999, she participated in the International Artists' Book Workshop and Symposium in Mor, Hungary. In addition to her full-time teaching at the State University of New York at Oneonta, Callahan has taught workshops at major book centers around the country, including the Center for Book Arts in New York City and The Women's Studio Workshop.

Diane Gallo (right in photo) is an award-winning writer and performance poet, as well as a master teacher. Her filmwork has received awards from American Women in Radio & Television and nominations from the American Film Institute. Gallo teaches creative writing and life-story workshops at universities and cultural institutes throughout the country and is a visiting poet with the Dodge Foundation Poetry Program, a humanist scholar with the National Endowment for the Humanities Poets in Person program, and co-founder of the newly formed Association of Teaching Artists.

Callahan and Gallo began working together in 1984 as a photographer/writer team for the Binghamton Press. As a result of many years of collaborative teaching, they became the first teaching artist team working with the Empire State Partnership project, jointly sponsored by the New York State Education Department and the New York State Council of the Arts. In 1996, they received fellowships to the Virginia Center for the Creative Arts, where they began working on a major project, which led to their selection by the Mid-Atlantic Foundation for their millennium project. Funded by the National Endowment for the Arts, the project—Artists & Communities: America Creates for the Millennium—named Callahan and Gallo as two of America's 250 most creative community artists.

MS: You've gained a lot of recognition for your recent text-based installations. Please describe *Storefront Stories*.

NC: Over the past two years we've had an extraordinary collaborative experience. As an extension of our writing, we developed a new type of text-based installation. One day as we worked on a story about ironing, we playfully hung a single wrinkled white shirt in the front window of our studio in Gilbertsville, New York. Below the shirt, we placed a small sign that said "No one irons anymore." As the lone shirt turned, it attracted attention, causing people on the sidewalk to stop, read the window, and react. *Storefront Stories* was born.

DG: Objects became words; words transformed objects. Week by week, using storefront windows as a public stage, we wrote and presented installments of autobiographical stories. In one town, a single window was changed every 10 days, creating an ongoing narrative. In another, we used five windows in a row, like pages in a book. Bits of text and symbolic objects were used to tell stories about personal change. Stories and objects—combined with the unexpected street location—sparked curiosity and started a community dialogue.

MS: How did members of the community become participants?

NC: They just began telling us their stories. An elderly woman on her way to the post office stopped to tell us the story of how she had learned to type on an old Smith typewriter, just like the one in the window. Eleven-year-old boys on bicycles stopped by. A mother brought her children to the windows each week to read the story aloud. Couples strolling by in the evening asked, "What's coming next?"

DG: People talked to us easily, asking questions and encouraging us. Many times, we'd return to find handwritten stories, comments, and suggestions. We watched passersby examine the windows and heard them laughing and talking to each other as they pieced together the story. When a viewer made a good suggestion, we incorporated the idea into the next window. When community members saw their ideas so quickly incorporated, they realized they were more than passive viewers. They were now active participants, with a vital involvement in the artistic process. The collaboration which began between two artists quickly expanded, engaging the entire town.

MS: In your household installations you create complete environments to frame your stories. To create these environments, you spend many hours scouting thrift shops and garage sales, searching for just the right objects to evoke an exact time and place. Why are these objects so important?

NC: Household objects are the vocabulary of the everyday world. Everyone feels comfortable with them. The objects are a bridge — they allow the viewer to cross easily from everyday life into the world of our installations.

DG: After the object is safely in the viewer's mind, it becomes a psychic spark which triggers associations and amplifies memories. For example, while we were doing the ironing installation, a delivery man who stopped for a moment to watch us work said, "I don't know anything about art," and began talking deeply and at length about how, when he was a boy, his mother took in ironing to make extra money so that he could have a bicycle.

NC: His narrative then created another layer of collaboration.

MS: When you began creating the installations, did you expect this kind of public reaction?

NC: No. It was a shock. From the moment we hung that first wrinkled shirt in the studio window, people on the street were responsive. The immediate feedback was exhilarating.

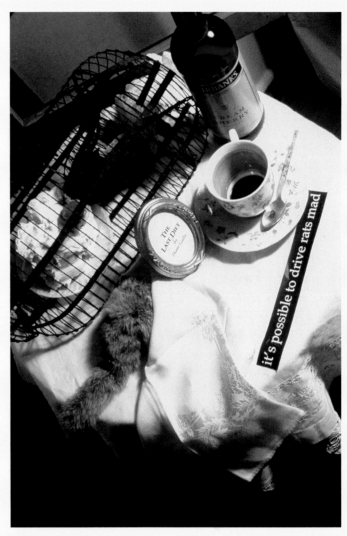

Diane Gallo and Nancy Callahan, *Storefront Stories*, **1999.** Mixed medium installation, 6 × 6 × 6 ft (1.83 × 1.83 × 1.83 m).

MS: What are the characteristics of a good collaboration?

DG: Quiet attention is crucial. We both have to really listen, not only to words but also to the implications.

NC: Always tell the truth. There can be no censoring. If something's bothering you, it's important to talk about it right away. Honesty and careful listening build trust. When you trust your partner, you can reveal more.

MS: When people first see your installations, many are almost overwhelmed. Why?

DG: We're balancing on a fine line between life and art, between the personal and the universal, the public and the private, the conscious and the unconscious. We're working on the edge of consciousness, looking for things you might only be half aware of under ordinary circumstances. It's like watching a horizon line in your mind, waiting for a thought or an answer to rise.

Problem Seeking and Problem Solving

Artworks are generally experienced visually. By learning the basic elements of design and exploring many approaches to composition, you can increase the visual power of your work. Composition, however, is only part of the puzzle. With the increasing emphasis on visual communication around the world, the ideas being expressed by artists and designers have become more varied and complex. Conceptual invention is just as important as compositional strength. New ideas invite development of new types of artwork. When the concept is fresh and the composition is compelling, expression and communication expand.

PROBLEM SEEKING

The Design Process

In its most basic form, the design process can be distilled down to four basic steps. When beginning a project, the designer asks

1. What is needed?
2. What existing designs are similar to the design we need?
3. What is the difference between the existing designs and the new design?
4. How can we transform, combine, or expand these existing designs?

By studying the classic Eames chair, we can see this process clearly. Charles and Ray Eames were two of the most innovative and influential designers of the postwar era. Trained as an architect, Charles was a master of engineering and had a gift for design integration. Trained as a painter, Ray contributed a love of visual structure, a sense of adventure, and an understanding of marketing. Combining their strengths, this husband-and-wife team designed furniture, toys, exhibitions, and architecture and directed over 80 experimental films.

Their first breakthrough in furniture design came in 1940, when they entered a chair competition sponsored by the Museum of Modern Art. Many architects had designed furniture, and the Eameses were eager to explore this field. Many similar products existed. The most common was the overstuffed chair, which continues to dominate American living rooms. Extensive padding on a boxy framework supported the sitter. Another popular design

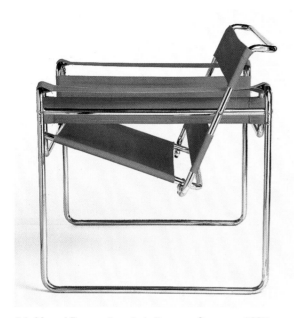

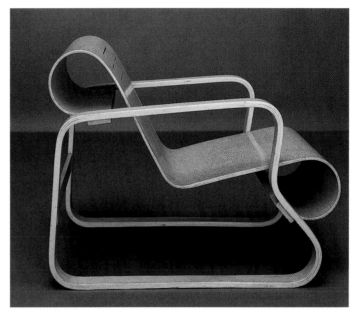

5.1 Marcel Breuer, Armchair, Dessau, Germany, 1925.
Tubular steel, canvas, 28¹¹⁄₁₆ in. h. × 30⁵⁄₁₆ in. w. × 26¾ in. d.
(72.8 × 77 × 68 cm).

5.2 Alvar Aalto, Paimio Lounge Chair, 1931–33. Laminated birch,
molded plywood, lacquered, 26 × 23¾ × 34⅞ in. (66 × 60.5 × 88.5 cm).

was the Adirondack chair, made from a series of flat wooden planes. Of greatest interest, however, were designs by architects such as Marcel Breuer (5.1) and Alvar Aalto (5.2). These designs used modern materials and clearly displayed their structure.

By comparing existing chairs with the chair they wanted, Charles and Ray could identify qualities they needed to retain and qualities that needed to be changed. The familiar overstuffed chair (5.3) was bulky and awkward, but it was comfortable. The Adirondack chair (5.4) was easy to mass-produce, but too large for interior use. The modern chairs were elegant and inventive but were expensive to produce and often uncomfortable. The Eameses wanted to create a modern chair that was comfortable, elegant, and inexpensive.

During World War II, the Eames team had designed and manufactured molded plywood splints, which were used by doctors in the U.S. Navy. After extensive research and experimentation, they had mastered the process of steaming and reshaping the sheets of plywood into complex curves. In developing their competition entry, they combined their knowledge of splints, love of modern chairs, understanding of painting, and mastery of architecture. Their plywood chair, designed in collaboration with architect Eero Saarinen, was awarded the first prize.

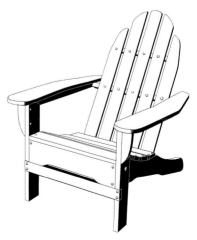

5.3 Overstuffed Chair

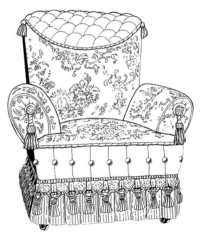

5.4 Adirondack Chair

PROBLEM SEEKING

129

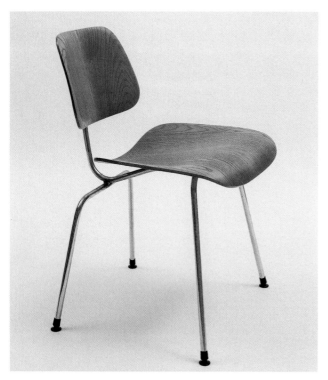

5.5 Charles and Ray Eames, Side Chair, Model DCM, 1946. Molded ash plywood, steel rod, and rubber shockmounts, 28¾ in. h. × 19½ in. d. × 20 in. w. (73 × 49.5 × 50.8 cm).

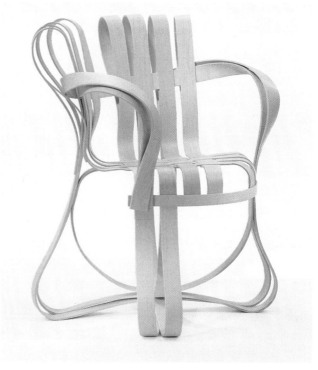

5.6 Frank Gehry, Cross Check Armchair, 1992. Maple, 33⅝ in. h. × 28½ in. d. × 28½ in. w. (85.3 × 72.4 × 72.4 cm).

A series of Eames designs followed, including a metal and plywood version in 1946 (5.5) and several cast plastic versions. One popular chair was mass-produced by the thousands.

By addressing a need, visualizing existing designs, making comparisons, and combining the best characteristics of existing chairs, the Eames team produced a new kind of chair and thus firmly established themselves as leaders in the design field.

The Fine Art Process

For a designer, the problem-solving process begins when a client requests help or the designer identifies a specific need. With the Eames chair, the museum competition provided the impetus for an experiment that reshaped an industry. Design is generally utilitarian, and the problem is usually determined by a client.

Contemporary sculptors, printmakers, filmmakers, and other fine artists generally invent their own aesthetic problems. Ideas often arise from personal experience and from the cultural context. Combining self-awareness with empathy for others,

many artists have transformed a specific event into a universal statement. For example, Picasso's *Guernica* (see figure 7.20, page 173) painted in response to the 1937 bombing of a specific Spanish village, is now revered as a universal statement about the horrors of war. Working more independently and with fewer deadlines, artists can explore ideas and issues of personal interest.

Sources of Ideas

Regardless of the initial motivation for their work, both artists and designers constantly scan their surroundings in an omnivorous search for images and ideas. As demonstrated by the profiles that appear throughout this book, the most improbable object or idea may provide inspiration. Memories of growing up in small-town America provide the stimulus for *Storefront Stories,* by Nancy Callahan and Diane Gallo. Biological systems inspire sculptor Heidi Lasher-Oakes. Ordinary vegetables and African vessels influence ceramicist David MacDonald. If you are at a loss for an idea, take a fresh look at your surroundings.

Transform a Common Object

Architect Frank Gehry based the exuberant armchair in figure 5.6 on the wood-strip bushel basket used by farmers (5.7). If you consider all the ideas that can be generated by a set of car keys, a pair of scissors, a baseball glove, or a compass, you will have more than enough to get a project started.

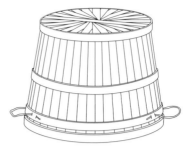

5.7 A Wood-Strip Bushel Basket

Study Nature

Ceramicist Ray Rogers is inspired by many natural forms, including mushrooms, stones, and aquatic life. His spherical pots (5.8) often suggest the colors, textures, and economy of nature. In figure 5.9, Vera Lisková used the fluidity and transparency of glass to create a humorous version of a prosaic porcupine. Through an inventive use of materials, both artists have reinterpreted nature.

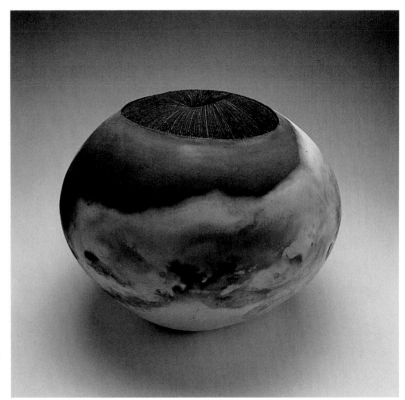

5.8 Ray Rogers, Vessel, New Zealand, 1984. Large, pit-fired (porous and nonfunctional) with "fungoid" decorative treatment in relief. Diameter approximately 21⅗ in. (55 cm).

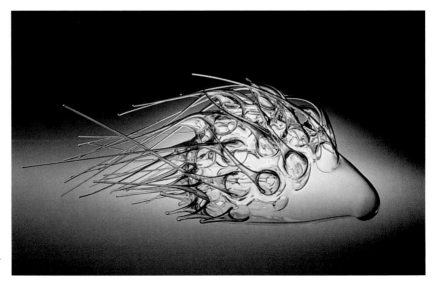

5.9 Vera Lisková, *Porcupine*, 1972–80. Flame-worked glass, 4¼ × 11 in. (10.8 × 28.2 cm).

Visit a Museum

Artists and designers frequently visit all kinds of museums. Carefully observed, the history and physical objects produced by any culture can be both instructive and inspirational. Looking at non-Western artwork is especially valuable. Unfamiliar concepts and compositions can suggest new ideas and fresh approaches. Beau Dick's *Mugamtl Mask* (5.10) is one example. First developed by a man who had revived from a deadly illness, it depicts the supernatural abilities (including flight) that he gained during his experience. His descendants now have the right to construct and wear this special mask. By understanding the story and studying the mask structure, you can more readily design a mask based on your own experiences.

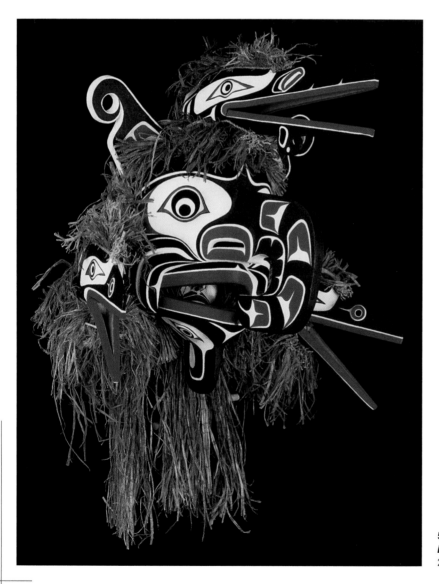

5.10 Beau Dick, *Mugamtl Mask (Crooked Beak)*, **1993.** Red cedar, cedar bark, paint, 24 × 26 × 16 in. (61 × 66 × 40.6 cm).

Characteristics of a Good Problem

Regardless of its source, the problem at hand must fully engage either the artist or the designer. By courageously confronting obstacles and seeking solutions, the artist or designer can develop increasingly ambitious work. Whether it is assigned or invented, a good problem includes many of the following characteristics.

Significant

When substantial amounts of time, effort, and money are being spent, it is wise to prioritize problems and focus on those of greatest consequence. Identifying and prioritizing your major goals can help you determine the significance of a job. Balancing this analysis with a sense of adventure can help you combine the best qualities of a risk-taker and a safe-keeper.

Socially Responsible

With the human population above 6 billion, it is unwise to pursue a project that squanders natural resources. In the past 20 years, designers have become increasingly aware of the environmental and social consequences of their actions. What natural resources will be required for a major project, and how will you dispose of resulting waste? Increasingly, designers consider the environmental as well as the economic implications of each project.

Comprehensible

It is almost impossible to solve a problem you don't understand. When working on a class assignment, ask questions if the assignment is unclear to you.

Open to Experimentation

It is important to distinguish between clear definition and restrictive limitations. Consider the following two assignment descriptions:

1. Organize at least 20 photocopies in such a way that they convey an idea or emotion.

2. Organize 20 photographs by American Civil War photographer Mathew Brady in order to tell a story about the life of Abraham Lincoln.

In the first case, the requirements of the project are clearly stated, but the solution remains open to invention. In the second case, the *solution* as well as the *problem* is described. For the inventive artist or designer, there are no "bad" problems, only bad solutions. Nonetheless, when limited to a narrow range of possible solutions, even the most inventive person will become ineffective. If you find yourself in a straitjacket, rethink the problem and try a new approach.

Ambitious yet Achievable

When the problem is too easy or the solution is too familiar, little is learned and nothing is gained. When the problem is too difficult or the solution is too time-consuming, completion is delayed and costs increase. Continued indefinitely, even the most exciting project can become a trap!

Authentic

Regardless of the source, every person approaches each problem on his or her own terms. Each of us has a unique perspective, and the connections, which are so important in design, will vary. Likewise, as a student, you will learn more when you really embrace each assignment and make it your own. Ask questions, so that you can understand the substance as well as the surface of each assignment. When you reframe the assignment in your own terms and plunge into the work wholeheartedly, the creative possibilities will expand and your imagination will soar.

CONVERGENT AND DIVERGENT THINKING

To see how it all works, let's work our way through an actual assignment, using two different problem-solving strategies.

> Problem: Organize up to 20 photocopies from the library so that they tell a story. Use any size and type of format as appropriate. Any image can be enlarged, reduced, cropped, or repeated.

Using Convergent Thinking

Convergent thinking involves the pursuit of a predetermined goal, usually in a linear progression and using a highly focused problem-solving technique. The word *prose* can help you remember the basic steps:

1. Define the *problem.*
2. Do *research.*
3. Determine your *objective.*
4. Devise a *strategy.*
5. *Execute* the strategy.
6. *Evaluate* the results.

In convergent thinking, the end determines the means. You know what you are seeking before you begin. For this reason, clear definition of the problem is essential: the most brilliant idea is useless if it doesn't solve the problem.

Convergent thinking is familiar to most of us through the scientific method, which follows the same basic procedure. It is orderly, logical, and empirical; there are clear boundaries and specific guidelines. Clearly focused on the final result, convergent thinking is a good way to achieve a goal and meet a deadline. Let's analyze each step.

Define the Problem

Determine the exact parameters of the assignment. Ask lots of questions, so that you understand the assignment objectives. Determine all of the physical and technical requirements and ask whether there are any stylistic limitations. Be sure that you understand the preliminary steps as well as the final due date.

Next, assess your strengths and weaknesses relative to the problem assigned, and determine your best work strategy. Let's consider the approaches taken by two hypothetical students, Jeremy (as a convergent thinker) and Angela (as a divergent thinker).

Jeremy begins by defining *story, images,* and *library.* From the dictionary, he finds that a *story* is shorter than a novel, that it may be true or fictitious, that a series of connected events is needed, and that it may take many forms, including a memoir, a play, or a newspaper article.

Next, he finds that an *image* is a representation of a person or thing, a visual impression produced by reflection in a mirror, or a mental picture of something: an idea or impression. This means that photographs from books or magazines and reproductions of paintings are fair game. Jeremy realizes that he can even include a mirror in the project, to reflect the viewer's own image.

Finally, by exploring the computer system in the *library,* he finds that Internet resources as well as books are available. He spends the first hour of class on brainstorming, then decides to develop a story about Irish immigration to America at the turn of the century.

Do Research

Creativity is highly dependent on seeking connections and making new combinations. The more information you have, the more connections you can make. Through research, you can collect and assess technical, visual, and conceptual information. For this assignment, Jeremy develops a plausible story based on immigrant diaries. He begins to collect images of ships, cities, and people.

Determine Your Objective

Jeremy now has the raw material needed to solve the problem. However, many questions remain unanswered, including

- What happens in this story? Is it fiction or nonfiction?

- Who is the storyteller? A 12-year-old boy will tell a very different story than a 20-year-old woman.

- What is the best format to use? A dozen letters, sent between fictitious brothers in Dublin and

Boston? A Website, describing actual families? A photo album?

At this point, Jeremy pauses to determine his objective, both as an artist and as a student. What does he really want to communicate? He considers:

- *Does it solve the problem?* He reviews the assignment parameters.

- *Is the solution conceptually inventive?* Is it really intriguing, or is it something we've all seen before, a cliché?

- *Is the planned solution visually compelling?*

- *Can this solution be completed by the due date?* To meet the due date, it may be necessary to distill a complex problem down to an essential statement. In this case, Jeremy decides to simplify his project by focusing on one main character.

Devise a Strategy

While some assignments can be done in an afternoon, three-dimensional projects and multiple-image works tend to take longer. Jeremy determines the supplies he needs and considers the best time and place to work on the project.

Execute the Strategy

Now, Jeremy just digs in and works. He has found it best to work with great concentration and determination at this point, rather than second-guessing himself.

Evaluate the Results

At the end of each work session, Jeremy considers the strengths and weaknesses of the work in progress. What areas in each composition seem timid or confusing? How can those areas be strengthened? He finally presents the project for a class critique.

Convergent Thinking Applications

Convergent thinking is most effective when

- The problem can be defined clearly.

- The problem can be solved rationally.

- The problem must be solved sequentially.

- Firm deadlines must be met.

Because many problems in science and industry fit these criteria, convergent thinking is widely used by scientists, businesspeople, and graphic designers.

Using Divergent Thinking

The advantages of convergent thinking are clarity, control, focus, and a strong sense of direction. For many tasks, convergent thinking is ideal. In some cases, however, convergent thinking can offer *too* much clarity and not enough chaos. Inspiration is elusive. Over-the-edge creativity is often messy and rarely occurs in an orderly progression. If you want to find something completely new, you will have to leave the beaten path.

In **divergent thinking,** the means determines the end. The process is more open-ended; specific results are hard to predict. Divergent thinking is a great way to generate ideas and move beyond preconceptions.

There are two major differences between convergent and divergent thinking. First, in divergent thinking, the problem is defined much more broadly, with less attention to "what the client wants." Research is more expansive and less tightly focused. Experimentation is open-ended: anything can happen. Second, because the convergent thinker discards weak ideas in the thumbnail stage, the final image is preplanned and predictable. The divergent thinker, on the other hand, generates many variables, is less methodical, and may have to produce multiple drafts of a composition in order to get the desired result.

While convergent thinking is usually more efficient, divergent thinking is often more inventive. It opens up unfamiliar lines of inquiry and can lead to a creative breakthrough. Divergent thinking is a high-risk/high-gain approach. By breaking traditional rules, the artist can explore unexpected connections and create new possibilities.

Let's try the same assignment again, now using Angela's divergent thinking.

> Problem: Organize up to 20 photocopies from the library so that they tell a story. Use any size and type of format as appropriate. Any image can be enlarged, reduced, cropped, or repeated.

Realizing that the strength of the source images is critical, Angela immediately heads for the section of the library devoted to photography. By leafing though a dozen books, she finds 30 great photographs, ranging from images of train stations to trapeze artists. She photocopies the photographs, enlarging and reducing pictures to provide more options. Laying them out on a table, she begins to move the images around, considering the stories that might be generated. Twenty of the images are soon discarded; they are unrelated to the circus story she begins to develop. She then finds 5 more images to flesh out her idea.

At this point, her process becomes similar to the final steps described in the preceeding section. Like Jeremy, she must clarify her objective, develop characters, decide on a format, and construct the final piece. However, because she started with such a disparate collection of images, her final story is more likely to be nonlinear. Like a dream, her images may suggest ideas rather than describe specific situations.

Divergent Thinking Applications

Divergent thinking is most effective when

- The problem definition is elusive or evolving.

- A rational solution is not required.

- A sequential work method is unnecessary.

- Deadlines are flexible.

Many creative people have used divergent thinking to explore the subconscious and reveal unexpected new patterns of thought. Surrealism, an art movement that flourished in Europe between the world wars, provides many notable examples of divergent thinking in art and literature. More interested in the essential substance of ideas and objects than in surface appearances, painter Yves Tanguy constructed *Multiplication of the Arcs* (5.11) from evocative abstract shapes. In *The Mystery and Melancholy of a Street* (5.12), Giorgio de Chirico used distorted perspective, relentless repetition, and threatening cast shadows to create a feeling of anxiety. More interested in stimulating the viewer's own response than in imposing a specific vision, the surrealists rejected rational thought.

Which is better—convergent or divergent thinking? A good problem-solving strategy is one

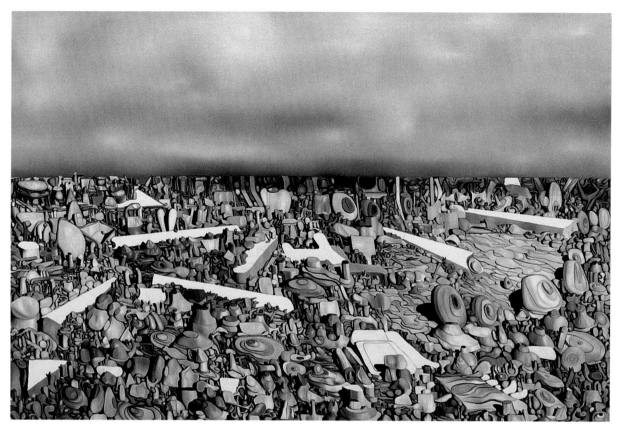

5.11 Yves Tanguy, *Multiplication of the Arcs,* **1954.** Oil on canvas, 40 × 60 in. (101.6 × 152.4 cm).

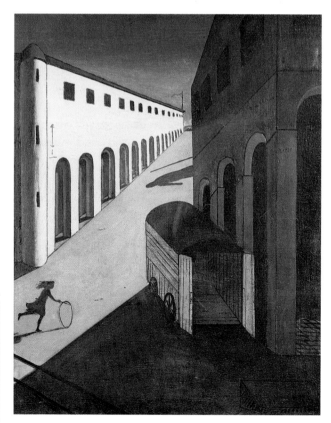

5.12 Giorgio de Chirico, *The Mystery and Melancholy of a Street,* **1914.** Oil on canvas, 24¼ × 28½ in. (62 × 72 cm).

that works. If five people are working on a Website design, a clear sense of direction, agreement on style, an understanding of individual responsibilities, and adherence to deadlines are essential. Such a design team will usually use convergent thinking. On the other hand, when an artist is working independently, the open-ended divergent approach can lead to a major breakthrough. By understanding both approaches, you can select the work method that is best for you.

BRAINSTORMING

Brainstorming plays an important role in both convergent and divergent thinking. It is a great way to expand ideas, see connections, and explore implications. The following are four common strategies.

Make a List

Let's say that the assignment involves visualizing an emotion. Start by listing every emotion you can, regardless of your interest in any specific area. Getting into the practice of opening up and actively exploring possibilities is crucial: just pour out ideas!

**joy   sorrow   anger   passion   jealousy
sympathy   horror   exaltation**

From the list of emotions, circle one that looks promising. To move from the intangible name of the emotion to a visual solution, develop a list of the *kinds*, *causes*, and *effects* of the emotion. Following is one example, using *anger* as a starting point.

KINDS	CAUSES	EFFECTS
annoyance	wrong-number phone call at 5 A.M.	slammed down phone
smoldering rage	friend gets award you want	argument with friend
desperate anger	fired from job	shouted at your child
anger at self	poor performance on test	major studying

By investigating specific kinds of anger and determining the causes and the effects, you now have some specific images to develop, rather than struggling with a vague, intangible emotion.

Use a Thesaurus

Another way to explore the potential of an idea is to use a thesaurus. Be sure to get a thesaurus that lists words conceptually rather than alphabetically. Use the index in the back to look up the specific word you need. For example, *The Concise Roget's International Thesaurus* has a section titled "Feelings," including everything from *acrimony* to *zeal*. Here is a listing of synonyms from the section on resentment and anger: *anger, wrath, ire, indignation, heat, more heat than light, dudgeon, fit of anger, tantrum, outburst, explosion, storm, scene, passion, fury, burn, vehemence, violence, vent one's anger, seethe, simmer,* and *sizzle!* Thinking about a wide range of implications and connections to other emotions can give you a new approach to a familiar word.

Explore Connections

By drawing a conceptual diagram, you can create your own thesaurus. Start with a central word. Then, branch out in all directions, pursuing connections and word associations as widely as possible. In a sense, this approach lets you visualize your thinking, as the branches show the patterns and connections that occurred as you explored the idea (5.13A).

In *Structure of the Visual Book*, Keith Smith demonstrates the value of verbal connections. Smith seeks immersion in his subject. He wants to know it

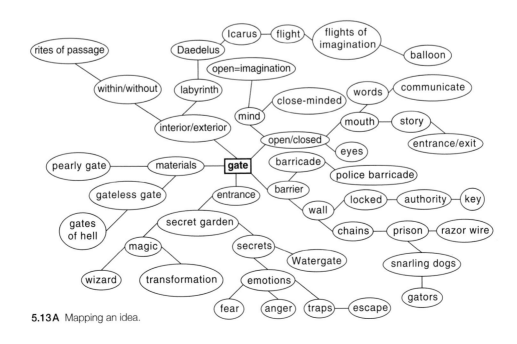

5.13A Mapping an idea.

If I am going to make drawings or photographs which include a bicycle, I might go for a bike ride, but more importantly I would fantasize about a bike. I would picture a bike in my mind. The most obvious depiction is the side view because this is the significant profile. I would then imagine a standing bicycle with no rider, looking from above, directly down on the bike, or from behind or in front of the standing bike with my eye-level midway between the ground and the handlebars. In these three positions the bicycle is seen from the least significant profile. It is a thin vertical line with horizontal protrusions of the pedals, seat and handlebars. The area viewed is so minimal that the bicycle almost disappears.

Before long in examining a bike I would become involved with circles. Looking at the tires, I think about the suspension of the rim and the tire, indeed, the entire vehicle and rider, by the thin spokes. It amazes me that everything is floating in space, connected only by thin lines. I imagine riding the bike through puddles and the trace of the linear journey from the congruent and diverging water marks left by the tread on the pavement. I might think about two friends together and separated. Symbolism.

I think about cycles of being with friends and apart. And again I would think literally of cycles, circles and tires.

I would think of the full moon as a circle and how in its cycle it turns into a line. I would see the tires from the significant profile and in my mind I would turn it in space and it would become an ellipse.

If I turned it further, until it was on an axis 90 degrees from the significant profile, it would no longer be a circle or an ellipse, but it would be a line. So again, line comes into my thoughts.

A circle is a line.

A circle is a straight line.[1]

5.13B

so well that, when he begins to work, he can pursue his images intuitively, with all the power and grace of a skillful cyclist. Try to follow the steps in figure 5.13B, as he explores the word *bicycle*.

Keep a Journal

Keeping a journal or sketchbook is an ideal way to record your ideas and create connections. In it, you can

- Classify, arrange, and record information.
- Brainstorm new ideas.
- Examine your current beliefs and analyze the beliefs of others.

- Record your responses to critiques.
- Make connections among your various classes.

Recording your ideas at the end of each class and reviewing them at the beginning of the next can help you construct your own learning process. Anything that expands your thinking is fair game, including

- Plans for projects, such as thumbnail sketches and rough drafts
- Comments on how your work can be improved
- Notes from textbook readings and clippings from magazines

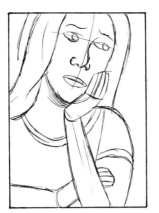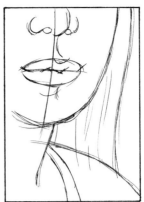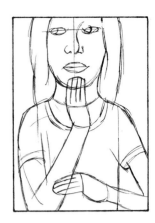

- Notes on visiting artists or gallery visits
- Technical notes or information on materials used in class
- Questions you want to pose in the next class meeting

Your record keeping can take many forms, including

- Drawings and diagrams
- Written ideas, descriptions, and lists
- Poetry or other excerpts from literature and song lyrics

Ask yourself the following questions:

- What was the most compelling image I saw today? What made it compelling?
- What was the most memorable or most offensive idea I heard expressed today? Why was it memorable or offensive?
- What similarities and differences were there among my studio classes this week?
- What connections were there between my lecture classes and studios?
- What do I know today that I didn't know yesterday?
- What do I need to know in order to push my ideas further?

Viewing the journal as a record of your creative process is liberating. Just let your ideas flow. A random idea today can help you solve a visual problem tomorrow. Indeed, it is wise to review the journal as you move into upper-level classes. Many ideas that were too ambitious for a first-year class are perfectly suited to further development in an upper-level class.

VISUAL RESEARCH

Thumbnail Sketches

Library research played a major role in Angela's divergent thinking as well as Jeremy's convergent thinking. We will now consider various approaches to visual research.

Return to your original list of emotions you developed in the brainstorming exercise. Circle the most promising words or phrases you have generated and look for connections between them. Start working on thumbnail sketches, about 1.5 × 2 in. in size (5.14). Be sure to draw a clear boundary for the sketches. The edge of the frame is like an electric fence; by using the edge wisely, you can generate a lot of power!

As with the verbal brainstorming, move fast and stay loose at this point. It is better to generate 10 to 20 possibilities than to refine any single idea. You may find yourself producing very different solutions, or you may make a series of multiple solutions to the same idea: either approach is fine. Just keep moving. An open, nonjudgmental attitude is essential.

Model Making

When working two-dimensionally, it is often necessary to make one or more full-sized rough drafts to

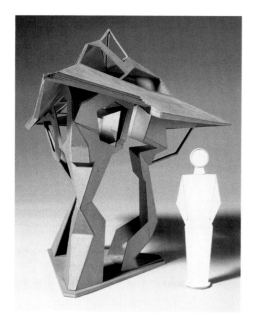

5.15A Peter Forbes, Models for *Shelter/Surveillance Sculpture,* 1994. Mixed media, 10½ × 9½ × 9 in. (27 × 24 × 23 cm).

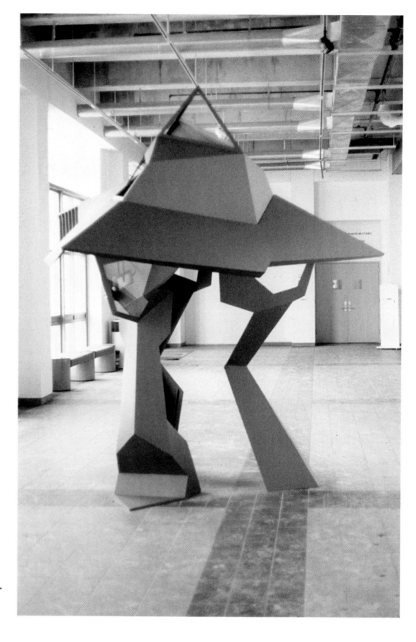

5.15B Peter Forbes, *Shelter/Surveillance Sculpture,* 1994. Mixed media, 11 ft 2 in. × 10 ft 4 in. × 10 ft (3.4 × 3.2 × 3 m).

see how the design looks when enlarged. Refinements made at this stage can make the difference between an adequate solution and an inspired solution.

Prototypes, models, and maquettes serve a similar purpose when you are working three-dimensionally. A **maquette** is a well-developed three-dimensional sketch. Figure 5.15A shows Peter Forbes' maquette for *Shelter/Surveillance Sculpture.* In this chipboard "sketch," Forbes determined the size of the sculpture relative to the viewer and developed a construction strategy. As a result, when he constructed the final, 11-foot-tall sculpture, Forbes was able to proceed with confidence. A **model** is a technical experiment. A **prototype** can be

quite refined, as with the fully functional test cars developed by automobile companies. In addition to the aesthetic benefit of these preliminary studies, it is often necessary to solve technical problems at this stage. Is the cardboard you are using heavy enough to stand vertically, or does it bow? Is your adhesive strong enough? If there are moving parts, is the action fluid and easy, or does the mechanism consistently get stuck?

By completing these preliminary studies, you can refine the idea, strengthen the composition, and improve the craft of the final piece. As with a well-rehearsed performance, the work you bring to the critique is now really ready for discussion.

VARIATIONS ON A THEME

When we work creatively, the idea develops right along with the image. As the project evolves, we see other implications that go beyond our initial intention. By courageously pursuing these implications, we can exceed our original expectations. Just as the landscape appears to expand when we climb a mountain, so an image can expand when our conceptual understanding increases.

One way to get a lot of mileage out of an idea is through variations on a theme. Professional artists rarely do just one painting or sculpture of a given idea — most do many variations before moving to a new subject. *Thirty-Six Views of Mount Fuji* is one example. Printmaker Katsushika Hokusai was 70 years old when he began this series. The revered and beautiful Mount Fuji appeared in each of the designs in some way. Variations in the time of year and size of the mountain helped Hokusai produce very different images while retaining the same basic theme (5.16A–C).

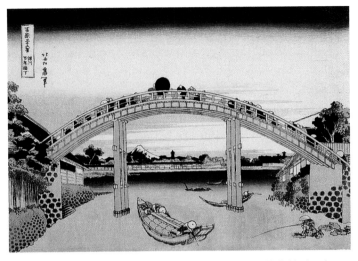

5.16A Katsushika Hokusai, *Thirty-Six Views of Mount Fuji: Under the Mannen Bridge at Fukagawa,* Edo Period, c. 1830. Color woodblock print, 10¹⁄₁₆ × 14¹¹⁄₁₆ in. (25.7 × 37.5 cm).

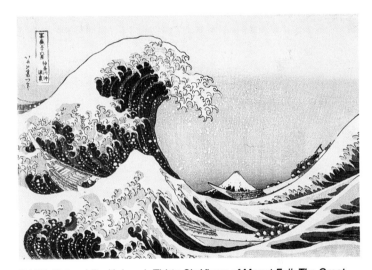

5.16B Katsushika Hokusai, *Thirty-Six Views of Mount Fuji: The Great Wave off Kanagawa,* Edo Period, c. 1830. Color woodblock print, 10³⁄₁₆ × 14¹⁵⁄₁₆ in. (25.9 × 37.5 cm).

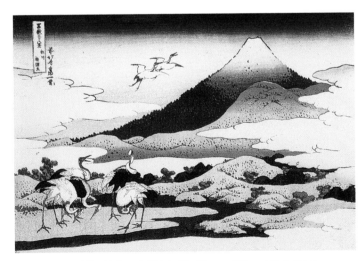

5.16C Katsushika Hokusai, *Thirty-Six Views of Mount Fuji: Near Umezawa in Sagami Province,* Edo Period, c. 1830. Color woodblock print, 10¹⁄₁₆ × 14⅞ in. (25.6 × 37.8 cm).

A very different series of variations is presented in figures 5.17 and 5.18. Here, the two artists offer very individual interpretations of the basic bracelet. Leslie Leupp's three bracelets present a playful dialogue between form and space. Lines, planes, and simple volumes dance around the wearer's wrist. In contrast, Lisa Gralnick's three bracelets are dark, massive, and threatening. The crisp angles, simple forms, and black acrylic are more suggestive of armor than of jewelry.

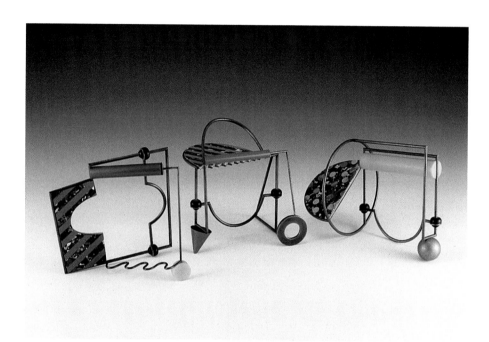

5.17 Leslie Leupp, Three Bracelets: Solidified Reality, Frivolous Vitality, Compound Simplicity, 1984. Steel, plastic, linoleum, laminate, aluminum. Constructed, each 3 × 4 × 3 in. (8 × 10 × 8 cm).

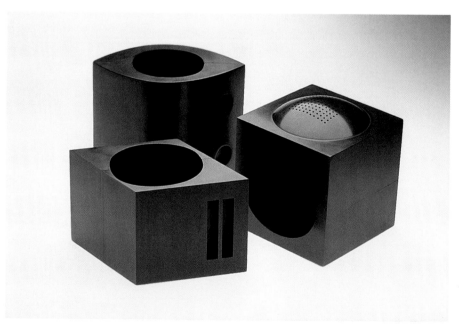

5.18 Lisa Gralnick, Three Bracelets, 1988. Black acrylic, gold, hollow construction, left to right: 3 × 3½ × 3½ in.; 4½ × 3½ × 3 in.; 3½ × 3½ × 3½ in. (7.6 × 8.9 × 8.9 cm; 11.4 × 8.9 × 7.6 cm; 8.9 × 8.9 × 8.9 cm).

AN OPEN MIND

As noted in Chapter Four, most creative people have a wide range of interests. The very best artists and designers are often accomplished in more than one field. For example, Michelangelo was acclaimed as a painter, sculptor, and poet, while da Vinci was a master of art, biology, and engineering. The study of philosophy has had a major impact on videographer Bill Viola and on installation artist Robert Irwin. Performer Laurie Anderson is equally an artist and a musician and derives many of her ideas from literature. Whenever the base of knowledge expands, the range of potential connections increases. When the islands of knowledge are widely scattered, as with interdisciplinary work, the imaginative leap is especially great.

The message is clear. The more you know, the more you can say. Read a book. Attend a lecture. Take a course in astronomy, archaeology, psychology, or poetry. Use ideas from academic courses to expand your studio work. Art and design require conceptual development as well as perceptual and technical skill. By engaging your heart, your eye, your hand, and your mind, you can fully use your emotional, perceptual, technical, and conceptual resources to create your very best work.

SUMMARY

- Concept and composition are equally important aspects of art and design.

- Designers usually solve problems presented by clients. Artists usually invent aesthetic problems for themselves.

- Ideas come from many sources, including common objects, nature, mythology, and history.

- Good problems are significant, socially responsible, comprehensible, achievable, and authentic. They provide basic parameters without inhibiting exploration.

- Convergent thinking is highly linear. The word *prose* can help you remember the steps.

- Divergent thinking is nonlinear and more open-ended than convergent thinking. It is less predictable and may lead to a creative breakthrough.

- Any idea can be expanded or enriched using brainstorming. Making lists, using a thesaurus, making a conceptual diagram, and creating connections are all common strategies.

- Visual and verbal research can provide the background information needed to create a truly inventive solution.

- Pursuing an idea through variations on a theme can help you realize its full potential.

Keywords

brainstorming	divergent thinking	model	prototype
convergent thinking	maquette		

Profile:
Heidi Lasher-Oakes, Sculptor

The Infinite Journey: Exploring
Ideas in Art and Science

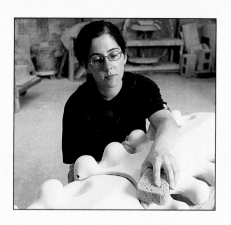

Heidi Lasher-Oakes is best known for her Biological Abstractions Series. Her exhibitions include "Seductive Matter, Sensual Form," which was installed in the Corcoran Art Gallery, and "In Three Dimensions: Women Sculptors of the 90's," which was held at the Snug Harbor Cultural Center. Educated at Reed College, the Pacific Northwest College of Art, and Syracuse University, Lasher-Oakes was awarded a residency at the Bemis Art Center in Omaha, Nebraska, and received a Pollock-Krasner Individual Artist Grant in 1997.

MS: What do art and science have in common?

HL: I have always believed that artistic and scientific methods are closely linked. A scientific experiment is aesthetically pleasing when it is simply and elegantly designed and takes into consideration all possible variables. On the other hand, the full exploration of an artistic idea requires the same rigor of inquiry and careful documentation as the exploration of a scientific hypothesis. In either discipline, if a process is aesthetically successful, it will lead to a coherent result. An aesthetic process requires that all components be ruthlessly considered and evaluated individually and as a unit. The aesthetic integrity of a process does not guarantee that the resulting artwork or experiment will be successful, but it does seem to guarantee that the subsequent work will not constitute a waste of time, either for the investigator or for the audience.

The Shakers have a philosophy of work that expresses this viewpoint simply: if you are going to do something, do it as well as you can.

MS: What is the connection between art and science in your work?

HL: The sculptures in my current Biological Abstraction Series are inspired by human anatomy and physiology, by the forms of cell and tissue structures as seen through an electron microscope, and by the relationships of these forms to manmade structures and objects. They also incorporate plant, animal, and rock forms. Science really provides the starting point for my artwork.

MS: Why are you a sculptor rather than a scientist?

HL: Art gives me a way to express my ideas and observations through the creation of physical objects. I am a haptic person, which means that I am as influenced by touch as I am by sight. I think this ties into a phrase common in our culture, "Let me see that!" which really means, "Give that to me: I want to hold it." To know a thing, I have to hold it, turn it over in my hands, take it apart, then put it back together.

MS: I'm intrigued by your strong emphasis on research, both in your own work and in the classes you teach. What is the value of research?

HL: Research is valuable for two reasons. It provides information for existing ideas and is a way of generating new ideas. Personally, I never know where research will take me. To my mind, the act of researching a subject is very much like exploring a hypertext site on the Internet — once you start clicking, you soon find that you have wandered far from your original reference point. While I understand the value of staying focused, it is the digressions and distractions that give me the best ideas, months or even years later.

Research is insurance. It provides context and fertilizes ideas. The more pieces of information you have, the more connections or associations you will be able to make. And associations are essential. Associative thinking is the ability to make original or unexpected connections. It is an essential part of creativity. Some people start out thinking this way, while for others it is a learned trait.

A wide range of interests seems to encourage associative thinking, so I keep my mind open. For example, I am currently reading a book on grasshoppers, two histories of military battle dress, a mystery novel by Antonia Fraser, three collections of American English proverbs, an introduction to chemistry, and a book by Jorge Luis Borges — and several others waiting in the wings!

MS: How do you get your ideas?

HL: Just about anything in my environment and experience can generate an idea — a book I read, a conversation, a walk in the woods.

MS: Your ideas are pretty complex. How do you communicate this information?

HL: Using association, I try to put as many ideas as possible into the forms I construct. For example, Biological Abstraction III, which depicts an ovary and associated seed structures, also embodies references to dandelion seeds, diving bells, and bomb casings. Each reference contains another piece of information which expands on a physical quality of the object and adds another layer of meaning. I'm not interested in making copies of the structures I study. Instead, I try to understand and express their essential forces and overriding themes.

MS: Please describe your working process.

HL: First, I identify a system for study. Since I am especially interested in human anatomy and physiology, I think of a system as an organ or group of organs in the human body. In this series, I have studied the female reproductive tract, the skin, the respiratory tract, and the inner ear.

Once I have chosen a system, I study it at microscopic and macroscopic levels to try to learn something about the relationship between its structure and function. Scale is really important: the microscopic view reveals an astonishing level

of complexity in the simplest of structures! During this phase, I also look for materials that share the structural and functional properties of my system's cellular building blocks. I experiment by combining these materials to see how they might work together. At the same time, I begin to make plans and drawings for different aspects of the piece. When I have gathered enough information to give me a solid foundation, I begin construction.

MS: It sounds so orderly! My creative process is much more chaotic.

HL: Actually, my process is definitely *not* as linear as it sounds! The research, while extensive, is never complete: all art-making requires a balance between analysis and intuition. The materials always have something new to teach me if I am willing to learn. This element of unpredictability can be frustrating and uncomfortable, but it is absolutely essential. If I play it safe, if I'm inflexible, too insistent on sticking to a set plan, the resulting piece will be dull and lifeless. For me, learning comes from experimenting and making mistakes. It is the desire to learn about my materials, myself, and the world around me that keeps me actively engaged during many hours of physical work.

MS: I think we can appreciate the function of science in our culture. What is the function of art?

HL: For me, art helps to stimulate thought, encourage contemplation, increase understanding, and express emotion. Like science, it gives us a way to see beyond everyday experience and embrace the complexity and beauty of our world.

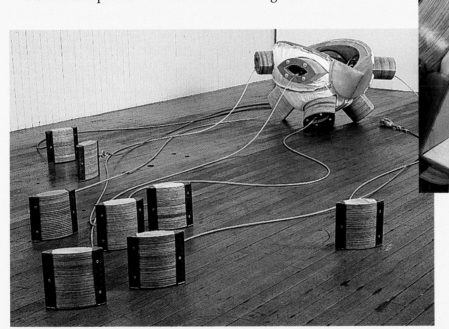

Detail

Heidi Lasher-Oakes, *Biological Abstraction III*, 1996. Wood, fiberglass, foam rubber, canvas, steel, dinghy anchors, rubber gasket material, fabricated and purchased hardware. Primary structure: 4 ft l. × 4 ft w. × 3½ ft h. (1.21 × 1.21 × 1.07 m), entire assembly approx. 15 ft l. (4.5 m).

Developing Critical Thinking

chapter six

Critical thinking combines

- Evaluation of all available information
- Analysis of visual relationships
- Exploration of alternative solutions

Never complacent, the best artists and designers continually seek to improve each image and expand each idea. Critical thinking is used to determine compositional strengths, develop concepts, and improve visual communication. Knowing what to keep and what to change is essential. By enhancing the best aspects of a design and deleting the weak areas, we can dramatically strengthen both communication and expression.

ESTABLISHING CRITERIA

Establishing the criteria on which judgments will be made is the first step. For example, if technical skills are being emphasized in an assignment, craftsmanship will be highly valued. Likewise, if the assignment must be done in analogous colors, a black-and-white painting will not meet the criteria, no matter how carefully it is composed. By determining the major questions being raised in each problem, we can understand the basis on which judgments will be reached. Consider the following questions:

- What is the purpose of the assignment? Does your teacher want you to learn any specific skills? What compositional and conceptual variables will you need to explore?
- What are the assignment parameters? Are there limitations in the size, style, or materials?
- When is the assignment due and in what form must it be presented?

It is important to distinguish between understanding assignment criteria and seeking the "right answer." In the first case, by determining the boundaries, you can fully focus your energy when you begin to work. Just as a magnifying glass can be used to focus sunlight into a powerful beam, so assignment parameters can help you focus creative energy. On the other hand, students who try to determine the "right answer" to a problem often simply want to know the teacher's solution. Such knowledge is rarely helpful. Any problem presented by a teacher simply sets a learning process in motion: you learn through your work. Since learning requires a personal process of investigation, finding your own answer is essential.

FORM, SUBJECT, AND CONTENT

The most effective compositions present a unified visualization of an idea or emotion. As a result, it is often difficult to dissect and analyze a design. Identifying three major aspects of an artwork can provide a beginning point for discussion.

Form may be defined as the physical manifestation of an idea or emotion. Two-dimensional forms are created using line, shape, texture, value, and color. The building blocks of three-dimensional forms are line, plane, volume, mass, space, texture, and color. Duration, tempo, intensity, scope, setting, and chronology are combined to create time-based art forms. For example, film is the form in which *Star Wars* was first presented.

The **subject,** or topic, of an artwork is most apparent when a person, an object, an event, or a setting is clearly represented. For example, the conflict between the rebels and the Empire provides the subject for *Star Wars.*

The emotional or intellectual message of an artwork provides its **content,** or underlying theme. The theme of *Star Wars* is the journey into the self. Luke Skywalker's gradual understanding of himself and acceptance of Darth Vader as his father provides an essential emotional undercurrent to the entire series.

STOP, LOOK, LISTEN, LEARN

Any of these three aspects of design can be discussed critically. A **critique** is the most common structure used. During the critique, the entire class analyzes the work completed at the end of an assignment. Many solutions are presented, demonstrating a wide range of possibilities. The strengths and weaknesses in each design are determined, and areas needing revision are revealed. These insights can be used to improve the current design or to generate possibilities for the next assignment.

Critiques can be extremely helpful, extremely destructive, or just plain boring, largely depending on the amount and type of student involvement. The main purpose of the critique is to determine which designs are most effective and why. Specific recommendations are most helpful: be sure to substantiate each judgment, so that your rationale is clear. Whether you are giving or receiving advice, come with your mind open, rather than your fists closed. A critique is not a combat zone! Listen carefully to any explanations offered and generously offer your insights to others. Likewise, receive their suggestions gracefully rather than defensively. You will make the final decision on any further actions needed to strengthen your design; if someone gives you bad advice, quietly discard it. An open, substantial, and supportive critique is the best way to determine the effect your design has on an audience, so speak thoughtfully and weigh seriously every suggestion you receive.

When beginning a critique, it is useful to distinguish between objective and subjective criticism. **Objective criticism** is used to assess how well a work of art or design utilizes the elements and principles of design. Discussion generally focuses on basic compositional concerns, such as

- The type of balance used in the composition and how it was created
- The spatial depth of a design and its compositional effect
- The degree of unity in a design and how it was achieved

Objective criticism is based on direct observation and a shared understanding of assignment parameters. Discussion is usually clear and straightforward. Alternative compositional solutions may be discussed in depth.

Subjective criticism is used to describe the personal impact of an image, the narrative implications of an idea, or the cultural ramifications of an action. Discussion generally focuses on the subject and content of the design, including

- The meaning of the artwork
- The feelings it evokes
- Its relationships to other cultural events
- The artist's intent

Because subjective criticism is not based on simple observation, it is more difficult for most groups to remain focused on the artwork itself or to reach any clear conclusions regarding possible improvements. The discussion may become more general and wide-ranging, as political or social questions raised by the works of art and design are analyzed. While these are important topics, because of the potential lack of clarity, subjective criticism may be used sparingly during the foundation year.

TYPES OF CRITIQUES

Description

The first step is to look carefully and report clearly. Without evaluating, telling stories, drawing conclusions, or making recommendations, simply describe the visual organization of the work presented. A **descriptive critique** can help you see details and heighten your understanding of the design. The student whose work you describe learns which aspects of the design are most eye-catching and readable and which areas are muddled and need work.

This is a particularly useful exercise when analyzing a complex piece, such as figure 6.1A. In an art history class you might write

Place de l'Europe on a Rainy Day is a rectangular painting depicting a street in Paris. A vertical lamppost and its shadow extend from the top edge to the bottom edge, neatly dividing the painting in half. A horizon line, extending from the left side and three-quarters of the way to the right, further divides the painting, creating four major quadrants. Because this horizon line is positioned just above center,

the bottom half of the composition is slightly larger than the top half.

A dozen pedestrians with umbrellas occupy the bottom half of the painting. At the right edge, a man strides into the painting, while next to him a couple moves out of the painting, toward the viewer. To the left of the lamppost, most of the movement is horizontal, as people cross the cobblestone streets.

When using description in a spoken critique, it is useful to consider the following compositional characteristics:

- What is the shape of the overall composition? A circle or sphere presents a very different compositional playing field than a square or a cube.

- What range of colors has been used? A black-and-white design is very different from a design in full color.

- What is the size of the project? Extremes are especially notable. A sculpture that is 10 feet tall or a painting that is 1-inch square will immediately attract attention.

- Is the visual information tightly packed, creating a very dense design, or is the design more spacious, with a lot of space between shapes or volumes?

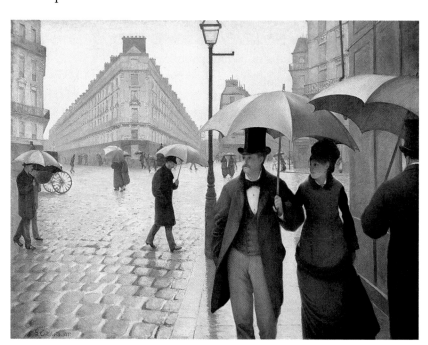

6.1A Gustave Caillebotte, *Place de l'Europe on a Rainy Day*, Paris Street, 1877. Oil on canvas, 83½ × 108¾ in. (212.2 × 276.2 cm).

Cause and Effect

A descriptive critique helps us analyze the compositional choices made by the artist. A **cause-and-effect critique** builds on this description. In a simple description, you might say that the design is primarily composed of diagonals. Using cause and effect, you might conclude that, *because* of the many diagonals, the design is very dynamic. In a cause-and-effect critique, you discuss consequences as well as choices. Analyzing the same painting, you might write

> *Place de l'Europe on a Rainy Day* depicts a city street in Paris near the end of the nineteenth century. A lamppost, positioned near the center, vertically dissects the painting in half. The horizon line creates a second major division, with 45 percent of the space above and 55 percent below this line.
>
> A dozen pedestrians in dark clothing cross the cobblestone streets from left to right, creating a flowing movement. To the right of the post, the pedestrians move in and out of the painting, from background to foreground. Both types of movement add compositional energy. Two men and one woman are the most prominent figures. The man at the far right edge pulls us into the painting, while the couple to his immediate left moves toward us, pushing out of their world and into our world. The movement that dominates each side of the painting is arrested by the lamppost. It is almost as if we are getting two paintings on one canvas.

As shown in figure 6.1B, a visual diagram can be used to support your written comments.

Compare and Contrast

In a **compare/contrast critique,** similarities and differences between two images are noted. We will use the Caillebotte painting one more time, now comparing the perspective used with the perspective in Raphael's *The School of Athens* (6.2).

> The city streets depicted in *The School of Athens* and *Place de l'Europe* demonstrate many differences between Renaissance and Impressionist perspective.
>
> The one-point perspective used in Raphael's painting leads our eyes to Plato and Aristotle, positioned just below the center of the composition. The other figures in the painting are massed in a

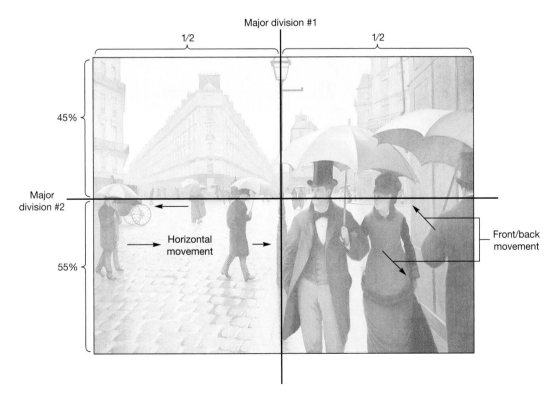

6.1B Gustave Caillebotte, *Place de l'Europe on a Rainy Day*, Paris Street, 1877. Compositional diagram.

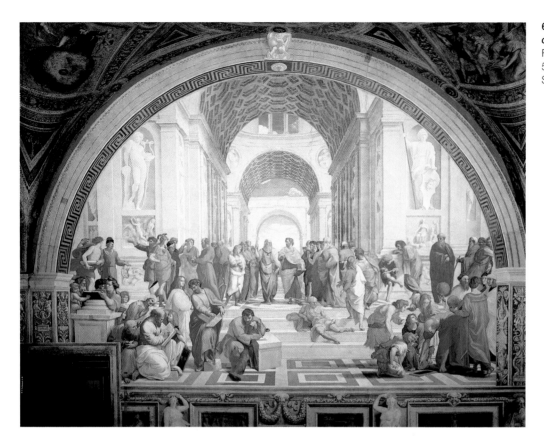

horizontal band from the far right to the far left side and in two lower groups, to the right and left of the central figures. Our eyes are led back to the philosophers by a man sprawled on the steps to the right and by the scribes' tables on the left. Like a proscenium arch in a theater, a broad arch in the foreground frames the scene. Overlapping arches add to the depth of the painting. This composition combines the stability of one-point perspective with a powerful illusion of space.

In the Caillebotte painting, a lamppost occupies center stage, rather than a philosopher. The perspective in the cobblestone street and in the buildings on the right is complicated by the perspective used for a large background building on the left. This unusual illusion of space, combined with the movement of the pedestrians, creates a feeling of instability.

Compare and contrast essays are often used in art history classes. This form of analysis helps demonstrate differences in historical periods or artistic styles. The same approach, however, may be used in the studio, for either spoken or written critiques. The following is an example, written by two students in a basic design class. The assignment was to complete an 18 × 24 in. design, transforming the music building (Crouse College) into a labyrinth.

Looking at Cally's design (6.3), Trish wrote

Cally's piece uses strong black-and-white contrast, with both negative and positive space clearly developed. On the other hand, my design is brightly colored, representing a kaleidoscope based on the stained glass windows in the building.

We both use the staircase as a major element. Cally's stair leads you in and around the building, creating a way to explore the space. My stair becomes part of the overall pattern.

I thought of the labyrinth as an abstract puzzle, a design you could draw your pencil through to find the ending. I wanted my design to be playful. Cally's design focuses on the psychological, creating an entry into the human mind. Cally's design is mysterious. Her staircases seem to lead nowhere.

We both use lines very deliberately. Where one line ends, another begins. Without lines in a labyrinth, it wouldn't be as puzzling or mysterious. It would just be another design, rather than a puzzle to solve or a fun house to explore.

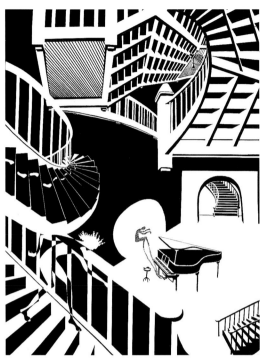

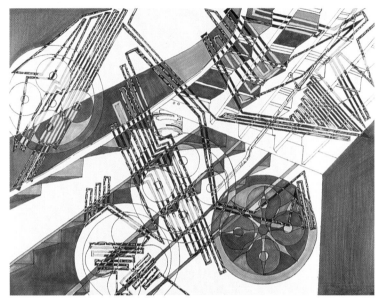

6.4 Tricia Tripp, *Transforming Crouse College into a Labyrinth.* Student work, 24 × 18 in.

6.3 Cally Iden, *Transforming Crouse College into a Labyrinth.* Student work, 18 × 24 in.

Looking at Trish's design (6.4), Cally wrote

The first difference I notice is that my labyrinth uses black and white to form a high-contrast composition, whereas Trish uses color to transform the building into a complex pattern. My vertical format helps suggest the height of the building, which is dominated by two amazing staircases. Trish's horizontal format contains a design that is as abstract as a computer circuit board.

Next, I notice conceptual differences between our solutions. My drawing is representational, depicting a psychological labyrinth, whereas Trish's turns the labyrinth into a puzzle. The space is essentially flat in her design: color is used to create a balanced composition rather than being used to create any illusion of space. On the other hand, because my design is representational, I used the illusion of space to create a convincing interior space.

One similarity between our drawings is in the inclusion of the staircase. Trish used the stairs as a *background* shape that adds dynamism to the composition. I used the stair as a primary motif, a means by which people using the building can explore their own minds.

For me, Trish's design creates a sense of alienation. There is no evidence of human experience here — it is a purely visual world, made up of complex shapes. It produces no strong emotion for me, no sense of mystery. It is purely visual.

On the other hand, there are hints of "the human" in my composition, but it is lost within the maze of repetitive stairs: only traces remain. I want to convey the feeling of being caught in a labyrinth, solving mysteries, and finding one's self.

Both critiques are honest without being abusive and offer a discussion of both concept and composition. While they are very different, each of the students clearly respects the approach taken by the other.

Greatest Strength/ Unrealized Potential

Many projects have one notable strength and one glaring weakness. To create a positive atmosphere, start by pointing out the strength in the work. Begin by looking for

- The level of unity in the design and how was it achieved
- The amount of variety in the design and how much energy it generates

- The visual rhythms used and their emotional effect
- The attention to detail. This could include craftsmanship, conceptual nuance, or compositional economy.
- A conceptual spark. We all love to see an unexpected solution that redefines the imaginative potential of a project.

Using figure 6.5A as an example, you could say,

> The primary strength of this project is unity. The use of black marker throughout gives the design a simple, clean, and consistent look. The repetition of the arches helps tie it all together. Vertical and horizontal lines dominate, creating a type of grid.

Next, consider ways to improve the project. Mentally arm yourself with a magic wand. If you could instantly transform the design, what single aspect would you change? How can the potential of the project be more fully realized? Some basic questions follow.

- Is it big enough? Is it small enough?
- Is it bold enough? Is it subtle enough?
- How rich is the concept? Can it be expanded?
- How can the concept be communicated more clearly? How can the concept be communicated more fully?

The assignment was to create a labyrinth. Figure 6.5A is spatially shallow. To strengthen the composition, you might suggest

> When I think about a labyrinth, I think of it as a mysterious place that I can enter and explore. As it now stands, this design is spatially flat: it gives me no place to go, so you might try increasing the illusion of space. Greater size variation in the arches, with larger ones in the front and smaller ones in the back, could help. Overlapping some of the arches could increase the space and add rhythm to the work. And have you considered

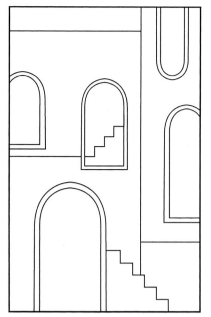

6.5A Design variation.

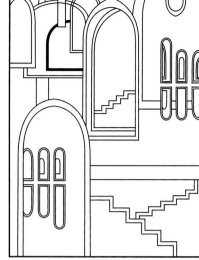

6.5B Design variation.

> using gray marker for the background shapes? This would reduce the contrast and push those shapes back in space.

The resulting design (6.5B) is more spatially complex.

DEVELOPING A LONG-TERM PROJECT

Critical thinking is useful at many points in a project, not just at the end. When working on a project for 10 hours or more, it is useful to assess progress at the beginning or the end of each work period. This may be done in a large-group critique, in small teams, in discussion with your teacher, or on your own. Several effective strategies follow.

Week One Assessment

Determine Essential Concept

As a project begins to evolve from brainstorming, to thumbnails, to rough drafts, the concept may also evolve. Your initial idea may expand or shift during the translation from the mind to the hand to the page. Stopping to reconsider your central concept and refine your image can bring great clarity and purpose to the work. What is the design *really* about? You can speak more forcefully when you know what you want to say.

Explore Polarities

Sometimes, the best way to strengthen an idea is to present the exact opposite. For example, if you want to show the *joy* a political prisoner feels on being released from jail, you may need to show the *despair* she felt before her release. To increase the *dynamism* in a design, add some emphatically *static* elements. The contrast created by polarities can heighten communication.

Move from General to Specific

"Be specific!" demands your writing teacher. Just as vague generalities weaken your writing, so vague generalities can weaken your designs. Details are important. "A bird watched people walk down the street" is far less compelling than "Two vultures hovered over University Avenue, hungrily watching the two hapless students stagger from bar to bar." Specifying the kind of bird, type of people, and exact location makes the image come alive.

Move from Personal to Universal

Autobiography is a particularly rich source for images and ideas. The authenticity of personal experience is extremely powerful. However, if you focus too tightly on your own family, friends, and experience, the viewer must know you personally in order to appreciate your design. Try expanding your field of vision. Use a story about your high school graduation to say something about *all* rites of passage from childhood to adulthood.

Week Two Assessment

A well-developed rough or a full-scale model may be presented at this stage. The purpose of this critique is to help the artist or designer determine ways to increase the visual and conceptual impact of an existing idea. Following are three major strategies.

Develop Alternatives

By helping someone else solve a problem, we can often solve our own problem. Organize a team of four or five classmates. Working individually, design 5 to 10 possible solutions to a visual problem using 3 × 4 in. thumbnail sketches. Then, have one person present his or her ideas verbally and visually. Each team member must then propose an alternative way to solve the problem. This can be done verbally; however, once you get going, it is more effective and stimulating if everyone (including the artist) draws alternative solutions. This process helps the artist see the unrealized potential in his or her idea. And, because of the number of alternatives presented, the artist rarely adopts any single suggestion. Instead, the exercise simply becomes a means of demonstrating ways to clarify, expand, and strengthen intentions already formed. Continue until everyone has made a presentation.

Edit Out Nonessentials

Have you ever found it difficult to determine the real point of a lengthy lecture and thus lost interest? In our zeal to communicate, teachers sometimes provide so many examples and side issues that students get lost. Likewise, if your design is overloaded with peripheral detail or if a secondary visual element is given the starring role, the result will be cluttered and impact will be lost. Look carefully at your design, focusing on visual relationships. Are there any extra shapes or volumes that can be deleted?

Amplify Essentials

Just as it is necessary to delete extraneous information, it is equally important to strengthen the essential information. Review the section on emphasis in Chapter Three and consider ways to increase your compositional power. Try "going too far," wildly exaggerating the size, color, or texture of an important visual element. The only way to get an extraordinary image is to make extraordinary compositional choices.

Developing a Self-Assignment

In the following two pages, Jason Chin describes the development of a month-long self-assignment he completed near the end of his freshman year. The original project proposal is given at the top of the first page. The rest of the text is devoted to Jason's analysis of his actual work process. This type of personal assessment can bring an extended project to a memorable conclusion.

Self-Assignment:
Jason Chin

The Mythological Alphabet

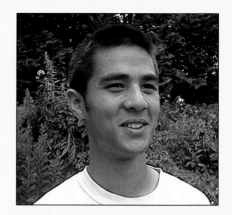

Original Proposal

Description: I plan to make an illustrated alphabet book with 32 pages and a cover. The theme of the book will be myths and heroes. I am interested in illustrating the essence of each hero's story. Specifically, how can I visually communicate the story of a tragic hero versus a triumphant one? Further concerns with the book will be making it work as a whole. That means keeping it balanced and making it flow: I don't want the images to become disjointed.

Primary Concerns

1. How do I communicate the individual nature of the characters?
2. How do I connect each hero to all the others?
3. How will the book affect the reader? I want to get the reader fully involved in the book.
4. How can I best use the unique characteristics of the book format?

Time Management

Week 1:   Research myths and heroes. Identify possible characters for the book.

Week 2:   Bring at least 20 thumbnail sketches to the first team meeting.

Week 3:   Bring finalized design/layout for book. Each page must have a final design in the form of thumbnails.

Week 4:   Complete half of the pages.

Week 5:   Finish remaining pages and present at the critique.

Commentary

The independent project was both a blessing and a curse. Given the freedom to do what I chose was liberating, but the burden of what to do with that freedom was great. Ultimately, it became one of the best learning experiences of my freshman year.

I had decided to pursue illustration as my major, because of my interest in storytelling. This interest in stories led me to choose to make a book for my project. The next step was to find a story to tell. To limit my workload, I looked for a story that had already been told, one that I could reinterpret, as opposed to writing my own story. At this point, I came across two books, one of Greek myths, and an alphabet book illustrated by Norman Rockwell, and my initial concept was born.

Once the idea was initiated, I set to work researching Greek myths. The idea was to find one character for each letter of the alphabet. It proved more difficult than I had first thought. I found about 20 names with no problem, but I soon realized that several letters in our alphabet did not exist in the Greek alphabet. To overcome this hurdle, I took some liberties on the original problem and did not limit myself strictly to characters from myths (for example, I included the White Island for the letter W). Once the subject of each illustration was chosen, I set about the task of doing the images and designing the format of the book.

Doing the illustrations and designing the format of the book all came together at about the same time.

As I was working out the drawings I made several key decisions that heavily influenced the outcome of the project. First, I decided that each picture would have to be black and white if I was going to pull this whole thing off. Second, I knew that they would have to be relatively small. Through my art history class, I gained a strong interest in Japanese woodblock prints and was especially attracted to their strong compositional sensibility. This became the focus of my attention while working out the illustrations. Finally, the decision to make the illustrations small helped determine the way I used text in the book, because it all but eliminated the possibility of overlaying text on image.

I designed each image in my sketchbook, doing thumbnails and comp sketches of all sizes and shapes, until I found the image that I felt best represented the character. For example, Zeus has the biggest and busiest frame in the book because he is the king of the gods, while the image of the White Island is quite serene because it is a burial ground.

When I had each individual image worked out, I redrew them in order in the pages of my sketch book as if they were in the real book. I could now see how each image would work as a double-page spread, as well as how well the book could flow visually. With this mockup of the book in front of me it was very easy to see obvious mistakes and correct them before going to final art.

I did the final illustrations in pen and ink, on illustration board, and when they were finished, it was time to drop in the text. My first concept for the text was to be very minimal; each page would read, "A is for," "B is for," and so on. However, I soon real-ized that making each page rhyme would drastically increase the reader's interest in the book. So I wrote a more extensive text and put the rhyming parts on opposite pages in order to give the reader one more incentive to turn the page.

The final touch for the book was putting the col-ored paper down. The decision to do this came when I went to place the type. The only means I had to get good type was to print it out on the computer, but I had no way to print it on the illustration board. So I had to put it on printer paper and cut and paste it. No matter how carefully I cut the paper and pasted it on, it just didn't look right. I came up with two solu-tions: one, print the words on colored paper and paste it on, or two, cut frames of colored paper to cover over the entire page except for the image and the text. I chose the latter and was pleased to dis-cover that the local art store had a vast selection of handmade and colored papers.

Today I look back on this project as a pivotal experience in my art education, because I had free range to pursue storytelling, something that has since become an essential aspect of my art. In the profes-sional world, bookmaking is rarely an individual process. It is a collaborative process, involving editors, artists, and writers, so for me to be able to pursue it on my own was in fact a blessing. I got to make a book the way that I thought it should be done, and pursue my own personal vision of what a Mythological Alphabet should be. By making this book, I discovered something that I love to do, and want to make a career of doing, and to me the vision that I have gained from this experience is invaluable.

Jason Chin, *A Is for Apollo* (left) and *U Is for Urania* (right). Student work.

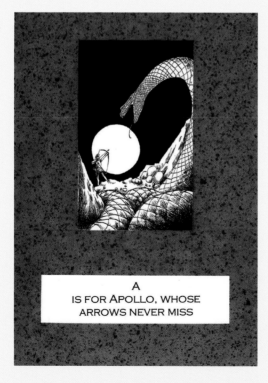

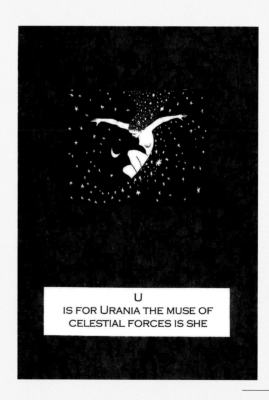

A
IS FOR APOLLO, WHOSE
ARROWS NEVER MISS

U
IS FOR URANIA THE MUSE OF
CELESTIAL FORCES IS SHE

TURN UP THE HEAT: PUSHING YOUR PROJECT'S POTENTIAL

Some compositions are so bold that they seem to explode off the page. Other compositions have all the right ingredients but never really take off. By asking the following questions you can more fully realize the potential of any assignment.

Basic Arithmetic

1. Should anything be *added* to the design? If your composition lacks energy, consider adding another layer of information or increasing the illusion of space. Notice how texture changes the composition in figures 6.6A and 6.6B.

2. Should anything be *subtracted?* If the composition is cluttered, try discarding 25 percent of the visual information. Then, use the remaining shapes more deliberately (6.7A–B). Get as much as possible from every visual element. Economy is a virtue.

3. What happens when any component is *multiplied?* As shown in figures 6.8A and 6.8B, repetition can unify a design, add rhythm, and increase the illusion of space.

4. Can the design be *divided* into two or more separate compositions? When a design is too complicated, it may become impossible to resolve. Packing 20 ideas into a single design can diminish rather than improve communication. In figures 6.9A and 6.9B, a complicated source image has been separated into several different designs, creating a series of stronger images.

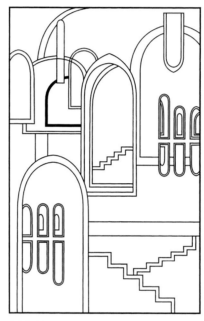

6.6A Linear design.

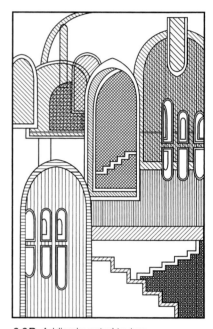

6.6B Adding invented texture.

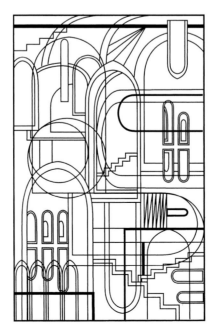

6.7A Visual clutter.

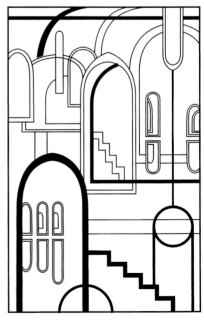

6.7B Visual clarity.

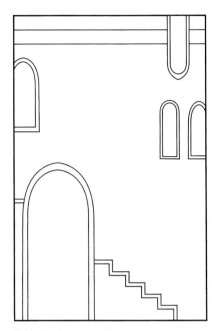

6.8A Basic composition.

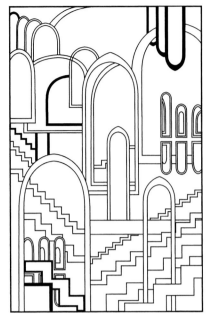

6.8B Elaborated composition.

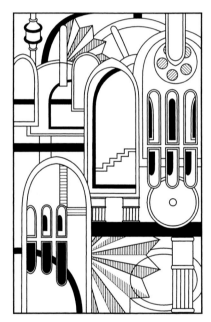

6.9A Completed labyrinth design.

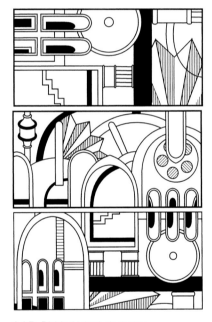

6.9B Divided labyrinth design.

Transformation

Works of art and design present ideas in physical form. Each composition is strongly influenced by the materials used, the relationships created, and the viewing context chosen. Consider the following alternatives:

1. What happens when the material is changed? Even when the shapes stay the same, a silver teapot is very different from a glass, steel, or ceramic teapot. Sculptor Claes Oldenburg has used transformations in material extensively, often changing hard, reflective materials into soft vinyl. This form of transformation is especially effective when the new material brings structural qualities and conceptual connotations that challenge our expectations.

2. What is the relationship of the piece to the viewer? What is the relationship between the artwork and its surroundings? What happens

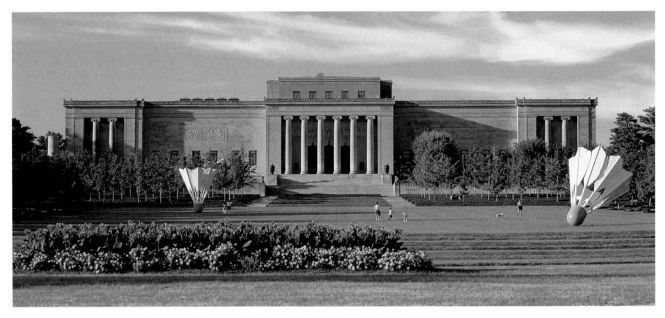

6.10 **Claes Oldenburg and Coosje van Bruggen,** *Shuttlecocks,* **1994.** South facade of the Nelson-Atkins Museum of Art and the Kansas City Sculpture Park. Aluminum, fiberglass-reinforced plastic, urethane paint, approx. 19 ft 2⅜ in. h. × 16 ft diameter (5.9 × 4.9 m).

when a chair is reduced to the size of a salt shaker? Or when a 20-foot-tall badminton shuttlecock (6.10) is placed in front of a museum? How does any image change, both visually and conceptually, when size is dramatically reduced or increased?

3. Can a change in proportion increase impact? Working with the same basic information, a seemingly endless number of solutions can be produced through variations in proportion (6.11).

4. Is a physical object compelling from all points of view? Does the composition of the artwork encourage the viewer to view it from other angles?

5. Will a change in viewing context increase meaning? The context in which a composition is seen can dramatically alter its meaning. For example, a side of beef has a very different meaning when it is hung in a gallery rather than staying in a slaughterhouse. Likewise, pop artists, such as Andy Warhol and Roy Lichtenstein, brought new meaning to soup cans and comic books by using them as subject matter in their paintings.

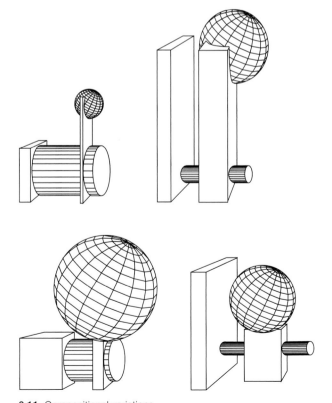

6.11 Compositional variations.

Reorganization

Time-based work, such as visual books, comic books, film, and video, is generally constructed from multiple images. Changing the organization of the parts of the puzzle can completely alter the meaning of the piece. For example, Angela contemplates entering the building in the sequence shown in figure 6.12. Using a different organization of the same three images, Angela now wonders what will happen when she opens the door at the top of the stairs (6.13). By repeating the image of Angela, we can present a dilemma: she is now in a labyrinth — which route should she take (6.14)?

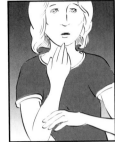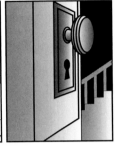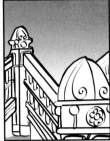

6.12

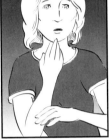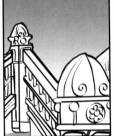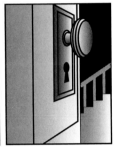

6.13

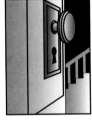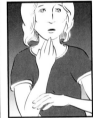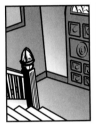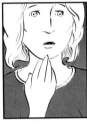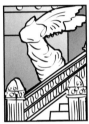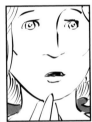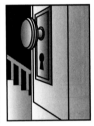

6.14

CONCEPT AND COMPOSITION

Any compositional change affects the conceptual impact of an artwork. Henry M. Sayre provides a striking example in *A World of Art*.[1] A distilled version of his ideas follows.

Robert Rauschenberg's Monogram (6.15) is constructed from a stuffed goat, an automobile tire, and a painted plywood base. Seeking to combine painting and sculpture, Rauschenberg created three different versions of this piece. In the first version (6.16), he placed the goat on a shelf that extended from the center of a 6-foot-tall painting. This created a connection between the painting and the goat but diminished its sculptural

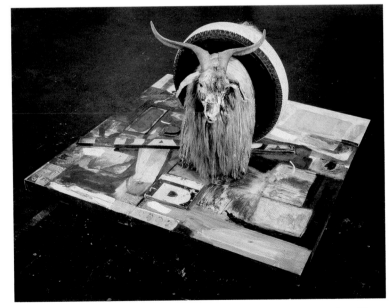

6.15 Robert Rauschenberg, *Monogram*, 1955–59. Freestanding combine, 42 × 63¼ × 64½ in. (106.7 × 160.7 × 163.8 cm).

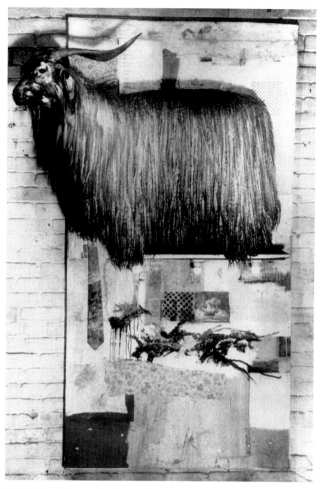

6.16 Robert Rauschenberg, *Monogram,* 1st State, c. 1955. Combine painting: oil, paper, fabric, wood on canvas, plus stuffed Angora goat and three electric light fixtures, approximately 75 × 46 × 12 in. (190.5 × 114.3 × 30.5 cm). No longer in existence.

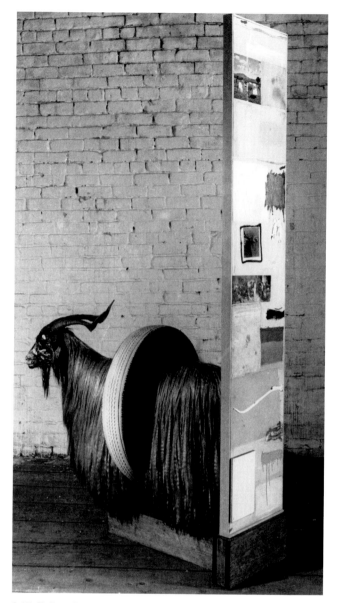

6.17 Robert Rauschenberg, *Monogram, 2nd State,* c. 1956. Combine: oil, paper, fabric, wood, plus rubber tire and stuffed Angora goat on wood, 115 × 32 × 44 in. (292 × 81.3 × 111.8 cm).

impact. In the second version, Rauschenberg placed a tire around the goat's midsection and moved the animal in front of the painting (6.17). This enhanced its three dimensionality but created too much of a separation between the animal and the painting. He finally hit on the right combination when he placed the painting on the floor and positioned the goat in the center. The painting retained its integrity as a two-dimensional surface, the goat retained its physical presence, and a highly unified combination of the two elements was achieved. The addition of the tire enhanced the goat's sculptural form and gave the artwork a humorous twist.

ACCEPTING RESPONSIBILITY

We have explored only a few of the many approaches to critical thinking in this chapter. Every assignment presents new possibilities for critiques, and each teacher invents his or her own way to address the needs of a specific class.

Regardless of the specifics, however, two facts are inescapable. First, you will learn only what you want to learn. If you reject out-of-hand the alternatives suggested, or if you avoid responsibility for your conceptual and compositional choices, you will gain nothing from the critique, no matter what strategy is used. Second, there are no free rides. Everyone in the class is responsible for the success of the session. It is often difficult to sustain your attention or honestly assess your work or the work of others. When you get a superficial response to a project, insisting on further clarification is not easy. Every critique demands sincere and sustained attention from each participant. And, when the responses are supportive and substantial, remarkable improvements in works of art and design can be made.

SUMMARY

- Using critical thinking, an artist or a designer can identify strengths and weaknesses in a project and determine the improvements that need to be made.

- Understanding the criteria on which a project will be judged helps focus critical thinking.

- Many artworks can be analyzed in terms of three basic aspects: form, subject, and content.

- Objective critiques focus on observable facts. Subjective critiques focus on feelings, intentions, and implications.

- Four common critique methods are description, cause and effect, compare and contrast, and greatest strength/unrealized potential.

- Many critique methods may be used when you are working on a long-term project. In every case, there are three primary objectives: explore alternatives, delete nonessentials, and strengthen essentials.

- It is only by pushing a project to the limit that its potential will be fulfilled. Basic arithmetic, transformation, and reorganization can be used to increase compositional power.

- Responsibility for the success of a critique rests with each participant. Come with your mind open rather than your fists closed.

Keywords

cause-and-effect critique	**critique**	**objective criticism**
compare/contrast critique	**descriptive critique**	**subject**
content	**form**	**subjective criticism**

Profile:
Bob Dacey, Illustrator

Tell Me a Story: Illustrating *Miriam's Cup*

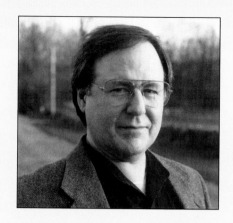

Bob Dacey is an internationally renowned artist whose drawings and paintings have been published as limited- and multiple-edition prints, as well as in a wide range of books and periodicals, including *McCall's,* Ballantine Books, Book-of-the-Month Club, *Playboy,* and Scholastic Publications. His commercial clients include The White House, ABC, CBS, NBC, PBS, Mobil Oil, Sony, the U.S. Post Office, Air Japan, and many others. Dacey has recently received a Silver Medal from the Society of Illustrators in New York for 1 of the 16 paintings he produced for Scholastic Publications illustrating a 32-page book, *Miriam's Cup,* which is themed on the Exodus of the Israelites from Egypt. The book tells the story of Miriam, the older sister of the prophet Moses. Dacey collected an extensive library of books on Egypt and spent almost a year on research. From costumes to musical instruments, Dacey insisted on getting all the details just right.

MS: Give me a bit of background on *Miriam's Cup.* What was the significance of this project, and what aspects of the story did you want to emphasize in the illustrations?

BD: *Miriam's Cup* gave me a chance to expand on my single-image work. I've always approached each illustration as a moment in time, as if it had a "before" and an "after." This book gave me a chance to push that much further. I started every painting by focusing on the emotion in the moment being depicted. I always ask myself: "What is the essence of this moment?" The composition follows. Shapes and values serve the emotional content, while movement is used to unify the composition.

MS: You have said that 75 percent of your work on this project was devoted to research. Can you describe your research and tell me why it was so important?

BD: For *Miriam's Cup,* I had to understand the culture of Egypt and the Jewish culture of the time. Fortunately, I've always had an extensive interest in both. My personal library contains more books on Egypt than the local library system. Research helped open new ideas, leading in some unexpected directions. Those bullrushes are one example. I looked up the word in three dictionaries and

two encyclopedias. One of these sources mentioned that the bullrushes of ancient Egypt are papyrus, those beautiful fan-shaped reeds that can be fashioned into a kind of paper. Without that knowledge, the image I arrived at would have been impossible.

MS: I understand that you have a seven-step process by which you refine and expand your ideas. Can you describe this process as it applies to the cover image for *Miriam's Cup?*

BD: I first consider the intent of each painting: what must this piece communicate? In this painting, I focused on Miriam's exuberance as she celebrates her escape from Egypt. Second, the composition must support my intent. The circular movement of the tambourine and flowers dominates this painting. The movement from the raised hand holding the tambourine, to Miriam's hair, to her face, and on to her cupped hand provides a secondary pattern. And that cupped hand repeats the curve of the flowers. Third, the shapes depend on both the intent and the composition. If I am painting a very stoic character, I use a lot of verticals. Diagonals are used when the character or event is very dynamic. Value is fourth on my checklist. I assign value according to the mood of the painting.

Lighter values are used for celebratory images, like this one; darker values dominate when the mood is somber. A mix of light and dark value is best. I base my compositions on the Golden Section [a classic use of proportion], and I often use a 60/40 proportion between light and dark values. Texture, step five, often results from the placement of shape and value — but it really deserves a place of its own, due to its importance as a constructive or destructive factor. When everything else works but the image still suffers, textural discord is usually the culprit! Color comes next. I really have to have the other questions resolved first. Color without composition, value, or intent just doesn't cut it. This painting is dominated by rich pastel colors, which help convey the exuberant emotion.

All of this contributes to the overall image, the final step. If all of the preceding factors serve my intent, the image can emerge naturally and effectively.

MS: In addition to the extensive research you did for *Miriam's Cup*, it seems that you have a very wide range of interests in general.

BD: Well, everything feeds into my work — and I've always been interested in everything! My under-graduate majors included theater and anthropology before I settled on ad design as the field in which I finally got my degree. Now, my readings range from archaeology to philosophy to psychology to paleontology, and more. I'm also developing my interest in writing and plan to pursue a master's in writing in order to increase my understanding of narrative.

MS: One of the questions my students often have is this: how do I get from where I am as a student to where you are as a professional?

BD: Focus on your goals and research the field. Talk to professionals you admire. Set high standards for yourself and be realistic about the level of professionalism and quality required.

MS: Any final bits of advice?

BD: Don't limit yourself. We all have great potential that serves the higher purpose of society. Pursue your goals with the knowledge that you can succeed. And remain flexible and open-minded, so that you can redirect your efforts as opportunities present themselves. Read everything! Draw everything!

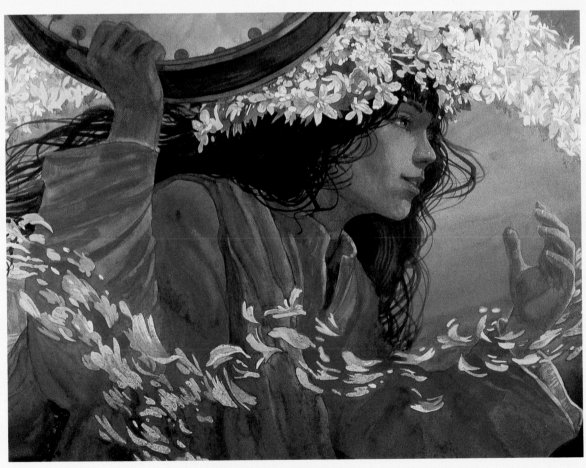

Bob Dacey, Cover of *Miriam's Cup*, by Fran Manushkin, 1988. Scholastic Press.

chapter seven

Constructing Meaning

Cultivating creativity, seeking and solving visual problems, and developing critical judgment all require hours of hard work. Why are these skills so highly valued by artists and designers and so strongly emphasized by college teachers?

The answer is simple. At a professional level, art and graphic design projects are done in order to communicate ideas and express emotions. Turning elusive concepts into effective communication is not easy. Clay, ink, metal, fabric, and other physical materials must somehow stimulate an audience to see, understand, and respond to a visual message. In this chapter, we will explore the essentials of visual communication and identify some of the strategies artists and designers use to construct meaning.

BUILDING BRIDGES

Shared Language

A shared language is the basis on which all communication is built. For example, if you are fluent in English and I am effective as a writer, the ideas I want to communicate in this chapter should make sense to you. On the other hand, if English is your second language, some of the vocabulary may be unfamiliar. In that case, you may have to strengthen the bridge between us by looking up words in a dictionary.

Figure 7.1 demonstrates the importance of shared language. For a reader of Chinese, the flowing brushstrokes form characters that communicate specific ideas. For those of us who know only English, the calligraphy is visually

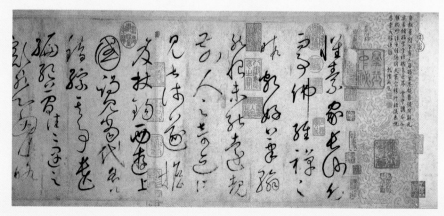

7.1 Huai-su, Detail of Autobiography, Tang dynasty, 7th – 10th centuries. Ink on paper.

enticing but conveys no specific message. We cannot understand the characters.

Iconography

Many visual images rely on cultural references to build meaning. **Iconography** (literally, "describing images") is the study of symbolic visual systems. Iconography plays a major role in all forms of visual communication.

Deborah Haylor-McDowell's *The Serpent Didn't Lie* (7.2) is loaded with cultural references. An anatomical diagram copied from Leonardo da Vinci's notebooks appears in the upper left corner, while the nude couple near the center is based on *The Kiss,* a sculpture by August Rodin. In the upper right corner, Haylor-McDowell has reproduced Einstein's computations for the theory of relativity, and, in the foreground, a baby takes his first steps. A snakeskin border surrounds the image. What does it all mean? Haylor-McDowell says:

> Ignorance may spare us the pain of difficult decisions. However, the price we pay is high. Can humankind's greatest gifts, emotion and intellect, mature in a world that is free of suffering? In the absence of adversity, will our humanness be lost?
>
> *The Serpent Didn't Lie* is based on a biblical text dealing with good and evil in the Garden of Eden. What is the price we pay for knowledge? The images I used in the composition deal with the complexities and responsibilities of our pursuit of knowledge.

Through a sophisticated use of iconography, the artist created a puzzle that is filled with ideas for us to unravel and explore. For those who understand the cultural references, this print presents a survey of types of knowledge in a compelling visual form. For those who do not understand the references, the print is simply a beautifully crafted collection of architectural and figurative fragments.

Graphic designers are especially aware of the importance of iconography. On a purely visual level, Milton Glaser's 1996 poster for the School of Visual Arts (7.3) is intriguing and evocative in itself. The hovering hat, shadowy figure, and curious text raise all sorts of questions. When we compare the poster with surrealist René Magritte's *Golconde* (7.4),

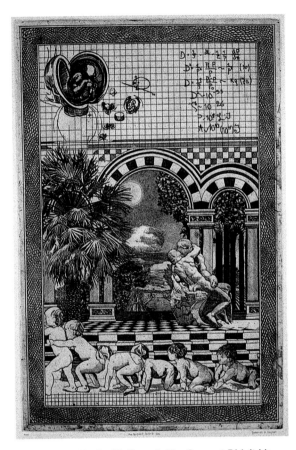

7.2 Deborah Haylor-McDowell, *The Serpent Didn't Lie*, **1997.** Etching, 15 × 23 in. (38.1 × 58.42 cm).

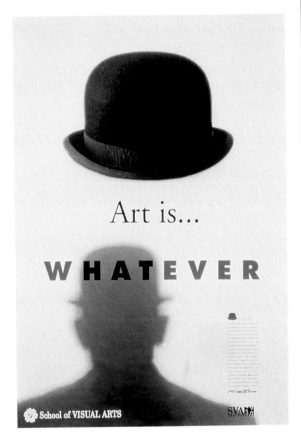

7.3 Milton Glaser, *Art is . . .*, **1996.** Poster.

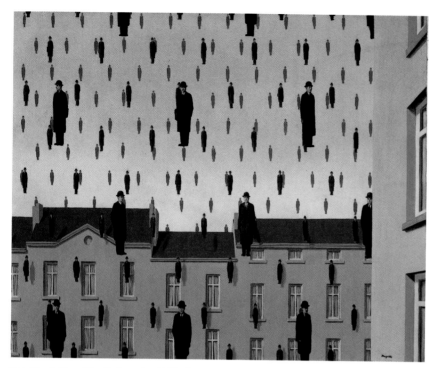

7.4 René Magritte, *Golconde*, 1953. Oil on canvas, 31¾ × 38⅝ in. (80.65 × 98.11 cm).

6.1A, page 148) presents yet another approach. It captures a quiet moment in time and space. There is minimal action, just the movement of groups of people within an architectural setting. This painting is compelling to a mature viewer yet lacks the action and excitement sought by a younger audience. To engage children, many museums use storytelling or other bridge-building activities when presenting paintings of this kind to school groups.

Immediacy

When the bridge between the image and the audience is explicit, communication can occur almost instantaneously. When the iconography is elusive or complex, communication takes longer and is more varied. Each approach can be effective in the right time and place. When driving a car, our lives depend on the immediate message we receive when a traffic light turns red. When visiting a museum, we often seek greater complexity and emotional resonance.

Graphic designers generally seek a combination of immediacy, clarity, and resonance. For them, an effective poster or billboard can be understood at a glance. Figure 7.7 is an excellent example. The bold, white hangman immediately attracts attention, and the book title itself is simple and direct. The position of the figure's head adds an additional layer of meaning to this critique of capital punishment.

By comparison, *Solstice Greetings* (7.8) by Georgiana Nehl and David Browne requires extended viewer involvement. The collage includes a map, international postage stamps showing birds in flight, various pieces of patterned paper, a color chart, and butterflies, both dimensional and drawn. A tiny watch, two insects, three globes, two cubes, a child's jack, a circle, and a spiral orbit around the egg at the center of the composition. The message here is neither explicit nor immediate. As with Haylor-McDowell's work, the viewer must piece together a complex set of

the ideas expand much further. In this and other paintings by Magritte, the man in the bowler hat represents anyone who is courageously navigating through the chaos of contemporary life. When we make the connection between Glaser and Magritte, the School of Visual Arts poster becomes poignant as well as provocative. Like the man in the bowler hat, each art student must find a path through the complexities of contemporary life in order to develop a meaningful approach to art and design.

Audience

Just as films are targeted and rated for specific audiences, so many forms of visual communication are designed for a particular type of viewer. Illustrator Kenny Kiernan specializes in cartoons for preteens (7.5). The subject matter is light-hearted; the iconography is simple; the drawing style is exuberant. A very different approach was used for figure 7.6. Realizing that disfigurement is of greater concern than death for many teenagers, the designers have focused on the scarred face of a traffic accident survivor. Seeking to discourage drunk driving, they have targeted the teenager's greatest fear in order to drive home their message. Caillebotte's *Place de L'Europe on a Rainy Day* (see figure

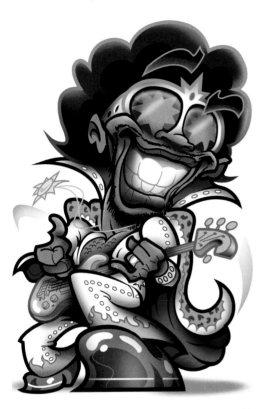

7.5 Kenny Kiernan, *Rock Stars.* Vector art created in illustrator.

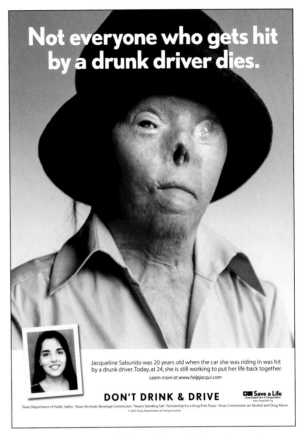

7.6 Sherry Matthews & Associates, photography, poster.

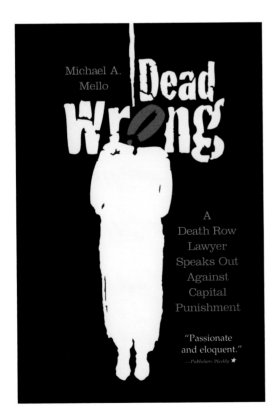

7.7 Mark Maccaulay, book jacket.

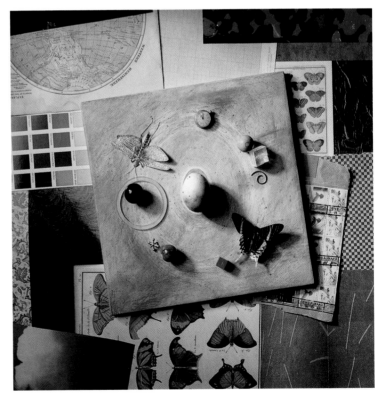

7.8 Georgiana Nehl and David Browne, *Solstice Greetings,* 1998. Color photograph of constructed assemblage, 5 × 5 in. (12.7 × 12.7 cm).

clues, then reach his or her own conclusions about journeys, the passage of time, and the transience of life. The message is conveyed using layers of iconography.

Stereotypes

A **stereotype** is a fixed generalization based on a preconception. On a benign level, when we use a stereotype, we ignore individual characteristics and emphasize group characteristics. For example, the broken wine glass in figure 7.9 is widely used on shipping crates to communicate fragility. Glass is actually a very versatile material that can be cast as bricks, spun into fiberoptic cables, and polished to create lenses. However, we are most familiar with fragile wine glasses and bottles. Relying on this *general* perception, the shipping label designer used a stereotype to communicate fragility.

Racial stereotyping, which is never benign, tends to exaggerate negative generalizations. Even when a positive assumption is made (such as "Asian-Americans are brainy overachievers"), the overall effect is demeaning. Rather than learning about an individual person, we make judgments based on our preconceptions.

Stereotypes are often used to create the bridge on which communication depends. Because they are based on preconceptions, stereotypes require little thought. The viewer responds automatically. In some situations, an automatic response is ideal. Four airport pictograms are shown in figure 7.10. Can you determine the meaning of each? If the designer is successful, even an exhausted traveler from New Zealand will be able to determine at a glance where to find a baggage locker, an elevator, or a toilet. Especially notice the use of the male and female stereotypes for the toilet pictograms. Despite the wide range of clothing worn by female travelers, the designer used a dress to create a stereotypical female.

Clichés

A **cliché** is an overused expression or a predictable treatment of an idea. Phrases such as "Let's level the playing field" and "Think outside the box" are powerful the first time we hear them. However, when we hear them repeatedly, they lose their impact and become clichés. Visual clichés are equally predictable. Skulls representing death and seagulls representing tranquility may be effective at first but tend to become worn out when used repeatedly.

Surprise

A shift in a stereotype or cliché upsets our expectations and challenges our assumptions. The resulting shock can surprise or delight an audience, making the message more memorable. Originally based on the cowboy stereotype, the Marlboro Man has been reinterpreted in figure 7.11. This ad, which begins like an ordinary cigarette commercial, quickly shifts from the heroic cowboy to a man with a hacking cough. At this point, the narrator suggests that "cowboys are a dying breed" because of the cancer caused by smoking. By breaking the stereotype, the designers attract the viewers' attention, challenge the conventional cigarette ad, and strengthen their nonsmoking message.

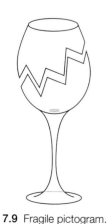

7.9 Fragile pictogram.

Baggage lockers
Elevator
Toilets, men
Toilets, women

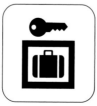 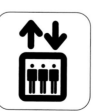 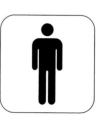 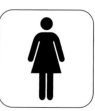

7.10 Roger Cook and Don Shanosky, images from a poster introducing the signage symbol system develped for the U.S. Department of Transportation, 1974.

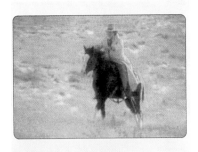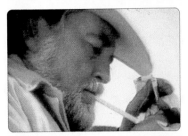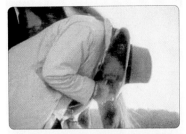
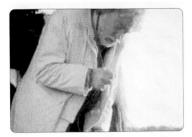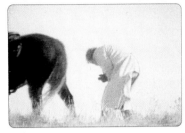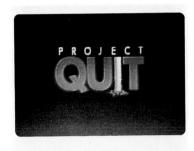

NARRATOR: No wonder cowboys are a dying breed. If

you need help quitting, tune into project QUIT, and take   control of your life.

7.11 Agency: Ruhr/Paragon, Minneapolis. Production: Lotter, Minneapolis. Details: TV, 30 seconds, color. First appearance: February 1988. Account Supervisor: Anne Bologna. Creative Director/Art Director: Doug Lew. Associate Creative Director/Copywriter: Bill Johnson. Agency Producer: Arleen Kulis. Production Company Director: Jim Lotter.

Key Questions

- Are there any symbolic meanings embedded in your composition? Are these meanings consistent with the message you want to convey?
- Have you used a stereotype or a cliché? Does this strengthen or weaken your message?
- What audience do you want to reach? Is the form and content of your design appropriate for that audience?

PURPOSE AND INTENT

Any number of approaches to visual communication can be effective. We simply choose the style, iconography, and composition best suited to our purpose.

Let's consider three very different approaches to human anatomy. *Arterial Fibrillation* (7.12) was developed for the cover of a medical journal. With equal training in art and science, medical illustrator Kim Martens combined anatomical accuracy with

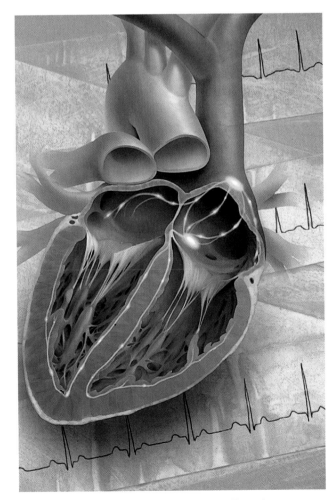

7.12 Kim Martens, *Arterial Fibrillation*, 2000. Photoshop.

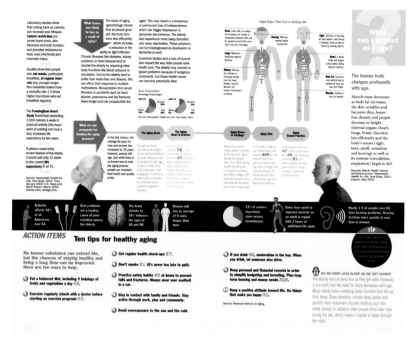

7.13 A page from *Understanding Healthcare* by Richard Soul Wurman. Design Firm: Pentagram Design.

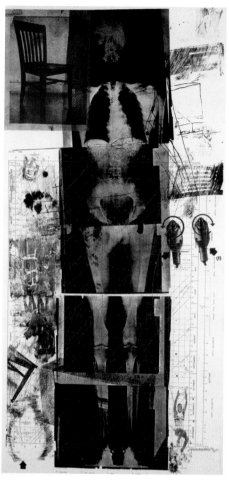

7.14 Robert Rauschenberg, *Booster*, 1967. Lithograph and serigraph, printed in color, composition 71⅜ × 35⅛ in. (181.7 × 89.1 cm).

artistic imagination to create this design. Intent on sales, the art director for the magazine requested an image that was both physically correct and visually enticing. Designed as an anatomical roadmap, *Understanding Healthcare* (7.13) had to present complex information in a clear and concise way. To make the text accessible to a general audience, the designers used a loose grid, dominated by vertical columns at the top and a strong horizontal band at the bottom. Arrows and other visual cues increase visual impact and help the reader navigate from page to page. *Booster* (7.14) is dominated by series of X-rays of the artist's body. In this unconventional self-portrait, Robert Rauchenberg combined a collection of personal X-rays with various examples of technological notation, including an astronomer's chart, diagrams analyzing the movement of drills and arrows, graphs, and an empty chair. The title adds further meaning, suggesting a connection to booster shots, booster rockets, and booster seats, which increase the height of an ordinary chair so that young children can sit at a table comfortably. Reduced to an X-ray image and surrounded by fragments of technological information, the artist becomes a cog in the machinery of mass culture.

CONTEXT

The compositional context in which any image appears profoundly influences meaning. In figure 7.15, the juxtaposition of a quiet line of hungry people with a propagandistic billboard makes us rethink the phrase "There's no way like the American way."

The social context in which an image appears is equally important. In figure 7.16, Winston Churchill, the prime minister most responsible for British victory during World War II, extends two fingers to create the "V for victory" gesture he used throughout the war. If we are familiar with Churchill and know about the desperate struggle of the British people during the war, we immediately make the correct connection. In figure 7.17, the same gesture communicates a very different idea. As part

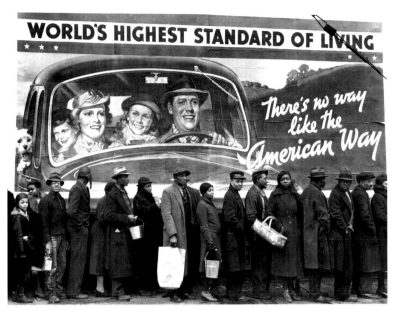

7.15 Margaret Bourke-White, *At the Time of the Louisville Flood*, 1937. Getalin silver print.

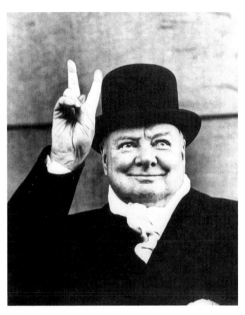

7.16 Alfred Eisenstadt, *Winston Churchill, Liverpool*, 1957. Getalin silver print.

of the signage for the Minnesota Children's Museum, the extended fingers now communicate the number two. Realizing that many young visitors to the museum may not be able to read, the designers used both a number and a gesture to communicate location. Finally, in Sean O'Meallie's *Out-Boxed Finger Puppets Perform the Numbers 1 Through 5 in No Particular Order* (7.18), the same gesture becomes a playful piece of sculpture as well as an indication of the number two. We now see the extended fingers in the context of a series of whimsical forms. In each of these three cases, the meaning of the two fingers depends on context.

CONNECTIONS

Analogies, similes, and metaphors are figures of speech that link one thing to another. An **analogy** creates a general connection between unrelated objects or ideas, while a **simile** creates the connection using the words *as* or *like*, as in "She has a heart as big as Texas." A **metaphor** is more explicit: speaking

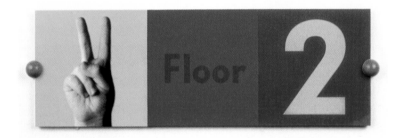

7.17 Minnesota Children's Museum, Pentagram design, NY, NY. Tracy Cameron and Michael Beirut, Designers.

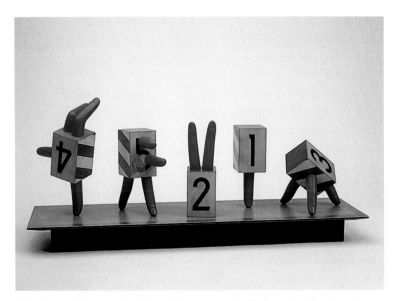

7.18 Sean O'Meallie, *Out-Boxed Finger Puppets Perform the Numbers 1 Through 5 in No Particular Order*, 1999. Polychromed wood.

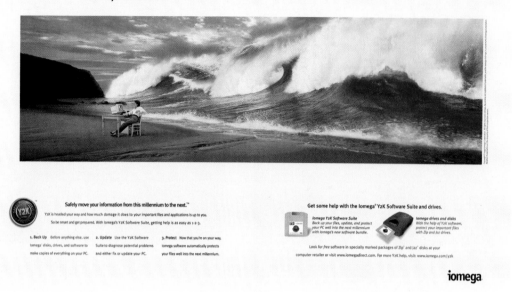

Y2K's coming.
Don't just sit there.

Safely move your information from this millennium to the next.™

Get some help with the Iomega® Y2K Software Suite and drives.

7.19 Iomega Corporation, "Y2K's coming. Don't just sit there."

metaphorically, we would say "Her heart *is* Texas." As you can see, the shift in meaning can be substantial when a metaphor is used.

In all cases, the original word is given the qualities of the linked word. For example, when Robert Burns wrote the simile "My love is like a red red rose," he gave the abstract concept of "love" the attributes of a glorious, colorful, fragrant, thorny, and transient rose.

Metaphorical thinking can be used to connect an image and an idea. Take the phrase, "I have butterflies in my stomach." This phrase is widely used to describe nervousness. Substitute other insects for butterflies, such as bees or wasps. How does this change the meaning? To push it even further, start with the phrase "My mind was full of clouds." What happens when "clouds" is replaced by mice on treadmills, rats in mazes, shadowy staircases, beating drums, screaming children — or even butterflies? When my mind is full of butterflies, I am happy, but butterflies in my stomach indicate fear. In addition to expanding your ideas, metaphors can help provide specific images for elusive emotions.

Metaphorical thinking and symbolism have always been used by artists and designers to strengthen communication. Exaggerated metaphors

are often used in advertising design. The massive wave that threatens the computer user in figure 7.19 is a metaphor for the destructive power of the Y2K computer bug that once seemed likely to create massive computer failures on January 1, 2000.

Picasso's *Guernica* (7.20) is also loaded with metaphors. In *A World of Art,* Henry Sayre offers the following description:

> The horse, at the center left, speared and dying in anguish, represents the fate of the dreamer's creativity. The entire scene is surveyed by a bull, which represents at once Spain itself, the simultaneous heroism and tragedy of the bullfight, and the Minotaur, the bull-man who for the Surrealists stood for the irrational forces of the human psyche. The significance of the electric light bulb at the top center of the painting, and the oil lamp, held by the woman reaching out the window, has been much debated, but they represent, at least, old and new ways of seeing.[1]

Rather than showing exploding bombs or collapsing buildings, Picasso filled his painting with abstracted animals, screaming humans, and various light sources. In so doing, he focused on the meaning and emotion of the event, rather than the appearance.

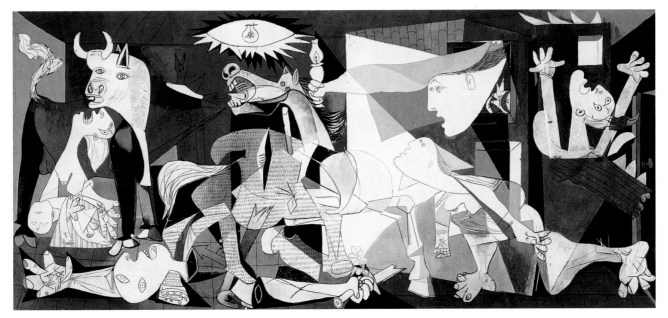

7.20 Pablo Picasso, *Guernica*, 1937. Oil on canvas, 11 ft 5½ in. × 25 ft 5¼ in. (3.5 × 7.8 m).

DRAMA

Regardless of the medium used or the message conveyed, all communication can be strengthened through dramatic delivery. Even Martin Luther King's "I Have a Dream" speech loses much of its power when delivered in a flat, monotonous tone of voice. Just as a playwright sets the stage for the story he or she seeks to tell, so an artist can set the stage for visual communication.

All of the elements and principles of design described in this book can be used to increase compositional drama. To increase conceptual drama, we can:

- *Personify the idea.* When we identify with a character in a play, we become more empathetic and involved in the story. Likewise, when we identify with a character in a painting or a poster, we are much more likely to remember the idea or emotion being conveyed. For example, the shattered face of the woman in figure 7.6 makes an immediate connection. We look her in the eye and feel her sorrow.

- *Focus on essentials.* It has often been said that theater is "life with the boring parts left out." To be meaningful to an audience, the characters and events in a play must have a strong relationship to direct experience. However, a

playwright rarely shows a character flossing his or her teeth. Too much detail clutters the composition, confuses the audience, and muddles the message. Including the right amount of information in just the right way can add drama to even the simplest idea.

- *Seek significance.* Any event, character, or time period can be used to create an effective play. Likewise, any object, event, or idea can be used in our quest for visual communication. A unique approach to a familiar subject or an insightful interpretation of personal and political events can add significance and increase impact.

AESTHETICS AND ANESTHETICS

In *Design in the Visual Arts,* Roy Behrens notes the difference between the words anesthetic and aesthetic (or esthetic). An *anesthetic* is used to induce insensitivity or unconsciousness. In an anesthetic state, we are numbed and disoriented. We may not be able to determine the size or location of objects or the sequence of events. On the other hand, *aesthetics* is the study of human responses to beauty. In an aesthetic experience, our feelings are enhanced and our understanding is expanded.

SUMMARY

- A shared language is the basis on which all communication is built.

- Iconography (the study of symbolic visual systems) provides us with a way to analyze the meaning of images and objects.

- Immediacy is often highly valued in graphic design. By comparison, many paintings require extended viewer involvement and longer viewing time.

- A stereotype is a fixed generalization based on a preconception. Stereotypes can easily create a bridge between the image and the audience.

- A cliché is an overused expression or predictable treatment of an idea. Even the most interesting image will lose its power if overused.

- A shift in a stereotype or cliché challenges our assumptions and can increase impact.

- Artists and designers choose the style, iconography, and composition best suited to their purpose. A mismatch between the type of image and its purpose creates confusion.

- The visual and social context in which an image appears will profoundly affect its meaning.

- Analogies, similes, and metaphors are figures of speech that link one thing to another. Metaphors are especially widely used in visual communication.

- Dramatic delivery of a message can enhance meaning.

Keywords

aesthetics	cliché	metaphor	simile
analogy	iconography	metaphorical thinking	stereotype

Profile:
Ken Botnick,
Graphic Designer

Landscape of the Page:
Conceiving and Composing Books

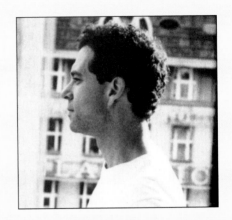

Ken Botnick has been making books for over 25 years. From 1979 to 1988, he and Steve Miller ran Red Ozier Press in New York City, producing over 50 limited-edition titles of contemporary poetry and fiction. From 1988 to 1993, Botnick was production and design manager of the art books at Yale University Press, with three of his book designs winning medals from the American Association of University Presses. He has also designed books for Princeton Architectural Press, Harry N. Abrams, Princeton School of Architecture, and the University of Alabama Press. Professor Botnick was Executive Director of the Penland School of Crafts in North Carolina for four years, has taught extensively.

MS: Some artists pursue a very linear career path. Other artists, who are equally or even more interesting, come to art and design through a more circuitous route. Please describe your path.

KB: My origin is in landscape design. I trained in this field and worked on a whole range of projects, from community gardens to artist-designed parks. I was fascinated by the relationship of the parts to the whole and love physical materials, such as plants, soil, and stone.

MS: How, and why, did you shift to book design?

KB: For me, landscape design became more and more about proposals and paperwork and less and less about the actual designs and the doing.

Since I had been involved with books since my undergraduate years at the University of Wisconsin, joining my friend Steve Miller at Red Ozier Press seemed like the right move. I began to think of the words as the soil and the paper, the type and ink as the plants that grow from it. In quick order, Steve and I were partners and publishers running a very active press in New York City, working with the most amazing writers and artists. We took our jobs very seriously and made careful choices as to whom we would publish. When you are setting type or printing 150 copies of a book, you see the text differently. You get to read in a way that you would never do ordinarily.

MS: "Landscape" is an unusual word to associate with book design. What is the meaning of this title?

KB: Like a landscape, a well-designed book is full of nuances and complex relationships. The page size, the weight and texture of the paper, the size and style of the type, and the layout of information on the page all contribute to the reading experience. For me, the page is a construct that you move through, literally and figuratively. Like the window on a train, the frame remains constant, while the landscape continually changes.

MS: Please talk us through your design process for *The Bicycle Rider*, a novel in 100 sections by Guy Davenport. which was produced as a limited edition at Red Ozier Press.

KB: In designing typography for a text, I first ask "What are my emotional responses to the content of the story?" Throughout *The Bicycle Rider*, Davenport refers to Dutch painter Piet Mondrian and the primary colors he used in his mature work. Like the bicycle rider, Mondrian was a master of proportion, balance, and daring. Reds and blues pop up throughout the text. So, instead of using illustration, I used various typographic embellishments and created a title page inspired by Mondrian's paintings. The book was bound in a subtle brown handmade paper, with simple typography and color in order to play off the idea of the plain wrappers of not-so-plain books. This brown text paper is filled with red and blue fibers that echo the color of the ink.

Next, I assess my current visual surroundings, including other design books, painting, sculpture, and so on. When working on *The Bicycle Rider,* I was looking at a pamphlet of poems by Kenneth Patchen that had been printed during World War II, with big red numbers in the margins of each poem. This book seems to do everything "wrong" typographically, yet because of its great energy, it is one of my favorite books. To emulate Patchen, I selected a clear and classic-looking typeface, then adapted his bold red numbers for the section numbers. Combined with the classic typeface, these numbers added a syncopated beat to the pages.

MS: It seems that a lot of planning is required and that everything in your design is intentional.

KB: The planning has to be there to support the spontaneity. I especially enjoy working with students who are planning their projects. Making the dummies of a book, exploring alternatives, and giving shape to the ideas are the most enjoyable part of the process. Most people are surprised at how much planning happens before production, yet that is where the magic really happens.

The beauty of craft is that there are all these repetitive functions one must go through in the studio: cutting paper, setting type, cleaning the presses, printing. These hours are vital to the creative process because they place you into direct contact with the materials, physically and sensually. That is the fertile time when many of the best ideas are formed. Creativity is not segmented out into "big-idea time" versus "boring production time"—it is all part of a fluid process. Ideas are elusive. The more you try to trap them, the more they escape.

MS: From whom did you learn the most?

KB: Even though I never took a book course, I worked closely with book artist Walter Hamady during my last year at the University of Wisconsin. I went to his house to plant trees, then stayed on to cook a meal and talk. It was really about building a life. I learned that a personal investment in life and a willingness to pour all of your energy into an activity is crucial.

My collaboration with Steve Miller was also pivotal. When it is working well, a partnership can be a wonderful mirror, reflecting what you do especially well and what your partner does especially well. It also taught me a great deal about transforming a vision into reality.

MS: What advice do you have for my students?

KB: First, keep your eyes open: don't limit yourself through rigid self-definitions. If I had limited myself to architecture, I would never have become a graphic designer. Mindless careerism can be the path to ruin. Be willing to take side trips: they may change your life. Second, read, read, and read some more! The opportunities for learning are endless and through books, you can access the wisdom of the masters in all fields.

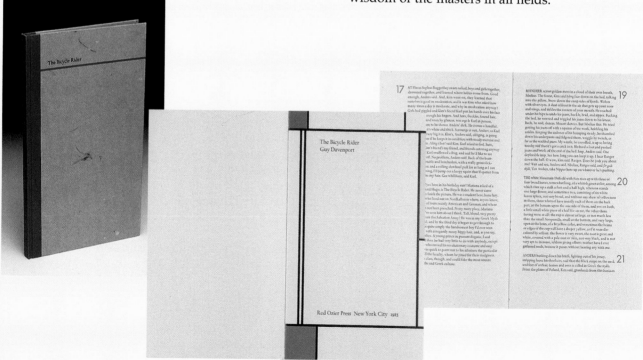

Ken Botnick, *The Bicycle Rider,* **1985.** Guy Davenport, author. Letterpress printing, 5½ × 9½ in. (14 × 24 cm).

Part Two
Multimedia Resources

Take advantage of the multimedia resources for Part Two in order to expand your understanding of how to generate ideas and manage your projects.

Resources

www.mhhe.com/launching2

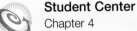

Student Center
Chapter 4
Chapter 5
Chapter 6
Chapter 7

Core Concepts in Art CD-ROM

Contents

Learning objectives for each chapter
Study outlines for each chapter
Quizzes with instant feedback
Flashcards for studying art vocabulary
Internet exercises for developing critical viewing skills
Book suggestions for your personal library and research projects

An Internet guide to help you maximize connectivity and avoid problems
A study skills primer to help you make the most of your courses

Studio projects for Part Two are described and illustrated for teachers on the Web and on a CD-ROM.

Resources

www.mhhe.com/launching2

Instructor Center
IM Part Two

Instructor's Resource CD-ROM

Part Two

Projects

Limited/Unlimited: Pushing beyond apparent limitations
Microcosmo/Macrocosmos: Connecting simple and complex forms
Poster Design: Integrating words and images; the importance of research
Collaborative Compositions: Digitally creating a collaborative collage
Expanding Escher: An exercise in collaborative creativity
Word/Image Synergy: Exploring juxtaposition
Build a Concept Generator: A basic cube turns into a conceptual toy
Capstone Assignment: Expanding creativity through in-depth exploration

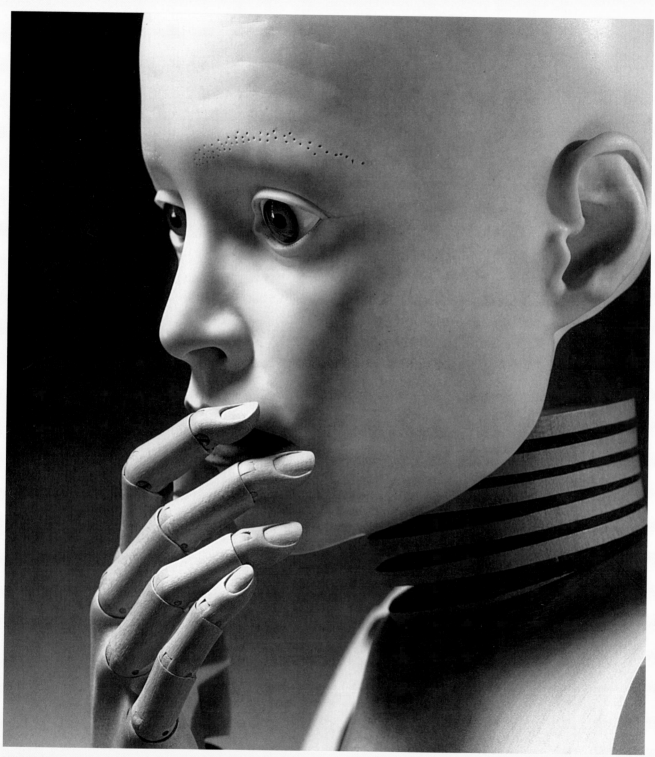

Katherine Wetzel (photograph), Elizabeth King (sculpture), *Pupil* from *Attention's Loop* (detail), **1987–90.** Installation at the Bunting Institute, Radcliffe College, 1997. Porcelain, glass eyes, carved wood, brass. One-half life size.

Three-Dimensional Design

Part Three

chapter eight
Elements of Three-Dimensional Design

chapter nine
Principles of Three-Dimensional Design

chapter ten
Materials and Methods

chapter eleven
Physical and Cerebral

As we begin our investigation of three-dimensional design, it is useful to consider both the similarities and differences between flat compositions and physical constructions. In both cases, basic design elements are organized to communicate ideas, express emotions, and create functional objects. The basic principles of design are used to create images and objects that offer an effective balance between unity and variety. And, in both two- and three-dimensional design, concept development and critical thinking are essential aspects of the creative process.

However, in two-dimensional design, we use our technical, perceptual, and conceptual skills to create flat visual patterns and convincing illusions. It is the viewer's *mental* response that gives the artwork meaning. By contrast, our experience in the three-dimensional world is physical and direct. As we traverse an architectural space, we alter our perception with each step we take. When we circle a sculpture, we encounter new information on each side. The materials used in the construction of a three-dimensional object determine its structural strength as well as its aesthetic appeal.

This physical connection gives three-dimensional design an inherent power. When we shift from an illusory world to a tangible world, a substantial shift in communication occurs. Confronted by the physical presence of a three-dimensional object, the viewer responds viscerally as well as visually.

This section is devoted to the elements, organization, and implications of three-dimensional design. The basic building blocks of three-dimensional design are discussed in Chapter Eight. In Chapter Nine, the principles of three-dimensional design are described. The unique characteristics of various materials are considered in Chapter Ten. Chapter Eleven is devoted to the ways in which artists have transformed their ideas into physical objects and to a discussion of differences between traditional and contemporary sculpture.

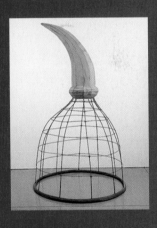

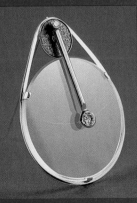

Elements of Three-Dimensional Design

When we paint a realistic seascape, we use our technical, perceptual, and conceptual skills to create a convincing illusion. In the painting, lines, shapes, colors, and textures are combined to represent a three-dimensional world. Based on these clues, each viewer mentally reconstructs the setting. Those who have walked on a beach can create a detailed mental image of sea, sand, and sky. Those who have never seen the sea may create a more fanciful world. For both viewers, however, it is the imagination that constructs the cosmos.

Our experience in the three-dimensional world is more direct. When we walk on an actual beach, we feel the wind, hear the waves, and smell the air. We can examine the marvelous creatures in a tidal pool and create castles in the sand. Tangible evidence of three-dimensional design surrounds and supports us. We use a cooler to transport a picnic lunch, recline in a folding chair, and construct a tent for shelter.

Line, plane, volume, mass, space, texture, light, color, and time are the basic building blocks from which three-dimensional designs are made. Just as oxygen and hydrogen are powerful both individually and when combined as H_2O, so these visual **elements** are powerful both individually and in combination. In this chapter, we will consider the unique characteristics of three-dimensional design and explore the primary uses of each of the basic elements.

DEFINING FORM

As noted in Chapter Six, **form** can be defined as the physical manifestation of an idea. **Content** refers to the idea itself, including the subject matter plus its emotional, intellectual, spiritual, and symbolic implications.

Form has an additional definition in three-dimensional design. In this context, *form* can refer to three-dimensionality itself. For example, a circle, a square, and a triangle are two-dimensional shapes, while a sphere, a cube, and a pyramid are three-dimensional forms.

To build a deeper understanding of three-dimensional design, we can expand this basic definition even further. Consider the following types of form.

- An empty three-dimensional form is generally defined as a **volume,** while a solid form is generally defined as a **mass.**

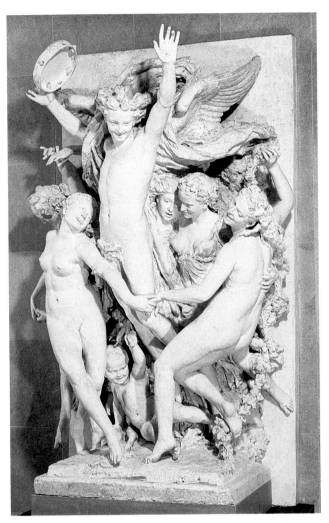

8.1 Jean-Baptiste Carpeaux, *The Dance* (after restoration), **1868–69.** Marble, 7 ft 6½ in. (2.3 m).

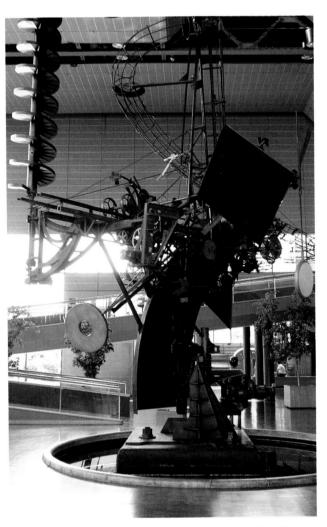

8.2 Jean Tinguely, *Chaos 1*, **1973–74.** Metal construction with moving balls on tracks, electric motors, 30 × 28 × 15 ft (915 × 854 × 458 cm).

- An effective three-dimensional composition balances **positive forms** (areas of substance) with **negative space.**

- **Organic forms** (forms that visually suggest nature or natural forces) create a very different effect than **geometric forms,** which are typically based on cubes, spheres, and other simple volumes.

- The degree of actual or implied movement in a form can expand our vocabulary even further. **Static forms** appear stable and unmoving. Designed to last forever, the Great Pyramids at Giza exemplify stability and repose. **Dynamic forms** imply movement. *The Dance* (8.1), by Jean-Baptiste Carpeaux, is a highly dynamic form. Dominated by rotating figures and curving lines, this sculpture swirls with energy.

Kinetic forms actually move. In Jean Tinguely's *Chaos 1* (8.2), a bowling ball on a track trips a series of movements in a massive metal mechanism.

As noted in Chapter Seven, determining the best form for our expressive content is one of the major challenges we face.

FORM AND FUNCTION

An artist seeks to express concepts and evoke emotions. For example, a sculptor explores an idea, chooses materials, and develops a composition based on his or her aesthetic intention. Public art projects, such as Eero Saarinen's *Jefferson National*

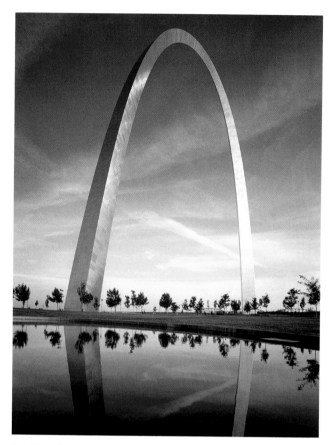

8.3 Eero Saarinen, *Jefferson National Expansion Memorial (Gateway Arch)*, St. Louis, 1966. 1868–69.

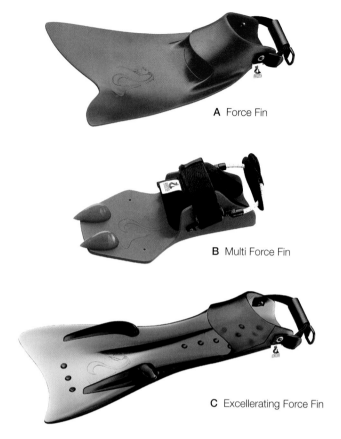

A Force Fin

B Multi Force Fin

C Excellerating Force Fin

8.4 A–C Bob Evans, *Force Fin Variations*, 1990–present. Molded polyurethane, size variable.

Expansion Memorial (8.3) and ritual objects, such as the Mugamtl mask (see page 132), often commemorate historical events or express social values.

A designer uses the same mastery of concept, composition, and materials to create an object that is functional as well as beautiful. For example, when designing aquatic gear, designer Bob Evans carefully analyzes the needs of swimmers and then creates equipment to best meet those needs. The basic *Force Fin* (8.4A) provides the maneuverability needed for snorkeling. The *Multi Force Fin* was designed as a training device to strengthen a swimmer's legs (8.4B), while the *Excellerating Force Fin* (8.4C) provides the extended power needed by scuba divers. For any designer, the form must fulfill a specific **function,** or purpose.

While the industrial designer has a different purpose than the sculptor, both use the same basic elements and principles of design. Both must organize line, plane, volume, mass, space, texture, and color into coherent form. The structural integrity of a sculpture is just as important as the structural

integrity of a wheelchair, and a teapot that is both beautiful and functional is ideal. By thoroughly understanding the elements of three-dimensional design, both the artist and the designer can create compelling compositions.

ORTHOGRAPHIC PROJECTION

Height, width, and depth are the three dimensions in three-dimensional design. In computer-aided design, these three dimensions are defined using the x, y, and z axes used in geometry (8.5). Using the cube as a basic building block, we can create many variations on these basic dimensions (8.6A–C).

There are many methods of depicting three-dimensional form on a two-dimensional surface. **Orthographic projection** is one of the most useful. Unlike perspective drawing, which relies on vanishing points to create the illusion of space,

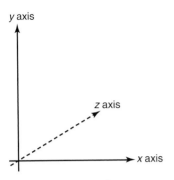

8.5 The three dimensions are defined through height, width, and depth.

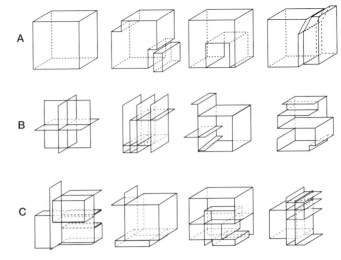

8.6 Variations on a Cube

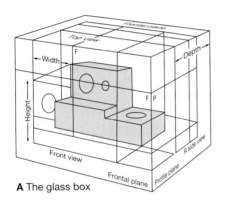

A The glass box

8.7A–C Orthographic projection can be used to define structural details.

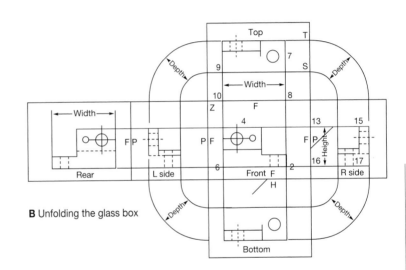

B Unfolding the glass box

orthographic projection uses parallel lines to define structural details.

An orthographic projection represents six views of a three-dimensional form. Imagine that your project is enclosed in a glass box (8.7A). As you look through the top, bottom, front, and back, then at the right and left sides, you can see six distinctive views. In effect, an orthographic drawing is created when you unfold and flatten this imaginary box (8.7B). Using orthographic projection, we can examine and record various surfaces of a three-dimensional object (8.7C).

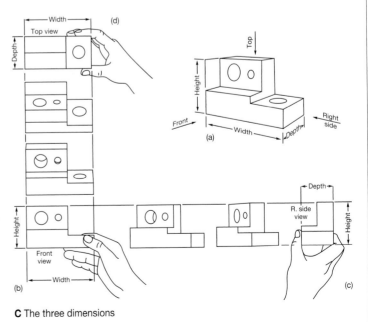

C The three dimensions

DEGREES OF DIMENSIONALITY

Our experience of a three-dimensional artwork is very different from our experience of a flat print or painting. We tend to construct an imaginary world when looking at a two-dimensional image, while our response to a three-dimensional object is generally more physical and direct. As a result, the degree of our physical involvement strongly affects our understanding of both the form and the content of the artwork. Four variations on dimensionality are described in this section.

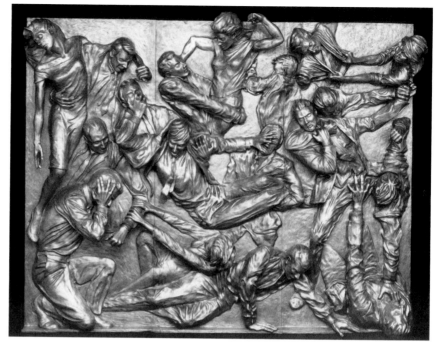

8.8 **Robert Longo,** *Corporate Wars* **(detail), 1982.** Cast aluminum, lacquer on wood relief, 7 × 9 × 3 ft (2.1 × 2.7 × .9 m).

Relief

When working in **relief,** the artist uses a flat backing (such as a wall or ceiling) as a base for three-dimensional forms. For example, Robert Longo's *Corporate Wars* (8.8) is like a sculptural painting. Using the boundaries created by the supporting wall and the four outer edges, it presents a group of white-collar warriors engaged in hand-to-hand combat. The figures are trapped, bound both to the backing and by their struggle for money.

Three-Quarter Works

A **three-quarter work,** such as Jean-Baptiste Carpeaux's *The Dance* (see figure 8.1) is more three-dimensional. We can walk around this piece, examining the front and two sides. As a result, the dancing figures create a vortex of implied motion.

Freestanding Works

Freestanding works are designed to be seen from all sides. When we circle August Rodin's *The Kiss* (8.9A–B), we capture every nuance in the movement of the two figures. Details (such as the man's stroking hand and the woman's raised heel) add energy to the inanimate marble.

Environmental Works

An **environmental work** (or **environment**) presents a space that can be physically entered. **Installations** (which are usually presented indoors) and **earthworks** (which are usually presented outdoors) are two major types of environments. Such works often require active audience participation and may present a series of images, ideas, and experiences that unfold over time.

Installations

Typically, an installation is an ensemble of images and objects that are presented within a three-dimensional environment. Surrounded by information, we become emotionally and physically involved in the artwork. For example, on entering Antoni Muntadas' *The Board Room* (8.10), the viewer confronts 13 chairs facing a long table. In a reference to the Last Supper described in the Bible, these chairs are accompanied by photographs of religious leaders, from the Ayatollah Khomeini to Billy Graham. Inserted in the mouth of each man, a small video monitor plays a film clip showing him in action. In this installation, religion becomes an extension of both business and politics.

The Board Room presents a series of clearly defined figures in a dramatic setting. In Christian

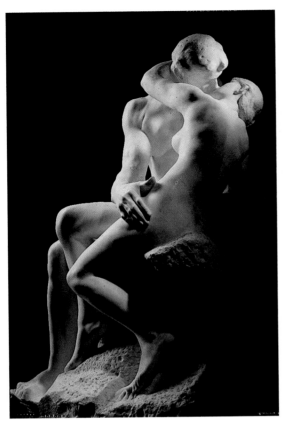

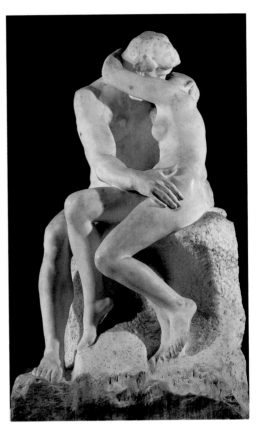

8.9A Auguste Rodin, *The Kiss,* 1886–98. Marble, over life size. Dramatic lighting accentuates form and can heighten emotion.

8.9B Auguste Rodin, *The Kiss,* 1886–98. Marble, over life size. A slight change in the viewer's position substantially changes the orientation of the two figures.

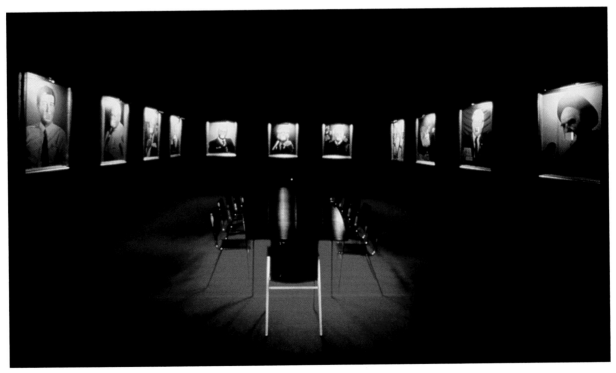

8.10 Antoni Muntadas, *The Board Room,* 1987. Installation at North Hall Gallery at Massachusetts College of Art, Boston. Thirteen chairs placed around a boardroom table. Behind each chair is a photo of a religious leader, in whose mouth a small video monitor shows the leader speaking. Subjects include Ayatolla Khomeini, Billy Graham, Sun Myung Moon, and Pope John Paul II.

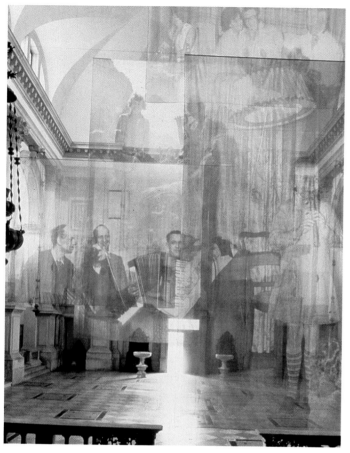

Marclay's *Amplification* (8.11), a series of translucent figures shift, merge, and divide, depending on the viewer's position within the room. Surrounded by images and enticed, enchanted, or assaulted by audio information, the viewer can become part of the artwork.

Earthworks

An earthwork is a large-scale outdoor installation. Often extending over great distances in time and space, earthworks may require substantial physical engagement by the artist, audience, and inhabitants of the site. Robert Smithson's *Spiral Jetty* (8.12) is an excellent example. This 1,500-foot-long coil of rock and earth extends from the shore into the water of the Great Salt Lake in Utah. For Smithson, the spiral created "a dot in the vast infinity of universes, an imperceptible point in a cosmic immensity, a speck in an impenetrable nowhere."[1] Remote and mysterious, this artwork evokes a cosmic connection that extends far beyond the walls of a museum or gallery.

8.11 Christian Marclay, *Amplification,* 1995. Mixed media with six found prints and six photographic enlargements on cotton scrim. Dimensions variable. Installation at the Chiesa di San Stae, Venice, Italy.

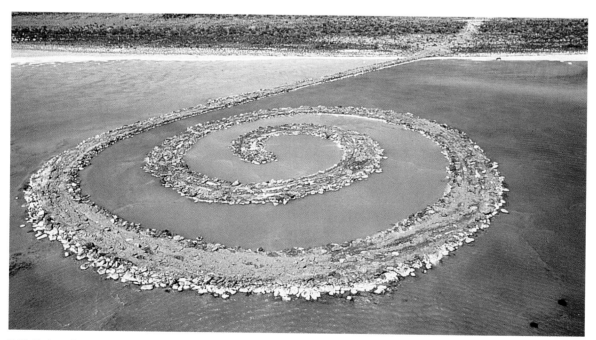

8.12 Robert Smithson, *Spiral Jetty,* Great Salt Lake, Utah, 1970. Rock, salt crystals, earth, algae, coil, 1,500 ft (457 m).

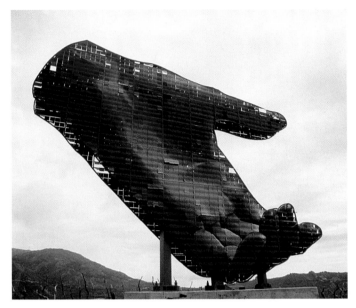

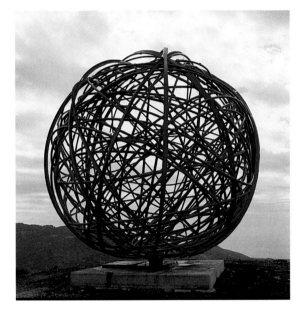

8.13 Todd Slaughter, *Mano y Balo* (details), 1997. Aluminum and steel, hand 27 × 40 × 4 ft (8.2 × 12.2 × 1.2 m), ball 20 ft (6 m) diameter. Overlooking the Straits of Gibraltar.

Site-Specific Artwork

A **site-specific** artwork is specifically designed and installed in a particular place. Commissioned by the port city of Algeciras in Spain, *Mano y Balo* (8.13) rests on a bluff overlooking the Straits of Gibraltar. The 40-foot-long hand may be catching or throwing the 20-foot-tall ball positioned roughly 50 feet away. Sculptor Todd Slaughter notes that "the implied action of the hand metaphorically alludes to the history of exchange of religion, art, power and conflict between the European and African continents." To heighten the metaphor, the hand has been designed to disappear when the wind blows. One thousand movable panels were covered with a photographic image of a hand, on the front and back. A strong wind shifts the panels from their vertical position to a horizontal position, causing the image to dissolve visually into the surrounding sky. In site-specific works such as *Mano y Balo*, the idea and the environment are inextricably intertwined. If moved to another location, this sculpture would lose much of its meaning.

LINE

In three-dimensional design, **line** can be created through

- *A series of adjacent points*. The cars that make up Ant Farm's *Cadillac Ranch* (8.14) are distinct objects in themselves as well as the points that create a line of cars. Commissioned by a rancher in Texas, this sculpture has been described as a requiem for the gas-guzzling American automobile.[2]

- *A connection between points*. *Free Ride Home*, by Kenneth Snelson (8.15) was constructed using two types of line. The aluminum tubes provide

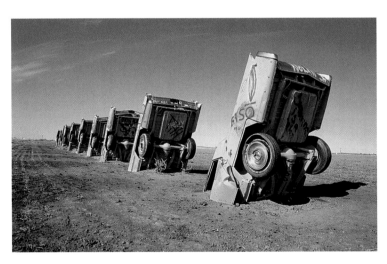

8.14 Ant Farm (Chip Lord, Hudson Marquez, Doug Michels), *Cadillac Ranch,* 1974. Ten Cadillacs. Amarillo, TX.

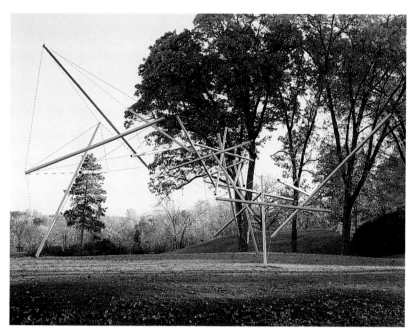

8.15 Kenneth Snelson, *Free Ride Home,* 1974. Aluminum and stainless steel, 30 × 30 × 60 ft (9.1 × 9.1 × 18.2 m). Storm King Art Center, Mountainville, NY.

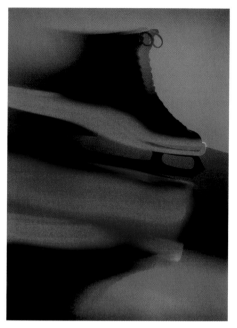

8.16 Moira North and Rudi Stern, *Neon Skates,* 1986. Battery-operated neon skates for performance by The Ice Theater of New York, Moira North, director.

a linear skeleton which becomes elevated when the connecting lines are attached. The resulting sculpture is compositionally dominated by diagonal lines that seem to defy gravity.

• *A point in motion.* When a skater wears the *Neon Skates* by Moira North and Rudi Stern, he or she can literally create lines from a moving point of light (8.16).

Line Quality

Each line has its own distinctive quality. This quality is largely determined by the line's orientation, direction, and degree of continuity, as well as the material used.

Orientation refers to the horizontal, vertical, or diagonal position of the line. Based on our experience in the natural world, we tend to associate horizontals with stability and diagonal lines with movement. Vertical lines tend to accentuate height and can make an object or interior appear more formidable and imposing.

All three types of line are used in Mark di Suvero's *Ik Ook Eindhoven* (8.17) and Peter Pierobon's *Ladderback Chair* (8.18). The di Suvero sculpture is

dominated by two horizontal I beams suspended from a vertical support. The diagonal lines that are connected to this primary structure emphasize the weight of the artwork and add visual movement. On the other hand, it is the tall vertical back that transforms Pierobon's chair into a whimsical sculpture. Its exaggerated height pulls our eyes upward and provides a support for the nine jagged lines that create the rungs of the ladder.

Curved lines can carve out more complex patterns in space and may encompass an object to create a harmonious whole. In José de Riviera's *Brussels Construction* (8.19), a single line of steel slices through space. As the sculpture slowly rotates on its motorized base, the movement suggested by the line is accentuated by its physical rotation.

Direction refers to the implied movement of a line. A line of consistent width tends to suggest equal movement in both directions. Varying line width can create a more specific sense of direction. For example, in *Jefferson National Expansion Memorial* (see figure 8.3, page 182), the massive lines at the bottom drive downward into the earth, while the tapered arch at the top lifts our eyes skyward.

Continuity, or linear flow, can increase movement and accentuate form. In *Brussels Construction,*

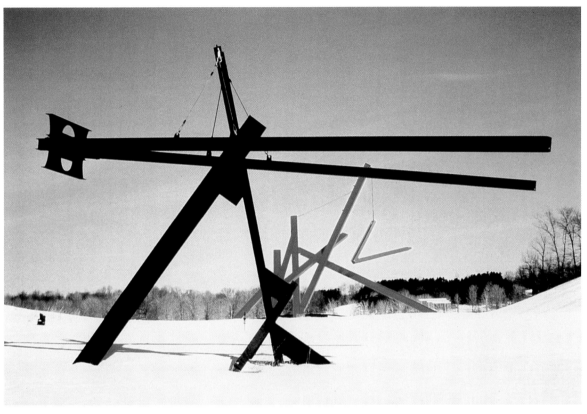

8.17 Mark di Suvero, *Ik Ook Eindhoven,* **1971–72.** Painted steel, 24 × 24 × 33 ft (7.3 × 7.3 × 10 m).
In the background: *Are Years What?* **(For Marianne Moore), 1967.** Painted steel, 40 × 40 × 30 ft (12.2 × 12.2 × 9.1 m).

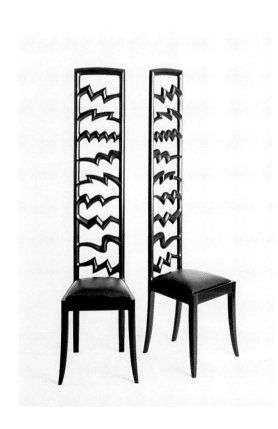

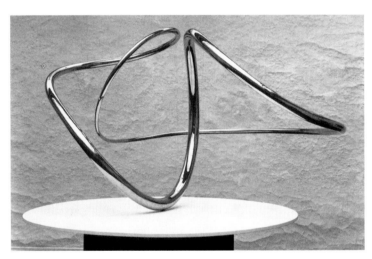

8.19 José de Riviera, *Brussels Construction,* **1958.** Stainless steel, 46½ × 79 in. (118.1 × 200.6 cm).

8.18 Peter Pierobon, *Ladderback Chair.*
Firm & Manufacturer: Snyderman Gallery.

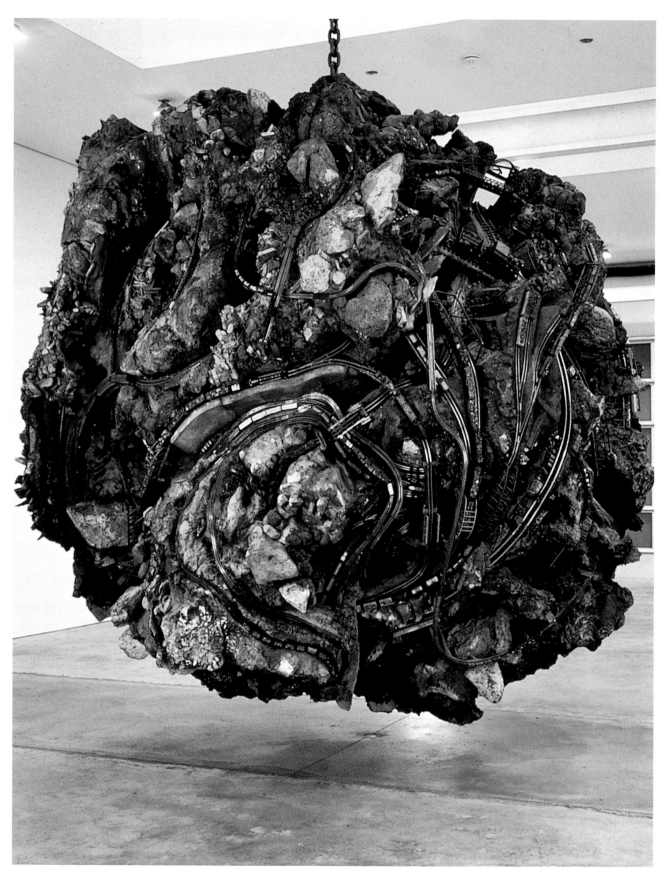

8.20 **Chris Burden,** *Medusa's Head,* **1989–92.** Cement, wood, train tracks, 16 ft. diameter, 5 tons.

the smooth steel line is as elegant and as energetic as a calligrapher's mark. The diagonal sections firmly position us in space, while the horizontal section accelerates our eye movement across the midsection of the piece. Continuity plays a very different role in Chris Burden's *Medusa's Head* (8.20). Here, a mad tangle of toy train tracks flows around and through the mass of rock, plywood, and cement. Representing the snakes that crowned the head of a mythical monster, these writhing lines accentuate the spherical mass and give us a fresh interpretation of an ancient Greek myth.

Actual Lines

Through their physical presence, **actual lines** can connect, define, or divide a design. *Laocoön and His Two Sons* (8.21) depicts a scene from the Trojan War. When the Greeks offer a large, hollow wooden horse to the Trojans, Laocoön warns against accepting the gift. The Greek goddess Athena then sends two serpents to attack and kill the seer, thus gaining entry into Troy for the soldiers hidden in the horse. The writhing serpent compositionally connects the terrified men while adding emotional intensity to this tale of Athena's wrath. In figure 8.22, dancers from the Nikolais Dance Theatre push against the elastic lines that define their space. The interaction between the lines and the dancers provides choreographic tension as well as visual energy. The line dividing Gordon Matta-Clark's *Splitting: Exterior* (8.23) changes an abandoned house into an evocative sculpture. Combining his background in architecture with a propensity for anarchy, Matta-Clark often sought to "undo" a building and thus challenge the social conditions that led to its construction.[3]

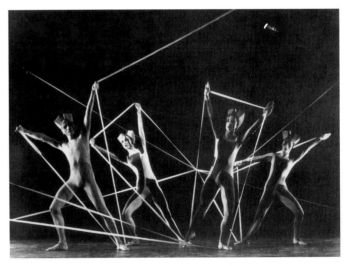

8.22 **The Nikolais Dance Theatre Performing** *Sanctum.* With Amy Broussard, Phyllis Lambat, and Murray Louis.

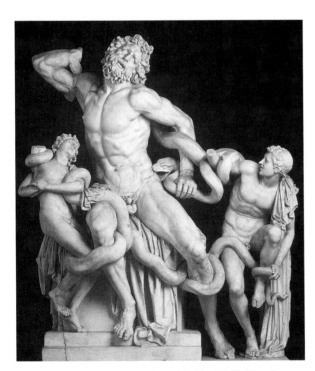

8.21 **Laocoön and His Two Sons.** Marble, 7 ft (2.13 cm).

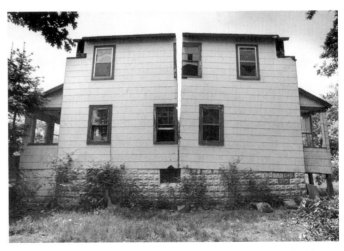

8.23 **Gordon Matta–Clark,** *Splitting: Exterior,* **1974.** Black-and-white photograph.

Implied Lines

Implied lines are created through mental rather than physical connections. *The Rape of the Sabine Women,* by Giovanni da Bologna (8.24), relies on a series of implied lines for its impact. Starting at the bottom and exploding upward, the repeated diagonals in the sculpture create a visual vortex as powerful as a tornado. At the bottom is the husband of the captured woman. In the center, a standing Roman soldier is intent on stealing a wife for himself. The agitated movement culminates at the top with the extended arm of the embattled woman.

A **sight line** activates Nancy Holt's *Sun Tunnels* (8.25). At first glance, the four 22-ton concrete tunnels seem static. Upon entering each tunnel, the viewer discovers a series of holes that duplicate the size and position of the stars in four major constellations. The light pouring in through these holes shifts as the sun rises and travels across the sky. During the winter and summer solstices, the sculpture is further transformed as light from the rising and setting sun is framed by an alignment in the circular tunnels. Like a telescope, the massive cylinders are more important for the visions they create than as objects in themselves.

Line Networks

Both artists and designers use linear networks in many different ways. In figure 8.26, interlocking metal lines form the woven mesh used on a fencer's mask. Due to its linear construction, it is light

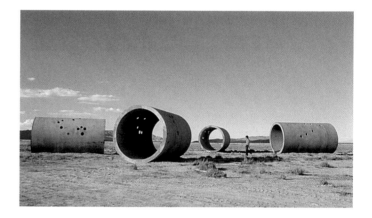

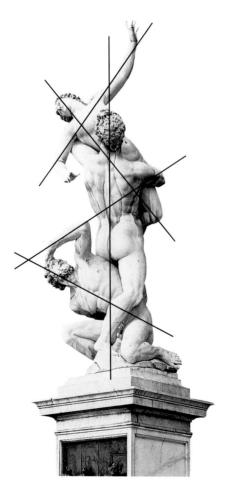

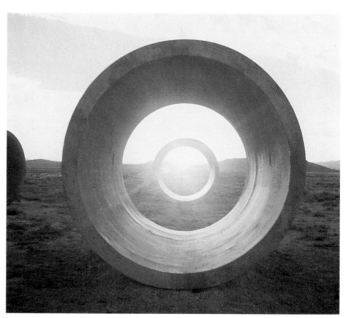

8.24 Giovanni da Bologna, *The Rape of the Sabine Women,* **completed 1583.** Marble, 13 ft 6 in. (4.1 m).

8.25 Nancy Holt, *Sun Tunnels,* **1973–76.** Great Basin Desert, UT. Four tunnels, each 18 ft long × 9 ft 4 in. diameter (5.5 × 2.8 m), each axis 86 ft long (26.2 m). Aligned with sunrises and sunsets on the solstices.

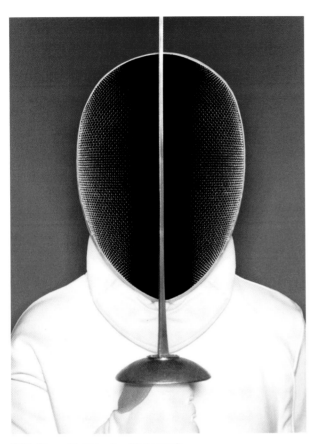

8.26 **Steve McAkkuster.** Photograph.

in weight and protects the athlete's face without blocking vision. As shown in Claire Zeigler's *Red Forest* (8.27), most fiber works are created through the organization of multiple lines of thread, yarn, or other materials. Single lines can bring a simple eloquence to a design, while multiple lines can be used to create strong, complex, and versatile forms.

Key Questions

- Vertical, horizontal, diagonal, and curving lines all have unique strengths. How can each type of line be used in your design most effectively?

- What can line continuity or discontinuity contribute to your design?

- What happens to your design when you increase or decrease the number of lines?

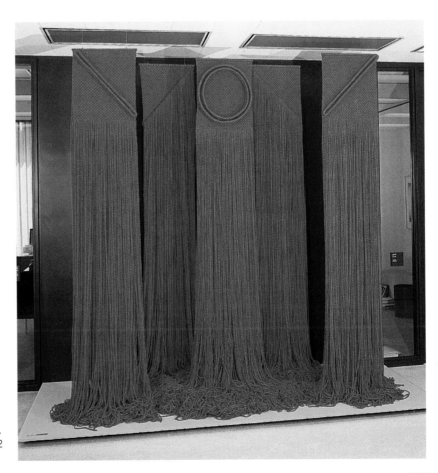

8.27 **Claire Zeisler,** *Red Forest*, **1968.** Dyed jute, 8 ft 2 in. h. × 7 ft 4 in. w. × 2 ft d. (249 × 224 × 61 cm).

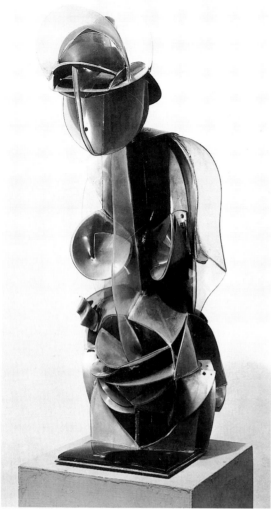

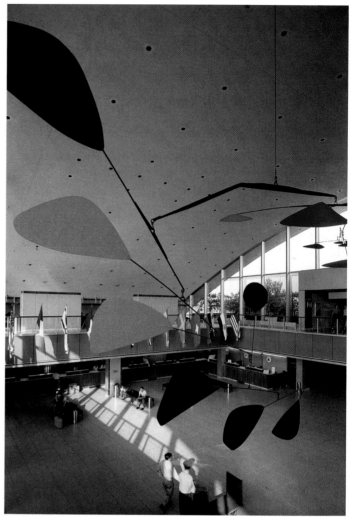

8.28 Antoine Pevsner, *Torso*, 1924–26. Construction in plastic and copper, 29½ × 11⅝ × 15¼ in. (74.9 × 29.4 × 38.7 cm).

8.29 Alexander Calder, *Untitled*, 1976. Painted aluminum and tempered steel, 29 ft 10½ in. × 76 ft (9.1 × 23.2 m). National Gallery of Art, Washington, DC.

PLANE

A **plane** is a three-dimensional form that has length and width but minimal thickness. Depending on the material used, planes can be transparent or opaque, rigid or flexible. Complex surfaces and enclosures can be constructed using folded or bent planes, and when slotted together, planes can be used to create a variety of sturdy forms.

Antoine Pevsner used all of these variables in *Torso* (8.28), one of the first major sculptures made using plastic. More interested in space than in mass, he essentially built the figure from the inside out. Cut and folded planes define anatomical details simply and clearly.

Alexander Calder was also a master of planar construction. In his famous mobiles (8.29), he put simple planes in motion. Inspired by the delicate weights and balances he saw in the paintings of Piet Mondrian, (see figure 3.34, page 76), Calder used these structures to represent the movement of heavenly bodies within the universe. Exquisitely balanced, the flat planes and curving lines can be activated by the slightest flow of air.

When slotted together, planes can create large-scale structures that are remarkably strong. With outdoor sculptures, such as Alexander Calder's *La Grande Vitesse* (8.30), structural integrity is especially important. Located in a public plaza, the sculpture must withstand wind, rain, and snow while presenting minimal risk to pedestrians. Intersecting planes, combined with a ribbed reinforcement at stress points, create this durable structure.

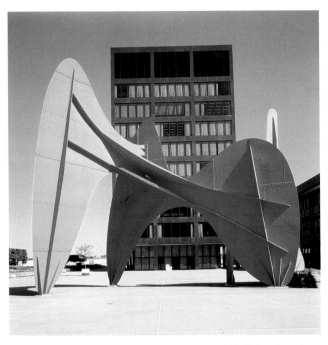

8.30 **Alexander Calder,** *La Grande Vitesse,* **1969.** Painted steel plate, 43 × 55 ft (13.1 × 16.8 m). Calder Plaza, Vandenberg Center, Grand Rapids, MI.

Key Questions

- Consider the limitations of the material you are using. Can it be cut or scored and folded to create curving planes?

- What are the structural and compositional advantages of curved or twisted planes versus flat planes?

- What happens to your design when you pierce or slot together any or all of the planes?

VOLUME

In general terms, volume is the amount of space an object occupies. In three-dimensional design, **volume** refers to an enclosed area of three-dimensional space.

Industrial designers often create functional objects using **polyhedra,** or multifaceted volumes (8.31). Such volumes can be surprisingly strong. In an assignment at Ohio State University (8.32), students used a variety of polyhedra to construct lightweight bristol board helmets.

Octahedron Net	Hexahedron Net	Dodecahedron Net
Octahedron	Hexahedron (cube)	Dodecahedron

8.31 A variety of polyhedra

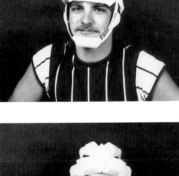
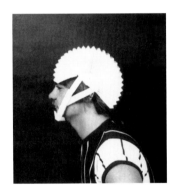
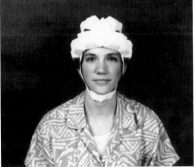
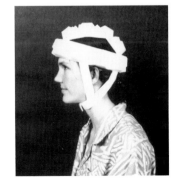

8.32 OSU students used a variety of polyhedra to construct bristol board helmets. Charles Wallschlaeger, professor emeritus, The Ohio State University, Department of Industrial, Interior, and Visual Communication Design.

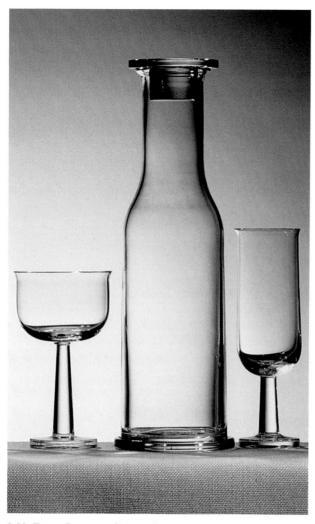

The specific amount of enclosed space is essential when we create any kind of container, from architecture to glassware. *The Ginevra Carafe,* by Ettore Sottsass (8.33), easily holds a liter of wine. This narrow cylinder requires little table space, and an extra disk of glass at the base increases weight and stability. An additional glass cylinder at the top ensures that the lid will remain firmly in place.

Weaving, folding, and slotting are a few of the strategies artists and designers use when creating volume. Defining an enclosed space while maintaining structural integrity is essential. If the structure fails, the volume will collapse and the space will be lost.

Each strategy has its advantages. As demonstrated by the fencer's mask on page 193, woven structures can be elegant, light in weight, and remarkably strong. Package designers generally create volume through folding. The heavy paper used for this purpose can be printed while flat, then scored, cut, and folded. The patterns used are mathematically specific and often structurally complex (8.34). And surprisingly strong volumes can be created using slotted planes. "Egg-crate" slotted structures (8.35) can be used to protect and separate fragile contents (such as wine bottles) and to hold them in a specific position.

8.33 Ettore Sottsass, *Ginevra Carafe,* **1997.** Manufactured by Alessi, Crusinallo, Italy.

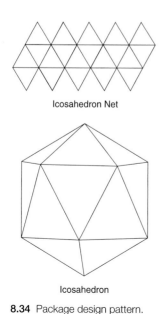

Icosahedron Net

Icosahedron

8.34 Package design pattern.

8.35 Example of "egg-crate" slotted structure.

MASS

A **mass** is a solid three-dimensional form. A massive object can be as dense and heavy as a bar of gold or as light and porous as a sponge.

Massive sculptures are often carved from a solid block of plaster, clay, or stone or are cast using bronze, glass, or other materials. Solid and imposing, they tend to dominate the environment in which they are placed.

Just as Alexander Calder took advantage of the buoyancy of a thin plane to create his mobiles, so Henry Moore took advantage of the power of mass when he created *Locking Piece* (8.36A). In such structures, the **primary contours** (or outer edges) are complemented by the **secondary contours** created by internal edges (8.36B). As the viewer circles the form, these contours visually alternate, as the primary contours become the secondary contours and the secondary contours become the primary contours.

Massive forms tend to suggest stability, power, and permanence. A series of colossal heads produced by the Olmec people of ancient Mexico combine the abstract power of a sphere with the specific power of a human head (8.37). The pyramids at Giza present an even more extreme example of permanence and stability. Built almost 5,000 years ago to memorialize and protect a deceased pharaoh, they continue to dominate the landscape and the human imagination.

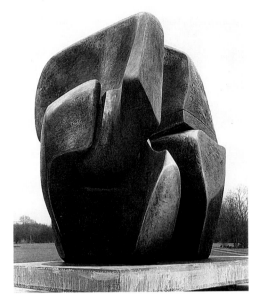

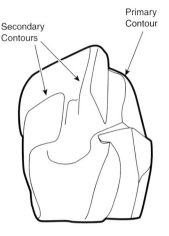

Secondary Contours

Primary Contour

8.36A-B Henry Moore, *Locking Piece*, **1963–64.** Bronze, 115 × 110¼ × 90½ in. (292 × 280 × 230 cm).

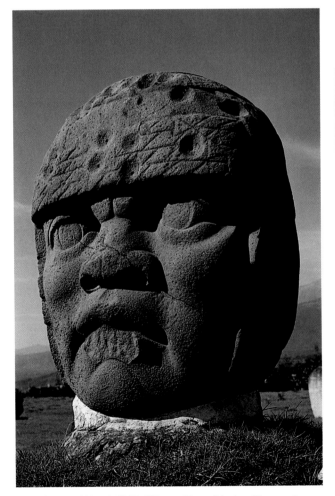

8.37 Colossal Head, 1300–800 B.C. Stone. Mexico, Olmec culture, Jalapa, Veracruz, Mexico.

Key Questions

- Experiment with various ways of creating volume, including folding, weaving, and using slotted structures. Which is most effective for your design?

- When should a closed volume (such as a cube) be used and when is an open, "egg-crate" structure preferable?

- What is the relationship between line, plane, volume, and mass in your design?

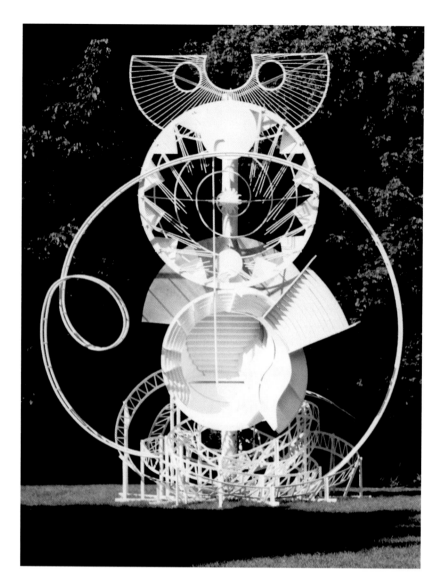

8.38 Alice Aycock, *Tree of Life Fantasy,*
Synopsis of the Book of Questions Concerning
the World Order and/or the Order of Worlds,
1990–92. Painted steel, fiberglass, and wood,
20 × 15 × 8 ft (6.1 × 4.6 × 2.4 m).

SPACE

In three-dimensional design, **space** is the area within or around an area of substance. A dialogue between a form and its surroundings is created as soon as an artist positions an object in space. Space is the partner to substance. Without it, line, plane, volume, and mass lose both visual impact and functional purpose.

The proportion of space to substance triggers an immediate response. The space in Alice Aycock's *Tree of Life Fantasy* (8.38) is defined by a filigree of delicate lines and planes. Inspired by the double-helix structure of DNA and by medieval illustrations showing people entering paradise through a spinning hole in the sky, Aycock combined a linear structure with a series of circular planes. The resulting sculpture is as open and playful as a roller coaster. By comparison, Burden's *Medusa's Head* (see figure 8.20, page 190) presents a relatively solid mass of tangled cement, wood, and metal. With sculptures of this kind, the *surrounding* space becomes more important than any enclosed space. Like a stone placed in a glass of water, the large, solid mass seems to displace the surrounding space, pushing it into the edges of the room.

Positive and Negative

The interrelationship between space and substance is demonstrated in every area of three-dimensional design. David Smith's *Cubi XXVII* (8.39) is dominated by a central void. The 10 gleaming geometric volumes are activated by the space they enclose.

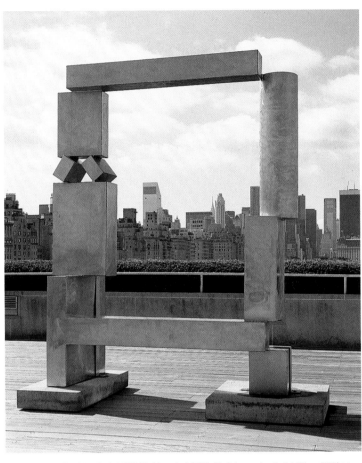

8.39 David Smith, *Cubi XXVII,* March 1965. Stainless steel, 111⅜ × 87¾ × 34 in. (282.9 × 222.9 cm).

Space plays an equally important role in representational work. The open mouth in *Model of a Trophy Head* (8.40) really animates the mask. No facial expression, however extreme, would be as lively if this mouth were closed.

Negative space is especially noticeable in designs that are dominated by positive form. Karen Karnes' *Vessel* (8.41) is a functional pot, with its internal bottom placed just above the vertical slit. In effect, the lower half of the design serves as a pedestal for the functional container at the top. This narrow slit of negative space presents a strong contrast to the solidity of the cylindrical form and helps energize the simple form.

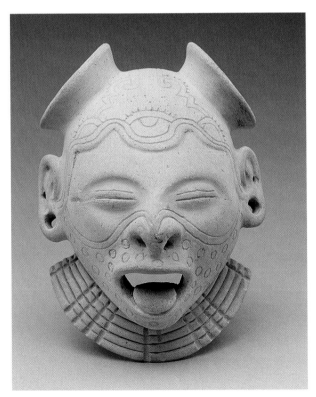

8.40 *Model of a Trophy Head,* Ecuador, La Tolita, 600 B.C.–A.D. 400. Ceramic.

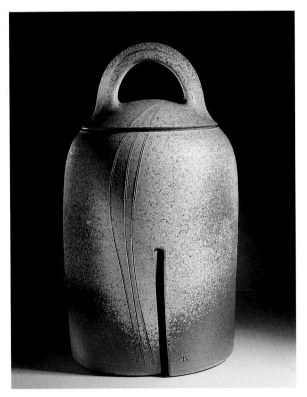

8.41 Karen Karnes, *Vessel,* 1987. Stoneware, wheel-thrown, glazed, and wood-fired, 16½ in. h. × 10½ in. d. (41.9 × 26.7 cm).

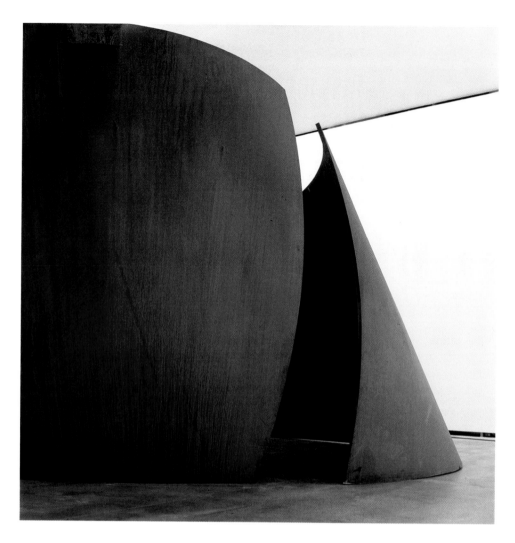

8.42 Richard Serra, *Torqued Ellipse VI,* 1998–99. Weatherproof steel, 13 ft 8 in. × 33 ft 5½ in. × 19 ft 8¼ in. © FMGB Guggenheim Bilbao Museoa. All Right Reserved.

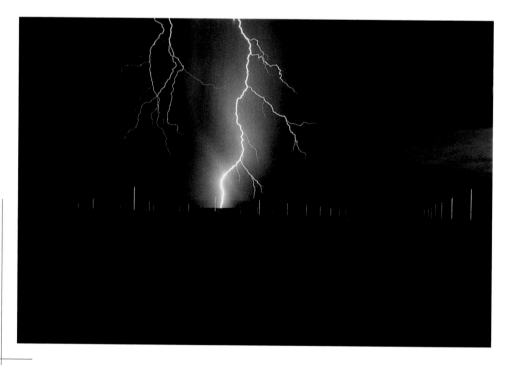

8.43 Walter de Maria, *The Lightning Field,* 1977. Near Quemado, NM. Stainless steel poles, average height 20 ft 7½ in. (6.1 m), overall 5,280 × 3,300 ft (1,609.34 × 1,005.84 m).

Compression and Expansion

Space is never passive or meaningless. It is just as important as the surrounding substance, and it can be manipulated very deliberately. The tangibility of space is especially apparent in the works of Richard Serra and Walter de Maria. Using four enormous steel plates, Serra created a sense of spatial compression in figure 8.42. Upon entering the piece, the viewer immediately becomes aware of the weight of the tilted planes and of the support the compressed space seems to provide. The space in de Maria's *Lightning Field* (8.43) is equally clearly defined yet is wonderfully expansive. Arranged in a grid over nearly 1 square mile of desert, 400 steel poles act as a collection of lightning rods. Impressive even in daylight, the site becomes awe-inspiring during a thunderstorm. Lightning jumps from pole to pole and from the sky to earth, creating a pyrotechnic display.

Activated Space

The space in an artwork may be contemplative, agitated, or even threatening. For example, a Japanese Zen garden is usually made from an enclosure containing several large rocks surrounded by carefully raked white sand. A few simple objects are used to create a contemplative space. By contrast, the space in Anish Kapoor's sculptures is often unsettling. Placed in the floor of a large, empty room, *Turning the World Inside Out II* (8.44) creates a sculptural whirlpool that seems to drain space, light, and energy from the surrounding room. Such activity becomes even more noticeable when the space itself is animated, as in *Lightning Field* during a thunderstorm.

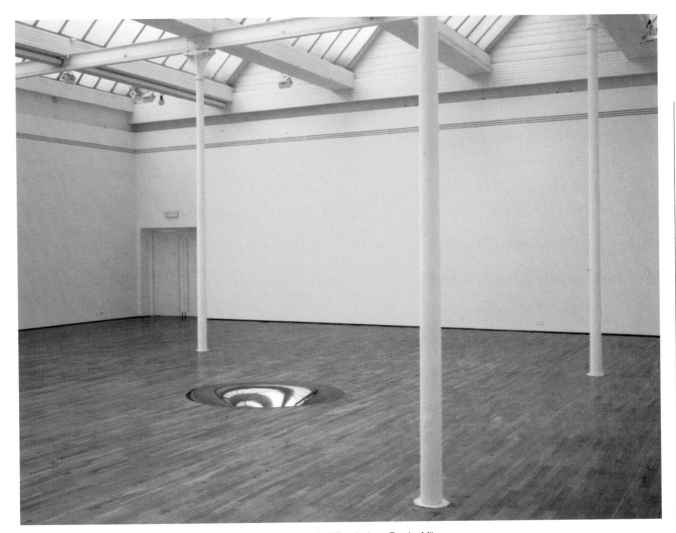

8.44 Anish Kapoor, *Turning the World Inside Out II*, 1995. Installed Fondazione Prada, Milan. Chromium-plated bronze, 57 × 73 × 73 in. (145 × 185 × 185 cm).

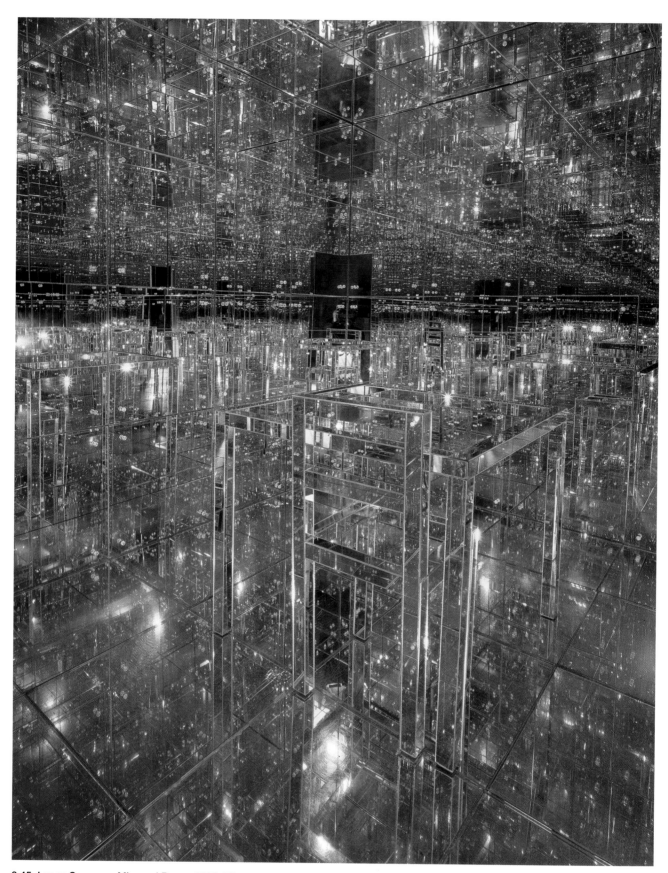

8.45 Lucas Samaras, *Mirrored Room,* **1966.** Mirrors on wooden frame, 8 × 8 × 10 ft (2.44 × 2.44 × 3 m).

8.46 Donna Dennis, *Subway with Silver Girders,* 1981–82. Wood, masonite, acrylic, enamel, cellulose compound, glass, electrical fixtures, and metal, 12 ft 2½ in. w. × 14 ft 3½ in. d. (31 × 36 cm).

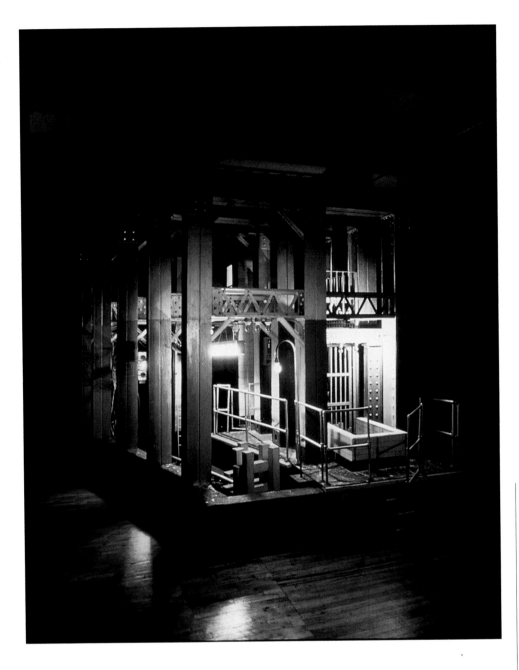

Entering Space

Some sculptures are designed to be entered physically. Lucas Samaras' *Mirrored Room* (8.45) multiplies and divides the reflection of each visitor who enters. Other sculptures can only be entered mentally. *Subway with Silver Girders* (8.46), by Donna Dennis, recreates in great detail the architecture and lighting we find in a subway station. Constructed at two-thirds the scale of an actual station, the sculpture presents a magical entry into a prosaic place. This subway station provides transportation for the mind, rather than the body.

Key Questions

- What is the relationship between substance and space in your design?

- What would happen if you substantially increased or decreased the amount of space? For example, would 70% space and 30% mass strengthen or weaken your design?

- How can the space play a stronger role in your design?

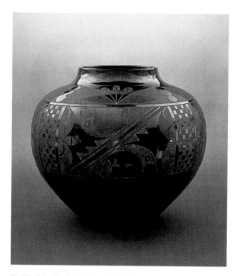

8.47 Maria Montoya Martinez and Julian Martinez, *Blackware Storage Jar*, 1942. Hopi, from San Ildefonso Pueblo, NM. Ceramic, 18¾ in. h. × 22½ in. d. (47.6 × 57.1 cm).

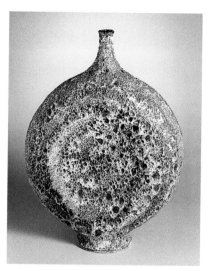

8.48 Gertrud Natzler and Otto Natzler, *Pilgrim Bottle*, 1956. Earthenware, wheel-thrown, and glazed, 17 × 13 × 5 in. (43.2 × 33 × 12.7 cm).

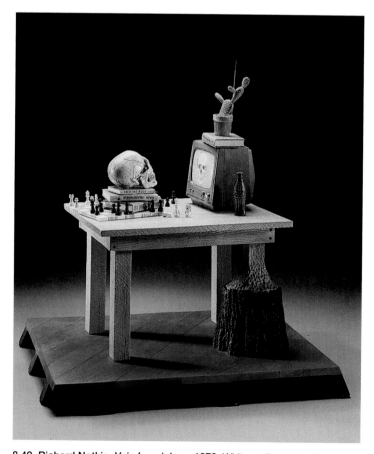

8.49 Richard Notkin, *Vain Imaginings*, 1978. White earthenware, glaze, brass, redwood, white cedarwood, 16 × 13½ × 16½ in. (40.6 × 34.3 × 41.9 cm).

TEXTURE

Texture refers to the visual or tactile quality of a form. The increased surface area of a three-dimensional form heightens the impact of texture. The surface shifts and turns, presenting many opportunities for textural elaboration.

Degrees of Texture

Variations in the surface of a volume may be subtle or pronounced. In *Blackware Storage Jar,* by Maria Montoya Martinez and Julian Martinez (8.47), a burnished, shiny surface was combined with a subtle matte surface. The visual effect is dramatic despite the minimal textural variation. The geometric patterns enhance the surface of the jar but never compete with the purity of the graceful form. Gertrud and Otto Natzler used a very different approach for *Pilgrim Bottle* (8.48). The volume as well as the textural surface is exaggerated. Between the narrow neck and compressed base, the jar bulges out in a circular shape, as magical and as pockmarked as the surface of the moon. The unusual union between volume and surface, combined with the intriguing title, invites intellectual speculation. Who is the pilgrim, and what might this bottle contain?

Characteristic and Contradictory Textures

Every material has its own inherent textural properties. Clay, glass, and metal can be poured, cast, or pressed to create a wide variety of textures. Gold, which may occur in nature as dust, in nuggets, or in veins, can be cast, hammered, enameled, and soldered. Despite the adaptability of most materials, however, we are accustomed to their use in specific ways. The reflective surface of a steel teapot, the transparency of glass, and the earthy functionality of clay fulfill our expectations.

When a material is used in an uncharacteristic way, or when strange textures are added to familiar forms, we must reappraise both the material and the object it represents. Except for the wooden platform and brass screws, Robert Notkin's *Vain Imaginings* (8.49) is made of clay. The textures of wood, plastic, glass, and bone have been skillfully imitated. Clay is very unlike any of these materials, and a purist may argue that such mimicry violates its inherent nature. On closer examination, however, we can see a perfect match between the image and the idea. The table, which symbolizes the world, supports a chess set, suggesting risk, and a television set, which presents an illusion. The ceramic skull is placed on top of four books titled *The Shallow Life, Moth and Rust, Vain Imaginings,* and *By Bread Alone.* The image on the screen repeats the skull. The clay itself suggests impermanence (as in "he has feet of clay") and mortality (as in "earth to earth, dust to dust," which is often said during funerals). In this masterwork of imitation, ceramicist Robert Notkin has created a "fake" sculpture for a false world.

Doormat, by Mona Hatoum (8.50), offers an even more disorienting interpretation of a familiar object. Constructed from steel pins, this mat is part of a series of political art projects by this Palestinian artist.

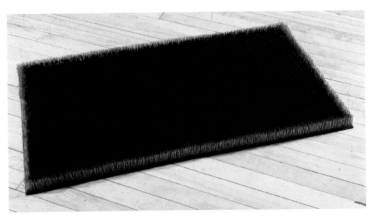

8.50 Mona Hatoum, *Doormat*, 1996. Stainless steel and nickel-plated pins, glue, and canvas, 1 × 28 × 16 in. (2.5 × 71 × 40.6 cm).

Commenting on the realities of racism, Hatoum suggests that for African-Americans, the opportunities offered by the Civil Rights movement may seem as illusory as a welcome mat made of pins.

The Implications of Texture

On a compositional level, texture can enhance or defy our understanding of a physical form. In figure 8.51, the lines carved into the surface of the vessel increase our awareness of its dimensionality. Concentric circles surrounding the knobs at the base of each handle create a series of visual targets that circle the globe, while additional grooves accentuate the surface of the sturdy handles. On a conceptual level, texture can add layers of meaning to art and design. In *Rock Bible* (8.52), Takako Araki used three kinds of

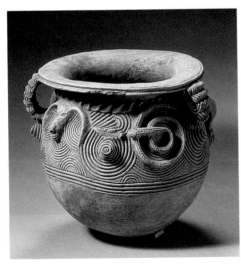

8.51 Globular Vessel with Inverted Rim, Tenth Century, Igbo, Nigeria. Terra-cotta, 16 in. (40.6 cm).

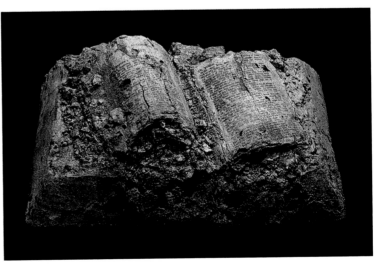

8.52 Takako Araki, *Rock Bible*, 1995. Ceramic, silkscreen, 8¼ × 23⅝ × 16½ in. (21 × 60 × 42 cm).

texture to animate an artwork and expand its meaning. The words on the pages of the Bible provide one texture, the rough surface of the disintegrating book provides a second, and the inherent texture of the clay provides a third.

In summary, texture can increase the surface area of an object, add contrast, and enrich our understanding of the physical and conceptual qualities of any three-dimensional object.

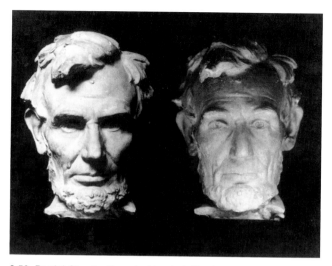

8.53 Daniel Chester French, *Head of Abraham Lincoln* (Detail of Seated Figure), 1911–22. Full-size plaster model of head of marble statue, Lincoln Memorial, Washington, DC, 1917–18. Head 50½ in. h. (128.3 cm), total figure 19 ft h. (5.8 m).

Key Questions

- How many textures can be created with the material you are using?

- What happens when a surface gradually shifts from a polished, smooth texture to a very rough texture?

- Can contradictory texture enhance or expand the idea you want to convey?

LIGHT

Light can enhance or obscure our perception of form. It can affect our emotions, entice us to enter a room, and create a mystery. It can even become a sculptural medium in its own right. Often overlooked, light is actually an essential aspect of three-dimensional design.

Value and Volume

A gradated series of highlights and shadows is produced whenever light pours across a surface. These **values,** or variations in light and dark, are our primary means of perceiving space. As demonstrated by two views of Daniel Chester French's *Head of Abraham Lincoln* (8.53), a surface that appears flat when lit from the front can become spatially rich when lit from the top or sides. Product designers are equally aware of the importance of light. A badly lit form will lack definition and impact, while even the simplest form will attract attention when it is dramatically lit. In figure 8.54, highlights, gradations and shadows give definition to each of Stan Rickel's *Teapot Sketches.*

Striking a Surface

Light is strongly affected by the substance it strikes. As demonstrated by the teapots in figure 8.54, light creates a continuous series of values when it strikes an opaque surface. Light behaves very differently when it strikes a transparent surface, such as clear plastic or glass. It is often refracted (or bent), creating a complex network of luminous shapes. Reflective surfaces can bounce light back into space. As a result, objects that are made from polished steel, mirrors, and other reflective materials can appear to emit their own light. A translucent surface is partially transparent. Neither fully opaque nor fully transparent, translucent surfaces can be mysterious and evocative.

Each type of surface can be used expressively. *The Dance* (figure 8.1) is dominated by the movement of seven opaque figures in and out of space. Light and shadow accentuate the action of the exuberant marble dancers. The same composition would dissolve into visual chaos if it were cast in transparent glass. On the other hand, the energy in Larry Bell's *The Iceberg and Its Shadow* (8.55) comes from the effects of light on a transparent and reflective surface. Multiple plates of glass create reflections, which continually shift, separate, and surround the viewer. Like a house of mirrors, the sculpture is both tangible and transient.

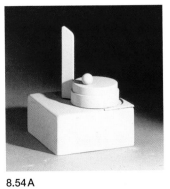

8.54 A

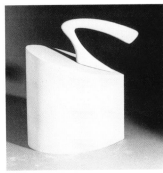

8.54 B

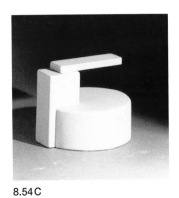

8.54 C

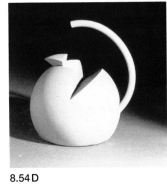

8.54 D

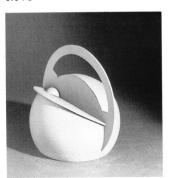

8.54 E

8.54 F

8.54 Stan Rickel, *Teapot Sketches*, 1991. Mixed medium, 12 × 12 × 12 in. (30.5 × 30.5 × 30.5 cm).

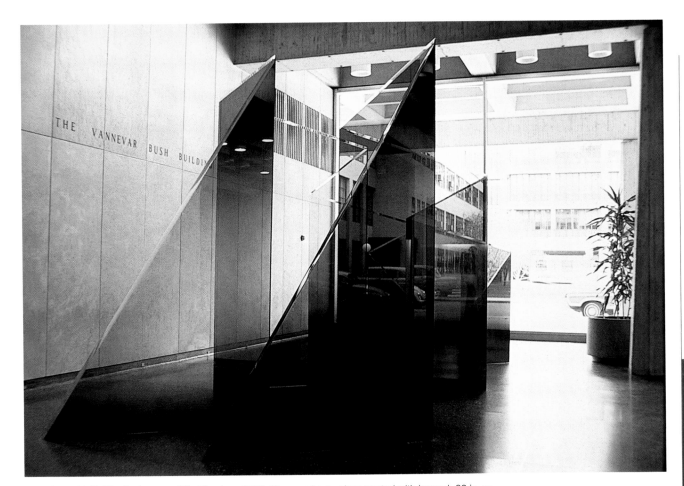

8.55 Larry Bell, *The Iceberg and Its Shadow,* 1977. Clear and gray glass coated with inconel, 60 in. w. (152.4 cm), 57 in. to 100 in. h. (144.8 to 254 cm). Busch Lobby, MIT Permanent Collection.

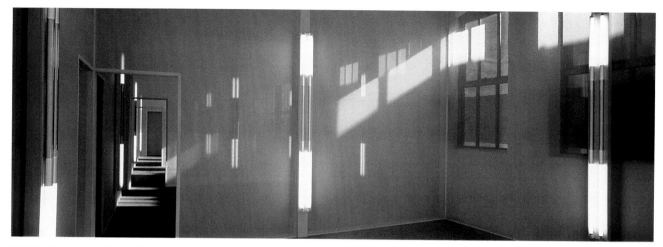

8.56 Robert Irwin, *Part II: Excursus: Homage to the Square*[3]. Installation at Dia Center for the Arts, New York. September 1998–June 1999.

Translucent materials can create even more complex effects. Robert Irwin's *Part II: Excursus: Homage to the Square*[3] (8.56) was installed at the Dia Center for the arts in New York in 1998–1999. This structure consisted of nine cubic rooms, defined by delicate walls of translucent cloth. The translucency of the fabric varied, depending on the amount and location of the light. Two vertical fluorescent lights illuminated each cube, creating subtle changes in color from room to room.

Entering the installation was both inviting and disorienting. From any point, all of the rooms were visible yet veiled. The layers of fabric and the variations in light made the most distant rooms appear to dissolve. The vertical fluorescent lights, which always remained visible, read first as individual, then as mirror, images, creating a hallucinatory experience similar to a carnival funhouse. All activity within the space was created by the visitors themselves, who entered, explored, and left the installation like ghostly silhouettes.

Ambient and Directed light

Ambient light encompasses an entire space or setting. For example, when we enter an open courtyard on a sunny summer afternoon, we are surrounded by warm ambient sunlight. Everything we see is colorful and brightly lit. **Directed light** is localized and focused, like a spotlight on a singer.

Exhibition designers are masters of light. They use directed light to focus the viewer's attention and increase visual drama. They use ambient light to create the underlying feeling. For example, the designers of a 1989 NASA exhibition used low ambient light to suggest the mystery of space travel. Bright pools of directed light were then used to emphasize individual displays (8.57).

Light as Sculpture

Many types of sculptural light are used by contemporary artists and designers. Some shape neon tubes into sculptural forms.

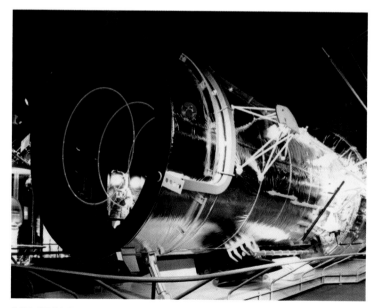

8.57 NASA Exhibit at the 1989 Paris Air Show. Designers: Bill Cannan, Tony Ortiz, H. Kurt Heinz. Design Firm: Bill Cannan & Co.

Others use commercial lighting fixtures and illuminated signs to convey aesthetic meaning. Still others project light onto various shapes and surfaces, creating effects that range from the humorous to the bizarre.

Projection and containment are two common ways to create sculptural light. James Turrell's *Afrum-Proto* (8.58) was created when a powerful beam of projected light struck the corner of an empty room. The resulting form was a complete illusion yet totally convincing: viewers *saw* a cube. Bill Parker's *Jewel of Enlightenment (Hashi-no Toma)* (8.59) demonstrates the power of containment. Measuring 40 inches in diameter, the transparent globe is both a container for electricity and a compelling volume in itself. Standing 5 feet from the floor, the sphere is slightly above ordinary eye level, making it even more awe-inspiring.

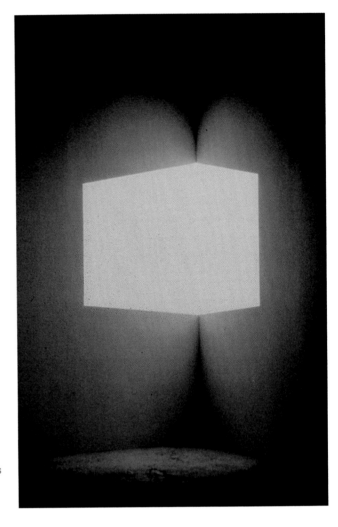

8.58 James Turrell, *Afrum-Proto*, 1966. Quartz-halogen projection, as installed at the Whitney Museum of American Art, New York, 1980.

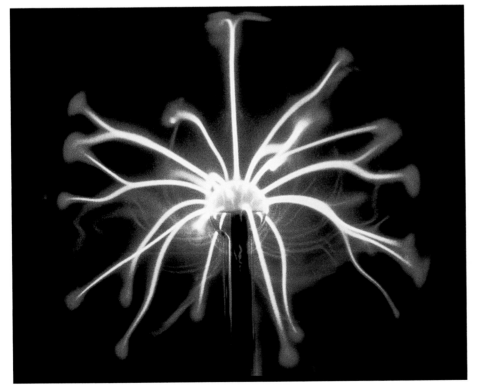

8.59 Bill Parker, *Jewel of Enlightenment (Hashi-no Toma)*, 1989. 40 in. (101.6 cm) diameter sphere standing 5 ft (1.5 m) from the floor, glass sphere, gas mixture, high voltage at high frequency.

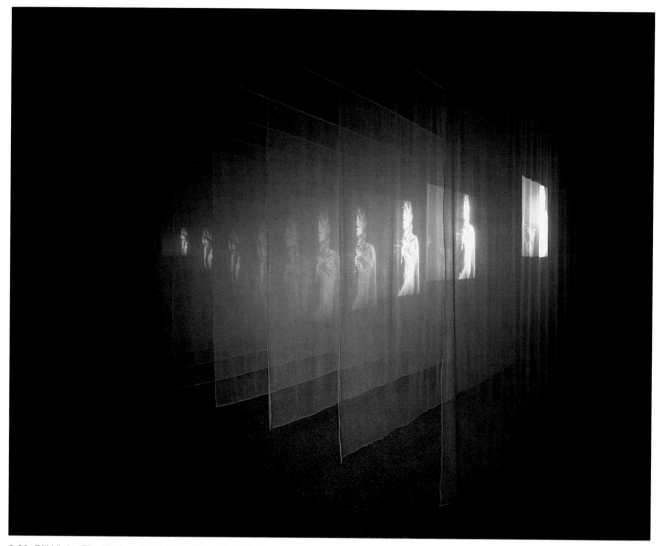

8.60 Bill Viola, *The Veiling*, 1995. Video/Sound Installation.

With the increasing use of new media, light has become an eloquent and versatile addition to the elements of three-dimensional design. In addition to its traditional role in accentuating form, it has now become a sculptural medium in itself. For example, in *The Veiling* (8.60), Bill Viola hung thin sheets of translucent fabric on parallel lines across the center of a darkened room. An image of a man was projected from one end, while an image of a woman was projected from the opposite end. These projections became increasingly diffused as they passed through the multiple layers of cloth. Finally, the two figures merged on a central veil as pure presences of light.

Key Questions

- How can lighting direction diminish or accentuate the dimensionality of your artwork?

- Does your object require special illumination, such as an internal light source, fiberoptics, or a video screen?

- How can light enhance the expressive content of your artwork?

- Can your object be redesigned to use light more effectively? If so, how?

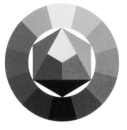

8.61A. Hue

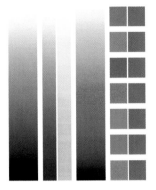

8.61B. Value

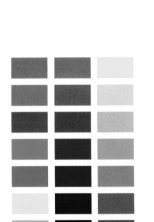

8.61C. Intensity

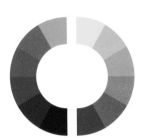

8.61D. Temperature

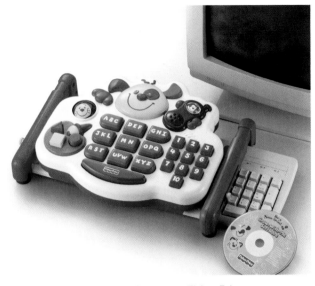

8.62 *Smartronics Learning System* by Fisher-Price

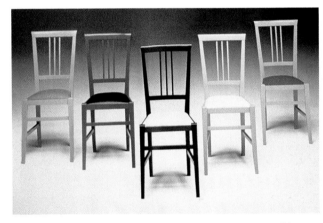

8.63 Toshiyuki Kita, *Kita Collection* of chairs with removable seats for Stendig International Inc. Beechwood frame and upholstered seat.

COLOR

Color definitions remain the same whether we are creating a three-dimensional or a two-dimensional composition. Each color has a specific **hue** (8.61A), which is determined by its wavelength. **Value** (8.61B), the lightness or darkness of a color, helps determine legibility. **Intensity,** or **saturation** (8.61C), refers to the purity of a color. **Temperature** (8.61D) refers to the psychological characteristics attributed to a color.

Degrees of Harmony

Selecting the right colors for a product and determining the degree of color **harmony** can make or break a design. The triadic harmony used in *Smartronics Learning System* by Fisher-Price (8.62) creates an attractive educational toy for young children. The large red, yellow, and blue buttons are easy to push and invite even the most skeptical child to play. A very different type of harmony is offered in *Kita Collection*, by Toshiyuki Kita (8.63).

These simple chairs with their removable seats can be color-customized to fit into any interior. The buyer can create his or her own sense of harmony.

Disharmony can also be used effectively. In figure 8.64, Keith Edmier portrays his pregnant mother on the day President Kennedy was assassinated. She is wearing the same Chanel suit pattern that Jackie Kennedy wore, and she pensively rubs her glowing belly. The orange-reds and purple-reds suggest traditional monochromatic harmony but seem skewed and off-key. While the surface of normalcy remained intact, the substance of American politics shifted after Kennedy's death. Likewise, while the artist's mother seems calm, the colors and materials used suggest an undercurrent of anxiety.

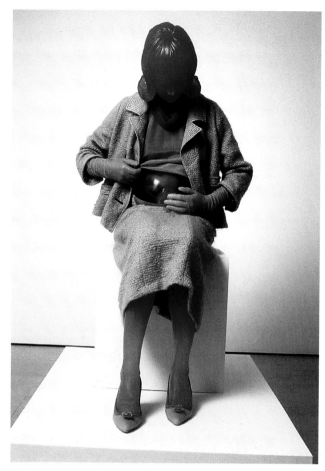

8.64 Keith Edmier, *Beverly Edmier*, 1967. Cast resin, silicone, acrylic paint, fabric.

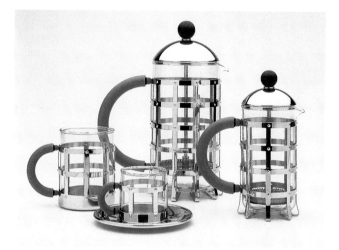

8.65 Michael Graves, *Alessi Coffee Set.* Glass, silver, mock ivory, and Bakelite.

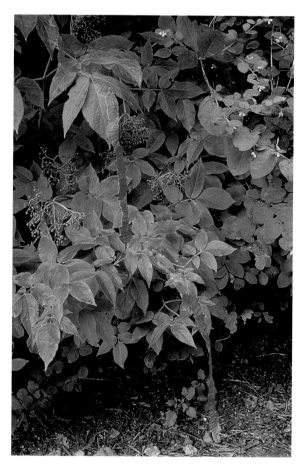

8.66 Andy Goldsworthy, *Poppy Petals*, August 1994. Leaves and flowers.

Contrast

Artists and designers often use contrasting colors to accentuate the function of a product or to create a distinctive image. Contrasting colors and contrasting materials distinguish Michael Graves' *Alessi Coffee Set* (8.65). The fragile, transparent glass is protected by metallic armor. These metal bands accentuate the cylindrical forms, while the blue handles and bright red accents further animate the set. Using natural materials in natural settings, Andy Goldsworthy often creates intense areas of red, green, or gold to alert the viewer to junctions, boundaries, or unusual configurations between objects in the landscape. These accents of color are especially powerful when the surrounding colors are subdued. The scarlet poppy petals in figure 8.66 create a glowing line, which cascades down the leaves of the host tree.

Color and Emotion

The emotional implications of color can be demonstrated by a visit to any car dealership. Bright red, black, or silver sports cars are often marketed as

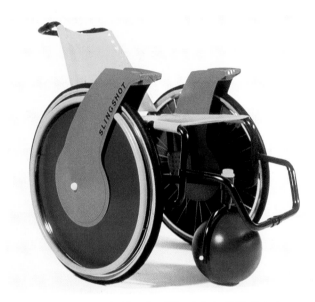

8.67 Adele Linarducci, *Slingshot Wheelchair,* 1989. Polystyrene, vinyl, PVC, and other materials, a nonworking model created while artist was a student at Rochester Institute of Technology.

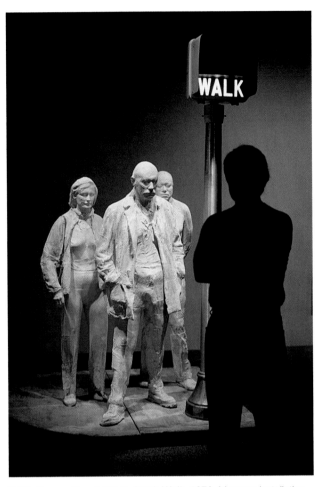

8.68 George Segal, *Walk, Don't Walk,* 1976. Museum installation, with viewer. Plaster, cement, metal, painted wood, and electric light, 104 × 72 × 72 in. (264.2 × 182.9 × 182.9 cm).

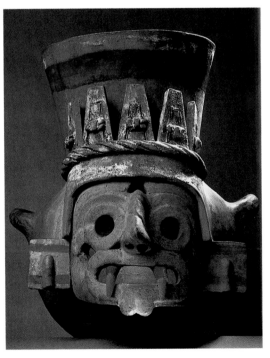

8.69 Ritual Vessel Depicting Mask of Tlaloc, Aztec, Mexico, Tenochtitlan, 1400–1521. Ceramic.

oversized toys for single drivers, while more subdued colors are often used for the minivans and station wagons favored by families. In figure 8.67, color is used to add a sporty look to quite a different vehicle. This manual wheelchair, designed by Adele Linarducci for children ages 6 to 11, gives the user a psychological boost while encouraging the development of physical strength and dexterity.

On the other hand, it is the absence of color that brings power to the life-size figures in George Segal's installations. Despite their proximity to the viewer and their large scale, the white figures in *Walk, Don't Walk* (8.68) are drained of color and emotionally distant. Here, an antiseptic white is used to suggest alienation.

Symbolic Color

Symbolic color is culturally based. Because each culture is unique, color associations vary widely. For example, yellow signifies the direction north in Tibet but the qualities of light, life, truth, and immortality to Hindus.[4] Blue represents mourning in Borneo, while in New Mexico it is painted on window frames to block entrance by evil spirits. In ancient times, blue represented faith and truth to the Egyptians yet was the color worn by slaves in Gaul.[5]

The blue face that dominates the mask of the Aztec god Tlaloc in figure 8.69 is both symbolically and visually appropriate. Symbolically, the blue represents sky and the rain that Tlaloc calls forth to nourish the crops. Visually, the contrast between the warm, reddish clay and the sky-blue paint increases the impact of the ferocious face.

Key Questions

- Which will work better in your design, a limited range of hues or a wide range of hues?

- Are all of the colors in your design similar in intensity? What would happen if you combined low-intensity colors with high-intensity colors?

- What is the proportion of warm and cool colors in your design — is it around 50/50, 70/30, 20/80? What would happen if these proportions were changed?

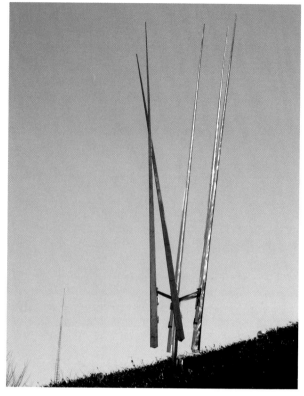

8.70 George Rickey, *Five Lines in Parallel Planes*, 1965. Stainless steel, 228 × 24 × 24 in.

TIME

Every object occupies a position in time as well as space. In some cases, the specific temporal location is of minor importance. For example, *Locking Piece* (see figure 8.36, page 197) is as meaningful now as it was when constructed in 1963. Formalist in approach, it makes no specific reference to social or political events. Constructed from durable bronze, it has effectively withstood the effects of time. In other cases, temporal location gives the object its meaning. As noted on page 192, Nancy Holt's *Sun Tunnels* creates a kind of celestial observatory. Light pours through the holes in the curving walls, creating projections that mark the movement of the planets. If the element of time were removed, the concrete tunnels would have no more meaning than drainage pipes at a construction site.

Two aspects of time are of particular importance to sculptors. **Actual time** refers to the location and duration of an actual temporal event. For example, it takes less than a minute for the bowling ball to roll down the ramps in Tinguely's *Chaos 1* (see figure

8.2, page 181). By contrast, **implied time** is the suggested location or duration of an event. The traffic light in Segal's *Walk, Don't Walk* changes, but the sculptural figures never move.

Actual motion and implied motion are equally important. The long metal lines in George Rickey's *Five Lines in Parallel Planes* (8.70) actually move, creating a seemingly endless variety of compositions over time. By contrast, all of the motion in Erwin Hauer's *Project California Condor* (8.71) is implied. We can almost hear the flapping wings, but the sculptural birds remain still.

Viewing time is a final basic consideration. The multiple surfaces presented by any three-dimensional object require extended analysis. We walk around Rodin's *The Kiss,* noting every nuance in form and texture; we rotate a ceramic vessel in our hands, savoring every detail. *The Board Room* (see figure 8.10, page 185), *Part II: Excursus* (see figure 8.56, page 208) and other installations require even more viewing time. To understand the artwork, the viewer must enter and fully explore the site.

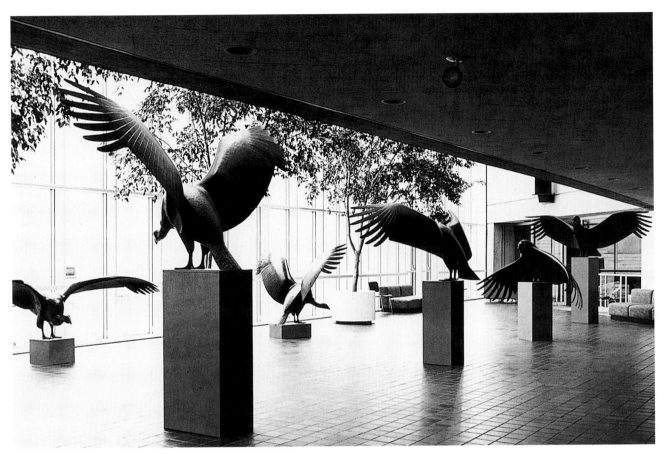

8.71 Erwin Hauer, *Project California Condor*, 1978–83. Plastic laminate, wingtip to wingtip 9 to 10 ft (2.75 to 3.05 m).

THE COMPLEXITY OF THREE-DIMENSIONAL DESIGN

Completing a new project every week or so is quite common in a basic two-dimensional design class. By contrast, a month of work may be devoted to a major project in a three-dimensional design class.

The materials are less familiar, the construction methods are more time-consuming, and the multiple surfaces of a physical object present a particular challenge. Used poorly, the elements of three-dimensional design can become adversarial, resulting in a disjointed composition. Used well, each design element contributes to a wonderfully complex and compelling artwork.

SUMMARY

- *Form* may be defined as the physical manifestation of an idea. *Content* refers to the idea itself, including the subject matter plus its emotional, intellectual, spiritual, and symbolic implications.

- In three-dimensional design, *form* also refers to dimensionality itself. Thus, a circle is a shape; a sphere is a form.

- The first step in creating a design is to understand its purpose. A sculptor seeks to convey ideas and express emotions. A craftsperson or designer is equally concerned with the function and the beauty of an object.

- Height, width, and depth are the three dimensions in three-dimensional design. Orthographic projection provides a means of clearly drawing these dimensions.

- Artworks can vary in dimensionality from relief, which uses a flat backing to support dimensional forms, to environmental works that the viewer can enter and physically explore.

- A line can connect, define, or divide a design. It can be static or dynamic, increasing or decreasing the stability of the form.

- A plane is a three-dimensional form that has length and width but minimal thickness.

- In three-dimensional design, *volume* refers to an enclosed area of three-dimensional space.

- A mass is a solid three-dimensional form. A massive object can be as dense and heavy as a bar of gold or as light and porous as a sponge.

- Space is the area within or around an area of substance. Space is the partner to substance. Without it, line, plane, volume, and mass lose both visual impact and functional purpose.

- *Texture* refers to the visual or tactile quality of a form. The increased surface area of a three-dimensional form heightens the impact of texture.

- Light can enhance our perception of a three-dimensional form, attract an audience, or be used as a material in itself.

- Hue, value, intensity, and temperature are the major characteristics of color.

- Every object occupies a position in time as well as space. Actual time, implied time, actual space, and implied space can be combined to create compelling objects of great complexity.

Keywords

actual line	freestanding work	mass	secondary contour
actual time	function	negative space	sight line
ambient light	geometric form	organic form	site specific
continuity	harmony	orientation	space
contrast	hue	orthographic projection	static form
directed light	implied line	plane	symbolic color
direction	implied time	polyhedra	temperature
dynamic form	installation	positive form	texture
environmental work	intensity	primary contour	three-quarter work
earthwork	kinetic form	relief	value
form	line	saturation	volume

Profile:
Rodger Mack, Sculptor

The Oracle's Tears: Conception, Composition, and Construction

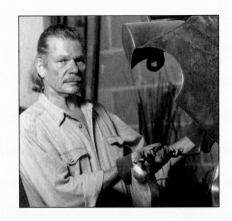

Rodger Mack was best known for his work in bronze and steel. His work is included in the collections of the Museum of Modern Art in Barcelona, Spain; the Grand Hotel in Guayaquil, Ecuador; the Arkansas Arts Center Museum, Little Rock; the Albrecht-Kemper Museum of Art in St. Joseph, Missouri; the Munson-Williams-Proctor Institute in Utica, New York; and the Everson Museum in Syracuse, New York. Mack, who always used travel as a major inspiration for his imagery, was the recipient of a Fulbright grant for study in Italy, grants from the National Endowment for the Arts and the New York State Council on the Arts, and workshop grants for projects in England, Barcelona, and South Africa.

My meeting with Mack in 2000 was delayed for almost a year, due to his many commissions and elaborate projects. We got together over lunch just before he left for Italy. I had always admired Mack's abstract sculptures that so elegantly combine power and grace. Indeed, I expected our conversation to focus on the elements and principles of design. As you will see, the conversation that actually developed was equally devoted to concepts and composition.

MS: One of the biggest questions my students have is this: how do I get from where I am, as a beginner to where you are, as a professional? Can you describe that path briefly?

RM: I always knew that I wanted to study art, and I began my undergraduate work at the Cleveland Institute of Art, planning to become an automotive designer. In the fourth year of the five-year BFA program, I had the good fortune of being picked by General Motors to participate in an experimental summer internship. It was an exciting time: I was well paid and directly involved in my intended career.

I realized, though, that automotive design limited my possibilities as an artist, and I turned instead to a major in sculpture, with a minor in ceramics. At Cleveland, ceramicist Toshiko Takaezu was a great influence. She taught me a level of professionalism and an understanding of a new level of quality, both in concept and in craft. I was further influenced by Toshiko's teacher, Maija Grotell, who had developed the ceramics program at Cranbrook, where I did my graduate work. At the age of 70,

she was continuing to do pioneering work with ceramic glazes.

Finally, as an apprentice to William McBey, I learned about working on commissions and the realities of day-to-day work in the studio. With sculpture, cleaning up is important: if you don't control your work space, it will control you!

MS: How do you get started on a sculpture?

RM: I don't have to get started, because I never stop! I'm always watching, listening, and thinking. When I do stop the merry-go-round long enough, I record my ideas in a notebook. I always carry this notebook on the plane: while others read, I draw. I always have many more ideas than I can handle: I wish I could build them as fast as I can think them up.

Whenever I stop generating new material, I just visualize the inventory of sculptural parts I already have in the studio. Putting them together in new ways provides even more possibilities: an idea gets me working with the metal, which then generates more ideas. I always try to have something ready for casting each month, if only to add to this inventory of parts.

I only make maquettes when they are required for a commission. The small scale of a maquette is so different from the actual scale of the piece, especially for a major project. I remember one maquette I made for a commission in North Little Rock, Arkansas. It was made of bronze, and I charged them $200 for the maquette. Before the meeting to review the project, one of the city councilors put a box of multi-colored sticks of plasticine in front of me and said, "Next time, make it out of this." He was annoyed that I had made the maquette in bronze. In fact, the city council was against the project — they just didn't want to spend the money — but a grassroots civic group saw the importance of the work, and the commission was approved.

MS: How do you choose which of the drawings to make into sculptures?

RM: I might choose a drawing because I can't see the other side. I get curious. There is something in the drawn side that compels me to spend the time and money on the sculpture, so that I can see the other side. Drawings that I really finish are the sculptures that I never make.

MS: It seems that you actually "draw" with the metal; that is, you approach it with the same openness with which I approach a sheet of paper. How malleable is it?

RM: Just malleable enough! I like it because it is NOT easy. It is hard, and you have to really commit yourself to the piece. I am most intuitive when I am working with existing fragments from my inventory, essentially collaging parts together. Starting with a collection of parts, I create connections, often heating a bar of bronze to just the right temperature and bending it to form a bridge or activate a space. I see the space around each volume as much as I see the volume itself.

MS: Please describe your latest piece, The *Oracle's Tears*.

RM: I've always been drawn to ancient cities and architectural forms and have been working with mythological themes for the past six years, with a series of maidens, a minotaur, a Trojan horse, and several oracles completed so far. When I visit these ancient civilizations, it saddens me that they are gone, destroyed to make way for new civilizations.

This sculpture is made from six major parts. The column is the dominant feature, structurally and conceptually. Just above it, I have placed a form which has reappeared in my work for 30 years, the Oracle. It is like an image on a tarot card, the hanging man, perhaps. A smaller piece, based on a shape I found in a market in Athens, connects the oracle and the column. On the top, the "capitol" repeats the triangular spaces seen throughout the sculpture. The tears are created by the three descending lines. The base is the final element. It provides a stable support and adds a sense of completion.

MS: How was the sculpture made?

RM: I used a combination of fabrication and casting. The oracle form was made by cutting out shapes from a sheet of 1/8-inch bronze and welding them together. The tears and the column were cast in sections, then welded. A potassium dichloride patina, applied using a blowtorch, gives the piece its golden color.

MS: This is an especially important piece for you, I think.

RM: You always hope your latest piece is the best! But yes, it combines ideas I've been working on for three years, with an overall theme, which first appeared in my work when I was in undergraduate school.

MS: What advice do you have for a beginning student?

RM: There's the old cliché: learn the rules before you break them. Always worked for me.

Rodger Mack died in September 2003. Hundreds of friends and former students from around the world attended his memorial service.

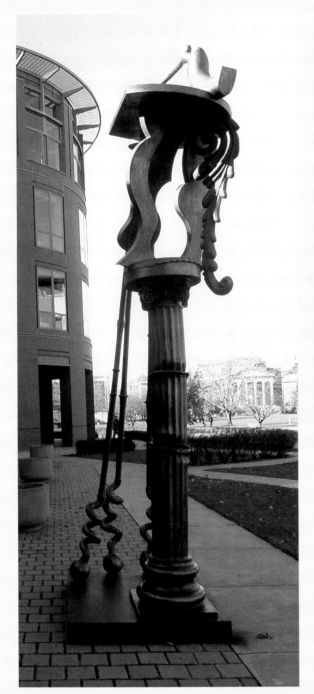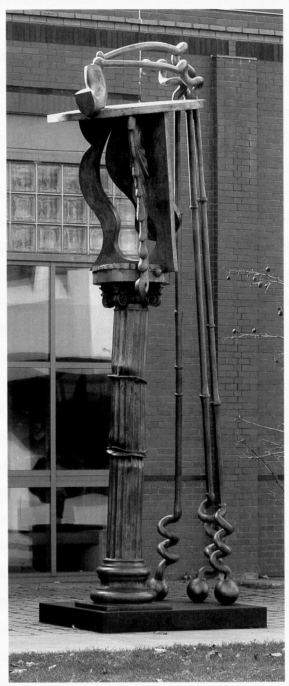

Rodger Mack, *The Oracle's Tears*, 1999. Cast and welded bronze, 17 × 6 × 4 ft (5.18 × 1.83 × 1.22 m).

chapter nine

Principles of Three-Dimensional Design

Composition can be defined as the combination of multiple parts into a unified whole. In a well-composed design, all of the elements work together, as a team. As one element becomes dominant, another element becomes subordinate. A dialogue is created between positive and negative forms, and opposing forces add vitality rather than causing confusion.

Each compositional part makes a positive contribution to an effective design. Graceful metal lines have been combined with a series of contoured masses to create the elegant and utilitarian form of Niels Diffrient's *Freedom Chair* (9.1). In Alice Aycock's *Tree of Life Fantasy* (see figure 9.9, page 224), line, plane, and space have been combined to create an exuberant dance. Every element is both dependent on and supportive of every other element. Martin Puryear's *Seer* (9.2) consists of a closed volume at the top and an open volume

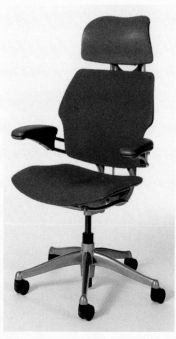

9.1 Niels Diffrient, *Freedom Chair*, 1999. Die-cast aluminum frame with fused plastic coating; four-way stretch black fabric.

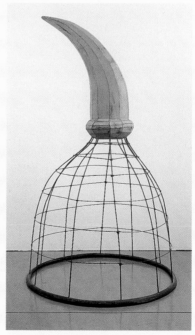

9.2 Martin Puryear, *Seer*, 1984. Water-based paint on wood and wire, 78 × 52¼ × 45 in. (198.2 × 132.6 × 114.3 cm).

at the bottom. The horn-shaped top piece is powerful and imposing, while the open construction at the bottom invites us to enter and visually explore the structure. A series of curving vertical "ribs" unifies the top and bottom sections, while the contrast between open and closed forms adds a touch of mystery. In both 9.1 and 9.2, the compositional parts work together to create a compelling whole.

The elements of design are the building blocks from which compositions are made. The principles of design describe ways in which these building blocks can be combined. Unity and variety are the overriding principles of three-dimensional design. Any composition gains when unity and variety are appropriately balanced. Balance, scale, proportion, emphasis, and rhythm are commonly listed as the other essential principles of design. These design principles can be used to create unity and variety.

UNITY AND VARIETY

Unity can be defined as similarity, oneness, togetherness, or cohesion. **Variety** can be defined as difference. Unity and variety are the cornerstones of composition.

Increasing Unity

We tend to scan an entire composition, then analyze the specific parts. A composition composed of units that are unrelated tends to appear random and unresolved. Evidence of deliberation and order tends to increase unity. Grouping, containment, proximity, continuity, repetition, and closure are six common strategies for increasing order.

Grouping

When presented with a collection of separate visual units, we immediately try to create order and make connections. **Grouping** is one of the first steps in this process. As noted in the discussion of Gestalt psychology in Chapter Three, we generally group visual units by location, orientation, shape, and color. *Many Times* (9.3), by Juan Muñoz, clearly demonstrates grouping by location. We first see a complete composition, comprised of seven figures. It is roughly triangular in shape, starting with the single seated figure on the right and extending to the standing figure at the far left. The division between the two sets of bleachers creates two subgroups, comprised of two figures on the right and five figures on the left. We can further group the three figures positioned on the top bleachers and the three figures on the bottom, with the single standing figure providing a visual exclamation point for the sculpture as a whole.

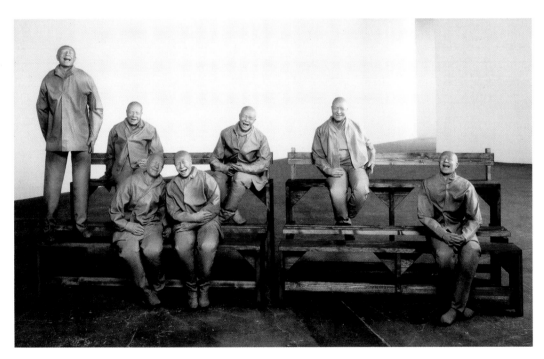

9.3 Juan Muñoz, *Towards the Corner*, 1998. Seven figures, wood, resin and mixed media.

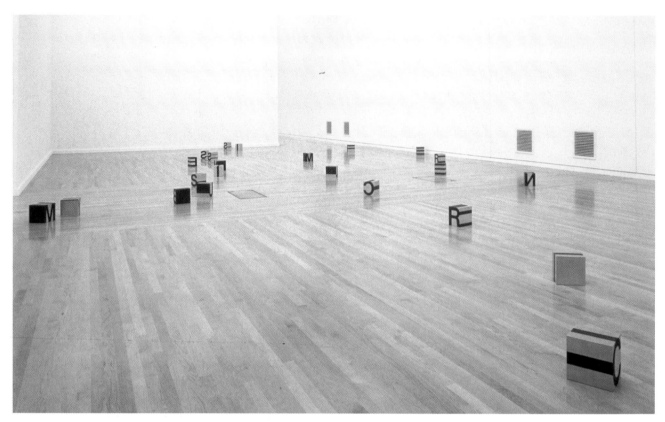

9.4 Roni Horn, *How Dickinson Stayed Home,* **1993.** Installation. Solid aluminum and plastic. 25 cubes, each 5 × 5 × variable lengths.

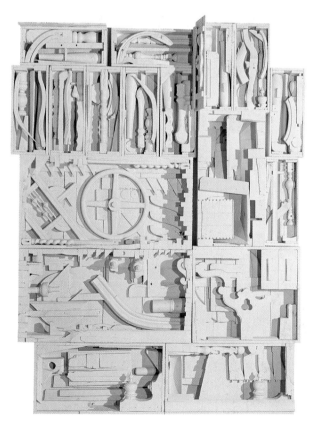

9.5A Louise Nevelson, *Wedding Chapel IV,* **1960.** Painted wood, height c. 9 ft. Private collection.

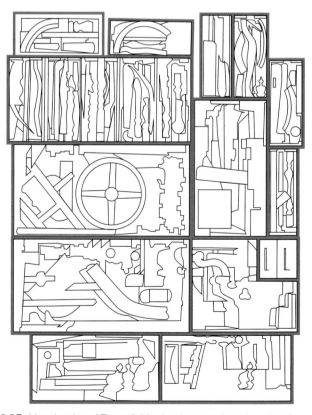

9.5B Line drawing of Figure 9.5A, showing containers in red and overall continuity in black.

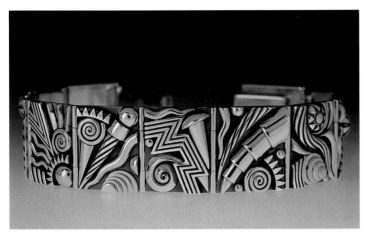

9.6 Aaron Macsai, *Panels of Movement.* Bracelet, 18K gold, sterling, copper, ⅞ × 7 in. (2 × 18 cm).

Containment

Containment is a unifying force created by the outer edge of a composition or by a boundary within a composition. A container encourages us to seek connections among visual units and adds definition to the negative space around each positive form. The room itself provides the container for Roni Horn's *How Dickinson Stayed Home* (9.4). Letters from the alphabet are presented on 25 small cubes. Like Emily Dickinson's poetry, the installation is both economical and expansive. A minimal amount of information evokes a wide range of interpretations. Contained by the white walls and dark floor of the room itself, the blocks create a unified statement, despite their seeming random distribution.

Proximity

In design, the distance between visual units is called **proximity.** Even the most disparate forms can become unified when they are placed in close proximity. For example, Louise Nevelson constructed *Wedding Chapel IV* (9.5A) from an improbable collection of wooden crates, staircase railings, dowels, chair legs, and other scrap. Organized into 14 rectilinear containers and placed in close proximity, the various pieces have become unified into a lively whole.

Continuity

Continuity can be defined as a fluid connection among compositional parts. When objects are placed in close proximity, continuity often happens naturally. As demonstrated by figure 9.5B, each form in

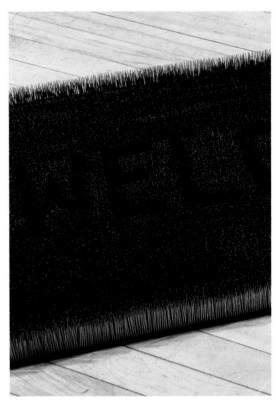

9.7 Mona Hatoum, *Doormat,* 1996. Stainless steel and nickel-plated pins, glue and canvas, 1 × 28 × 16 in. (2.5 × 71 × 40.6 cm).

Wedding Chapel IV touches several other forms. As a result, our eyes move easily from section to section, increasing connections among the parts.

Repetition

Repetition occurs when we use the same visual element or effect any number of times within a composition. In Aaron Macsai's *Panels of Movement* (9.6), similar lines, shapes, textures, and colors were used in each of the 10 panels from which the bracelet was constructed. A spiral shape, a wavy line, a sphere, and at least one triangular shape appear repeatedly. Despite their variations in size, texture, and location, these repeated forms create a strong connection from panel to panel.

Closure

Closure is the mind's inclination to connect fragmentary information to produce a completed form. In Mona Hatoum's *Doormat* (9.7), we must visually connect hundreds of steel pins to create the word *welcome.* Closure makes it possible to communicate using implication. Freed of the necessity to provide every detail, the artist or designer can convey an idea

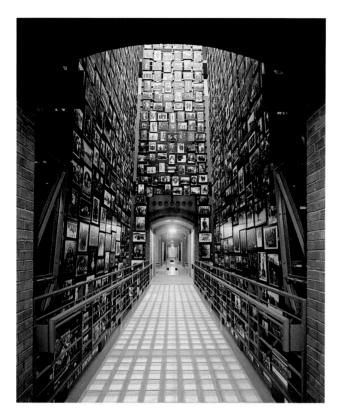

9.8 *Tower of Photos* **from Ejszyszki, Completed in 1993,** United States Holocaust Memorial Museum, Washington, DC. James Ingo Freed, lead designer.

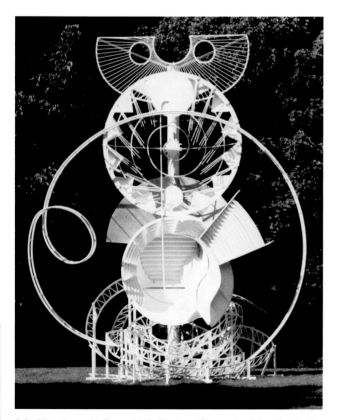

9.9 Alice Aycock, *Tree of Life Fantasy,* **Synopsis of the Book of Questions Concerning the World Order and/or the Order of Worlds, 1990–92.** Painted steel, fiberglass and wood, 20 × 15 × 8 ft (6.1 × 4.6 × 2.4 m).

through suggestion, rather than description. When the viewer completes the image in his or her mind, it is often more memorable than an explicit image.

Combining Unifying Forces

James Ingo Freed used all of these unifying forces to create the *Tower of Photos* in the Holocaust Museum in Washington, DC (9.8). His design team wanted to demonstrate the number of lives lost in one Polish village while honoring the individuality of the inhabitants. They collected and framed thousands of photographs, including groups of schoolchildren, weddings, and family snapshots. Placed in close proximity and relentlessly repetitive, the photographs personalized the victims while emphasizing their connection to the lost community. Based on the chimneys used to burn the bodies of the dead, the tower itself provides the dominant structure for the exhibition, both structurally and emotionally.

Increasing Variety

Difference in any aspect of a design increases variety. By reviewing the elements of design described in Chapter Eight and the principles of design described in this chapter, you can quickly create a checklist of areas for variation, such as

- *Line variation.* Lines of different diameter were combined with double linear "train tracks" in Aycock's *Tree of Life Fantasy* (9.9).

- *Variation in texture.* Combining smooth and textured surfaces can add energy and interest to even the simplest form.

- *Variation in pattern.* The Pacific island mask shown in figure 9.10 is unified through symmetrical balance. This underlying order freed the artist to experiment with many colors and patterns.

Degrees of Unity

Creating an effective partnership between unity and variety is essential. Excessive unity can be monotonous, while excessive variety can be chaotic. As noted in Chapter Seven, our compositional choices must support our conceptual intentions. Some

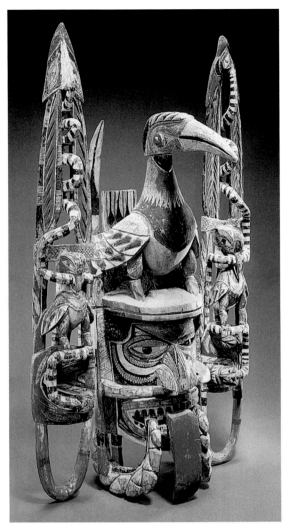

9.10 Mask (Wanis), New Ireland. 37 × 20⅞ × 19 in. (94 × 53 × 48.3 cm).

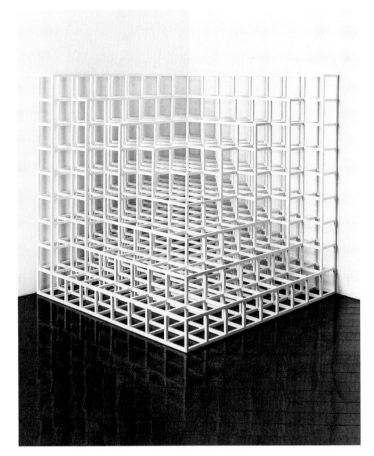

9.11 Sol LeWitt, *Wall/Floor Piece #4*, 1976. White painted wood, 43¼ × 43¼ × 43¼ in. (109.9 × 109.9 × 109.9 cm).

designs require a high level of unity. Based on a grid, Sol Lewitt's *Wall/Floor Piece #4* (9.11) provides a methodical transition from the horizontal floor to the vertical wall. Other designs require a high level of variety. The lines, shapes, volumes, and masses in Judy Pfaff's *Rock/Paper/Scissor* (9.12) ricochet off the floor, walls and ceiling with an almost chaotic energy.

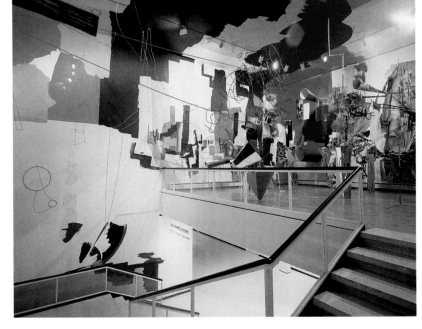

9.12 Judy Pfaff, *Rock/Paper/Scissor*, 1982. Mixed media installation at the Albright-Knox Art Gallery, Buffalo, NY, September 1982.

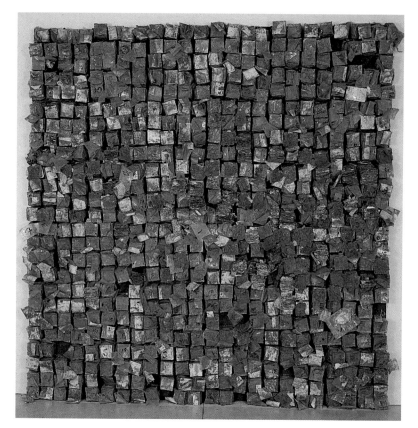

9.13 **Leonardo Drew,** *Number 56,* **1996.** Rust, plastic, wood, 113 × 113 in. (287 × 287 cm).

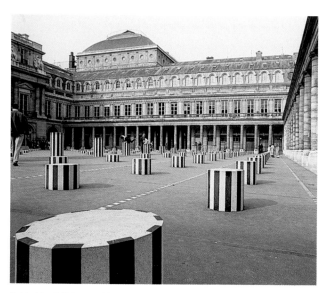

9.14 **Daniel Buren,** *The Two Plateaus,* **1985–86.** 1,000-square-foot sculpture for the Cour d'Honneur, Palais Royal, Paris. Black marble, granite, iron, cement, electricity, water.

Grid and Matrix

A **grid** is created through a series of intersecting lines. A **matrix** is a three-dimensional grid. Both can unify a design by creating containment, continuity, and proximity.

In *Number 56* (9.13), Leonardo Drew poured rust into hundreds of plastic bags, which were then connected to a wooden support. The rust and the relentlessly numbered plastic specimen bags create a dialogue between the orderly grid and the decaying metal. The resulting combination of order and disorder balances monotony and mystery.

Daniel Buren's *The Two Plateaus* (9.14) offers another variant on the grid. This public art project, located in the Palais Royal in Paris, covers a 1,000-square-foot plaza. The striped cylinders range in height from about 2 to 6 feet. Mimicking the columns in the building and organized on the pavement like players on a checkerboard, they bring both energy and humor to the site.

In *Current Disturbance* (9.15), Mona Hatoum used a matrix for unity and a sequence of lights for variety. A single clear lightbulb has been placed in each compartment within the structure. Controlled by a computer, these lights flicker in various patterns, from near darkness to a crescendo of illumination when all are lit. A single lit bulb in the center of the piece and the matrix itself are the only constants.

Key Questions

• What strategies have you used to unify your composition?

• What gives your composition variety?

• Is the balance between unity and variety appropriate for the ideas you want to express?

• What would happen if your composition were constructed using a pattern or grid?

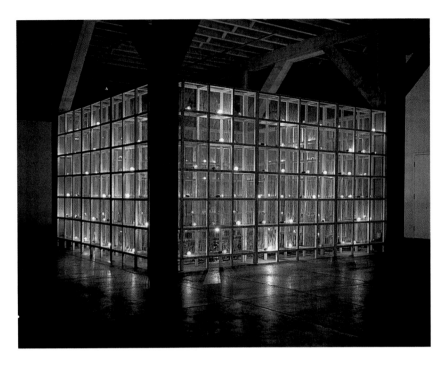

9.15 Mona Hatoum, *Current Disturbance,* 1996. Wood, wire mesh, lightbulbs, timed dimmer unit, amplifier, four speakers, 9 ft 2 in. × 18 ft × 16 ft 6 in. (279 × 550.5 × 504 cm).

BALANCE

In design, **balance** refers to the distribution of weight or force among visual units. For the architect, sculptor, and industrial designer, physical balance is a structural necessity, while a degree of visual balance is an aesthetic necessity. As with physical balance, visual balance requires equilibrium, or equality in size, visual weight, and force. Especially in three-dimensional design, visual balance can be created through the absence as well as the presence of form.

There are three major types of balance.

In **symmetrical balance,** forms are mirrored on either side of a central axis. The resulting form is generally physically and visually stable. The central face in figure 9.16A is an example of symmetrical balance.

With **radial symmetry,** design elements extend out from a central point, as with the spokes of a wheel. Radiating in all directions while remaining anchored at the center, this type of balance tends to generate a great deal of energy while retaining a high level of unity. The outer ring in figure 9.16 is an example of radial balance. Diagram 9.16B shows both of these forms of symmetry.

Asymmetrical balance creates equilibrium among visual elements that do *not* mirror each other

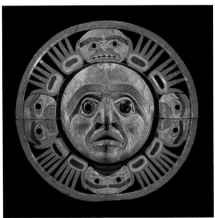

9.16A Bella Coola Mask Representing the Sun, from British Columbia, before 1897. Wood, diameter 24¾ in. (63 cm).

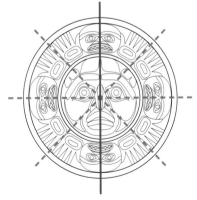

9.16B Diagram of Bella Coola mask. The central face is an example of symmetrical balance. The outer ring is an example of radial symmetry.

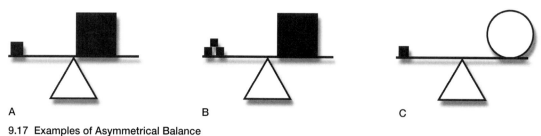

9.17 Examples of Asymmetrical Balance

on either side of an axis. Depending on the degree of asymmetry, the resulting design may be quite stable, very dynamic, or nearly chaotic. Many strategies can be used to create asymmetrical balance:

- A large form is placed close to the fulcrum, while a small form is placed farther away. Just as a child at the end of a seesaw can balance an adult near the center, so large and small forms can be balanced in a design (9.17A).

- Multiple small forms can balance a single large form (9.17B).

- A small, solid form can balance a large, open form. The solidity and stability of the square give it visual weight as well as physical weight (9.17C).

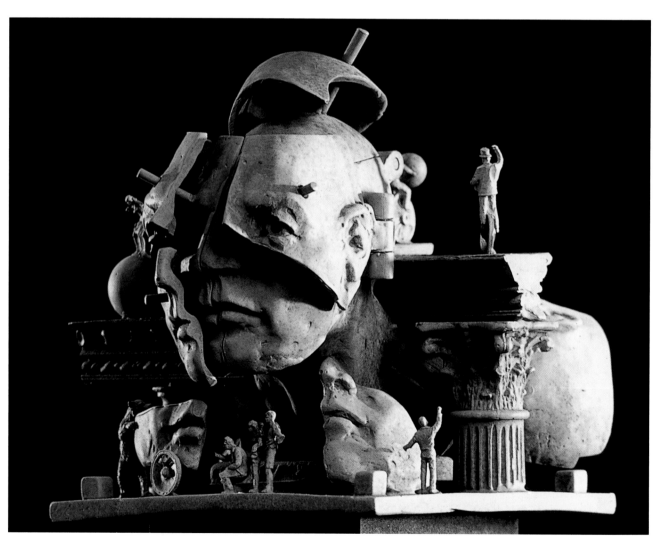

9.18 Theodore Gall, *Plaza Facets,* 2001. Cast bronze, 6 × 6 × 6 in. (15.2 × 15.2 × 15.2 cm).

Most artworks are constructed from multiple parts. Size variations among the parts affect both the physical balance and expressive impact. A **dominant,** or primary, form is often balanced by one or more **subordinate,** or secondary, forms. For example, in Theodore Gall's *Plaza Facets* (9.18), the large head on the left is balanced by the column and fragmentary heads on the right. The seven smaller figures create yet a third compositional level. Using these compositional hierarchies, artists and designers can create unified designs using distinctly individual parts.

Two contrasting interpretations of a single figure further demonstrate the expressive power of balance. Figures 9.19 and 9.20 both represent St. Bruno, an eleventh-century Catholic saint who founded an austere, contemplative religious group known as the Carthusian Order. Members lived in caves and devoted their time to manuscript transcription, meditation, and prayer.

The first statue, completed by Michel-Ange Slodtz in 1744, dramatizes a pivotal moment in Bruno's life. Preferring his contemplative existence to the power and prestige of a more public life, Bruno rejects promotion to the office of bishop. Slodtz used asymmetrical balance to express this dramatic moment. The small bishop's hat, proffered by the angel in the lower right corner is the focal point of the entire sculpture. The much larger figure of St. Bruno recoils when confronted by this symbol of authority. As a result, the small hat matches the power of the saint.

A very different interpretation of the life of St. Bruno is given in the second sculpture. Completed by Jean-Antoine Houdon in 1766, it emphasizes the contemplative nature of the Carthusian Order and its founder. Using symmetrical balance, Houdon presents a dignified, introspective man. If we divide the figure in half from top to bottom, the two sides basically mirror each other. This saint is a philosopher, very much at peace with the choices he has made. Just as asymmetrical balance is appropriate for the dramatic moment represented by Slodtz, so symmetrical balance is ideal for the serenity shown by Houdon.

Exaggerated weight or buoyancy can shift the balance in an artwork and enhance meaning. In Chuichi Fujii's *Untitled* (9.21), a cedar log seems to have been crushed by the weight of a second log.

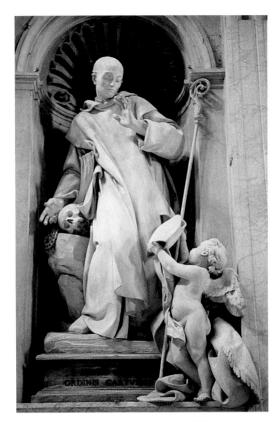

9.19 Michel-Ange Slodtz, *St. Bruno*, 1744. Marble.

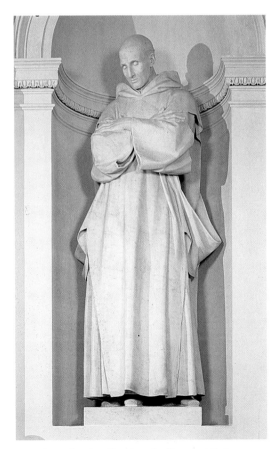

9.20 Jean-Antoine Houdon, *St. Bruno of Cologne*, 1766. Stucco.

The combination of the rough logs and the exaggerated weight seems to bring a powerful natural force into the pristine gallery. At the other extreme, Patricia A. Renick's *Life Boats/Boats About Life* (9.22) seems to float on air, as weightless as a dream. Dramatic lighting and cast shadows heighten the magical effect. This artwork derives its power from the denial of gravity.

Key Questions

- Which form of balance is most effective for the ideas you want to express?

- Which is the dominant form in your design? Is its dominance conceptually justified?

- What happens when an unexpected part of the design plays the dominant role?

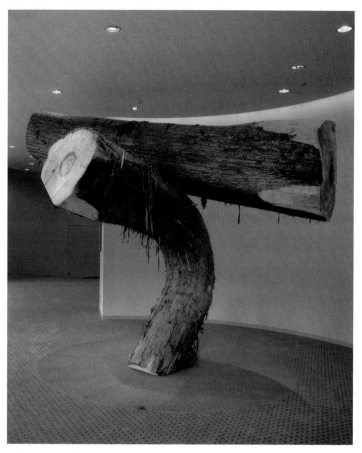

9.21 Chuichi Fujii, *Untitled,* 1987. Japanese cedar, 10 ft 6 in. × 13 ft ½ in. × 11 ft 6 in. (320 × 400 × 350 cm).

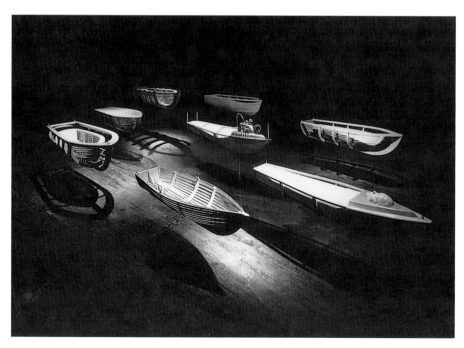

9.22 Patricia A. Renick, *Life Boats/Boats About Life,* 1979–80. 1 to 1½ ft high × 5 to 6½ ft long × 1 to 1½ ft deep (30.5 to 45.7 cm high × 152.4 to 198.1 cm long × 30.5 to 45.7 cm deep).

SCALE

Scale commonly refers to the size of a form when compared with human size. Using our bodies as a constant, we can identify three major types of scale relationships. Small-scale objects can be **hand-held,** while **human scale** refers to designs that are roughly our size. Very large objects and installations are **monumental** in scale.

Returning to Thomas Gall's sculpture, we can explore the implications of each scale type. The actual artwork is roughly 6 × 6 × 6 in. and can be hand-held. At this scale, we are invited to enter and explore the artwork mentally rather than physically (9.23A). At triple this size (18 × 18 × 18 in.), the dominant head in the design would be about the size of our own head (9.23B). This would create a very different dialogue between the audience and the artwork. Expanded to monumental scale — say, 32 × 32 × 32 feet — the artwork would invite physical entry (9.23C). We could now stand beside the sculptural figures in the piece. Simply by changing the scale, the artist could create three very different responses to the same composition.

PROPORTION

Proportion refers to the relative size of visual elements *within* an image. When we compare the width of the head with its height, or divide a composition into thirds, we are establishing a proportional relationship.

In industrial design, changes in proportion can enhance or diminish function. The five gardening tools in figure 9.24 are all based on the same basic combination of handle, blades, and a simple pivot. Variations in proportion determine their use. The short-handled pruner in the lower left corner is used to trim twigs and small branches from shrubs. It must fit comfortably in a single hand. The proportions of the lopper in the opposite corner are much different. Its 20-inch-long handle provides the leverage needed to cut heavier branches from small trees. For the industrial designer, function often determines proportion.

In sculpture, variations in proportion can increase aesthetic impact. Three proportional variations

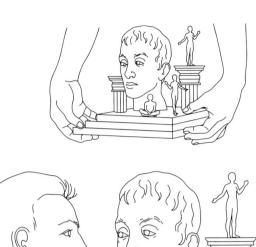

A

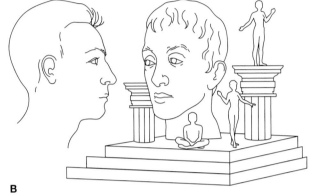

B

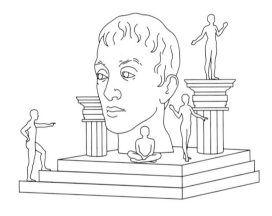

C

9.23 A–C Scale variations, from hand-held to monumental.

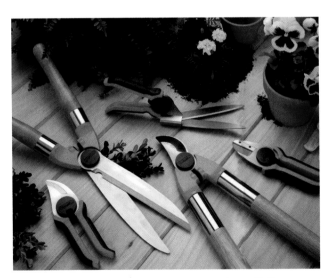

9.24 Home Pro Garden Tool Line. Designers: James E. Grove, John Cook, Jim Holtorf, Fernando Pardo, Mike Botich. Design Firm: Designworks/USA.

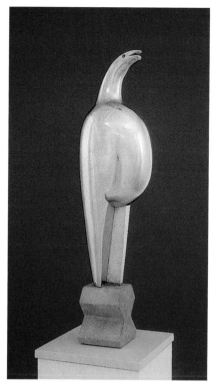

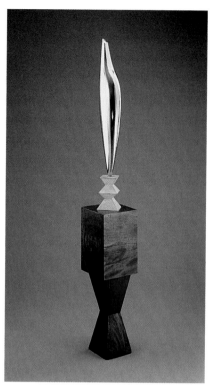

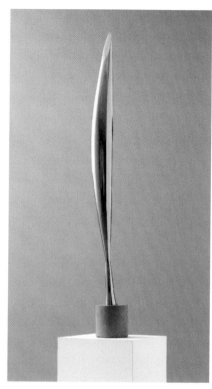

9.25 Constantin Brancusi, *Maiastra*, 1912. Polished brass, 29⅞ × 7¼ × 7½ in. (75.7 × 18.5 × 19 cm).

9.26 Constantin Brancusi, *Golden Bird*, 1919, Pedestal c. 1922. Bronze, stone, and wood, 37¾ in. h. (95.9 cm), base 48 in. h. (121.9 cm).

9.27 Constantin Brancusi, *Bird in Space*, 1928. Bronze (unique cast), 54 × 8½ × 6½ in. (137.2 × 21.6 × 16.5 cm).

of Constantin Brancusi's *Bird in Space* are shown in figures 9.25 through 9.27. In *Maiastra* (9.25), the abstract bird form is dominated by the egg-shaped torso, which tapers into the folded wings at the bottom and the raised head at the top. This bird is approximately 3 times taller than it is wide. Brancusi further abstracted *Golden Bird* (9.26) and elongated the body. The bird is now 7 times taller than it is wide, and an elaborate base adds even more height to the sculpture. With *Bird in Space* (9.27), Brancusi elongated the form even more and added an expanding "foot" below the folded wings. This bird is almost 10 times taller than it is wide. By lengthening the columnar structure in this final version and carefully tapering the sculpture near the base, Brancusi made this simple sculpture fly.

As with all design decisions, choosing the right scale and proportion greatly increases expressive power. Giovanni Bologna's *Apennine* (9.28) is scaled to overwhelm the viewer with a sense of the mountain spirit's presence. His human frame is monumental, and the surrounding trees and cliff appear to diminish by comparison.

Proportional extremes can be equally expressive. Standing just over 5 feet tall, Alberto Giacometti's *Chariot* (9.29) offers a somber analysis of the human condition. The solitary figure is delicately balanced on gigantic wheels, which then rest on two small pedestals. The entire form is linear, as if distilled down to the barest essentials. Both the chariot and the life it transports are precariously balanced and seem fragile and vulnerable.

Key Questions

• What would happen to your composition if you dramatically changed its scale?

• What would happen if you dramatically changed the proportions in your composition?

• Imagine that your design can be stretched or compressed in any direction. What are the advantages of a very tall, thin composition, compared with a short, cubic composition?

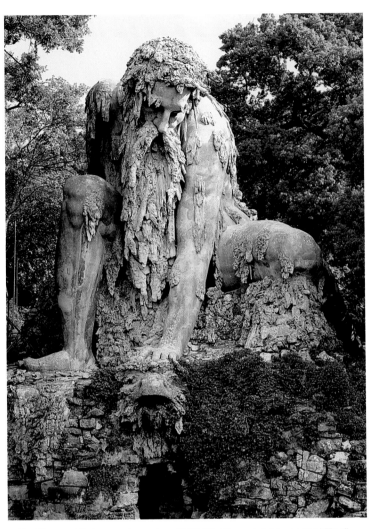

9.28 Giovanni Bologna, *Apennine*, 1580–82. Stone, bricks, mortar. Villa di Pratolino, Florence region, Italy.

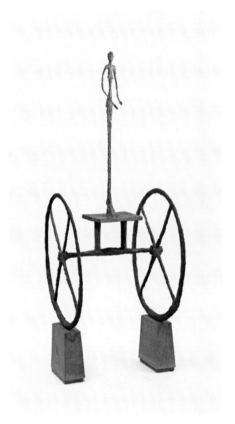

9.29 Alberto Giacometti, *Chariot*, 1950. Bronze, 57 × 26 × 26⅛ in. (144.8 × 65.8 × 66.2 cm).

EMPHASIS

Emphasis gives particular prominence to part of a design. A **focal point** is a compositional device used to create emphasis. For example, the bishop's hat in Slodtz's version of St. Bruno (figure 9.19, page 229) is the focal point of the composition. Both emphasis and focal point are used to attract attention and increase visual and conceptual impact.

Emphasis by Isolation

Any **anomaly,** or break from the norm, tends to stand out. Because we seek to connect the verbal and visual information we are given, a mismatched word or an isolated object immediately attracts attention. In *I Never Liked Musical Chairs* (9.30), metalsmith Joana Kao established the norm through

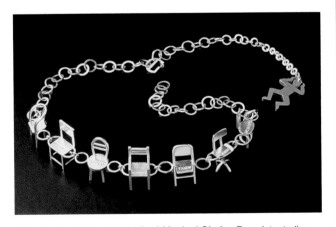

9.30 Joana Kao, *I Never Liked Musical Chairs.* Bracelet, sterling, 24K, 2¾ × 1¾ in. (7 × 4 cm).

seven tiny chairs connected by a silver chain. The figure at the end of the chain breaks the pattern. This break conveys the isolation felt by a child who has been ejected from the game.

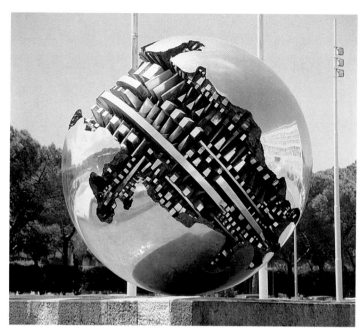

9.31 **Arnaldo Pomodoro**, *Sphere*, **1965**. Bronze, 47 in. (119.4 cm) diameter. Ministero degli Esteri, Rome.

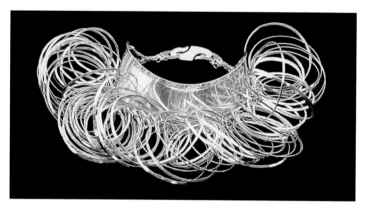

9.32 **Mary Ann Scherr**, *Loops*, **1988**. Sterling silver neckpiece, 8½ × 4¾ × 5 in. (21.6 × 12.1 × 12.7).

Emphasis Through Contrast

Contrast is created when two or more forces operate in opposition.

By reviewing the elements and principles of design discussed thus far, we can quickly create a long list of potential adversaries, including static/dynamic, small/large, smooth/textured, and curvilinear/rectilinear. When the balance is just right, powerful compositions can be created from any such combination. Many artists and designers devote most of their compositional area to one force and a much smaller amount to a contrasting force. The larger force sets the standard, while the smaller force creates the exception.

Contrast can appear in many forms and in varying degrees. Two opposing forces dominate Arnaldo Porudoro's *Sphere* (9.31). The imposing spherical form seems to have been eaten away by an external force, leaving a pattern of rectilinear teeth across its equator. This creates a strong contrast between the massive structure and the invading space, and adds rhythm and texture to the spherical form.

Loops (9.32), by Mary Ann Scherr, presents a contrast between movement and constraint. A curving plane encircles the user's throat, providing protection but restricting

9.33 **Pol Bury**, *Fountains at Palais Royal*, Paris, 1985.

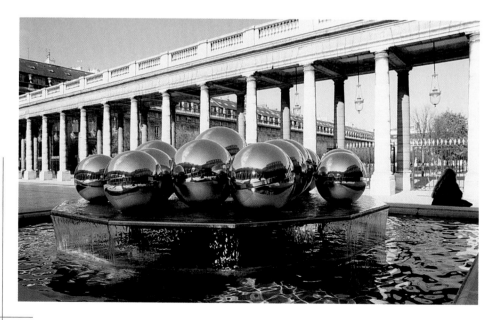

motion. Below, the suspended rings sway with every movement of the body, creating a dynamic counterpoint to the constraining collar.

Water animates Pol Bury's *Fountains at Palais Royal* (9.33). The design relies on three major elements. The site itself is dominated by the regularly spaced columns that are so characteristic of neoclassical architecture. The polished steel spheres, poised within the bowl of each foundation, reflect these columns and the shimmering water, which provides the third element in the design. In a sense, the spheres serve as mediators between the rigid columns and the silvery water. Like the columns, they are simple volumes, arranged in a group. Like the water, they seem fluid as they reflect the moving water and the passing clouds. In this project, unity and variety have been combined to create an elegant and ever changing sculpture.

Key Questions

- Is there a focal point in your composition? If not, should there be?

- What is the most prominent form in your composition? If so, is it the form you most *want* to emphasize?

- What would happen to your composition if you dramatically increased the amount of contrast?

REPETITION AND RHYTHM

As noted at the beginning of this chapter, *repetition* occurs when we use the same visual element or effect any number of times within a composition. **Rhythm** can be defined as the organization of these multiple elements or effects into a deliberate pattern. Just as a musician creates a deliberate pattern connecting sound and silence, so the artist can create rhythm using positive form and negative space. Using the CD-ROM, you can experiment with regular, alternating, progressive, and complex rhythm.

As with music, the number and distribution of beats create the rhythm. In David Watkins' *Torus 280*

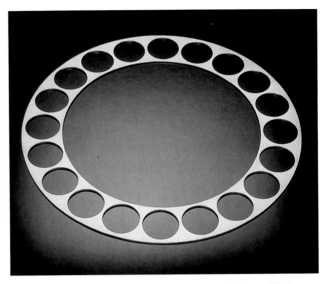

9.34 David Watkins, *Torus 280 (B2)*, 1989. Neckpiece, gilded brass, 11 in. (28 cm).

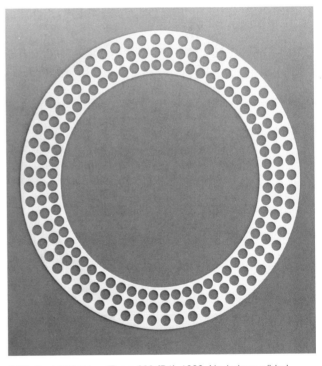

9.35 David Watkins, *Torus 280 (B1)*, 1989. Neckpiece, gilded brass, 11 in. (28 cm).

(B2) (9.34), the consistent order of the circular shapes creates a slow, regular pattern. When the number of circles multiplies in *Torus 280 (B1)* (9.35), the tempo, or pace, increases. As the neckpiece expands outward, the space between the circular openings also expands, creating greater variety in form. Rhythm plays an even greater role in figure

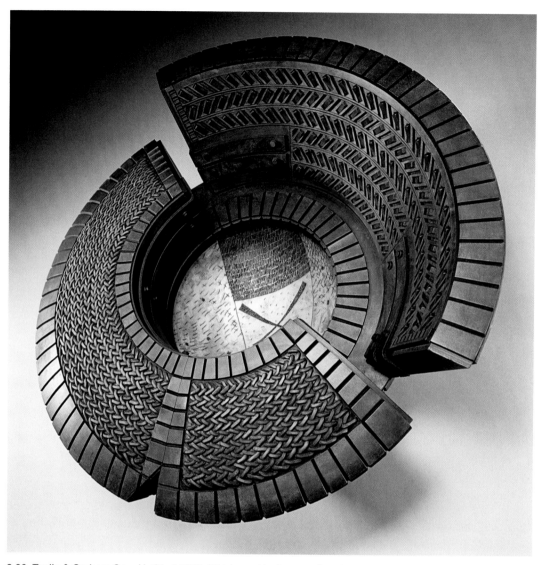

9.36 Tanija & Graham Carr, *Untitled,* **2001.** Wet-formed leather, acrylic paint, 13¾ × 29¼ × 29¼ in. (35 × 74 × 74 cm).

9.36. The woven herringbone pattern in the bottom suggests first a clockwise then a counterclockwise visual movement. A similar pattern at the top accentuates the spatial variations in the piece. Tapered rectilinear shapes create a border, around both the interior and the exterior edges. Like a complex musical piece, three types of rhythm have been skillfully woven together.

The multiple views offered by physical objects accentuate the importance of rhythm. The movement of four women around an exuberant musician creates a joyous dance in Jean-Baptiste Carpeaux's *The Dance* (9.37). Our eyes follow the turning heads, clasped hands, and swirling arms as they move in, out, and around in space. A similar rhythm ani-

mates Steve Woodward's *Model of Proposal for Concourse Commission* (9.38). The plywood vortex seems to rise out of the floor to collect in a spinning disk at the top, then descend again, in an endless pattern. When combined with the spinning effect, this up-and-down movement gives the design great vitality.

Repetition is often used to increase compositional unity. It can also be used to quantify an elusive idea. For example, the 30 statues in Magdalena Abakanowicz's *Standing Figures* (9.39) are unified by their similarity in size, shape, and solemnity. Variations in each cast bronze surface provide a degree of individuality. Often interpreted as victims of war, the hollow, headless figures seem frozen in time, offering a silent testimony to a tragic past. The 6,000

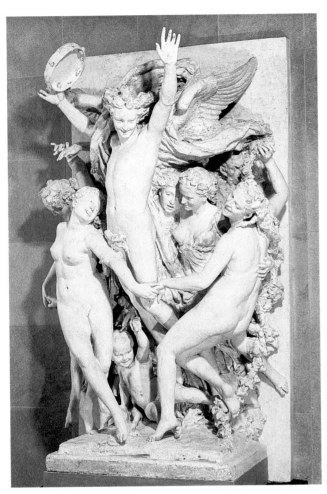

9.37 Jean-Baptiste Carpeaux, *The Dance (After Restoration),* **1868–69.** Marble, 7 ft 6½ in. (2.3 m).

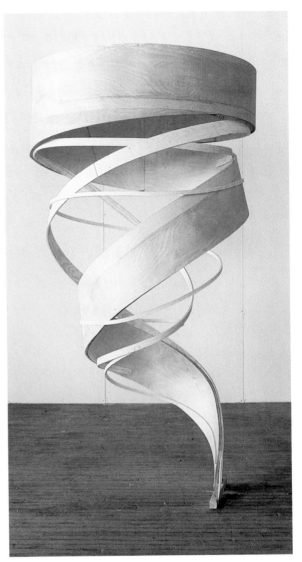

9.38 Steve Woodward, *Model of Proposal for Concourse Commission,* **1987.** Wood, 13¾ × 8 × 7½ in. (34.9 × 20.3 × 19 cm).

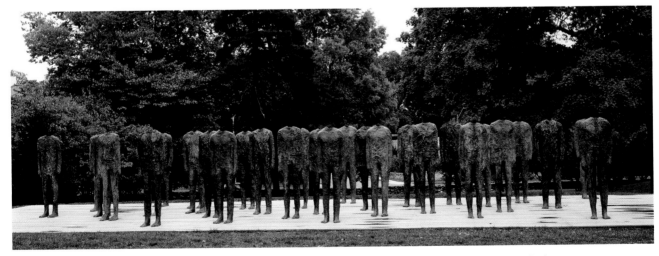

9.39 Magdalena Abakanowicz, *Standing Figures (30),* **1994–99.** Bronze, overall 54 ft 3 in. × 19 ft 8 in. (16.55 × 6 m).

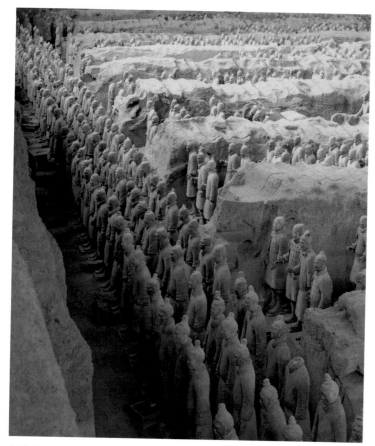

9.40 Tomb of Emperor Shih Huang Ti, 221–206 B.C. Painted ceramic figures, life size.

clay soldiers filling the tomb of Emperor Shih Huang Ti (9.40) demonstrate a different use of repetition. As he faced his death, the emperor may have sought companionship or protection from his army. Sherrie Levine's *La Fortune* (9.41) demonstrates a third use of repetition. Our sense of reality is challenged when we encounter these four pool tables. The identical arrangement of the balls seems impossible: the balls would be randomly distributed in four actual games. Here, a very ordinary scene becomes mysterious, even nightmarish, due to relentless repetition.

Key Questions

- Try repeating any element in your design. What does this repetition contribute, conceptually and compositionally?

- What happens when simple repetition is changed to specific rhythm?

- Does the rhythm remain constant in your design, or is there a change in pace? What is the advantage of each approach?

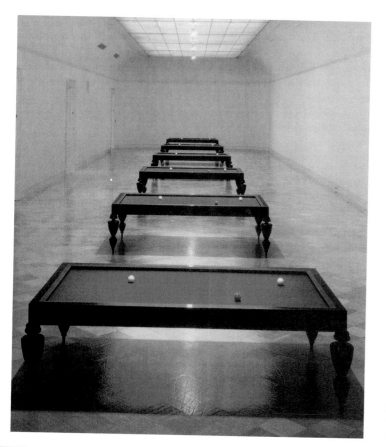

9.41 Sherrie Levine, *La Fortune* **(After Man Ray) 1–6, 1990.** Felt, mahogany, resin, 33 × 110 × 60 in. (84 × 280 × 153 cm).

SUMMARY

- Through composition, we can combine multiple parts to create a unified whole.

- Grouping, containment, proximity, repetition, continuity, and closure are six common strategies for increasing unity. Difference in any aspect of a design increases variety.

- A grid is created through a series of intersecting lines. A matrix is a three-dimensional grid.

- Symmetry, radial symmetry, and asymmetry are three common forms of balance. A dominant, or primary, form is often balanced by one or more subordinate, or secondary, forms.

- Scale and proportion are two types of size relationships. Proportion refers to size relationships within an image, while scale involves a size comparison with our physical size.

- Emphasis gives prominence to a specific part of a design. A focal point is a compositional device used to create emphasis.

- Contrast is created when two or more forces operate in opposition. Many artists and designers devote most of their compositional area to one force and a much smaller amount to a contrasting force. The larger force sets the standard, while the smaller force creates the exception.

- Repetition occurs when we use the same visual element or effect any number of times within a composition. Rhythm is the organization of these multiple elements or effects into a deliberate pattern. Just as a musician creates a deliberate pattern connecting sound and silence, so the artist can create rhythm using positive form and negative space.

Keywords

anomaly	contrast	human scale	rhythm
asymmetrical balance	dominant	matrix	scale
balance	emphasis	monumental	subordinate
closure	focal point	proportion	symmetrical balance
composition	grouping	proximity	unity
containment	grid	radial symmetry	variety
continuity	hand-held	repetition	

Profile:
David MacDonald, Ceramicist

A Passion for Pottery

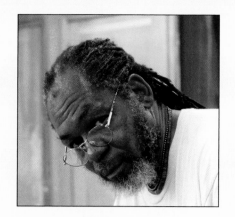

Internationally renowned ceramicist David MacDonald is best known for his work with utilitarian vessels. His work has been included in over 60 exhibitions, including the Torpedo Factory Art Center in Alexandria, Virginia; The Studio Museum in Harlem; and the Afro-American Historical and Cultural Museum in Philadelphia. He is also renowned as community leader, with work in an adult literacy program, a summer ceramics intensive program for high school students, and work with inmates at the Green Haven Maximum Security Correctional Facility in New York State to his credit.

MS: How did you start making art?

DM: Initially, it was a way to create some private space. As the third in a family of nine children, I always shared a bedroom with at least three of my brothers. I would help my parents unpack the groceries, then unfold the paper bags so that I could use the inside as drawing paper. Through hours of drawing, I was able to create my own little world.

MS: In our conversations and in viewing your work, I am struck by your passion for ceramics in general and functional vessels in particular. What is special about clay?

DM: I was introduced to ceramics during my second year in college. I was immediately fascinated by clay: it is responsive to the slightest pressure and can record the finest impression. After my first mug came out of the kiln and I made my first cup of tea, I was hooked. The idea of turning a lump of dirt into a useful object amazed me. Since I grew up with very little material wealth, I loved the idea of transforming nothing into something.

Now, I am drawn to functional ceramics because I like playing with the interaction between the object and the user. Having to produce a functional object makes the creative act much more interesting and challenging for me. When a teapot has just the right weight, balance, and proportions, it makes the act of pouring tea a celebration of the physical world.

MS: What is the source of your ideas?

DM: Anything can become a conscious or unconscious inspiration. I can get lost in the produce section of the supermarket: the shapes and colors of the vegetables give me all sorts of ideas.

On a more scholarly level, I was influenced by Japanese and Chinese ceramics during college, and for the past 20 years, I have been strongly influenced by African art and culture.

MS: Yes, I notice that a dramatic change in your work occurred around 1978. Before that time, your work was sculptural, representational, and highly charged politically; afterward, it became more utilitarian and abstract. What happened?

DM: At the opening for a solo show in Syracuse, I was asked a question by an elderly white woman that dramatically changed my attitude about my work. She innocently asked if there was anything positive about being black in America or was it just one frustration and humiliation after another. The question haunted me for months afterward. I realized that my creative work had been based on anger and a feeling of victimization. As I matured as an individual, I realized that my experiences weren't limited to anger — there is much more to my life than that! I then decided to tap the rich and varied cultural and artistic tradition to which I am heir. Now I am most interested in expressing the magnificence and nobility of the human spirit and in celebrating my African heritage.

MS: What distinguishes a great pot from a mundane pot?

DM: There is no simple answer to this question. We can talk endlessly about form, surface, line, and so forth and still not gain any real insight into what makes one pot great and another mundane, yet we immediately feel it when the mixture of physical elements is just right. Out of the 30 similar bowls a potter produces, 2 or 3 always seem to stand apart, as something special.

The search for this elemental quality makes my art magical and compels me to make the next piece. Ironically, if I ever identify exactly what it is that makes an exceptional piece, the excitement will be sucked out of the creative process. The search is as compelling as the solution.

MS: Tell me about the vessel pictured here.
DM: *Carved Stoneware Jar* was inspired by the bulbous form of a melon or gourd. The body is full and round and the lid handle is suggestive of a stem. I like the sense of an internal force or energy stretching the outer shell almost to the point of bursting.

First, I considered the function of the jar. To a large extent, the function determines the form. A certain size range facilitates everyday use. If the size is increased, the object is more suitable for ceremonial use, or as a decorative object. Certain shapes offer more storage capacity and better accessibility to whatever is being stored. Finally, the base must be big enough to provide stability.

The surface was carved when the jar was leather-hard, a couple of days after being thrown on the potter's wheel. A form this large can "carry" a fairly complex pattern, composed of smaller shapes in combination with larger design areas. By leaving some areas uncarved, I was able to create an overlapping effect and increase the illusion of space. The slashing diagonal lines help to unify the design and move the viewer's eye around the form, reinforcing the spherical volume.

MS: What were the most valuable lessons you learned from your teachers?
DM: From Joseph Gilliard at Hampton University, I learned the history and technique of ceramics and gained greater patience and self-control. I developed my self-awareness and passion for communication through my work with Robert Stull at the University of Michigan. From Henry Gernhardt, my Syracuse University colleague for 24 years, I learned that teaching is also an art. In nearly 40 years of teaching, Henry's commitment to his art and his students never faltered.

MS: Is there any advice you would like to give to my students?
DM: An artist has to believe in him- or herself. The dedication, courage, and energy my students bring to the classroom are more important than anything I can offer. If you want to stand above the crowd, your passion for your art must be manifest through a willingness to work harder than anyone else. The students who succeed see their art as a way of life and not simply as a way of earning a living. My job as a teacher is to help my students realize their potential and to bring eloquence to their unique voice.

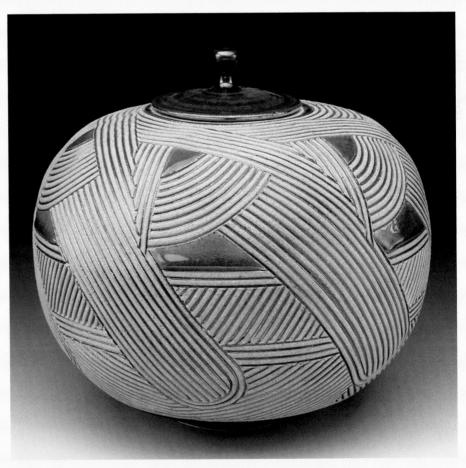

David MacDonald, *Carved Stoneware Storage Jar*, 1997. 15 in. (38.1 cm).

Materials and Methods

An incredible range of materials and methods can be used to produce three-dimensional objects. Paper, metal, fibers, clay, and plastic are among the most versatile materials used by artists and designers; folding, casting, carving, weaving, and stamping are just a few of the production methods. A separate course specifically devoted to materials would be needed if we were to explore this subject in depth.

The purpose of this chapter is more pragmatic. As a beginner, you need both practical advice and a basic introduction to the aesthetic implications of various materials. We will begin with a discussion of the essential characteristics of materials, then consider ways in which contemporary artists use traditional materials. The last section is devoted to student materials used in many three-dimensional design courses.

CHOICE OF MATERIALS

Each material has specific strengths and limitations. For example, rubber cement is a temporary adhesive for ordinary paper, while white glue is an effective permanent adhesive for heavier paper and cardboard. Carpenter's glue works well for wood, while hot glue is an effective adhesive for assemblage materials. Misuse of any material can ruin a great design. By understanding the physical characteristics of common materials, we can produce better work in less time and at less cost. The following considerations are crucial:

- *Strength.* How much weight can a given material support? What is its breaking point when twisted, folded, or bent?

- *Workability.* How difficult is it to alter the shape of a material? Does it cut and bend easily? Can it be melted and cast or dripped to create a new form?

- *Durability.* What range of forces can this material withstand and for how long? Is it impervious to heat, water, wind, and ultraviolet light?

- *Weight.* A material that is too light for a given purpose can be as problematic as a material that is too heavy. What is the function of the project, and how can material weight serve that function?

- *Cost.* Can the material chosen be obtained easily and at a reasonable cost? If your budget is limited, expensive materials may have to be removed from consideration.

- *Toxicity.* Many plastics produce toxic gases when cut, etched, or burned. Paints and solvents may require the use of masks and gloves and often present significant disposal problems. Is the ventilation of your workplace appropriate for your work process? Are less toxic materials available?

- *Function.* Most important, how appropriate is a given material for a particular purpose? A teapot will be useless if the material used is porous, and a chair that is too difficult to construct will never be mass-produced. Any material chosen must serve the structural and aesthetic needs of the object you plan to produce.

Increasing Material Strength

Composites

A **composite** is created when two or more materials of differing strengths are fused together. Fiberglas (which combines glass filaments with plastic resin) and ferro-concrete (which is made from metal mesh embedded in concrete) are familiar examples. Foamcore (which is made from a sheet of polystyrene sandwiched between sheets of coated paper) and duct tape (constructed from three layers of "skin") are composites that are commonly used in three-dimensional design classes. Composites are often used when light weight, low cost, and increased strength are required.

Structural Strength

After years of experimentation, nature has developed an amazing array of effective structures. Two major types are skeletons (also called endoskeletons) and exoskeletons. A **skeleton** provides the internal structure needed by mammals and fish, while insects and many sea creatures rely on an external **exoskeleton** for support.

Architects are masters of both skeletal and exoskeletal structures. In his Guggenheim Museum Bilbao (10.1), architect Frank Gehry created a complex "skeleton" to support the building's gleaming titanium skin. The Gothic cathedral in figure 10.2 demonstrates the use of an exoskeleton. To increase

10.1 Computer-generated Catia image used for the Solomon R. Guggenheim Museum Bilbao, finished 1997.

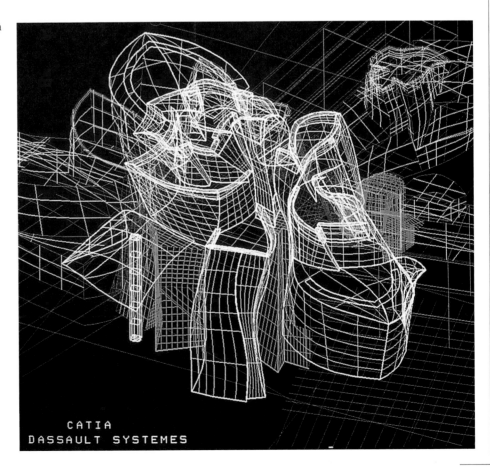

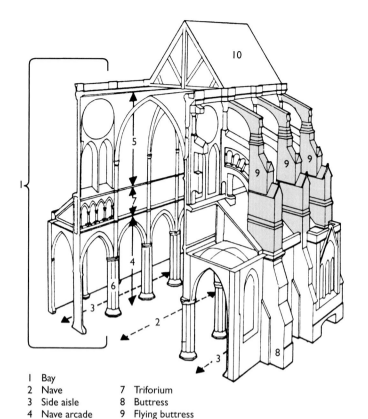

1	Bay
2	Nave
3	Side aisle
4	Nave arcade
5	Clerestory
6	Cluster pier with colonettes
7	Triforium
8	Buttress
9	Flying buttress
10	Wooden roof

10.2 Perspective diagram and cross-section of Chartres Cathedral.

building height while reducing mass, medieval architects developed the **flying buttress** used in hundreds of cathedrals throughout Europe. These external structures provided the primary support for many remarkable buildings.

Artists and designers often use an **armature** to create internal structure. For example, a wire or wooden armature is often used to support the cloth or paper used in lampshades. Designers from around the world have created an amazing range of variations on this simple object (10.3). Engineer Gustav Eiffel developed a much more elaborate armature to support Auguste Bartholdi's *Statue of Liberty* (10.4). Standing over 150 feet tall and weighing 225

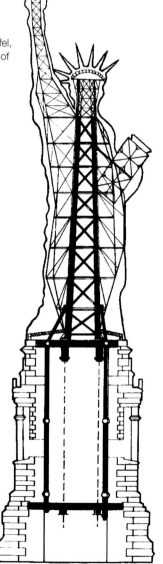

10.4 Alexander-Gustave Eiffel, diagram of the construction of the Statue of Liberty.

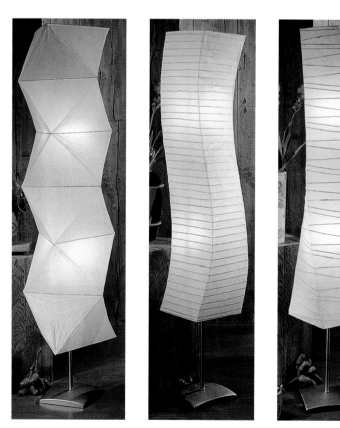

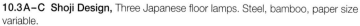

10.3 A–C Shoji Design, Three Japanese floor lamps. Steel, bamboo, paper size variable.

tons, this monumental sculpture has to withstand wind, rain, and brisk sea winds. Without a strong internal structure, the statue could never have been built.

Distributing Force

As shown in figure 10.5, the five major forces are **compression, tension, bend, torque,** and **shear.** The equilateral triangle is the linear shape that best resists deformation by all of these forces, and the tetrahedron, or pyramid, is the strongest three-dimensional form. A triangular support, such as a corner brace on the back of a painting, can distribute force effectively and greatly increase strength. On a larger scale, a network of crossbeams in Thorncrown Chapel (10.6) adds both strength and beauty to a sacred space. R. Buckminster Fuller's geodesic

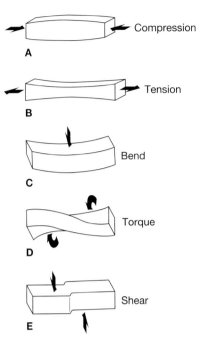

10.5A–E Major physical forces.

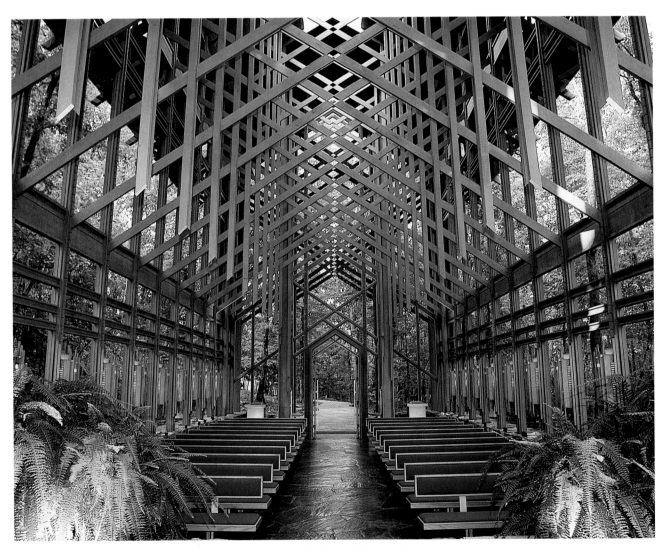

10.6 E. Fay Jones & Associates, Thorncrown Chapel, Eureka Springs, Arkansas, 1981.

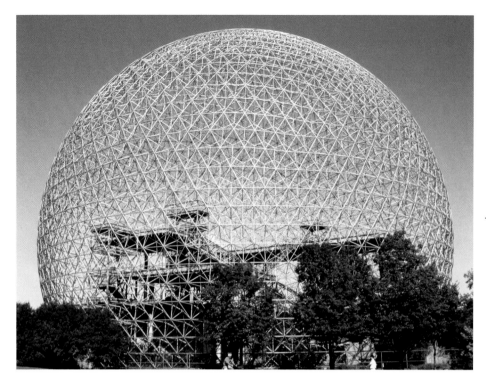

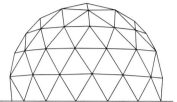

10.7 R. Buckminster Fuller, U.S. Pavilion, Expo-67, Montreal, 1967.

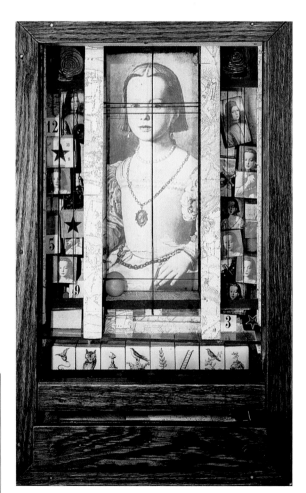

10.8 Joseph Cornell, *Untitled (Medici Princess)*, c. 1948. Construction, 17⅞ × 11⅛ × 4⅜ in. (44.8 × 28.3 × 11.1 cm).

dome (10.7) expands this idea even further. Typically constructed using hundreds of tetrahedrons, the dome is relatively easy to build and creates a large volume using a minimal amount of mass. A model of beauty and efficiency, the geodesic dome has been widely used for large, open buildings, such as greenhouses and airplane hangars.

Methods of Construction

Compositional choices are strongly influenced by the method of construction. The two most common methods are addition and subtraction.

In **additive sculpture,** the artwork is created from separate parts that have been connected, usually using glues, joints, stitching, or welds. **Assemblage** is one additive method. Using objects and images that were originally designed for another purpose, Joseph Cornell created a whole series of evocative box structures (10.8). Many of these assemblages were designed to honor specific people, past or present. **Modeling** is an additive process often used by ceramicists. Pinching and pushing the pliable clay, skillful ceramicists can make both functional and sculptural objects of great complexity. To create his *Head Series* (10.9), Jean-Pierre Larocque stamped slabs of clay with various textures from cloth, then modeled and carved a head that is both activated and imposing.

In **subtractive sculpture,** the artist removes materials from a larger mass. Carving, drilling, cutting, and turning on a lathe are all subtractive processes. The Tlingit man shown in figure 10.10 follows a methodical process, beginning by drawing on the cedar pole, making a rough cut, then refining and finishing the totem pole.

Plastic and metal forms are often produced using two additional methods. With **solidification,** a liquid material is poured into a mold or extruded through a pipe, then allowed to harden. For example, when we squeeze cake frosting through a shaped nozzle, we can create a wide range of extruded forms. This same basic principle can be applied to materials that are more permanent and less tasty. With **displacement,** a solid material is physically forced into a new configuration. The stamping process used to mint coins is a familiar example of displacement.

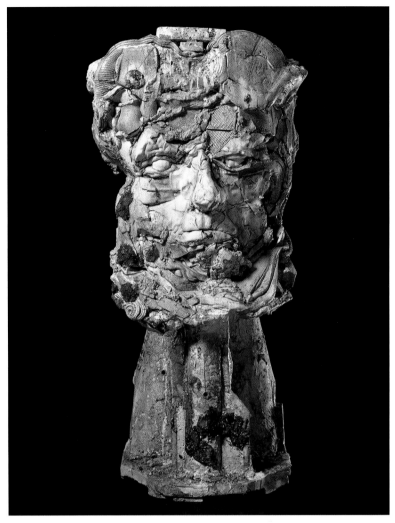

10.9 Jean-Pierre Larocque, *Untitled (Head series),* **2002.** Stoneware, 36¾ × 21 in. (93.3 × 53.3 cm).

10.10 **Tlingit Totem Carver, 1996.** Southeast Alaska.

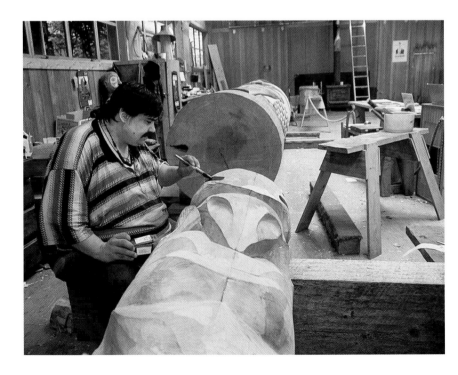

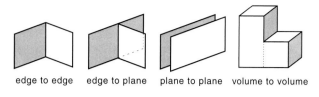

edge to edge edge to plane plane to plane volume to volume

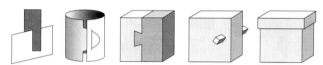

edge to edge edge to plane plane to plane mass to mass

10.11A Connections Through Contact.

10.11B Connections Through Junctions.

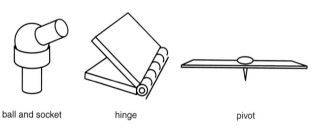

ball and socket hinge pivot

10.11C Connections Through Joints.

CONNECTIONS

Physical and visual connections are equally important in three-dimensional design. Visual connections compositionally unify multiple surfaces, while physical connections can increase strength, flexibility, functionality, and stability. Connections can be created

- Through contact (10.11A)
- Through junctions (10.11B)
- Through joints (10.11C)

Physical connections are especially important to woodworkers. Carpenters and furniture designers learn dozens of specific joints, hinges, and splices. Mary Miss's *Staged Gates* (10.12A) was largely constructed using three types of joints (10.12B). Nails, screws, bolts, or glue is required when lap or butt joints are used. Interlocking joints can often create a simple connection without such additional reinforcement.

Employed to create functional objects, industrial designers pay particular attention to all types of connections. Because of the various joints used,

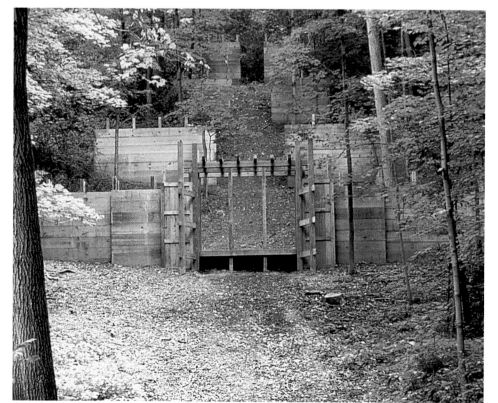

10.12A Mary Miss, *Staged Gates*, 1979. Wood, 12 × 50 × 120 ft (3.6 × 15.2 × 36.6 m).

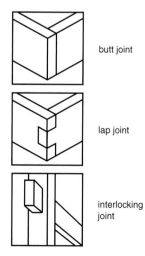

butt joint

lap joint

interlocking joint

10.12B Three Types of Joints.

the simple camera tripod can be expanded or collapsed, and the top can be rotated and reoriented. A model of a human figure (10.13) presents an even wider array of possibilities. Ball-and-socket joints at the shoulders and hips create rotating forms, while the hinge joints in the fingers, knees, and elbows permit a folding and unfolding movement. The spine is a marvel of engineering. Comprised of 24 stacked vertebrae, it provides a highly flexible framework for the entire torso.

Visual connections are just as important as physical connections. A split yellow-orange circle dominates the center of John Okulick's *Wind Wizard* (10.14). Through closure, we mentally connect the halves, despite their physical separation. A second broken circle echoes the interior circle and creates a dynamic boundary for the composition as a whole. The two gold spheres at the upper left and lower right seem poised for movement. Every form is connected to at least one other form, enhancing overall continuity.

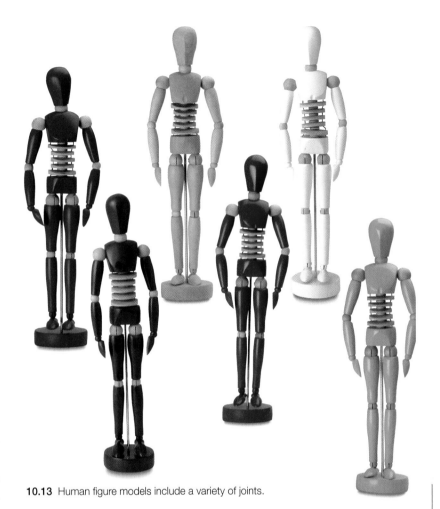

10.13 Human figure models include a variety of joints.

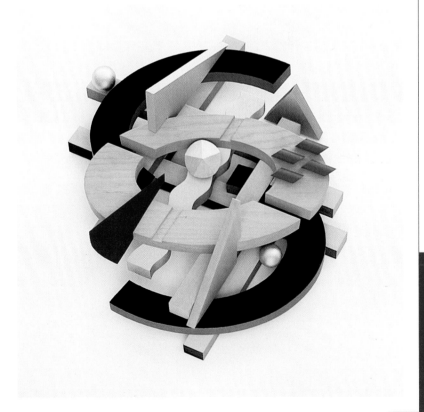

10.14 John Okulick, *Wind Wizard*, **1987.**
Painted wood, gold leaf, oil stick, 22 × 25 × 6 in.
(55.9 × 63.5 × 15.2 cm).

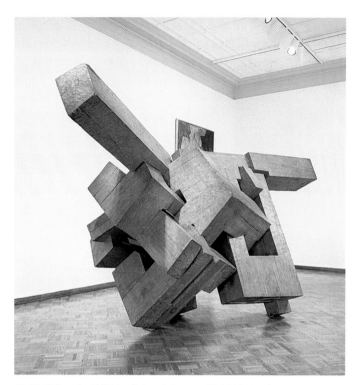

10.15 **Eduardo Chillida,** *Asbesti Gogora III*, **1962–64.** Oak, 81½ × 136⅜ × 73⅛ in. (207.3 × 346.4 × 184.2 cm).

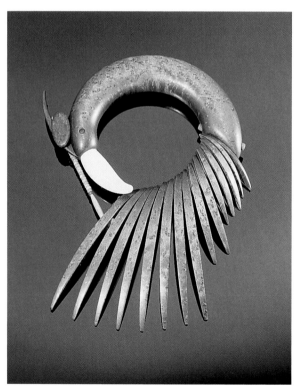

10.16 **Liv Blåvarp,** *Bird*, **1991.** Neckpiece, birdseye maple, satinwood, whaletooth, 12½ × 10¼ in. (32 × 26 cm).

TRANSITIONS

Many types of transitions can be created in three-dimensional design. The various angles and joints in Eduardo Chillida's *Asbesti Gogora III* (10.15) create an abrupt transition from surface to surface, while a fluid transition helps unify the various sections of Liv Blåvarp's *Bird* (10.16). Fluid transitions are often created through gradual change from one form or surface to another. Such **gradation** creates sequential change within a consistent pattern. Figure 10.17 shows a few of the many types of gradation.

TRADITIONAL MATERIALS, CONTEMPORARY USES

Stone

Limestone, basalt, marble, and other dense, fine-grained stones have been used since prehistory to create durable and imposing objects. Hand-held stone amulets have been worn to ward off evil, while monumental sculptures, such as Mount Rushmore and the pyramids at Giza, have been used to commemorate political and religious figures and beliefs. Using chisels, mallets, and rasps, stone carvers can create remarkably delicate forms using an amazing array of textures.

Contemporary artist Anish Kapoor is especially intrigued by the relationship between space and substance. Rather than viewing these forces as simple opposites, he often creates sculptures and installations exploring the essential connection between the two. *Void Field* (10.18) is one example. Kapoor notes:

> It's a work about mass, about weight, about volume, and then at the same time seems to be weightless, volumeless, ephemeral; it's really turning stone into sky. The darkness inside the stones is the darkness of black night, the darkness of sky.[1]

By drilling small, cylindrical openings into 16 massive block of sandstone, Kapoor was able to exaggerate the physicality of a durable stone and emphasize the significance of the interior space.

Wood

Traditional cultures worldwide use wood to create functional structures, such as buildings, furniture, and utensils, as well as sculptural objects, such as masks, ancestor poles, and walking sticks. Readily available in most areas, wood is inherently beautiful, easily painted, relatively light-weight, and surprisingly versatile. It can be carved, steam-formed, and assembled using various hinges and joints.

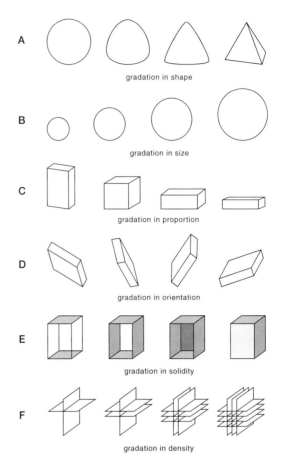

A   gradation in shape

B   gradation in size

C   gradation in proportion

D   gradation in orientation

E   gradation in solidity

F   gradation in density

10.17A–F Examples of Gradation.

10.18 Anish Kapoor, *Void Field*, **1989.** Sixteen sandstone elements.

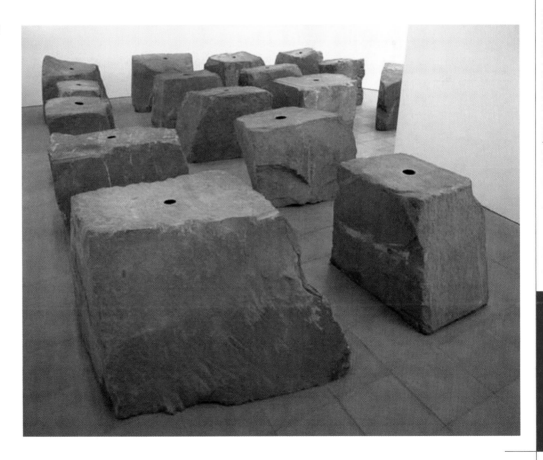

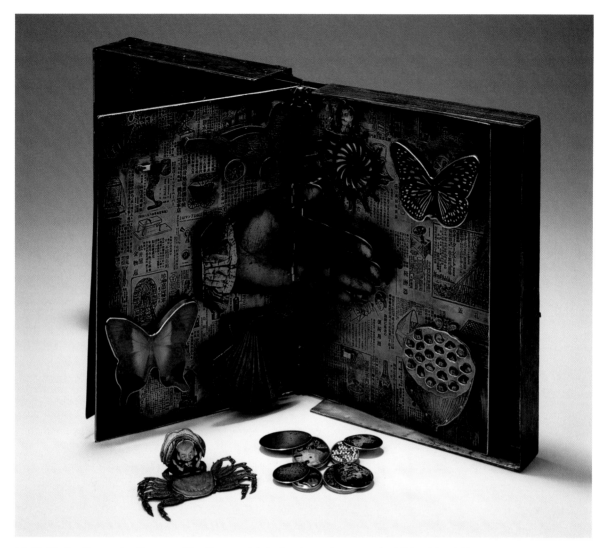

10.19 Mariko Kusumoto, *Tansu no Oku.* Copper, nickel, silver, brass, bronze, resin, 15½ × 14 × 14 in. (39.4 × 35.6 × 35.6 cm) open.

Metals

Bronze casting, refined during the Renaissance, has traditionally been used for large-scale sculptures of all kinds. Gold, silver, copper, pewter, and brass are more commonly used for jewelry and utensils. Most metals can be cast, forged, soldered, etched, and stamped.

Mariko Kusumoto used copper, nickel silver, sterling silver, resin, bronze, and brass to create *Tansu no Oko* (10.19). A lotus blossom, seashells, butterflies, and an open hand extend out from an etched sheet of turn-of-the-century advertisements. A plastic resin adds color and sparkle to the butterflies. The structure is based on a children's pop-up book, while the images recall the Victorian fascination with mechanical and natural objects.

Clay

Clay is perhaps the most basic and versatile of all materials. Essentially made from refined earth, it can be hand-formed using coil, slab, and carving techniques; poured into molds; and "thrown," using a potter's wheel. When fired, it becomes extremely durable and can be decoratedwith beautiful colored glazes. All of these qualities are exploited fully by contemporary ceramicists and potters.

Glass

Glass, which is made primarily from silica, has been used for containers of all kinds since the time of the pharaohs. It can be transparent or opaque and, with the addition of copper, cadmium, cobalt, and other materials, can take on a complete range of colors. In its molten state, it can be poured, blown, pressed into molds, drawn into threads, stamped, and extruded.

The transparency of glass is emphasized in Eric Hilton's *Innerland* (10.20). Constructed from 25 cubes of clear glass, the sculpture appears to shift with each change in the viewer's position. Hilton combined the transparency and brilliance of glass with its density and mass to create an artwork that is both formidable and evocative.

Fibers

The term *fibers* covers a wide range of linear materials, including strips of willow, bamboo, and reeds, as well as the more familiar cotton, linen, silk, and wool. As with the other traditional materials, fibers have been used for basketry, quilts, clothing, and other commonplace objects, as well as prayer rugs and ritual clothing, from shrouds to wedding dresses. Most fibers can be painted or dyed and can be constructed in many ways, including weaving, braiding, knotting (as with macramé), knitting, and felting.

Two qualities most distinguish contemporary fibers. First, the traditional separation between

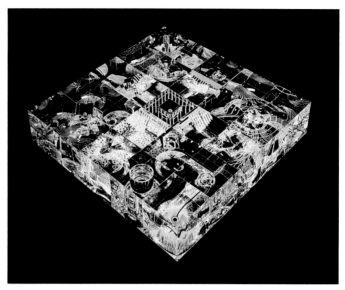

10.20 Eric Hilton, *Innerland*, 1980. Engraved by Ladislav Havlik, Lubomir Richter, Peter Schelling, and Roger Selander, cut by Mark Witter. Cast, cut, engraved, sandblasted, and polished, 3⅞ × 19⅜ × 19⅜ in. (9.9 × 49.3 × 49.3 cm).

sculpture and fiber arts has largely disappeared. As demonstrated by Red Forest (see figure 8.27, page 193), fibers are often used for large-scale designs. Second, the definition of *fibers* has become increasingly broad. For example, Cathy Strokowsky wove together glass, wire, artificial sinew, and horsehair to create *Glass Pod with Hair*, shown in figure 10.21.

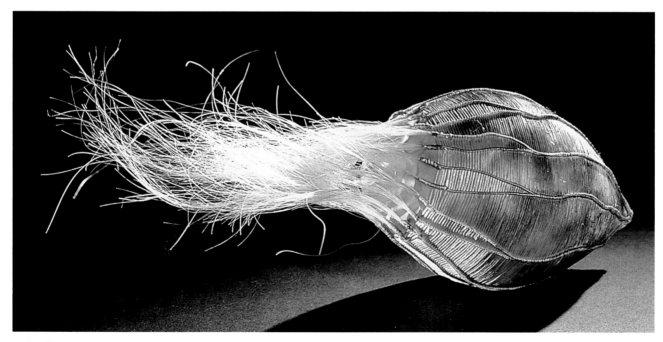

10.21 Cathy Strokowsky, *Glass Pod with Hair*, 2001. Blown glass, sand-blasted, woven artificial sinew, wire, horse hair, 4¾ × 12½ × 4¾ in. (12 × 31.75 × 12 cm).

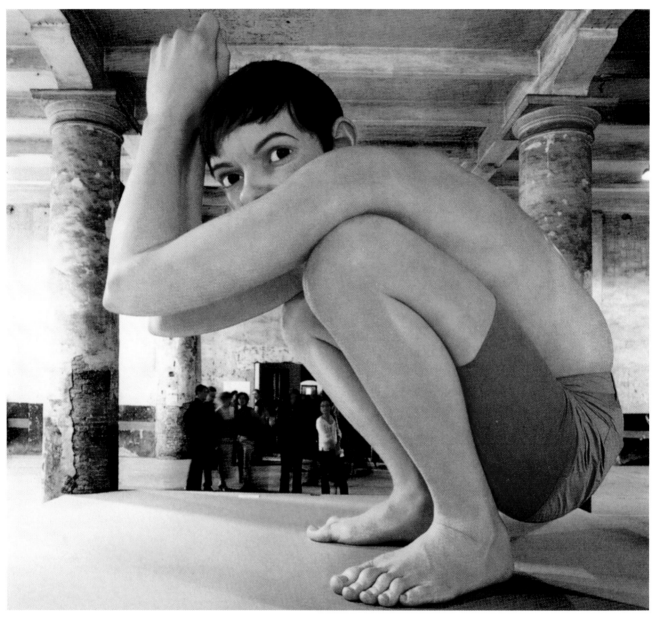

10.22 **Ron Mueck,** *The Boy,* **1999.** Site-specific work installed in the Mind Zone at the Millenium Dome, London, United Kingdom. 16 ft (190 in, 490 cm).

Plastics

Since the 1920s, plastics have provided a plethora of possibilities for both artists and designers. Transparent, translucent, or opaque, plastics can be formed into sheets and then cut and assembled. Many types of plastic can be extruded, cast, vacuum-formed, and stamped. Light in weight, varied in color, and relatively cheap to produce, plastics have fueled a revolution in the design and distribution of household products.

Using a variety of plastics, Ron Mueck has made many large-scale sculptures of human figures. One of the most compelling is *The Boy* (10.22), installed in London's Millennium Dome. Nearly 20 feet high, the adolescent boy seems vulnerable and defensive, despite (or perhaps because of) his enormous size. As with all of Mueck's work, the details are astounding: every hair is defined, and the eyes seem to glisten with moisture as well as apprehension.

STUDENT MATERIALS

To minimize cost and expedite exploration, three-dimensional design projects are often constructed from common materials, such as bristol board, corrugated cardboard, plywood, wire, plaster gauze, and plaster. The following section describes the most basic types of boards and adhesives.

Boards

Bristol board is like thick, stiff paper. It is available in various thicknesses from 1-ply (similar to drawing paper in weight) to 5-ply (which is similar in weight to illustration board). A *cold-pressed* (or vellum) surface is slightly textured, while a *hot-pressed* (or plate) surface is very smooth. The vellum surface is best for graphite, charcoal, pastels, and colored pencils. The smooth surface is good for felt markers and pen and ink. Either can be used for model building, book arts, and planar structures.

Chipboard is a dense, gray, uncoated board made from recycled paper. Most drawing pads have a chipboard backing. Single-thickness chipboard can be cut with an exacto knife or a heavy-duty paper cutter; use a utility knife for all heavier board.

Foamcore is light, strong, and rather unforgiving. It must be cut with a very sharp exacto knife or a scroll saw, and dents in the surface or cutting errors are difficult to repair.

Corrugated cardboard is strong, light-weight, cheap, and amazingly versatile. It is often used for large-scale projects. Through careful planning, you can use the grain (corrugation direction) to create curving planes or even expose it to add texture.

Glues

White glue is nontoxic and water-soluble when wet. It can be used with most porous materials, including all of the boards described in the previous section. It is not suitable for paper-to-paper adhesion, as most papers adhered with white glue will buckle when dry.

Glue stick is water-soluble, acid-free, and nontoxic. Designed as an adhesive for thin paper, glue stick is generally ineffective for gluing any kind of board.

Rubber cement is a traditional paper adhesive that can be "erased" when misapplied, using a special pick-up tool. However, because rubber cement is highly toxic, flammable, and impermanent, it has limited use in three-dimensional design classes.

Hot glue is a wax-based, translucent material that is heated in a gun and applied as a hot, viscous fluid. It is most effective in adhering nonporous materials, and it provides a quick way to create an assemblage. It can also be used to tack cardboard structures together while the white glue dries.

Dry mounting tissue is distributed in sheets of thin, clear plastic. Adhesion occurs when this material is heated, either in a drymount press or using an iron. This is an excellent adhesive for most papers and light-weight cloth, and it is widely used in photography and bookarts.

Tapes

Transparent tape ("Scotch tape") is an all-purpose, light-weight, temporary adhesive for paper. It is not an effective adhesive for boards.

Masking tape is tough, flexible crepe-paper tape. It is designed to mask off unpainted areas, as with painting a car. It is a good temporary adhesive for boards, especially during the model-building stage.

Drafting tape and *artist's tape* are similar to masking tape but with less glue. They can be removed without damaging the surface to which they are applied.

Double-sided encapsulating tape has acrylic adhesive on both surfaces. A layer of thin paper protects one side until the tape is actually applied. An archival version of this material is sold by bookbinding stores, and it can be used for well-crafted final projects.

MATERIALS AND MEANINGS

The materials used in most three-dimensional design classes are inexpensive, can be easily manipulated and are conceptually neutral. As you begin to expand your ideas through more advanced assignments, you can more fully explore the meaning of materials.

Every material has unique psychological associations as well as physical properties. Mirrors are fragile, reflective surfaces commonly used for observation of the self and others. A pile of autumn leaves suggests decay and exudes an earthy aroma. Powdered turmeric spice is yellow and pungent and suggests both cooking and travel.

Whether we are making sculpture or designing products, materials have meaning. For example, the thorny branches at the base of Michele Oka Doner's *Terrible Table* (10.23) are sure to change the emotional atmosphere of any room this table occupies. The wood and wire Deborah Butterfield used to create *Large Horse #4* (10.24) forces us to reconsider our understanding of both horses and nature. A love of materials and an understanding of their characteristics are essential aspects of all three-dimensional work.

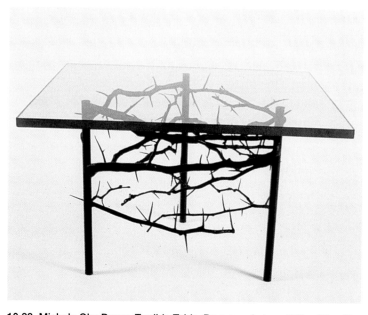

10.23 Michele Oka Doner, *Terrible Table.* Bronze and glass, 15¾ × 26 × 22 in. (40 × 66 × 56 cm).

Key Questions

- Why did you choose a particular material for your project? Considering its strength, workability, cost, and so forth, is it really the best material for your purpose?

- What would your project look like if it were done in a different material?

- How would a change in material affect the meaning of your project?

- What nontraditional materials could you use? How can they enhance meaning?

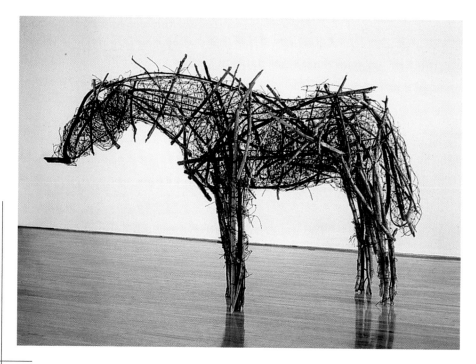

10.24 Deborah Butterfield, *Large Horse #4*, 1979. Steel, wire, sticks, 77 × 124 × 33 in. (195 × 315 × 84 cm).

SUMMARY

- Choice of material substantially affects both the structure and the meaning of a three-dimensional object.

- Strength, workability, durability, weight, cost, toxicity, and function are major considerations when an artist or a designer chooses a material.

- Materials can be strengthened by using composites, by distributing force, and by using skeletons or exoskeletons.

- Common construction methods include addition, subtraction, solidification, and displacement.

- Connections and transitions can increase visual impact as well as structural strength.

- Traditional materials, such as stone, wood, metal, clay, glass, fibers, and plastics, are used by contemporary artists to express a wide range of ideas.

- Student materials, including various types of boards and adhesives, work best when used for the purpose intended.

Keywords

additive sculpture	compression	gradation	solidification
armature	displacement	modeling	subtractive sculpture
assemblage	exoskeleton	shear	tension
bend	flying buttress	skeleton	torque
composite			

Profile:
Todd Slaughter, Sculptor
Materials and Metaphors

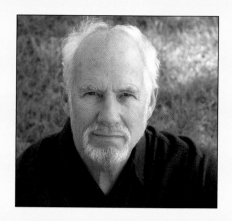

Todd Slaughter was born in Memphis, Tennessee, in 1942. After majoring in chemistry and then in mathematics, he transferred into the art program at University of Texas where he earned a BSA (Bachelor of Science in Art) degree. He subsequently earned a Masters degree in Industrial Design at Pratt, in New York City, and is now a professor in the sculpture program at The Ohio State University. He has had solo shows at the Wexner Center for the Arts, PS 1, and the Chicago Cultural Center, and his major commissions include "The Body of Lake Michigan," in Chicago, Illinois, and La Mano y La Balo (figure 8.13, page 187) near Algeciras, Spain.

MS: Abstract forms dominated your early work. For the past fifteen years, you have shifted more toward representational and narrative work. What is the advantage of each approach?

TS: There is a simple beauty in formal relationships. Like music, lines, planes, volumes and spaces can be organized into wonderful and expressive visual patterns.

However, as I have gotten older, I have become more attuned to human relationships and more interested in the power of metaphor. Metaphors can create a bridge between an object and an idea. Using metaphor, I can add layers of meaning to physical structures.

Representational imagery helps the viewer understand the metaphor in a specific way. For example, the 150 aluminum milkweed castings I used for *Hospice* may suggest a single season of growth, the richness of mundane objects around us, and both the fragility and tenacity of life. A roomful of non-referential forms would not carry the same specificity and layering of meaning.

MS: I'm fascinated by your use of everyday objects, such as hats and domestic objects such as sofas, chairs, and houses.

TS: I want to create the strongest, most personal connection possible between the audience and the artwork. Transforming known objects has become more effective for me than introducing forms that are outside of common experience. I am interested

in exploring complex relationships within this world rather than in creating an escape into an alternative world.

MS: Your use of materials is especially distinctive. Many of your works have been constructed using graphite, sulfur, salt, paprika, and turmeric. Why use these unusual materials?

TS: They carry meanings and references that I want my artwork to reflect. I am especially interested in transience. Nothing is permanent; even the most massive chunk of steel changes over time. When I cast a thousand pounds of salt to create a full-sized sofa and then place it in a steam room, or set two opposing graphite fists in motion grinding each other to a powder (figure 8.13, page 187), the rate of change becomes accelerated and highly visible. Work is produced and the hands are consumed.

Materials have their own unique physical and conceptual properties based on how they are commonly used. Ancient spices such as turmeric and paprika bring a particular sense of human experience to an artwork in a way that a red chalk could not. With its ability to both preserve and to corrode, salt has long been used as a metaphor for the human body, and can have the delicate appearance of marble.

MS: You have recently used video, taxidermied birds, plastic and rubber-like materials. Why are you using these materials now?

TS: I am attempting to use these synthetic materials to comment on synthetic realities of our time. In my mind, artificial aspects of our life are proliferating and expanding. We are becoming excessively self-protective, seeking perfectly imagined and constructed fantasy homes, malls, theme parks, religious cults, and Internet relationships. I believe these constructions are without vitality, and are simulated reality.

The Upstate Dream Home: Domestic Fortress is a critical symbol of a fantasy home. This work is an isolated, home defensive complex of buildings and walkways protected by three synthetically constructed guard-swans, set atop a cake stand. The cake stand, paved with a landscape of siicone berries and elevated by a circular plinth, protectively isolates a domestic world.

MS: *Protected Comforts* seems to embody many of your major concerns in one complex installation. Please talk us through this piece.

TS: The house's foundation is constructed of brick-like cast graphite pairs of hands. The interior of the foundation walls is felt padded. There is just enough room for a single chair within this interior space. A three-minute looped video, projected onto the translucent roof and seen from within, depicts an increasing number of people "on" the roof; the blue light gradually decreases and the strong bass sound track intensifies. This scenario culminates in a blackening out of the projection and the interior of the house.

This artwork is a dramatization of our often itself-isolating and self-destructive attempts to create comfort and security within an uncomfortable and insecure world. We say that "a man's home is his castle," which suggests that a man is in control and that the home is powerful and protected. But we need only to read a newspaper to see that domestic tensions and external forces insure a level of insecurity.

MS: I'm intrigued by your placement of the viewer inside of the artwork.

TS: Direct experience is very powerful. By placing the viewer in a chair inside the bottom room, I created a primary experience rather than a secondary, symbolic experience. The viewer is held in place, feeling both isolation and an enclosing external threat.

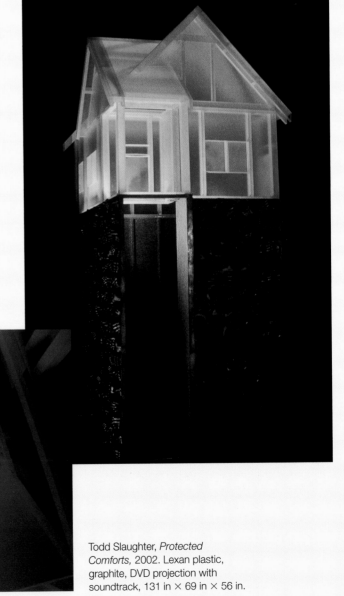

Todd Slaughter, *Protected Comforts*, 2002. Lexan plastic, graphite, DVD projection with soundtrack, 131 in × 69 in × 56 in.

Physical and Cerebral

What is the difference between the pile of wood in figure 11.1 and the sculpture in figure 11.2? The size, orientation, and location of the pile of wood are based on its purpose. It provides the raw material needed for building a house. Positioned at the edge of a construction site, the boards are arranged in a roughly parallel position so that workers can easily grasp and remove individual planks. The pile of wood is purely functional. Its organization has no aesthetic intention.

At first glance, figure 11.2 may seem very much like a pile of wood. The rough planks are clustered together, in close proximity to the house and in a parallel position. On closer examination, we see the perpendicular boards that elevate the structure. Balanced on stilts, the mass of wood seems suspended and in transition. It continues around the house and into the windows. Is the house expelling or inhaling the boards? The entire structure seems poised, ready to shift at any moment.

How and why was this sculpture made? Sculptor Tadashi Kawamata begins by collecting scrap wood from demolished buildings. He then constructs temporary installations, which he describes as "cancers," on conventional buildings. With no predetermined end point, the structures grow like weeds, often enveloping the building. At the end of the exhibition, Kawamata continues onward, dismantling the construction to create another sculpture else-

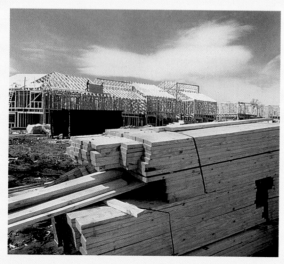

11.1 Pile of Wood from a Construction Site.

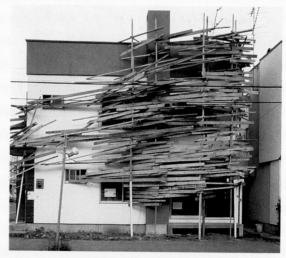

11.2 Tadashi Kawamata, *Tetra House N-3, W26 Project,* **1983.** Sapporo, Japan.

where. Using scrap material to build temporary structures, his work demonstrates the fluidity and circulation of urban structures. His design is based on aesthetic rather than functional criteria.

All three-dimensional work gains power from its physical presence. Sculpture, however, is much more than brute force. It is through the transformation of tangible material into ideas and emotions that a sculpture gains significance. The planks in figure 11.1 begin and end as physical material. A pile of wood is just a pile of wood. By contrast, sculpture, such as *Tetra House N-3, W26 Project,* uses physical material to explore and express ideas.

CONSTRUCTED THOUGHT

From Life to Art

Contemporary sculpture is constructed from a wide range of materials, including ice, fire, blood, spools of thread, and crushed automobiles. In her *Ceremonial Arch* (11.3), Mierle Ukeles combined the metal and wood used in traditional sculpture with gloves, lights, metal springs, and asphalt to create an artwork that is both visually exuberant and structurally sound. Sculpture is now shown in parks, subway stations, and public plazas, as well as in galleries and museums. Because contemporary sculpture is so reliant on familiar materials and public settings, the relationship between art and life has become especially close.

This can be an advantage or a disadvantage. Connection to life gives art its vitality. Authenticity is essential. For example, when a play expresses actual feelings in a compelling way, it connects to our personal experience. Too direct a connection is deadly, however. A pile of wood is just a pile of wood. For art to have meaning, commonplace experiences must be distilled, reexamined, or transformed. It has often been said that a play is "life

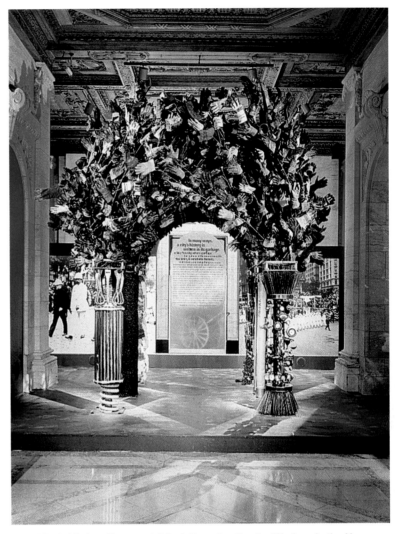

11.3 Mierle Ukeles, *Ceremonial Arch Honoring Service Workers in the New Service Economy,* 1988. Steel arch with materials donated from New York City agencies, including gloves, lights, grass, straps, springs, and asphalt; overall structure 11 ft × 8 ft × 8 ft 8 in. (3.35 × 2.43 × 2.44 m), plus glove branches ranging from 2 to 4 ft long (61 × 122 cm).

with the boring parts left out." A play that simply replicates everyday experience can never transport an audience beyond the commonplace. Likewise, sculpture requires a heightened experience, *beyond* everyday life. Through a combination of insight and hard work, the sculptor transforms even the most resistant material into compelling communication. When all elements in a sculpture support the central concept, the viewer is simultaneously connected by the reality of the material and transported by the power of the idea.

Degrees of Representation

Representational artworks often depict persons or objects in such exquisite detail that they seem to come to life. Michelangelo's *Pietà* (11.4) is a good example. In this massive sculpture, Mary grieves as she cradles the dead Jesus. Every crease in the fabric is defined and every nuance of gesture is deliberate. Mary's right hand extends Jesus' flesh as she gently lifts his right shoulder. She tilts her head slightly, and her left hand echoes the position of his feet. Sculptures such as the *Pietà* seem to embody life. They engage our thoughts and emotions through their compelling realism and narrative implications.

Nonobjective artworks can be appreciated for their pure physical form. For example, the simple metal rings Sandra Enterline constructed for her *Caged Sphere Bracelet Series* (11.5) work beautifully as ends in themselves. We can appreciate their economy and grace without knowing a story or pursuing any additional ideas they may suggest.

Most sculptural objects fall somewhere between these two extremes. These **abstract artworks** have been distilled down from a recognizable source. Myra Mimlitsch-Gray's *Timepiece* (11.6) simultaneously suggests the mechanism and movement of a clock, a pendulum, and a musician's metronome. By reducing these familiar timepieces to their essential form, she was able to create an economical design that conveys a universal sense of time.

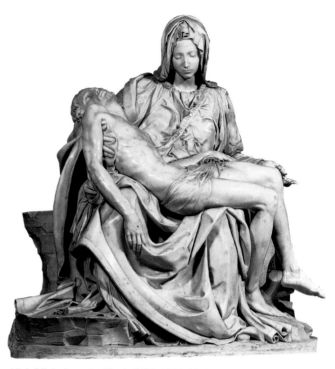

11.4 Michelangelo, *Pietà*, 1498–1500. Marble, 5 ft 8 in. (1.74 m) h.

Each approach has its advantages. Nonobjective forms are often used in situations that require universality or simplicity. Barnett Newman's *Broken Obelisk* (11.7) is a monochromatic structure constructed from a simple pyramid and an inverted

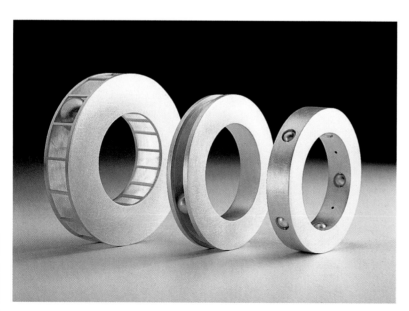

11.5 Sandra Enterline, *Caged Sphere Bracelet Series,* 1992. Sterling silver, 18-karat gold, hollow-formed, fabricated. Left to right, 5 × 5 × 1⅛ in. (12.7 × 12.7 × 3 cm), 4 × 4 × ¾ in. (10.2 × 10.2 × 1.9 cm), 4 × 4 × ¾ in. (10.2 × 10.2 × 1.9 cm).

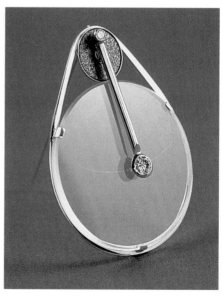

11.6 Myra Mimlitsch-Gray, *Timepiece,* 1988. Kinetic brooch, 14-karat gold, lens, diamonds, abrasive disk. Fabricated, 2¼ × 1½ × ¼ in. (6 × 4 × .5 cm).

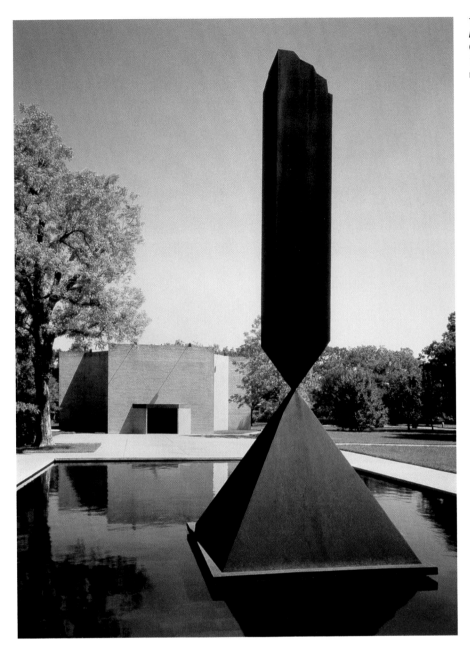

obelisk. The point of contact between the two sections becomes charged with energy, as the top half seems to balance on the point of the pyramid. Caught in this moment of equilibrium, the sculpture is as carefully balanced as a ballerina on point.

On the other hand, the representational approach can stimulate the imagination by providing a fresh interpretation of a familiar object. In *Of Bodies Born Up by Water* (11.8), Walter Martin and Paloma Muñoz used a similar structure to create a very different effect. The poised obelisk is now a grandfather clock. When it topples, time, memory, and family history may be erased.

**11.8 Walter Martin and
Paloma Muñoz,** *Of Bodies
Born Up by Water,* **1987.**
Plaster, oil paint, sheet metal,
and wood, 111½ × 20 ×
16½ in. (283 × 51 × 42 cm).

CONSTRUCTED THOUGHT

263

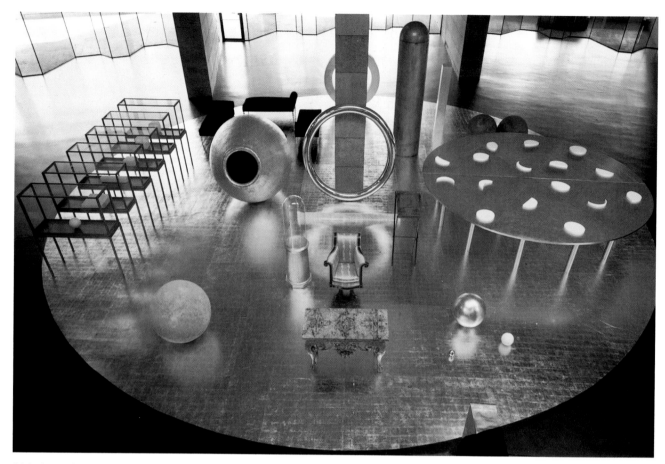

11.9 James Lee Byars, *The Perfect Thought*, 1990 (installation shot). Various objects covered with gold leaf, composed in one of two circles of gold leaf, large circle 40 ft (12.2 m) diameter, small circle 27 ft (8.2 m) diameter.

Boundaries

Because the art/life connection is so important, sculptors must be especially attentive to the physical and psychological boundaries in each piece. As the dividing line between objects, images, or experiences, the boundary is charged with energy. It can serve three major purposes.

Boundaries Can Connect

A simple shape can create a boundary. To define *The Perfect Thought* (11.9), James Lee Byars painted two gold-leaf circles on the floor. The larger circle enclosed 23 separate works from earlier exhibitions, while the smaller circle remained empty. This simple strategy unified a collection of individual artworks while leaving a second space open, to be filled by the viewer's imagination.

A physical boundary is used to create a psychological connection in *My Mother 3,* by Cho Duck-

Hyun (11.10). The strip of fabric that extends out from the drawing and rolls onto the floor enters our space. Combined with the gentle gesture of the woman, the unfurled fabric invites our entry into her world. Here, the tangible world of sculpture and the illusory world of drawing work in perfect harmony.

Boundaries Can Separate

Constructed from nine 12-foot-wide bushes within the median of a busy highway, Maya Ying Lin's *Topo* (11.11) uses a boundary to separate as well as to connect. Enclosed within the mile-long median, the bushes provide a series of visual steppingstones, inviting us to move down the line diagonally. Shifting circles at either end of the sculpture appear to rotate the last two bushes, directing our attention back down the line. Through this illusion of per-

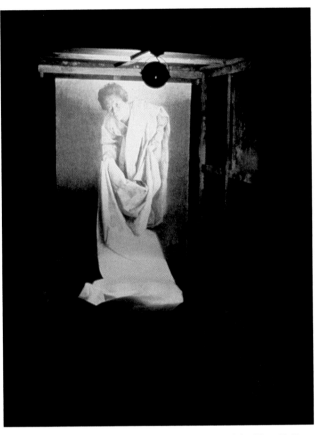

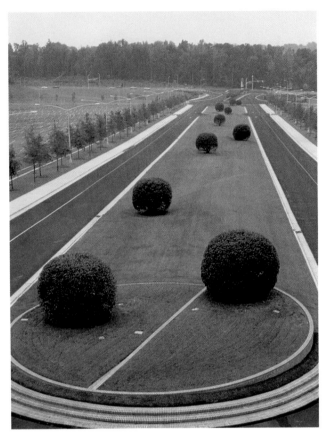

11.10 Cho Duck-Hyun, *My Mother 3* (Memory of the Twentieth Century), **1996.** Graphite and charcoal on canvas, Halogen light, 48 × 57 in. (122 × 145 cm).

11.11 Maya Ying Lin, *Topo,* 1991.

petual motion, the simple design becomes highly activated.

Psychological separation adds power to George Segal's *The Subway* (11.12). Developed as a three-dimensional painting, Segal's construction replicates a familiar setting, using actual subway seats, handrails, and a window, which flashes with the lights of "passing" trains. The ghostly white plaster figure seems familiar but remains distant, the shell of a living, breathing person. Here, a psychological boundary transforms the commonplace into an expression of alienation.

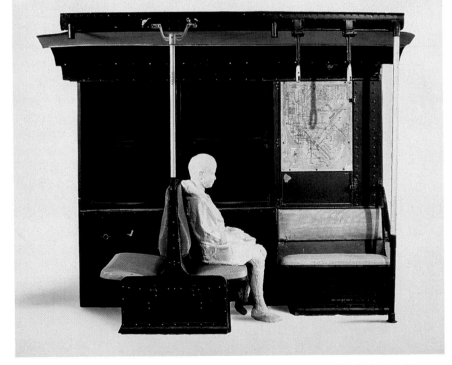

11.12 George Segal, *The Subway,* **1968.** Plaster, metal, glass, rattan, electrical parts with lightbubs, and map. 7 ft 4 in. × 9 ft 5 in. × 4 ft × in. (2.25 × 2.88 × 1.3 m).

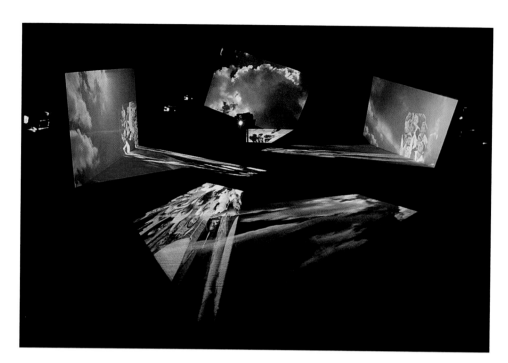

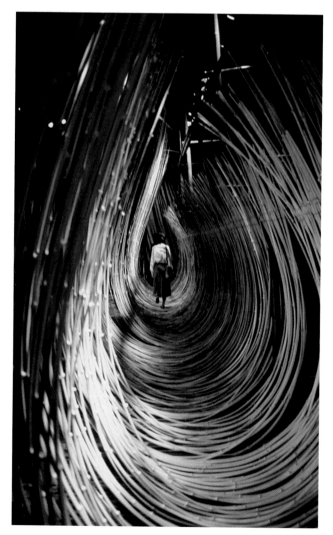

11.14 Hiroshi Teshigahara, One-Man Show Bamboo Installation at Metropolitan Plaza in Ikebukuro, Tokyo, June 10–15, 1993.

Boundaries Can Enclose

Increasingly, sculptors are using every square inch of gallery space and surface to create complex installations. In *Blue Skies* (11.13), Susan Trangmar used the gallery walls as four large projection surfaces. Surrounded by the projections and by his or her own cast shadow, the viewer becomes a participant in the installation.

The sculpture itself can also envelop the viewer. The boundaries in Hiroshi Teshigahara's *Monumental Ikebana* (11.14) create a passage through a bamboo maze. The patterns of light and shadow combined with the graceful arch entice and enchant the visitor. The physical sensation of enclosure brings magic to the delicate structure.

Bases and Places

Traditional sculpture is generally mounted on a **plinth,** which provides a horizontal base, or on a **pedestal,** which provides a vertical base. Either can serve three purposes:

- To physically separate the sculpture from the surrounding space

- To provide strength and structural stability

- To elevate an object psychologically, distinguishing it from its surroundings and increasing its impact

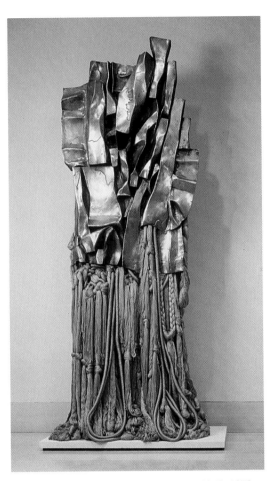

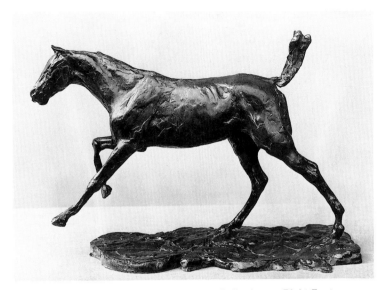

11.16 Edgar Hilaire Germain Degas, *Horse Galloping on Right Foot*, c. **1881.** Bronze cast of wax model, 11⅛ in. (30 cm).

11.17 Benvenuto Cellini, *Perseus and Medusa,* **1545–54.** Bronze, 18 ft h.

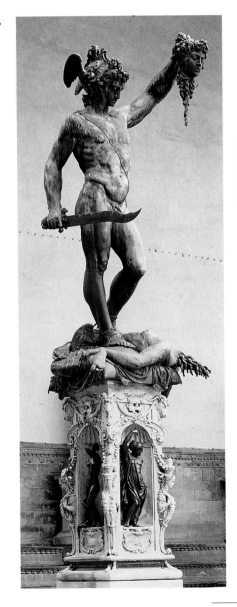

11.15 Barbara Chase-Riboud, *Malcolm X #3*, 1970. Polished bronze and silk.

Seemingly insignificant, the plinth or pedestal can actually become an essential component of three-dimensional design, both physically and aesthetically. In figure 11.15, the marble base adds elevation as well as a marked contrast in material. As a result, Barbara Chase-Riboud's *Malcolm X #3* now has a solid platform from which to speak. The plinth in *Horse Galloping on Right Foot* (11.16), by Edgar Degas, provides a visual context for the galloping horse, as well as physical stability. The sculpture would collapse, physically and aesthetically, if the base were removed. The pedestal for Benvenuto Cellini's *Perseus and Medusa* (11.17) elevates the heroic statue and creates an architectural connection to the surrounding buildings.

For Constantin Brancusi, the base was an essential element rather than a passive support. He used a specific pedestal form to enhance the power and grace of each of his variations on birds (figures 9.25, 9.26, 9.27, page 232), Seeking dynamism rather than stability, Umberto Boccioni split the base in half

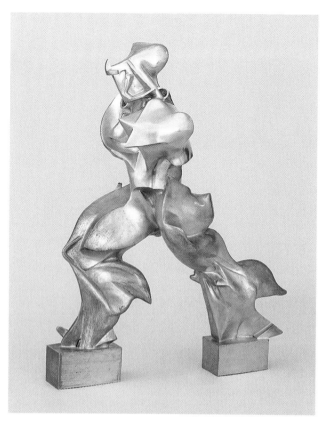

11.18 Umberto Boccioni, *Unique Forms of Continuity in Space,*
1913. Bronze (cast in 1931), 43⅞ × 34⅞ × 15¾ in. (111.2 × 88.5 × 40 cm).

when he composed *Unique Forms of Continuity in Space* (11.18). The abstracted figure strides forward in space, too energetic to be constrained by conventional boundaries.

In contemporary sculpture, the base often extends to include an entire architectural site. Resting directly on the surface of the plaza, the granite boulders in Elyn Zimmerman's *Marabar* (11.19) are intended to suggest continents, while the channel of water suggests the ocean. Combining large scale with a "baseless" design, the artist has dissolved the traditional boundary between the stones and the surroundings. The entire plaza is thus transformed into a sculptural site.

Key Questions

- How is your artwork similar to everyday life? How is it different?

- What can a boundary or base add to your design?

- How will the content change if your project is placed in a specific setting?

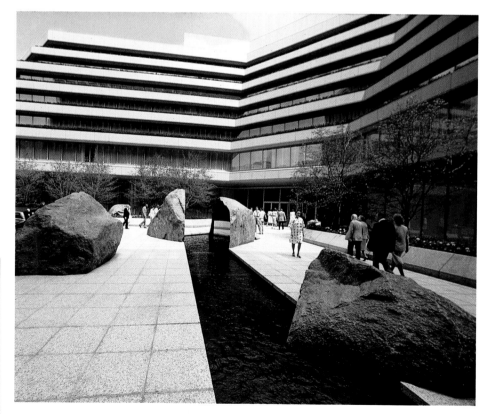

11.19 Elyn Zimmerman, *Marabar,*
1984. Boulders (natural cleft and polished granite) and water. Plaza: 140 × 60 ft (42.7 × 18.3 m). Pool: 60 ft × 6 ft × 18 in. (18.3 m × 1.8 m × 45.7 cm). Boulders: 2 to 10½ ft. (61 cm to 3.2 m).

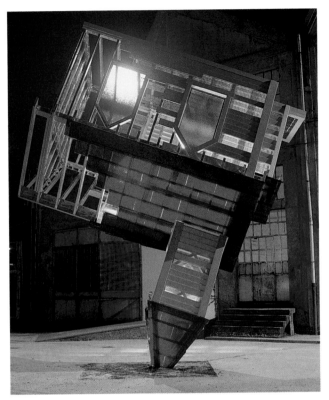

11.20 Dennis Oppenheim, *Device to Root Out Evil*, 1997. Galvanized structural steel, anodized perforated aluminum, transparent red Venetian glass, concrete foundations, 20 × 15 × 8 ft (6.1 × 4.57 × 2.44 m).

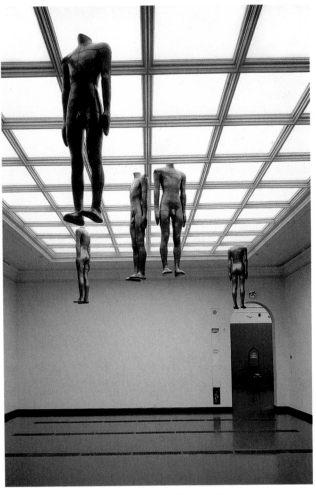

11.21 Antony Gormley, *Learning to Think*, 1991. Lead, fiberglass and air, five figures, each 68 × 41¾ × 122 in. (173 × 106 × 310 cm).

PHYSICAL FORCES

Weight and Gravity

Of the forces of nature, gravity is the most immediately noticeable when we begin to construct a three-dimensional structure. Lines, spaces, and volumes must be organized according to the laws of physics while simultaneously meeting our aesthetic objectives. Balance is a structural necessity as well as a compositional force. After watching several prototypes collapse, it is easy to conclude that gravity is our enemy, to be conquered at all costs. But is it?

When we begin to analyze the uses of gravity in sculpture, we soon find that it is an asset rather than a liability. Just as a ballet dancer relies on gravity to provide a solid launching pad for each leap and a predictable support for each landing, so the sculptor uses gravity to express ideas and generate emotions.

Downward gravity animates *Device to Root Out Evil* (11.20). The inverted church structure seems to have been propelled aloft, finally driving into the ground upon landing. As noted by sculptor Dennis Oppenheim, this inversion of a familiar structure creates a reversal of content. The steeple is now pointing to hell rather than to heaven. Even without any cultural associations, however, we would still respond to the improbable balance and intense color in this large piece.

A combination of weight and weightlessness gives Antony Gormley's *Learning to Think* (11.21) its impact. Constructed from a mold made from the artist's own body, the hollow lead figures are basically identical. Hovering 10 feet off the ground, they seem weightless. At the same time, because they are suspended from the ceiling, each figure seems as heavy as a convict at the end of a hangman's noose. This paradox gives the sculpture great physical force and communicates an elusive concept. Clearly, the knowledge embodied in this sculpture is not easy to attain!

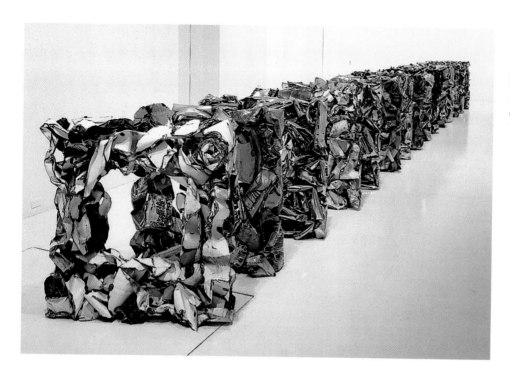

11.22 John Chamberlain, *The Hedge*, 1997. Painted milled steel, chromium-plated steel, and stainless steel, overall installed 44½ in. × 44½ in. × 46 ft 4 in. (113 cm × 113 cm × 14.12 m); 16 units, each 44½ × 44½ × 12 in. (113 × 113 × 30.5 cm).

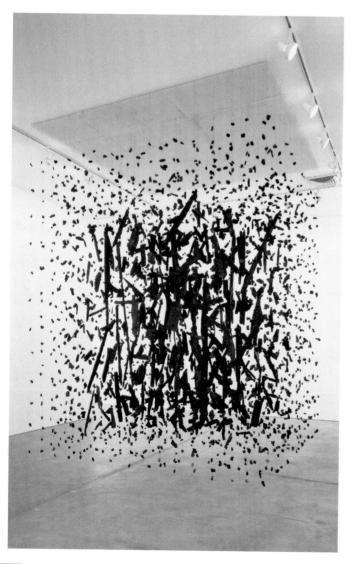

Compression and Expansion

Most materials tend to compress as weight increases. As shown in figure 9.21 (on page 230), physical compression can be used to evoke a visceral response. We feel the pressure as the top log pushes down on the log below. Compression plays an especially important role in the works of John Chamberlain, who began making sculptures from crushed automobiles in the 1960s. In *The Hedge* (11.22), crushed pieces of metal have been transformed into an improbable garden. The contradiction between the materials and the meaning suggests a new definition of *nature*.

Expansion is an equally compelling force. Constructed from the charred fragments of a church that had been struck by lightning, Cornelia Parker's *Mass* (11.23) seems to present the event in suspended animation. Supported by fine steel wire and cotton thread, the hovering sculpture appears weightless, caught at the moment of explosion.

11.23 Cornelia Parker, *Mass (Colder Darker Matter)*, 1997. Charcoal retrieved from a church struck by lightning, suspended from steel wire and cotton thread, 10 × 10 × 10 ft (3.5 × 3.5 × 3.5 m).

Tension and Torsion

Tension can be used to stretch or bend an object, while torsion creates a twisting movement. Either can add physical and cerebral strength to a sculpture. Stretched taut, the steel cables in Kenneth Snelson's *Free Ride Home* provide the force needed to elevate the aluminum tubes that dominate the sculpture. Tension is equally important for the designer. It is the tension in the bent metal rods that creates the structure in the *Peregrine Tent* from The North Face (11.24). In Maren Hassinger's *12 Trees No 2* (11.25), cables and wires have been twisted together, then clamped at the top. Based on our experience in the physical world, we can feel the force in the twisted strands and imagine the explosive result if this power were released.

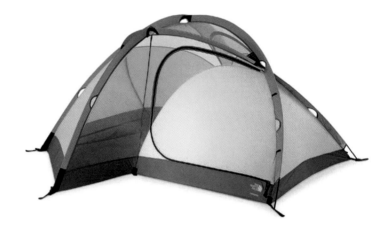

11.24 *Peregrine Tent* by The North Face, San Leandro, CA

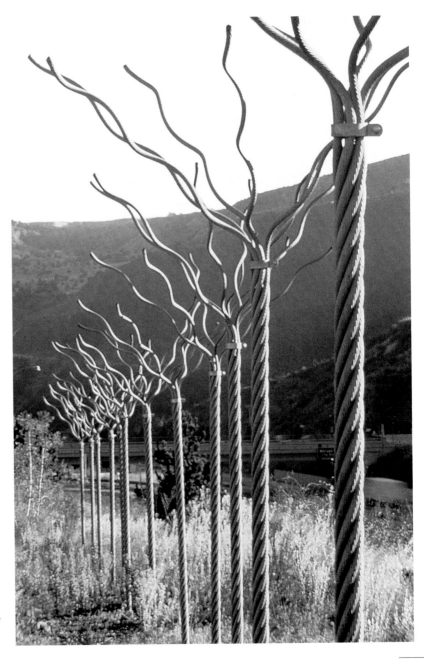

11.25 Maren Hassinger, *12 Trees No 2,* 1979. Galvanized wire rope, 10 × 150 × 5 ft (3.1 × 45.7 × 1.5 m).

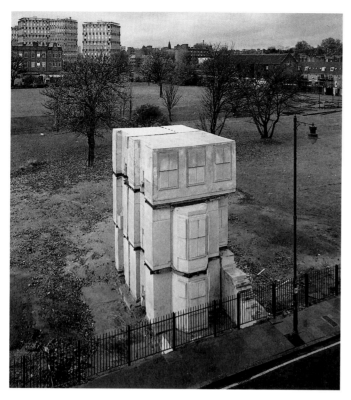

11.26 Rachel Whiteread, *House*, 1993. Commissioned by Artangel Trust and Beck's (corner of Grove Rd. and Roman Rd., London, destroyed 1994).

Presence and Absence

Presence is another important aspect of physicality. When we confront a massive sculpture, like the Olmec portrait on page 197, it exudes a strength that is far beyond anything a small photograph can convey. Equally, the space surrounding a sculpture or the absence of an anticipated object can have great impact.

Many sculptors have used this quality of presence and absence to explore the passage of time and the nature of memory. British sculptor Rachel Whiteread explores presence and absence in many of her works. Using hundreds of gallons of cement to create a solid cast from an empty house, she accentuates absence by making the space within the house very solidly present (11.26). In his *Writing on the Wall* series, Shimon Attie used slide projections to remind us of shops and families destroyed during the Holocaust. Figure 11.27 shows one of the many slides from the 1930s that he projected onto various buildings in Berlin. The actual bookstore depicted disappeared long ago.

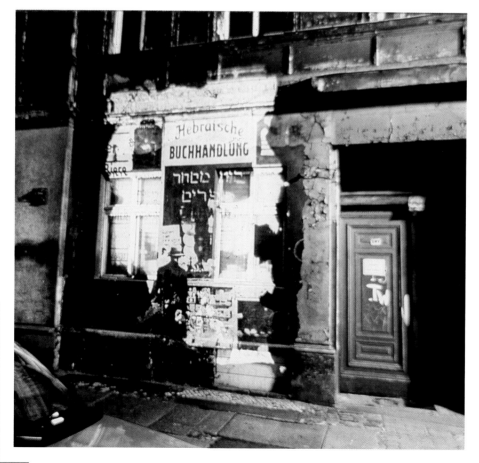

11.27 Shimon Attie, *Almstadtstrasse 43 (formerly Grenandierstrasse 7): Slide Projection of Former Hebrew Bookstore, Berlin*, 1930, from the series *The Writing on the Wall*, 1992. Ektacolor print of site-specific slide-projection installation, 20 × 24 in. (50.8 × 60.9 cm).

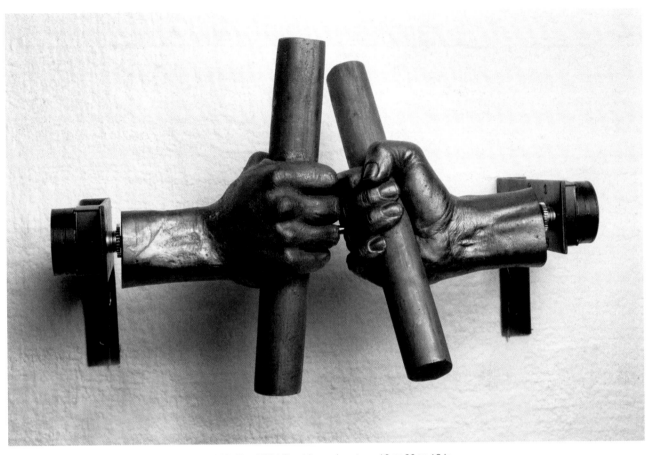

11.28 Todd Slaughter, *Grinding Knuckles*, 1993. One RPM Graphite and motors, 12 × 20 × 12 in.

Process and Product

In the past 50 years, sculptors have expanded their choice of materials to include many physical and chemical processes:

- *Friction.* The graphite hands in Todd Slaughter's *Grinding Knuckles* (11.28) slowly rotate, grinding the sculpture away every time this artwork is displayed.

- *Condensation.* Sealed inside the Hans Haacke *Weather Cube* (11.29), water evaporates or condenses based on the ambient temperature inside the gallery.

- *Oxidation.* Ronald Dahl transformed the familiar ladder when he placed his sculpture in the

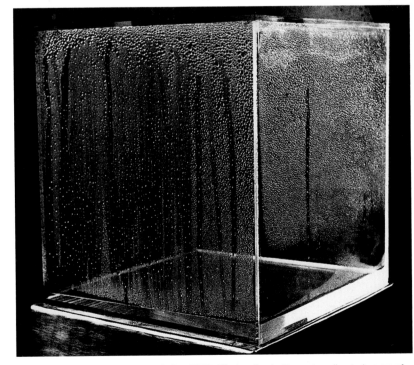

11.29 Hans Haacke, *Weather Cube,* 1963–65. Acrylic plastic, water, climate in area of display, 12 in. cube (30.5 cm).

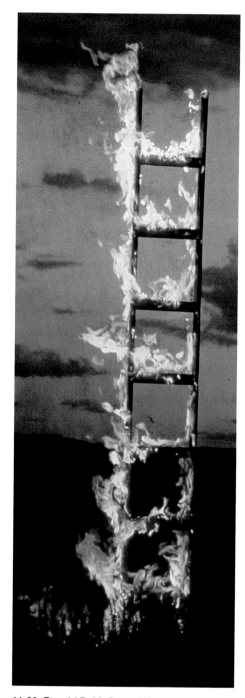

Nevada desert and set it aflame to create *Seven Windows to a Sky on Fire* (11.30).

- *Filtration.* Located next to a wastewater treatment plant, Lorna Jordan's *Waterworks Gardens: The Grotto* (11.31) purifies up to 2,000 gallons of oil-laced storm water per minute. The 8-acre site includes stone mosaics, natural filtration systems, and colorful bands of sedges, yellow irises, and red-twig dogwoods.

11.30 Ronald Dahl, *Seven Windows to a Sky on Fire,* **1982.** Wood/flame, 9 × 12 × 3 in. (22.7 × 30.5 × 7.6 cm).

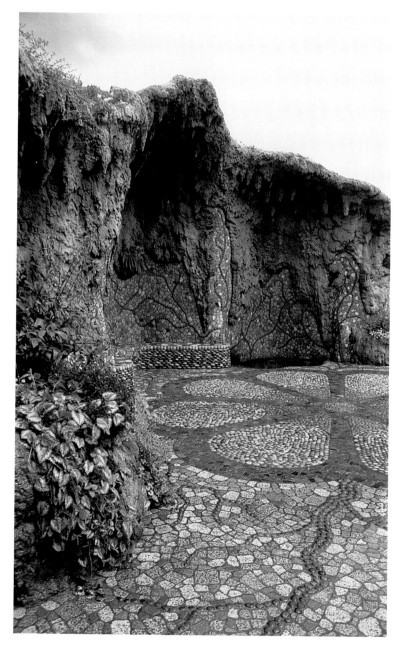

11.31 Lorna Jordan, *Waterworks Gardens: The Grotto,* **1996.** Third of five public garden rooms in the King County East Division Reclamation Plant, Renton, WA.

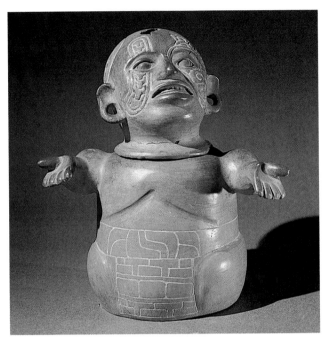

11.32 **Covered Effigy Jar with Removable Head.** From Teotihuacan, Mexico. Ceramic, 10¾ in. (27.3 cm).

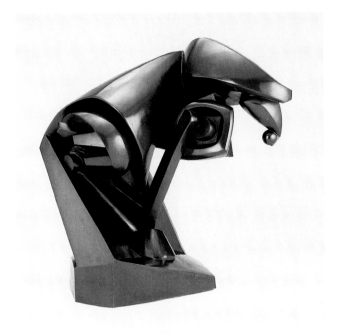

11.33 Raymond Duchamp-Villon, *The Great Horse*, 1957 version of a 1914 work. Bronze, 39¼ × 24 × 36 in. (99.7 × 60.9 × 91.4 cm).

CEREBRAL QUALITIES OF SCULPTURAL OBJECTS

Building on a Tradition

Traditional sculpture has been characterized by four qualities. First, mass, or solid substance, rather than open space, is the primary concern. Traditional sculptures, such as Michelangelo's *Pietà* (see 11.4, page 262), are relatively solid. In this masterpiece, a sense of profound resignation is created through the use of gravity. The mother has fully accepted her grief. The position of the limbs and the folds in the fabric create a dynamic surface on a stable pyramidal mass. Second, the human figure is the primary subject. Sculptors have long sought to capture in wood, metal, or stone the vitality of a living person. Third, as a means to this end, traditional sculpture is overwhelmingly representational. Indeed, attention to detail and the ability to animate marble have long been the hallmarks of Western sculpture, from the Renaissance to Romanticism. Even a less detailed pre-Columbian effigy jar (11.32) gains eloquence from the use of representation.

Finally, traditional sculptures often tell stories. Public monuments have often been commissioned by kings or by communities of ordinary people to tell national stories. For example, the Statue of Liberty, designed to embody the democratic ideal shared by France and the United States. It was financed through a public lottery, theatrical events, and even prizefights. The poem describing "huddled masses yearning to breathe free," combined with the heroic figure, distills the history of immigration to America into a few words.

Reinventing Sculpture

In Europe, the four qualities of traditional sculpture reached their climax during the nineteenth century. Seeking fresh ideas and new approaches, artists in Russia, Italy, and France then began a process that would transform sculpture forever.

Four major changes followed. First, space became a major concern. As shown in Antoine Pevsner's *Torso* (see 8.28, page 194), sculpture began to be constructed from the inside out, rather than being carved from the outside in. Second, abstraction and transformation became more important than description and representation. For example, Raymond Duchamp-Villon's *The Great Horse* (11.33), constructed from a mix of organic and mechanical parts, bears little resemblance to an actual horse. Third, while the human figure continued to dominate early-twentieth-century sculpture, by mid-century almost any subject matter could be used.

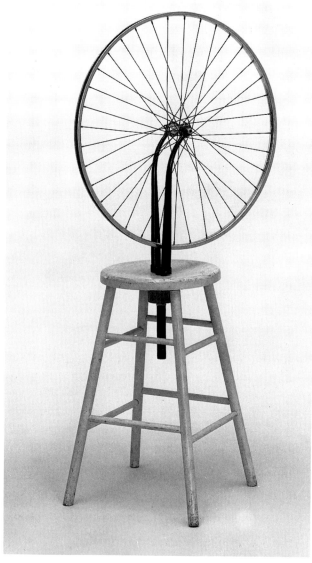

11.34 Marcel Duchamp, *Bicycle Wheel*, 1951. (Third version, after lost original of 1913.) Assemblage, metal wheel, 25½ in. (63.8 cm) diameter, mounted on painted wood stool 23¾ in. (60.2 cm); overall 50½ × 25½ × 16⅝ in. (128.3 × 63.8 × 42 cm).

Indeed, many significant artworks from this period, including Mark de Suvero's *Ik Ook Eindhoven* (see figure 8.17, page 189), are nonobjective, without external subject matter. Weight, balance, and the dynamics of space are the only content such works require. Most importantly, sculptors began to break down the traditional separation between art and life. Commonplace objects, such as Marcel Duchamp's *Bicycle Wheel* (11.34), were placed in galleries and defined as art.

CONTEMPORARY QUESTIONS, CONTEMPORARY ANSWERS

The evolution of sculpture has accelerated in the past 30 years. Earthworks, which transform natural sites into sculptural settings, have become a powerful force in both art and ecology. An installation, which may combine time, space, and sound, can present both artist and audience with new opportunities for communication and expression. Performance art (which is discussed at greater length in Chapter Fourteen), combines art, technology, and theater. The traditional has become the transformative. Four of the manifestations of change are described in the following sections.

Sculpture as Place

Traditionally permanent, sculpture has always been placed in a wide variety of significant settings. Stonehenge (11.35), constructed from massive limestone blocks weighing up to 50 tons, may have been used as a gigantic sundial by its Neolithic builders. The avenue approaching the stone circle is carefully aligned to the summer solstice, while stones within the circle are aligned with the northernmost and southernmost paths of the rising moon.

Likewise, contemporary sculptors add meaning to their work by exploring the physical, psychological, and temporal characteristics of each site. Glen Onwin's *Nigredo* (11.36) is one of four works in a series titled *As Above, So Below*. Placed in an abandoned chapel, this concrete pool, filled with water,

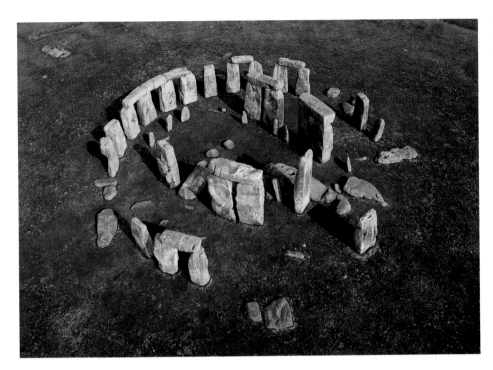

11.35 Stonehenge (Aerial View), Salisbury Plain, England, c. 2800–1500 B.C.

11.36 Glen Onwin, *Nigredo,* 1992.
Installation view of exhibition *As Above, So Below,* at the Square Chapel, Halifax, May 9–June 15, 1992. Exposed timbers of the roof reflected in an artificial concrete pool filled with black brine and wax.

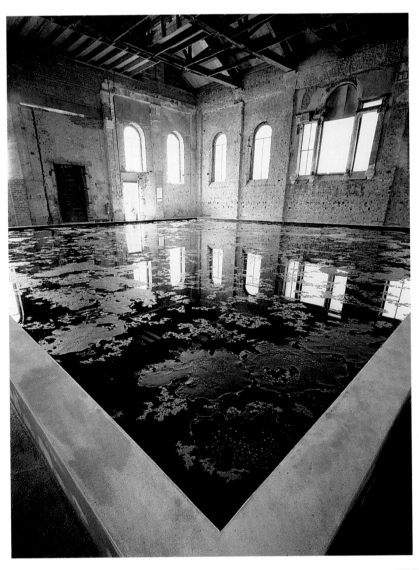

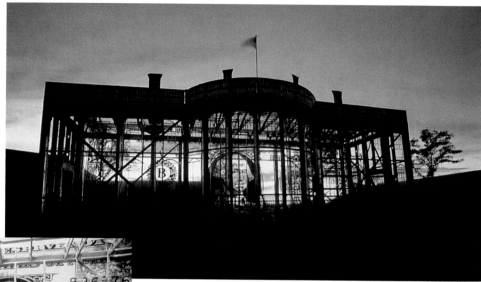

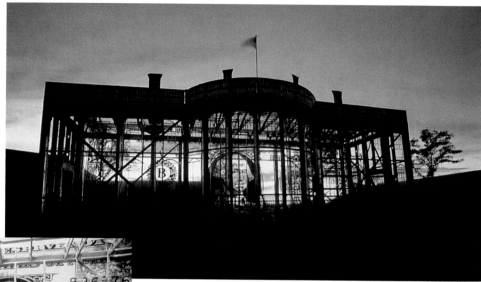

11.37 Karen Giusti, *White House/Greenhouse,* New York City, 1996. Recycled steel beams, vinyl, Plexiglas, and rose bushes, 40 × 15 × 14 ft (12 × 4.5 × 4.3 m).

black brine, and wax, seems especially ominous in the once-sacred site. The personal and the political were combined in Karen Giusti's *White House/Greenhouse* (11.37). Placed in Battery Park in New York City, the transparent one-quarter scale model of the White House had both Wall Street and the Statue of Liberty in the background. Made of recycled steel beams, clear vinyl, and large paintings on Plexiglas, the structure presented a scathing commentary on American politics while providing a greenhouse for 200 rose bushes.

Sculpture as Journey

As sculptures have expanded in size, the manner in which the viewer enters, exits, and explores the site has become increasingly important. When the audience participates, a sculpture can be transformed from an object into an experience.

Christopher Janney's *Sonic Plaza* (11.38) at Eastern Carolina University is an especially enticing example. Composed of four distinct sculptures, the site offers a variety of sensory experiences. Various melodic sounds greet participants at the *Sonic Gates.* The 64 water jets on the *Percussion Water Wall* spew forth complex patterns of water to a percussive accompaniment. Four smaller sculptures emerge from the large doors of the *Media Glockenspiel* each day. Finally, a cloud of water vapor created by *Ground Cloud* hovers over the plaza, responding to pedestrian movement and wind direction.

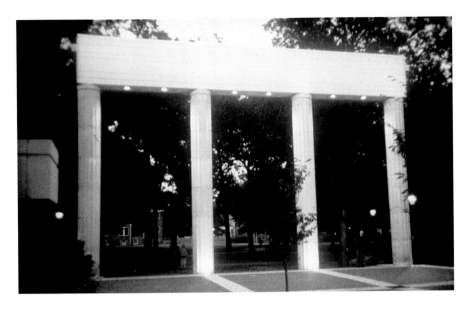

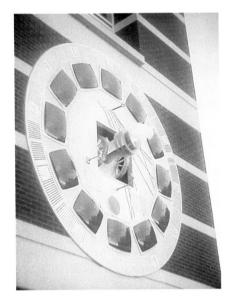

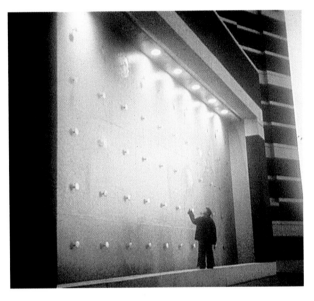

11.38 Christopher Janney, *Sonic Plaza,* Eastern Carolina University, 1998. Sound, light, water, and interactive elements, total length 400 ft (122 m). Top: *Sonic Gates;* middle row left to right: *Media Glockenspiel* and *Percussion Water Wall;* bottom, *Ground Cloud.*

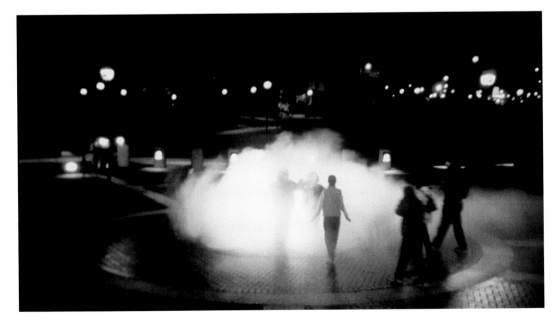

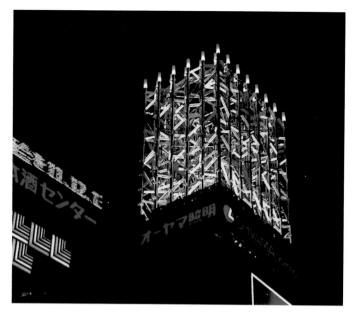

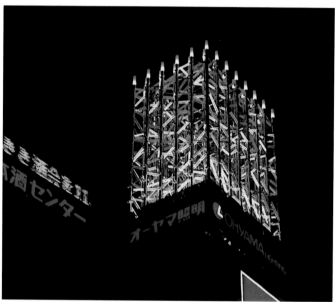

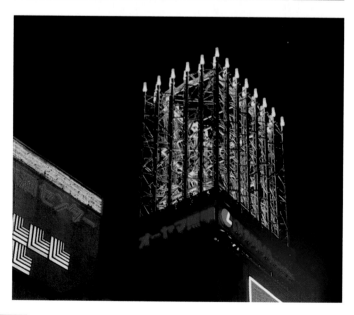

Sculpture as Time

A fascination with time pervades contemporary sculpture. Many sculptures demonstrate the changes that occur as time passes. The amount, frequency, and means of change vary widely. Placed atop the corporate offices of a lighting company, Fumaki Nakamura's *Light Communication* (11.39) presents a simple metamorphosis in a spectacular way. The 88 neon poles gradually illuminate the interior of the structure in three 30-second cycles. The beauty of the light, combined with the hypnotic sequence of change, animates and illuminates the night sky.

Sculpture is also used to demonstrate the impermanence that is an essential characteristic of time. To create *curcuma sul travertino* (11.40), Shelagh Wakely covered the entrance hall to a British school with a thin layer of yellow turmeric spice. As visitors passed through the room, they gradually erased the dust. Thus, during the week-long exhibition, visitors were marked by their passage through the room, and, with spice on their shoes, subsequently marked each new room they entered.

Time itself is the subject of Jim Campbell's *Digital Watch* (11.41). An ominous ticking noise accompanies the installation. On the massive screen, viewers see themselves twice — in real time to the left of the clock and in a 2-second delay on the clock face itself. The repetition and delay create a disturbing psychological effect. The persistent sound of the watch freezes time with each tick while pushing time forward in a relentless pattern.

11.39 Fumaki Nakamura, *Light Communication,* **Oyama Lighting.** Installed at Ginza 4-chome (main intersection). Eighty-eight poles on a box frame with 400 flashing lamps and projection lights underneath, front 26 ft 3 in. w. × 19 ft 8 in. d. × 29 ft 4 in. h. (8 × 6 × 12 m). Neon tube total length 546 ft 2 in. (1,500 m).

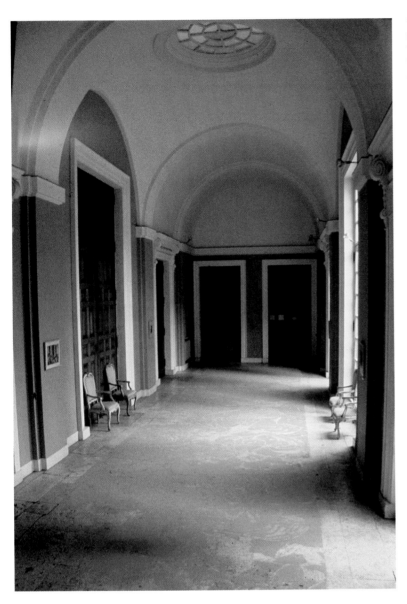

11.40 Shelagh Wakely, *curcuma sul travertino*, 1991. Turmeric powder on travertine marble floor (smell of turmeric filled the space), swept up after three weeks, 46 ft × 11 ft 6 in. (14 × 3.5 m).

11.41 Jim Campbell, *Digital Watch*, 1991. Watch, camera, video cameras, electronics. Dimensions variable.

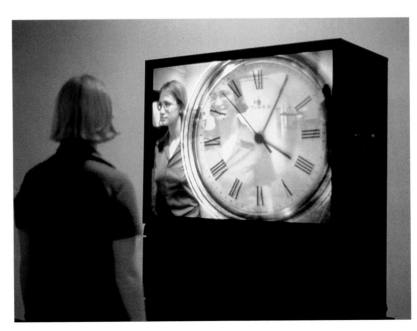

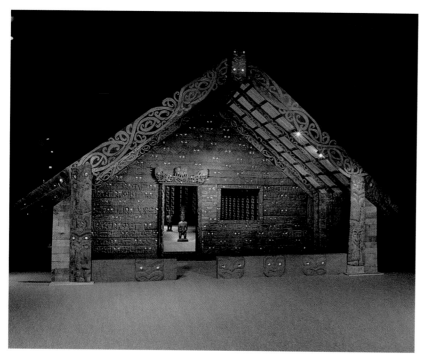

11.42 *Maori Meeting House,* called "Rautepupuke," New Zealand, 1881. 56 ft × 13 ft 10 in. (17 × 4 m).

Sculpture as Self

It has often been said that all artwork is autobiographical. This is especially true of sculpture. As the physical manifestation of thought, sculpture has an immediacy similar to that of a living person.

Both traditional and contemporary sculptors have explored this theme in many marvelous ways. The indigenous people of New Zealand, the Maori, have often combined sculpture with architecture to create a genealogical self-portrait. The face of a prominent ancestor is placed on the front gable of the sacred meeting house (11.42). The ridge at the top of the roof is the ancestor's backbone, the rafters form his ribs, and the four

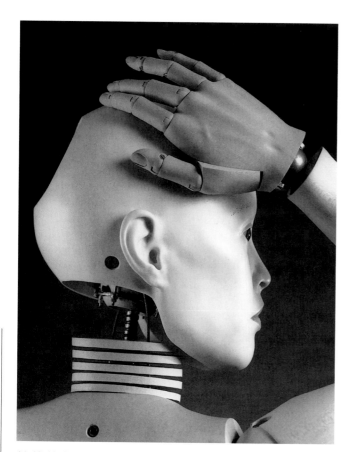

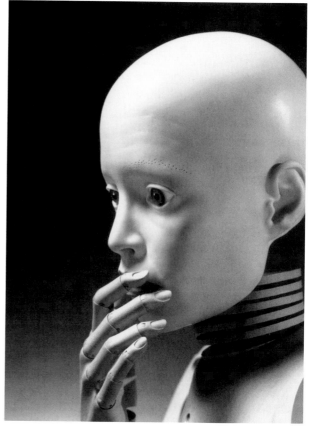

11.43 Katherine Wetzel (photograph), Elizabeth King (sculpture), *Pupil* from *Attention's Loop,* 1987–90. Installation at the Bunting Institute, Radcliffe College, 1997. Porcelain, glass eyes, carved wood, brass. One-half life size.

corner posts represent his arms and legs. Faces of other ancestors are carved on the exterior of the building and on interior posts. Finally, carvings of the Earth Mother and Sky Father are placed over the porch. Through a combination of representation and symbolism, every aspect of the building is designed to honor the past and inspire the present people.

Attention's Loop (11.43), by Elizabeth King, offers another type of self-portrait. In this installation, six highly detailed mannequins are presented in a variety of poses. Carefully articulated arms and hands in three additional display cases line the back wall of the gallery, while an 11-minute video loop shows the mannequins moving. The combination of supreme craftsmanship, robotic machinery, and fluid animation communicates a complex range of ideas. The mannequins are both fascinating and disturbing. It appears that human consciousness has been trapped in a sculptural body.

Eva Hesse's *Laocoön* (11.44) is a more abstract self-portrait. As noted in Chapter Seven, the ancient Greek sculpture *Laocoön and His Two Sons* (see figure 8.21, page 191), depicts a scene from the Trojan War. Laocoön warns against accepting the large wooden horse the Greeks offer as a gift. The Greek goddess Athena sends two serpents to attack and kill Laocoön, thus gaining entry into Troy and victory for the Greeks hidden in the horse. Like the snakes that bind Laocoön and his sons, the cords in Hesse's sculpture are messengers of death. They choke the ladder structure and foreshadow Hesse's own death at age 34 from a brain tumor. As she noted, "My life and art have not been separated."[1]

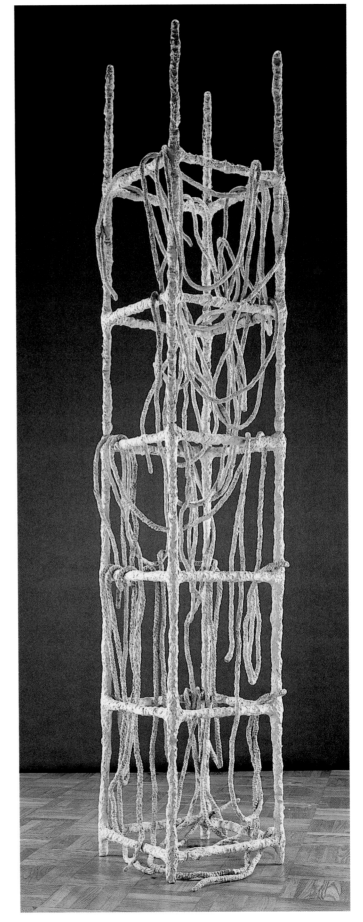

11.44 Eva Hesse, *Laocoön*, 1966. Acrylic paint, cloth-covered cord, wire, and papier-mâché over plastic plumber's pipe, bottom 130 × 23½ × 23 in. (330.2 × 59.7 × 58.4 cm), top 130 × 21½ × 21½ in. (330.2 × 54.6 × 54.6 cm).

EXPRESSING IDEAS IN PHYSICAL FORM

The combination of tangible material and aesthetic complexity gives sculpture a unique power. Like an alchemist, the sculptor transforms ordinary materials into conceptual gold. Tadashi Kawamata's pile of wood becomes a metaphor for urban change. In Mierle Ukeles' *Ceremonial Arch,* the gloves and lightbulbs used by sanitation workers are transformed into a sculpture. A burning ladder becomes a metaphor for a spiritual passage in Ronald Dahl's *Seven Windows to a Sky on Fire.* Through a miracle of invention, the best sculptures simultaneously embrace and transcend their physical nature.

Key Questions

• How might physical forces, such as gravity, tension, and compression, expand the meaning of your artwork?

• How would a change in material affect your artwork, both physically and conceptually?

• What does your artwork reveal about yourself and the world around you?

SUMMARY

• A pile of wood at a construction site is stacked for convenience and accessibility. A pile of wood in a sculpture is designed to communicate ideas and emotions.

• Art gains power from its connection to life. Through art, commonplace experiences are distilled, reexamined, and transformed.

• Physical and psychological boundaries can connect or separate art and life.

• A base can distinguish a sculpture from its surroundings, provide structural stability, and expand aesthetic content.

• Physical forces, such as gravity, compression, expansion, tension, and torsion, can be used to express ideas while providing structural strength.

• The materials a sculptor selects can both heighten and deepen the meaning of the artwork.

• Traditional Western sculpture is massive, representational, figurative, and narrative.

• Contemporary sculpture is often more spatial, abstract, and nonfigurative than traditional sculpture.

• Many contemporary sculptors use specific sites, audience participation, temporal change, and explorations of the self to create powerful artworks.

Keywords

abstract artwork
installation
nonobjective artwork

pedestal
performance art

plinth
representational artwork

Profile:
Rick Paul, Sculptor
Physical, Virtual, and Cerebral

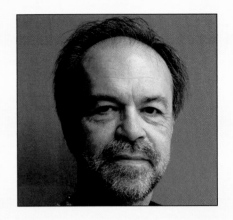

Rick Paul is a professor in the Department of Visual and Performing Arts at Purdue University and chairperson of the Art and Design division. Paul has been involved with foundations design courses throughout the entire 30 years of his teaching career, and for 10 years, he was foundations design coordinator at Purdue.

Paul received his BFA in sculpture from the University of Florida and his MFA in sculpture from Pennsylvania State University. During the 1980s, he made room-sized architectural installations, including exhibitions at The Contemporary Arts Center, Cincinnati; The Cultural Center, Chicago; The Fort Wayne Museum of Art; and The Institute of Contemporary Art, Philadelphia. In 1992, Paul was awarded a Master's fellowship by the National Endowment for the Arts.

Paul's earliest computer work dates from 1974. It was the advent of the personal computer and CAD software that prompted him to use computers to make sculpture. His current work is almost entirely virtual but still maintains many of the characteristics of earlier, site-related sculptures. The relationship between structure and form, the use of environmental context, and the significance of symbolic substitution continue to be issues addressed by his art.

MS: How and why did you start making art?

RP: I started making art as a sophomore in college. At that time I was majoring in another creative area, chemistry, and taking art courses as electives. The first two art courses I enrolled in were photography and three-dimensional design. I enjoyed these classes so much that I continued to take at least one art course each subsequent semester. It took me five years of undergraduate school to decide my major. Once I realized that art could be as creative and challenging as the sciences, I changed my major from chemistry to art and finished my BFA in two semesters.

MS: You have been making sculpture for some 35 years. What qualities attract you to three-dimensional art and design?

RP: As a child I found building my own toys much more interesting than playing with packaged toys. The raw materials for my projects came from the neighborhood trash cans. I had a large walk-in closet full of all sorts of mechanical and electrical parts cataloged and stored in columns of shoeboxes. I was totally fascinated with the variety of materials and forms used by industry and the many ways to combine the parts.

I also made large dioramas and miniature architectural structures. These were often based on the book I was reading at the time. My father forbade me to use his workshop and tools but that did not stop me from using them when he was not around. Looking back, I am convinced that these childhood experiences helped me to develop my intuitive sense of space and dexterity. It also led me to understand the specific physical properties of each material (strength, hardness, malleability, color, texture, grain), which every sculptor uses to advantage.

I have always enjoyed posing questions and solving complex problems. I enjoy the challenges of construction — how can I design an object which possesses structural integrity and withstands the forces of gravity? And, every sculptural question has an ideal as well as a pragmatic answer. When and where do you compromise the ideal solution to get the job done?

MS: Tell me about your creative process. How do you generate, develop, and implement an idea?

RP: My creative process starts with an initial spark usually a response to an intriguing idea, site, material, or process. Ideas usually come from looking at an ordinary everyday experience from an unusual viewpoint. For example, my 10 years of working with Gatorfoam started with a scrap I carried with me in my truck for over a year. Occasionally I would examine it while stopped at a red light. I was convinced that it had very special properties that I could take advantage of to make very special sculptures. I was right. Gatorfoam, which is like foamcore with a hard surface, permitted me to construct very large, light structures very easily. *Kepler's Dream* at The Contemporary Arts Center in Cincinnati (1981) was the first piece I built with this material.

My virtual objects usually start as sketches. Some of my best ideas occur when I am traveling. During travel, I am physically and psychologically free of my usual daily routine and obligations. I have time for new ideas and more freedom to explore. I have one simple rule for using my sketchbook: there are no rules! Drawings are combined with text and computer pseudocode. My sketchbook is a record of where my head has been and where ideas might lead me in the future. Brainstorming on paper is a great way of generating new ideas.

MS: What do you do when you hit a wall?

RP: I guess I am a contrarian. Often I deliberately turn left where other people would go forward. I make a point of searching for the less obvious. In the process I am willing to obliterate or discard an approach I've worked on for hours.

MS: What is the importance of scale?

RP: I consider two kinds of scale when building a sculpture. The first is the scale of the work itself. How big is it relative to the viewer or space it occupies? If I use architectural elements, they are two-thirds scale. This scale makes for a more intimate environment and can provide for more information within a limited space. Rarely is the viewer aware that such elements as stairs are subhuman

Rick Paul, *DC Object*, 1998. Virtual sculpture, wood and canvas (virtual materials), 36 × 13 × 13 ft (virtual size).

in scale. In this way they accept the various architectural elements as larger than they really are.

The second kind of scale is "material scale." Material scale is actually a scale range that is defined by the physical characteristics of the material. For example, corrugated cardboard works fine for small-scale constructions, but it is an unlikely material for a tiny matchbox sculpture or for construction of an object 20 feet tall. You learn what the scale range of a material is by working with it. Typically students are unaware of the potential of a material. This is why I encourage them to study and experiment with unfamiliar materials before using them.

MS: In our discussions of teaching, you talked a lot about the advantages of limitations, which can help students focus their energy and explore an idea more deeply. What are the limitations in your own work? How do you push past the boundaries?

RP: I accept the limits of a problem as a challenge rather than a hindrance. The most significant limits to creativity are self-imposed, rather than external. Knowing yourself and how to work around self-imposed limits is an important asset to creativity that takes a long time to develop.

MS: How do you compare your tangible art with your virtual objects?

RP: For me there is no boundary separating the material world from the virtual world. My work moves back and forth between the two, drawing from both. I am currently working on a series of virtual objects built for specific real environments. Compare *Object at Rest* and *DC Object*, for example. Both were conceived with a specific site in mind. They are roughly equal in size. They are made of the same materials (wood and fabric). Both were conceived as floating objects to be exhibited in an out-of-context environment. There are advantages and disadvantages to both ways of working.

MS: Do you have any advice for my students?

RP: Realize that there is no substitute for experience. Art and design require mastery of many skills, investigation of many emotions, and exploration of many ideas. There are no shortcuts. Persistence is much more important than talent. No matter how much talent you have, nothing will happen without a sincere and sustained commitment to your work.

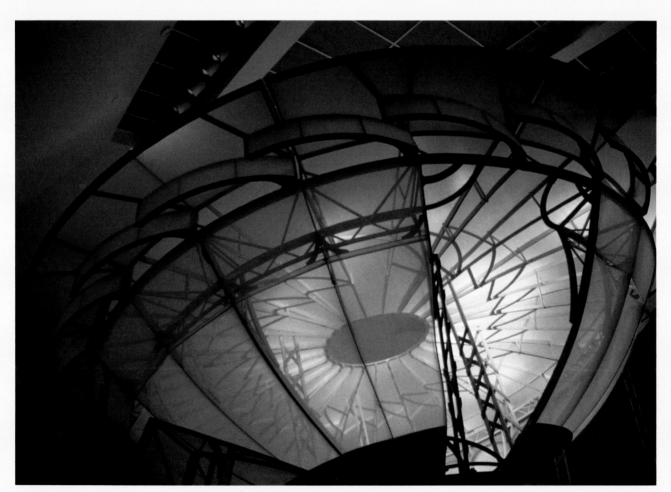

Rick Paul, *Querschnitt*, 1989 installation. Gator foam™, wood and fabric, 36 × 24 × 20 ft.

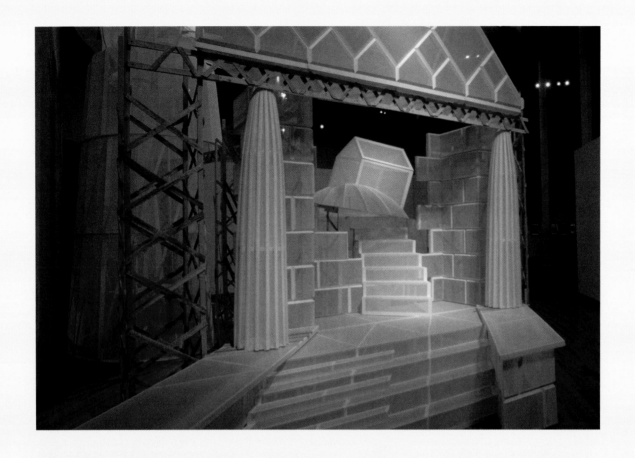

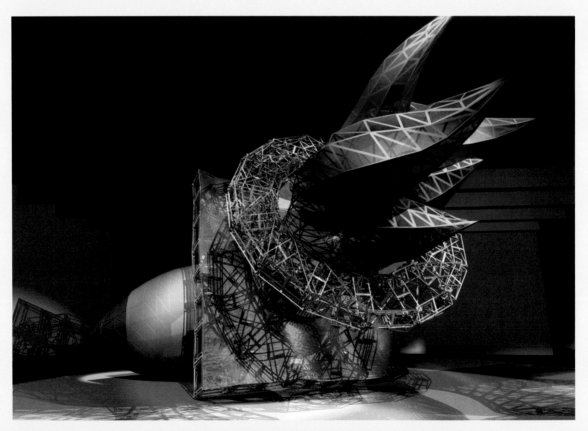

Top: Rick Paul, *Object at Rest*, 1994 installation. Wood and fabric, 24 × 24 × 12 ft. Bottom: Rick Paul, *Expanding History*, 2000. Virtual sculpture, wood and fabric (virtual materials), 36 × 26 × 14 ft (virtual size).

Part Three
Multimedia Resources

Take advantage of the multimedia resources for Part Three in order to test and expand your understanding of three-dimensional design elements.

Resources

www.mhhe.com/launching2

Student Center
Chapter 8
Chapter 9
Chapter 10
Chapter 11

Core Concepts in Art CD-ROM

Contents

Learning objectives for each chapter
Study outlines for each chapter
Quizzes with instant feedback
Flashcards for studying art vocabulary
Internet exercises for developing critical viewing skills
Book suggestions for your personal library and research projects

Exercises to explore how 3D elements are used to create works of art
Videos illustrating sculpture, glass, and jewelry-making techniques

Studio projects for Part Three are described and illustrated for teachers on the Web and on a CD-ROM.

Resources

www.mhhe.com/launching2

Instructor Center
IM Part Three

Instructor's Resource CD-ROM

Part Three

Projects

Spheres of Influence #1 and #2: Planar construction problems
Head Case: Planar construction and tunnel books
Calderesque Self Portrait: A linear problem using wire
Linear Athlete: Gesture, balance, and implied motion
Becoming Borg: The skin and the skeleton of human and machine
Discovering Mass: Modeling a sculptural object and carving a form
Wooden Wizardry: Transforming a wooden plank into a wizard's staff
Superhero Mask/Headgear Design: From the personal to the improbable
Audio Assemblage: Creating a sculptural musical instrument
Myths and Masks: Exploring concept and construction
Book Transformed: Content based construction
Abstracted Object, Fragmented: Work with scale, craft, and concept

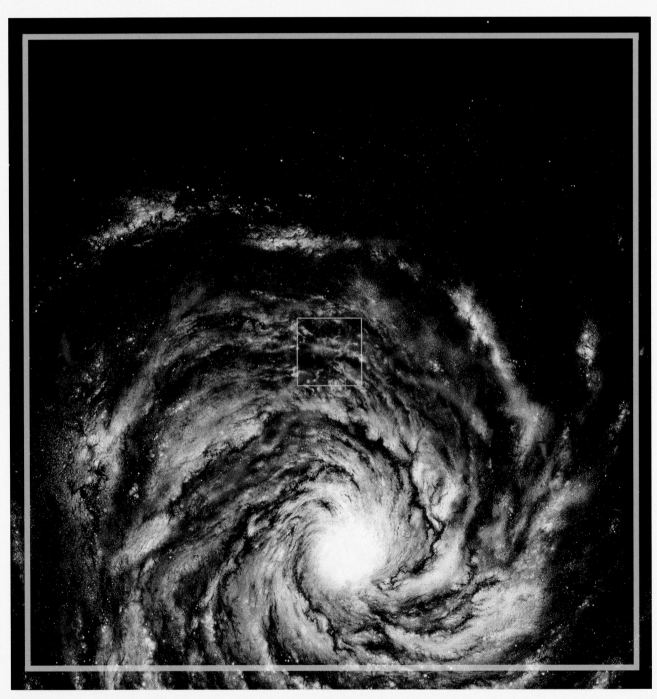

Charles and Ray Eames, *Powers of Ten,* **1977.** Film frame.

Time
Design

From prehistory to the present, artists have sought to create images, objects, and architectural works that embody and express the most profound aspects of human experience. Expressions of love and hate, life and death, and dominance and subordination fill the walls of any art museum. As we study art and design, we encounter a remarkable variety of images and objects that express thoughts and feelings in imaginative form.

This compulsion to create has always compelled artists and designers to seek new avenues of expression. In contemporary art, innovation and experimentation have become the rule, rather than the exception. Actions and ideas once considered taboo dominate many exhibitions. Separations among music, theater, and art become blurred when interdisciplinary artworks are created.

In this final major part, we will consider time as a dimension of art and design. While all areas of visual communication are affected by time, it is the sequential arts — such as film, computer graphics, visual books, and performance art — that most depend on the manipulation of time.

Chapter Twelve offers an overview of time design and a description of its basic aspects and elements. Various forms of storytelling are discussed in Chapter Thirteen. We conclude with an exploration of interdisciplinary art and design, including an extended discussion of visual books, installation art, and performance art.

Part
Four

chapter twelve
**Aspects and
Elements of Time**

chapter thirteen
**Narrative and
Non-Narrative**

chapter fourteen
Interdisciplinary Arts

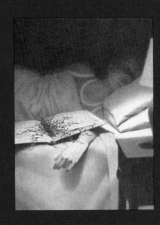

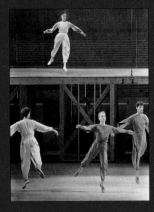

Aspects and Elements of Time

Abe Morell quietly sets up a large camera in an empty New York apartment. Except for a single small opening, he blocks the light coming in the windows. Ghostly and inverted images of the surrounding city begin to appear on the walls. At just the right moment, he releases the shutter.

In 1998, Nancy Callahan and Diane Gallo created *Storefront Stories* in Cherry Valley, New York. A combination of words, images, and everyday objects was installed in an unused storefront window. Every 10 days, the installation was changed, presenting the next chapter in a story. Over a six-week period, an entire narrative was revealed to the people in the town.

An unusual advertisement was shown during the 1984 Super Bowl game. The 60-second commercial begins as gray-faced workers in a futuristic city trudge into a huge theater and shuffle into their seats (12.1). From the screen, a grim "Big Brother" intones: "From today we celebrate the first anniversary of the information purification directions." A woman athlete is then shown, carrying a sledgehammer and sprinting toward the theater, with guards in hot pursuit (12.2). On arrival, she hurls the hammer into the screen, which explodes. As the words appear on the screen, an announcer reads, "On January 24, Apple Computer will introduce Macintosh. And you'll see why 1984 won't be like *1984*."

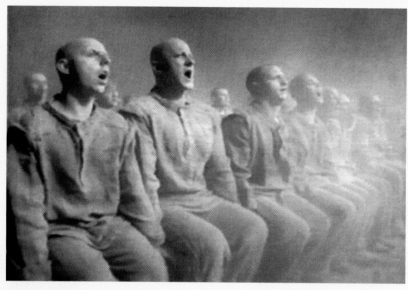

12.1 Apple Computer television Ad Introducing the Macintosh Computer. Shown during the 1984 Super Bowl game.

What is the connection? What do these artworks have in common?

In each case, an understanding of time is an essential aspect of the work. Like gravity, time itself is intangible. It is easy to overlook a force that we cannot see, yet the *effects* of time are critically important in all areas of art and design. An illustrator working on a track meet poster seeks the most dramatic moment in each event. The action shown in a narrative painting such as *Raft of the Medusa* (see 3.13, page 67) is as important as the composition created. And, through variations in texture and color, a ceramicist invites us to examine a bowl slowly, revealing each nuance as we rotate the form.

Photographers, book artists, and filmmakers are especially sensitive to the importance of time. When news photographer Sam Shere captured the moment at which the dirigible *Hindenburg* exploded, he created an indelible image (12.3). In *The Mysteries of Harris Burdick*, illustrator Chris Van Allsburg suggested a series of complex stories using a single drawing and a fragment of text (12.4). And, after shooting many reels of footage, a filmmaker spends months editing the film down to the essentials.

Meanings unfold through the passage of time. By selecting and composing each moment, we can turn the most mundane event into a memorable experience. Connections made through the juxtaposition of images can create a visual rhythm, express an idea, or tell a story. While these aspects of time are most clearly demonstrated through film, video, and photography, the implications for all areas of art and design are profound.

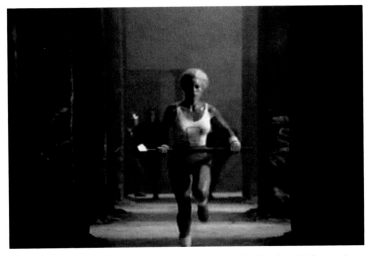

12.2 Apple Computer Television Ad Introducing the Macintosh Computer. Shown during the 1984 Super Bowl game.

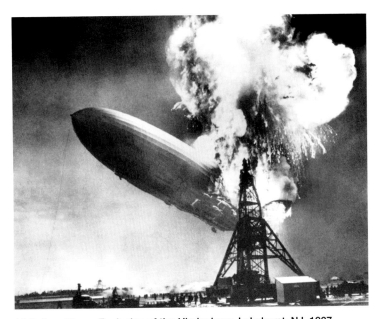

12.3 Sam Shere, Explosion of the *Hindenburg*, Lakehurst, NJ, 1937. Photograph.

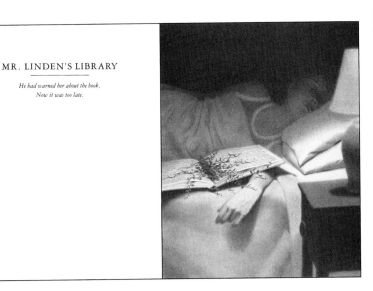

12.4 Chris van Allsburg, "Mr. Linden's Library" from *The Mysteries of Harris Burdick*, **Houghton Mifflin, 1984.**

MR. LINDEN'S LIBRARY

He had warned her about the book.
Now it was too late.

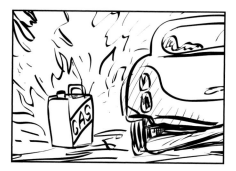

12.5A Single Frame, Close-Up

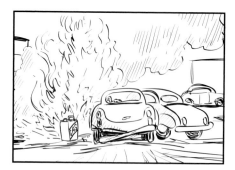

12.5B Single Frame, Medium Shot

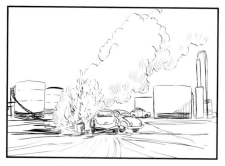

12.5C Single Frame, Long Shot

BUILDING BLOCKS

Transforming temporal experience into expression or communication may seem daunting at first. The compositional skills needed for two-dimensional design and the spatial skills needed for three-dimensional design become even more complex when time is added to the mix.

We are surrounded by time design, however, and, with some basic definitions and a sense of direction, can build on our existing vocabulary and begin to work. We are all familiar with television, movies, and comic books. Generally, sequential structures are composed using four basic units: frame, shot, scene, and sequence. The **frame** is a single static image. Projected onto a flat screen, a film frame is governed by the same compositional forces as a painting, a poster, or a photograph. As shown in figures 12.5A, 12.5B, and 12.5C, the boundaries of the frame determine the meaning of the image. The **close-up** in the first frame shows the gasoline can that is the source of the fire. The **medium shot** in the second frame shows the parking lot in which the fire has been set. The **long shot** in the final frame shows the fire in a larger context. We now see that this fire at an oil refinery could spark an explosion.

In filmmaking, a **shot** is a continuous group of frames. In figure 12.6, the first shot consists of eight frames, the second shot consists of six frames, and the third shot consists of four frames. In traditional films, the eight-frame shot would last for one-third of a second, while the six-frame shot would last for one-quarter of a second.

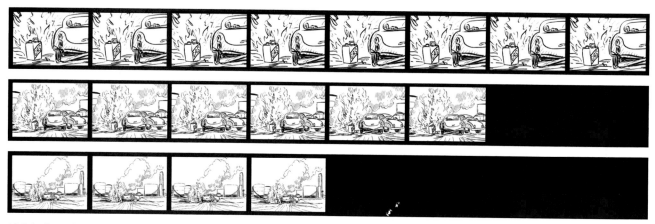

12.6 In filmmaking, a shot is a continuous group of frames.

By combining these shots, we can create a scene. A **scene** is usually constructed from continuous action in continuous time and continuous space. Shots of various length are combined to strengthen expression.

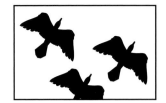

12.7A Doves symbolize peace.

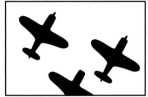

12.7B Bombers symbolize war.

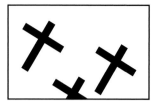

12.7C Crosses symbolize death.

A **sequence** is a collection of related shots and scenes that constitute a major section of action or narration. To understand the expressive potential of a sequence, we will now examine four major ways in which shots can be related.

Relationships

In *Film Art: An Introduction,* David Bordwell and Kristin Thompson describe four types of shot-to-shot relationships.

A **graphic relationship** connects two or more images through visual similarity. Because the images of doves, airplanes, and crosses in figures 12.7A, 12.7B, and 12.7C are graphically similar, a visual connection is made when they are shown together. In this case, a visual connection can be used to communicate a political idea. Doves symbolize peace, bombers symbolize war, and crosses symbolize death. The juxtaposition of these shots shows that the transition from peace to war leads to death.

A **spatial relationship** can expand or compress the stage on which an action occurs (12.8A–C).

Through a combination of close-ups and distance shots, the filmmaker can imply movement and can increase or decrease the emotional connection between the actor and the audience.

A **temporal relationship** can establish **chronology,** the order in which events occur. A story may be told through a simple sequence of events or reorganized, using **flashbacks,** which refer to previous events. The 1993 movie *The Fugitive* uses flashbacks extensively. The film begins with the murder of Dr. Kimball's wife. Wrongly accused of the crime and sentenced to death, Kimball must discover the actual killer if he is to clear his name. Flashbacks to the murder, which occur throughout the story, show Kimball's recollection of the event that shattered his life.

When many shots are combined, a deliberate **rhythmic relationship** can be developed. Rhythm is often based on an interplay between static and dynamic, on a contrast between light and dark, or on a combination of shots of different duration.

In *The Birds,* Alfred Hitchcock used all these relationships to create a suspenseful sequence that

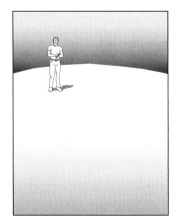

12.8A Long shot.

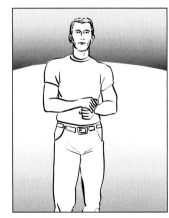

12.8B Medium shot.

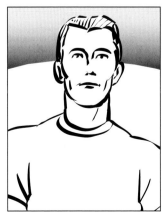

12.8C Close-up.

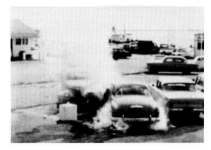

12.9A

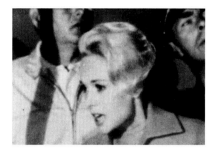

12.9B

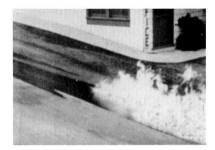

12.9C

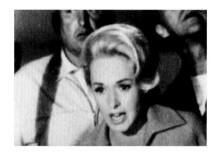

12.9D

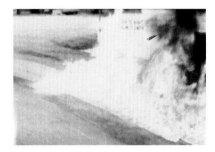

12.9E

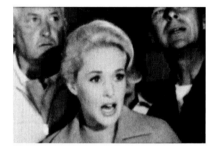

12.9F

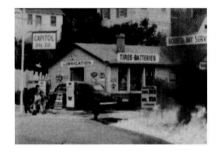

12.9G

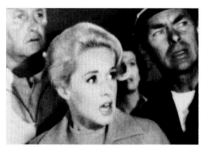

12.9H

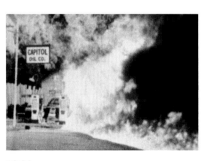

12.9I

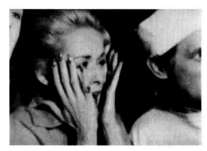

12.9J

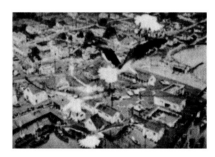

12.9K

builds to an explosive climax (12.9A–K). In *Film Art,* David Bordwell and Kristin Thompson describe an especially impressive example.[1] Melanie, the central character in the sequence, watches in horror as a line of flaming gasoline advances across the pavement, then ignites a gasoline station. The shots of her face create one graphic relationship, while the shots of the flame create a second graphic relationship. By **crosscutting,** or alternating between the two, Hitchcock created a relentless rhythm and established a simultaneous temporal relationship: Melanie is watching the gasoline as it advances toward the gas station. In a final aerial view (12.9k), we shift our spatial position to watch the final explosion from a seagull's point of view. Graphic, rhythmic, temporal, and spatial relationships were combined to create a cinematic tour de force.

Transitions

The four most common transitions in film are the cut, fade, dissolve, and wipe (12.10). A **cut** is an abrupt transition that may connect very different images or very similar images, depending on the effect required. Fades and dissolves are gradual transitions. In a **fade,** the shot slowly darkens or lightens. In a **dissolve,** as one shot fades, an-

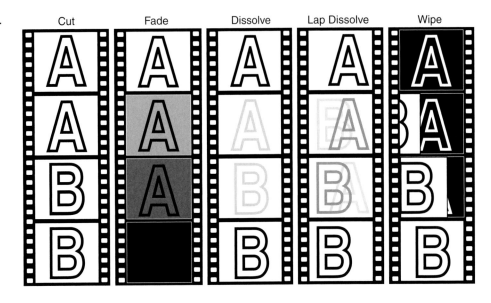
12.10 Common Transitions.

Cut | Fade | Dissolve | Lap Dissolve | Wipe

other appears. Two shots are superimposed briefly in a **lap dissolve.** A **wipe** is more abrupt than a fade but softer than a cut. In a wipe, the first shot seems to be pushed off the screen by the second.

As described by Scott McCloud in *Understanding Comics,* comic books rely on six additional transitions.[2] American comics rely heavily on **action-to-action transitions** (12.11). Capturing sequential moments within an event, the action-to-action transition is clear and straightforward.

In a **subject-to-subject transition** (12.12), two shots within the same scene are juxtaposed. The combination may provide crucial information, as in this explosive story.

A **scene-to-scene transition** (12.13) requires more reader involvement. Depending on the images used, this type of transition can transport us across great distances in time and space.

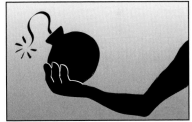
12.11 Action-to-Action Transition.

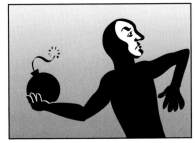

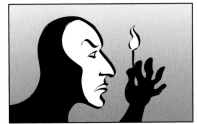
12.12 Subject-to-Subject Transition.

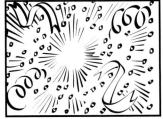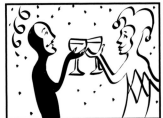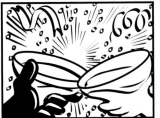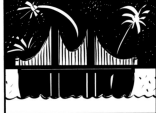
12.13 Scene-to-Scene Transition.

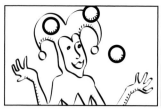 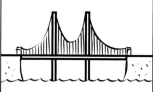

12.14 Non-Sequitur Transition.

A **non-sequitur transition** (12.14) requires even more reader involvement. Because there is no logical relationship between shots, meaning must be invented.

Two additional transitions often appear in Japanese comic books. A **moment-to-moment transition** (12.15) is used when a character or situation is simply being observed over time.

An **aspect-to-aspect transition** (12.16) is used to record different views within a scene. The passage of time is slowed as we scrutinize our surroundings.

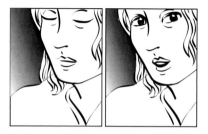

12.15 Moment to Moment Transition.

Key Questions

- Will a graphic relationship among the shots in your artwork add meaning to your project?
- Where are you using close-ups, medium shots, and long shots? Why?
- Would rhythmic variation strengthen communication?

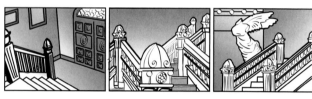

12.16 Aspect-to-Aspect Transition.

DURATION

Duration refers to the running time of a film, video, or performance; to the events depicted in the story; and to the overall span of time the story encompasses. For example, the viewing time of *Star Wars* is 118 minutes. The **plot duration** (from the capture of Princess Leia to the destruction of the Death Star) is about a month. The overall **story duration,** however, extends back to Darth Vader's betrayal of the Jedi warriors and his alliance with the dark side of the Force.

Matching the duration to the message is essential. Tolstoy's *War and Peace* cannot be fully communicated in a 25-minute film. Equally, a 10-second rocket launch may lose rather than gain power when the duration is increased. Every moment has its own power. A 15-second soft drink ad uses time just as carefully as a 2-hour film.

Determining the plot duration is equally important. Following the principles of drama described by Aristotle, ancient Greek plays (such as *Oedipus Rex*) generally occur over a one- or two-day period.

Even though the characters often refer to previous events, the action on stage is brief. *Hamlet, Romeo and Juliet,* and most other Shakespearean plays are equally brief. By limiting the time frame, the playwright focuses our attention on a few events and thus increases the impact of the play.

Key Questions

- What is the actual duration of the event on which your artwork is based? What is the duration of your edited version?

- How can temporal compression or expansion strengthen your artwork?

TEMPO

Tempo refers to the speed at which time passes. Despite the apparent constancy of real time, our perception of events in our lives varies widely, depending on the nature of the activity and the rate of change. Consider this story. Once upon a time, six coal miners were trapped by the collapse of a mine shaft. Based on the size of their shelter and the number of trapped men, the miners determined that there would be enough oxygen for a four-hour wait. Beyond that point, rescue would be futile: they would run out of oxygen. A miner with a fluorescent watch was asked to call out the hours as the time passed. He did so but modified his report, cutting in half the actual length of time passed. Eight hours passed. All the miners survived, except the man with the watch. He alone knew that they were out of oxygen.

Tempo is equally determined by the movement of the actors and by the editing of the film. In *Star Wars,* the fight between Darth Vader and Obi-Wan Kenobi began as staged combat between two actors (12.17). To provide director

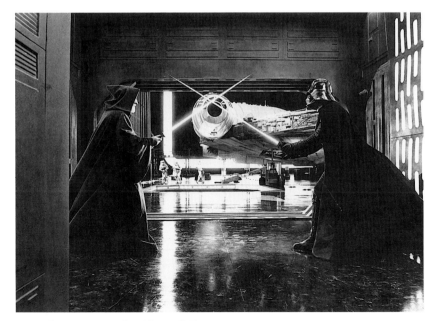

12.17 George Lucas, *Star Wars*, 1977.

George Lucas with enough raw material, many versions, or **takes,** were filmed, using multiple cameras. The final tempo was determined through editing. By connecting fragments from many different views, Lucas was able to increase or decrease the fight tempo.

As with film, tempo in a comic book is largely determined by the organization of multiple images. Vertical panels placed in close proximity tend to speed up the tempo, while horizontal panels tend to slow down the tempo. The tragic conclusion to the myth of Orpheus is shown in a double-page spread from Essential Vertigo's *The Sandman Special #1* (12.18). To retrieve his dead wife, the musician Orpheus has descended into the Underworld. Through his song, he persuades the god Hades to release his beloved Eurydice. They may leave unharmed, but, if Orpheus looks back before they

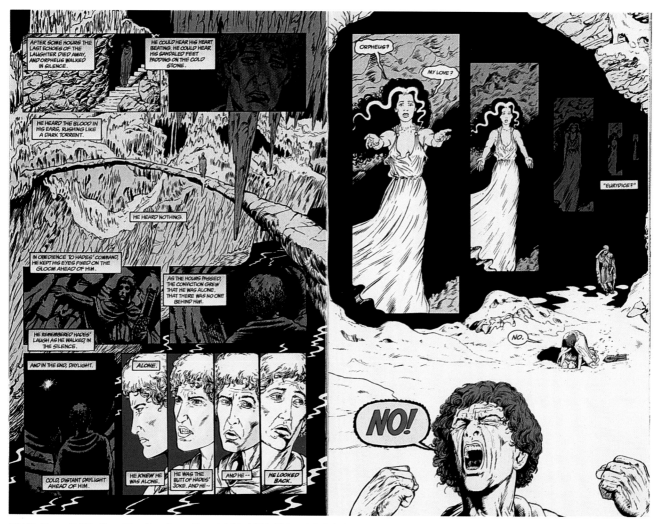

12.18 Essential Vertigo, *The Sandman Special #1,* **1991.** TM and © DC Comics. All Rights Reserved. Used with Permission.

reach the surface, Eurydice will again be lost. At the bottom of the left page, multiple frames show his desire to look back. The frames at the top of the right page show the result. He looked, and Eurydice fell back into Hades.

In a visual book, tempo can be created in two ways. First, by increasing the number and frequency of images, the artist can increase the tempo. Second, by turning the page, the reader controls viewing speed.

In a flip book, actions can pass slowly or quickly, depending on the pace set by the viewer. In a more elaborate book called *Cover to Cover* (12.19), Michael Snow presents multiple views of a room interior and the surrounding landscape. There is no text: photographs of walls, doorways, and streets re-create the environment within the book format. The viewer can run or stroll through the house, depending on the speed with which the pages are turned.

Key Questions

- How quickly does time pass in your artwork?
- Are there any changes in tempo?
- When and why do these changes occur?

INTENSITY

Intensity refers to the level of energy in a performance or the quality of observation of an event. For example, to win an Olympic gold medal, an ice skater must spin rapidly, fully extend each move, and exude both athletic skill and emotional conviction. Likewise, even an ordinary glass of water becomes fascinating when observed closely. The glass itself offers a graceful interplay between line and shape, while light passing through droplets of water breaks into a prismatic array of color.

Intensity of performance is an essential aspect of theater. We can feel the concentration the actors bring to the stage and, when a dramatic or dangerous event occurs, we can share their emotion. In *Cleaning the House* (12.20), Yugoslavian artist Marina Abramovic combined intensity with metaphor to

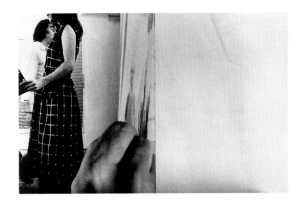

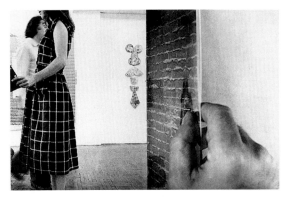

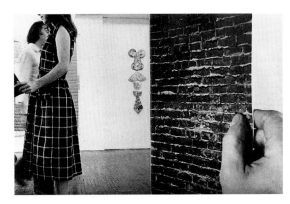

12.19 Michael Snow, from *Cover to Cover*, 1975. Press of the Nova Scotia College of Art and Design. New York University Press.

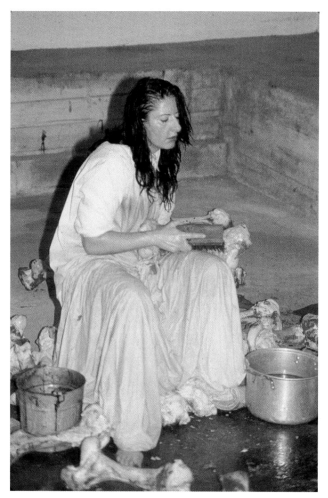

12.20 Marina Abramovic, *Cleaning the House,* **1995.** Performance at Sean Kelly Gallery. Duration, two hours.

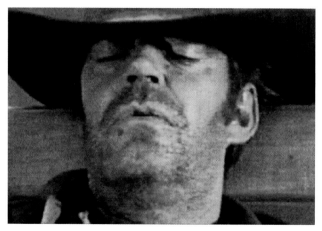

12.21 Sergio Leone, *Once upon a Time in the West,* **1968.** Detail.

make a political statement. Wearing a white dress and sitting in a poorly lit New York City basement, she repeatedly scrubbed the dirt and blood off a collection of massive cow bones. Like the bones, various ethnic groups in her homeland have been "cleansed," bringing trauma and bleached bones to the once prosperous country.

The opening sequence in Sergio Leone's *Once Upon a Time in the West* provides a cinematic example of observational intensity. Three bandits await the arrival of their leader by train. For nearly 15 seconds, the film focuses on the face of the most disreputable of the men, recording every twitch and swat as a fly repeatedly alights and investigates every florid detail (12.21). Finally, the train does arrive — and just in time, for the bandit has pulled his gun and is preparing to shoot the fly (and himself). No expansion or contraction of the actual running time is needed. The very act of filming the sequence in such detail gives it significance, as well as humor.

Key Questions

- What is the intensity level of your artwork or performance? How will a change in intensity affect the expressive power of your artwork?

- How are you communicating this intensity to the audience?

- What is the most important moment in your work? Is it the most intense moment?

- Should the intensity remain constant, or will a change in intensity enhance meaning?

SCOPE

Scope can be defined in two ways. Conceptually, it is the extent of our perception or the range of ideas our minds can grasp. Temporally, scope refers to the range of action within a given moment.

The earliest films, such as *The Arrival of a Train at La Ciotat Station* (12.22), are limited in scope. A single event is seen from a fixed viewpoint. By positioning his camera carefully, director Louis Lumière created a dynamic, diagonal composition. The train

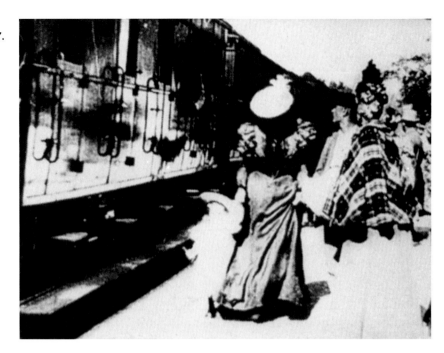

12.22 Louis Lumière, *The Arrival of a Train at La Ciotat Station*, 1897.

and passengers seem to come out of the screen and into the theater. Some audience members were so convinced of the illusion that they ran from the theater to avoid being hit by the train. In the early days of cinema, any moving image fascinated the audience, and the dramatic composition made this film especially popular.

As directors gained experience, they expanded the temporal scope of their films. In *The Great Train Robbery* (1903), a gang of bandits holds up a train; a telegraph operator alerts the authorities; a posse is gathered from men at a local dance; the posse captures the thieves. Director Edwin S. Porter used only 11 shots and the editing is quite simple. Nonetheless, it is clear that the robbery, the telegrapher's message, and the dance are roughly simultaneous events.

With *Intolerance*, director D. W. Griffith expanded conceptual scope to the limit. Using intolerance throughout history as a theme, Griffith developed four simultaneous stories: the fall of Babylon, Jesus' final days, the St. Bartholomew's Day Massacre in France, and a labor strike in modern-day America. These stories are intercut throughout the film, with the image of a woman rocking a cradle as a further recurrent theme. Each story concludes in an attempted rescue. Weaving the four narratives together in an accelerating rhythm (12.23), Griffith brings the film to a breathtaking conclusion.

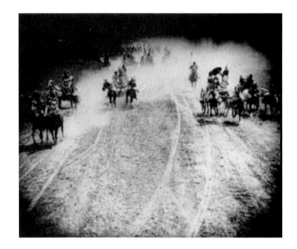

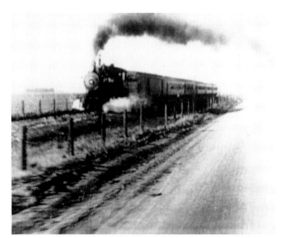

12.23 D. W. Griffith, *Intolerance*, 1916.

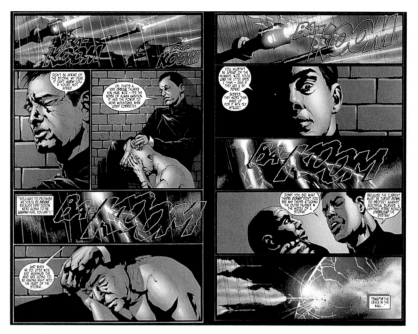

12.24 Paul Jenkins, Writer, and Jae Lee, Artist, *Inhumans: "First Contact,"* Volume 2, Issue 5, March 1999. Marvel Comics.

Complex stories require complex editing, and Griffith became a master of the art. By alternately showing two or more events, he created a connection between simultaneous actions. Comic book artists use many of the same skills. This technique of crosscutting is repeatedly used in *Inhumans* (12.24), by Paul Jenkins and Jae Lee. Moving from cannon fire to a quiet conversation between two men, the artists show that the events are concurrent.

Scope is equally important in traditional narrative painting. In Nicolas Poussin's *The Rape of the Sabine Women* (12.25), a complex event is shown in a single image. Seeking wives, the Romans have invited the Sabines to a festival. They then attack their guests and abduct the women. Many actions occur at once. In the left corner, Romulus raises his cloak as a signal to attack. As the courtyard swirls with struggles between the women and their captors, an old woman and two children watch in terror.

Key Questions

• Is your artwork limited or broad in scope?

• If it is broad in scope, how can you create continuity among multiple events?

• If it is narrow in scope, how can a "small" story become meaningful?

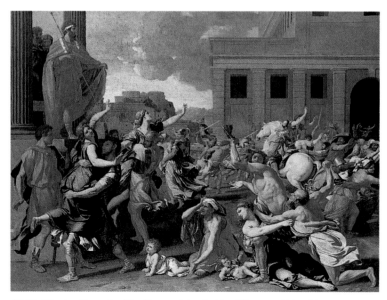

12.25 Nicolas Poussin, *The Rape of the Sabine Women*, 1634. Oil on canvas, 5 ft ⅞ in. × 6 ft 10⅝ in. (154.6 × 209.9 cm).

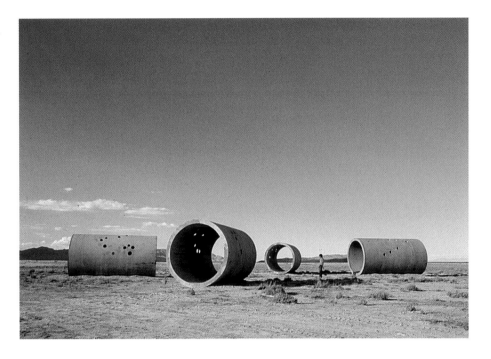

12.26 Nancy Holt, *Sun Tunnels*, 1973–76. Great Basin Desert, UT. Four tunnels, each 18 ft long × 9 ft 4 in. diameter (5.5 × 2.8 m), each axis 86 ft long (26.2 m). Aligned with sunrises and sunsets on the solstices.

SETTING

Setting is one of the most complex aspects of time. It includes the physical and temporal location of a story, its props and costumes, and the use of sound.

The physical setting of an event has an extraordinary impact on meaning. An action that is appropriate in one context may be appalling in another. As a drum major, you will be applauded when you strut down Main Street during a Fourth of July parade. At a different time of day (such as Monday morning rush hour) or in a different location (such as an airport), you are likely to be arrested.

The temporal setting is equally significant. Most of the action in *Gone with the Wind* is derived from romantic conflict involving Scarlett O'Hara, Ashley Wilkes, and Rhett Butler. While each of the three characters is interesting, the love triangle itself is commonplace. It is the temporal setting of the novel during the American Civil War that shifts the story from soap opera to epic.

Likewise, Nancy Holt's *Sun Tunnels* (12.26) would be meaningless if removed from its site in western Utah. Constructed from four 22-ton concrete tunnels, this sculpture is aligned with the rising and setting sun during the winter and summer solstices. The arrangement of stars in four constellations is shown using holes cut in the walls of each tunnel. Designed to heighten awareness of our place in the universe, this work relies on both time and place for its impact.

Objects and Implications

Props and costumes can have an equally dramatic effect in a narrative. The top hat and tuxedo worn by Fred Astaire in many films helped convey a formal elegance, while the leather jacket worn by Michael Jackson in *Beat It* clearly placed him on a contemporary city street. In James Cameron's *Titanic*, the diamond known as the Heart of the Ocean and the drawing of Rose wearing this jewel are essential to the overall narrative.

Fifty Years of Silence (12.27 A–C), a visual book by Tatana Kellner is even more dependent on objects and their meanings. The simple pine crate that houses the book seems innocuous, until we see the small, five-digit number burned into the lid. When the lid is removed, a papier-mâché arm is revealed, bearing the same number. It is a cast of the arm of Kellner's mother, a survivor of Auschwitz. The book pages, cut out around the arm, tell the story of the family before and during the Holocaust. As the pages are turned, the actual arm and the cut-out

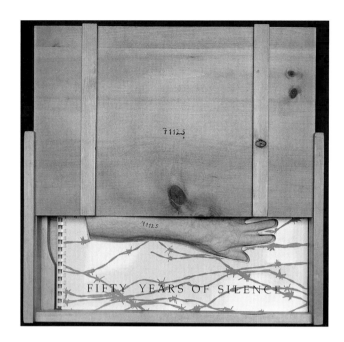

arm are as inescapable as the repressed memories of a Holocaust survivor. By placing it in such a prominent position in the book, Kellner provides us with a sculptural close-up of the indelible tattoo.

The wooden crate suggests a container for expensive wine or a shipping crate for a valuable object. The arm is an even more compelling sculptural object. By using these "props," Kellner gives her book greater immediacy and transforms the familiar story of a Holocaust survivor into a highly personal event.

12.27A Tatana Kellner, *Fifty Years of Silence,* **1992.** Cover, 14 × 22⅝ × 3 in. (35.5 × 57.3 × 7.6 cm).

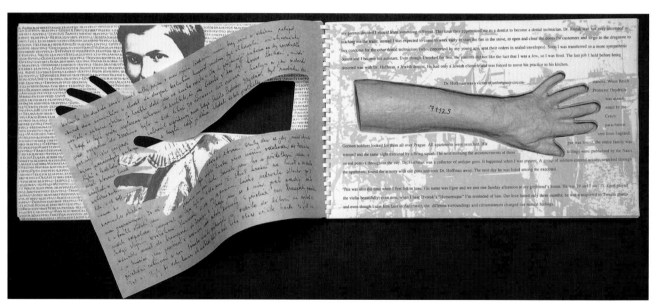

12.27B Tatana Kellner, *Fifty Years of Silence,* **1992.** 12 × 20 × 1½ in. (30.5 × 50.8 × 3.8 cm).

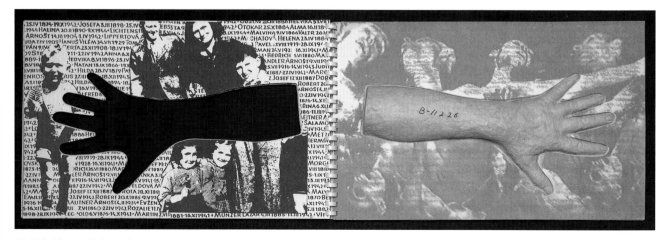

12.27C Tatana Kellner, *Fifty Years of Silence,* **1992.** 12 × 20 × 1½ in. (30.5 × 50.8 × 3.8 cm).

Setting and Actor

Relationships between an actor and a setting can substantially affect our interpretation of an action or event. As shown in figures 12.28 through 12.34, placement of a single figure within a setting offers a wide range of possibilities.

First, we must decide where to place the dancer within the frame. Three alternatives are shown in figure 12.28. Positioned at the far left edge, she faces an empty stage, which invites her entry. Positioned in the center, she commands attention. She can move to the right, left, forward, or back with ease. She is now in a more commanding position. Facing right, and positioned at the right, she seems ready to leave the frame, perhaps to join other dancers offstage.

What happens when the size of the dancer is varied? As shown in figure 12.29, changing the size of the figure in relationship to the frame helps define the distance between the dancer and the viewer. When the dancer is reduced in size and placed in the upper half of the frame, she seems distant, far from the viewer. When she moves far into the foreground, with her torso filling the frame, she seems to push past the boundary and into our space.

The addition of an illusionistic setting (12.30) dramatically changes the amount of space available to our dancer. Even a simple line can be used in various ways. It may be the ground, providing a resting place for the dancer. When the dancer overlaps the line, it recedes, suggesting a horizon. The addition of a second line can expand the space even further. We can now show two grounds at the same time: the foreground and the background.

In figure 12.31, the addition of perspective lines further enhances the space. A long corridor in one-point perspective gives the dancer an expansive stage that invites movement from the background to the foreground. The space can be extended beyond the edge of the frame by the repeating chairs and the lines in the floor. Despite her small size, the dancer's central placement makes her the focus of both images.

The setting can become even more significant when the dancer is viewed from above or below (12.32). Looking up from the front row gives the figure a commanding presence. Looking down from the balcony makes her seem insignificant.

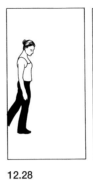
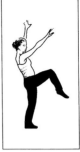
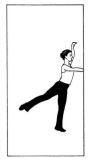

12.28

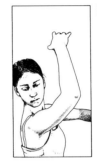
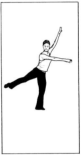
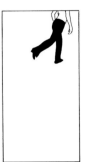

12.29

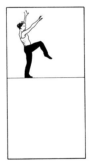
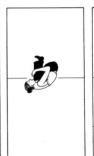
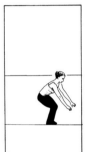

12.30

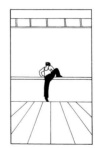
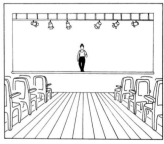

12.31

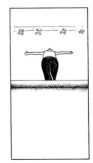
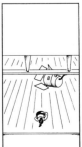
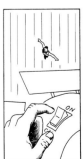

12.32

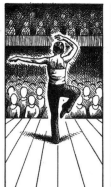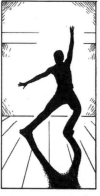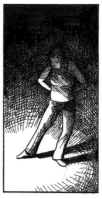

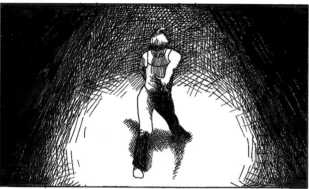

12.33

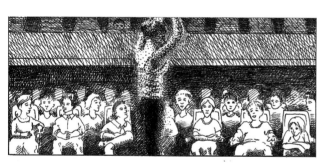

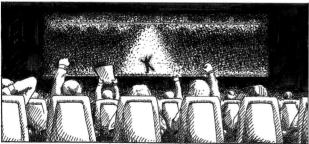

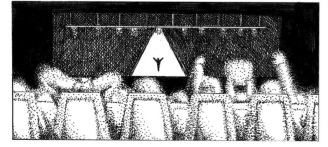

12.34

Turning on the lights greatly increases the compositional and emotional possibilities (12.33). Sidelighting accentuates the dimensionality of both the figure and the setting. When we backlight the dancer, she becomes a silhouette. We lose information about her volume but gain a striking graphic image and an impressive cast shadow. Spotlighting the dancer can direct attention to a specific part of her body or eliminate the rest of the stage altogether.

Variations in focus (12.34) can affect both spatial location and emotional impact. When the foreground figure is out of focus, she is less dominant, and we quickly look past her into the more tightly focused audience. A more traditional use of focus is shown in the second drawing. Clear focus in the foreground gradually diminishes as we approach the distant stage. However, do we really want to focus on the back of the audience? By focusing on the distant stage, we can watch the dancer end her performance and accept the applause.

Sound: The Hidden Dimension

Two versions of a clip from *Chariots of Fire* were shown during the 1996 Academy Awards ceremony. In the first, a group of young men ran along a beach, accompanied by the sounds of their feet splashing in the water. It was a pleasant but prosaic scene, showing ordinary men on an ordinary beach. The same footage was then shown as it appeared in theaters around the world. Accompanied by the famous theme music, these Olympic runners became graceful, even godlike. They were transformed by the music.

Despite its invisibility, the soundtrack is as important to a film as the images we see. Sound engages another of our senses and heightens our emotion. A well-written score can set the stage for an action and help unify a complex film. And sound heightens our expectations. Consider the importance of squeaky doors in any horror movie or our feeling of expectation when the *Star Wars* theme is played. As we begin to study film, we find that the example from *Chariots of Fire* is not an isolated case. Sound can make or break a film.

Four types of sound dominate time design: speech (as delivered by an actor or generated from the audience), music, ambient sound, and sound effects. Each sound has seven qualities.

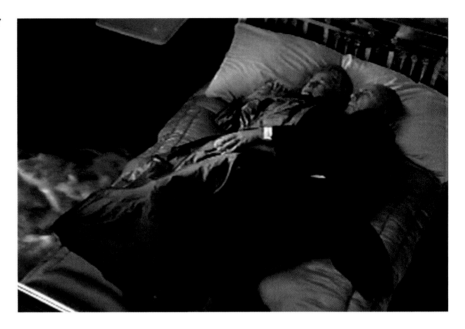

Loudness is determined by the size of the oscillations in a sound wave. Just as Beethoven varied the volume (or loudness) within his symphonies, so the astute filmmaker or performance artist learns to use a full range of sound, from a whisper to a scream.

Pitch is determined by wave frequency, as compression and expansion occur within the sound wave. The higher pitch of most female voices is generally less threatening than the lower pitch of most male voices. Not surprisingly, the hero is a tenor, while the villain is a bass or a baritone in most operas.

Timbre refers to the unique quality of each instrument. For example, a note of the same volume and pitch is quite different when it is generated by a trumpet rather than a violin.

Duration refers to the length of time the sound can be heard. A sound that persists over a long period of time is often used as a bridge between two or more film clips, while a brief, explosive sound may jolt us out of our seats.

Rhythm is determined by three qualities: the **beat,** or pulse, of the sound; the **pace** (or tempo), at which the sound is played; and the **accents,** or areas of emphasis, within the sound. We encounter rhythm in every conversation as we listen to the speed of our friend's speech and note his or her emphasis on particular words. Rap music, which in some ways is a heightened form of speech, greatly emphasizes the beat, through both a rhythmic use of words and the strong definition of each syllable.

In film, **fidelity** refers to the connection between a sound and its source. The arrival of a helicopter at the end of the musical *Miss Saigon* is accompanied by the loud sound of a churning propeller. Here, the sonic and visual information matches. In *Apocalypse*

Now, Richard Wagner's "Ride of the Valkyries" is played as a group of helicopters arrives. As with *Chariots of Fire,* this mismatch between the visual and sonic information substantially changes our interpretation of the event.

Finally, all forms of sound operate within a **spatial context.** The bagpipe, designed to rally troops in war, is an excellent instrument to play outdoors. When played in a small room, the same instrument can very nearly blast plaster off a wall. Likewise, a whispered conversation in a closet may be more compelling than a shouted conversation on a beach. Even when we have no image at all, sound alone can define space and create a sense of anticipation or dread.

In a film, the spatial dimension of sound becomes even more significant. **Diegetic** sound, or sound that is part of the world we see on the screen, can be generated by a visible event or can come from an invisible, offscreen source. Both onscreen and offscreen sound are critically important and, in many cases, a director will shift between the two. For example, in *Titanic,* a quartet of musicians begins to play "Nearer My God to Thee" as the ship sinks lower and lower. The music continues as we see an elderly couple in their cabin, embracing (12.35), and a mother comforting her child. The combination of the music and the images heightens the emotion of the moment.

Key Questions

- What is the setting for your artwork? Why did you choose that setting?

- Consider all aspects of setting: sound, props, physical space, and lighting. Have you used each aspect fully?

- How can changes in setting add meaning to your artwork?

- What will happen if the setting changes during the performance?

CHRONOLOGY

Chronology refers to temporal order. In real time, a foot race begins with the athletes lining up in position (action A), the firing of the starting gun (action B), the running of the race (action C), and the conclusion at the finish line (action D). These actions can be organized in various ways, from a disorienting ABACADA pattern to the familiar ABCD pattern of the actual race.

In *Structure of the Visual Book,*[3] Keith Smith demonstrates the narrative possibilities of multiple images. Changes in chronology completely change meaning. In each case, relationships among the

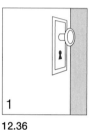 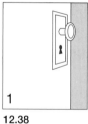

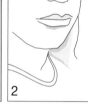

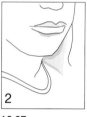 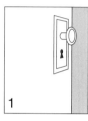

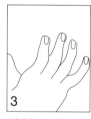 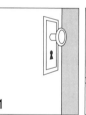

12.36–12.45 Keith Smith, Excerpt from *Structure of the Visual Book,* **1995.**

12.36 — Start with a door.

12.37 — Add a figure. Here, a woman opens the door.

12.38 — Here, the door opens and we meet a woman.

12.39 — Adding a close-up of a hand creates a confrontation, . . .

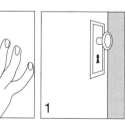 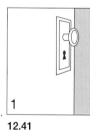

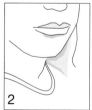 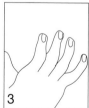

12.40 — . . . while this order creates a sense of anticipation.

12.41 — Here, we create a mystery.

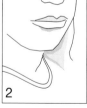

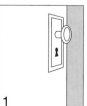 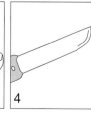 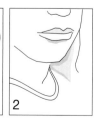

12.42 — With the introduction of a knife, a new meaning emerges. It is now becoming threatening.

continued

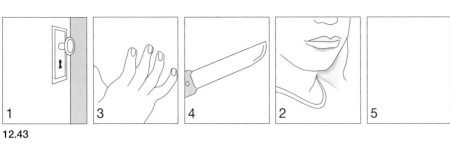
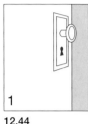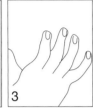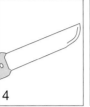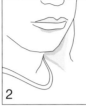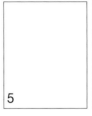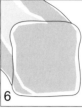

12.43

And now even more so. Our imaginations provide a wide range of horrors for panel 5.

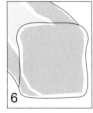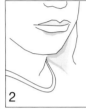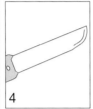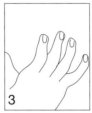

12.44

Addition of a loaf of bread, however, diffuses the tension. It is not a murder after all, just a sandwich being made.

12.45

The woman still has to take care, however; this final version suggests that she has cut herself!

images create the sequence of events needed to tell a story.

Chronology is created when shots are combined. A filmmaker combines shots through **editing.** Editing serves six basic purposes.

First, the film editor must select the most compelling images from the total footage shot. No matter how carefully a scene is rehearsed, variations in performance quality occur, especially when there are many actors on the set. Even more footage is shot for a documentary film. In filming the 1936 Olympic Games in Berlin, Leni Riefenstahl devoted 10 solid weeks of work just to watching the raw footage. Editing this material down to a 3½-hour film took another 2 years!

Second, the raw film must be organized into a cohesive whole. Multiple cameras are often used to provide plenty of rough footage. Constructing a coherent conversation using both close-up and distant shots is often the first step.

Third, through editing, a temporal framework for the film is developed. Time can expand, contract, or move in a dizzying spiral. When using crosscutting, the editor shifts back and forth between two or more events, thus suggesting the simultaneous occurrence of multiple actions. *A Tale of Two Cities*, by Charles Dickens, is a literary example of crosscutting. The narrative reaches a climax as Sydney Carton, in Paris, is led to the guillotine, while his double, who was actually condemned to die, is drugged and transported to London. Chapter after chapter, the story shifts between the two men, increasing the sense of urgency while presenting the simultaneous events. This novel offers simultaneous action at its best. Indeed, pioneer film director D. W. Griffith used Dickens as an example when challenged for his innovative editing of *Intolerance*.

Fourth, tempo in a film is largely determined by the number of cuts made. For example, an introspective drama may be constructed from 1,000 shots, while an action film may be made of 2,000 shots or more. Variations in tempo help sustain interest. If there is too little variation, a fast-paced film is just as monotonous as a slow-paced film. To develop momentum gradually, many filmmakers use a slow-paced beginning, which builds to a fast-paced climax, which returns to a slow-paced conclusion.

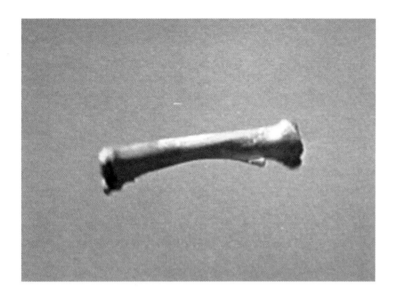

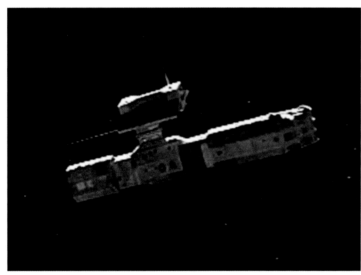

12.46 Stanley Kubrick, *2001: A Space Odyssey*, 1968.

Fifth, connections made through editing can heighten emotion and suggest the real motivation for a character's actions. In a famous experiment, early Soviet filmmaker Lev Kulesov demonstrated the emotional impact of editing. He combined a neutral shot of an actor's face with four very different images, including a bowl of soup, scenes from nature, a baby, and a dead woman.[4] When the film was shown, the audience praised the actor's skill: he looked hungry when the soup appeared, longed for freedom when the landscape was shown, was filled with joy at the sight of the baby, and felt grief at the sight of the woman. In each case, however, the shot of the actor's face was exactly the same. The emotions were created by the audience's response to the editing, not by any change in the actor's expression.

Finally, connections made through editing can substantially change or enhance the meaning of a film. By cutting from a bone spinning in the air to a space station orbiting the earth (12.46), Stanley Kubrick connected prehistory to space travel in *2001: A Space Odyssey*.

Key Questions

- Do events in your project occur in linear (ABCD) or nonlinear order?

- What would happen if this order were changed?

- What would happen if you deleted half of the information in your project? Would the artwork as a whole gain, or lose power?

SCHINDLER'S LIST: CONTENT AND COMPOSITION

All these aspects of editing are used brilliantly in *Schindler's List*. Mixing contemporary images with black-and-white images of wartime Poland, director Steven Spielberg tells a harrowing tale of the survival of over 1,000 Jews during the Holocaust. Based on historical events, the film shows the transformation of Nazi Oskar Schindler from a single-minded war profiteer to a compassionate man who finally bought the lives of his enslaved workers. It is an incredible story, and any skillful filmmaker could have made a good film based on this event. However, to show the complexities of each character and to turn the story into a truly compelling film required another level of insight. Spielberg and his collaborators had that insight.

The critical importance of editing is apparent from the start. A contemporary scene of a Jewish family at home ends with a trail of smoke rising from an extinguished candle (12.47). We cut to the smokestack on a train in wartime Krakow (12.48) and are transported back in time.

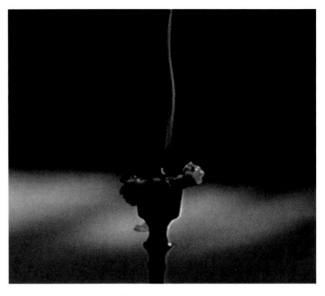

12.47 *Schindler's List.* Extinguished candle.

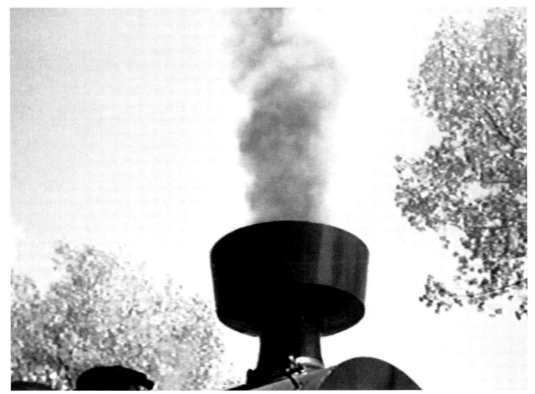

12.48 *Schindler's List.* Train's smokestack.

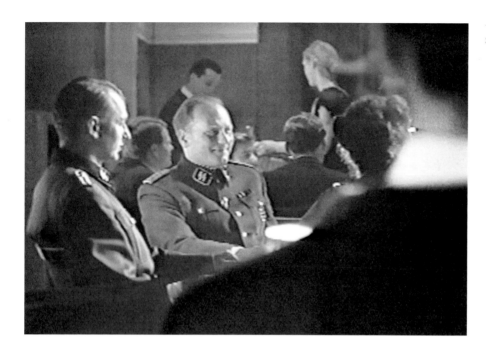

12.49 *Schindler's List.*
Schindler in a cafe.

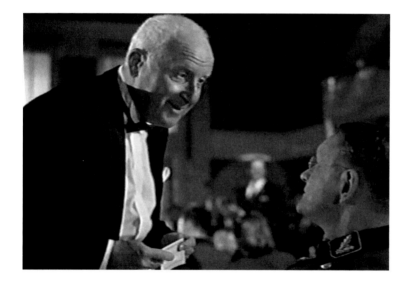

Editing also establishes Schindler's motivation and gives us insight into his personality. When he arrives at a cafe favored by Nazi officers, the maitre d' seats him, then asks a waiter who he is. Neither one knows his name.

Schindler carefully positions himself at the center of the room. Through a series of close-ups, we follow his gaze, as he notes the SS insignia on an officer's uniform and assesses the importance of the reserved table across the room. Using Schindler as the axis, the camera pans around the room (12.49).

Positioned just over his shoulder, we watch Schindler as he observes the soldiers. He did not come to this restaurant to eat. He intends to meet the most influential Nazis in the area and establish himself as a man of consequence. As the scene continues, Schindler joins the Nazis and leads a song. Finally, the highest-ranking officer asks the maitre d' about this newcomer. He now enthusiastically replies, "Why, that is Oskar Schindler!" (12.50A). Schindler (who entered the restaurant as a nobody) is now well defined: he has become the center of attention. The evening has been a success (12.50B).

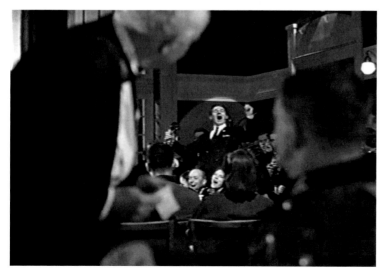

12.50A and B *Schindler's List.* Maitre d' points out Schindler.

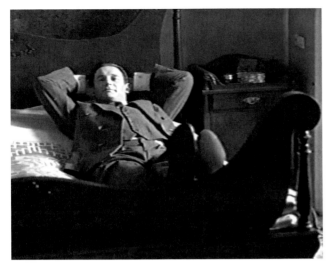

12.51 *Schindler's List.* New home.

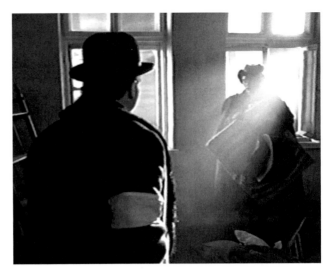

12.52 *Schindler's List.* New home, shared by three families.

Crosscutting is used throughout the film, both to establish a connection and to emphasize separation. Eviction of a Jewish family from their spacious home is immediately followed by images of Schindler surveying the same space, now his new home. He reclines on a large bed and exclaims, "It couldn't be better!" (12.51). We then cut to the evicted family, struggling up the stairs of their new house, which will be shared with many other families. As they sit down in the single room they have been assigned, the wife notes, "It could be worse."

Her angry husband replies, "How could it *possibly* be worse?" (12.52). Just then, another large family apologetically moves into the cramped space. It is now worse.

The destruction of the Krakow ghetto is a masterpiece of storytelling. Sound is especially important in this sequence, and variations in pacing substantially increase the visual impact. The sequence begins as Nazi commandant Goeth gives his assembled troops a brief history lesson (12.53). As he describes the arrival of the Jews in Poland in the fourteenth

12.53 *Schindler's List.* Commandant Goeth.

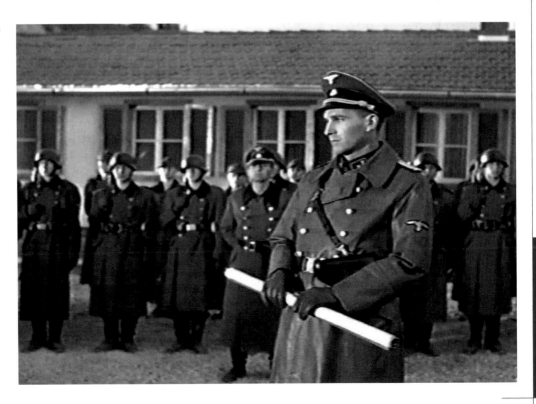

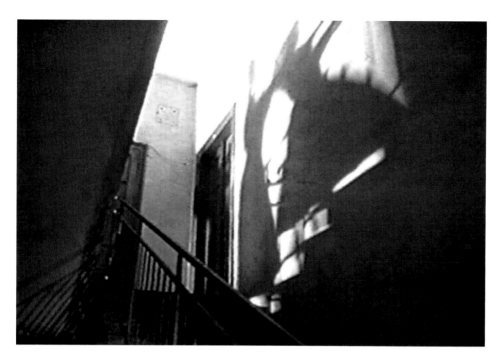

century, we cut from the soldiers to scenes of ghetto families quietly eating and preparing for the day ahead, unaware of the terror to follow. We return to Goeth as he concludes his speech, noting that "by this evening, those six centuries are a rumor. They never existed."

An explosion of violence follows. The family at breakfast is now wrapping jewels in bread and eating them, in the hope of retaining something of value when the pogrom ends. Stern, the overworked accountant upon whom Schindler depends, desperately searches his pockets for his identity papers as a soldier screams in his face. The camera is jostled as terrified people are evicted from their apartments. Diagonal staircases and extreme camera angles increase compositional dynamism (12.54).

A contrast between violence and compassion, fast and slow pace, heightens the impact of this sequence. An old woman, walking slowly down a foggy street, is ignored by the soldiers, who run past, determined to clear the ghetto. A doctor methodically adds poison to cups of water, then gently administers it to his patients (12.55), rather than leave them for the soldiers to kill. A young Polish boy, assigned to report any survivors, instead saves the life of a woman and her daughter.

We now see a small girl in a red coat walking through the streets (12.56) and observed by Schindler, who surveys the action from a nearby hill. Accompanied by angelic music, she is the symbol of all the innocent deaths on this horrible day. We last see her as she scoots under a bed, seeking a place to hide. We will not see her again until much later in the film, when her red coat appears as the corpses from the ghetto liquidation are gathered to be burned.

Quiet finally descends on the city. The soldiers are now using stethoscopes to listen for survivors who may have hidden in apartment walls. In a final burst of violence, one soldier plays a vigorous Bach toccata while other soldiers explode into action, firing their machine guns into the walls and urging their dogs to attack.

The calm before the storm makes this sequence even more frightening. It would be impossible to sustain a fast pace throughout the film. Incessant horror would have simply left us numb. The editing and use of contrast has greatly enhanced the power of the ghetto sequence, leaving us with an indelible impression.

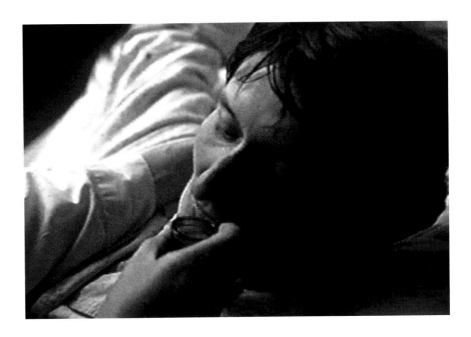

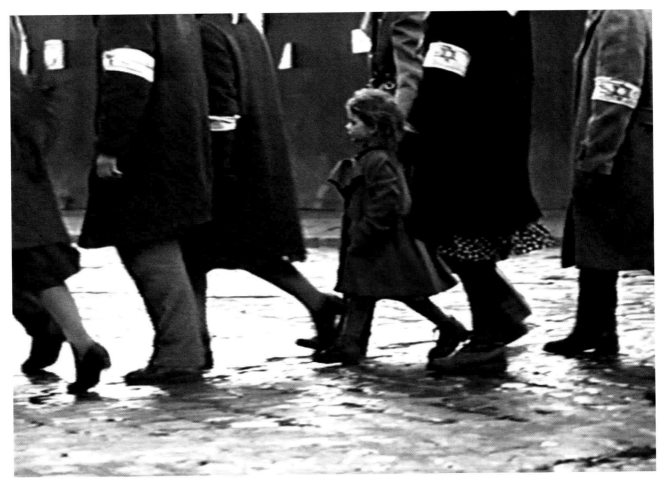

12.56 *Schindler's List.* Girl in a red coat.

SUMMARY

- An understanding of time is an essential aspect of any artwork, Photographers, filmmakers, and performers use time directly; painters, illustrators, ceramicists, and other artists generally use time indirectly.

- The building blocks of film are the frame, the shot, the scene, and the sequence.

- Shots can be related graphically, spatially, temporally, and rhythmically.

- The cut, fade, dissolve, and wipe are the most common transitions in film.

- Comic books use six additional transitions: action-to-action, subject-to-subject, scene-to-scene, moment-to-moment, non-sequitur, and aspect-to-aspect.

- Duration, tempo, intensity, scope, setting, and chronology are the six major elements of time design.

Keywords

accent
action-to-action transition
aspect-to-aspect transition
beat
chronology
close-up
crosscutting
cut
diegetic
dissolve
duration

editing
fade
fidelity
flashback
frame
graphic relationship
intensity
lap dissolve
long shot
loudness
medium shot
moment-to-moment transition

non-sequitur transition
pace
pitch
plot duration
rhythm
rhythmic relationship
scene
scene-to-scene transition
scope
sequence
setting
shot

spatial context
spatial relationship
story duration
subject-to-subject transition
take
tempo
temporal relationship
timbre
wipe

Profile:
Sharon Greytak, Filmmaker
Resilient Spirit

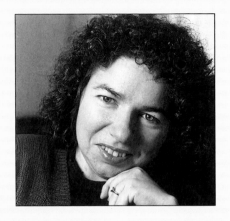

Sharon Greytak is writer, producer, and director of two award-winning features, *The Love Lesson* (1996) and *Hearing Voices* (1990), as well as the documentary *Weirded Out and Blown Away* (1985). Her films have been screened theatrically and at numerous festivals and showcases, including the Museum of Modern Art, Lincoln Center, Kennedy Center for the Performing Arts, George Eastman House, WNET-13, The Wexner Center, and Films de Femmes in Creteil, France. She won a Silver Award at the Houston International Film Festival and first prize at the Athens International Film Festival. She recently finished *Losing It*, a feature-length documentary, and is now writing her third fiction screenplay.

MS: You studied painting at CalArts and were always interested in literature. How, then, did you become a filmmaker?

SG: Film seemed to suit my personality. I was beginning to feel that art shown primarily in galleries reached a specific audience, but not the general public where discussion and change should occur. I felt an urgency about the social issues I wanted to address and the unconventional stories I knew only I could tell. I knew as a filmmaker I could reach a very wide audience.

Furthermore, the process of painting is mainly solitary, while filmmaking is absolutely a collaborative art. There's an energy in film production that doesn't exist anywhere else, an energy toward what the mind's eye sees, toward what the camera will record. I guess I'm able to hold an idea and an image in my mind for a very long time. Communicating my vision and staying on track as the piece becomes more refined is the essence of what drives any artist.

MS: You write the screenplay, hire the crew, produce and direct the film, then market the result, yet it all seems to start with a story you want to tell. What stories interest you most?

SG: All of my screenplays are original. A film is a visual story — very different than a written story. I write pictures. The script is the blueprint, providing the visual and emotional tone as well as the dialogue.

I explore unconventional human relationships in my stories — relationships that are overlooked by the mass media. I am interested in stories that haven't been told. In any film, I am always aware of the facet or angle of a story that is unique. The space between one's public and private identity has always fascinated me. I want to give voice to people whose voices are rarely heard.

MS: You've said that you are good at spotting the nuggets, the most telling images and human interactions. What makes an image or an exchange of dialogue compelling?

SG: It's very hard to explain. For me, it's a combination of all the senses, plus one or two unnamed senses, maybe instinct. I guess you're looking for the essence of what you're trying to communicate but never naming it precisely. If you name it directly, it's dead. It comes back to trusting the viewer and leaving space for interpretation. When I'm directing actors and doing several takes, I look for something that shimmers, or wavers in the air around them, where all of us, cast and crew, have created an ephemeral moment aside from the actor's lines or anything tangible. It's something that lingers in the air for a moment. It is resonant yet unsaid.

MS: Film constantly changes, and, if the viewer doesn't "get" it the first time, the story can be lost. How do you determine what to say? What is essential?

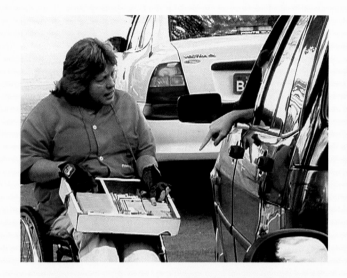
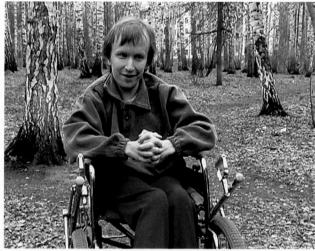
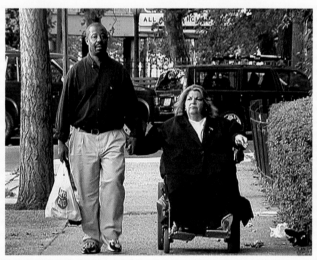
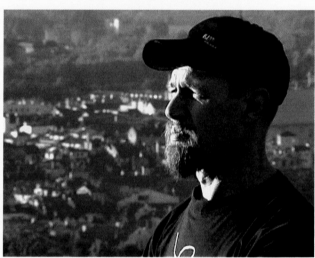

Stills from *Losing It*, Documentary Film by Sharon Greytak, Writer, Producer, Director, 2000

SG: In any artform, it is so easy to overstate an idea. When I was in my twenties, I studied with painter David Salle. At that time, I was painting and drawing. I showed a series of mixed media works in David's experimental studio class. David cocked his head, stared a long time, then turned and said, "What do you think I am, stupid?" I was stunned. He went on about signs and symbols, the indexical and the iconic, a priori knowledge, and underestimating your audience. He then rattled off a list of books and articles I should be reading.

I made no art for three months. I read. I read aesthetics and politics, semiotics. I skulked around the edges of my classes, listening and watching. It was the turning point in my life as an artist, exactly the right thing. And I picked up the camera, Super-8 at first. I realized I had been always talking about my abstract drawings in a very narrative way. I wondered what I would do if I had to choose an image in the world. Inspiration had never come from life

before. It had always been formal properties of line and color, mark-making, and the gesture. It was from that point that my films and drawings began to have an undertone, something of their own, combined with a respect for the intelligence of my audience.

MS: I am impressed by the immediacy of film. A good film draws me in: I feel that I am right there.

SG: A base in reality is essential: when you have that, anything is possible to write. And small things can illuminate big ideas. When I screened my short films at a festival in Krakow, Poland, we were invited to visit Auschwitz. Since I have a physical disability, I was not able to follow the tour group to the second level of the barracks. The irony of the situation was comical, and powerful. Had it been 50 years earlier, I wouldn't have lasted a day there. Just by fate, the scenario would have been very different.

As the rest of the tour went upstairs, I stayed alone on the ground floor of the barracks. In silence, I was able to look at the scratches on the door, scratches that had been made by human hands. By sitting still, alone, I could touch where so many other lives had been. I could make a more authentic connection through the remnants of a real life, through the energy I did not expect to find.

MS: Tell me about your current film.

SG: *Losing It* is an international film exploring the quality of life for people with disabilities. It's about how people navigate social stereotypes within their culture to carve out a sense of purpose and worth despite physical limitations. I traveled in the U.S., Brazil, Hong Kong, Russia, and Italy to interview people about the way they view themselves and the way in which society views them. It's also a story of personal search and human nature with regard to disability.

MS: What advice do you have for my students?

SG: Cultivate a diverse circle of friends and colleagues. Build a career slowly. Making art means a life in the arts. Not a year or two but a lifetime of observing and questioning in order to create something unique. When I find myself having to do something or go somewhere out of obligation, a thing that at the time seems totally a waste of time, fate often finds a way of adding that experience or person to further my creative work. Most of the time, I end up seeing an angle I wouldn't have recognized before. I guess what I'm saying is, stay open enough for life to show you things. Let life take you where you're supposed to go.

Narrative and Non-Narrative

As with any other form of art or design, a film, a performance, or an installation is designed to communicate ideas, express emotions, record action, and explore vision. Just as a poet uses a few words to evoke a complex idea, so artists can communicate a wide range of thoughts and feelings through a single image. On the other hand, the sequential artist can act like a novelist. Since the verbal and visual information is distributed over many images, ideas and emotions can be expanded when sequential art is used.

TELL ME A STORY

Like the novelist, many sequential artists use collections of images to tell stories. Storytelling is one of the most ancient and effective forms of communication. It can serve four basic purposes.

- *Stories can increase self-awareness.* When we record our own story in an autobiography, we become more conscious of the patterns in our lives and can gain a better understanding of the individual events that break or reinforce these patterns.

- *Stories can provide inspiration.* By researching the life of another artist or discussing the past with an elderly relative, we find that our personal problems and conflicts are not unique. Everyone experiences a wide range of emotions, from exhilaration to despair. In reading another person's story, we can learn from his or her solution to a problem.

- *Stories can supply information.* News stories and documentary films provide us with information on current events and analysis of their implications. Art never occurs in a vacuum. Developing an understanding of the world around us can strengthen our ideas.

- *Stories can encourage understanding.* Abstract numbers and dry statistics are rarely as compelling as human experience. When we hear the story of a particular refugee in a specific war, the horrible effect of combat on civilians becomes personal. Such stories can help us understand the emotional meaning of an event.

To increase our understanding even further, we may explore the biggest questions of all, through myths. A **myth** is a traditional story collectively composed by many members of a society. The creation of the world, sources of evil, the power of knowledge, and even the nature of reality may be explained through these grand expressions of the imagination. The *Star Wars* series, most comic books, and many types of performance art are inspired by myths.

WORKING WITH MULTIPLE IMAGES

In all forms of storytelling, multiple images can provide many advantages over an individual image. In Jacques-Louis David's *Oath of the Horatii* (13.1), both the action and the emotion must be expressed within a single frame. To avoid mass slaughter, two warring Roman clans, the Horatii and the Curatii, have each agreed to send three warriors into a fight to the death. This heroic moment of self-sacrifice is demonstrated by the three young Horatii warriors on the left. A tragic complication to this plan is borne by the wives of the warriors, who are huddled together in a triangular shape on the right. They are members of the opposing Curatii clan and will lose either their brothers or their husbands in the battle. The children in the background are caught in the middle.

Through skillful composition and careful selection of an emotionally charged moment in the narrative, Jacques-Louis David created a masterpiece that caused a sensation when it was first shown in 1786 and continues to be studied today. The use of gesture, composition, and technique in this painting is stunning. Nonetheless, it is difficult to appreciate

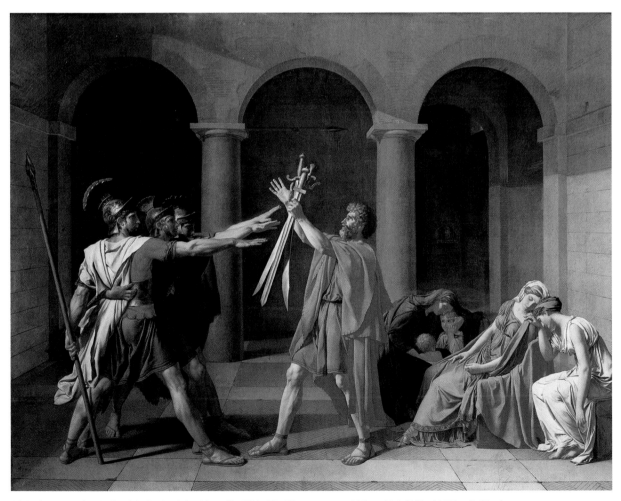

13.1 Jacques-Louis David, *Oath of the Horatii*, 1784–85. Oil on canvas, 14 ft × 10 ft 8¼ in. (4.27 × 3.26 m).

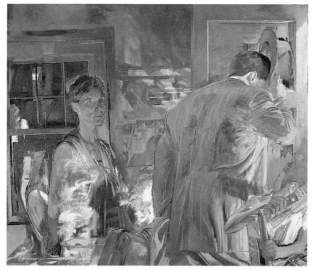

Left

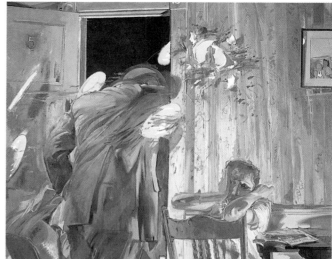

Middle

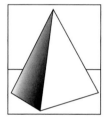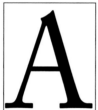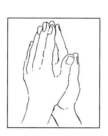

13.3 Grouping by Shape.

the painting fully or to understand the story without explanation. With only a single image, David had to rely on his audience for some knowledge of the event shown.

By contrast, in the three paintings that constitute *Division Street* (13.2), Jerome Witkin tells a story sequentially. Like David, he selected the colors, gestures, and actions most appropriate to the narrative and composed each frame with great care. Unlike *Oath of the Horatii*, however, *Division Street* requires little explanation. The argument in the first frame, the man's explosive departure in the second frame, and the angry woman in the third frame tell the story. This multiple-image narrative can speak for itself.

Multiple-Image Structures

In *Structure of the Visual Book,* Keith Smith describes three multiple-image structures commonly used by printmakers, photographers, and book artists.[1] A **group** is a collection of images that are related by subject matter, composition, or source. In figure 13.3, images of a pyramid, the letter *A,* and a pair of praying hands can be grouped by shape. Each is dominated by a triangle. The individual illustrations in figures 13.4, 13.5, and 13.6 can be grouped by subject. All are part of the *Frog Folio,* a calendar produced by Dellas Graphics to showcase the work of contemporary illustrators. In a group, image order is unimportant.

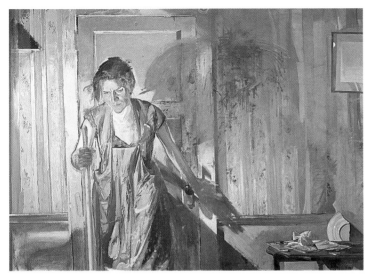

13.2 Jerome Witkin, *Division Street* [A Story Told in 3 Panels], **1984–85.** Oil on canvas, triptych. Top panel, 75⅛ × 63¼ in. (190.9 × 160.7 cm); middle panel, 81⅛ × 63 in. (206.2 × 160 cm); bottom panel, 87⅛ × 63 in. (221.3 × 160 cm).

Right

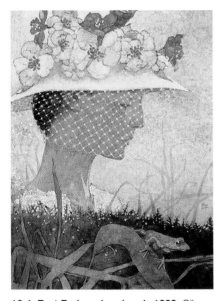

13.4 Bart Forbes, *Landmark,* **1999.** Oil on canvas, 14 × 19 in. (35.6 × 48.3 cm).

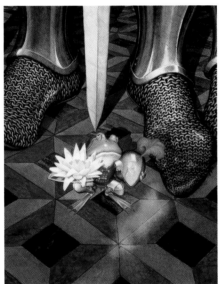

13.5 Charles Santore, Cover of *William the Curious, Knight of the Water Lilies,* **1997.** Watercolor, front cover 9 × 12 in. (22.8 × 30.5 cm).

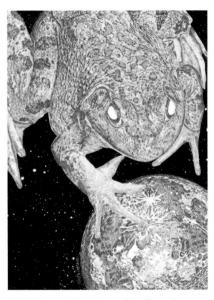

13.6 Murray Tinkelman, *The Frog Jumps over the Moon.* Colored ink crosshatch, 9 × 12 in. (22.9 × 30.5 cm).

A **series** links multiple images together sequentially. Each image builds on the previous image and leads to the subsequent image. As a result, events are linked together like boxcars on a train. *Chance Meeting,* by Duane Michals (13.7), is a series of photographs. Like a short film, it tells a simple story using multiple images.

Simple narratives, such as fairy tales and fables, often use serial construction. Indeed, numerical repetition may be an essential part of the story. For example, when Goldilocks enters the house of the three bears, she samples three bowls of porridge. One is too hot, the second is too cold, the third is just right. She tries sitting on the three chairs, with a similar result. Finally, when she decides to take a nap, she finds the first bed too hard, the second too soft, and the third just right. As a story for children, "Goldilocks" and other such tales are simple and straightforward. Flashbacks, crosscutting, and other narrative complexities are avoided.

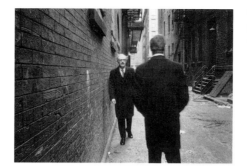

13.7 Duane Michals, *Chance Meeting*, 1969. Six prints, each 4⅞ × 3¼ in. (12.4 × 8.3 cm).

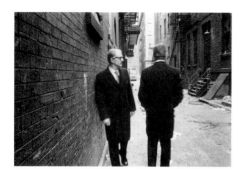
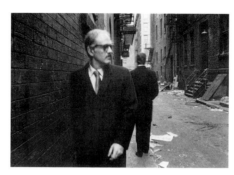

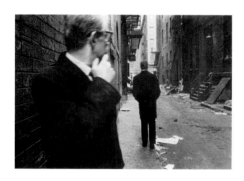
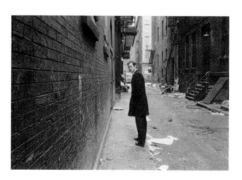

As defined by Smith, a **sequence** is the multiple-image structure used by most popular filmmakers and comic book artists. In a sequence, multiple images are organized by *cause and effect*. In a simple sequence, action number two is caused by action number one. In a complex sequence, there may be a considerable delay between the cause and the effect. Actions five, six, and seven may all be caused by action number one. Rather than film a simple line of boxcars in a train, we may now move among the cars, showing the conductor napping, two passengers playing cards, the engineer steering, and another passenger reading. These human actions may be combined with images of the landscape through which the train is traveling, the setting sun, or even images of the construction of the original train track. To understand a sequence, viewers may have to mentally connect many fragments of information.

From Scene to Screenplay

With a run time of an hour or more, a film or television show is constructed from many sequences, each building the story using cause and effect. Let's analyze one example.

Jeremy and Angela are spending their honeymoon on the Orient Express. On the third morning of the trip, they awake to the sound of drunken singing in the adjoining cabin. Angela wants to confront the revelers, while Jeremy cautions her against getting involved. They begin to argue. Angela accuses Jeremy of indifference, while Jeremy says Angela is overreacting. Now focused on their own quarrel, they ignore the singers and instead continue their argument over breakfast in the dining car. Finally, Angela threatens to leave. Jeremy ridicules her threat, saying that she isn't capable of traveling alone in a foreign country. Angela punches Jeremy in the nose. Jeremy then shoves his grapefruit into her face. Their fight disrupts the dining car. At the next stop, the conductor throws both of them off the train. Sitting in a deserted train station, they both begin to laugh at their ridiculous response to the drunken singers.

As described in *Story* by Robert McKee, the **beat** is the most basic element in a story.[2] A beat is an exchange of behavior, based on action and reaction. There are five beats in this story.

1. Angela responds to the singers: "I am not going to listen to those drunken louts for one more minute!" Then, Jeremy responds to Angela: "Oh, take it easy. Let's get some breakfast; I bet they will be asleep when we return."

2. As they walk to the dining car, Angela says to Jeremy: "You really don't care, do you? If someone punched you in the nose, you would just walk away." Jeremy responds to Angela: "Don't be such a hothead. There is no reason to get angry about every little thing."

3. Over breakfast, Angela retorts : "If you can't take the heat, get out of the kitchen! I suggest we split up at the next station." Jeremy responds: "Are you kidding? You wouldn't last a day on your own."

4. Angela punches Jeremy, who shoves his grapefruit into her face.

5. The conductor reacts by throwing both of them off the train. Sitting on their suitcases in the empty station, they finally respond to the situation by laughing.

Beats build **scenes.** Scenes generally occur in a single space in continuous time. Scenes build sequences. In filmmaking, a sequence is made from a series of scenes, which generally increase in emotional impact. In this story, a minor disagreement escalates into a major battle. Each action results in a stronger reaction, culminating in the couple's ejection from the train. Sequences build **acts.** An act is an even longer sequential structure. The **screenplay,** which is the written blueprint for the film, is constructed from multiple acts.

ESTABLISHING BOUNDARIES

When just starting college, few of us have the time, money, or expertise necessary to write a screenplay or direct a film. However, we can use the same storytelling principles to develop storyboards, videos, and visual books.

Conceptual Boundaries

It is wise to begin by defining the conceptual breadth of an idea. An idea that is overly ambitious or is ill defined will be impossible to communicate well.

You already have extensive experience with conceptual boundaries. Just consider the questions you face when planning a 10-page art history paper.

- *What is the topic?* What historical period interests you most? In a course devoted to Western art from the Renaissance to Impressionism, you have many excellent choices and a dazzling array of images. Choosing a topic that is manageable and interesting is essential.

- *How should the topic be approached?* If the paper is on Impressionism, you could

  - Analyze the work of a single artist, such as Cassatt or Degas

  - Compare and contrast paintings by Cassatt and Degas

  - Explore the impact of photography on Impressionist painters

By focusing on one aspect of a complex topic, you can develop an effective research strategy and complete the paper on time.

Defining conceptual boundaries is equally important in sequential art. Just as Impressionism is too big a topic to explore thoroughly in a 10-page paper, so reality is too big to record fully in a 10-minute video. The following questions can help you define the conceptual frame of an artwork.

- *What to see?* Start with an interesting and easily accessible site. Explore several of the buildings on campus; then select one and begin your research. Find out the history of the building, look for distinctive architectural details, and find out what happens each day in the building.

- *When to see it?* Each time of day is distinctive, both visually and emotionally. How does the building look at sunset? What is its appearance at midnight? Select the moments in time that are charged with meaning, then watch closely.

- *And then, what happens?* To answer this question, you must become a storyteller.

Developing a Story

In 1908, the White Star Line began construction of three identical Atlantic ocean liners. The *Olympic* was launched in 1910; the *Titanic* was launched in 1911; the *Gigantic* was never completed. The *Titanic* struck an iceberg during her maiden voyage and sank on April 15, 1912. She had lifeboat capacity for 1,178 people; there were 2,201 on board. The *Californian,* less than 10 miles away, did not respond to her distress signals. The *Carpathia,* 58 miles away, sped to the scene. Arriving four hours later, *Carpathia* rescued 711 people from the freezing lifeboats. The *Olympic, Titanic's* sister ship, provided reliable service until she was scrapped in 1937.

These are the basic facts. No narrative, however, is limited to facts. Even a newspaper reporter must make choices about the organization of facts and determine the most important aspects of a story. Fiction offers even more options. Using a familiar journalistic device, let's list the most basic questions.

- *Whose story is it?* That of ship designer Thomas Andrews, who perished? Of J. Bruce Ismay, director of the White Star Line, who survived? Of the captain of the *Carpathia,* who became a hero? Of the captain of the *Californian,* who was reviled?

- *When should the story begin and end?* We know that the iceberg was spotted at 11:40 P.M. and that the collision occurred soon after. A storyteller, however, can start at any point in time. How does the story change when we begin with initial planning of the "unsinkable" ship? What happens when we start the story just as a

survivor comes to consciousness after being rescued?

- *Where does the story occur?* Each cabin, deck, and lifeboat contains its own specific characters and its own particular story.

- *Why did the tragedy occur?* Was the captain pressured to complete the crossing in record time, which caused him to increase the ship's speed, despite the danger? Was faulty construction the cause?

- *What is the story really about?* Courage? Arrogance? Injustice? Sixty-two percent of the 325 first-class passengers survived, while only 25 percent of the 706 third-class passengers survived. While the sinking itself is the most obvious event, this tale contains many stories.

Knowing where to start the story is essential. If the story is devoted to the construction of the ship and the arrival of the passengers, the most dramatic events (the sinking itself, the rescue, and the inquiry into the cause) will be lost.

Emotional Boundaries

In theater and performance art, communication often depends on a connection between the imaginary world on stage and the tangible world of the audience. This was demonstrated beautifully in Wole Soyinka's *Death and the King's Horseman,* performed by Syracuse Stage in 1999. The play explores a range of cultural conflicts between the native Yoruba population of Africa and a group of British colonizers. The king has died, and the king's horseman, a powerful leader in his own right (13.8), must commit suicide, so that he can guide the king in the world beyond life. Attempts by the British government to stop this ritual are disruptive and tragic.

To feel the full impact of the event, the audience must emotionally connect to the Yoruba world, which revolves around a village market. As we enter the theater, a dramatically lit stage piled with fruit, colorful baskets, and bolts of fabric invites us into this world. One by one, seven female actors enter, assume the poses of various vendors, then freeze. The play begins with the sound of drum-

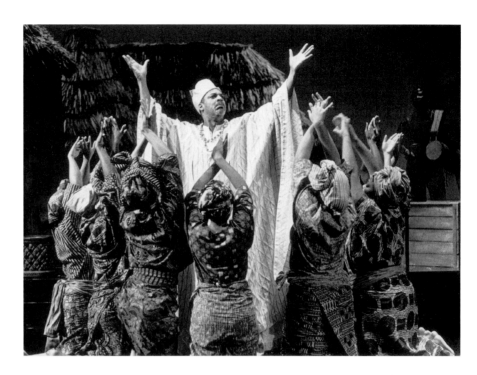

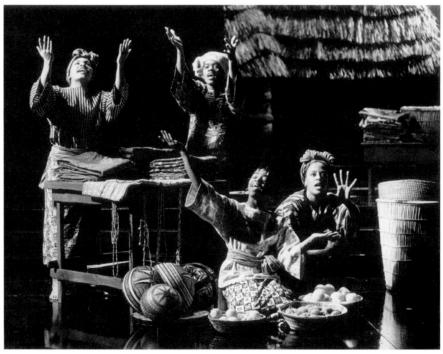

ming coming from behind the audience. As the women become animated and the market comes to life (13.9), we are enveloped in the Yoruba world. Additional actors sing and dance down the aisles, finally joining the company on stage.

Establishing an emotional connection between the image and the audience is even more important in filmmaking. When we see a play, the entire stage is visible and each member of the audience frames the scene a bit differently. In a film, the image is created by a flickering beam of light rather than by a live actor. The film frame is defined by the director. By using a close-up, the director can place the actor directly in front of us. A distance shot pushes the actor away, reducing the emotional connection.

ESTABLISHING BOUNDARIES

329

Style

Just as any setting offers a wide range of compositional possibilities, so any story can be told in many ways. Three cinematic interpretations of William Shakespeare's *Romeo and Juliet* provide a striking example of the importance of style. Zeffirelli's *Romeo and Juliet* (13.10) is closest to the written play in style and interpretation. There is some editing of the original text, but the lines spoken were written by Shakespeare. While the musical score is a distinctly modern interpretation of Renaissance music, the beautiful settings, opulent costumes, and graceful dancing that fill the screen are based on historical models.

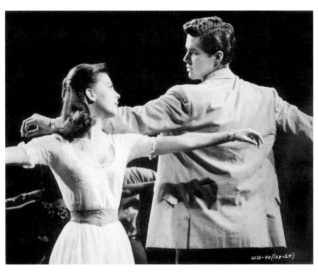

13.10 Franco Zeffirelli, *Romeo and Juliet*, 1968. Romeo and Juliet.

West Side Story (13.11) offers a very different interpretation of the story of Romeo and Juliet. Set in contemporary New York City, this film uses warfare between rival gangs to create the tragedy, rather than the familiar conflict between the Capulets and the Montagues. While the story is based on Shakespeare's play, the dialogue is distinctly American. The spirit and emotion of the original were retained, but the dialogue, setting, and specific actions are contemporary. Even the characters have new names, as Romeo becomes Tony, the leader of the Polish Jets, and Juliet becomes Maria, affiliated with the Puerto Rican Sharks.

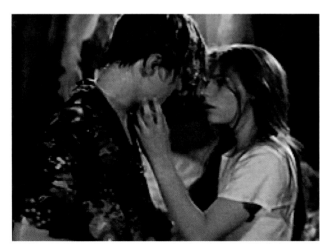

13.11 *West Side Story*, 1961. Tony and Maria.

An unusual combination of these two sensibilities occurs in *William Shakespeare's Romeo and Juliet* (13.12). Now set in contemporary California as a struggle between the skinhead Montagues and the leather-clad Capulets, the film begins with a prologue delivered from a television screen by a newswoman. The words of Shakespeare are often delivered as a scream, and familiar characters are transformed in amazing ways. For example, when we first meet Mercutio, he is wearing high heels, a silver-sequined miniskirt with a halter top, and a white wig. The words of Shakespeare have been retained, but the setting, characters, and action have been shifted to create a bizarre contemporary version of a sixteenth-century play.

13.12 William Shakespeare's *Romeo and Juliet*, 1996.

CAUSALITY

Every story is constructed using a chain of events. In traditional narrative, the first event causes the second, which results in the third, and so on until the conclusion is reached. This chain of events is called **causality.** Like a crossword puzzle, the storyteller presents us with a series of clues, which we construct into meaning.

When the relationship between cause and effect is clear, the puzzle is easy to solve. When there is an extended delay between cause and effect, or when relationships among events seem arbitrary, the solution becomes much more elusive.

Un Chien Andalou (An Andalusian Dog), by Salvador Dali and Luis Bunuel, presents such a puzzle. A quarrel between two lovers is presented through a bizarre sequence of illogical events. As the film opens, a man smoking a cigarette calmly sharpens a straight razor. A sliver of cloud passes across the full moon. The man grasps a woman's face (13.13) and slits her left eye with the razor. He then bicycles down the street wearing a nun's uniform. The uninjured woman welcomes him to her apartment. Ants crawl out from a hole in his hand. A severed hand appears on the street below. A crowd gathers. A policeman gives the severed hand to a woman, who places it in a box. The crowd disperses. The woman, still standing in the street, is then hit by a car.

As the film continues, the man harnesses himself to a piano filled with slaughtered mules (13.14), shoots a double image of himself, and strolls along a beach with the woman, collecting, then discarding, debris. While these two characters dominate the story, the film as a whole is as mysterious and disturbing as a surrealist painting.

In contrast, a series of very clear cause-and-effect relationships fuels the lovers' quarrel in James Cameron's *Titanic.* The film begins with a prologue showing a contemporary expedition to salvage a

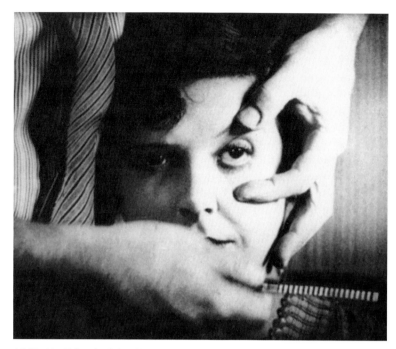

13.13 *Un Chien Andalou.* Woman's eye being slit.

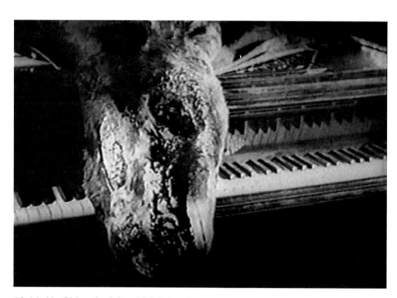

13.14 *Un Chien Andalou.* Mule's head on piano.

precious diamond from the sunken wreck. Rose, an elderly woman who survived the disaster, then describes the voyage she remembers. Through her memories, we meet the primary characters. Young Rose is a pampered society woman betrothed to the rich and arrogant Cal. Jack is an independent but impoverished artist who has won his passage back to America in a poker game.

Conflicts between Cal and Rose are apparent from the start. Rose is intelligent and strong-willed,

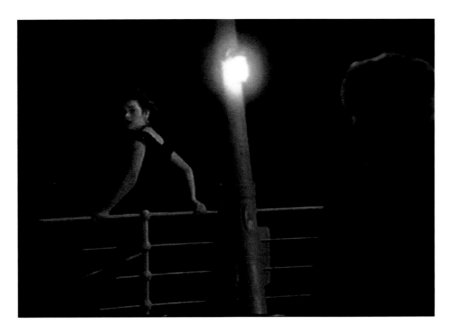

with a love of art and ideas. Cal is arrogant and domineering; he demands obedience. Rose feels trapped, and, in despair, she climbs over a railing on the ship and prepares to jump (13.15). Jack saves her. The resulting romance develops through a sequence of cause-and-effect events and reaches a climax with a battle between Cal and the lovers on the sinking ship. Rose survives, and in a classic **denouement,** or summation, the film ends as the elderly Rose again climbs a ship's railing and flings a diamond back into the sea (13.16). Beautifully filmed and carefully edited, the three-hour film easily sustains our interest. In this case, the traditional narrative structure served the director's purpose. There is no ambiguity: the actions and emotions of all of the characters are shown clearly.

Each film has its own purpose and its own power. *Un Chien Andalou* is suggestive, rather than descriptive; mystery is an essential part of its meaning. *Titanic* gains meaning from the escalating conflict between Cal and Rose. In each case, the director made the right choice for the film content.

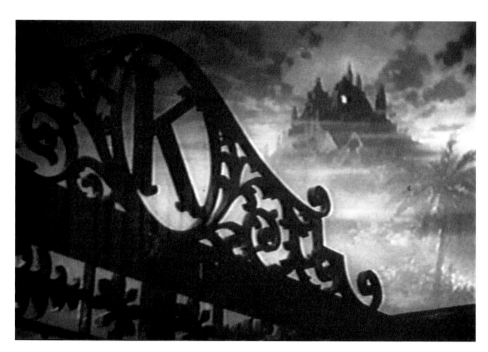

STORY AND STYLE IN
CITIZEN KANE

The Opening Sequence

Because most narratives are so dependent on the interplay between cause and effect, the first image shown substantially affects each subsequent action. As a result, many directors use the opening sequence to create the sense of anticipation that will pull the viewer into the story.

Citizen Kane, widely hailed as one of the finest films ever made, actually uses three opening sequences to set the story in motion. Each builds on the previous sequence, creating a powerful domino effect. From the very beginning, we are swept into a complex story.

In the first opening, we see the dim silhouette of a castle behind a gate dominated by a "No Trespassing" sign. Through a series of dissolves, we move in closer (13.17), accompanied by slow, ominous music. As the music reaches a climax, a light in a window blinks off. The camera zooms in on a glass globe containing a tiny cabin in a snowy landscape. In an extreme close-up, we now see a man's lips move (13.18), as he whispers the word *rosebud*. The globe falls to the floor

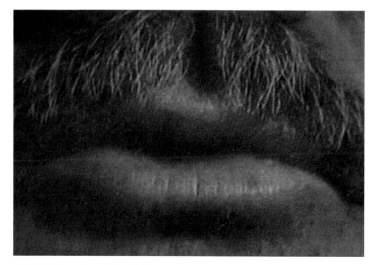

13.18 *Citizen Kane.* Kane's lips.

and shatters. A nurse enters the distorted room and, after taking his pulse, pulls a sheet over the face of the man. Charles Foster Kane is dead.

The second opening is dramatically different, in style, narration, and pacing. It is a newsreel, showing the major events in Kane's life (13.19). All the basic information about the man is presented through the narrator's brisk voice-over: Kane's fortune came from a Colorado gold mine, he was a powerful newspaper editor, he had an affair with a shopgirl, and he failed in his attempt to be elected governor. This sequence presents the facts of his life but misses the meaning. A reporter named Thompson is sent to solve the mystery, to determine who, or what, was "rosebud."

We get closer to Kane in the third opening. Thompson begins his search at the Thatcher library, a forbidding place of echoing rooms and silent sentries. Walter Thatcher was both Kane's guardian and his nemesis. As Thompson reads Thatcher's journal, the words dissolve into a snowy scene in Colorado. When the scene ends, young Charlie is taken from his parents to begin his new life in Chicago. Each of the openings tells us more about Kane and each expands the sense of anticipation.

Conflict

Inner conflict or conflicts between characters often generate the cause-and-effect relationships on which a narrative is built. *Citizen Kane* relies on both types of conflict. The pivotal mystery, which is set in motion by Kane's death, is reinforced when Thompson is given his assignment to "find rosebud: dead or alive." Who was Kane, and why was "rosebud" so important to him? As the story unfolds, we are offered a wide variety of opinions.

1. In "News on the March," Kane is called a communist by Thatcher, a fascist by a man in a labor rally, and finally "an American" by Kane himself.

2. The Thatcher diaries, read by Thompson and shown in close-ups on the screen, include a confrontation between the newspaperman and the banker. Thatcher is appalled by Kane's support for the working class and points out that, as a capitalist, Kane has much to lose if reforms

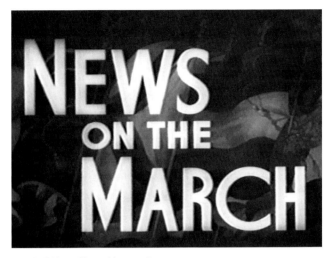

13.19 *Citizen Kane.* Newsreel.

occur. Here, Kane defines himself more emphatically: "You don't realize that you're talking to two people. As Charles Foster Kane, who has two thousand, six hundred and thirty-one shares of Metropolitan Transfer, I sympathize with you. Charles Foster Kane is a dangerous scoundrel; his paper should be run out of town. . . . On the other hand, I am the publisher of the *Inquirer.* As such, it is my duty to see that decent, hardworking people are not robbed blind by a bunch of money-mad pirates." Kane clearly realizes that his motivations are contradictory. Welles uses a series of increasing close-ups to demonstrate the increasing tension between Kane and Thatcher (13.20–13.22).

3. Thompson next visits Bernstein, Kane's business manager. His memories reveal two critical aspects of Kane's character. First, with the publication of his first edition of the *Inquirer*, Kane inserts a "Declaration of Principles" pledging honest reporting and support for the working man. For Bernstein, Kane was a man of principles.

4. Leland, once Kane's best friend, offers quite a different assessment of the man. Kane, he says, "wasn't a brutal man — he just did brutal things." Kane "never had a conviction, besides himself." Kane "never actually gave you anything — he just left you a tip." At the end of the interview, Leland offers a more compassionate assessment: "He did everything for love. All he ever wanted was love. He just didn't have any to give."

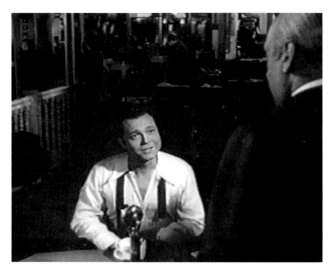

13.20 *Citizen Kane.* Kane and Thatcher.

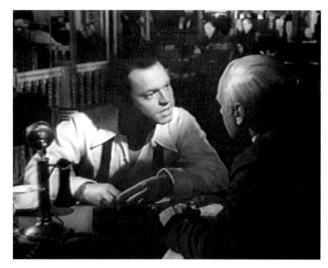

13.21 *Citizen Kane.* Kane and Thatcher.

5. Two final interviews complete our picture of Kane. His former wife, Susan, focuses on Kane's attempt to transform her into an opera singer. Susan is initially excited by this prospect but is soon overwhelmed by the gap between her modest ability and the demands of the profession. It is only after she attempts suicide that Kane allows her singing lessons to end. Raymond, the butler, offers a final memory. When Susan finally walks out on him, the elderly Kane awkwardly lunges around her bedroom, ferociously destroying mirrors and hurling books to the floor. He stops only when he picks up the snow globe seen at the beginning of the film, and for a second time in the film, he utters the word *rosebud*. He then departs, endlessly mirroring himself as he walks through his castle. (13.23)

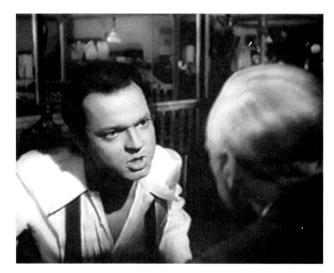

13.22 *Citizen Kane.* Kane and Thatcher.

While the mystery is revealed to the audience at the end of the film, Thompson never does learn the meaning of "rosebud." Nonetheless, the memories of Kane's associates have deepened his understanding of a complex and contradictory character and provided us with a remarkable film.

The Closing Sequence

Especially with a mystery story, the closing sequence is as important as the opening sequence. A powerful closing can reveal an

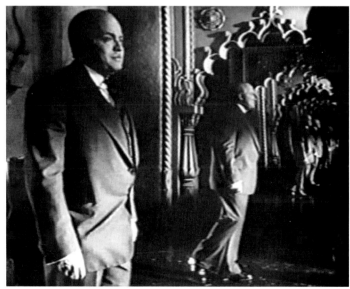

13.23 *Citizen Kane.* Mirror.

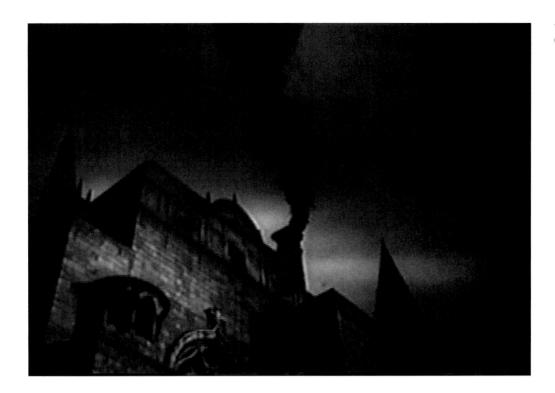

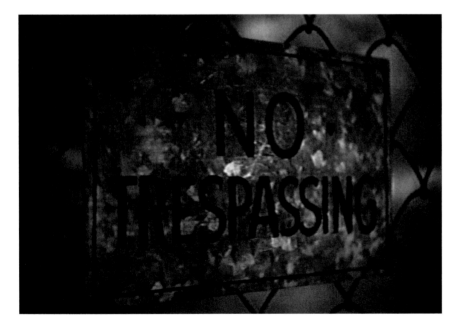

13.25 *Citizen Kane.* "No trespassing."

elusive truth, resolve outstanding conflicts, pose a question, or hammer home an important point.

In *Citizen Kane,* three closing sequences mirror the film's beginning. In the first, Thompson summarizes his search for Kane. In the second, the true identity of "rosebud" is revealed to the viewer. The third ending is a reprise of the opening shot. The mysterious outline of Kane's castle is shown, now with smoke billowing from the chimney (13.24). This change is significant. To clear out the castle, workmen are burning most of Kane's possessions, including rosebud. The camera slowly tilts downward, resting once more on the "No Trespassing" sign (13.25). After two hours of film, the mystery is only partially resolved: we can never fully enter another person's life.

THE 15-SECOND NARRATIVE

Duration, framing, editing, and narration become especially charged with meaning when a television commercial is designed. Lasting only 15 seconds, the ad must immediately command attention, make a favorable impression, and influence consumer behavior. Whether you are selling soap or discouraging smoking, your approach must be clear, concise, and compelling.

Ads must appeal to the emotions as well as the intellect. The **hard-sell** approach, shown in figure 13.26, relies on rational argument and clearly presents one major point. The narrative is linear, and the message is explicit: drinking and driving can kill a friendship. Words underscore the ideas that are being communicated visually.

Soft-sell ads focus on emotion. While the message is still sharply focused, the designer may seek a sensory response rather than a rational response. An ad for a Jeep Cherokee (13.27) shows a car driving through the woods. The song "Row, Row, Row Your Boat" provides the sound track. There is no obvious connection between the song and the car, but phrase "life is but a dream" certainly implies that a Jeep can provide a carefree vacation.

13.26 Agency: Leber Katz Partners, New York. Production: Phil Marco Productions, New York. Editing Company: Cinemetric, New York. Music Production: Roy Eaton Productions, New York. Details: TV, 30 seconds, color. First appearance: December 12, 1983. Advertiser's Supervisor: Eleanor Hanley. Account Supervisor: Susan Wershba. Creative Director: Jack Silverman. Copywriter: Lou Linder. Art Director: Len Fink. Agency Producer: Herb Miller. Producer: Catherine Bromley. Director/ Cameraman/Lighting Director: Phil Marco. Editor: Larry Plastrik. Music Director: Roy Eaton. Music Composers: Roy Eaton/Joe Hudson. Performers: Jon Carthay, Laurence White, Bobby Hudson. Voice: Doug Jeffers.

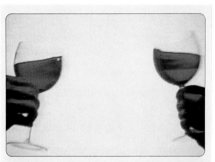
NARRATOR: When friends don't stop friends from drinking and driving

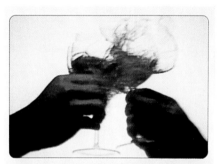
[TIRES SCREECH AND CRASH]

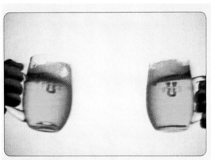
friends die from drinking and driving.

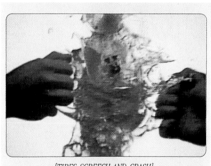
[TIRES SCREECH AND CRASH]

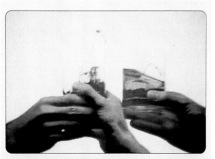
Friends die from drinking and—

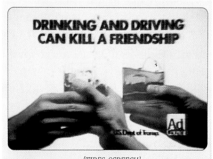
DRINKING AND DRIVING CAN KILL A FRIENDSHIP

Ad

[TIRES SCREECH]
Drinking and driving can kill a friendship.

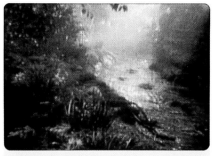
[BIRDS CHIRPING]

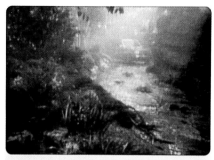
CHORUS: Row, row, row your boat,

13.27 Agency: Campbell-Mithun-Esty, Southfield. Production: Bill Hudson Films, New York. Editing Company: Editors Gas, New York. Music Production: Elias & Associates, New York. Details: TV, 30 seconds, color. First appearance: October 1, 1988. Creative Director/Copywriter: Mike Belitsos. Art Director: Steve Goldsworthy. Agency Producer: Craig Mungons. Production Company Director: Dickson Sorenson.

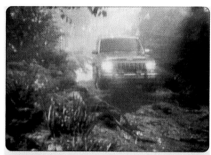
gently down the stream.

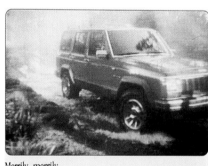
Merrily, merrily,

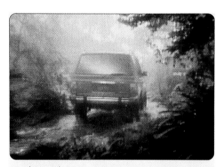
merrily, merrily,

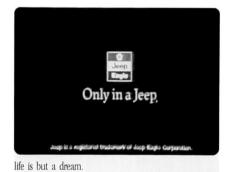
life is but a dream.

Feeling good is not enough: the viewer must feel good about the specific product being sold. Because viewer response is triggered by clues rather than literal content, designers using the soft-sell approach pay particular attention to details, such as the soundtrack and lighting.

All ads rely on a clear message, strong imagery, and simple communication. However, very different strategies can be used to convey an idea, and the skillful designer carefully matches the communication style to the message content. Following are six contrasting strategies.

1. **Rational.** A rational ad provides the viewer with specific information. When the message is compelling in itself or the product is truly unique, a straightforward demonstration can be effective. A 1985 commercial for Cheer detergent (13.28) combined a rational demonstration with deadpan humor, which attracts our attention while conveying the message.

2. **Emotional.** When the product is not unique or the message lacks urgency, an emotional approach may be more effective. For example, to a dog owner, all dog food is pretty much alike. Neither the product nor the message is compelling in itself. When the dog food becomes a manifestation of love for the dog, however, the appeal is heightened. In figure 13.29, the emotion of love is more powerful than any rational argument.

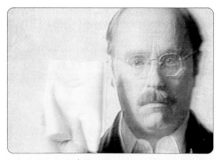

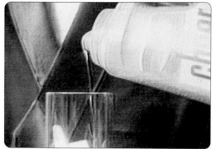

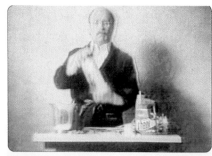

[TANGO MUSIC]

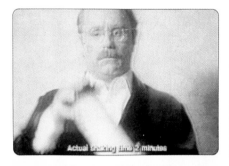

Actual drinking time 2 minutes

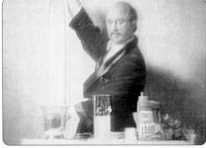

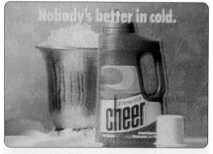

Nobody's better in cold.

cheer

NARRATOR: Nobody's better in cold, than All-Temperature Cheer.

13.28 Agency: Leo Burnett, Chicago. Production: Leroy Koetz Company, Chicago. Editing Company: Cutters, Chicago. Music Production: Colnot-Fryer Music, Chicago. First appearance: 1988. Account Supervisor: Ray DeThorne. Creative Director: Gerry Miller. Associate Creative Director/Copywriter: Alex Goslar. Art Director: Bob Ribits. Agency Producer: Angelo Antonucci. Production Company Producer: George Lakehomer. Production Company Director: Leroy Koetz. Editor: R. J. Music Composer: Cliff Colnot. Casting Director: Bonnie Murray. Performer: Jobe Cerny. Voice: Jim McCance.

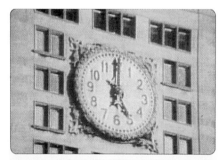

[SFX: CLOCKS CHIMING 5 PM]

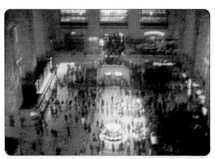

[MUSIC]

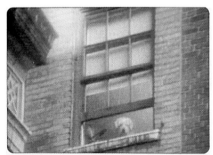

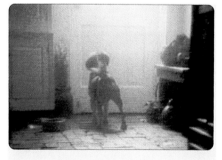

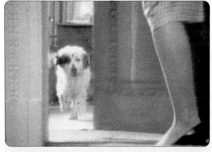

NARRATOR: When you think about the unique joy your dog brings you, why would you ever want to feed him anything less than America's finest dog food? New Reward,

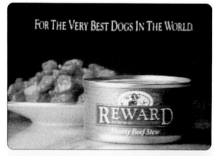

FOR THE VERY BEST DOGS IN THE WORLD

REWARD
Hearty Beef Stew

for the very best dogs in the world. What may just be the very best dog food.

13.29 Agency: Goodby, Berlin & Silverstein, San Francisco. Production: Griner, Custa & Associates, New York. Editing Company: Straight Cut, Los Angeles. Music Production: Piece of Cake, Los Angeles. Details: TV, 60 seconds, color. First appearance: July 18, 1988. Advertiser's Supervisor: Tom Branky. Account Supervisor: Pam Malone. Creative Directors: Jeff Goodby, Rich Silverstein. Copywriter: Jeff Goodby. Art Director: Rich Silverstein. Agency Producer: Debbie King. Production Company Producer: Chris Stefani. Production Company Director/Cameraman: Norm Griner. Lighting Director: William Coleman. Editor: Tom Schacte. Music Director/Composer: Don Pierstrup. Casting Director: Kathy Sorkin.

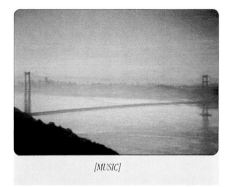

[MUSIC]

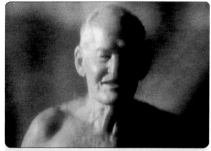

WALT STACK: I run 17 miles every morning. People ask

13.30 Agency: Wieden & Kennedy, Portland. Production: PYTKA, Venice. Details: TV, 30 seconds each, color. First appearance: August, 1988. Advertiser's Supervisor: Scott Bedbury. Creative Directors: Dan Wieden, David Kennedy. Copywriters: Dan Wieden, Jim Riswold. Art Director: David Jenkins. Agency Producers: Bill Davenport, Elinor Shanklir. Production Company Director: Joe Pytka. Editor: Steve Wystrach.

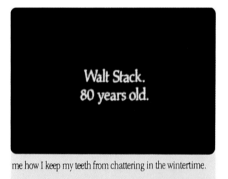

Walt Stack.
80 years old.

me how I keep my teeth from chattering in the wintertime.

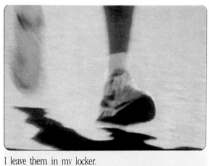

I leave them in my locker.

Just do it.

NIKE
A I R

3. **Serious.** A serious approach is often best when you have a serious message. Public service announcements dealing with AIDS, drunk driving, or drug abuse are rarely funny. However, the ad will succeed only if it is seen. Horrific images of starving children or tortured prisoners may so repel viewers that they change the channel and lose the message. Finding the right balance between serious content and engaging imagery is crucial.

4. **Humorous.** In a society saturated with sales pitches, an ad that makes us laugh is an ad we will remember. Since any ad is designed to encourage a change in behavior, memory is important. The message we receive while watching the nightly news must be retained when we buy a tube of toothpaste two days later. To be effective, however, a humorous ad must truly be funny, without insulting the viewer or demeaning the product. By showing the strength as well as the weakness of an elderly runner, the ad in figure 13.30 strikes just the right balance.

5. **Realistic.** Communication requires connection. For a commercial to succeed, the viewer must feel connected to the ideas and images presented. For example, few adults will pay attention to an ad for the latest rock band, while few teenagers will pay attention to an ad for denture adhesive. In either case, there is no connection to the message conveyed. Similarly, when we like a character in an ad, we are more likely to listen to his or her argument.

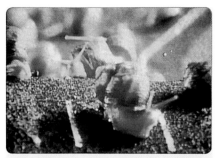

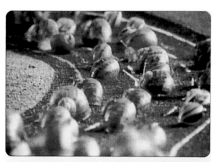

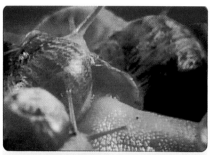

[TRAFFIC NOISE]
TRAFFIC REPORTER: I've never seen traffic like this. The traffic down there today is unbelievable.

[OTHER DRIVERS' VOICES]
NARRATOR: Remember what it was like the last time you drove yourself to the airport. Next time take Massport's

Logan Express Bus from Quincy or Framingham. It's fast, convenient, and comfortable. For more information, call Massport, at 1-800-23LOGAN.

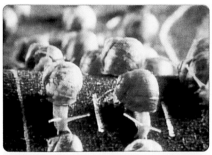

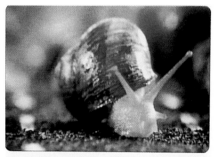

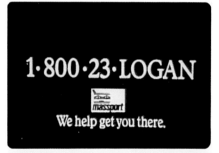

MAN: Move it, buddy!

WOMAN: I can walk faster than this.

1·800·23·LOGAN
massport
We help get you there.

13.31 Agency: Rossin, Greenberg, Seronick and Hill, Boston. Production Company: Cavanaugh & Co., Boston. Details: TV, 30 seconds, color. First appearance: November 1988. Advertiser's Supervisor: Teresa McAlpine. Account Supervisor: Neal Hill. Creative Directors: Gary Greenberg, Peter Seronick. Copywriter: Peter Seronick. Art Director: Gary Greenberg. Agency Producer: Julie Lauerman. Production Company Producer: David Norman. Production Company Director: Steve Cavanaugh. Set Designer: Bob Field. Cameraman/Lighting Director: Dan Stoloff. Editor: George Mauro. Voice: Chris Murney.

A common form of realism is **testimonial.** In a testimonial, a trustworthy character (often a celebrity) addresses us directly. The 1998 Aleve medicine commercial is a good example. An ordinary-looking middle-aged man wearing blue jeans tells us that two Aleve pills do the same job as a fistful of pills from a competing company. When he ends the ad by saying simply, "It works for me," we assume that it will also work for us.

6. **Exaggerated.** Exaggeration can be a great strategy when the product is commonplace or the message is uninteresting, To be effective, an ad must be seen and remembered. Exaggeration tends to be memorable. Even if the event shown is ludicrous, the ad can be effective if the basic message is believable. We know that the snails shown in figure 13.31 are not literally stuck in traffic; they represent frustrated drivers who are moving at a "snail's pace." The metaphor is unexpected and, when combined with the voice-over, becomes humorous. Through exaggeration, a mass transit message becomes memorable.

NON-NARRATIVE

Titanic is a familiar type of popular film. It tells a fictitious story, based on a series of actions and reactions. The opening and closing sequences provide an effective framework for the story of Rose, Jack, and Cal. The characters are believable, and the plot is plausible.

Many forms of sequential art, however, are non-narrative in structure. For example, the elegant contours and gleaming chrome of an expensive car provide both the form and the content in figure 13.32. There is no story: viewers are simply shown a series of beautiful close-ups. Evocative artworks of this kind often require more audience participation and encourage an open-ended response.

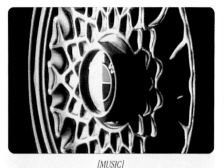
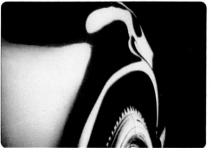
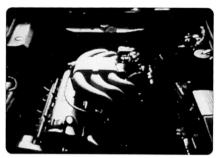

[MUSIC]

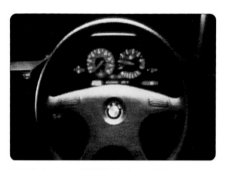
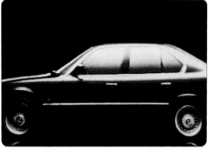
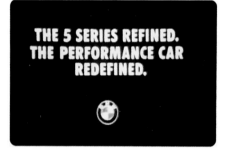

THE 5 SERIES REFINED.
THE PERFORMANCE CAR
REDEFINED.

13.32 Agency: WCRS Mathews Marcantonio, London. Production: Park Village Productions, London. Music Production: Jeff Wayne Music, London. Details: TV, 60 seconds, color. First appearance: June 3,1988. Country: England. Language: English. Advertiser's Supervisor: Martin Hainge. Account Supervisor: Hugh Smiley. Creative Director: Alfredo Marcantonio. Art Director: Paul Garret. Agency Producer: Simon Wells. Production Company Producer: Chris Harvey. Production Company Director: Roger Woodburn. Cameraman: Joe Coe. Lighting Director: Keith Goddard. Editor: Patrick Moore. Music Composer: Trevor Jones.

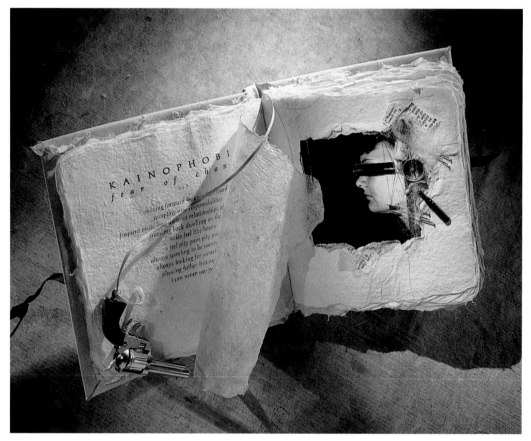

13.33 Susan Kae Grant, *Kainophobia, Fear of Change,* from *Giving Fear a Proper Name: Detroit,* **The Black Rose Press, 1982–85.** Edition of 15, printed letter press with silver prints. Mixed media, handmade paper, simulated bullet-proof case, 5 × 5 in. (12.7 × 12.7 cm).

Three common approaches to non-narrative are the categorical approach, the rhetorical approach, and the abstract approach. A **categorical** approach is based on the exploration of a single concept, action, or emotion. *Giving Fear a Proper Name,* a visual book by Susan Kae Grant, uses text from a diary to explore fear. Contained within a clear plexiglass box, the book itself is like a fetish. Handmade paper and inserted objects cause the book to open on its own, and the tiny toy revolver that dangles from a bookmark string simultaneously suggests self-protection and self-annihilation.

This catalogue of terror begins with kainophobia, the fear of change (13.33). From the diary, we learn that Grant has moved to Detroit, a profoundly foreign environment for her. On the first page of a double-page spread, she writes of "moving forward looking backward . . . I can never say good-bye." On the facing page, she is shown in profile, facing left, with her face pierced by straight pins and accompanied by a tiny compass and a plastic groom, suggesting a wedding cake. Topophobia, the fear of place, comes next. Grant now writes that she "stares in disbelief out smashed vacant beauties/violet oppressive depression surrounds me/people are angry, filled with hate." Her face in the photograph has now become a target. Eremophobia, the fear of solitude, follows. A close-up of her ear is shown, pierced by pins, while a plastic toy phone dangles like an earring. The book continues, with pages devoted to the fear of sleep, fear of being alone, fear of being observed, and so forth. In each case, increasingly painful words accompany a photographic self-portrait of some kind. The book ends with the fear of infinity. Now in profile facing right, Grant is accompanied by a pair of dice and a map of Texas, which will become her new home. Using fear as a category, then relentlessly exploring various types of fear, Grant transformed her personal experience into powerful communication.

In a **rhetorical** approach, sequential images are used to present an argument. One example is *Powers of Ten,* by Charles and Ray Eames (13.34). This 9½-minute film provides an elegant exploration of "the relative size of things in the universe." The central image is framed by a dark border, which includes information on the spatial position of each shot on the right and its numerical equivalent on the left. Beginning with a shot of a man asleep in a park, the

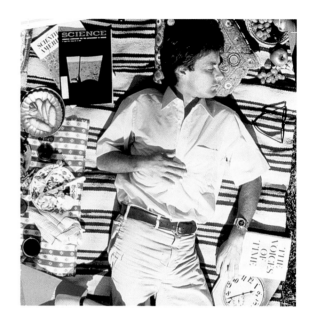

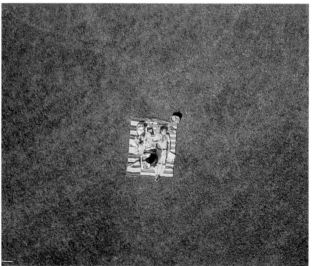

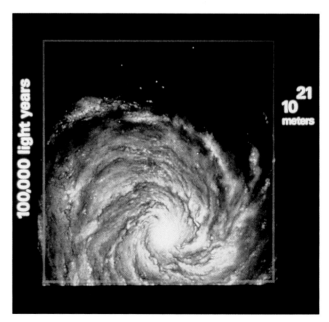

13.34 Charles and Ray Eames, *Powers of Ten*, 1977. Film frames.

camera gradually moves out to the farthest reaches of the known universe. Physicist Philip Morrison provides the narration, describing the meaning of the image at each step.

The process is then reversed, and the speed is greatly accelerated. Returning to the sleeping man, the camera now moves through his skin, into his blood, down to a cell, and finally into an atom in the man's right hand. The beautiful images entice us while the mathematical narration teaches us. Moving from astrophysics to nuclear physics, this film presents an analysis of the distance between the largest and smallest spaces known.

Words for the World, by Ed Hutchins, presents a social argument using equally simple means. By filling a small metal pencil box with 16 special pencils, he makes a plea for tolerance and peace. A map of the world is printed on the top of the box. Various texts are printed on the pencils, in languages ranging from Arabic to Zulu, each accompanied by an English translation. The phrases are simple: "It doesn't hurt to listen." "The time is always right for justice." "We all live under the same sky." The message, however, is compelling. What words will we write with these pencils? What words can we say to each other? Hutchins is promoting a change in behavior rather than knowledge of the cosmos.

Finally, sequential art may be purely **abstract.** In a well-designed book or film, changes in color, shape, texture, and movement can provide all the information needed for a compelling piece. *Blacktop,* another experimental film by Charles and Ray Eames, provides one example. An outdoor basketball court has been washed. As the residue is rinsed away, the film records the movement of soap bubbles and water over the asphalt surface. The delicate Bach harpsichord music that is used as the sound track suggests that this act of washing the asphalt is as elegant as a Balanchine ballet. And, in the hands of these inventive filmmakers, it is.

Key Questions

- Whose story is it? a 7-year old girl? a 17-year old boy? a priest? a thief?

- What is the point of view? Does the main character tell his/her own story (first person narrative) or does someone else tell the story? How does this affect meaning?

- What are the strengths and weaknesses of each character?

- What conflicts occur? Why? How do the characters deal with conflict?

- To what degree and by what means is the conflict resolved at the end?

SUMMARY

- Multiple-image structures can be used to express complex ideas using narrative and non-narrative approaches.

- Storytelling is one of the most ancient and effective forms of communication. Stories can increase self-awareness, provide inspiration, supply information, and encourage understanding.

- The group, series, and sequence are the multiple-image structures most commonly used by printmakers, photographers, and book artists.

- The beat, scene, sequence, and act are used by filmmakers and playwrights to create screenplays.

- By establishing effective boundaries, we can develop more effective stories. Common questions include the following: Whose story is it? When should the story begin and end? Where does the story occur? Why did it happen? What is the underlying theme or message in the story?

- A change in style can substantially affect communication.

- Ideas and emotions can be communicated through a straightforward series of causes and effects or through a series of seemingly unrelated images.

- The opening and closing, personal perspective, and characters used can make or break a story.

- Television advertisements can present complete ideas in 15 seconds. Hard-sell, soft-sell, rational, emotional, serious, humorous, realistic, and exaggerated approaches are the most common strategies.

- Categorical, rhetorical, and abstract are common non-narrative approaches.

Keywords

abstract	group	scene
act	hard-sell advertising	screenplay
beat	humorous advertising	sequence
categorical	myth	series
causality	rational advertising	serious advertising
denouement	realistic advertising	soft-sell advertising
emotional	rhetorical narrative	testimonial advertising
exaggerated advertising		

Profile:
Jerome Witkin, Painter

Life Lessons: Exploring the
Human Condition

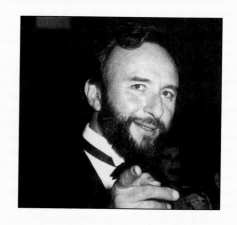

Jerome Witkin is an internationally renowned figurative painter. He has had over 50 solo exhibitions, including shows at Greenville County Museum of Art in South Carolina; Delaware Art Museum; Columbia College Art Gallery in Chicago; Arkansas Art Center; Munson-Williams-Proctor Institute in Utica, New York; and three shows at Sherry French Gallery in New York City. Witkin is the recipient of numerous awards, including a Guggenheim Fellowship and two Ford Foundation fellowships. His work is in over 40 public collections, including the Butler Institute of American Art in Youngstown, Ohio; Hirshhorn Museum and Sculpture Garden in Washington, DC; the Cleveland Museum of Art; and the Metropolitan Museum of Art in New York City. Witkin's work has been reviewed extensively in major periodicals, and a book on his work, titled *Life Lessons: The Art of Jerome Witkin,* by Sherry Chayat, was published in 1989.

Three aspects of Witkin's work exemplify the importance of narrative in painting. First, there is a theatrical use of setting, character, and movement. Using a stage he has constructed in his studio, Witkin uses space and lighting as deliberately as a film director. Second, he has a heightened awareness of time, often focusing on the "decisive moment" as described by photographer Henri Cartier-Bresson. Witkin often makes narratives of four or more paintings, which help him convey complex ideas dramatically. Third, Witkin is a technical virtuoso, using light, color, and illusionistic space with extraordinary energy.

MS: To what extent is painting a narrative art form?

JW: It depends on the painter. For me, the story is very important. As a child, I was fascinated by the stories I heard on the radio. They occurred in episodes, and, while waiting for a week between programs, I could image settings, situations, and characters. The words provided the beginning point, then my imagination took over. I approached comic books in the opposite way. I tended to ignore the word balloons and instead made up my own dialogue to accompany the images.

MS: What is the advantage of multiple images?

JW: I really think Francis Bacon was right when he said that a painting should attack the nervous system. With multiple pictures, you can create an emotional overcharge based on the interplay between images. The viewer gets more fully involved. This can extend the meaning of the painting.

MS: To what extent are you influenced by other forms of narrative, such as films or novels?

JW: As a painter, I shouldn't separate myself from other media, such as dance or theater. My world involves choreography, human gesture, human physicality, all of which is integrated into the play I am creating in paint. The trouble with art today is that we have so taken the meat off the bones that there is often nothing left. I am drawn to paintings that have a real emotional depth as well as a breadth of ideas.

MS: How did *Division Street* evolve, both as an image and as an idea?

JW: *Division Street* is based on an actual and very, very psychologically charged memory. I saw my father turn to leave; I saw my mother launch plates at him; I saw her come back through the door. I wanted my father to be fairly anonymous: his face remains hidden. The color in the first two images is heightened. It is the color of night, or of a nightmare.

MS: Why was it done as a triptych?

JW: A triptych can be like a symphony, with the first image presenting the essential theme, the second developing the theme, and the third providing a conclusion.

The center is especially important in each of these paintings. The center of the first panel is at the edge of my father's tricep. To the left, there is a gap, a division. In the middle panel, the division occurs at the space between the door jamb, the father, the plates, and the kid. In the last panel, the center of gravity has shifted, to the edge of the closed door.

The space also shifts from panel to panel. It is fairly deep in the first, begins to flatten in the second, and becomes very shallow in the third. You are finally confined, closed in. While working on the paintings, I wrote in my notebook that "the use of telephoto can crush the form to help express the boy's emotional take on the scene, his surprise and shock."

MS: So many visual storytellers use film or video to express their ideas. Why do you use paint?

JW: At its core, painting is an exploration of the mystery of reality. Painting can make the world real: if I paint it, I can see it, if I can see it, I can hold it. With each mark of the brush, you respond to reality and create a new reality.

Painting is a summation of experience, requiring a level and degree of sustained attention that is unlike anything else. It offers us a dialogue with reality. A still life is a meditation on order, at very close range. Figurative painting engages us in a different way: in effect, we are always seeing ourselves, whether we are painting a self-portrait or working from the model.

Painting requires an appreciation of intonation — the nuances of light, space, and gesture. It is so much more than the accumulation of perceptual detail.

MS: What advice do you have for my students?

JW: Choose your images carefully. We are inundated by millions of images, on television, in magazines, on city streets. In this age of careless images, seek and produce your images with care. It is when painting becomes a necessity rather than a diversion that you begin to become an artist.

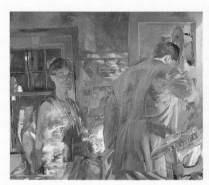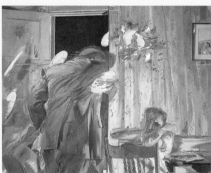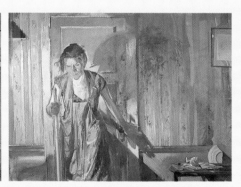

Jerome Witkin, *Division Street* [A story told in 3 panels], 1984–85. Oil on canvas, triptych. Left panel, 75⅛ × 63¼ in. (190.9 × 160.7 cm); middle panel, 81⅛ × 63 in. (206.2 × 160 cm); right panel, 87⅛ × 63 in. (221.3 3 160 cm).

Interdisciplinary Arts

In this final chapter, we explore three forms of interdisciplinary art. In **interdisciplinary art,** two or more disciplines are fused to create a hybrid art form. The first section focuses on visual books, which combine words and images in a wide variety of structures. The next section is devoted to **installation art,** which presents an ensemble of images and objects within a three-dimensional environment. The final section is devoted to **performance art,** which can be broadly defined as live art performed by artists.

EXPLORING THE VISUAL BOOK

What is a visual book?

A **visual book** is an experimental structure that conveys ideas, actions, and emotions using multiple images in an integrated and interdependent format. Every image is connected in some way to every other image. In a sense, there are no single pages in a visual book. It is the combination of the multiple pages that creates the complete artwork.

Any material may be used for pages, from the bags of tea Nancy Callahan used for her *Daybook* (14.1) to the sheets of lead Anselm Kiefer used for *Breaking of the Vessels* (14.2). Pages may be of any size or shape, from the 3-inch triangles Daniel Kelm and Tim Ely used in *Rubeus* (14.3) to 8-foot-tall screens.

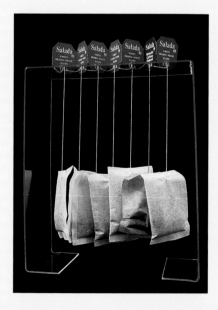

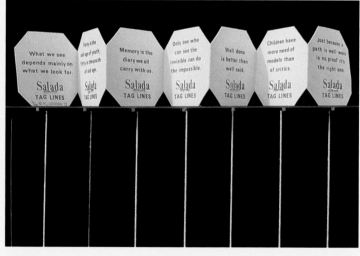

14.1 Nancy Callahan, *Daybook,* 1988. Artist's book, screen printing, and hand-fabricated tea bags, 16 × 12 × 6 in. (40.6 × 30.5 × 15.3 cm).

14.2 Anselm Kiefer, *Breaking of the Vessels,* **1990.** Lead, iron, glass, copper wire, charcoal, and aquatec. 12 ft 5 in. × 11 ft × in. × 4 ft 9 in. (378.5 × 343 × 144.8 cm).

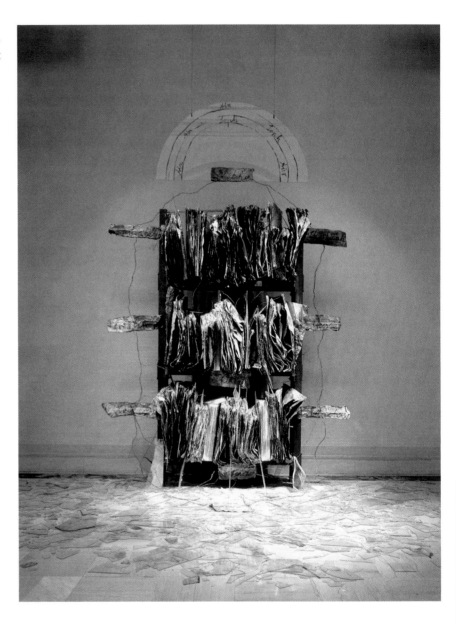

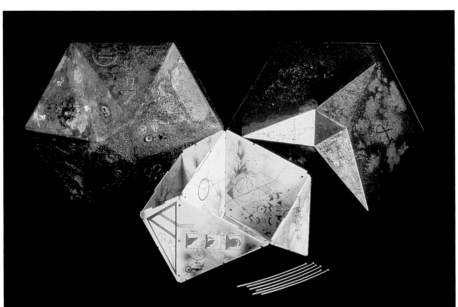

14.3 Daniel E. Kelm and Timothy C. Ely, *Rubeus,* **1990.** Book: Flexahexahedron (six cyclically linked tetrahedra with a circular axis of rotation), Arches paper, museum board, stainless steel wire, aluminum tubing, brass beads, cotton-covered polyester thread, with drawings using airbrush acrylics and ink, 5 × 10½ × 10½ in. (12.7 × 26.7 × 26.7 cm). Box: high faceted structure with hexagonal base and felt pad; paper consolidated paperboard and medium-density fiberboard, finished with polymer medium, copper leaf, plastic, metal bits, and sand from sacred sites, 6.25 in. (15.9 cm) high, 13 × 13 in. base (33 × 33 cm).

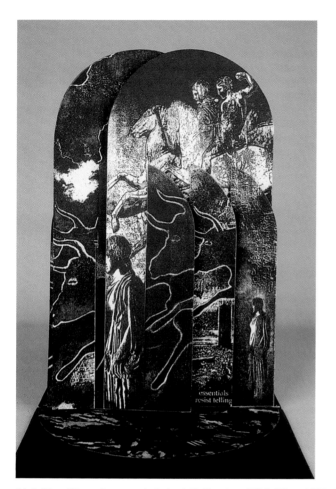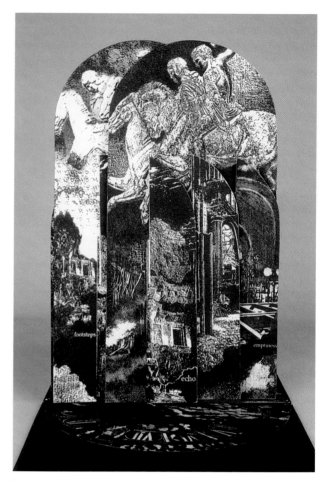

14.4 Mary Stewart, a page in *Labyrinth,* **Front and Side View, 1999.** Intaglio, 13 × 18 × 39 in. (33 × 45.7 × 99 cm).

14.5 Keith Smith, Bound-Edged Codex Structure.

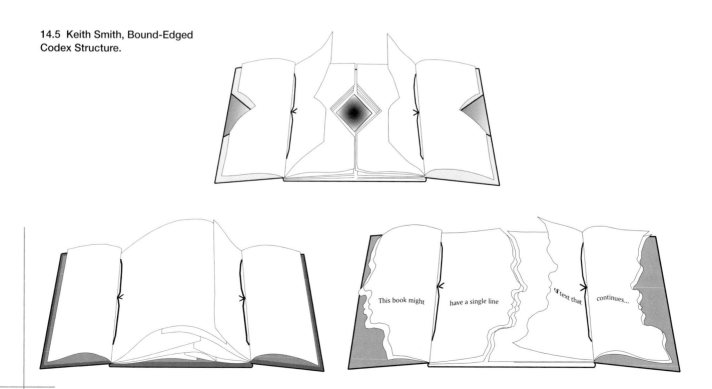

14.6 Tom Phillips, *A Humument,* 1980. From *The Cutting Edge of Reading: Artists' Books,* R. R. Hubert and J. D. Hubert. Granary Books, New York, 1999.

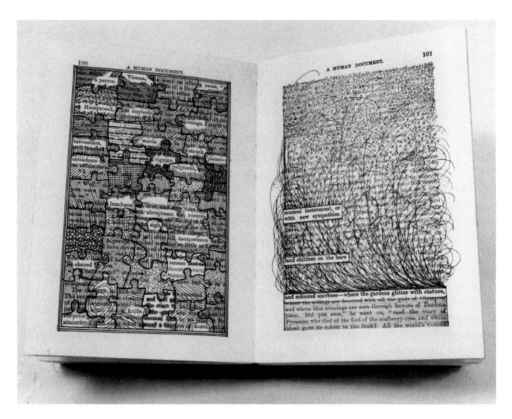

The subject matter can be painfully personal, as in Susan Kae Grant's *Giving Fear a Proper Name* (see 13.33), profoundly philosophical, or fiercely political. Images can be generated using photography, print-making, drawing, or other techniques.

Visual books combine two-dimensional composition and three-dimensional structure. For example, each page in my own *Labyrinth* (14.4) was composed individually, then slotted together to create a complex three-dimensional object. Even when a more traditional bound-edged **codex** structure is used (as shown in figure 14.5), variations in the page length and shape can substantially affect meaning.

Visual books may be entirely visual, as in Michael Snow's *Cover to Cover* (see 12.19); primarily verbal, as in Tom Phillips' *A Humument* (14.6); or entirely conceptual, as in Keith Smith's *Book 50* (14.7). Generally seen by one person at a time, a visual book can create a very direct connection between the audience and the artist. This contact is especially important with pop-up books, which come to life when the pages are turned and the tabs are pulled.

BOOK NUMBER 50
(Turning the page creates and destroys the image.)
Autumnal Equinox 1974

Construct a Western Codex book consisting of images on thirty transparencies. Process the film-positives by developing, short stop but no fix. Wash, dry and under proper safelight, hand bind as a leather case bound book. Place completed book in light-tight box.

Present the boxed book to the viewer. Upon opening the box and viewing, the entire book will not fog at once. Opening to the first page, the viewer will glimpse the image as it quickly blackens. The black will protect the remainder of the book from light. Upon turning each page, the viewer will momentarily see the image as it sacrifices itself to protect the remaining pages.

KE◉TH

14.7 Keith Smith, *Book 50,* 1974. A conceptual book.

Selecting a Text

Generative Potential

An evocative text can act as a springboard for the book artist, while an overly descriptive text may become a trap. More than verbal polish, a text must provide an opening for further development.

The labyrinth book project I assign to my students provides such generative potential, both visually and conceptually. The students begin by developing a labyrinthine drawing of a complex building (14.8). Because this drawing will act as a stage set for the narrative, careful use of lighting, balance, and the illusion of space is encouraged.

After a critique of the work, students expand their ideas and refine their images, finally creating two rough drawings, one on the front and one on the back of a 22 × 30 in. sheet of sturdy paper. This sheet is then cut apart to create four 7½ × 22 in. strips, which are finally folded and sewn to create sixteen 7½ × 11 in. pages.

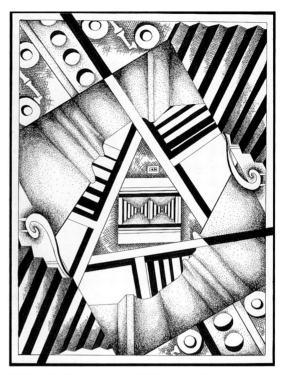

14.8 Emily Frenkel, *Labyrinth Drawing.* Pen and ink, 18 × 24 in. (45.6 × 61 cm).

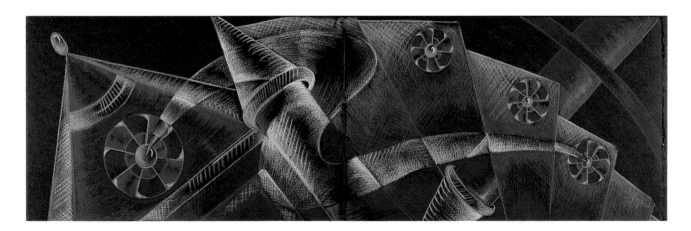

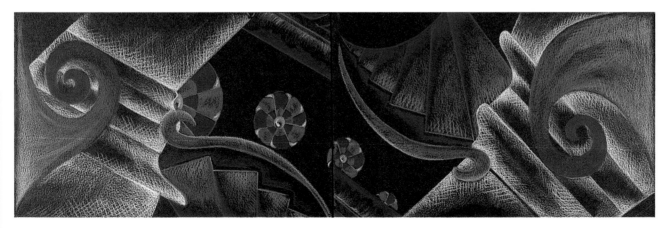

14.9 Emily Frenkel, *Labyrinth Book,* Two Double-Page Spreads. Colored pencil on black paper, 11 × 7½ in. (28 × 19 cm).

The book final is developed from this raw material. We consider dictionary definitions:

lab-y-rinth: 1: a structure full of intricate passageways that make it difficult to find the way from the interior to the entrance or from the entrance to the center (for example, the labyrinth constructed by Daedalus for Minos, king of Crete, in which the Minotaur was confined); 2: a maze in a park or garden formed by paths separated by high, thick hedges; 3: something bewilderingly involved or tortuous in structure: a complex that baffles exploration; 4: a situation from which it is difficult to extricate oneself; 5: the internal ear, or its bony or membranous part; 6: a body structure made up of a maze of cavities and channels; 7: intricate, sometimes symbolic pattern, spec. such a pattern inlaid in the pavement of a medieval church; 8: in metallurgy, series of troughs in a stamping mill through which water passes for washing pulverized ore.[1]

We read the story of Theseus, the Greek hero who conquered the half-man, half-bull Minotaur, and meet the princess Ariadne, who provided him with a ball of golden thread that aided in his escape from the maze. We investigate labyrinths as described by archaeologists, physiologists, and psychologists.

This assignment consistently results in an astonishing array of inventive books. Some students introduce characters into the setting, creating a simple narrative. Others use the illusion of space to move the viewer through mysterious corridors and down precipitous staircases. Others use light and pattern to create a world of enchantment and beauty (14.9). All are valid solutions to the problem. Because the word *labyrinth* is so open to interpretation, the assignment has great generative potential.

Divisions and Connections

A text that easily breaks apart can suggest connections or divisions between book pages. An alphabet

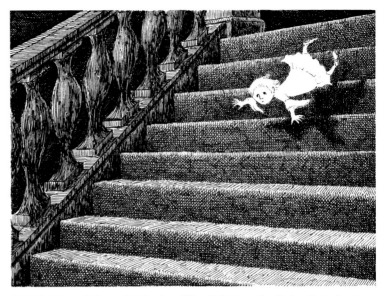

14.10A Edward Gorey, *A is for Amy Who Fell Down the Stairs.* Illustration from *The Gashlycrumb Tinies or, After the Outing.*

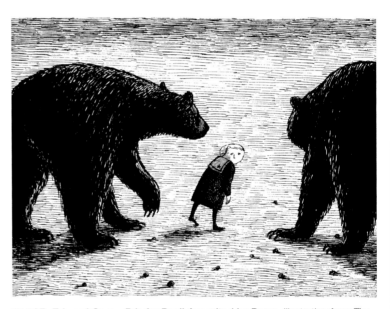

14.10B Edward Gorey, *B is for Basil Assaulted by Bears.* Illustration from *The Gashlycrumb Tinies or, After the Outing.*

provides the page divisions in Edward Gorey's *The Gashlycrumb Tinies or, After the Outing* (14.10A–B). Each letter is accompanied by a rhythmic and rhyming text describing assorted accidents and childhood fatalities, beginning with "A is for Amy who fell down the stairs, B is for Basil assaulted by bears, C is for Clara who wasted away, D is for Desmond thrown out of a sleigh," and so forth. The alphabet provides a sense of anticipation, as we wonder what wild expression of humor we will encounter on the next page, while the singsong rhythm and clever rhymes help unify the separate pages.

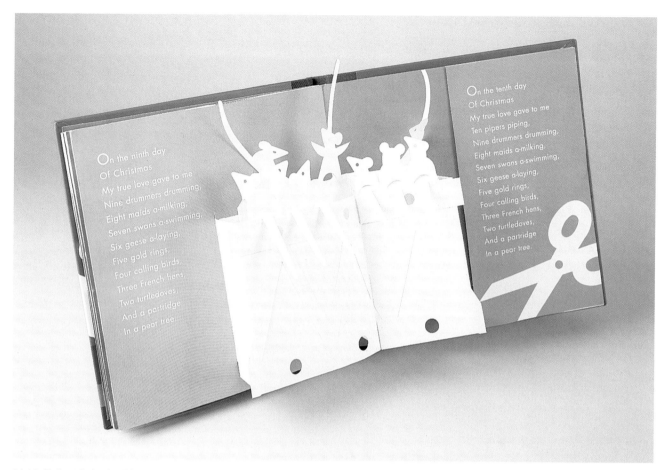

14.11 Robert Sabuda, "Nine Drummers Drumming." Reprinted from *The 12 Days of Christmas, a Pop-Up Celebration.* Simon & Schuster.

Similarly, a traditional song provides the structure for *The Twelve Days of Christmas,* by Robert Sabuda. This song has become a holiday cliché, and a conventional drawing of the familiar partridge in a pear tree would have been deadly. Sabuda overcame the cliché by using a lively imagination combined with elegant and elaborate pop-ups. The "six geese-a-laying" sit atop a slice of gooseberry pie, while the "seven swans-a-swimming" fill a crystal ball. For "eleven ladies dancing," nine ballerinas dance atop a music box and a mirror is used to multiply some of the figures. And the "nine drummers drumming" (14.11) are mice, with their tails tapping out a lively beat! Imagination conquers cliché, every time.

Music

Each language has a distinctive aural quality, or music, as well as a distinctive grammatical structure. English, which is dominated by words derived from Latin and Germanic languages, provides at least two ways to say almost anything. For example, a Viking warrior is *strong* (a word that is derived from the Anglo-Saxon word for strength), while a Roman warrior is *vigorous* (a word that is derived from the Latin word for strength). Spanish provides great grammatical clarity, and similar word endings encourage rhyme, while Chinese is literally musical — the meaning of words changes when the inflection and the tone of voice change.

Each text also has music. When words are poorly chosen, the text is discordant and painful to read. When the words are used thoughtfully, however, both the meaning and the music improve. *Kubla Khan,* by Coleridge, uses wonderfully musical language.

In Xanadu did Kubla Khan
A stately pleasure dome decree:
Where Alph, the sacred river, ran
Through caverns measureless to man
Down to a sunless sea.[2]

You simply must read this aloud. A combination of rhyme, repetition, and alliteration makes the words sing.

Rachel Carson's *Under the Sea Wind* provides many examples of musical prose.

> By September the eels of the sound country had begun to drop downstream to the sea. The eels came down from the hills and the upland grasslands. They came from cypress swamps where black-watered rivers had their beginnings; they moved across the tidal plain that dropped in six giant steps to the sea. In the river estuaries and in the sound they joined their mates-to-be. Soon, in silvery wedding dress, they would follow the ebbing tides to the sea, to find — and lose — themselves in the black abysses of mid-ocean.[3]

As with an alphabetic or a traditional song, the music of the text may suggest page divisions while simultaneously providing conceptual unity to the book as a whole.

Writing a Text

At some point, most book artists and illustrators decide to generate their own texts. The ideas and emotions they want to express are not available in a traditional text, and copyright laws may limit the use of a contemporary text.

Taking a creative-writing course is a good place to start. As with art courses, a well-designed writing course can provide a solid base of information and encourage the beginner to try various approaches. Try writing a page or two in response to any of these assignments:

- *Memory amplifier.* Describe an object, a sensation, or a setting that summarizes or epitomizes an event, a feeling, or an idea in your life. Looking at family photographs, childhood toys, or everyday objects is a good place to start.

- *Moment of truth.* Describe an event that clarified or transformed your life.

- *Homeworld.* Describe the physical or psychological place that is your home. Is it a particular house? A forest? The World Wide Web?

- *Build a memory bank.* Triggering questions can help you start. Just fill in the blanks: (a) "the first time I ever____"; (b) "the best day of my life was___"; (c) list memorable events, such as theater, trips, or concerts; (d) list companions in triumph and adversity; (e) consider the greatest gift you ever received or ever gave.

- *Concept generator.* Research a single word, using a thesaurus, a dictionary, an encyclopedia, the Internet, and so on. Collect all of the resulting meanings into a book.

Selecting or writing an appropriate text can increase the impact of the book. The best texts are of personal interest, offer room for experimentation in the book format, and are meaningful to your audience. Ask yourself the following questions as you assess the potential of several texts.

- *What is the conceptual, psychological, or political power of the text?* Does it embody ideas and emotions you find personally compelling? The stronger your connection to the text, the more effective the book will be.

- *Does the text include any verbal patterns that can help unify the book?* Rhythm, repetition, and rhyme can be used to create a stronger connection among the pages.

- *How resonant are the words?* Do they gain or lose strength through multiple readings?

- *How accessible is the text?* Is the language comprehensible to the intended audience? How wide an interest is there in the book's subject matter?

- *How long is the text?* Generally, texts of 30 or fewer words are easiest to use effectively. Extended texts can get long-winded and crowd out the images.

Any source, from graffiti to Shakespeare, can be used. Indeed, many visual books derive their power from an unexpected selection of words.

Text and Type Style

After a text is chosen, book construction can begin. Each page you design raises many questions. Let's concentrate on three major questions, using an 11 × 17 in. double-page spread. Ask yourself the following questions.

- *What type style and type size is most appropriate to the ideas expressed?*

Each type style has a significant effect on communication. Let's experiment with a simple phrase: "Footsteps echoed emptiness."

Impact type has an industrial look: perhaps it is the echo of boots descending a factory staircase that we hear (14.12).

FOOTSTEPS ECHOED EMPTINESS

14.12

Garamond type, especially when italicized, is flowing and graceful. The footsteps we now hear may be those of a child descending a staircase in a Victorian house on Christmas Eve (14.13).

footsteps echoed emptiness

14.13

Madrone type paints a much grimmer picture. A gang war has concluded, and the survivors are slowly leaving the deserted parking lot where it occurred (14.14).

FOOTSTEPS ECHOED EMPTINESS

14.14

- *Can more than one type style be used effectively?*

Multiple texts are used in many books to communicate the distinctive voices of multiple speakers or to convey multiple perspectives on the same event. *Sticky Buns: An Overnight Roll* uses this approach (14.15). This book was developed by a team of 12 artists during a workshop organized by the Paper and Book Intensive, a national book-arts

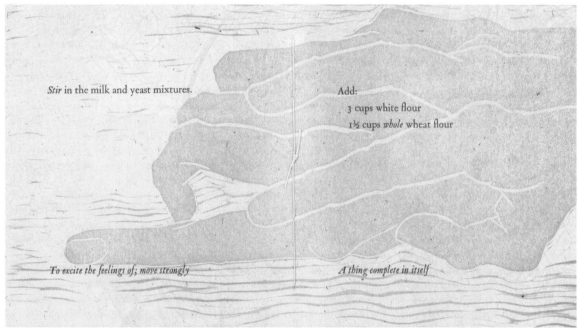

14.15 *Sticky Buns: An Overnight Roll,* **1996.** A collaborative book developed by 12 artists participating in a letterpress workshop at the Paper and Book Intensive. Kathy Keuhn, instructor.

group. An actual recipe for cinnamon buns is provided near the top of each page, while a **gloss,** or commentary on the text, is written in italics along the bottom. Words carefully selected from the recipe are thereby reinterpreted, suggesting a romantic afternoon in the kitchen as the emotions (as well as the dough) begin to rise.

• *How should the words be positioned on the page?*

In figure 14.16, position combined with size emphasizes the acute hearing we develop in threatening situations.

The mysterious implications of the phrase are emphasized in figure 14.17.

With the addition of two more pages, figure 14.18 communicates the loneliness of the journey.

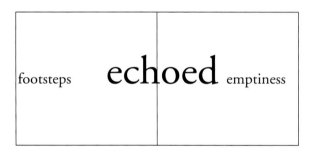

14.16

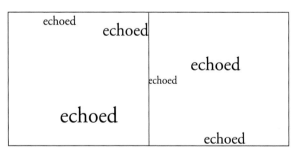

14.17

footsteps	echoed		e m p t i n e s s

14.18

Word and Image Relationships

Things get even more interesting when words and images are used together.

The organization in figure 14.19 suggests the woman's memory of a past event.

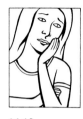 footsteps 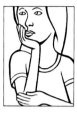 echoed 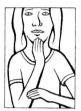 emptiness

14.19

The same phrase describes a walk into the future in figure 14.20.

 footsteps 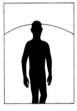 echoed 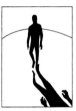 emptiness

14.20

Finally, the combination of word and image in figure 14.21 puts us back into a labyrinth.

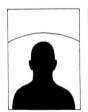 footsteps 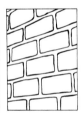 echoed 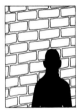 emptiness

14.21

Advantages of Visual Books

Through a combination of words and images, visual books can convey complex ideas and emotions to a broad audience. In some books, the words provide direct, explicit communication, while the images are more implicit and evocative. In other books, the words are evocative, while the images are explicit and direct. In either case, layers of meaning can be created through a contrast between the visual and the verbal. Instead of overexplaining an image, words can be used to suggest alternative ideas and implications. For artists with big ideas, this interplay between words and images greatly expands communication.

Key Questions

When designing a visual book, consider

- What thoughts and emotions do you most want to express?
- What thoughts and emotions are best expressed in words, or through images?
- What balance between words and images is best?
- Will a change in tempo increase impact? Try adding some blank pages to slow down the tempo or putting multiple frames on a single page to speed up the tempo.

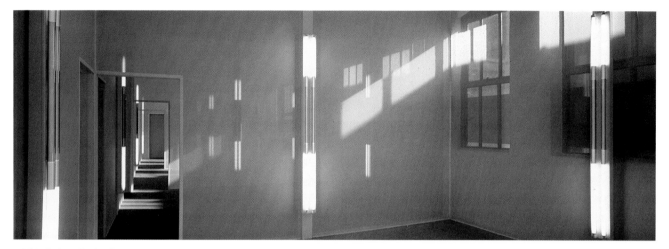

14.22 Robert Irwin, *Part II: Excursus: Homage to the Square³.* Installation at Dia Center for the Arts, New York. September 1998–June 1999.

INSTALLATION ART

An installation is an ensemble of images and objects that are presented within a three-dimensional environment. Because we occupy the actual time and space of the artwork, we become physically engaged in an installation, and the aesthetic experience becomes heightened.

Uses of Space and Time

Some installations are primarily spatial. For example, many installations by Robert Irwin emphasize direct experience within a constructed space. By creating a series of entrances, exits, and environments, Irwin creates a framework that is activated by each visitor. His *Part II: Excursus: Homage to the Square*³ (14.22) was installed at the Dia Center in New York in 1999. This structure consisted of nine cubic rooms, defined by delicate walls of cloth. The opacity and transparency of the fabric varied, depending on the amount and location of the light. Two vertical fluorescent lights illuminated each cube, creating subtle changes in color from room to room.

Entering the installation was both inviting and disorienting. From any point, all of the rooms were visible, yet veiled. Multiple layers of cloth and the variations in light made the most distant rooms dissolve. The vertical fluorescent lights, which always remained visible, first read as individual, then as mirror images, creating a hallucinatory experience similar to a carnival fun house. All activity within

the space was created by the visitors themselves, who entered, and explored, the installation like ghostly silhouettes.

By contrast, *Floodsong,* by Mary Lucier, was primarily temporal. Six video monitors were installed in a narrow room at the Museum of Modern Art. Each showed an interview with a survivor of the 1995 Grand Forks flood. A young girl, an old woman, an old man, a minister, and a farmer told the story of the terrifying event. In the enclosed space, the individual voices were indistinct. They echoed and merged, creating a litany of fortitude and grief, resilience and fear. In sharp contrast to the straightforward interviews, an enormous projection on the back wall of the gallery took the audience through wrecked houses and piles of debris.

Bill Viola's *Hall of Whispers* (14.23), was equally temporal and spatial. In his catalogue for a retrospective exhibition of Viola's work, David Ross wrote:

Viewers enter a long, narrow, dark room, and must pass between ten video projections arranged in two rows along the side walls, five on either side of the room. The projections are life-sized black and white images of people's heads facing the viewer, with their eyes closed and their mouths tightly bound and gagged. They are straining to speak, but their muffled voices are incomprehensible, and mingle in the space in a low, indecipherable jumble of sound.[4]

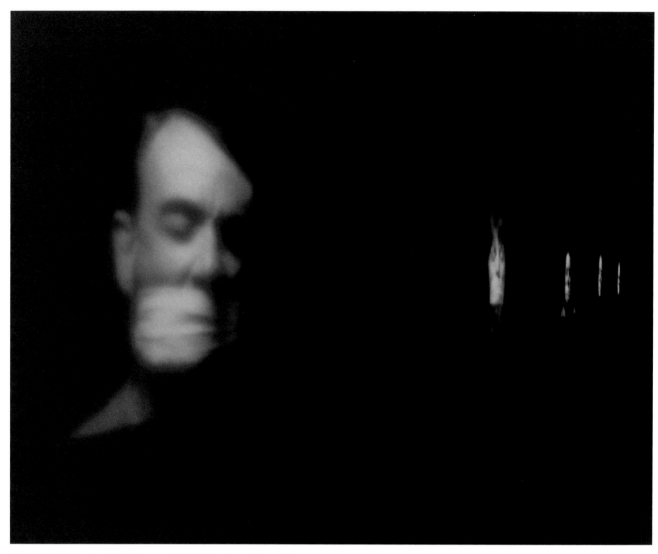

14.23 Bill Viola, *Hall of Whispers*, 1995. Video/sound installation.

This installation, while similar to *Floodsong* in layout, created an entry into a nightmare. Lucier's installation evoked a range of emotions: fear, pity, and respect. Viola's *Hall of Whispers* was claustrophobic and terrifying.

The Importance of Context

Installations must be seen in context. Spatial variations from site to site require changes in an installation whenever it is moved. More important, each site adds its own meaning to the artwork. No site is neutral. Each imparts its own emotional and spatial charge.

When the context is used fully, a powerful connection can be made between art and life. For exam-
ple, our associations with the interior and the objects used in Sandy Skoglund's *Walking on Eggshells* (14.24) are essential to the meaning of the piece. For most of us, there is no place more private than a bathroom and there are few animals more insidiously frightening than snakes. This combination alone is sure to create tension. The addition of a floor covered with delicate eggshells, twin female figures, and playful rabbits expands the expressive range further. Even the wall tiles are deliberate. Dominated by hieroglyphics from the Egyptian Book of the Dead and other ancient images, they add to the sense of mystery. The women in this space seem like goddesses from antiquity, and the bathroom becomes loaded with conflicting emotions.

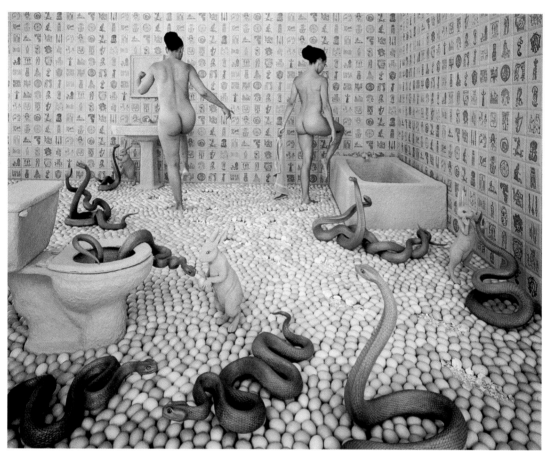

14.24 Sandy Skoglund, *Walking on Eggshells*, 1997.
Cibachrome print, 47 × 60 in. (119 × 152 cm).

A site may also be used to expand the audience for art. In *Storefront Stories* (14.25), Nancy Callahan and Diane Gallo (see "Profile," page 126) transformed empty shop windows in several small towns into a series of vignettes based on childhood memories. When shown in Cherry Valley, New York, a single window was changed every day over a six-week period. In this project, personal experience became public communication through the use of a nontraditional exhibition space.

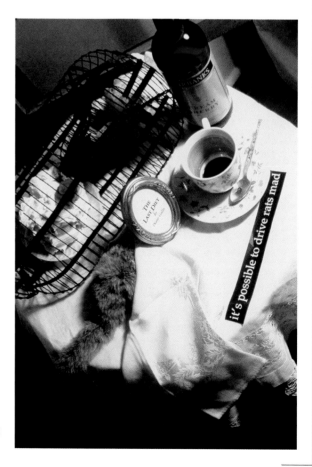

14.25 Diane Gallo and Nancy Callahan, *Storefront Stories*, 1999. Mixed medium installation, 6 × 6 × 6 ft (1.83 × 1.83 × 1.83 m).

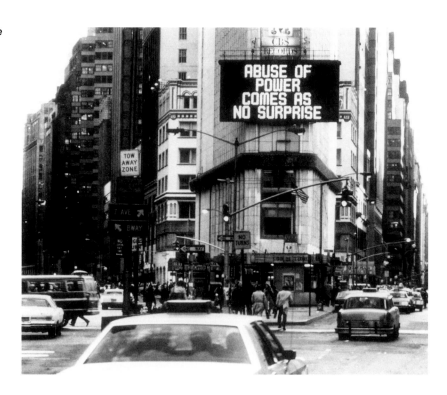

Through *Truisms* (14.26), Jenny Holzer brought public art to an urban audience for a more political purpose. Printing various proverbs on posters, flyers, T-shirts, hats, and finally electronic signs, Holzer used mass-marketing techniques to convey messages such as "Abuse of power comes as no surprise" and "Raise boys and girls the same way." Shown next to the flashing neon signs in New York City's busy Times Square, these seemingly banal messages took on new importance and reached many viewers unfamiliar with contemporary art.

Advantages of Installation Art

For the artist seeking new and expanded means of expression, installation art offers

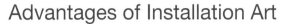

- *A fresh perspective on a familiar setting or situation.* The site itself is an essential component of the piece. We must see familiar settings afresh. Any aspect of reality can become a staging area for art. Our expectations may become shifted, inverted, or upended.

- *A large scale.* Most installations are made in a size that invites physical entry. Thus, the distance between viewer and image is eliminated: we become one with the artwork. The principles of time, space, and gravity that rule our everyday life can be used deliberately in an installation to heighten impact or to create a sense of disorientation.

- *Increased viewer involvement.* No longer a bystander, the viewer must physically enter and consciously interact with the artwork.

Key Questions

When designing an installation, consider

- What ideas do you most want to express? What emotions do you most want to evoke?

- What is the advantage of a confined space as opposed to an expansive space?

- How much lighting is needed, and what is the most appropriate light source?

- What sounds will you provide? What sounds can be generated by the audience?

- How can you invite viewers into your artwork? What will they discover? What might they know on leaving that they didn't know on entering?

PERFORMANCE ART

Mixing dance, theater, music, and art with politics, philosophy, and other disciplines, performance art pushes the possibilities of interdisciplinary work even further. As with any other art form, performance art is designed to communicate ideas and express emotions. Unlike traditional art forms, performance art is immediate and direct. Rather than paint an image on a canvas, the performers generally present images directly, on a stage, in a gallery, or outdoors. The wood, bronze, or marble of traditional figurative sculpture is replaced with the flesh and blood of the artist's own body. The stage becomes a laboratory for aesthetic experimentation, and both the audience and the artist may determine the outcome of an event.

Historical Background

Performance art has become especially prominent in the past 10 years. The current surge in interest is often traced to the Happenings developed by Allan Kaprow and others in the 1950s and 1960s. In a **Happening,** the time, place, materials, and general theme for the event were determined by the artist. Upon arrival, the audience created the artwork through their actions. Unrehearsed, these events were often chaotic as well as exhilarating.

The roots of contemporary performance art may actually extend back in time to the Futurists, a group of Italian poets, musicians, and artists most active from 1911 to 1915. Determined to develop a new approach to art, they created revolutionary paintings and sculptures based on dynamism, wrote inflammatory manifestos, and staged theatrical performances that were both frenetic and shocking. In word and deed, the Futurists rebelled against good taste, traditional subject matter, compositional rules, and established institutions, such as museums.

Characteristics of Performance Art

To some extent, contemporary performance art shares many of the basic characteristics of Futurism. Four qualities are especially notable.

Ephemeral

Just as a symphony ceases to exist as soon as the last note fades, so performance art is inherently ephemeral. The performance may persist in the memory of each member of the audience, but the full force of the event disappears as soon as the audience leaves the site. While any well-trained classical violinist can perform a given Beethoven sonata, roles in performance pieces are rarely played by new actors. Generally, a piece written by Laurie Anderson must be performed by her. Even when a new production is planned, difficulty in transferring information about the role may make it impossible to re-stage the piece.

As a result, time is always of particular importance in performance art. In 1952, musician John Cage deleted pitch, timbre, and loudness from one composition, leaving duration as the only remaining aspect of the music. The resulting work, titled *4 minutes 33 seconds (4'33")* was therefore silent for 4 minutes and 33 seconds.

Time was also a major component of Dan Graham's *Past Continuous Pasts*, installed in a New York City gallery in 1974. The walls were covered with mirrors, and time-delayed video monitors were positioned at each end of the room. Upon entering, viewers first viewed themselves in the present, then, watching the video monitors, viewed themselves in the past.

Collaborative

Working collaboratively, artists can expand their ideas and explore new modes of expression. Despite their interest in live art, few visual artists have extensive training in dance and theater. It may be physically impossible for them to perform a movement themselves. And, just as an amateur's drawing is very different from a drawing done by a professional, so amateur dance differs greatly from professional dance. By working collaboratively, artists, actors, musicians, and dancers can combine forces to create powerful new pieces.

Furthermore, a collaboration tends to extend the ideas generated by each of the participants. Despite their similarities, art, theater, music, and dance are also distinctively different. Each has a long and complex history, an extensive theoretical background, and particular aesthetic values. By sharing information and discussing alternative approaches to an idea, each participant in a performance has an opportunity to rethink his or her own creative process.

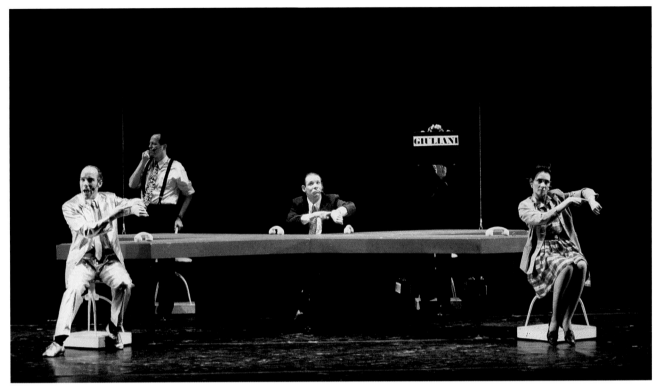

14.27 Karole Armitage, *Predator's Ball,* 1996. Brooklyn Academy of Music. Sets by David Salle, animation videos by Erica Beckman, costumes by Hugo Boss, Pila Limosner & Debra Moises Co.

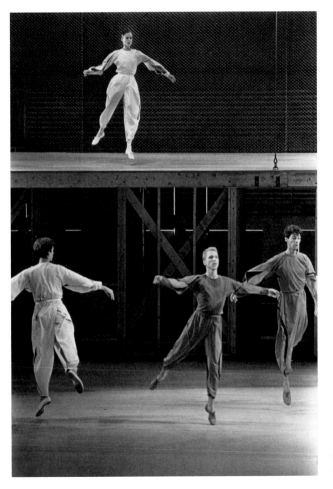

Many disciplines have been combined successfully. In *Predator's Ball* (14.27), Karole Armitage combined her choreography with sets by painter David Salle and videos by Erica Beckman. This tale about Wall Street junk bond dealer Michael Milken is both stark in its staging and frenzied in its energy. In *Available Light* (14.28), choreographer Lucinda Childs sought a pulse in the spaces designed by architect Frank Gehry and the music composed by John Adams. And, in *L.O.W. in Gaia* (14.29), Rachel Rosenthal presented a meditation on art, feminism, and ecology.

Blurred Boundaries

During a performance, separations between art and life are often dissolved. For some artists, performance art is a way to work outside the rarefied world of the art museum or the competitive world of the commercial gallery. Viewing art as a creative process and a life-affirming philosophy rather than as a product, such artists seek new venues and new

14.28 Lucinda Childs, Image from *Available Light,* 1983. Performed at the Brooklyn Academy of Music.

audiences. Separations between high art and mass culture may become blurred. Graffiti, popular music, or television advertisements may provide more inspiration than a masterpiece in a museum. Indeed, in describing his approach to a Happening, Allan Kaprow said that "the line between art and life should be kept as fluid and perhaps as indistinct as possible."

Many contemporary artists pursue this goal with a vengeance. In John Cage's *First Construction in Metal,* automobile brake drums, cowbells, and sheets of metal are used along with conventional percussion instruments in a highly rhythmic piece. In *Imaginary Landscape #4,* Cage broke the concert-hall barrier even more vigorously. Twelve ordinary radios, tuned to various stations, were the major instruments played. Any advertisement, news, or music each radio played became part of the concert.

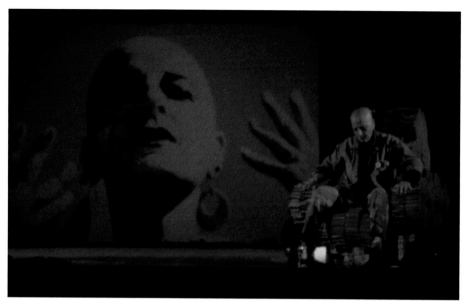

14.29 Rachel Rosenthal, *L.O.W. in Gaia.* First performance, Marquette University, WI. 1986.

The Artist and the Audience

When barriers between art and life are removed, separations between artist and audience also become blurred. Indeed, many artists deliberately involve the audience in the work. In *Performance/Audience/Mirror,* Dan Graham confronted his audience directly, describing their appearance and commenting on their participation in the performance. In *Cut Piece,* musician Yoko Ono knelt on the stage, as a traditional Japanese woman. Throughout the half-hour performance, members of the audience approached and, using a large pair of scissors provided, cut off her clothing. And, with *Pull,* Mona Hatoum created a humorous interaction between audience and artist. Viewers were invited to pull on an actual braid of hair, then watch the artist's reaction on the video monitor. No longer an observer, each member of the audience helped create the artwork.

Key Questions

When designing a performance, consider

- When working collaboratively, what can you offer to your partner and what can your partner offer to you? What similarities and differences are there in your creative processes? What is the best way to handle differences of opinion?

- How many performers are needed?

- What is the relationship between the performer(s) and the set? Should all of the performers appear live, or can some appear via slides or video projections?

- How can sound and light heighten emotion or expand meaning?

- How much change must occur during the performance? Is repetition a virtue?

- What role will the audience play?

PERFORMANCE ART

ADVANTAGES OF INTERDISCIPLINARY ART

Visual books, installations, and performance art all require interdisciplinary integration. The connections created offer new opportunities for creative thinking and complex communication. Ideas and emotions outside the mainstream can become accessible to both artists and audiences. Furthermore, because each of these new media requires a substantial amount of audience participation, relationships between artist and audience become redefined. An active audience can contribute more to the experience than a passive audience. When artist and audience share the same time and space, as in a performance piece, this connection is especially strong.

With performance art, boundaries dissolve, not only between art and theater, but also between art and life.

SUMMARY

- A visual book is an experimental structure that conveys ideas, actions, and emotions in an integrated and interdependent format. Each page is connected in some way to the preceding page and the following page.

- Visual books combine two-dimensional composition with three-dimensional structure and may use time and narrative very deliberately. They may be entirely visual, may be entirely verbal, or may mix words and images.

- In selecting a text, consider its potential to generate ideas, how a text will be divided and distributed over multiple pages, the rhythm and music of the words, and the significance of the ideas.

- Every type style has its own distinctive quality, which can add or detract from the meaning of the book.

- The combination of words and images in a visual book can encourage the development of complex ideas using layers of meaning.

- An installation is an ensemble of images and objects that is presented within a three-dimensional environment. When the viewer enters an installation, he or she is physically surrounded and aesthetically engaged.

- An installation may be primarily spatial, may be primarily temporal, or may use both equally. The context in which an installation occurs can add to, subtract from, or expand its meaning.

- Installation art offers a fresh perspective on a familiar setting or situation, is usually done in large scale, and requires some viewer involvement.

- Performance art is live art designed by artists. Combining aspects of theater, music, art, and dance, it offers both the artist and the audience a laboratory for aesthetic experimentation.

- Many performance artists use time very deliberately, expand their ideas through collaboration, and seek to blur the boundaries between art and life.

- Each of the interdisciplinary arts described in this chapter requires substantial audience participation. As a result, relationships between the artist and the audience are constantly being redefined by contemporary artists.

Keywords

codex	installation art	performance art
gloss	interdisciplinary art	visual book
Happening		

Profile:
Abelardo Morell, Photographer

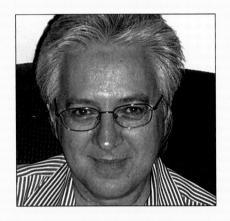

Born in 1948 in Havana, Cuba, Abelardo Morell moved to New York City with his family at the age of fourteen.

Morell is best known for his photographs of everyday objects, room interiors, and all kinds of books. Using traditional photography, he transforms even the most mundane subject matter into an evocative image. An ordinary pencil becomes a monumental object, a rumpled newspaper becomes a complex landscape, and we can almost feel the pages, spines, and bindings of the books he photographs.

Morell has exhibited widely, including solo shows at the Boston Museum of Fine Arts, the Museum of Photographic Arts in San Diego and the Isabella Stewart Gardner Museum in Boston. His monographs include *A Camera in a Room, Alice's Adventures in Wonderland,* and *The Book of Books.* When we met, he was preparing work for a major exhibition at the International Center for Photography in New York City. He published two new books in the fall of 2004, and is currently exploring the ways in which evidence of time can be found in everyday objects.

Use of the camera obscura is a major aspect of Morell's artwork. Using a darkened room with just a pinhole of light, he creates projected images of external events on the interior walls of ordinary rooms. *Camera Obscura Image of Brookline View in Brady's Room, 1992,* is one example.

MS: When did you realize the power of photography?

AM: Right away, with my first two rolls of film. As an exile, a teenager in New York with no English, I badly needed a way to express myself. Moving to the frozen tundra of Maine was equally as strange. I felt isolated and scared, and saw no real way to fit in. My initial photographs were very bold and expressive. For the first time I could communicate the alienation I was feeling.

MS: How did you express that alienation?

AM: There were all kinds of crazy juxtapositions in my work. Generally, I saw the world around me through a surreal lens. Absurdity was everywhere. It became fun to seek it out in common places. I think I just wanted the world around me to match my own inner world.

MS: It sounds like a surrealist extravaganza, reminiscent of poet Andre Breton's comment about putting a sewing machine on a hospital operating table. The Surrealists used irrational juxtapositions so expressively.

AM: I don't know who said it, but I half believe this. "The problem with surrealism is that it invents everything, but discovers nothing." You have to be careful with how much you invent. You want your work to be fueled by some sense of being in the world, in reality.

Photographically, I was most influenced by Robert Frank's book *The Americans,* and by the work of Diane Arbus and Cartier-Bresson. Cartier-Bresson let me see the poetry of the street. Frank took that poetry and made it more expressionistic and psychological. And Arbus made the psychological aspect even more intense. Her photographs of twins, circus performers and ordinary people went beyond simple curiousity. They became both poignant and disturbing. Through these artists' work, I learned that straight photography can often pack more surrealism into an image than I can create through collage.

MS: Your camera obscura work seems especially to embody a sense of wonderment, the extraordinary qualities of everyday events. How did you begin this body of work?

AM: As a teacher at Massachusetts College of Art, I use the camera obscura to demonstrate the basics of optics to beginning students. Camera obscuras have been used for over five hundred years as a way to bring exterior images into darkened rooms. The entire room is darkened, except for a ⅜" hole looking out on an interesting view. My students are always amazed to see projections of people on Huntington Avenue walking upside down on the classroom walls.

Light Bulb, 1991, was also initially made to demonstrate this effect. I constructed a small camera obscura from a simple cardboard box with a lens held in place with duct tape. When I printed the image, I was amazed by the detail and magical effect from these ordinary materials. This picture helped me rediscover the mystery of the medium and encouraged me to think of new ways to share it with others.

MS: Tell me about *Camera Obscura Image of Brookline View in Brady's Room.*

AM: That is one of the early camera obscuras I made. Part of the enjoyment was collaborating with my son Brady. He set up animals, dinosaurs, a battle scene. It was nice to have my own child invent the inside while I brought the outside in. It was a great meeting place for both of us.

MS: What constitutes a great photograph for you?

AM: One that you feel like you can't add or take away anything from it.

MS: What advice do you give to your students? What seem to be the characteristics of a great photographer?

AM: Perseverance — staying with it for the long run, no matter what. I believe that the medium gives you something back if you stay with it. Ultimately, you should be true to your feelings, no matter what they may be.

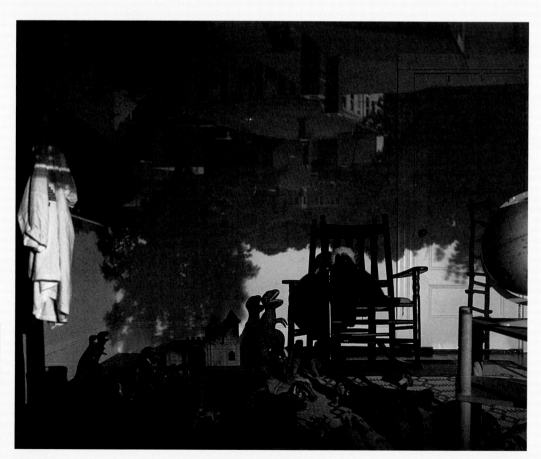

Abe Morrell, Camera Obscura Image of Brookline View in Brady's Room, 1992. Silver getalin print, 20 in × 24 in.

Part Four
Multimedia Resources

Take advantage of the multimedia resources for Part Four in order to test and expand your understanding of time design.

Resources	Contents

www.mhhe.com/launching2

Student Center
Chapter 12
Chapter 13
Chapter 14

Learning objectives for each chapter
Study outlines for each chapter
Quizzes with instant feedback
Flashcards for studying art vocabulary
Internet exercises for developing critical viewing skills
Book suggestions for your personal library and research projects

Core Concepts in Art CD-ROM

Exercises to explore how time is used as an element of art
Videos illustrating new media techniques

Studio projects are described and illustrated for teachers on the Web and on a CD-ROM.

Resources

www.mhhe.com/launching2

Instructor Center
IM Part Four

Instructor's Resource CD-ROM

Part Four

Projects

Time Observed: Increasing awareness of time through careful attention.
Sequences: Using graphic, temporal, rhythmic, and spatial relationships
Tempo: Exploring variations in the rate of change
Chronology: A simple demonstration of the impact of chronology on narrative
Intensity: Demonstrating the significance of an elusive concept
Countdown: Exploring ways to compress, expand, and accelerate time
Changing the Scene Changes the Story: An exploration of setting and narrative
Scope: Creating a composition that is spatially and temporally complex
Strata: Increasing complexity through layers of space
Arrested Time: Implied time and captured moments
Time Piece: Exploring kinetic time
Homage to Hockney: An exploration of time, space, and movement
Causality and Duration: An introduction to narrative
True Lies: Designing Fiction: An introduction to linear narrative
Before and After: Understanding narrative implications of objects and interiors
Build a Concept Generator: Exploring non-linear and associative approaches

Visual Organization

Arnheim, Rudolph. *Art and Visual Perception: A Psychology of the Creative Eye.* Berkeley: University of California Press, 1974.

Arnheim, Rudolph. *Power of the Center.* Berkeley: University of California Press, 1999.

Berger, Arthur Asa. *Seeing Is Believing: An Introduction to Visual Communication*, 2nd ed. New York: McGraw-Hill.

Berger, John. *Ways of Seeing.* London: British Broadcasting Corporation, 1987.

Dondis, Donis. *A Primer of Visual Literacy.* Cambridge, MA: MIT Press, 1973.

Two-Dimensional Design

Behrens, Roy R. *Design in the Visual Arts.* Englewood Cliffs, NJ: Prentice-Hall, 1984.

Cheathan, Frank, Jane Hart Cheathan, and Sheryl A. Haler. *Design Concepts and Applications.* Englewood Cliffs, NJ: Prentice-Hall, 1983.

Graham, Donald W. *Composing Pictures.* New York: Van Nostrand Reinhold, 1970.

Kepes, Gyorgy. *Language of Vision.* Chicago: Paul Theobald, 1944.

Lauer, David A., and Stephan Pentak. *Design Basics*, 5th ed. Orlando, FL: Harcourt, Brace and Company, 2000.

Myers, Jack Fredrick. *The Language of Visual Art: Perception as a Basis for Design.* Orlando, FL: Holt Rinehart and Winston, 1989.

Ocvirk, Otto G., Robert E. Stinson, Philip R. Wigg, Robert O. Bone, and David L. Cayton. *Art Fundamentals: Theory and Practice*, 10th ed. New York: McGraw-Hill, 2006.

Color Theory

Albers, Josef. *Interaction of Color.* New Haven, CT: Yale University Press, 1963.

Birren, Farber. *Light, Color and Environment.* New York: Van Nostrand Reinhold, 1982.

Gerritsen, Frans. *Theory and Practice of Color.* New York: Van Nostrand Reinhold, 1975.

Hornung, David. *Color: A Workshop Approach.* New York: McGraw-Hill, 2005.

Itten, Johannes. *The Art of Color.* New York: Van Nostrand Reinhold, 1974.

Kuppers, Harald. *Color: Origin, Systems, Uses.* New York: Van Nostrand Reinhold, 1972.

Linton, Harold. *Color Model Environments.* New York: Van Nostrand Reinhold, 1985.

Munsell, Albert H. *A Grammar of Color: A Basic Treatise on the Color System of Albert H. Munsell.* New York: Van Nostrand Reinhold, 1969.

Norman, Richard B. *Electronic Color.* New York: Van Nostrand Reinhold, 1990.

Pile, John F. *Interior Design.* New York: Harry N. Abrams, 1988.

Zelanski, Paul, and Mary Pat Fisher. *Color.* Englewood Cliffs, NJ: Prentice Hall, 1989.

Creativity

Bohm, David. *On Creativity.* New York: Routledge, 2000.

Briggs, John. *Fire in the Crucible: Understanding the Process of Creative Genius.* Grand Rapids: Phanes Press, 2000.

Csikszentmihalyi, Mihaly. *Creativity: Flow and the Psychology of Discovery and Invention.* New York: Harper Collins, 1996.

Dewey, John. *Art as Experience.* New York: Capricorn Books, 1958.

Gardner, Howard. *Art, Mind and Brain: A Cognitive Approach to Creativity.* New York: Basic Books, 1982.

Gardner, Howard. *Creating Minds: An Anatomy of Creativity Seen Through the Lives of Freud, Einstein, Picasso, Stravinsky, Eliot, Graham, and Gandhi.* New York: Basic Books, 1993.

Gardner, Howard. *Frames of Mind: The Theory of Multiple Intelligences.* New York: Basic Books, 1985.

Lamott, Anne. *Bird by Bird: Some Instructions on Writing and Life.* New York: Anchor Books, 1998.

Le Boeuf, Michael. *Imagineering.* New York: McGraw-Hill, 1980.

Prince, George. "Creativity and Learning as Skills, Not Talents," *The Philips Exeter Bulletin,* 1980.

Shekerjian, Denise. *Uncommon Genius: How Great Ideas Are Born.* New York: Penguin Books, 1991.

Wallace, Doris B., and Howard E. Gruber, eds. *Creative People at Work.* New York: Oxford University Press, 1989.

Concept Development

Adams, James L. *Conceptual Blockbusting.* Reading, MA: Addison-Wesley, 1986.

de Bono, Edward. *Lateral Thinking.* London: Ward Educational Limited, 1970.

Grear, Malcolm. *Inside/Outside: From the Basics to the Practice of Design.* New York: Van Nostrand Reinhold, 1993.

Johnson, Mary Frisbee. *Visual Workouts: A Collection of Art-Making Problems.* Englewood Cliffs, NJ: Prentice Hall, 1983.

Lakoff, George, and Mark Johnson. *Metaphors We Live By.* Chicago: University of Chicago Press, 1981.

Shahn, Ben. *The Shape of Content.* Cambridge, MA: Harvard University Press, 1957.

Von Oech, Roger. *A Kick in the Seat of the Pants.* New York: Harper and Row, 1963.

Von Oech, Roger. *A Whack on the Side of the Head.* New York: Harper and Row, 1986.

Wilde, Judith and Richard. *Visual Literacy: A Conceptual Approach to Graphic Problem Solving.* New York: Watson-Guptil, 2000.

Critical Thinking

Barnet, Sylvan. *A Short Guide to Writing About Art,* 6th ed. New York: Addison, Wesley, Longman, 2000.

Barrett, Terry. *Criticizing Photographs: An Introduction to Understanding Images,* 3rd ed. New York: McGraw-Hill, 2000.

Barrett, Terry. *Interpreting Art.* New York: McGraw-Hill, 2003.

Sayre, Henry M. *Writing About Art,* 3rd ed. Upper Saddle River, NJ: Prentice Hall, 1999.

Smagula, Howard, ed. *Re-visions: New Perspectives of Art Criticism.* Englewood Cliffs, NJ: Prentice Hall, 1991.

Tucker, Amy. *Visual Literacy: Writing About Art.* New York: McGraw-Hill, 2002.

Three-Dimensional Design

Andrews, Oliver. *Living Materials: A Sculptor's Handbook,* Berkeley: University of California Press, 1988.

Bachelard, Gaston. *The Poetics of Space,* trans. Maria Jolas. Boston: Beacon Press, 1969.

Beardsley, John. *Earthworks and Beyond: Contemporary Art in the Landscape.* New York: Abbeville Press, 1998.

Ching, Frank. *Architecture: Form, Space, and Order,* 2nd ed. New York: Van Nostrand Reinhold, 1996.

de Oliveria, Nicolas, Nicola Oxley, and Michael Petry. *Installation Art.* Washington, DC: Smithsonian Institution Press, 1994.

Dormer, Peter, and Ralph Turner. *The New Jewelry: Trends and Traditions.* London: Thames and Hudson, 1985.

Frantz, Suzanne. *Contemporary Glass: A World Survey from the Corning Museum of Glass.* New York: Harry N. Abrams, 1989.

Koplos, Janet. *Contemporary Japanese Sculpture.* New York: Abbeville Press, 1991.

Lane, Peter. *Ceramic Form: Design and Decoration,* rev. ed. New York: Rizzoli, 1998.

Lewin, Susan Grant. *One of a Kind: American Art Jewelry Today.* New York: Harry N. Abrams, 1994.

Lidstone, John. *Building with Wire.* New York: Van Nostrand Reinhold, 1972.

Luecking, Stephen. *Principles of Three Dimensional Design.* Upper Saddle River, NJ: Pearson Education, 2002.

Lynn, Martha Dreyer. *Clay Today: Contemporary Ceramicists and Their Work.* Los Angeles: Los Angeles County Museum of Art, and San Francisco: Chronicle Books, 1990.

Manzini, Ezio. *The Material of Invention: Materials and Design.* Cambridge, MA: MIT Press, 1989.

Miller, Bonnie J. *Out of the Fire: Contemporary Glass Artists and Their Work.* San Francisco: Chronicle Books, 1991.

Nunley, John W., and Cara McCarty. *Masks: Faces of Culture.* New York: Harry N. Abrams in association with the Saint Louis Art Museum, 1999.

Penny, Nicholas. *The Materials of Sculpture.* New Haven: Yale University Press, 1993.

Selz, Peter Howard. *Barbara Chase-Riboud, Sculptor.* New York: Harry N. Abrams, 1999.

Wallschlaeger, Charles, and Cynthia Busic-Snyder. *Basic Visual Concepts and Principles for Artists, Architects and Designers.* New York: McGraw-Hill, 1992.

Williams, Arthur. *Sculpture: Technique, Form, Content.* Worcester, MA: Davis, 1993.

Wong, Wucius. *Principles of Form and Design.* New York: Van Nostrand Reinhold, 1993.

Wyatt, Gary. *Spirit Faces: Contemporary Native American Masks from the Northwest.* San Francisco: Chronicle Books, 1994.

Time Design

Baldwin, Huntley. *How to Create Effective TV Commercials,* 2nd ed. Lincolnwood, IL: NTC Business Books, 1989.

Bordwell, David, and Kristin Thompson. *Film Art: An Introduction,* 7th ed. New York: McGraw-Hill, 2004.

Goldberg, Roselee. *Performance: Live Art Since 1960.* New York: Harry N. Abrams, 1998.

Johnson, Lincoln F. *Film: Space, Time, Light and Sound.* Orlando, FL: Holt, Rinehart and Winston, 1974.

Katz, Stephen D. *Film Directing, Shot by Shot: Visualizing from Concept to Screen.* Studio City, CA: Michael Wiese Productions, 1991.

McCloud, Scott. *Understanding Comics.* New York: Harper-Perennial, 1994.

McKee, Robert. *Story: Substance, Structure, Style and the Principles of Screen Writing.* New York: HarperCollins, 1997.

Riordan, Steve, ed. *Clio Awards: A Tribute to 30 Years of Advertising Excellence, 1960–1989.* Glen Cove, NY: PBC International, 1989.

key readings

Ross, David. *Bill Viola*. New York: Whitney Museum of American Art, 1998.

Vogler, Christopher. *The Writer's Journey: Mythic Structure for Storytellers and Screenwriters*. Studio City, CA: Michael Wiese Productions, 1991.

Zettl, Herbert. *Sight, Sound, Motion: Applied Media Aesthetics*, 3rd ed. Belmont, CA: Wadsworth, 1999.

Book Arts

Drucker, Johanna. *The Century of Artists' Books*. New York: Granary Books, 1995.

La Plantz, Shereen. *Cover to Cover*. Asheville, NC: Lark Books, 1995.

Lyons, Joan. *Artists' Books: A Critical Anthology and Sourcebook*. Rochester, NY: Visual Studies Workshop Press, 1985.

Smith, Keith A. *Structure of the Visual Book*. Fairport, NY: The Sigma Foundation, 1992.

Smith, Keith A. *Text in the Book Format*. Fairport, NY: The Sigma Foundation, 1991.

Gordon, Stephen F. *Making Picture-Books: A Method of Learning Graphic Sequence*. New York: Van Nostrand Reinhold, 1970.

key readings

Works Cited, Chapter Two

1. Johannes Itten, *The Art of Color* (New York: Van Nostrand Reinhold, 1974), p. 16.
2. Alexander Theroux, *The Primary Colors: Three Essays* (New York: Henry Holt and Company, 1994), p. 6.

Works Cited, Chapter Three

1. Jean L. McKechnie, *Webster's New Universal Unabridged Dictionary* (New York: Simon and Schuster, 1983), p. 373.

Works Cited, Chapter Four

1. Mihaly Csikszentmihalyi, *Creativity: Flow and the Psychology of Discover and Invention* (New York: HarperCollins), pp. 55–76, 1996.
2. George Prince, "Creativity and Learning as Skills, Not Talents," *The Philips Exeter Bulletin*, June-October, 1980.
3. Anne Lamott, *Bird by Bird: Some Instructions on Writing and Life* (New York: Anchor Books, 1998), pp. 18–19.

Works Cited, Chapter Five

1. Keith A. Smith, *Structure of the Visual Book* (Fairport, NY: The Sigma Foundation, 1991), pp. 17–18.

Works Cited, Chapter Seven

1. Henry M. Sayre, *A World of Art*, 3rd ed. (Upper Saddle River, NJ: Prentice Hall, 2000), p. 496.

Works Cited, Chapter Eight

1. John Beardsley, *Earthworks and Beyond: Contemporary Art in the Landscape* (New York: Abbeville Press, 1998), p. 31.
2. Johathan Fineberg, *Art Since 1940: Strategies of Being* (Englewood Cliffs, NJ: Prentice-Hall, 1995), p. 383.

3. Anish Kapoor, interview with Constance Lewallen, *View VII*, no. 4, San Francisco, 1991.
4. Alexander Theroux, *The Primary Colors: Three Essays* (New York: Henry Holt and Company, 1994), p. 86.
5. Theroux, p. 6.

Works Cited, Chapter Twelve

1. David Bordwell and Kristin Thompson, *Film Art: An Introduction*, 5th ed. (New York: McGraw-Hill, 1997), pp. 277–78.
2. Scott McCloud, *Understanding Comics* (New York: HarperPerennial, 1994), pp. 70–74.
3. Keith A. Smith, *Structure of the Visual Book* (Fairport, NY: The Sigma Foundation, 1991), pp. 102–4.

Works Cited, Chapter Thirteen

1. Keith A. Smith, *Structure of the Visual Book* (Fairport, NY: The Sigma Foundation, 1991), p. 106.
2. Robert McKee, *Story: Substance, Structure, Style and the Principles of Screen Writing* (New York: HarperCollins, 1997), pp. 37–41.

Works Cited, Chapter Fourteen

1. Jean L. McKechnie, *Webster's New Universal Unabridged Dictionary* (New York: Simon and Schuster, 1983), p. 1011.
2. Maynard Mack, *World Masterpieces* (New York: W.W. Norton and Company, 1965), p. 478.
3. Rachel Carson, *Under the Sea Wind* (New York: Viking Penguin, 1996), p. 23.

notes

Glossary
by Mary Stewart and Peter Forbes

A

abstract form 1. a form derived from visual reality that has been distilled or transformed, reducing its resemblance to the original source. 2. a multiple image structure, such as a film, in which the parts are related to each other through repetition and visual characteristics, such as shape, color, scale or direction of movement.

abstract shape a shape that is derived from a visual source, but is so transformed that it bears little visual resemblance to that source.

abstraction the reduction of an image or object to an essential aspect of its form or concept.

accent a specific shape, volume, color, musical note, etc. that has been emphasized. Using an accent, a designer can bring attention to part of a composition and increase rhythmic variation within a pattern.

accent color a color that stands out from its surroundings. Often used to attract attention to a specific part of a design.

achromatic color a color (such as black and white) that has no hue.

act a major division in a film or theatrical event. Acts are generally constructed from a group of sequences that increase in intensity.

action-to-action transition in comic books, the juxtaposition of two or more panels showing a sequence of actions.

actual lines lines which are physically present in a design.

actual motion motion that physically occurs in a design.

actual time the duration of an actual temporal event. For example, it takes less than a minute for the bowling ball to roll down the ramps in Jean Tinguley's *Chaos 1*.

additive color color created by combining projected beams of chromatic light. The additive color primaries are red, green and blue and the secondaries are cyan, magenta, and yellow.

additive sculpture a physical object constructed from separate parts that have been connected using glues, joints, stitching, welds and so on.

aesthetics the study of human responses to art and beauty.

afterimage in color theory, a ghostly image that continues to linger after the actual image has been removed.

ambient light the quality of light within an entire space or setting. For example, when we enter an open courtyard on a sunny summer afternoon, we are surrounded by warm ambient sunlight. Everything we see is colorful and bright.

amplified perspective the exaggerated use of linear perspective to achieve a dramatic and engaging presentation of the subject. Amplified perspective is often created using an unusual viewing position, such as a bird's eye view, accelerated convergence, or some form of distortion.

analogy a similarity or connection between things which are apparently separate and dissimilar. For example, when a teacher describes wet plaster as having the "consistency of cream," she is using an analogy.

analogous color a color scheme based on hues that are adjacent on a color wheel, such as red, red-orange and orange.

anesthetic a chemical or action used to induce insensitivity or unconsciousness.

anomaly an obvious break from norm in a design.

approximate symmetry a form of balance that occurs when roughly similar imagery appears on either side of a central axis.

aspect-to-aspect transition in comic books, the juxtaposition of two or more panels showing different views of a single setting or event. This transition is often used in Japanese comic books.

armature an internal structure created to strengthen and support a three-dimensional object.

assemblage an additive method in which the artist or designer constructs the artwork using objects and images which were originally created for another purpose. Essentially, assemblage can be defined as three-dimensional collage.

asymmetrical balance equilibrium among visual elements that do not mirror each other on either side of an axis.

atmospheric perspective a visual phenomenon in which the atmospheric density progressively increases, hazing over the perceived world as one looks into its depth. Overall definition lessens, details fade, contrasts become muted and, in a landscape, a blue mist descends.

attached shadow a shadow that directly defines a form.

B

backlight a light source positioned behind a person or object that can either create a silhouette or separate the person or object from the background.

balance the equal distribution of weight or force among visual units.

base a horizontal support for a physical object, such as a stone block supporting a bronze sculpture.

beat 1. a unit of musical rhythm which creates the pulse of a sound, 2. in acting, the most basic element in a story. A beat is an exchange of behavior, based on action and reaction.

bend one of the five major forces affecting structural strength.

Bezold effect a change in a single color that substantially alters our perception of the entire composition.

boundary the dividing line or edge between objects, images, or experiences.

brainstorming any of a number of problem solving techniques which are designed to expand ideas and encourage creativity. List making, mapping, associative thinking, and metaphorical thinking are common strategies used.

calligraphic line derived from the Greek words for beautiful and writing, a flowing, and expressive line that is as personal as handwriting. Calligraphic lines generally vary in thickness and velocity.

camera angle the angle at which an object or event is viewed. An aerial view can provide the sweeping panorama needed to convey the enormity of a battle, while a low camera angle can provide an expansive view of the sky.

carving the removal of materials from a larger mass, gradually revealing an image or object. Carving is a subtractive process.

cast shadow a dark shape that results from placement of an opaque object in the path of a light source.

causality the interrelation of cause and effect, based on the premise that nothing occurs without cause. Narrative film is based on causality: because the starting pistol was shot, the footrace began.

cause/effect critique a critique in which the viewer seeks to determine the cause for each visual or emotional effect in a design. For example, the dynamism in a design may be caused by the diagonal lines and asymmetrical balance used. Also known as formal analysis.

categorical form in film, a multiple image structure that is based on categories, or subsets of a topic. For example, a film on predators might begin with a discussion of wolves, then move on to lions, and conclude with a discussion of hawks.

centricity as identified by Rudolph Arnheim, a compressive compositional force.

characteristic texture the inherent or familiar texture of a material. The gleaming reflective surface of a steel teapot, the transparent and reflective qualities of glass, and the gritty texture of clay are all characteristic textures.

chiaroscuro (from Italian meaning **"light-dark"**). The gradual transition of values to create the illusion of light and shadow on a three-dimensional form.

chroma the purity, intensity, or saturation of a color.

chromatic gray a gray made from a mixture of various hues, rather than a simple blend of black and white.

chronology the order in which events occur.

cliché an overused expression or a predictable visual treatment of an idea.

close-up in film, a type of framing in which the scale of the object shown is relatively large, as in a close-up of an actor's face.

closure the mind's inclination to connect fragmentary information to produce a completed form. Closure is an essential aspect of Gestalt psychology.

collage an image constructed from visual or verbal fragments initially designed for another purpose.

color harmony use of compatible colors to help unify a composition.

color interaction the way colors within a composition influence one another.

color key a color that dominates an image and heightens its psychological and compositional impact.

color overtone a secondary hue "bias" in a primary color. For example, alizarin crimson is a red with violet overtones, while scarlet is a red with orange overtones.

color theory the art and science of color interaction and effects.

compare/contrast critique a critique in which similarities and differences between two designs are analyzed. Often used in art history classes to demonstrate differences in approach between artists.

comparison recognition of similarity in two or more compositions. Often used in art history to demonstrate connections between images done by different artists or in different periods.

complementary color hues that oppose one another on a color wheel. When paired in a composition, complementary colors create contrast; when mixed, complementary colors produce a wide range of browns.

composite a new material created when two or more materials of differing strengths are fused together. Examples include fiberglas and formcore.

composition the combination of multiple parts into a unified or harmonious whole.

compression the forcing or crushing of material into a smaller, denser condition and its visual dynamics and implied psychological effects.

condensation to be reduced to a denser form, as with the transition from a vapor to a liquid.

cone of vision in perspective drawing, a hypothetical cone of perception originating at the eye of the artist and expanding outward to include whatever he or she wishes to record in an illusionistic image, such as a perspective drawing. The cone's maximum scoping angle is 45-60 degrees anything outside of the cone of vision is subject to distortion.

contact the meeting point between visual or structural elements in a design.

containment a unifying force created by the outer edge of a composition or by a boundary within a composition.

content the emotional and/or intellectual meaning or message of an artwork.

continuity degree of connection or flow among compositional parts.

contradictory texture the unfamiliar use of a texture or the addition of an unusual texture to the surface of an object.

contrast the degree of difference between compositional parts or between one image and another. Contrast is created when two or more forces operate in opposition.

contrasting colors colors that are substantially different in hue, value, intensity or temperature.

contour line a line that describes the edges of a form and suggests three-dimensional volume.

convergent thinking a problem-solving strategy in which a predetermined goal is pursued in a linear progression using a highly focused problem-solving process. Six steps are commonly used: 1. define the problem, 2. do research, 3. determine your objective, 4. devise a strategy, 5. execute the strategy, 6. evaluate the results.

critique any means by which the strengths and weaknesses of designs are analyzed.

cropping the manner in which a section of an image or a fragment of observed reality has been framed. For example, photographers select a fragment of reality every time they look through the view finder of the camera. Part of the scene is included, while the remainder is cut away. Photographs are often cropped further in the darkroom, leaving only the most significant information.

cross contour multiple lines running over the surface of an object horizontally and/or vertically which describe its surface configuration topographically, as in mapping. This process is much like wire-framing in three-dimensional computer modeling. Cross contours can also be used in drawing to suggest three-dimensional form through tonal variation.

cross–hatching a technique used in drawing and print-making to shade an object using two or more networks of parallel lines. Darker values are created as the number of networks increases.

crosscut in film, an abrupt alternation between two or more lines of action.

curvilinear shape a shape whose contour is dominated by curves and flowing lines.

cut in film, the immediate change from one shot or frame to another.

D

definition 1. the degree to which a shape is distinguished from both the ground area and from other shapes within the design. 2. the degree of resolution or focus of an entire image. Sharply defined shapes tend to advance while blurred shapes tend to recede.

denouement the outcome, solution or point of clarification in a story.

density the extent to which compositional parts are spread out or crowded together. Visual connections generally occur easily in high-density compositions, while visual connections may be less obvious in low-density compositions.

depth of field the range of focus in a photographic image, from foreground to background. In a photograph with great depth of field, an object that is fifteen feet from the camera is in focus, as well as an object that is ten feet from the camera.

descriptive shape a shape that is derived from specific subject matter and strongly based on perceptual reality.

diegesis the world created in a film or video.

descriptive critique a critique in which the viewer carefully describes what he or she sees when observing a design.

directed light localized and focused light, such as a spotlight on a singer.

direction actual or implied movement of an element within a design.

displacement a forming method in which a solid material is physically forced into a new configuration. The stamping process used to mint coins is an example of displacement.

dissolve a transition between two shots during which the first image gradually disappears while the second image gradually appears.

dissonance the absence of harmony in a composition. Often created using disharmonious colors, shapes, textures or sounds.

distribution the manner in which colors, shapes or other visual elements are arranged within the format.

divergent thinking an open-ended problem-solving strategy. Starting with a broad theme, the artist or designer expands ideas in all directions.

dominance the principle of composition in which certain elements assume greater importance than others. Also see **emphasis.**

duration 1. the length of time required for the completion of an event; as in the running time of a film, video, or performance. 2. the running time of events depicted in the story (plot duration), 3. the overall span of time the story encompasses (story duration).

dynamic energetic, vigorous, forceful; creating or suggesting change or motion.

dynamic form a form that implies change.

E

earthwork Commonly, an artwork that has been created through the transformation of a natural site into an aesthetic statement.

eccentricity as identified by Rudolph Arnheim, an expansive compositional force.

economy distillation of a design down to the essentials in order to increase impact.

editing in film, selecting and sequencing the details of an event to create a cohesive whole.

elements of design basic building blocks from which designs are made. For example the essential elements of two-dimensional design are line, shape, texture, color and value.

environmental work (or environment) an artwork that must be entered physically. Installations, (which are usually presented indoors) and earthworks (which are usually presented outdoors) are two major types of environmental works.

emotional advertising use of emotion to sell a service, product, or idea. This strategy is often used when a product is neither unique nor demonstrably better than a competing product.

elevation in orthographic projection, the front, back and side views of an object or architectural structure.

emphasis special attention given to some aspect of a composition to increase its prominence.

exaggerated advertising pushing an idea to an extreme to make a point.

exoskeleton an external support structure.

expansion the extending outward of materials to fill more space.

eye level or eye line in linear perspective, the eye level is determined by the physical position of the artist. Sitting on the floor creates a low eye level while standing at an easel creates a higher eye level. Also know as the horizon line. All vanishing points in one and two point perspective are positioned on the eye level.

fade a gradual transition use in film and video. 1. In a fade-in, a dark screen gradually brightens as a shot appears. 2. In a fade-out, the shot gradually darkens as the screen goes black.

fidelity the degree of connection between a sound and its source. For example, when we hear the sound of a helicopter and see a helicopter on the screen, the sound matches with image, creating tight fidelity.

figure the primary or positive shape in a design; a shape which is noticeably separated from the background. The figure is the dominant shape in a figure-ground relationship.

figure/ground reversal an arrangement in which positive and negative shapes alternatively command attention.

fill light a diffused light used to lower the contrast between light and dark areas in cinematic and theatrical lighting.

filtration the process of separating a solid from a liquid by passing it through a porous substance such as cloth, charcoal or sand.

flashback in film, an alternation in chronology in which events that occur later in a story are shown first.

floodlight a softly defined light with a broad beam.

flying buttress a type of exoskeleton commonly used by medieval architects in creating cathedrals.

focal point primary point of interest in a composition. A focal point is often used to emphasize an area of particular importance or to provide a strong sense of compositional direction.

format the outer edge or boundary of a design.

form 1. the physical manifestation of an idea, as opposed to the content, which refers to the idea itself. 2. the organization or arrangement of visual elements to create a unified design 3. a three-dimensional composition or unit within a three-dimensional composition. For example, a sphere, cube and pyramid are all three-dimensional forms.

formalism an approach to art and design that emphasizes the beauty of line, shape, texture, etc. as ends in themselves rather than as means to express content. Strictly formalist works have no explicit subject matter.

fractured space discontinuous space that is created when multiple viewpoints are combined within a single image.

frame a single static image in film or video.

freestanding work an artwork that is self-supporting and is designed to be viewed from all sides.

function the purpose of a design or the objective which motivates the designer. For an industrial designer, the primary purpose of a design is often utilitarian. For example, he or she may be required to design a more fuel-efficient automobile. For a sculptor, the primary purpose of a design is aesthetic: he or she seeks to create an artwork that engages the viewer emotionally and intellectually.

fusion the combination of shapes or volumes along a common edge.

geometric form a three-dimensional form derived from or suggestive of geometry. Examples include cubes, spheres tetrahedrons, etc.

geometric shape a shape derived from or suggestive of geometry. Geometric shapes are characterized by crisp, precise edges and mathematically consistent curves.

Gestalt psychology a theory of visual perception that emphasizes the importance of holistic composition. According to this theory, grouping, containment, repetition, proximity, continuity, and closure are essential aspects of visual unity.

gesture drawing a vigorous drawing that captures the action, structure and overall orientation of an object, rather than describing specific details. Often used as a basis for figure drawing.

gloss 1. in writing, words of explanation or translation inserted into a text. 2. a secondary text within a manuscript that provides comments on the main text.

gradation any gradual transition from one color to another or from one shape or volume to another. In drawing, shading created through the gradation of grays can be used to suggest three-dimensional form.

graphic relationship the juxtaposition of two or more separate images that are compositionally similar. For example, if a basketball is shown in the first panel, an aerial view of the round free-throw zone is shown in the second, and the hoop of the basket itself is shown in the third, a graphic relationship based on circles has been created.

gravity the force that tends to pull all bodies toward the center of the Earth.

grid a visual or physical structure created from intersecting parallel lines.

grisaille a gray underpainting, often used by Renaissance artists, to increase the illusion of space.

group in sequential structure, a collection of images that are related by subject matter, composition, or source. For example the trombone, trumpet and tuba are all members of the group know as the brass section in an orchestra.

grouping visual organization based on similarity in location, orientation, shape, color and so on.

gutter in bookbinding, the center line of a book, where the two pages are joined.

Happening an assemblage of improvised, spontaneous events performed by the artist and audience alike, based on a general theme. There is no rehearsal and any location, from a parking lot to a factory interior can be used. The Happening is most commonly associated with Alan Kaprow and is a precursor to Performance Art.

hard sell advertising an advertising approach in which a major point is presented in a clear, direct manner. The narrative is usually linear, and the message is usually explicit.

harmony a pleasing or soothing relationship among colors, shapes, or other design elements.

hatching A technique used in drawing and printmaking to create a range of gray tones using multiple parallel lines.

high definition sharply focused visual information that is easily readable. High definition creates strong contrast between shapes and tends to increase clarity and immediacy of communication.

horizon line in linear perspective, the line on which all vanishing points are positioned. More accurately described as the eye line or eye level.

hue the name of a color (such as red or yellow) that distinguishes it from others and assigns it a position in the visual spectrum.

human scale a design that is roughly our size.

humorous advertising use of humor to sell a service, product, or idea. By entertaining the viewer, the designer can make the message more memorable.

Iconography the study of symbolic visual systems.

illusionary space the representation of an object or scene on a two-dimensional surface so as to give it the appearance of three-dimensionality.

imbalance the absence of balance.

implied line 1. a line that is suggested by the positions of shapes or objects within a design. 2. a line that is suggested by movement or by a gesture rather than being physically drawn or constructed.

implied motion the suggested change in location of a figure or object.

implied time the suggested location or duration of an event.

installation an artwork or a design that presents an ensemble of images and objects within a three-dimensional environment.

intensity 1. the purity, saturation, or chroma of a color. For example, fire engine red is a high intensity color, while brick red is a low intensity color. 2. in time design, the power, concentration and energy with which an action is performed or the quality of observation of an event.

interdisciplinary art the combination of two or more different disciplines to create a hybrid artform.

interdisciplinary thinking use of skills and knowledge from more than one discipline.

in the round a three dimensional object that is self-supporting and is designed to be viewed from all sides, as in free-standing sculpture.

invented texture a form of visual texture that has been created without reference to perceptual reality.

joint a physical connection between elements or parts in a three-dimensional object. Some joints are fixed, such as ones that are bolted together, while others can be moved, as with a hinge or a ball and socket joint.

junction 1. the place at which objects or events meet. 2. a physical intersection between elements or parts in a three-dimensional object.

key light a primary source of illumination.

kinetic form a form that actually moves.

kinesthetics the science of movement.

lap dissolve in film, a dissolve in which two shots are temporarily superimposed.

layed space compositional space that has been deliberately separated into foreground, middle ground and background.

line 1. a point in motion, 2. a series of adjacent points, 3. a connection between points, 4. an implied connection between points. Line is one of the basic elements of design.

line weight variation in line thickness.

linear perspective a mathematical system for projecting the apparent dimensions of a three-dimensional object onto a flat surface. Developed by artists during the Renaissance, linear perspective is one strategy for creating the illusion of space.

long shot in film, a type of framing in which the scale of the subject shown is relatively small, as with an image of a human figure within a landscape.

loudness the amplitude of a sound wave; the volume of a sound.

low definition blurred or ambiguous visual information. Low definition shapes can increase the complexity of the design and encourage multiple interpretations.

maquette a well developed three-dimensional sketch, comparable to a two-dimensional thumbnail sketch.

matrix a three-dimensional grid.

mass a solid three-dimensional form.

medium shot a type of framing in which the scale of the subject shown is of moderate size, as in view of an actor from the waist up.

meter the basic pattern of sound and silence in music or positive and negative in design.

metaphor a figure of speech in which one thing is directly linked to another dissimilar thing. Through this connection, the original word is given the qualities of the linked word. For example, when we say "she's a diamond in the rough" we attribute to a woman the qualities of an unpolished gem.

metaphorical thinking the use of metaphors or analogies to create visual or verbal bridges.

model in three-dimensional design, a model is a technical experiment or a small-scale version of a larger design.

modeling the process of manipulating a pliable material (such as clay) to create a three-dimensional object.

moment-to-moment transition in comic books, a transition in which a character or situation is simply being observed over time. This transition is often used in Japanese comic books but rarely in American comic books.

monochromatic color scheme a color scheme based on variations in a single hue. For example, a light, pastel blue, a medium navy blue and a dark blue-black may be used in a room interior.

monumental objects objects that are much larger than humans.

movement in design, the use of deliberate visual pathways to help direct the viewer's attention to areas of particular interest.

myth a traditional story collectively composed by many members of a society. The creation of the world, sources of evil, the power of knowledge and even the nature of reality may be explained through these grand expressions of the imagination.

N

negative shape (or **space**) 1. a clearly defined area around a positive shape or form 2. a shape created through the absence of an object rather than through the presence of an object.

non-objective shape shapes created without reference to specific visual subject matter.

non-sequitur transition the juxtaposition of multiple frames or shots that have no obvious conceptual relationship.

O

objective criticism the assessment of strengths and weakness in a design solely based on the visual information presented.

one-point perspective a form of linear perspective in which the lines receding into space converge at a single vanishing point of the eye level or horizon line.

opponent theory an explanation for the electric glow that occurs when two complementary colors are placed side by side.

orientation the horizontal, vertical, or diagonal position of a composition or design element.

organic shape a shape that visually suggests nature or natural forces. also know as biomorphic shape.

organizational lines lines used to create the loose linear "skeleton" on which a compositional can be built. Also know as structural lines.

orthographic projection a drawing system widely used by artists and designers to delineate the top, bottom and four side views of a three-dimensional object. Unlike perspective drawing, which is designed to create the illusion of space, an orthographic projection is constructed using parallel lines that accurately delineate six surfaces of an object.

overlap placement of one shape in front of another to create the illusion of space.

oxidation a common form of chemical change used in creating a patina (or colored surface) on a metal sculpture.

P

panel a single frame in a comic book.

pattern a design created through systematic repetition. Many patterns are based on a module, or repeated visual unit.

pedestal a vertical support for a sculptural object.

performance art a live presentation, often including the artist, usually combining elements from a variety of art forms, such a film, video, theater and dance.

permanence the degree of durability, or resistance to decay, in a given material or design.

physical texture actual variation in a surface.

picture plane in linear perspective, the flat surface on which a three-dimensional image is mentally projected.

pitch in music, the relative highness or lowness of a sound. Pitch is determined by wave frequency, as compression and expansion occurs within the sound wave.

plane a three-dimensional form that has length and width but minimal thickness.

plan view the top view of a three-dimensional object or architectural structure, drawn orthographically or freehand.

plinth horizontal support for a sculptural object.

plot duration the running time of the events depicted in a story.

polyhedra (or **polyhedrons**) multi-faceted volumes.

positive form an area of physical substance in a three-dimensional design.

positive shape the principle or foreground shape in a design and the dominant shape or figure in a figure-ground relationship.

primary colors colors from which virtually all other colors can be mixed. The additive (or light) color primaries are red, green and blue. The subtractive (or pigment) color primaries are yellow, magenta red and cyan blue.

primary contour the defining edges of a physical object, such as the extremities of a carved sculpture.

principles of design the means by which visual elements are organized into a unified and expressive arrangement. Unity and variety, balance, scale and proportion, rhythm, illusion of space and illusion of movement are commonly cited as the principles of two-dimensional design.

proportion the relative size of visual elements within an image.

prototype a well-developed model, as with the fully-functional prototype cars developed by automobile companies.

proximity the distance between visual or structural elements or between an object and the audience.

pure forms circles, spheres, triangles, cubes and other forms created without reference to specific subject matter.

R

radial symmetry a form of balance that is created when shapes or volumes are mirrored both vertically and horizontally, with the center of the composition acting as a focal point.

glossary

rational advertising a type of advertising in which logic and comparisons of quality are used to sell a service, product, or idea. A rational approach is most effective when the message is compelling in itself or the product is truly unique.

realistic advertising use of a familiar setting or situation to involve the viewer and relate a product, service or idea to use in everyday life.

rectilinear shape a shape composed from straight lines and angular corners.

refracted light light that has been bent as it passes through a prism.

relief sculpture in which forms project out from a flat surface. The degree of projection ranges from low to high relief.

repetition the use of the same visual element or effect a number of times in the same composition.

representation commonly, the life-like depiction of persons or objects.

representational shape a shape derived from specific subject matter and strongly based on visual observation.

rhetorical form a type of sequential organization in which the parts are used to create and support an argument. Often used in documentary films.

rhythm 1. presentation of multiple units in a deliberate pattern. 2. in filmmaking, the perceived rate and regularity of sounds, shots, and movement within the shots. Rhythm is determined by the beat (pulse), accent (stress) and tempo (pace).

rhythmic relationship the juxtaposition of multiple visual elements or images to create a deliberate pulse or beat.

S

saturation the purity, chroma, or intensity of a color.

scale a size relationship between two separate objects, such as the relationship between the size of the Statue of Liberty and a human visitor to the monument.

scene in film, continuous action in continuous time and continuous space.

scene-to-scene transition in comic books, the juxtaposition of two or more frames showing different scenes or settings.

scope conceptually, the extent of our perception or the range of ideas our minds can grasp. temporally, scope refers to the range of action within a given moment.

screenplay the written blueprint for the film; commonly constructed from multiple acts.

secondary colors hues mixed from adjacent primaries. In paint, the secondary colors are violet, green and orange.

secondary contour the inner edges of a physical object, such as the internal design and detailing of a carved sculpture.

section in orthographic projection, a slice of an object or architectural structure that reveals its internal structure and detail.

sequence 1. in filmmaking, a collection of related shots and scenes that comprise a major section of action or narration, 2. in narrative structure, any collection of images that have been organized by *cause and effect*. In a simple sequence, action number two is caused by action number one. In a complex sequence, there may be a considerable delay between the cause and the effect.

series in sequential structure, a collection of images that are linked simply, as with cars in a train.

setting the physical and temporal location of a story, the props and costumes used in a story, and the use of sound.

serious advertising advertising which treats a topic in a somber or solemn manner. Often used for public service announcements, such as drunk driving commercials.

shape a flat, enclosed area created when a line connects to enclose an area, an area is surrounded by other shapes, or an area is filled with color or texture.

shade a hue that has been mixed with black.

shading in drawing, a continuous series of grays that are used to suggest three-dimensionality and create the illusion of light.

shear a force that creates a lateral break in a material.

shot in film, a continuous group of frames.

side light a light positioned to the side of a person or object. Can be used to dramatically increase the sense of dimensionality.

sight line 1. a viewing line that is established by the arrangement of objects within one's field of vision, 2. a straight line of unimpeded vision.

simile a figure of speech in which one thing is linked to another dissimilar thing using the word "like" or "as." Through this connection, the original word is given the qualities of the linked word. For example, when we say "he's as strong as an ox," we attribute to a man the strength of an animal.

simultaneous contrast the optical alteration of a color by a surrounding color.

site-specific artwork an artwork is specifically designed for and installed in a particular place.

skeleton (or endoskeleton) a structure that provides internal support.

soft sell advertising an advertising approach that uses emotion, rather than reason, to sell a service, product, or idea. The narrative is often non-linear and ideas or actions may be implied.

solidification a forming method in which a liquid material is poured into a mold or extruded through a pipe, then allowed to harden.

space the area within or around an area of substance The artist/designer defines and activates space when constructing a three dimensional object.

spatial context the space in which a sound is generated. A sound that is played outdoors behaves differently than a sound that is played in a small room.

spatial relationship the juxtaposition of two or more images that are spatially different, such as a close-up, medium shot, and a long shot.

split complementary a complementary color plus the two colors on either side of its complement on the color wheel.

spotlight a light that creates a small, clearly defined beam.

story duration the overall length of a story.

static a composition that is at rest or an object that appears stationary.

static form a form that appears to be stable and unmoving.

stereotype a fixed generalization based on a preconception.

subordinate of secondary importance. See **emphasis.**

subtractive color hue created when light is selectively reflected off a colored surface.

subject the person, object, event or idea on which an artwork is based.

subject-to-subject transition in comic books, the juxtaposition of two or more frames showing different subject matter.

subjective criticism the assessment of strengths and weaknesses in a design based on non-objective criteria, such as the narrative implications of an idea, the cultural ramifications of an action or the personal meaning of an image.

subtractive sculpture a forming method in which materials are removed from a larger mass, Carving, drilling, cutting and turning on a lathe are all subtractive processes.

symbolic color a color that has been assigned a particular meaning by the members of a society. For example, in the United States, the white color of a wedding gown symbolizes purity, while in Borneo, white symbolizes death.

symmetrical balance a form of balance that is created when shapes are mirrored on either side of a central axis, as in a composition that is vertically divided down the center.

tangibility the substantiality of an object or the degree to which an object or a force can be felt.

take in film or video, one version of an event.

temperature the physical and psychological heat suggested by a color's hue.

tempo the pace at which time-based art and music occurs. A fast tempo is generally used in action films while a slow tempo is usually used in a dramatic film.

temporal relationship how the shots in a film relate in time.

tension the extension of an object through stretching or bending.

tertiary color a hue that is mixed from a primary color and an adjacent secondary color.

testimonial advertising use of a trust worthy character or celebrity to provide endorsement for a product, service or idea.

texture the visual or tactile quality of a form. Texture can be created visually using multiple marks, physically, through surface variation, or through the inherent property of a specific material, such as sand as opposed to smooth porcelain.

timbre the unique sound quality of each instrument. For example, a note of the same volume and pitch is quite different when it is generated by a flute rather than a violin.

three-point perspective a form of linear perspective in which the lines receding into space converge at a two vanishing points of the eye level (one to the left of the object being drawn and one to the right of the object being drawn) plus a third vanishing point above or below the eye level. Used when the picture plane must be tilted to encompass an object placed above or below the eye level.

three-quarter work a physical object that is designed to be viewed from the front and sides only.

tint a hue that has been mixed with white.

tone a hue that has been mixed with black and white.

torque the distortion of an object through a twisting movement. Also know as **torsion.**

transition the process of changing from one state or form to another. For example, the surface of a metal sculpture as it shifts from a smooth to a rough surface or the manner in which a computer drawing morphs from one form to another.

triadic harmony a color scheme based on three colors which are equidistant on a color wheel.

tromp l'oeil a flat illusion that is so convincing the viewer believes the image is real. From a French term meaning "to fool the eye."

two-point perspective a form of linear perspective in which the lines receding into space converge at a two vanishing points of the eye level (or horizon line), one to the left of the object being drawn and one to the right of the object being drawn.

typestyle the distinctive quality of the letterforms within a given font. For example, Helvetica has a very different look than Palatino type.

unity compositional similarity, oneness, togetherness, or cohesion.

value the relative lightness or darkness of a surface.

value distribution the proportion and arrangement of lights and darks in a composition. Also know as **value pattern.**

value scale a range of grays that are presented in a consistent sequence, creating a gradual transition from white to black.

variety the differences which give a design visual and conceptual interest; notably, use of contrast, emphasis, differences in size, and so forth.

vanishing point in linear perspective, the point or points on the eye line at which parallel lines appear to converge.

viewing time the time an audience devotes to watching or exploring an artwork.

glossary

visual book an experimental structure which conveys ideas, actions and emotions using multiple images in an integrated and interdependent format. Also known as an artist's book.

visual movement use of continuity to create deliberate visual pathways. Often used to direct the viewer's attention to areas of particular importance in the composition.

visual texture texture created using multiple marks or through a descriptive simulation of physical texture.

visual weight 1. the inclination of shapes to float or sink compositionally 2. the relative importance of a visual element within a design.

vitalistic sculpture a sculpture which appears to embody life in an inanimate material, such as Fiberglas, stone or wood.

volume 1. an empty three-dimensional form. 2. in two-dimensional design, a three-dimensional form that has been represented using the illusion of space. 3. in time design, the loudness of a sound.

volume summary a drawing which communicates visual information reductively, using basic volumes, such as sphere, cubes and cylinders to indicate the major components of a figure or object.

W

weight the visual or physical heaviness of an object.

wipe in film, a transition in which first shot seems to be pushed off the screen by the second. Wipes were used extensively in *Star Wars*.

introduction

i.1, Collection: Edition 1: Museo Nacional Centro de Arte Reina Sofia, Madrid. Edition 2: Los Angeles County Museum of Art, Modern and Contemporary Art Council Fund. Photo: Gary McKinnis.

i.2, Collection Toni Greenbaum, NY. Photo: Keith E. LoBue.

i.3, Designers: Bill Cannan, Tony Ortiz, H. Kurt Heinz. Design Firm: Bill Cannan & Co. Client/Mfr. NASA Public Affairs

i.5, Installation,Venice Bienniale, Chiesa de San Stae, Venice, Italy. Courtesy of Paula Cooper Gallery, NY.

i.6, Photograph © The Museum of Modern Art, Film Stills Archive. By permission of the Estate of Alfred Hitchcock.

i.7, Designers: James E. Grove, John Cook, Jim Holtorf, Fernando Pardo, Mike Boltich. Design Firm: Designworks/USA. Client/Mfr: Corona Clipper Co.

i.9, Denver Art Museum Collection: Funds from Helen Dill bequest, 1935.14. © Denver Art Museum 2005.

i.10, © 2005 The Estate of Sam Francis/Artists Rights Society (ARS), NY.

i.11, Collection, University of Illinois at Urbana, Champaign. Photo courtesy of the artist © Alice Aycock, 1994.

i.12, TM & © 2005 Marvel Characters, Inc. Used with permission.

i.13, Courtesy of the author.

part one

Page 16: The Solomon R. Guggenheim Museum, New York. Gift, Solomon R. Guggenheim, 1941 (41.283). © 2005 Artists Rights Society (ARS), NY.

Page 17 T: Collection of David Geffen, Los Angeles. © Jasper Johns/Licensed by VAGA, NY.

Page 17 B: Courtesy Scott Hull Associates.

chapter one

1.03, The Sidney and Harriet Janis Collection, Digital Image © The Museum of Modern Art, NY/Licensed by Art Resource, NY. © 2005 Artists Rights Society (ARS), NY.

1.04, AP/Wide World Photos.

1.05, National Gallery of Art, Washington, DC, Robert and Jane Meyerhoff Collection, 1986.65.1. Photograph © 2001 Board of Trustees, National Gallery of Art. © 2005 Barnett Newman Foundation/Artists Rights Society, (ARS), NY.

1.06, Iris & B. Gerald Cantor Center for Visual Arts at Stanford University, Gift of Dr. and Mrs. Louis J. Rattner.

1.07, Courtesy of the Estate of Rico Lebrun and Koplin Del Rio Gallery, West Hollywood, CA.

1.08, © British Museum.

1.09, The Nelson-Atkins Museum of Art, Kansas City, Missouri. Gift of Mrs. George H. Bunting, Jr., 73-27.

1.10, Spencer Museum of Art, Gift of Rhodes and Leona B. Carpenter Foundation, 91.3.

1.11, © Alfred Leslie.

1.13, Reproduction courtesy The Minor White Archive, Princeton University. © 1982 by The Trustees of Princeton University. All Rights Reserved.

1.14 A-B, Vatican Museums, Vatican State. Scala/Art Resource, NY.

1.15, The Museum of Modern Art, New York. Gift of Victor S. Riesenfeld. Photograph © 2005 The Museum of Modern Art. © 2005 Artists Rights Society (ARS), NY/ADAGP, Paris. Art Resource, NY.

1.16, Courtesy of David Mach.

1.17, Musée du Louvre, Paris. © Réunion des Musees Nationaux/Art Resource, NY.

1.18, The Museum of Modern Art, The Sidney and Harriet Janis Collection. Photograph © 2001 The Museum of Modern Art, NY/Art Resource, NY. © 2005 The Pollock-Krasner Foundation/Artists Rights Society (ARS), NY.

1.19, PATH Station Maps, Louis Nelson Associates Inc, NY. Artist: Jennifer Stoller, Louis Nelson. © Louis Nelson Associates for the Port Authority of New York & New Jersey.

1.20, Courtesy of Joel Peter Johnson.

1.21, Courtesy of Pentagram Design.

1.24, Art & Artifacts Division, Schomburg Center for Research in Black Culture, The New York Public Library, Astor, Lenox and Tilden Foundations.

1.25, Diego M. Rivera, *Detroit Industry*, North Wall, 1932-1933. Gift of Edsel B. Ford, Photograph © 2001 The Detroit Institute of Arts.

1.26, Carin Goldberg, Cover of *Ulysses*, by James Joyce, 1986. Random House Vintage Books. Art Director: Edith Loseser.

1.27, Courtesy Bantam Books.

1.28, Galleria Moderna Venice, Italy/Cameraphoto/Art Resource, NY.

1.30, Philadelphia Museum of Art: Purchased with the Edward and Althea Budd Fund, the Adele Haas Turner and Beatrice Pastorius Turner Memorial Fund, and with funds, 1981-94-a, b.

1.31, Bill Brandt Archive, Ltd.

1.32, The Museum of Modern Art, New York. Acquired throught the Lillie P. Bliss Bequest. Photograph © 2005 The Museum of Modern Art, New York. Artists Rights Society (ARS), NY.

1.33, © 2005 Cordon Art B. V. Baarn, Holland.

1.34, © 2005 The Estate of Sam Francis/Artists Rights Society (ARS), NY.

1.35, The Department of Theater Arts, California State University, Los Angeles, David McNutt, 1985.

1.37, The Stapleton Collection, Bridgeman Art Library, NY.

1.38, © Robert Rauschenberg/Licensed by VAGA, NY.

1.39, © Valerie Jaudon/Licensed by VAGA, NY.

1.40, San Francisco Museum of Modern Art, Gift of the Women's Board.

1.41, © Zhou Brothers.

1.42, Photograph © Ansel Adams Publishing Rights Trust/CORBIS.

1.43, Courtesy Joseph Helman Gallery, New York (#BH 1912).

1.44, Art Institute of Chicago, Gift of Georgia O'Keeffe, (1948.650).

1.45, © Robert Frank, Courtesy Pace/MacGill Gallery, New York. The Museum of Fine Arts Houston; The Target Collection of American Photography, museum purchase with funds provided by Target Stores.

1.46, The Museum of Modern Art, New York. Gift of Mr. and Mrs. Walter Bareiss. Photograph © 2005 The Museum of Modern Art/Art Resource, NY.

1.47, Courtesy Marian Goodman Gallery, NY.

1.48, Art Director & Designer: Gary Goldsmith, Copywriter: Neal Gomberg, Agency: Goldsmith/Jeffrey, Client: Citizens Against Cocaine Abuse.

1.49, The Museum of Modern Art, New York. Blanchette Rockefeller Fund. Photograph © 2005 The Museum of Modern Art, NY. © Romare Bearden/Licensed by VAGA, NY.

1.50, Collection of David Geffen, Los Angeles. © Jasper Johns/Licensed by VAGA, NY.

1.51, Reproduced with permission of AT & T Archives.

1.53, Client GSX Corporation. © Douglas Smith, 2005.

1.54, Whitney Museum of American Art, New York, Gift of Norman Dubrow, 77.98.

1.55, Courtesy of the artist.

1.56, © Peter Mauss/Esto. All rights reserved. © Richard Haas/Licensed by VAGA, NY.

1.57, The Baltimore Museum of Art, Thomas E. Benesch Memorial Collection, BMA 1970.4.19.

1.58, Courtesy of Dugald Stermer.

1.59, The British Museum, London/HIP/Scala/Art Resource, NY.

1.60, © Anselm Kiefer. Gift of the Friends of the Philadelphia Museum of Art in celebration of their twentieth anniversary, 1985. Philadelphia Museum of Art/Art Resource, NY.

1.61, Courtesy of the artist.

1.62, Photograph by Ellen Page Wilson, Courtesy of Pace Wildenstein Gallery. © 2005 Chuck Close.

1.63, The Museum of Modern Art, New York, acquired through the Lillie P. Bliss Bequest. © 2005 The Museum of Modern Art/ Art Resource, NY.

1.66, © Deborah Remington/Licensed by VAGA, NY.

1.67, Sony Music Creative Services, Santa Monica, CA. Graphic Interface Designer: Mary Maurer.

1.68, Art Institute of Chicago, The Alfred Steiglitz Collection, (1949.706).

1.69, National Museum of American Art, Washington, DC/Art Resource, NY.

1.70, © Conley Harris; Courtesy of the Boston Public Library.

1.72, Courtesy of Paul M. R. Maeyaert, Belgium.

1.73, Courtesy, the Colorado Historical Society (978.06/P871es).

1.74, The Detroit Institute of Arts, Gift of Mr. Leslie H. Green.

1.75, Photos: John Veltri.

1.76, Photofest.

Profile, page 50-51: Courtesy of the artist.

chapter two

2.01, Guerrilla Girls.

2.04, Courtesy of Louis K. Meisel Gallery, NY.

2.10, Courtesy of the artist and Cheim & Read, NY.

2.13-2.15, Courtesy of Louis K. Meisel Gallery, NY.

2.14, School of Art, Ohio University.

2.16, © Kenneth Noland/Licensed by VAGA, NY.

2.17, MANUAL/Suzanne Bloom/Ed Hill.

2.20, © Nicora Gangi.

2.21, © David Hockney/Gemini G.E.L.

2.22, National Museum of American Art, Washington, DC/Art Resource, NY.

2.23, © 2005 Succession H. Matisse, Paris/Artists Rights Society (ARS), NY.

2.25, Courtesy of National Trust for Historic Preservation.

2.26, Collection, Albright-Knox Art Gallery, Buffalo, NY. Gift of Seymour H. Knox, 1956. © 2005 Estate of Arshile Gorky/Artists Rights Society (ARS), NY.

photo credits

3.21 A-B, Digital Image © The Museum of Modern Art, NY/Licensed by Scala/Art Resource, NY. © 2005 Artists Rights Society (ARS), NY.

3.23, © Berenice Abbott/Commerce Graphics Ltd, Inc.

3.24, © British Museum.

3.25, © Ansel Adams Publishing Rights Trust/ CORBIS.

3.27, © Anthony Kersting.

3.28, Courtesy of the Allan Stone Gallery, NY.

3.30, San Francisco Museum of Modern Art, Gift of Tracy O'Kates. © 2005 Judy Chicago/Artists Rights Society (ARS), NY.

3.31, Wadsworth Atheneum, Hartford, CT. The Ella Gallup Sumner and Mary Catlin Sumner Collection Fund (1952.52).

3.34, Hirshhorn Museum and Sculpture Garden, Smithsonian Institution, Washington, DC. Gift of Joseph H. Hirshhorn Foundation, 1972 (HMSG 72.205). © 2005 Mondrian/Holtzman Trust, c/o Beeldrecht/Artists Rights Society (ARS), NY.

3.35, Courtesy of Frank Miller, Edina, MN.

3.36, Museo de Arte Moderno, Mexico. D.F. Photo: Bob Schalkwijk/Art Resource, NY.

3.37, Courtesy of the artist and Mary Boone Gallery, NY.

3.39, Michael Bierut, Design Firm: Pentagram, NY. Client: Designing New York Committee. © Pentagram.

3.40, Albright-Knox Art Gallery, New York. Gift of Seymour H. Knox, 1967.

3.41, Courtesy of the National Museum of American Art, Smithsonian, Washington, DC, and Charles Cowles Gallery, NY.

3.42, Photo: David Caras.

3.43, Philadelphia Museum of Art/Bridgeman Art Library. © 2005 Artists Rights Society (ARS), NY/ ADAGP, Paris/Estate of Marcel Duchamp.

3.44, Publisher: Art Center: College of Design, Pasadena, CA.

3.45, Photo: Doug Yaple.

3.46, © Jacey, Shannon Associates.

3.48, © Robert Crawford.

3.49, Wadsworth Atheneum, Hartford, CT. Ella Gallup Sumner and Mary Catlin Sumner Collection (1951.40).

3.51, Trinity College Library, Dublin.

3.52, Alte Pinakothek, Munich. Scala/Art Resource, NY.

3.53, Stanza della Segnatura, Vatican Palace, Vatican State/Scala/Art Resource, NY.

3.56, Museo del Prado, Madrid. Giraudon/Art Resource, NY.

3.57, The Metropolitan Museum of Art, Rogers Fund, 1907 (07.123). Photograph © 1996 The Metropolitan Museum of Art.

3.58, National Palace Museum, Taipei, Taiwan.

3.59, Glasgow Museums: The St. Mungo Museum of Religious Life and Art. © 2005 Kingdom of Spain, Gala-Salvador Dali Foundation/Artists Rights Society (ARS), NY.

3.60, © David Hockney.

3.62, Collection, AXA Financial, Inc. through its subsidiary The Equitable Life Assurance Society of the U. S. © AXA Financial, Inc.

3.63, © Disney Enterprises, Inc.

3.64, Albright-Knox Art Gallery, Buffalo, James S. Ely Fund, 1980.

3.65, Museo Nazionale Romano delle Terme, Rome, Italy. Scala/Art Resource, NY.

3.66, Henri Cartier-Bresson/Magnum Photos.

3.67, © 1984 by Chris van Allsburg. Reprinted by permission of Houghton Mifflin Co.

3.68, The Historical and Interpretive Collections of The Franklin Institute, Philadelphia, PA.

3.69, The Cleveland Museum of Art, Bequest of Leonard C. Hanna, Jr., 1946.83.

Profile, pages 112-113: Photo: Don House.

part two

Page 114: © 1996 Georgiana Nehl. Photo by David Browne.

Page 115: Courtesy of Jason Chin.

chapter four

4.2, © 2005 Cordon Art B. V. Baarn, Holland.

Page 125: © 1996 Georgiana Nehl. Photo by David Browne.

Profile, pages 126-127: © Nancy Callahan and Diane Gallo.

chapter five

5.1, Cooper-Hewitt National Design Museum, Gift of Gary Laredo, 1956.10.1 Smithsonian Institution/Art Resource, NY.

5.2, The Museum of Modern Art, New York. Gift of Edgar Kaufman, Jr. Photo © 2005 Art Resource, NY.

5.5, The Museum of Modern Art, New York. Gift of Herman Miller Furniture Company. Photo © Museum of Modern Art/Art Resource, NY.

5.6, Photo courtesy of Knoll, Inc.

5.8, Courtesy of Ray Rogers.

5.9, The Corning Museum of Glass, Gift of Vera Liskova.

5.10, Courtesy of Chronicle Books.

5.11, The Museum of Modern Art, New York. Mrs. Simon Guggenheim Fund. Photograph © 2005 The Museum of Modern Art/© 2005 Estate of Yves Tanguy/Artists Rights Society (ARS), NY.

5.12, © 2005 Artists Rights Society (ARS), NY, SIAE, Rome. Allan Mitchell Photography.

5.15 A-B, Courtesy of the author.

5.16 A-C, Honolulu Academy of Arts, Gift of James Michener, 1991 (21.971). Photo © Honolulu Academy of Arts.

5.17, Photo: Leslie Leupp.

5.18, Private Collection; Collection Stedelijk Museum, Amsterdam. Photo: George Erml.

Profile, pages 144-145: © Heidi Lasher-Oakes.

chapter six

6.1 A-B, © The Art Institute of Chicago, Charles H. and Mary F. S. Worcester Collection. All Rights Reserved.

6.2, Stanza della Segnatura, Vatican Palace, Vatican State. Scala/Art Resource, NY.

Self Assignment, pages 154-155: Courtesy of Jason Chin.

6.10, The Nelson-Atkins Museum of Art and The Kansas City Sculpture Park including Shuttlecocks, by Claes Oldenburg and Coosje van Bruggen, 1994; Purchase: acquired through the generosity of the Sosland Family. Photograph: E.G. Schempf, F94-1/2-4 .

6.15, Moderna Museet, Stockholm. © Robert Rauschenberg/Licensed by VAGA, NY.

6.16, © Robert Rauschenberg/Licensed by VAGA, NY. Photo: Harry Shunk.

6.17, © Robert Rauschenberg/Licensed by VAGA, NY.

Profile, page 162: Courtesy of the artist.

Page 163: From a cover of *Miriam's Cup* by Fran Manushkin, illustrated by Bob Dacey. Published by Scholastic Press, a division of Scholastic Inc. Illustration © 1998 by Bob Dacey. Used by permission.

chapter seven

7.1, Collection of the National Palace Museum, Taipei, Taiwan.

7.2, Courtesy of the artist.

7.3, © Milton Glaser.

7.4, The Menil Collection, Houston.

7.5, © Kenny Kiernan, Mendola Ltd.

7.6, Courtesy of Jacqui & Sherry Matthews Advocacy Marketing.

7.7, Michael A. Mello, *Dead Wrong: A Death Row Lawyer Speaks Out Against Capital Punishment.* © 1997. Cover design and illustration by Mark MacCaulay. Reprinted by permission of The University of Wisconsin Press.

7.8, Courtesy of Georgiana Nehl.

7.10, Courtesy of the artists.

7.11, Ruhr/Paragon, Minneapolis.

7.12, Courtesy of the artist.

7.13, Courtesy of Richard Saul Wurman, wurmanrs@aol.com and Pentagram.

7.14, © Robert Rauschenberg/Licensed by VAGA, NY.

7.15, Margaret Bourke-White/TimePix/Getty Images.

7.16, Alfred Eisenstadt/TimePix/Getty Images.

7.17, Michael Bierut & Tracey Cameron/Pentagram. Photo: Don F. Wong.

7.18, Courtesy of Sean O'Meallie. Photo: Ric Helstrom.

7.19, © 1999 Iomega Corporation.

7.20, Museo Nacional Centro de Arte Reina Sofia, Madrid/Bridgeman Art Library, NY. © 2005 Estate of Pablo Picasso/Artists Rights Society (ARS), NY.

Profile, page 176: Courtesy of the artist.

Profile, page 177: *The Bicycle Rider*, author Guy Davenport, 1985, Red Ozier Press. Letterpress printing, 5 x 5 x 9.5 inches. Courtesy of the artist.

part three

Page 178: Collection of the Hirshhorn Museum, Washington, DC. Photo © 1997 Katherine Wetzel, of Sculpture "Pupil" by Elizabeth King.

Page 179 T: Solomon R. Guggenheim Museum, New York, purchased with funds contributed by the Louis and Bessie Adler Foundation, Inc., Seymour M. Klein, President, 1985 (85.3276).

Page 179 B: Private Collection. Photo: M. Mimlitsch-Gray.

8.55, Busch Lobby, MIT Permanent Collection, Gift of the Albert and Vera List Family Collection.

8.56, September 1998-June 1999 Installation at Dia Center for the Arts, NY.

8.57, Designers: Bill Cannan, Tony Ortiz, H. Kurt Heinz. Design Firm: Bill Cannan & Co. Client/Mfr. NASA Public Affairs.

8.58, As installed at the Whitney Museum of American Art, New York, 1980. Courtesy of Barbara Gladstone, NY.

8.59, © 2005 Artists Rights Society (ARS), NY/ADAGP, Paris.

8.60, Edition 1: Collection of Marion Stroud Swingle. Edition 2: Collection of the Artist. Photo: Roman Mensing.

8.62, Courtesy of Fisher-Price.

8.63, Courtesy of Toshiyuki Kita/IDK Design Laboratory, LTD, Japan.

8.64, © Keith Edmier. Courtesy of Sadie Coles HQ, London.

8.65, Courtesy of Michael Graves & Associates. Photo: William Taylor.

8.66, © Andy Goldsworthy.

8.67, Photo by Robert Stave, 1989. © Adele Linarducci, 1989.

8.68, Whitney Museum of Art, NY. Purchase, with funds from the Louis and Bessie Adler Foundation, Inc., Seymour M. Klein, President, the Gilman Foundation, Inc., the Howard and Jean Lipman Foundation, Inc., and the National Endowment for the Arts (79.4). Photo: Duane Preble. © The George and Helen Segal Foundation/Licensed by VAGA, NY.

8.69, Museo del Templo Mayor, Mexico City. Instituto Nacional de Antropologia e Historia (INAH).

8.70, © University of Cincinnati Fine Arts Collection.

8.71, Courtesy of Erwin Hauer.

Profile, pages 217-219: Courtesy of the artist.

chapter nine

9.1, Courtesy of Humanscale, NY.

9.2, Solomon R. Guggenheim Museum, New York, purchased with funds contributed by the Louis and Bessie Adler Foundation, Inc., Seymour M. Klein, President, 1985 (85.3276).

9.3, Courtesy Marian Goodman Gallery, NY.

9.4, Courtesy of Matthew Marks Gallery, NY.

9.5, Giraudon/Art Resource, NY. © 2005 Estate of Louise Nevelson/Artists Rights Society (ARS), NY.

9.6, © Aaron Macsai.

9.7, Courtesy of Alexander and Bonin, NY.

9.8, Photo: Timothy Hursley. Holocaust Memorial Museum, Washington, DC.

9.9, Collection, University of Illinois at Urbana, Champaign. Photo courtesy of the artist © Alice Aycock, 1994.

9.10, UCLA Fowler Museum of Cultural History. Photo: Don Cole.

9.11, Detroit Institute of Arts, Detroit, MI. © 2005 Sol Le Witt/Artists Rights Society (ARS), NY.

9.12, Mixed media installation at the Albright-Knox Art Gallery, September 1982. Albright-Knox Art Gallery, Buffalo, NY.

9.13, Courtesy of Mary Boone Gallery, NY.

9.14, Superstock.

9.15, Installation: Capp Street Project, S.F. Courtesy of Alexander and Bonin, NY.

9.16a, Courtesy the Library, American Museum of Natural History, NY, Trans. 2104(2)

9.18, Courtesy of Theodore Gall.

9.19, Ludovica Canali De Rossi, Milano, Italy.

9.20, Santa Maria degli Angeli, Rome, Italy/Mauro Magliani/Superstock.

9.21, Kukje Gallery, Chrong Ku, Seoul, Korea.

9.22, Courtesy of Patricia A. Renick.

9.24, Designers: James E. Grove, John Cook, Jim Holtorf, Fernando Pardo, Mike Boltich. Design Firm: Designworks/USA. Client/Mfr: Corona Clipper Co.

9.25, Solomon R. Guggenheim Foundation, New York, Peggy Guggenheim, Venice (76.2553.50). © 2005 Artists Rights Society (ARS), NY/ADAGP, Paris. Photo: David Heald, © Solomon R. Guggenheim Museum Foundation, NY.

9.26, Art Institute of Chicago. Partial gift of the Arts Club of Chicago; restricted gift of various donors, through prior bequest of Arthur Rubloff; through prior restricted gift of William Hartmann; through prior gifts of Mr. and Mrs. Carter H. Harrison, Mr. and Mrs. Arnold H. Maremont through the Kate Maremont Foundation, Woodruff J. Parker, Art Institute of Chicago. Photo © 2005 Art Institute of Chicago. All Rights Reserved. © 2005 Artists Rights Society (ARS), NY/ADAGP, Paris.

9.27, The Museum of Modern Art, New York, given anonymously. © 2005 Artists Rights Society (ARS), NY/ADAGP, Paris. Photograph © Museum of Modern Art/Art Resource, NY.

9.28, Fratelli Alinari/Superstock.

9.29, The Museum of Modern Art, New York/ Art Resource, NY. © 2005 Artists Rights Society (ARS), NY.

9.30, Photo: Doug Yaple.

9.31, Ludovica Canali De Rossi, Milano, Italy.

9.32, Courtesy of the National Ornamental Metal Museum, Memphis, TN. Collection of the artist.

9.33, © 2005 Artists Rights Society (ARS), NY/ADAGP, Paris. Photo © CNAP Command Publique, Ministére de la Culture, Paris.

9.34, Museum fur Kunst und Gewerbe, Hamburg.

9.35, Private Collection.

9.36, Courtesy of Tanija & Graham Carr. Photo: Victor France.

9.37, Musée d'Orsay, Paris. Réunion des Musées Nationaux/Art Resource, NY.

9.38, Collection Walker Art Center, Minneapolis. Acquired with Lannan Foundation support in conjunction with the exhibition Sculpture Inside Outside, 1991.

9.39, The Nelson-Atkins Museum of Art, Kansas City, Missouri. Gift of the Hall Family Foundation, F99-33/1 A-DD. Photo: E. G. Schempf.

9.40, Photo: Don Hamilton.

9.41, San Francisco Museum of Modern Art. Courtesy of Paula Cooper Gallery, NY.

Profile, pages 240-241: Photos courtesy of the artist.

chapter ten

10.1, Guggenheim Bilbao © 1997, The Solomon R. Guggenheim Foundation, Bilbao. © FMGB Guggenheim Bilbao Museo, 2001. All rights reserved.

10.3, Courtesy of Shoji Design.

10.6, Photo: Whit Slemmons, Courtesy of Thorncrown Chapel.

10.7, © Lee Snider/CORBIS.

10.8, Courtesy Agnes Gund Collection. © The Joseph and Robert Cornell Memorial Foundation/Licensed by VAGA, NY.

10.9, Courtesy of Garth Clark Gallery, NY. Photo: Pierre Longtin.

10.10, Photo: Don Pitcher. Alaska Stock.

10.12, Wright State University, Dayton, OH.

10.13, Photo supplied by Blick Art Materials.

10.14, Collection Majorie & Arnold Platzker.

10.15, Art Institute of Chicago, Grant J. Pick Purchase Fund (1967.386). © 2005 Artists Rights Society (ARS), NY/VEGAP, Madrid.

10.16, Kunstindustrimuseet I Oslo (Museum of Decorative Arts & Design) Norway.

10.18, Courtesy Anish Kapoor and Lisson Gallery, London.

10.19, Private Collection.

10.20, Corning Museum of Glass, Corning, NY (86.4.180).

10.21, Courtesy Galerie Elena Lee, Montreal.

10.22, Courtesy of James Cohan Gallery.

10.23, Collection of the Art Institute of Chicago. Courtesy of the artist.

10.24, Courtesy of Deborah Butterfield.

Profile, pages 258-259: Courtesy of Todd Slaughter.

chapter eleven

11.1, George Glod/Superstock.

11.2, Photo: Shigeo Anzai, Tokyo.

11.3, Courtesy of Ronald Feldman Fine Arts.

11.4, Saint Peter's Basilica, Vatican, Rome. Alinari/Art Resource, NY.

11.5, Private Collection; Collection Martha Stewart; Collection Oakland Museum of Art.

11.6, Private Collection. Photo: M. Mimlitsch-Gray.

11.7, Collection: Rothko Chapel, Houston, dedicated to Reverend Martin Luther King, Jr. © 2005 Barnett Newman Foundation/Artists Rights Society, NY.

11.8, Courtesy of P.P.O.W., NY.

11.9, University of California, Berkeley Art Museum. Photographed for the UC Berkeley Art Museum by Ben Blackwell.

11.10, Kukje Gallery, Chrong Ku, Seoul, Korea.

11.11, Photo: Henry Arnold, © Maya Lin.

11.12, Private collection. © The George and Helen Segal Foundation/Licensed by VAGA, NY.

11.13, Courtesy of Susan Trangmar.

11.14, Courtesy of the Sogetsu Foundation.

11.15, On loan to The Philadelphia Museum of Art, Philadelphia, PA.

11.16, The Metropolitan Museum of Art, Bequest of Mrs. H.O. Havemeyer, 1929. The H.W. Havemeyer Collection.

11.18, The Museum of Modern Art, New York. Acquired through the Lillie P. Bliss Bequest. Photograph © The Museum of Modern Art/Art Resource, NY.

11.19, National Geographic Society Headquarters, Washington, DC.

11.20, Collection of The Denver Art Museum, Denver, CO. Gift of Ginny Williams. Photo: Edward Smith. Courtesy Joseph Helman Gallery, NY (BH 1912).

11.21, Courtesy Jay Jopling Gallery/White Cube, London. © Antony Gormley.

11.22, Courtesy of Pace Wildenstein. Photo: Ellen Page Wilson. © 2005 John Chamberlain/Artists Rights Society (ARS), NY.

11.23, Installation at SITE Santa Fe, 1999.

11.24, Courtesy of The North Face, San Leandro, CA.

11.25, Collection: Caltrans, City of Los Angeles, San Diego Freeway Northbound, Mulholland Drive Exit, Los Angeles.

11.26, (Corner of Grove Rd. and Roman Rd., London, destroyed 1994). Commissioned by Artangel Trust and Beck's.

11.27, Courtesy of Jack Shainman Gallery, NY. © 2005 Artists Rights Society (ARS), NY/VG Bild-Kunst, Bonn.

11.28, Courtesy of Todd Slaughter.

11.29, © 2005 Artists Rights Society (ARS), NY/VG Bild-Kunst. Bonn.

11.30, © Ronald Dahl.

11.31, Third of five public garden rooms in the King County East Division Reclamation Plant, Renton, WA.

11.32, Courtesy of the Library, American Museum of Natural History, NY, Trans. 1448(4).

11.33, Art Institute of Chicago, Gift of Margaret Fisher in memory of her parents, Mr. andMrs. Walter L. Fisher (1957.165), view 1.

11.34, The Museum of Modern Art, New York. The Sidney and Harriet Janis Collection. Art Resource, NY. © 2005 Artists Rights Society (ARS), NY/ADAGP, Paris/Estate of Marcel Duchamp.

11.35, © Skyscan Balloon Photography.

11.36, Courtesy of the Henry Moore Foundation and the artist.

11.37, Nikolai Fine Art, New York.

11.38, © PhenomenArts,Inc. Christopher Janney, Artistic Director.

11.39, Courtesy of Rudi Stern.

11.40, The British School at Rome. Photo: Shelagh Wakely.

11.41, San Francisco Museum of Modern Art. Doris and Donald G. Fisher Fund. Courtesy Hosfelt Gallery.

11.42, © The Field Museum of Natural History, Chicago. Photo: White & Dorman, Front view, neg #A112518.C.

11.43, © Allen Memorial Art Museum, Oberlin College, OH. Fund for Contemporary Art and gift of the artist and the Fischbach Gallery, 1970.

11.44, Collection of the Hirshhorn Museum, Washington, DC. Photo © 1997 Katherine Wetzel, of Sculpture "Pupil" by Elizabeth King.

Profile, pages 286-289: Courtesy of the artist.

part four

Page 290: © 2005 Eames Office/ www.eames office.com.

Page 291 T: © 1984 by Chris van Allsburg. Reprinted by permission of Houghton Mifflin Co.

chapter twelve

12.1-12.2, © Apple Computer, Inc. Used with permission. All rights reserved. Apple ® and the Apple logo are registered trademarks of Apple Computer Inc.

12.3, Photo: © Sam Shere/Hulton/Archive/Getty Images.

12.4, © 1984 by Chris van Allsburg. Reprinted by permission of Houghton Mifflin Co.

12.17, Photofest.

12.18, The Sandman Special #1, TM and © DC Comics, 1991. All Rights Reserved. Used with Permission.

12.19, Michael Snow, *Cover to Cover*, 1975. The New York Public Library, Astor, Lenox and Tilden Foundations.

12.20, © 2005 Artists Rights Society (ARS), NY/VG Bild-Kunst, Bonn.

12.24, TM & © 2005 Marvel Characters, Inc. Used with permission.

12.25, The Metropolitan Museum of Art, New York, Harris Brisbane Dick fund, 1946 (46.160).

12.26, © Nancy Holt/Licensed by VAGA, NY.

12.27, Courtesy of Tatana Kellner and the Syracuse University Library, Department of Special Collections.

Profile, page 319: © Joanna Eldredge Morrisey.

Profile, page 320: From *Losing It*, documentary film by Sharon Greytak.

chapter thirteen

13.1, Musée du Louvre, Paris. © Réunion des Musees Nationaux/Art Resource, NY.

13.2, Courtesy of the artist and Munson Williams Proctor Arts Institue (96.14 a-c). G.R. Farley Photography.

13.4, From Frogfolio 10, Dellas Graphics, Syracuse, NY. © Bart Forbes, 2005.

13.5, Dellas Graphics, Syracuse, NY.

13.6, From Frogfolio 10, Dellas Graphics, Syracuse, NY.

13.7, © Duane Michals.

13.8-13.9, © Douglas Wonders.

13.10-13.11, Photofest.

13.13-13.14, © 2005 Kingdom of Spain, Gala-Salvador Dali Foundation/Artists Rights Society (ARS), NY.

13.26, Used with permission Greenberg, Seronick, O'Leary & Partners, Boston.

13.27, Used with permission Jeep/Daimler Chrylser.

13.28, Used with permission Procter & Gamble.

13.29, Used with permission Goodby, Silverstein & Partners.

13.30, Used with permission Nike and the estate of Walt Stack.

13.31, Used with permission Greenberg, Seronick, O'Leary & Partners, Boston.

13.32, Used with permission BMW and WCRS Matthews Marcantonio, London.

13.33, Susan Kae Grant, Black Rose Productions.

13.34, © 2005 Eames Office/www.eamesoffice.com.

Profile, page 346: Courtesy of the artist.

Profile, page 347: Courtesy of the artist and Munson Williams Proctor Arts Institue (96.14 a-c). G.R. Farley Photography.

chapter fourteen

14.1, © Nancy Callahan, 2005.

14.2, The Saint Louis Art Museum. Funds given by Mr. and Mrs. George Schlapp, Mrs. Francis A. Mesker, the Henry L. and Natalie Edison Freund Charitable Trust, The Arthur and Helen Baer Charitable Foundation, Sam and Marilyn Fox, Mrs. Eleanor J. Moore, Mr and Mrs. John Wooten Moore, Donna and William Nussbaum, Mr. and Mrs. James. E. Schneithorst, Jain and Richard Shaikewitz, Mark Twain Bancshares, Inc., Mr. and Mrs. Gary Wolff, Mr. and Mrs. Lester P. Ackerman Jr., the Honorable and Mrs. Thomas F. Eagleton, Alison and John Ferring, Mrs. Gail K. Fischmann, Mr. and Mrs. Solon Gershman, Dr. and Mrs. Gary Hansen, Mr. and Mrs. Kenneth S. Kransberg, Mr. and Mrs. Gyo Obata, Jane and Warren Shapleigh, Lee and Barbara Wagman, Anabeth Calkins and John Weil, Museum Shop Fund, the Contemporary Art Society, and Museum Purchase; Dr. and Mrs. Harold J. Joseph, estate of Alice P. Francis, Fine Arts. Associates, J. Lionberger Davis, Mr. and Mrs. Samuel B. Edison, Mr. and Mrs. Morton D. May, estate of Louise H. Franciscus, an anonymous donor, Miss Ella M. Boededker, by exchange.

14.4, Courtesy of the author.

14.6, © 2005 Artists Rights Society (ARS), NY, DACS, London.

14.8-14.9, Courtesy of the author.

14.10 A-B, Illustration from The Gashlycrumb Tinies or, After the Outing. Harcourt, Inc.

14.11, Reprinted with permission of Little Simon, an imprint of Simon & Schuster Children's Publishing Division, from The 12 Days of Christmas, a Pop-up Celebration, by Robert Sabuda. © 1996 by Robert Sabuda.

14.22, September 1998-June 1999 Installation at Dia Center for the Arts, NY. © 2005 Robert Irwin/Artists Rights Society (ARS), NY.

14.23, Collection of the artist. Photo: Roman Mensing.

14.24, © 1997 Sandy Skoglund.

14.25, © Nancy Callahan and Diane Gallo.

14.26, © 2005 Jenny Holzer/Artists Rights Society (ARS), NY.

14.27, Photo © Dan Rest. Courtesy of Brooklyn Academy of Music.

14.28, Paula Court Photography.

14.29, Courtesy of The Rachel Rosenthal Company. Photo: Lothar Schmitz.

Profile, page 368-369: Courtesy of the artist.

A

A is for Amy Who Fell Down the Stairs (Gorey), *353*

A Is for Apollo and *U Is for Urania* (Chin), *155*

Aalto, Alvar
Paimio Lounge Chair, *129*

Abakanowicz, Magdalena
Standing Figures, 236, *237*

Abbott, Berenice
Exchange Place, *88*

Abramovic, Marina
Cleaning the House, 301–302, *302*

Absence, in sculpture, 272

Abstract art, 262

Abstract shapes, 32

Accent color, 68

Accents, 309

Achromatism, 55

Action-to-action transition, *297*

Acts (narrative), 327

Actual lines, 20, 191

Adams, Ansel
Monolith, The Face of Half Dome, Yosemite Valley, 32, *33*, 103
Moonrise, Hernandez, New Mexico, *89*

Adams, John, 364

Additive color, 53, 54–55

Additive sculpture, 246

Adirondack chair, 128, *129*

Advertisement, Citizens Against Cocaine Abuse, 35, *37*

Advertising, 337–341

Aesthetics, 173–174

Afrum-Proto (Turrell), 208–209, *209*

Afterimages, 56

Albers, Joseph, 6

Alessi Coffee Set (Graves), *212*

Aleve advertisement, *341*

Alice in Chains Website, 43, *44*

Almstadtstrasse 43 (Attie), 272

Altdorfer, Albrecht
Battle of Alexander, *99*

Ambient light, 208

American Institute of Graphic Artists
"Design 2 Business" brochure, *25*

Amnesty International leaflet (Dubkin), *86*, 86–87

Amplification (Marclay), *186*

Amplified perspective, 103

Analogous color schemes, 62

Analogy, 171

. . . And the Home of the Brave (Demuth), *34*

Anderson, Laurie, 143

Annette (Giacometti), *19*, 21

Anomaly, 96, 233

Ant Farm
Cadillac Ranch, *187*

Apennine (Giovanni da Bologna), 232, *233*

Apocalypse Now (film), 309

Apple Computer Television Ad, 292, *293*

Approximate symmetry, 90

Araki, Takako
Rock Bible, 205

Arbus, Diane, 368

Aristotle, 298

Armature, 244

Armitage, Karole
Predator's Ball, 364

Arnheim, Rudolf, 97

The Arrival of a Train at La Ciotat Station (film), 302–303, *303*

Art is . . . (Glaser), *165*, 165–166

Arterial Fibrillation (Martens), *169*

Asbesti Gogora III (Chillida), *250*

Aspects of Negro Life: From Slavery Through Reconstruction (Douglas), *26*

Aspect-to-aspect transition, *298*

Assemblage, 247

Asymmetrical balance, *91*, *92*, 91–93, 227–228, *228*

At the Time of the Louisville Flood (Bourke-White), 170, *171*

Atmospheric perspective, 46, 103

Attached shadows, 46

Attention's Loop (King), *282*, 283

Attie, Shimon
Almstadtstrasse 43, *272*

Audience, 166

Automobile advertisement, 341, *342*

Available Light (Childs), 364

Aycock, Alice
Tree of Life Fantasy, *9*, 198, *224*

Aztec Ritual Vessel Depicting Mask of Tlaloc, *213*

B

B is for Basil Assaulted by Bears (Gorey), *353*

Bacon, Francis
Four Studies for a Self-Portrait, *63*, 109
Triptych, *66*

Balance, 87–94, 227–230
asymmetrical, *91*, *92*, 91–93, 227–228, *228*
color and, 68
defined, 87
expressive uses of, 93
symmetry, 89–91, 227
weight and gravity, 87–89

Barbeque (Fischl), *93*

Bartholdi, Auguste
Statue of Liberty, construction diagram by Eiffel, *244*

Basic elements of two-dimensional design; *see* Elements of two-dimensional design

Battle of Alexander (Altdorfer), *99*

Baudelaire (Villon), *23*

Bearden, Romare
The Dove, *36*

Beardsley, Aubrey
Salomé with the Head of John the Baptist, 30–31, *31*

Beat
in narrative, 327
in sound, 309

Beckman, Erica, 364

Beethoven, Ludwig von, *84*

Behrens, Roy, 173

Bell, Larry
The Iceberg and Its Shadow, 206, *207*

Bella Coola Mask Representing the Sun, *227*

Bend, 245

Benton, Thomas Hart
City Building, *105*

Bertrand Russell (Stermer), *40*, 41

Beverly Edmier (Edmier), *211*, 212

Bezold effect, 55–56, *56*

Bezold, Wilhelm, 55

The Bicycle Rider (printed by Ken Botnick), *177*

Bicycle Wheel (Duchamp), *276*

Bierstadt, Albert
The Rocky Mountains, Landers Peak, 102, 103

Bierut, Michael
Minnesota Children's Museum signage (with Tracy Cameron), 170, *171*
Save Our City, *94*

Billy Budd (Davis), *95*

Biological Abstraction III (Lasher-Oakes), *145*

Bird (Blåvarp), *250*

Bird in Space (Brancusi), *232*

The Birds (film), *5*, 296

Blacktop (film), 344

Blackware Storage Jar (M. M. Martinez and J. Martinez), *204*

Blåvarp, Liv
Bird, *250*

Blue Skies (Trangmar), *266*

The Board Room (Muntadas), 184, *185*

Boards, 255

Boccioni, Umberto
Unique Forms of Continuity in Space, *268*

Book 50 (K. Smith), *351*

Book of Kells: Opening page, St. Luke's Gospel, *99*

Booster (Rauschenberg), *170*

Bordwell, David, 295–296

Botnick, Ken (printer), 176–177
The Bicycle Rider, *177*

Bourke-White, Margaret
At the Time of the Louisville Flood, 170, *171*

The Boy (Mueck), *254*

Brace (Rauschenberg), *31*

Bradbury, Ray, 72

Brainstorming, 136–139

Brancusi, Constantin
Bird in Space, *232*
Golden Bird, *232*
Maiastra, *232*

Brandt, Bill
Nude, 28–29, *29*

Braque, Georges
Man with a Guitar, *29*

Bravo, Claudio
Package, *40*

Breaking of the Vessels (Kiefer), *349*

Breuer, Marcel
Armchair, *129*

Brilliant Scape (Blue) (Sawada), *88*

Bristol board, 255
Broken Obelisk (Newman), 262–263, *263*
Brooks, Romaine
  Self-Portrait, 60
Brotherhood Building mural (Haas), 40
Browne, David
  Solstice Greetings (with Georgiana Nehl), 166, *167*, 168
Brussels Construction (De Riviera), 188, *189*
Bunuel, Luis
  Un Chien Andalou (with Salvador Dali), *331*
Burden, Chris
  Medusa's Head, 190, 191
Buren, Daniel
  The Two Plateaus, 226
Burns, Robert, 172
Bury, Pol
  Fountains at Palais Royal, 234, 235
Bush Cabbage Dreaming at Ngarlu (Japaljarri, A. N. Granites, and R. J. Granites), 64, *65*
Butterfield, Deborah
  Large Horse #4, 256
Butterfly Maiden (Hopi Kachina), 72, *73*
Byars, James Lee
  The Perfect Thought, 264

Cadillac Ranch (Ant Farm), *187*
Cage, John
  4 minutes 33 seconds (4'33"), 363
  First Construction in Metal, 365
  Imaginary Landscape #4, 365
Caged Sphere Bracelet Series (Enterline), 262
Caillebotte, Gustave
  Place de l'Europe on a Rainy Day, 148, 149, 148–150, 166
Calder, Alexander
  La Grande Vitesse, 194, 195
  Untitled, 194
Callahan, Nancy, 126–127
  Daybook, 348
  Storefront Stories (with Diane Gallo), 127, *292, 361*
Calligraphic lines, 21
Camera angles, 105–106
Camera Obscura Image of Brookline View in Brady's Room (Morell), *369*
Cameron, James
  Titanic, 305, 309, 331–332, *332*
Cameron, Tracy
  Minnesota Children's Museum signage (with Michael Bierut), 170, *171*
Campbell, Jim
  Digital Watch, 280, 281
Cannan, Bill, & Co.
  NASA's Participating Exhibit at the 1989 Paris Air Show, *3, 208*
The Canterbury Tales, illustration (Morris), *85*

Capra (Remington), 43, *44*
Caravaggio
  The Deposition, 22
Carpeaux, Jean-Baptiste
  The Dance, 181, 236, 237
Carr, Tanija & Graham
  Untitled, 236
Carson, Rachel
  Under the Sea Wind, 355
Cartier-Bresson, Henri, 368
  Valencia, 107–108, *108*
Carved Stoneware Storage Jar (MacDonald), *241*
Casablanca (film), *48*
Cast shadow, 46
Cause-and-effect critique, 149
Cellini, Benvenuto
  Perseus and Medusa, 267
Celmins, Vija
  Untitled (Ocean), 79
Centricity, 97
Ceremonial Arch Honoring Service Workers in the New Service Economy (Ukeles), *261*
Cézanne, Paul
  Houses in Provence, 62
Chamberlain, John
  The Hedge, 270
Champollion, Jean-François, 117
Chance Meeting (Michals), 326, *327*
Chaos 1 (Tinguely), *181*
Chariot (Giacometti), 232, *233*
Chariots of Fire (film), 308
Chartes Cathedral, perspective diagram and cross-section, *244*
Chase-Riboud, Barbara
  Malcolm X #3, 267
Cheer detergent advertisement, 338, *339*
Chiaroscuro, 46
Chicago, Judy
  Rejection Quintet: Female Rejection Drawing, 90, *91*
Un Chien Andalou (film), *331*
Childs, Lucinda
  Available Light, 364
Chillida, Eduardo
  Asbesti Gogora III, 250
Chin, Jason, 153–155
  A Is for Apollo and *U Is for Urania, 155*
Chipboard, 255
Cho Duck-Hyun
  My Mother 3, 264, 265
Christ of St. John of the Cross (Dali), 103, *104*
A Christmas memory (Quinn), *66*
Chroma, 60
Chromatic grays, 64–65
Chronology, 310–312
Churchill, Winston, 170, *171*
Citizen Kane (film), *104,* 333–336
Citizens Against Cocaine Abuse, advertisement, 35
City Building (Benton), *105*
City Life (Hartigan), *60, 61*
Clay, 252

Cleaning the House (Abramovic), 301–302, *302*
Clichés, 168
Close, Chuck
  Self-Portrait, 42
Closure, 22, 84, 223–224
Codex, *351*
Coleridge, Samuel Taylor
  Kubla Khan, 354
Collaboration, 122–123
Collage, 37
Color, 52–75
  accent, 68
  additive, 53, 54–55
  analogous, 62
  balance, 68
  chromatic grays, 64
  color wheel, 57
  complementary, 56, 63
  composing with, 67–69
  contrast, 212
  defined, 57–58
  disharmony, 65–66
  distribution, 68
  earth colors, 64–65
  emotion and, 70–74, 212–213
  emphasis, 69
  expressive, 74
  harmony, 62–64, 211
  hue, 57–58, 211
  intensity, 60, 211
  interaction of, 55–56
  key, 72
  light and, 54
  monochromatic, 62
  overtones, 55
  primaries, 53, 57
  process, 53
  proportion, 68
  secondaries, 57
  spectrum, *54*
  split complementary, 63
  subtractive, 53, 55
  symbolic, 72, 213
  temperature, 57–58, 211
  tertiaries, 57
  theories of, 52–53
  triadic, 64
  value, 58–60, *59,* 211
  weight, 68
Common objects, transformation of, 131
Communication, visual; *see* Constructing meaning
Compare/contrast critique, 149–151
Complementary colors, 56, 63
Composites, 243
Composition, 78–110, 220–239
  balance, 87–94, 227–230
  color, 67–69
  defined, 220
  emphasis, 96–99, 233–235
  movement, illusion of, 107–109
  priorities in, 109–110
  proportion, 94, 231–232
  repetition, 235–238
  rhythm, 95–96, 235–238

Index

scale, 94, 231
spatial illusion, 99–107
unity and variety, 78–87, 221–226
Composition with Blue and Yellow
(Mondrian), *92*
Compression (force), 245, 270
Computerized Nude (Knowlton and
Harmon), *38*
Conceptual diagrams of ideas, *137*,
137–138
Cones (eye), 56
Constructing meaning, 164–174
aesthetics, 173–174
audience, 166
clichés, 168
connections, 171–172
context, 170–171
drama, 173
iconography, 165–166
immediacy, 166–167
language, 164–165
purpose and intent, 169–170
stereotypes, 168
surprise, 168
Containment, 81, 223
Content, 147, 180
Context for communication, 170–171
Continuity
in composition, 82–84, 223
of line, 19, 188, 191
Contour lines, 20
Contours, 197
Contrast
color and, 212
emphasis through, *97*, 97–98,
234–235
simultaneous, 55
value and, 43–44
Convergent thinking, 133–135
Cook, Roger
signage symbol system poster (with
Don Shanosky), *168*
Cornell, Joseph
Untitled (Medici Princess), 246
Corporate Wars (Longo), 184
Corrugated cardboard, 255
Cover to Cover (Snow), 301
Covered Effigy Jar with Removable
Head, *275*
Cowboy smoking advertisement, 168,
169
Crawford, Robert
Jamie Sleeping, 98
Creation of Adam (Michelangelo), 82
Creative Club of Orlando, illustration
for, *81*
Creative process, 115
constructing meaning, 164–174
creativity, 116–125
critical thinking, 146–161
exploring project's potential,
156–160
long-term projects, 152–155
problems, 128–143
Creativity, 116–125; *see also* Problems
design and, 116
goal setting and, 118–120
open mind and, 143

seven characteristics of, 116–118
sources of ideas, 130–132
time management and, 120–123
Critical thinking, 146–161
critiques, 147–152
establishing criteria, 146–147
long-term projects, 152–155
realizing project's potential, 156–160
Critiques
conducting, 147
elements of, 147–148
personal responsibility and, 160–161
types of, 148–152
Cross contours, 23
Cross-hatching, 23
Crow, Nancy
Double Mexican Wedding Rings 1, 68
Csikszentmihalyi, Mihaly, 117
Cubi XXVII (D. Smith), 198, *199*
Cubism, 29
curcuma sul travertino (Wakely), 280,
281
Current Disturbance (Hatoum), 226, *227*
Curtiz, Michael, 48
Curvilinear shapes, *30*, 30–31
Cut, 296, *297*
Cut Piece (Ono), 365
Cut with a Kitchen Knife (Höch), 79
Cyclone Design
Turn of the Screw, *84*, 84–85

Da Vinci, Leonardo, 143
Dacey, Bob, 162–163
Cover of *Miriam's Cup*, *163*
Dahl, Ronald
Seven Windows to a Sky on Fire, 274
Dali, Salvador
Christ of St. John of the Cross, 103, *104*
Un Chien Andalou (with Luis
Bunuel), *331*
The Dance (Carpeaux), *181*, 236, *237*
Davenport, Guy
The Bicycle Rider, 177
David, Jacques-Louis
Oath of the Horatii, 323
Davis, Gene
Billy Budd, 95
Day at the Beach (Riedy), 78, *79*
Daybook (Callahan), 348
De Chirico, Giorgio
*The Mystery and Melancholy of a
Street*, 135, *136*
De Kooning, Willem
Door to the River, 68, *69*
De Maria, Walter
The Lightning Field, 200, *201*
De Riviera, José
Brussels Construction, 188, *189*
Death and the King's Horseman
(Soyinka), 328–329, *329*
Decisive moment, 107–108
Definition, degrees of, 34
Degas, Edgar
Frieze of Dancers, 109
Horse Galloping on Right Foot, 267

Dellas Graphics
Frog Folio, 324, *325*
Demuth, Charles
. . . And the Home of the Brave, 34
Dennis, Donna
Subway with Silver Girders, 203
Denouement, 332
The Deposition (Caravaggio), 22
Deposition (Van der Weyden), *102*, 103
Descriptive critique, 148
Design, defined, 5–6
Design process, 128–130
"Design 2 Business" brochure, 25
Designworks/USA
Home Pro Garden Tool Line, *6*, 231
Detroit Industry, north wall (Rivera), 27
Device to Root Out Evil (Oppenheim),
269
Di Suvero, Mark
Ik Ook Eindhoven, 188, *189*
Dick, Beau
Mugamtl Mask (Crooked Beak), 132
Dickens, Charles
A Tale of Two Cities, 311
Dickinson, Eleanor
Study of Hands, 20
Diebenkorn, Richard
Interior with Book, 70, *71*
Diegetic sound, 309
Diffrient, Niels
Freedom Chair, 220
Digital Watch (Campbell), 280, *281*
Directed light, 208
Direction of line, 19, 188
Discus Thrower (Diskobolos) (Myron),
107
Disharmony (color), 65–66
Displacement, 247
Dissolve, 296, *297*
Distributing force, 245–246
Distribution, color and, 68
Divergent thinking, 135–136
Division Street (Witkin), 324–325, *347*
"Do women have to be naked . . ."
(Guerilla Girls), *52*
Dog food advertisement, 338, *339*
Dominant form, 229
Door to the River (De Kooning), 68, *69*
Doormat (Hatoum), 205, 223
Las Dos Fridas (Kahlo), 93
Double Jump (Eakins), 108
Double Mexican Wedding Rings 1
(Crow; quilted by Marie Moore),
68
Doubles/Triples, Italy (Harris), 44, *45*
Douglas, Aaron
*Aspects of Negro Life: From Slavery
Through Reconstruction*, 26
The Dove (Bearden), 36
Drama, 173
Drew, Leonardo
Number 56, 226
Drift No. 2 (Riley), 95
Drinking and driving advertisement,
337
Dry mounting tissue, 255

index

Dubkin, Joan
  leaflet for Amnesty International,
    86, 86–87
Duchamp, Marcel
  Bicycle Wheel, 276
  Nude Descending a Staircase, No. 2, 96
Duchamp-Villon, Raymond
  The Great Horse, 275
Duration
  as design element, 298–299
  in sound, 309
Dürer, Albrecht
  The Knight, Death and the Devil, 41
Dynamic forms, 181

E. Fay Jones & Associates
  Thorncrown Chapel, Eureka
    Springs, Arkansas, 245
Eakins, Thomas
  Double Jump, 108
Eames, Charles and Ray, 128–130
  Blacktop, 344
  Powers of Ten, 290, 343, 343–344
  Side Chair, Model DCM, 130
Earth colors, 64–65
Eccentricity, 97
Eckow (Mach), 23
Edison, Thomas, 122
Editing, 311
Edmier, Keith
  Beverly Edmier, 211, 212
Eiffel, Alexander-Gustave
  Statue of Liberty, construction
    diagram, 244
Einstein, Albert, 29
Eisenstadt, Alfred
  Winston Churchill, Liverpool, 170, 171
Elements of three-dimensional design,
    180–216
  color, 211–214
  degrees of dimensionality, 184–214
  environmental works, 184, 186–187
  form, 180–182
  freestanding works, 184
  light, 206–210
  line, 187–193
  mass, 197
  orthographic projection, 182–183
  plane, 194–195
  relief, 184
  space, 198–203
  texture, 204–206
  three-quarter works, 184
  time, 214
  volume, 195–196
Elements of two-dimensional design,
    17–49
  color, 52–75
  line, 17–26
  shape, 26–37
  texture, 37–42
  value, 43–48
Ely, Timothy C.
  Rubens (with Daniel E. Kelm), 349
Emotion, color and, 70–74, 212–213
Emphasis, 96–99, 233–235

color and, 69
by isolation, 96–97, 233
by placement, 97
through contrast, 97, 97–98, 234
Enterline, Sandra
  Caged Sphere Bracelet Series, 262
Environmental works, 184, 186–187
  earthworks, 186
  installation art, 184, 186, 359–362
  site-specific works, 187
Escher, M. C.
  Metamorphosis II (detail), 29, 122
Essential Vertigo
  The Sandman Special #1, 300
Estes, Richard
  Miami Rug Company, 90
Evans, Bob
  Force Fin Variations, 182
Exchange Place (Abbott), 88
Exoskeleton, 243
Expansion (force), 270
Explosion of the Hindenburg (Shere), 293
Eye
  eye level, 100
  rods and cones, 56
Eye level, 100

Fade, 296, 297
Fibers, 253
Fidelity (sound), 309
Fifty Years of Silence (Keller), 306
Figure, 28, 28–30
Figure/ground reversal, 29–30
Fine art process, 130
Fischl, Eric
  Barbeque, 93
Fisher, Vernon
  Objects in a Field, 69, 70
Flack, Audrey
  Wheel of Fortune, 53 (detail), 57
Flag (Johns), 72, 73
Flash Point (Francis), 8, 30, 97
Flashbacks, 295
Floodstage (Lucier), 359
Flying buttress, 244
Flying Cranes and Poetry (attributed to
    Sôtatsu; calligraphy by Koetsu),
    21
Foamcore, 255
Focal point
  color and, 69
  emphasis and, 233
  line and, 83
Forbes, Bart
  Landmark, 325
Forbes, Peter
  Shelter/Surveillance Sculpture and
    models, 140
Force Fin Variations (Evans), 182
Form
  defined, 147, 180
  types of, 180–181
Formal Relationships (Exercise), 11
Fountains at Palais Royal (Bury), 234,
    235

4 minutes 33 seconds (4'33") (Cage), 363
Four Studies for a Self-Portrait (Bacon),
    63, 109
Fractured space, 103–104
Fragile pictogram, 168
Frames, 294
Francis, Sam
  Flash Point, 8, 30, 97
Frank, Robert, 368
  Movie Premiere, Hollywood, 34
Frankenthaler, Helen
  Interior Landscape, 32
Free Ride Home (Snelson), 187–188, 188
Freed, James Ingo
  Tower of Photos, 224
Freedom Chair (Diffrient), 220
Freestanding works, 184
French, Daniel Chester
  Head of Abraham Lincoln, 206
Frenkel, Emily
  Labyrinth Book, two double-page
    spreads, 352
  Labyrinth Drawing, 352
Frieze of Dancers (Degas), 109
Frog Folio (Dellas Graphics), 324, 325
The Frog Jumps over the Moon
    (Tinkelman), 325
The Fugitive (film), 295
Fujii, Chuichi
  Untitled, 229–230, 230
Fuller, R. Buckminster
  U.S. Pavilion, Expo-67, 246
Function, 182
Fusion, 82
Futurists, 363

Gall, Thomas T.
  Plaza Facets, 228, 229, 231
Gallo, Diane, 126–127
  Storefront Stories (with Nancy
    Callahan), 127, 292, 361
Gangi, Nicora
  Vision, 58, 59
Garden design, 6
The Gashlycrumb Tinies, or After the
    Outing (Gorey), 353
Gehry, Frank, 364
  Cross Check Armchair, 130, 131
  Guggenheim Museum Bilbao,
    computer-generated image, 243
Gentileschi, Artemesia
  Judith and Her Maidservant with the
    Head of Holofernes, 47
Geometric forms, 181
Geometric shapes, 32
Gericault, Théodore
  Raft of the Medusa, 83, 83–84
Gernhardt, Henry, 241
Gestalt psychology, 80–85
  closure, 84
  combining principles of, 84–85
  containment, 81
  continuity, 82–84
  grouping, 80, 80–81
  proximity, 82
  repetition, 82

index

Gesture drawing, 20
The Ghent Altarpiece (closed) (Van Eyck), 46
Giacometti, Alberto
 Annette, 19, 21
 Chariot, 232, 233
Gilliard, Joseph, 241
Ginevra Carafe (Sottsass), *196*
Giovanni da Bologna
 Apennine, 232, 233
 The Rape of the Sabine Women, 192
Giusti, Karen
 White House/Greenhouse, 278
Glaser, Milton
 Art is . . . , 165, 165–166
Glass, 252–253
Glass Pod with Hair (Strokowsky), *253*
Globular Vessel with Inverted Rim, Igbo, Nigeria, *205*
Glues, 255
Goal setting, 118–120, *119*
Golconde (Magritte), *166*
Goldberg, Carin
 Cover of *Ulysses,* 27
Golden Bird (Brancusi), *232*
Goldsmith, Gary
 Advertisement, Citizens Against Cocaine Abuse, 35, *35,* 37
Goldsworthy, Andy
 Poppy Petals, 212
Gone with the Wind (film), 305
González-Torres, Felix
 Untitled (Death by Gun), 87
Goodman, Sidney
 Man Waiting, 35
Goodwin, Guy
 Tracers–Side Order, 62
Gorey, Edward
 A is for Amy Who Fell Down the Stairs, 353
 B is for Basil Assaulted by Bears, 353
Gorky, Arshile
 The Liver is the Cock's Comb, 60, *61*
Gormley, Antony
 Learning to Think, 269
Gradation, 26, 250, *251*
Graham, Dan
 Past Continuous Pasts, 363
 Performance/Audience/Mirror, 365
Gralnick, Lisa
 Three Bracelets, *142*
La Grande Vitesse (Calder), 194, *195*
Granites, Alma Nungarrayi
 Bush Cabbage Dreaming at Ngarlu (with Japaljarri and R. J. Granites), 64, *65*
Granites, Robin Japanangka
 Bush Cabbage Dreaming at Ngarlu (with Japaljarri and A. N. Granites), 64, *65*
Grant, Susan Kae
 Kainophobia, Fear of Change, 342, 343
Graves, Michael
 Alessi Coffee Set, 212
Gravity
 in sculpture, 269
 visual, 87–89
The Great American Dream (Indiana), *39*

The Great Horse (Duchamp-Villon), *275*
The Great Train Robbery (film), 303
Green Stripe (Madame Matisse) (Matisse), *60*
Greytak, Sharon, 319–321
 Losing It, 320
Grids, 85–87, 226
Griffith, D. W.
 Intolerance, 303, 311
Grinding Knuckles (Slaughter), *273*
Grisaille, 46
Ground (shape), *28,* 28–30
Grouping, *80,* 80–81, 221, 324
GTS Companies Website, 109, *110*
Guerilla Girls
 "Do women have to be naked . . . ," *52*
Guernica (Picasso), 172, *173*
Guggenheim Museum Bilbao, computer-generated image (Gehry), *243*
Gumiring Garkman (Onus), *86*

Haacke, Hans
 Weather Cube, 273
Haas, Richard
 Mural on Brotherhood Building, Cincinnati, Ohio, *40*
Hall of Whispers (Viola), 359–360, *360*
Hamady, Walter, 177
Hand (Lebrun), *20*
Hand-held scale, 231
Happenings, 363, 365
Hard-sell advertising, 337
Harmon, Leon and Kenneth Knowlton
 Computerized Nude, 38
Harmony (color), 62–64, 211
Harris, Conley
 Doubles/Triples, Italy, 44, *45*
Hartigan, Grace
 City Life, 60, *61*
Hassinger, Maren
 12 Trees No 2, 271
Hatching, 23
Hatoum, Mona
 Current Disturbance, 226, 227
 Doormat, 205, 223
 Pull, 365
Hauer, Erwin
 Project California Condor, 214, *215*
Haylor-McDowell, Deborah
 The Serpent Didn't Lie, 165
Head of Abraham Lincoln (French), *206*
Head of a Satyr (Michelangelo), *23*
The Hedge (Chamberlain), *270*
Helmets, bristol board, *195*
Henry Moore Much Hadham 23rd July 1982 (Hockney), *104*
Hesse, Eva
 Laocoön, 283
High-definition shapes, 34
Hilton, Eric
 Innerland, 253
Hitchcock, Alfred
 The Birds, 5, 296

Höch, Hannah
 Cut with a Kitchen Knife, 79
Hockney, David
 Henry Moore Much Hadham 23rd July 1982, 104
 Mist, 59
Hofmann, Hans
 Magnum Opus, 67
Hokusai, Katsushika
 Thirty-Six Views of Mount Fuji (three prints), *141*
Holt, Nancy
 Sun Tunnels, 192, 305
Holzer, Jenny
 Truisms, 362
Home Pro Garden Tool Line (Designworks/USA), *6,* 231
Horizon line, 100
Horn, Roni
 How Dickinson Stayed Home, 222, 223
Hornung, David, 55
Horse Galloping on Right Foot (Degas), *267*
Houdon, Jean-Antoine
 St. Bruno of Cologne, 229
House (Whiteread), *272*
Houses in Provence (Cézanne), *62*
How Dickinson Stayed Home (Horn), 222, *223*
Huai-su
 Autobiography, 164
Hue, 57–58, 211
Human figure models, 249
Human scale, 231
A Humument (Phillips), *351*
Hutchins, Ed
 Words for the World, 344

I Never Liked Musical Chairs (Kao), *96, 97, 233*
Icarus (Matisse), *68*
The Iceberg and Its Shadow (Bell), *206, 207*
Iconography, 165–166
Iden, Cally
 Transforming Crouse College into a Labyrinth, 150–151, 151
Ik Ook Eindhoven (Di Suvero), 188, *189*
Illusionistic art
 meaning and, 34
 space, 99–107
 surface and, 28
 texture and, 40
 value and, 46
Illustrated Man (Spadaford), *72*
Imaginary Landscape #4 (Cage), 365
Imbalance, 93
Immediacy, in visual communication, 166–167
Implied lines, 22, 192
Indiana, Robert
 The Great American Dream, 39
Inhumans: "First Contact" (Jenkins and Lee), *10,* 304
Inner Sanctum Waterfall (Steir), *56*
Innerland (Hilton), *253*

Installation art, 184, 186, 359–362
    context, 360–362
    space and time, 359–360
Intensity
    of color, 60, 211
    time and, 301–302
Intent of communication, 169–170
Interdisciplinary arts, 348–366
    advantages of, 366
    installation art, 359–362
    performance art, 362–365
    visual books, 348–358
Interior Landscape (Frankenthaler), 32
Interior with Book (Diebenkorn), 70, 71
Intermission (Stout), 94, 113
Intersection II (Sierra), 200, 201
Intolerance (film), 303, 311
Invented texture, 37–38
Iomega Corporation
    "Y2K's coming. Don't just sit
        there.," 172
Irwin, Robert, 143
    *Part II: Excursus: Homage to the
        Square³*, 206, 208, 359
Itten color wheel, 57
Itten, Johannes, 52, 57

Jack in the Pulpit No. V (O'Keeffe),
    63, 64
Jackson, Reggie, 122
James, Michael
    Rhythm/Color: Improvisation, 95
Jamie Sleeping (Crawford), 98
Janney, Christopher
    Sonic Plaza, 278, 279
Japaljarri, Cookie Stewart
    Bush Cabbage Dreaming at Ngarlu
        (with A. N. Granites and R. J.
        Granites), 64, 65
Japanese floor lamps, 244
Jaudon, Valerie
    Tallahatchee, 32
Jeep Cherokee advertisement, 337, 338
Jefferson National Expansion Memorial
    (Saarinen), 182, 188
Jenkins, Paul
    Inhumans: "First Contact" (with Jae
        Lee), 10, 304
Jewel of Enlightenment (Hashi-no Toma)
    (Parker), 209
Jinks, John
    Cover of *The Penguin Pool Murder*,
        27
Joel Katz Design Associates
    Cover of *Philadelphia Architecture*, 64
Johns, Jasper
    Flag, 72, 73
    Target with Plaster Casts, 37
Johnson, Joel Peter
    Self Portrait, 25
Joints, 248–249
Jordan, Lorna
    Waterworks Gardens: The Grotto, 274
Journals, for exploring ideas, 138–139
Joyce, James
    Ulysses, 27

*Judith and Her Maidservant with the
    Head of Holofernes* (Gentileschi), 47
Junctions, 248
Just in Time (Murray), 28

K

Kachina doll, 72, 73
Kahlo, Frida
    Las Dos Fridas, 93
Kahn, Wolf
    The Yellow Square, 67
Kainophobia, Fear of Change (Grant),
    342, 343
Kandinsky, Wassily
    Several Circles, 16
Kao, Joana
    I Never Liked Musical Chairs, 96, 97,
        233
Kapoor, Anish
    Turning the World Inside Out II, 201
    Void Field, 250–251, 251
Kaprow, Allan, 363, 365
Karnes, Karen
    Vessel, 199
Kawamata, Tadashi
    Tetra House N-3, W26 Project, 260,
        260–261
Keister, Ann Baddley, 76–77
    Memory, 77
Kellner, Tatanya
    Fifty Years of Silence, 305–306, 306
Kelm, Daniel E.
    Rubens (with Timothy C. Ely), 349
Kennedy, Jackie, 211
Kennedy, John F., 211
Key, color, 72
Kiefer, Anselm
    Breaking of the Vessels, 349
    Wayland's Song (with Wing), 41
Kiernan, Kenny, 166, 167
The Killing Cycle(#5) (Leslie), 21, 22
Kinesthetics, 107
Kinetic forms, 181
King, Elizabeth
    Attention's Loop, 282, 283
King, Larry, 117
The Kiss (Rodin), 185
Kita, Toshiyuki
    Kita Collection of chairs, 211
Klimt, Gustav
    Salomé, 27, 27–28
The Knight, Death and the Devil (Dürer),
    41
Knowlton, Kenneth and Leon
    Harmon
    Computerized Nude, 38
Koetsu, Hon'ami
    Flying Cranes and Poetry, 21
Kollwitz, Käthe
    Selbstbildnis in Profil Nach Rechts, 74
    Selbstbildnis und Akstudien, 74
    Self-Portrait in Profile, 74
Kubla Khan (Coleridge), 354
Kubrick, Stanley
    2001: A Space Odyssey, 312
Kulesov, Lev, 312

Kusumoto, Mariko
    Tansu no Oku, 252

Labyrinth Book, two double-page
    spreads (Frenkel), 352
Labyrinth Drawing (Frenkel), 352
Labyrinth, page from (Stewart), 350,
    351
Lac Laronge IV (Stella), 83
Ladderback Chair (Pierobon), 188, 189
Lamott, Anne, 121
Landmark (Forbes), 325
Laocoön (Hesse), 283
Laocoön and His Two Sons, 191, 283
Lap dissolve, 297
Large Horse #4 (Butterfield), 256
Larocque, Jean-Pierre
    Untitled (Head Series), 246–247, 247
Lasher-Oakes, Heidi, 144–145
    Biological Abstraction III, 145
Layered space, 104
Lazuka, Robert
    Thoughts of Summer, 57
Learning to Think (Gormley), 269
LeBoeuf, Michael, 116, 119
Lebrun, Rico
    Hand, 20
Lee, Jae
    Inhumans: "First Contact" (with Paul
        Jenkins), 10, 304
Leonardo da Vinci, 143
Leone, Sergio
    Once Upon a Time in the West, 302
Leslie, Alfred
    The Killing Cycle(#5), 21, 22
Leupp, Leslie
    Three Bracelets, 142
Levine, Sherri
    La Fortune, 238
LeWitt, Sol
    Wall/Floor Piece #4, 225
Lichtenstein, Roy, 158
Life Boats/Boats About Life (Renick), 230
Life-art boundary, 261, 364–365
Light, 206–210
    ambient, 208
    color and, 54
    directed, 208
    as sculpture, 208–210
    striking a surface, 206, 208
    value and volume, 206
Light Communication (Nakamura), 280
Lighting, 47–48
Lighting techniques (Veltri), 47
The Lightning Field (De Maria), 200,
    201
Ligon, Glenn
    Untitled, 39
Lin, Maya Ying
    Topo, 264, 265
Linarducci, Adele
    Slingshot Wheelchair, 213
Lincoln, Abraham, 206
Line, 18–26, 187–193
    actual, 20, 191
    calligraphic, 21

index

contour, 20
defined, 18
implied, 22, 192
medium and instrument, 19
networks, 23–24, 192–193
organizational, 21
quality, 18–19, 188, 191
using, 25–26
Linear perspective, 100–101
Lisková, Vera
   Porcupine, 131
Lists, for generating ideas, 136–137
The Liver is the Cock's Comb (Gorky),
   60, *61*
LoBue, Keith E.
   Where the Music Dwells, 2
Locking Piece (Moore), 197
Longo, Robert
   Corporate Wars, 184
   Untitled, 107
Long-term projects, 152–155
Loops (Scherr), 234
Lord, Chip, 187
Losing It (Greytak), 320
L.O.W. in Gaia (Rosenthal), 364, *365*
Low-definition shapes, 34
Lucas, George
   Star Wars, 299
Lucier, Mary
   Floodstage, 359
Lumière, Louis
   *The Arrival of a Train at La Ciotat
      Station*, 302–303, *303*

MacDonald, David, 240–241
   Carved Stoneware Storage Jar, *241*
Mach, David
   Eckow, 23
Macintosh Computer Ad, *292*, 293
Mack, Rodger, 217–218
Macsai, Aaron
   Panels of Movement, 82, *223*
Magnum Opus (Hofmann), 67
The Magpie (Monet), 64, *65*
Magritte, René
   Golconde, 166
Maiastra (Brancusi), 232
Malcolm X #3 (Chase-Riboud), *267*
Man Waiting (Goodman), 35
Man with a Guitar (Braque), 29
Mano y Balo (Slaughter), *187*
MANUAL
   Quinault, 58
Manushkin, Fran
   Miriam's Cup, 163
Many Times (Muñoz), 221
Maori Meeting House, 282, *282–283*
Maquettes, 140
Marabar (Zimmerman), *268*
Marclay, Christian
   Amplification, 186
Marquez, Hudson, 187
Marra, Benjamin
   Self-Portrait, 42
Martens, Kim
   Arterial Fibrillation, 169

Martin, Walter
   Of Bodies Born Up by Water (with
      Paloma Muñoz), *263*
Martinez, Maria Montoya and Julian
   Blackware Storage Jar, *204*
Mask (Wanis), *225*
Mass, 180, 197
Mass (Colder Darker Matter) (Parker),
   270
Mass transit advertisement, *341*
"Master Harold" . . . and the Boys
   (McNutt), *30*
Materials, 242–257
   boards, 255
   clay, 252
   connections, 248–249
   considerations for, 242–243
   contemporary uses of, 250–254
   fibers, 253
   glass, 252–253
   glues, 255
   meaning and, 255–256
   metals, 252
   methods of construction, 246–247
   plastics, 254
   stone, 250–251
   strength, 243–246
   student, 255
   tapes, 255
   transitions, 250, *251*
   wood, 251
Matisse, Henri
   Green Stripe (Madame Matisse), 60
   Icarus, 68
Matrices, 226
Matta-Clark, Gordon
   Splitting: Exterior, 191
McCloud, Scott, 297
McKee, Robert, 327
McNutt, David
   "Master Harold" . . . and the Boys, 30
Meaning, construction of; *see*
   Constructing meaning
Medusa's Head (Burden), *190*, 191
Memory (Keister), 77
Metals, 252
Metamorphosis II (detail) (Escher),
   29, *122*
Metaphor, 171–172
Metaphorical thinking, 172
Methods of construction, 246–247
Metzker, Ray K.
   Philadelphia, 44, *45*
Miami Rug Company (Estes), 90
Michals, Duane
   Chance Meeting, 326, *327*
Michelangelo, 143
   Creation of Adam, 82
   Head of a Satyr, 23
   Pietà, 262
Michels, Doug, 187
Michelson, Harold
   Storyboard for Alfred Hitchcock's
      The Birds, 5
Mickey Mouse, 19
Milken, Michael, 364
Miller, Frank
   Untitled, 92, 93

Miller, Steve, 176–177
Mimlitsch-Gray, Myra
   Timepiece, 262
Minnesota Children's Museum
   signage (Cameron and Bierut),
      170, *171*
Miriam's Cup, cover of (Dacey), 163
Mirrored Room (Samaras), 202, *203*
Miss, Mary
   Staged Gates, 248
Miss Saigon (film), 309
Mist (Hockney), 59
Model making, 139–140
Model of a Trophy Head, 199
*Model of Proposal for Concourse
   Commission* (Woodward), 236, *237*
Modeling, 247
Moment-to-moment transition, *298*
Mondrian, Piet, 177
   Composition with Blue and Yellow, 92
Monet, Claude
   The Magpie, 64, *65*
   Waterlily Pond, 7
Monochromatic color schemes, 62
Monogram (Rauschenberg), *159–160*
*Monolith, The Face of Half Dome,
   Yosemite Valley* (Adams), 32,
      33, 103
Monumental Ikebana (Teshigahara), *266*
Monumental scale, 231
Moonrise, Hernandez, New Mexico
   (Adams), 89
Moore, Henry
   Locking Piece, 197
Moore, Larry
   illustration for Creative Club of
      Orlando, 81
Moore, Marie, 68
Moran, Thomas
   Noon-Day Rest in Marble Canyon, 46
Morell, Abelardo, 292, 368–369
   *Camera Obscura Image of Brookline
      View in Brady's Room*, 369
Morris, William
   illustration from *The Canterbury
      Tales*, 85
Morrison, Philip, 344
Moskowitz, Robert
   Seventh Sister, 32, *33*
Movement
   before and after, 108
   in composition, 82–84
   decisive moment, 107–108
   illusion of, 107–109
   kinesthetic response, 107
   multiplication, 108–109
Movie Premiere, Hollywood (Frank), 34
*"Mr. Linden's Library," from The
   Mysteries of Harris Burdick* (Van
      Allsburg), 293
Mueck, Ron
   The Boy, 254
Mulan (film), 105–107, *106*
Multiplication, movement shown
   through, 108–109
Multiplication of the Arcs (Tanguy), 135,
   136

index

Muñoz, Juan
    Many Times, 221
    Raincoat Drawing, 35
Muñoz, Paloma
    Of Bodies Born Up by Water (with
        Walter Martin), 263
Muntadas, Antoni
    The Board Room, 184, 185
Murray, Elizabeth
    Just in Time, 28
Museums, as sources of ideas, 130–132
Music, in language, 354–355
My Mother 3 (Cho Duck-Hyun), 264,
    265
Myron
    Discus Thrower (Diskobolos), 107
The Mysteries of Harris Burdick (Van
    Allsburg), 108, 293
The Mystery and Melancholy of a Street
    (De Chirico), 135, 136
Myths, 322–323

N

N Lines Vertical (Rickey), 214
Nakamura, Fumaki
    Light Communication, 280
Narrative, 322–345
    advertising, 337–341
    boundaries, 327–330
    causality, 331–332
    multiple images, 323–327
    non-narrative, 341–344
    purposes of, 322
    story development, 328, 333–336
    style, 330, 333–336
NASA's Participating Exhibit at the
    1989 Paris Air Show (Bill Cannan
    & Co.), 3, 208
Natzler, Gertrud and Otto
    Pilgrim Bottle, 204
Negative shape, 28–29
Negative space, 181, 198–199
Nehl, Georgiana
    Solstice Greetings (with David
        Browne), 166, 167, 168
    Sun/Star (detail), 114, 125
Neon Skates (North and Stern), 188
Nevelson, Louise
    Wedding Chapel IV, 222, 223
Newman, Barnett
    Broken Obelisk, 262–263, 263
    Stations of the Cross, 19, 20
Nigredo (Onwin), 276, 277
Nike advertisement, 340
Nikolais Dance Theatre
    Sanctum, 191
"Nine Drummers Drumming"
    (Sabuda), 354
No. 15 (Zhou and Zhou), 32, 33
No Turning (D. Smith), 38
Noland, Kenneth
    A Warm Sound in a Gray Field, 58
Nonobjective art, 262
Nonobjective shapes, 32
Non-sequitur transition, 298
Noon-Day Rest in Marble Canyon
    (Moran), 46

North, Moira
    Neon Skates (with Rudi Stern), 188
Notkin, Richard
    Vain Imaginings, 204, 205
Nude (Brandt), 28–29, 29
Nude Descending a Staircase, No. 2
    (Duchamp), 96
Number 56 (Drew), 226

O

Oath of the Horatii (David), 323
Objective criticism, 147
Objects in a Field (Fisher), 69, 70
Of Bodies Born Up by Water (Martin
    and Muñoz), 263
Oka Doner, Michele
    Terrible Table, 256
O'Keeffe, Georgia
    Jack in the Pulpit No. V, 63, 64
Okulick, John
    Wind Wizard, 249
Oldenburg, Claes, 157
    Shuttlecocks (with Coosje Van
        Bruggen), 158
Olmec Colossal Head, 197
O'Meallie, Sean
    *Out-Boxed Finger Puppets
        Perform . . .* , 171
Once Upon a Time in the West (film),
    302
One-point perspective, 101
Ono, Yoko
    Cut Piece, 365
Onus, Lin
    Gumiring Garkman, 86
Onwin, Glen
    Nigredo, 276, 277
Open mind, creativity and, 143
Oppenheim, Dennis
    Device to Root Out Evil, 269
Opponent theory, 56
Organic forms, 181
Organic shapes, 32
Organizational lines, 21
Orientation of line, 18–19, 19, 188
Orthographic projection, 182–183, 183
The Other Side (Yi), 51
Out-Boxed Finger Puppets Perform . . .
    (O'Meallie), 171
Overstuffed chair, 128, 129

P

Pace, 309
Package (Bravo), 40
Package designs, 196
Palmer, Stuart
    The Penguin Pool Murder, 27
Panels of Movement (Macsai), 82, 223
Parker, Bill
    *Jewel of Enlightenment (Hashi-no
        Toma)*, 209
Parker, Cornelia
    Mass (Colder Darker Matter), 270
Parsifal (Syberberg), 3
Part II: Excursus: Homage to the Square³
    (Irwin), 206, 208, 359

Past Continuous Pasts (Graham), 363
PATH Station Maps, 25, 69
Patterns, 85–86
Paul, Rick, 286–289
Pedestal, 266
The Penguin Pool Murder (Skalski and
    Jinks), 27
Pentagram Design, 96
Peregrine Tent, 271
The Perfect Thought (Byars), 264
Performance art, 362–365
    artist-audience boundary, 365
    background of, 363
    collaboration, 363–364
    ephemeral character, 363
    life-art boundary, 364–365
Performance/Audience/Mirror
    (Graham), 365
Perseus and Medusa (Cellini), 267
Perspective
    amplified, 103
    atmospheric, 46, 103
    linear, 100–101
    one-point, 101
    three-point, 101
    two-point, 101
Pevsner, Antoine
    Torso, 194
Pfaff, Judy
    Rock/Paper/Scissor, 225
Philadelphia Architecture, 64
Philadelphia (Metzker), 44, 45
Phillips, Tom
    A Humument, 351
Photography, definition in, 34
Physical texture, 37, 40–41
Picasso, Pablo
    Guernica, 130, 172, 173
Picture plane, 100
Pierobon, Peter
    Ladderback Chair, 188, 189
Pietà (Michelangelo), 262
Pilgrim Bottle (G. Natzler and
    O. Natzler), 204
Pine Spirit (Wu Guanzhong), 21
Pitch, 309
Place de l'Europe on a Rainy Day
    (Caillebotte), 148, 149, 148–150,
    166
Plane, 194–195
Plastics, 254
Plaza Facets (Gall), 228, 229, 231
Plinth, 266
Pollock, Jackson
    White Light, 24
Polyhedra, 195
Pomodoro, Arnaldo
    Sphere, 234
Poppy Petals (Goldsworthy), 212
Porter, Edwin S.
    The Great Train Robbery, 303
Portrait of Paris von Gütersloh (Schiele),
    72, 73
Positive forms, 181, 198–199
Positive shape, 28–29
Poussin, Nicolas
    The Rape of the Sabine Women, 304

index

Powell, J. W.
  Engraving after *Noon-Day Rest in Marble Canyon* (Moran), *46*
Powers of Ten (film), *290*, 343, 343–344
Predator's Ball (Armitage), *364*
Presence, in sculpture, 272
Primary colors, 53, 57
Primary contours, 197
Prince, George, 118
Principles of design; *see* Composition; Composition
Problems, 128–143
  brainstorming on, 136–139
  characteristics of good, 132–133
  convergent and divergent thinking for, 133–136
  design process, 128–130
  fine art process, 130
  open mind and, 143
  and sources of ideas, 130–132
  variations on a theme, 141–142
  visual research on, 139–140
Process colors, 53
Profiles
  Abelardo Morell, 368–369
  Ann Baddley Keister, 76–77
  Bob Dacey, 162–163
  David MacDonald, 240–241
  Heidi Lasher-Oakes, 144–145
  Jerome Witkin, 346–347
  Ken Botnick, 176–177
  Ken Stout, 112–113
  Nancy Callahan and Diane Gallo, 126–127
  Phillia Yi, 50–51
  Rick Paul, 286–289
  Rodger Mack, 217–218
  Sharon Greytak, 319–321
  Todd Slaughter, 258–259
Project California Condor (Hauer), 214, *215*
Proportion
  color and, 68
  in composition, 94, 231–232
Prototypes, 140
Proximity, 82, 223
Pull (Hatoum), *365*
Pure forms, 32
Purpose of communication, 169–170
Puryear, Martin
  Seer, 219–220, *220*

Quinault (MANUAL), *58*
Quinn, Steve
  A Christmas memory, 66

Radial symmetry, *90*, 90–91, 227
Radioactive Cats (Skoglund), 70, 71
Raft of the Medusa (Gericault), 83, 83–84
Raincoat Drawing (Muñoz), *35*
Rama and Laskshmana Bound by Arrow-snakes (Sahibdin and workshop), *80*, 80–81

Rand, Paul, 76
The Rape of the Sabine Women (Giovanni da Bologna), *192*
The Rape of the Sabine Women (Poussin), *304*
Raphael
  The School of Athens, *100*, 100, 149–150, *150*
Rauschenberg, Robert
  Booster, *170*
  Brace, *31*
  Monogram, 159–160
Realism
  meaning and, 34
  in sculpture, 261–262
  space, 99–107
  surface and, 28
  texture and, 40
  value and, 46
Rectilinear shapes, *30*, 30–31
Red Forest (Zeigler), *193*
Rejection Quintet: Female Rejection Drawing (Chicago), 90, *91*
Relief sculpture, 184
Rembrandt van Rijn
  Two Women Helping a Child to Walk, *20*
Remington, Deborah
  Capra, 43, *44*
Renick, Patricia A.
  Life Boats/Boats About Life, *230*
Repetition, 82, 223, 235–238
Representation
  in sculpture, 261–263
  shape and, 32–34
Research, visual, 139–140
Rhythm
  in sound, 309
  in three-dimensional design, 235–238
  in time-based art, 295
  in two-dimensional design, 95–96
Rhythm/Color: Improvisation (James), *95*
Rickel, Stan
  Teapot Sketches, *207*
Rickey, George
  N Lines Vertical, *214*
Riedy, Mark
  Day at the Beach, 78, *79*
Riefenstahl, Leni, 311
Riley, Bridget
  Drift No. 2, *95*
Ringgold, Faith
  Tar Beach, *85*
Rivera, Diego M., 93
  Detroit Industry, north wall, *27*
Rock Bible (Araki), *205*
Rock/Paper/Scissor (Pfaff), *225*
The Rocky Mountains, Landers Peak (Bierstadt), *102*, 103
Rodin, Auguste
  The Kiss, *185*
Rods (eye), 56
Rogers, Ray
  Vessel, *131*
Romeo and Juliet (film), *330*
Rosenthal, Rachel
  L.O.W. in Gaia, *364*, 365

Ross, David, 359
Rubber cement, 255
Rubens (Kelm and Ely), *349*
Rubens, Peter Paul
  Tiger Hunt, *91*

Saarinen, Eero, 129
  Jefferson National Expansion Memorial, *182*, 188
Sabuda, Robert
  "Nine Drummers Drumming," *354*
Sahibdin and workshop
  Rama and Laskshmana Bound by Arrow-snakes, *80*, 80–81
Saint Serapion (Zurbarán), *98*
Salle, David, 320, 364
Salomé (Klimt), *27*, 27–28
Salomé with the Head of John the Baptist (Beardsley), 30–31, *31*
Samaras, Lucas
  Mirrored Room, 202, *203*
Sanctum (Nikolais Dance Theatre), *191*
Sandblaster (White), *22*
Santore, Charles
  Cover of *William the Curious, Knight of the Water Lilies*, *325*
Saturation, 60, 211
Save Our City (Bierut), *94*
Sawada, Tetsurō
  Brilliant Scape (Blue), *88*
Sayre, Henry M., 159, 172
Scale, 94, 231
Scenes, 295, 327
Scene-to-scene transition, *297*
Scherr, Mary Ann
  Loops, *234*
Schiele, Egon
  Portrait of Paris von Gütersloh, 72, *73*
Schindler's List (film), *98*, 313–317
The School of Athens (Raphael), *100*, 100, 149–150, *150*
Scope, 302–304
Screenplays, 327
Sculpture, 260–284
  additive method, 246
  bases and places, 266–268
  boundaries, 264–266
  compression and expansion, 270
  as journey, 278
  life and art, 261
  light as, 208–210
  as place, 276–278
  presence/absence, 272
  process and product, 273–274
  reinvention of, 275–276
  representation, 261–263
  as self, 282–283
  subtractive method, 247
  tension and torsion, 271
  as time, 280
  traditional, 275
  weight and gravity, 269
Secondary colors, 57
Secondary contours, 197
Seer (Puryear), 219–220, *220*

index

Segal, George
  The Subway, 265
  Walk, Don't Walk, 213
Selbstbildnis in Profil Nach Rechts
    (Kollwitz), 74
Selbstbildnis und Akstudien (Kollwitz),
    74
Self-assignments, 153–155
Self-Portrait (Brooks), 60
Self-Portrait (Close), 42
Self Portrait (J. P. Johnson), 25
Self-Portrait (Marra), 42
Self-Portrait in Profile (Kollwitz), 74
Sequences, 295, 326
Series, 325
The Serpent Didn't Lie (Haylor-
    McDowell), 165
Serra, Richard
  Intersection II, 200, 201
Setting, 305–309
  actor and, 307–308
  objects and implications, 305–306
  sound and, 308–309
Seven Windows to a Sky on Fire (Dahl),
    274
Seventh Sister (Moskowitz), 32, 33
Several Circles (Kandinsky), 16
Shade, 58, 59
Shading, 26
Shadows, 46
Shanosky, Don
  signage symbol system poster (with
    Roger Cook), 168
Shape, 26–37
  abstract, 32
  curvilinear, 30, 30–31
  defined, 26, 26–28
  definition of, 34–35
  figure, 28, 28–30
  figure/ground reversal, 29–30
  geometric, 32
  ground, 28, 28–30
  negative, 28–29
  nonobjective, 32
  organic, 32
  positive, 28–29
  rectilinear, 30, 30–31
  representational, 32–34
  types of, 28–32
  using, 35–37
Shear, 245
Shelter/Surveillance Sculpture (Forbes),
    140
Shere, Sam
  Explosion of the Hindenburg, 293
Shots, 294
Shuttlecocks (Oldenburg and van
    Bruggen), 158
Sight lines, 192
Signage symbol system poster (Cook
    and Shanosky), 168
Simile, 171
Simultaneous contrast, 55
Site-specific works, 187
Skalski, Krystyna
  Cover of *The Penguin Pool Murder*,
    27
Skeleton, 243

Skoglund, Sandy
  Radioactive Cats, 70, 71
  Walking on Eggshells, 360, 361
Slaughter, Todd, 258–259
  Grinding Knuckles, 273
  Mano y Balo, 187
Slingshot Wheelchair (Linarducci), 213
Slodtz, Michel-Ange
  St. Bruno, 229
Slowly Turning Narrative (Viola), 2
Smartronics Learning System, 211
Smith, David
  Cubi XXVII, 198, 199
Smith, Douglas
  No Turning, 38
Smith, Keith, 137–138, 324, 350
  Book 50, 351
  from *Structure of the Visual Book*,
    310–311
Smithson, Robert
  Spiral Jetty, 186
Snelson, Kenneth
  Free Ride Home, 187–188, 188
Snow, Michael
  from *Cover to Cover*, 301
Social responsibility, 132
Soft-sell advertising, 337
Solidification, 247
Sonic Plaza (Janney), 278, 279
Sôtatsu, Tawaraya (attributed)
  Flying Cranes and Poetry, 21
Sottsass, Ettore
  Ginevra Carafe, 196
Sound, 308–309
Soyinka, Wole
  Death and the King's Horseman,
    328–329, 329
Space, 99–107, 198–203
  activated, 201
  color and, 58, 67, 103
  compression and expansion, 201
  dynamic, 105–107
  entering, 203
  illusion of, 99–107
  in installation art, 359–360
  linear perspective, 100–101
  location and, 103
  negative, 181, 198–199
  overlap and, 103
  shape definition and, 103
  size variation and, 103
  sound and, 309
  texture and, 38, 38–39
  using illusion of, 103–105
  value and, 46–47
Spadaford, Joseph
  Illustrated Man, 72
Spectrum of colors, 54
Sphere (Pomodoro), 234
Spielberg, Steven
  Schindler's List, 98, 313–317
Spiral, 90–91
Spiral Jetty (Smithson), 186
Split complementary color schemes,
    63
Splitting: Exterior (Matta-Clark), 191
St. Bruno (Slodtz), 229

St. Bruno of Cologne (Houdon), 229
Staged Gates (Miss), 248
Standing Figures (Abakanowicz), 236,
    237
Star Wars (film), 299
Starry Night (Van Gogh), 42, 43
Static forms, 181
Stations of the Cross (Newman), 19, 20
Statue of Liberty, construction diagram
    (Eiffel), 244
Steir, Pat
  Inner Sanctum Waterfall, 56
Stella, Frank
  Lac Laronge IV, 83
Stereotypes, 168
Stermer, Dugald
  Bertrand Russell, 40, 41
Stern, Rudi
  Neon Skates (with Moira North), 188
Stewart, Mary
  Expanded Escher Collaboration, 123
  Formal Relationships (Exercise), 11
  page from *Labyrinth*, 350, 351
Sticky Buns: An Overnight Roll
    (collaborative book), 357
Stieglitz, Alfred
  The Terminal, 44
Stoller, Jennifer
  PATH Station Maps, 25, 69
Stone, 250–251
Stonehenge, 276, 277
Storefront Stories (Callahan and Gallo),
    127, 292, 361
Stout, Ken, 112–113
  Intermission, 94, 113
Strength/potential, as critique topic,
    151–152
Stress, 124
Strokowsky, Cathy
  Glass Pod with Hair, 253
Structural strength, 243–245
Structure of the Visual Book (Smith),
    310–311
Study of Hands (Dickinson), 20
Stull, Robert, 241
Subject, 147
Subjective criticism, 147–148
Subject-to-subject transition, 297
Subordinate form, 229
Subtractive color, 53, 55
Subtractive sculpture, 247
The Subway (Segal), 265
Subway with Silver Girders (Dennis),
    203
Sun Tunnels (Holt), 192, 305
Sun/Star (detail) (Nehl), 114, 125
Surface
  of illusionistic painting, 28
  light striking, 206, 208
Surprise, in visual communication,
    168
Surrealism, 135
Syberberg, Hans-Jürgen
  Parsifal, 3
Symbolism, color and, 72, 213
Symmetry
  approximate, 90

Index

asymmetry, *91, 92,* 91–93
radial, *90,* 90–91, 227
symmetrical balance, 89, 227

T

Taj Mahal, Agra, India, *89*
Takes, 300
A Tale of Two Cities (Dickens), 311
Tallahatchee (Jaudon), *32*
Tanguy, Yves
    Multiplication of the Arcs, 135, 136
Tapes, 255
Tar Beach (Ringgold), *85*
Target with Plaster Casts (Johns), *37*
Temperature, 57–58, 211
Tempo, 299–301, 311
Tension (force), 245, 271
The Terminal (Stieglitz), *44*
Terrible Table (Oka Doner), *256*
Tertiary colors, 57
Teshigahara, Hiroshi
    Monumental Ikebana, 266
Tetra House N-3, W26 Project
    (Kawamata), *260,* 260–261
Text style, 356–357
Texture, 37–42, 204–206
    characteristic and contradictory,
        204–205
    combinations of, 40–41
    creating, 38
    defined, 37
    degrees of, 204
    implications of, 205–206
    space and, *38,* 38–39
    trompe l'oeil, 40
    types of, 37–38
    using, 42
The Sandman Special #1 (Essential
    Vertigo), *300*
Theroux, Alexander, 72
Thesaurus, as source of ideas, 137
Thirty-Six Views of Mount Fuji (three
    prints) (Hokusai), *141*
Thompson, Kristin, 295–296
Thoughts of Summer (Lazuka), *57*
A Thousand Peaks and Myriad Ravines
    (Wang Hui), *103*
Three Bracelets (Gralnick), *142*
Three Bracelets (Leupp), *142*
Three-dimensional design
    complexity of, 214–215
    composition, 220–239
    elements, 180–216
    materials and methods, 242–257
    sculpture, 260–284
    two-dimensional versus, 179
Three-point perspective, 101
Three-quarter works, 184
Thumbnail sketches, 139
Tiger Hunt (Rubens), *91*
Timbre, 309
Time
    artistic building blocks of, 294–295
    aspects and elements, 292–318
    chronology, 310–312
    content and composition, 313–317
    duration, 298–299

    in installation art, 359–360
    intensity, 301–302
    in interdisciplinary arts, 348–366
    narrative and, 322–345
    relationships, 295–296
    scope, 302–304
    sculpture as, 280
    setting, 305–309
    tempo, 299–301
    in three-dimensional design, 214
    transitions, 296–298
Time management, 120–123
Timepiece (Mumlitsch-Gray), *262*
Tinguely, Jean
    Chaos 1, 181
Tinkelman, Murray
    The Frog Jumps over the Moon, 325
Tint, 58, *59*
Titanic (film), 305, *309,* 331–332, *332*
Tlingit totem carver, 247
Tomb of Emperor Shih Huang Ti, *238*
Tone, 58, *59*
Topo (Lin), *264, 265*
Torque, 245
Torsion, in sculpture, 271
Torso (Pevsner), *194*
Torus 280 (B1) (Watkins), *235*
Torus 280 (B2) (Watkins), *235*
Tower of Photos (Freed), *224*
Tracers–Side Order (Goodwin), *62*
Trangmar, Susan
    Blue Skies, 266
Transforming Crouse College into a
    Labyrinth (Iden), 150–151, *151*
Transforming Crouse College into a
    Labyrinth (Tripp), 150–151, *151*
Tree of Life Fantasy (Aycock), *9, 198,*
    224
Triadic color schemes, 64
Tripp, Tricia
    Transforming Crouse College into a
        Labyrinth, 150–151, *151*
Triptych (Bacon), *66*
Trompe l'oeil, 40
Truisms (Holzer), *362*
Turn of the Screw (Cyclone Design), *84,*
    84–85
Turning the World Inside Out II
    (Kapoor), *201*
Turrell, James
    Afrum-Proto, 208–209, *209*
The Twelve Days of Christmas (Sabuda),
    354
12 Trees No 2 (Hassinger), *271*
The Two Plateaus (Buren), *226*
2001: A Space Odyssey (Kubrick), 312
Two Women Helping a Child to Walk
    (Rembrandt), *20*
Two-dimensional design
    basic elements, 17–49
    color, 52–75
    composition, 78–110
    three-dimensional versus, 179
Two-point perspective, 101
Type style, 356–357

U

Ukeles, Mierle
    Ceremonial Arch Honoring Service
        Workers in the New Service
        Economy, 261
Ulysses, cover of (Goldberg), *27*
"Under the Rug," from *The Mysteries*
    of Harris Burdick (Van Allsburg),
    108
Under the Sea Wind (Carson), 355
Understanding Healthcare, 170
Unique Forms of Continuity in Space
    (Boccioni), *268*
Unity and variety, 78–87, 221–226
    closure, 84, 223–224
    combining forces, 224
    combining Gestalt principles, 84–85
    containment, 81, 223
    continuity, 82–84, 223
    defined, 78, 221
    degrees of unity, 224
    Gestalt psychology, 80–85
    grids, 85–87, 226
    grouping, *80,* 80–81, 221
    increasing variety, 224
    matrices, 226
    patterns, 85–86
    proximity, 82, 223
    repetition, 82, 223
Untitled (Calder), *194*
Untitled (Fujii), 229–230, *230*
Untitled (Ligon), *39*
Untitled (Longo), *107*
Untitled (Miller), *92, 93*
Untitled (T. Carr and G. Carr), *236*
Untitled (Death by Gun) González-
    Torres, *87*
Untitled (Head Series) (Larocque),
    246–247, *247*
Untitled (Medici Princess) (Cornell), *246*
Untitled (Ocean) (Celmins), *79*
U.S. Pavilion, Expo-67 (Fuller), *246*

V

Vain Imaginings (Notkin), *204, 205*
Valencia (Cartier-Bresson), 107–108,
    108
Value, 43–48
    color and, 58–60, *59,* 211
    contrast, 43–44
    defined, 43
    distribution, 44
    lighting, 47–48, 206
    relative, 43
    space, 46–47
    volume, 46
Value scale, 43
Van Allsburg, Chris
    "Mr. Linden's Library," from *The*
        Mysteries of Harris Burdick, 293
    "Under the Rug," from *The*
        Mysteries of Harris Burdick, 108
Van Bruggen, Coosje
    Shuttlecocks (with Claes Oldenburg),
    158

index

Van der Weyden, Rogier
    Deposition, 102, 103
Van Eyck, Jan
    The Ghent Altarpiece (closed), 46
Van Gogh, Vincent
    Starry Night, 42, 43
Vanishing point, 100
Variations on a theme, 141–142
Variety; *see* Unity and variety
The Veiling (Viola), 210
Veltri, John
    Lighting techniques, 47
Vessel (Karnes), 199
Villon, Jacques
    Baudelaire, 23
Viola, Bill, 143
    Hall of Whispers, 359–360, 360
    Slowly Turning Narrative, 2
    The Veiling, 210
Vision (Gangi), 58, 59
Vision, rods and cones, 56
Visual books, 348–358
    advantages of, 358
    defined, 348
    selecting text, 352–355
    word-image relationship, 358
    writing text, 355–357
Visual communication; *see*
    Constructing meaning
Visual research, 139–140
Visual texture, 37, 40–41
Void Field (Kapoor), 250–251, 251
Volume
    shading and, 26
    in three-dimensional design, 180,
        195–196
    value and, 46
Volume summary, 21
Von Oech, Roger, 115

Wakely, Shelagh
    curcuma sul travertino, 280, 281

Walk, Don't Walk (Segal), 213
Walking on Eggshells (Skoglund),
    360, 361
Wall/Floor Piece #4 (LeWitt), 225
Wang Hui
    *A Thousand Peaks and Myriad
        Ravines*, 103
Warhol, Andy, 158
A Warm Sound in a Gray Field
    (Noland), 58
Waterlily Pond (Monet), 7
Waterworks Gardens: The Grotto
    (Jordan), 274
Watkins, David
    Torus 280 (B1), 235
    Torus 280 (B2), 235
Watson, Thomas, 122
Wayland's Song (with Wing) (Kiefer), 41
Weather Cube (Haacke), 273
Website design, 109
Wedding Chapel IV (Nevelson), 222,
    223
Weight
    color and, 68
    in sculpture, 269
    visual, 87–89
West Side Story (film), 330
Wetzel, Katherine (photographer)
    Pupil from *Attention's Loop*
        (Elizabeth King, sculptor),
        282, 283
Wheel of Fortune (Flack), 53 (detail), 57
Where the Music Dwells (LoBue), 2
White House/Greenhouse (Giusti), 278
White Light (Pollock), 24
White, Minor
    Sandblaster, 22
Whiteread, Rachel
    House, 272
William Shakespeare's Romeo and Juliet
    (film), 330
*William the Curious, Knight of the Water
    Lilies* (Santore), 325

Wind from the Sea (Wyeth), 70
Wind Wizard (Okulick), 249
Winston Churchill, Liverpool
    (Eisenstadt), 170, 171
Wipe, 297
Witkin, Jerome, 346–347
    Division Street, 324–325, 347
Wood, 251
Wood-strip bushel basket, 131
Woodward, Steve
    *Model of Proposal for Concourse
        Commission*, 236, 237
Word-image relationships, 358
Words for the World (Hutchins), 344
Wu Guanzhong
    Pine Spirit, 21
Wummer, Jesse
    Expanded Escher Collaboration, 123
Wyeth, Andrew
    Wind from the Sea, 70

Y

The Yellow Square (Kahn), 67
Yi, Phillia, 50–51
    The Other Side, 51

Z

Zeffirelli, Franco
    Romeo and Juliet, 330
Zeigler, Claire
    Red Forest, 193
Zettl, Herbert, 47
Zhou brothers
    No. 15, 32, 33
Zimmerman, Elyn
    Marabar, 268
Zurbarán, Francisco de
    Saint Serapion, 98